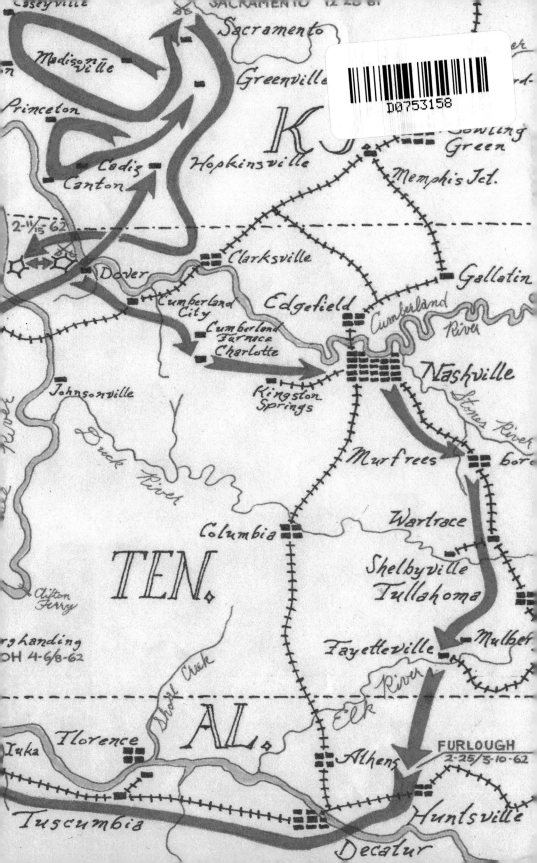

# NATHAN BEDFORD FORREST

# NATHAN BEDFORD FORREST

## IN SEARCH OF THE ENIGMA

**EDDY W. DAVISON AND DANIEL FOXX**
**FOREWORD BY EDWIN C. BEARSS**

PELICAN PUBLISHING COMPANY
GRETNA 2007

THE WORD "PELICAN" AND THE DEPICTION OF A PELICAN
ARE TRADEMARKS OF PELICAN PUBLISHING COMPANY, INC., AND
ARE REGISTERED IN THE U.S. PATENT AND TRADEMARK OFFICE.

**Library of Congress Cataloging-in-Publication Data**

Davison, Eddy W.
  Nathan Bedford Forrest : in search of the enigma / Eddy W.
Davison and Daniel Foxx ; foreword by Edwin C. Bearss.
    p. cm.
  Includes bibliographical references and index.
  ISBN-13: 978-1-58980-415-9 (hardcover : alk. paper)
  1. Forrest, Nathan Bedford, 1821-1877. 2. Forrest, Nathan
Bedford, 1821-1877—Military leadership. 3. Generals—
Confederate States of America—Biography. 4. Confederate States
of America. Army—Biography. 5. United States—History—Civil
War, 1861-1865—Cavalry operations. I. Foxx, Daniel. II. Title.
  E467.1.F72D385 2006
  973.7'3092—dc22
  [B]
                                        2006031938

*Maps illustrated by Tom Tatum.*

Printed in the United States of America
Published by Pelican Publishing Company, Inc.
1000 Burmaster Street, Gretna, Louisiana 70053

*For our parents:*

*Bill and Marie Davison*

*Roy and Lois Foxx*

# CONTENTS

# FOREWORD

Many longtime Civil War aficionados know that my interest in the Civil War dates to the winter of 1935-36, when my father, a World War I Marine, then a Montana cattle rancher, read to me John W. Thomason's *Jeb Stuart*. I was hooked, and until 1940, the "Plumed Cavalier" and his horse soldiers were my heroes. By the latter date, having read Lloyd Lewis's *Sherman, Fighting Prophet*, Robert Selph Henry's *The Story of the Confederacy*, Howard Swiggett's *The Rebel Raider: A Life of John Hunt Morgan*, and other Civil War-related books, I expanded my horizons. The exploits of Morgan and his raiders had entranced me even before my introduction to Jeb Stuart. In 1933 I had visited my Peru, Indiana, relatives. There I had listened wide-eyed as my great-grandfather's youngest brother recalled the summer of 1863, when the Bearss brothers answered Gov. Oliver P. Morton's call for militia to turn back Morgan and his "terrible men." It didn't matter, as I later learned, that though they never got nearer than a hundred miles of the raiders, for Uncle Frank this was one of the high points in a long and distinguished life that began before the war with Mexico and extended through the attack on Pearl Harbor.

Then combat in World War II as a Marine ground-pounder gave me a different perspective on the Civil War, particularly what makes a good leader. Twenty-six months in army and navy hospitals, especially the fifteen months spent as a patient in San Diego Naval Hospital, with its extensive library, gave me hundreds of hours to immerse myself in such books as Douglas Southall Freeman's multi-volume *R. E. Lee* and *Lee's Lieutenants*. Subsequently, I learned that the "Marine's Marine," then Col. Lewis "Chesty" Puller, was reading *Lee's Lieutenants* on the eve of the invasion of Pelelieu.

During the months from June 1944 to October 1945, I also read my first Forrest biography, Andrew W. Lytle's *Bedford Forrest and his*

9

*Critter Company,* my introduction to Forrest and his way of war. Further readings highlighting Forrest were postponed until the years following my September 1955 joining the National Park Service and entering duty as historian at Vicksburg National Military Park. This assignment enabled me to expand my focus, allowing me to devote more time and energy to the war in Mississippi, Louisiana, and west Tennessee and related Civil War sites. It was during these years that I immersed myself in following Forrest's paper trail, reading such major works as Henry's *As They Saw Forrest: Some Recollections and Comments of Contemporaries* and *"First With the Most": Nathan Bedford Forrest,* Thomas Jordan and Joseph Pryor's *The Campaigns of Lieut. Gen. N. B. Forrest,* J. Harvey Mathes' *Bedford Forrest,* Eric W. Sheppard's *Bedford Forrest, the Confederacy's Greatest Cavalryman,* and John A. Wyeth's *Life of Lieutenant-General Nathan Bedford Forrest.*

In the late 1950s, Mississippi governor James P. Coleman, a student of the Civil War, historian, and preservationist, secured an appropriation from the state legislature for identifying and marking the Brice's Cross Roads battlefield. Local historian and raconteur Claude Gentry, versed in the battle story, prepared the texts and located the interpretive markers. I visited Brice's Cross Roads and other north Mississippi and west Tennessee Forrest-related 1863-64 sites before my 1966 transfer to the National Park Service's Washington office.

In 1969, as an element of the National Park Service's ongoing research program, I prepared a resource study on the Battle of Tupelo and in 1971 authored the service's *Protecting Sherman's Lifeline: The Battles of Brice's Cross Roads and Tupelo.* Although long interested in Forrest as the ideal leader of troops in combat, coupled with the attributes of Marine Corps legends like Merritt "Red Mike" Edson, Chesty Puller, and Herman Hanneken, whose exploits dated from the Banana Wars through World War II, I had never considered an in-depth study of Forrest's leadership style and battles until the 1970s. It was then that my friend and Civil War guru Robert "Bob" Younger asked me to author a book on the Wizard of the Saddle. By the spring of 1979, my manuscript was finished and published by Morningside Bookshop under the title *Forrest at Brice's Cross Roads and in North Mississippi in 1864.*

Since then I have kept abreast of publications (books and monographs) with a focus on Forrest and his way of war. I have also led a number of tours, most of which are five days and six nights, highlighting Forrest and his command for Travel America, a history-oriented Texas company that guides people where they can walk in the footsteps of history. I have also spoken before a number of workshop symposia on Forrest, a soldier described by the late Shelby Foote as one of "our Civil War's" geniuses, the other being President Lincoln. In addition to keeping current with the academic treatment of this Civil War figure, I have authored featured articles in *Blue and Gray* on Forrest, titled "Brice's Cross Roads: Forrest Puts the Skeer on the Yankees" and "Charge Them Both Ways! The Battle of Parker's Cross Roads."

Most of the Forrest monographs that have appeared since John L. Jordan's definitive work in the *Tennessee Historical Quarterly*'s 1947 spring edition have dealt with the Fort Pillow Massacre. Eleven years later Albert Castel addressed this controversy in his 1958 monograph in *Civil War History* titled "The Fort Pillow Massacre: A Fresh Examination of the Evidence." The December 1982 issue of *Civil War History* revisited what would prove to be an increasingly acrimonious issue as late-twentieth-century historians waded in with their interpretations of the evidence. First to do so were editors John Cimprich and Robert C. Mainfort, with "Fort Pillow Revisited: New Evidence to an Old Controversy," *Civil War History,* published in December 1982. Zeroing in on Forrest again, the spring 1985 issue of the *Tennessee Historical Quarterly* carried a Cimprich and Mainfort monograph titled "Dr. Fitch's Report on the Fort Pillow Massacre," supporting Castel's massacre thesis. Historian Lonnie Mannes came to Forrest's support in the pages of the spring 1987 issue of the *Tennessee Historical Quarterly* with "The Fort Pillow Massacre: Fact or Fiction." Cimprich and Mainfort held their ground with "The Fort Pillow Massacre: A Statistical Note," published in the December issue of the *Journal of American History.* Against this backdrop of attack and counterattack, Brian Steel Wills authored in 1992 an outstanding Forrest biography titled *A Battle from the Start*, which was republished in 1998 as *The South's Greatest Cavalryman: Nathan Bedford Forrest.* No one will ever understand and better appreciate what made Forrest tick or document that his way of war and leadership is one that many soldiers aspire to but very few achieve.

Some five years ago I became aware of two historians who had accepted the challenge broached by Mannes fourteen years before: was Fort Pillow a Massacre? Eddy W. Davison and Daniel Foxx chose as their venue the *Confederate Veteran* and their article carried the title "A Journey to the Most Controversial Battlefield in America." Long familiar with the site and the literature concerning the "massacre" controversy, I read the Davison-Foxx article with more than passing interest.

By this time Brian Wills and I had shared time as talking heads on the Forrest segment of *Civil War Journal* and *Booknotes.* We had also co-hosted many History America tours to Fort Pillow. Brian and I were in agreement that if Forrest had intended a "massacre" there would have been few, if any, survivors. His practice heretofore was to lead. But uncharacteristically Forrest had absented himself from the field when his bugler sounded the charge. Today he would be held responsible for the actions of his men pending his return to the field, resuming command, and restoring order. It took some twenty minutes after the United States flag was cut down and Forrest had reached the strand fronting Coal Creek and called on his men to cease fire for order to be restored.

Within a year of reading the Davison-Foxx monograph, I traveled to Arizona for what has become my annual program before the Scottsdale Civil War Roundtable. There I was introduced to Davison, and I told him that I was impressed with his and Foxx's monograph. He informed me that he and Foxx were writing a book on Forrest and inquired whether I would like to see the manuscript on its completion. Recalling the superior quality of the *Confederate Veteran* article, I agreed.

Some two years ago I received the manuscript titled "Nathan Bedford Forrest: In Search of the Enigma." A careful reading satisfied me that the draft was of the same superior quality as "A Journey to the Most Controversial Battlefield in America." With the space given to battle actions, Davison and Foxx's book complements Wills' critically applauded Forrest biography. After returning this draft with my comments, I urged the coauthors to seek a publisher. When he replied, Davison asked, if they found an interested party, would I prepare the foreword. Yes, I answered. Now another Forrest biography will be out to enlighten us on the life and career of one of the Civil War's most remarkable and, at the same time, most controversial soldiers.

The word "enigma" in the title is inspired, as demonstrated in the various elements of his persona: his Scots-Irish frontier heritage, sometime participation in the slave trade, and role as a successful businessman, civic leader, and soldier who rose in rank from private to lieutenant general. A soldier far in advance of his time, who knew that war means fighting, and fighting means killing, he also recognized that getting the bulge on the foe was vital to success. The Fort Pillow massacre and his postwar leadership in the Ku Klux Klan raise hackles today as they did then and as such constitute part of the Forrest enigma.

Supplementing the book are a series of troop movements that document the marches, engagements, and battles of Forrest and his critter cavalry. Eddy Davison and Daniel Foxx are to be commended on their research and writing skills in seeking out the enigma that was Forrest. It, along with the Wills biography, is recommended as must reading for those who want to know Forrest and his way of war.

—EDWIN C. BEARSS
Historian Emeritus
National Park Service

# ACKNOWLEDGMENTS

A work of this magnitude could not have reached completion without the assistance of many talented and committed people, and the gratitude we feel for a special group of such people and for their interest and support must be expressed. In attempting to do so, we realize that we risk leaving someone out in this acknowledgment and apologize in advance if this is the case.

Edwin C. Bearss, historian emeritus of the United States Park Service, has been particularly kind in his support of this project, and we no doubt owe him an apology for imposing on him, as we sought a liberal outpouring of his wisdom and expertise on the Civil War era. Those who have made the Civil War their special field of study know the legend of Ed Bearss, a man who has a passion for detail and the human connection in our national story. He has walked the trails and battlefields, retold the stories in virtually countless publications, held audiences spellbound as he weaves the tapestry of America's cast of historical characters as if he knew them personally, and, as an energetic octogenarian himself, continues to lead battlefield tours in the United States and Europe. All of this is impressive beyond words, yet there is another side to Ed Bearss that endears him to us: he took the time out of his almost impossible schedule not only to encourage us in our work, but also to spend hours reading and correcting our manuscript and making invaluable suggestions, for which we are humbly grateful.

We also owe a special debt to a man we have never met: Robert Selph Henry. In our early reading, and later in our serious research, and finally in the writing of this book, it was Henry who inspired us through the pages of his works on Forrest, the result of a lifetime of labor and scholarship. Indeed all who have followed him in studying the life and times of Nathan Bedford Forrest truly navigate the same waters he charted in his own research and writing.

Our first research trip into Forrest country took us to Oxford, Mississippi, where we were guests of novelist Lawrence Wells and his gracious wife, Dean, niece of southern literary icon William Faulkner. Larry had written an intriguing novel in which Forrest played a major role, and he spun fabulous stories for us as together we walked the fields of Shiloh and Brice's Cross Roads. We will never forget the wonderful evening we spent in Larry and Dean's kitchen, swapping stories and laughing until way too late in the night. For these unforgettable memories and for their advice and support we thank them.

Closer to home we must thank Neil Humphreys for his relentless criticism of the manuscript, from syntax to format. The readability of this book is due, in no small part, to his willingness to allow us to strain his patience and our willingness to let him bruise our egos from time to time for the sake of the work.

The Scottsdale Civil War Roundtable was a friendly refuge during the long process of research, writing, and revision. Past president Dean Becraft shared our interest in this project and from the beginning remained enthusiastic about the outcome when discouragement often knocked on our door. We thank him for his encouragement and support. Also, thanks to the 2006 president of the Roundtable, Mack Stanley, for his help and support.

Many others assisted in more ways than we can possibly recount here. Dr. Fred Zook, Mike Kading, and Dr. Woody Woodward never lost faith and kept our spirits up when we wavered. Thanks also to Mary-Helen Foxx for the hand-holding, invaluable research, literary suggestions, and immeasurable kindnesses when we felt overwhelmed. Jordan Davis, Jack Windham, and D. F. Hillsheim selflessly shared their computer expertise with us and spent many hours teaching us those handy little computer tricks that made our work more manageable. We're not sure what they said about us to their computer-savvy buddies, but we thank them not only for their help, but for making us feel we were worth it.

Lindsey Reynolds, in editing this work for publication, made invaluable suggestions and called to our attention a number of inconsistencies that we were able to set right. Her hard work and dedication have added to the accuracy and readability of this book, and we thank her for all she has done.

Though unnamed, we are also grateful to the many librarians, archivists, webmasters, association and foundation members, park rangers, and helpful correspondents who graciously responded to our many requests for information and assistance. And thanks also to our students, who cheered us on and called many facts and sources to our attention, which we might otherwise have missed.

# Chapter One

# A HEART THAT KNEW NO FEAR

*—Joseph Garnet Wolseley*

## 1800-1861

The United States had nearly doubled its size with the purchase of the Louisiana Territory in 1803, a vast new domain of big skies and long horizons that seemed so limitless there did not seem to be Americans enough to fill it. But within a hundred years it was done. A hundred years of astonishing growth and expansion saw the United States of America roll forth aboard the *Manifest Destiny Express* all the way to the Pacific coast and beyond. Along the way America fought a second war with Great Britain, settled boundary disputes with three European nations, making all of the Pacific Northwest American, wrested enough land from Mexico to make five new states, and nearly destroyed itself by Civil War.

America was in its first blush of nationalism following the War of 1812 against Britain, the end of which ironically had been negotiated just days before Andrew Jackson led his countrymen to one of the most staggering military victories in their history at Chalmette, downstream from New Orleans, on January 8, 1815. The young country had finally won a measure of respect from Europe, and the next decade would be known as the "Golden Age of American Diplomacy" as the United States assumed its place among the family of nations. Newly elected congressmen came to Washington from the recently added western states of Tennessee and Kentucky, demanding recognition for their rapidly growing section and calling for the expenditure of federal funds for internal improvements to the infrastructure of the new nation.

South Carolina's John C. Calhoun, who had allied himself with the western Warhawks, calling for war against Great Britain after his election to Congress in 1810, became the champion of American nationalism when the war was over. His voice led the chorus calling for the federal government to underwrite great transportation projects like the National Road, bridges, and canals that would, in his words, "cement this nation together." As a committed nationalist he went on to serve as secretary of war to one president, vice president to two others, and even flirted seriously with the presidency himself. Yet, when he ended his public career on the floor of the United States Senate in 1850, he did so calling for an end to compromise between the states that had already resolved themselves into two separate sections, each with its own culture and set of political demands. He died the symbol of that sectionalism. The great "ism" he had expressed at the beginning, however, had been achieved, but that nation then stood at the edge of an abyss too horrible for many Americans to name: Civil War.

Perhaps the journey to that point had been too rapid, too filled with great, epochal change. The Erie Canal Project, completed in 1825, made New York City a port through which the world connected with the great waterways of North America. Very quickly other canals tied rivers and lakes and cities together over thousands of miles of water highways. Passengers and cargo could travel on the Erie Canal from New York City to Buffalo, thence to the Lake Erie shore of northern Ohio, where the Wabash and Ohio Canal could be taken southwest across the entire state of Indiana to connect with the Ohio River at Evansville. From there passengers could travel the Mississippi River to connections with a dozen other major rivers branching off east and west before finally reaching New Orleans and the Gulf of Mexico beyond.

Great steamboats plied the rivers carrying cargoes of cotton, trade goods, and food staples. Freight wagons fanned out from the river ports to share the bounty with villages and hamlets across the land. The introduction and expansion of railroad transportation added greatly to the mobility of America's citizens and to the movement of goods back and forth, as each stage of development added more layers of complexity to the national fabric. The combination of improved roadways, canals, river travel, and railroads continued to bind the country together, providing farmers, merchants, and manufacturers with unprecedented access to markets and the exchange of commodities and ideas.

However, as America was evolving and coming together in new ways, the old ways were driving her people and states apart. In the early nineteenth century, politicians struggled to contain the expansion of slavery, while growing numbers of moralists called for its extinction. The first attempt at maintaining a balance had come in 1820, with the Missouri Compromise, which offered that balance through Missouri's admission to the Union as a slave state against Maine's as a free state. The Missouri Compromise further attempted to draw a new line, permanently separating slave territories from free. America had become, in a sense, two nations: one coming and one going. The one coming was a nation bound to become the greatest in history. The nation going was one that could not find a way to put the baggage of the old world behind and rise to the promises made in its birth certificate, the Declaration of Independence. At the crossroads where those two nations met, Abraham Lincoln stood and declared, "A nation divided against itself cannot stand."[1]

On the frontier of these two nations, and forty years from the fulfillment of Lincoln's words, a future military genius was born on July 13, 1821, in the wilderness of middle Tennessee. His name was Nathan Bedford Forrest; Nathan after his grandfather and Bedford for the county of his birth. He would draw his first breath in a world where survival was a daily task and opportunity a birthright. The frontier in which he was bred and born was not only remote, but also more violent than the more cultured tidewater regions of the South. The daily struggle for survival produced self-reliant, independent men who carried with them, just barely tethered by a slim cord of civility, a rough sense of justice and a quick temper. The land of his birth was a beautiful but unforgiving place inhabited by wild beasts and often wilder men.

The Forrest genealogy was not uncommon in that place and time. The family boasted no kings in their family tree, not in recent generations, at least. Bedford, as he was more commonly called, came from ancestors who had emigrated from England and Scotland and, on this side of the ocean, had been mainly traders in horses, cattle, and mules. Shadrack Forrest, Bedford's great-grandfather, who had immigrated to North Carolina, eventually moved to middle Tennessee in 1806.[2]

Shadrack Forrest owned 471 acres near Caney Spring Creek in Bedford County, and he also owned at least one slave. His second son, Nathan, produced a son named William, the father of Nathan Bedford Forrest, whose name is immortalized in military history. Bedford arrived in the world with a twin sister, Fanny, and they were the first of eleven children born to Miriam Beck and William Forrest.

William was a blacksmith and a small-time farmer struggling to survive on the edge of civilization. The family lived in a primitive log cabin consisting of two small rooms and struggled with the frontier on its own uncompromising terms. Typhoid fever ravaged the Forrest family, taking two of Bedford's eight brothers and all three of his sisters. Bedford also contracted the disease but survived. It was an early demonstration of the tenacity for which he would become famous. These circumstances required that Bedford work like a man at a young age.[3]

When the Chickasaw nation was relocated to the new Indian Territory, opening up land for white settlement, William moved the family to Tippah County, just below the Tennessee line, in Mississippi. Soon after the family relocated, and for causes lost to history, William died, leaving Bedford the dubious charge of head of the family. He was fifteen years old.[4] If it is difficult to imagine Nathan Bedford Forrest as a teenager there is a reason; he never really was one except in age. After his mother gave birth to his last brother, Jeffery, two months after his father, William, had died, Bedford had the responsibility of feeding eight mouths and managing a hardscrabble farm.[5] With an eye for detail and a formidable will, he took control of the situation. Hard work, frugality, and good management had the family on a solid footing within three years. From age sixteen to nineteen Forrest was required to work the fields during the day and spend the nights helping his mother sew the family clothes and make footwear out of buckskins.

In his premature role as father figure and vigilant protector, as well as big brother, he became well acquainted with the realities of frontier life, which often included sudden death from a variety of causes. Bedford learned early on that a man must rely solely upon himself, and, if necessary, he must kill to protect his own. Growing up as he did in an arena ruled by law similar to that of the jungle, Bedford's primal instincts would have been magnified in his formative years of hard and fast experience.

That he learned his lessons well was demonstrated when he was sixteen years old. The Forrest family's neighbor allowed his bull to roam freely, and often the bull would get into the Forrests' field, breaking down the fence as it went. Once on Forrest land the bull would rampage through the recently planted field. Those crops were the currency of survival for the Forrest family, and whatever the neighbor might have thought about his bull's freedom to roam, such behavior just could not be tolerated on the Forrest side of the fence. Bedford went to the neighbor to complain and put the man on notice. If the bull got into the Forrests' crops again, Bedford warned him fairly, he would shoot the animal.

When the bull once again trespassed into his fields, young Bedford backed up his words. His neighbor heard the shot and surmised what had happened. He grabbed his gun and went running toward the Forrest homestead. Seeing Forrest standing over his dead bull, the man shouted out a threat and came forward, climbing over a fence to close the distance between him and the audacious young man. As the outraged neighbor was straddling the fence, Forrest, who had already reloaded, fired a shot that whizzed by the man's ear, sending him back over the fence in a hurried retreat to the sanctuary of his own farm.[6]

Both men learned a valuable lesson that day, but to young Forrest it would become a motto of sorts throughout his life: during violent confrontation with man or beast, immediate and fierce action is the key to success. Once he established a reputation as a dangerous individual, he could use that notoriety as a weapon or a shield. As a weapon it could make an enemy flinch or blink at the moment of truth. As a shield it could subvert his enemy's confidence. When he recognized the psychological edge this gave him during a fight, intimidation became an integral part of Forrest's arsenal.

Forrest always attributed his inclination to seize the initiative to an experience during his formative years. He was out riding through the woods one day when he and his horse were suddenly attacked by a pack of wild dogs. Startled, the horse reared and threw Forrest directly into the group of snarling animals. When he landed among the pack of dogs, an amazing thing happened. As it turned out, the dogs were as scared as Bedford was. They broke and ran. Bedford never forgot that lesson, either.[7]

With all the burdens upon the young man's shoulders, there was little time for formal education. He never attended school beyond the fourth grade, and Forrest's borderline illiteracy would be an irritation for years to come. His speech and expressions would always carry the mark of his limited education, and writing became a difficult thing for him. He once said, "I cannot think of a time when I looked upon a pen and did not think of a snake." Later, most of his battle reports and letters were dictated and then read back to him so he could decide if the words "had the right pitch."[8]

Ray Allen Billington, noted historian of the American frontier experience, found this attitude toward life common among the pioneers. "These people understandably had little time to devote to luxuries such as education when other concerns, not the least of which was food and shelter, occupied most of their time." Nevertheless, Billington observed, "they developed a practical mind that served them well in their circumstances."[9]

Bedford's single-mindedness was probably inherited, as was his size. By the time he was eighteen, Bedford had grown to a height of six feet, one inch, and he weighed 190 pounds. His mother, Miriam, was nearly six feet tall herself and a fighter in her own right. Once when returning from a neighbor's farm where she had just purchased a basket of baby chicks, a cougar attacked the horse she was riding as she was fording a creek. Miriam's horse bolted, and she was thrown into the water. Although the wild cat clawed her leg, she did not relinquish her hold on the basket of chicks and nearly drowned attempting to reach the creek bank.

When she made it back home and young Forrest saw his mother's condition, he went into action. The panther's accustomed role of hunter was about to be reversed, as the cat became the prey of vengeful young Bedford. Miriam tried to talk her son out of stalking the panther, but he would not be deterred. "I am going to kill that beast if it stays on the earth," he said. Taking his hunting dogs with him, Forrest began to track the cat through the woods until his dogs had the animal treed. By then it was growing dark, so Forrest took his time. He waited all night so that he would have a clear shot. One shot might be all he would have time for. When the sun began to rise, Forrest took careful aim, and with a single ball dropped the panther from the boughs of the tree. To verify his kill he cut off the panther's ears and brought them home as a trophy for his mother.[10]

Side-by-side, Miriam and Bedford worked and fought to hold the family together until all the younger Forrest brothers were sufficiently grown to allow Bedford time to venture away from home. From early on in his life the future Wizard of the Saddle had been drawn to a fight like a moth to the flame, and in February 1841, he heard the faint beckoning of a distant bugle. Since Texas had won its independence from Mexico in 1836, rumors had circulated of an impending war between the United States and her southern neighbor. In that late winter of 1841, the stories coming out of Texas suggested that Mexico was threatening the Texas town of Houston. In Holly Springs, Mississippi, that kind of threat was taken seriously, and Capt. Wallace Wilson raised a company of volunteers to support their Southern compatriots in Texas. Forrest joined this unit with high hopes, and perhaps a yen for adventure, but the short-lived campaign soon turned into a comedy of errors. By the time the company of volunteers arrived by steamer at New Orleans, poor management had left them busted and stranded.

Their resolve drained, most of the men found their own way home, but Forrest doggedly led a few of the others into Texas. Upon arriving in Houston, Forrest found that he was five years early. The war with Mexico would not begin until 1846. There he was, first with the most, so to speak, but with no one to fight. Soon he was broke and forced to take a job splitting fence rails at fifty cents per one hundred to earn enough money to go back home.[11]

When Forrest returned to the old homestead, he continued to run the farm until his mother was remarried to Joseph Luxton in 1843. With his yoke of responsibility thus lifted, Bedford left home for good.

By the early 1800s, slavery had become the natural order of things, especially in the southern United States. The two-hundred-year legacy of slavery was well entrenched in the Southern psyche. It was a way of life, the only way of life that several generations of Southerners had known. In reality, slavery predates the United States of America, for Europeans brought the seeds with them across the Atlantic and planted the American hybrid in the 1600s.

The South became more defensive concerning slavery as Forrest was growing into manhood. By the time he was ready to strike out on his own, the South, with respect to slavery, had become a closed society with a closed mind. After two centuries of white domination and control, the "peculiar institution" had become a determining factor in driving a wedge between the North and the South.

Though slavery was a deeply seated establishment, its foundation was beginning to crack. The year before Bedford's birth, the bloody slave revolt of San Domingo had occurred. By the time Forrest was ten years old, the South's own worst nightmare became reality with the slave uprising in Southampton County, Virginia. Nat Turner's rebellion in 1831 was only one of many such revolts since the turn of the century, but its ferocity rattled the complacency of whites across the South. Soon after, a series of new laws was enacted that sought to create more control over both slaves and free blacks. Among other things, these laws forbade them to gather in large groups without a white man's supervision and prohibited them from learning to read and write. This embattled attitude of oppression swept across Dixie like a prairie fire, matching the moral outrage of the abolitionists to the north. Like the times into which he'd been thrust, Forrest's future was written against a crimson sky.

*the Transformation / The Workup / The Change that came over him When angry*

## Law of the Gun

In the winter of 1844, Forrest moved to Hernando, Mississippi, a small hamlet of less than four hundred inhabitants, twenty-five miles south of Memphis. There he hoped to go into business with his uncle, Jonathan Forrest, who owned a store and had some trading interests in livestock and land. In the nine years he resided in Hernando he became a successful businessman, but not without hardships and setbacks. As it had been since he was a child, nothing seemed to come easy to Nathan Bedford Forrest. He would later lament, "My life was a battle from the start."[12]

Shortly after arriving in Hernando he found himself in the middle of a quarrel that had been brewing between Forrest's Uncle Jonathan and a local man named William Matlock. The quarrel, the seriousness of which even Jonathan might not have fully realized, had grown out of a misunderstanding with William Matlock concerning a "security" bond issue. The situation turned violent on March 10, when William Matlock came to town to settle the matter. He obviously intended that the outcome should be in his favor, for he brought with him his two brothers, James and Jefferson Matlock, and a man named Bean, the overseer on the Matlock plantation. Apparently, they were not looking to parley with the sixty-year-old Jonathan Forrest.

It is uncertain whether the men knew of Bedford's presence in town or his association with Jonathan, and they certainly had no idea how protective the young Forrest felt toward his family members. However, it seems clear that they had not counted on any intervention from Jonathan's hot-blooded nephew. Before the day ended the new Forrest in town would have a reputation as a dangerous man capable of violence and swift to take life.[13]

The details of how the gunfight broke out are sketchy. In one fashion or another, Bedford intervened as the three Matlocks and the overseer were looking to confront Jonathan. Very quickly, heated words were exchanged and guns were drawn. According to some versions, Jefferson Matlock fired upon Bedford, who immediately returned fire, hitting two of the Matlock brothers. Other accounts had Forrest drawing and firing first when one of the Matlocks raised a stick to strike his uncle. Approximately thirteen shots were fired during the gun battle.

When Bedford ran out of ammunition a bystander tossed him a bowie knife. Brandishing the weapon, he charged his last two opponents, Bean and James Matlock, who were reloading. The sight of young Forrest bearing down on them with the wicked-looking knife at the ready must have been an unsettling image. Both men quickly withdrew, to put a romantic twist to it, but in fact they were unceremoniously chased out of town by a fierce young fighter who understood the value of determined pursuit. The Matlocks were not the last to be routed so ignominiously. In a few years Forrest would regularly be doing the same thing to professionally trained soldiers.[14] In battles to come Forrest would call this tactic "getting the bulge" on the enemy and "keeping up the 'skeer.'"

The brief brawl had been costly. By the time the smoke cleared, Bedford had discovered he was suffering from a minor flesh wound, but his Uncle Jonathan was dead, shot by one of the Matlocks during the lethal exchange. Jefferson Matlock was soon under the surgeon's knife and had his right arm amputated. The other brother died later from complications of the chest wound he suffered at the hands of young Forrest.

The following account was published on March 21, 1845, in the *Memphis Eagle:*

> T.J. Matlock, Esq., and his brother and overseer on one side . . . had a dispute with another person when a young Mr. Forrest made some interfering remarks; sometime after which he and the Matlocks met, some exciting language rose and one of the Matlocks raise[d] a stick to strike Forrest, who immediately drew a pistol and set it to work as fast as possible, shooting both of the Matlocks through; the younger T.J., through the shoulder and upper part of the breast, and the other through the arm, which since has been amputated; Mr. T.J. Matlock lies in a doubtful state; young Forrest received a slight wound in his arm.[15]

The article goes on to mention that Jonathan Forrest was also killed. A few days later, Bedford was arrested and held briefly. He was released, however, upon the testimony of witnesses who said that Forrest had acted in self-defense.

In the months following the gunfight, Bedford took control of Jonathan's business, which entailed the sale of farm equipment, horses, cattle, and sheep. He also inherited his first six slaves.[16] However, his new interests and responsibilities did not come without strings attached. His uncle had been in considerable debt, which required Bedford to quickly find other sources of income. His immediate solution was to expand his business with a new brickyard in Hernando and to take one of his first business gambles by opening a new stage-coach line between Memphis and Hernando. Within a year he was well on his way to building his business into a thriving enterprise.

As an up-and-coming member of the business community, all he seemed to need to continue his rise was a wife at his side to cement a public picture of steadfastness and honesty. It is not known if Forrest was actively looking for a bride, but he certainly made the most of the opportunity when it came. His courtship of Mary Ann Montgomery during the summer of 1845 was not unlike his future military campaigns. He got there "first with the most" and put the "skeer" into the opposition.

While riding in the countryside Forrest came upon Mary Ann, her mother, and their slave team-driver with their carriage stuck in the muddy bottom of a shallow creek. As Forrest rode up he noticed two local men sitting on the creek bank. The two men were having a few laughs at the expense of the Montgomery women but were offering no assistance. Forrest charged up and quickly dismounted. Wading into the hip-deep water, Bedford carried Mary Ann and her mother to the creek bank. Then he gave the driver some terse instructions and went around to the rear of the carriage. Upon the given signal, Forrest lifted the carriage while the teamster whipped the horses, and the job was soon completed. Quick introductions were made and before the Montgomery ladies were sent on their way, permission was granted to call upon Mary Ann in the near future. Bedford then turned his attention to the two spectators who were still amused by the situation. Mounting his horse, he rode up to the two hecklers and blasted them for being big-mouthed no-accounts and advised the men not to cross his path again or he would whip hell out of both of them.

The next Sunday, Bedford rode to the Montgomery home to ask for Mary Ann's hand in marriage. Forrest wasted no time taking action when he saw something he wanted, and he wanted Mary Ann for his bride. When he arrived at the Montgomery place he spotted the same two men from the incident at the creek. They too had come to ask permission to court the popular Miss Montgomery. One of the suitors was said to be studying for the ministry. Competition and confrontation were issues from which Forrest never shrank. Still mounted, he approached the two men and this time made his threat more emphatic. They were to immediately withdraw or face the consequences. Undoubtedly, the two men had already heard of Bedford's prowess with gun and knife and decided not to push their luck. They, like Bedford, may have considered Mary Ann a prize, but not one worth dying for. That was the difference. Forrest was ready to fight to the death for what he wanted; most men were not.

Once he was invited inside the Montgomery home, Bedford asked for Mary Ann's hand in marriage, mentioning during his proposal his willingness to fight for what he wanted. This was only the second time Mary Ann had spoken with him, and she naturally hesitated. Forrest told her that he would always take care of her, while men such as those whom he had just chased off could never protect her, as their cowardice demonstrated. On his third visit she accepted the marriage proposal; however her uncle and guardian proved to be a harder sell.[17]

The Reverend Samuel Montgomery, of the Cumberland Presbyterian Church, was Mary Ann's uncle and foster father, and he initially declined when Forrest asked for Mary Ann's hand. Forrest's reputation had obviously reached the reverend's ear. He had no doubt that Forrest could protect Mary Ann; however, he had some other issues with his potential "son-in-law." The reverend told Forrest, "Why Bedford, I couldn't consent, you cuss and gamble, and Mary Ann is a Christian girl." Forrest's reply was smart and "theologically unassailable." "I know it," he said, "and that's just why I want her."[18]

Marriage to Mary Ann Montgomery was a step up the social ladder for Forrest. Her family was well respected and could trace their roots to Gen. Richard Montgomery, who had been killed at Quebec in 1775 during the failed attack in which Col. Benedict Arnold was wounded. They owned 350 acres near Cowan, Tennessee, in Franklin County. The Montgomerys were also slave owners who were associated with planters throughout the region. Such connections could be useful to a young businessman.[19]

Bedford and Mary Ann were married on Thursday evening, September 25, 1845, and wasted no time starting their own family. In 1846, William "Willie" Montgomery Forrest was born, and on June 26, 1847, Mary Ann gave birth to a baby girl, Frances "Fanny" Forrest, named for Bedford's twin sister who had died of typhoid fever when she was only five. Tragically, Fanny would die of dysentery in 1854 at the age of six.

Forrest continued to reside in Hernando for the next seven years as his business became more and more profitable. However, he soon discovered that the real money was in the slave trade. Unlike established planters, who in many cases came from old money and eschewed slave traders and their ilk, Forrest would indulge in the buying and selling of slaves to fund his move upward, into the planter class of wealthy landowners. To this end, in the spring of 1852, he moved his family to "establish himself in Memphis as a broker in real estate and a dealer in slaves."[20]

*Trader & planter*

## The Peculiar Institution

Slavery and slave trading was a monumental dilemma for Southern whites. White Southerners benefited from slavery, but they were simultaneously intimidated by it and ashamed of it, a part of the psychological burden attached to white supremacy. Memphis was the largest slave-trading boomtown in the South. By 1845, the population of Memphis had grown to twenty-three thousand and attracted commerce of all kinds from miles around. From his farm supply trade Forrest became familiar with planters and farmers throughout the region and these customers also demanded slaves. He was in the right place at the right time, and possessing a good instinct for business, he was poised to become one of the more prolific slave traders in Tennessee.[21]

The growing business took Forrest on many wide-ranging business trips, and it was during the time he was establishing himself as a major player in the Memphis slave trade that he narrowly escaped disaster in a spectacular steamboat accident on such a trip to Houston, Texas. Heading home in the spring of 1852 aboard the steamboat *Farmer*, from Houston to Galveston, Bedford retired early one night but was awakened by the rowdy festivities of the drunken gamblers on board. After having a few words with some of the men responsible for the noise, Forrest stepped out on the deck for some fresh air. Once outside, he noticed that the steamboat chimneys were red hot and ready to explode. He immediately hustled to the pilothouse to speak to the captain. There Forrest found the captain drunk and engaged in a race with another vessel. He advised the captain that the boat was on a suicide course, but the captain's drunkenness had overtaken him, and he would not relent. He told Forrest that he would win this race to Galveston "or blow the old tub and every soul on board to hell."[22]

Forrest no sooner had moved to the extreme rear of the boat when suddenly it happened. An explosion tore the *Farmer* nearly in half. Debris and bodies were thrown into the air and scattered across the water. Forrest was tossed around violently by the blast and received a bruised shoulder, but he was able to lend a hand in the rescue efforts. The accident occurred as the two competing steamboats were passing by Rockfish Bar, where luckily the water was shallow. The other boat came alongside to help with the rescue and transfer of the wounded to the medical facilities at Galveston. It was said to have been gruesome work, as more than one hundred of the passengers on board were mangled and burned. Sixty of these victims "were swept from mortal existence by this dreadful affair, including the wretched captain." Once again Forrest proved to be a survivor. Fate seemed to be saving him for something singular.[23]

Back in Memphis a few months later the following advertisement ran in the July 27, 1853, *Local Eagle Inquirer* on behalf of the Forrest & Maples slave trading company:

> Five hundred negroes wanted. We will pay the highest cash price for all good negroes offered. We invite all those having negroes for sale, to call on us, at our Mart, opposite Hill's old stand, on Adams Street. We will have a lot of Virginia negroes on hand, for sale, in the fall. Negroes bought and sold on commission.[24]

By 1853, Forrest also owned two extensive plantations in Coahoma County, Mississippi, each producing upward of one thousand bales of cotton. Forrest was not afraid of being accused of nepotism and eventually brought all of his brothers into the business. Jesse, William ("Bill"), Aaron, and Jeffrey helped expand his holdings into Tennessee and Alabama. Very soon Forrest was able to buy his way into the upper crust of the planter elite.[25] As Forrest's reputation as a prominent citizen was solidified, the slave trader stigma seemed to fade in the minds of the people in west and middle Tennessee. Soon he was taking part in the civic life of Memphis. Forrest's election as city alderman of Memphis three times running seemed to blur any memories of his origins. The rest of the nation, however, would not demonstrate the same selective amnesia or forgiving attitude. *Alderman*

Although Forrest had many similarities with the slave trader stereotype, he also had his differences. Whenever possible he attempted to keep slave families together. And he clothed and fed them well. The slaves whom Forrest bought and sold could expect better medical treatment than was the norm for the time. However, these considerations for his slave property were only good business practices. Dealing with a trader who had a reputation for being humane could ease the consciences of aristocratic plantation owners who viewed slave traders as low-class barbarians. They naturally preferred dealing with a reputable company.

When pondering the depth of Forrest's racism, one must consider the man's personality, which, with the slavery issue aside, was dominating and explosive. But one thing he was not was a hypocrite. He never attempted to hide his personal position behind the smoke screen of states' rights or tradition. He was a businessman who looked at a situation or obstacle with a cold, deliberate practicality. The South's economy depended on slaves and Forrest supplied the goods. No less guilty, the plantation owners who purchased slaves from Forrest and the consumers who purchased the cotton and tobacco produced by a slave-driven economy may have looked down their noses at slave traders, but their noses were breathing the same corrupt stench.

A recurring quote found in several Forrest biographies states: "Forrest was reported to have been kind to his slaves yet taught them to fear him exceedingly." The quote has been used to indicate that Forrest was a caring slave owner. It also has been interpreted as a blatant contradiction indicating that there was no possible way he could be kind and instill fear at the same time. His biographers, Jordan and Pryor, who wrote the first account of his life in 1868, had Forrest looking over their shoulders as they wrote the book. Their assessment of Forrest's relationship with his slaves is that "they were strongly attached to him."[26] Strongly attached or not, his slaves probably recognized that Forrest was a fair and responsible owner in comparison to many others. Undoubtedly they resented him, but perhaps they also realized that these might very well be the best circumstances they were likely to find themselves in while remaining in bondage.

Slavery was a "peculiar institution" in more ways than one, and the relationships between slaves and their masters often extended beyond the literal chains that bound them together. Was this the case with Forrest and his slaves? Perhaps. If anyone might have been able to pull off this contradictory style of supervision, it was Forrest. The soldiers and officers who fought with him in the war could easily attest to the loyalty and kindness he felt for the men he led. But, to a man, they all knew he could be terrifying and unforgiving when he lost control of his mercurial temper.

Between the year of Forrest's birth and the eve of the Civil War, the number of slaves in the American South nearly tripled, from 1.5 million in 1820 to 4 million in 1860. This increase mirrored the expansion of commerce and wealth in the South. Forrest rode this wave of unparalleled growth in the Southern economy, and by anyone's standard he had become an astounding success. In fact, by 1860, Nathan Bedford Forrest had become a millionaire. Having experienced and survived the poverty of his childhood, he was driven to ensure that his family would have a secure and comfortable life. On the eve of the Civil War in 1861, it looked as though he had accomplished that task.

# Chapter Two

*Private to General* (handwritten)

# YOUNGBLOODS OF THE SOUTH

—*William Tecumseh Sherman*

## June 1861-January 1862

When the Democratic convention met in Charleston, South Carolina, in 1860, the Southern delegates were determined that Sen. Stephen A. Douglas of Illinois would be denied the party's presidential nomination. Their solidarity led to both sections of the country nominating a candidate; thus, Douglas became the candidate of the Northern Democrats, and the Southern delegates nominated John C. Breckinridge. Making the situation even more precarious for the Democrats, John Bell of Tennessee was nominated by a third party, the Constitutional Unionists. By dividing their party the Democrats virtually assured that Republican Abraham Lincoln would be the next president of the United States, a prospect that South Carolina would not accept. If a Republican were to be elected, South Carolinians warned late in the race, their state would leave the Union.

War talk reverberated through the South even before the election of 1860 split the Democratic Party along sectional lines and threatened to confirm that split by means of secession. Memphis had become a center of military activity in Tennessee as recruiters swept the countryside looking for volunteers to fill the militia ranks. Tennessee did not become known as "The Volunteer State" by accident. Tennesseans turned out in great numbers to join up, just as they had during the war with Mexico.

Following the election and throughout the winter of 1860-61, appeals for conciliation were intended to pressure the North to reach yet another compromise that would prolong the agony of a nation growing apart. Such attempts at concession were in vain. The embers of mistrust and sectional aggrandizement had been smoldering too long to hold back the coming firestorm. After unanimously adopting an ordinance of secession on December 20, 1860, the South Carolina Convention issued a Declaration of the Causes of Secession. This document presented arguments that proved, to South Carolina's satisfaction, the sovereignty of the states and offered evidence that the Northern states had violated the federal "compact," i.e., the Constitution. By the end of the year six other states had withdrawn from the Union: Georgia, Florida, Alabama, Mississippi, Louisiana, and Texas.

Across the nation war seemed imminent, when on April 12, at 4:30 in the morning, the thunder of big guns rocked Charleston Harbor. The opening barrage that lit up the predawn sky awoke Mary Chesnut, who made a note that day in her diary, which she would continue to write throughout the war. Her very first record- ed observation of the war reflected on the shelling of Fort Sumter: "April 12 . . . The heavy booming of a cannon—I sprang out of bed, and on my knees, prostrate, I prayed as I have never prayed before."[1]

On April 15, George Templeton Strong of New York wrote, "Events multiply. The President is out with a proclamation calling for 75,000 volunteers. . . . It is said 200,000 more will be called with- in a few days." Subsequent to Lincoln's call to arms in the North, Virginia, Arkansas, North Carolina, and Tennessee followed South Carolina out of the Union and into open rebellion.

Before Lincoln's proclamation, Tennesseans had voted against secession, but enough dissension existed in Tennessee that in June a second referendum on the secession issue was held, and this time the vote was two to one to leave the Union. "Woe to those who began this war if they were not in bitter earnest," wrote Mary Chesnut. And although Nathan Bedford Forrest had remained silent throughout the preliminaries, once the war started he would wage it in the most bitter and earnest manner that could possibly be imagined.[2]

Though not even Forrest could have foretold it, a new chapter in the history of mounted warfare was about to be written when, on June 14, 1861, he walked into the headquarters of Capt. Josiah White's Tennessee Mounted Rifles. Bedford enlisted as a private, along with his youngest brother, Jeffrey, and his fifteen-year-old son, Willie. As raw recruits, the new privates were ordered to Camp Yellow Jacket, a training camp sixty-five miles north of Memphis, which the soldiers there had appropriately named for a wasp infestation that plagued the area. The soldiers gathering there to form Captain White's command would eventually evolve into the famous Seventh Tennessee Cavalry, which would fight until the end of the war under Forrest's leadership.

John Milton Hubbard, a private in Hardeman's Avengers, which would later be attached to the Seventh Tennessee Cavalry, was stationed at Camp Yellow Jacket in those early days and remembered meeting Forrest there:

> Two cavalry companies from Memphis were in camp near us—Logwood's and White's. In riding near these one day I met a soldier speeding a magnificent black horse along a country road as if for exercise, and the pleasure of being astride of so fine an animal. On closer inspection I saw it was Bedford Forrest, only a private like myself, whom I had known ten years before down in Mississippi. I had occasion afterward to see a good deal of him.[3]

Hubbard's last sentence is a remarkable understatement, for he would find himself under Forrest's command at numerous engagements, including Union City, Fort Pillow, Brice's Cross Roads, Harrisburg or Tupelo, the Memphis raid, Athens, Nashville, and finally, Selma. Private Hubbard's observations were published in Memphis in 1909 and provide valuable insight into the ways and the minds of the men who rode with Forrest.

Whether it was Bedford's status before the war or a visionary recognition of his potential that decreed it, Private Forrest was not destined to remain at that lowliest of ranks for long. A private in June, he became a lieutenant colonel the next month, and on July 10, Forrest was called back to Memphis to meet with Gov. Isham G. Harris, who commissioned him to raise a battalion of mounted rangers under the authority of the Confederate states.

Though Forrest embarked upon his recruitment drive under the authority of the Confederate States, it was with his own money that he would accomplish the task. The young Confederacy had shaky and uncertain sources of supplying the needs of its commanders, so even before his first combat action, Forrest learned to depend on his own resources to get the job done. He would find himself in virtually the same situation time and again until he finally surrendered in May 1865, one of the last significant Confederate commanders to do so. That tenacious independence, though necessary to provide the needs of his soldiers from time to time, often alienated him from his fellow commanders as the war progressed.

Forrest began his recruiting drive with vigor as shown by a call for volunteers, which appeared on July 24 in the *Memphis Appeal:*

Having been authorized by Gov. Harris to raise a battalion of mounted rangers for the war I desire to enlist five hundred able bodied men, mounted and equipped with such arms as they can produce (shot-guns and pistols preferable), suitable to service. Those wishing to enlist are requested to report to the Gayoso Hotel, where quarters will be assigned until such time as the battalion is raised.

Nathan Bedford Forrest

His preference for weapons used most effectively in close quarters combat should have warned recruits of their new commander's partiality for war waged at an intimate and personal level.

Three days before Forrest's recruiting advertisement ran in the Memphis newspaper, the first great battle of the war was fought a mere twenty-five miles from Washington, at Manassas Junction, Virginia, on July 21, where the rebels stunned the Union army and drove it ignominiously from the field. Neither side yet realized the enormity of the struggle to come, nor that nearly four years of carnage lay ahead. In the East, skirmishing and maneuvering would occupy both armies for the rest of the year.

But, as yet, in the more thinly settled wilderness that stretched between the Appalachians and the Mississippi, the two armies were kept tenuously apart by the proclaimed neutrality of Kentucky. Both sides aggressively courted Kentucky's allegiance, as well as its young men. Forrest was more interested in Kentucky's potential to provide arms and other supplies. It was obvious to him that the demand placed on the new government far outweighed what it could produce, so he set out to supply himself. He first sent agents into middle and west Tennessee, northern Mississippi, and Alabama to recruit for his new command. Then he started for Louisville on horseback in hopes of establishing an underground supply line that could tap into Northern-produced weapons and equipment.[4] Cautiously avoiding large towns like Frankfort, Lexington, and Louisville, where Union sentiment was keen, he conducted his clandestine activities at the homes of Southern sympathizers in outlying areas of the Ohio River country. Materials and weapons were purchased and transported south on back roads, usually under cover of darkness. Some of the equipment was stored prior to shipment in a livery in the suburbs of Louisville.

Years after the war C. W. Button remembered details of this activity:

At Louisville I was introduced to Forrest by my father. He had bought a large number of navy pistols, saddles, and other cavalry equipments, which had been stored in a livery stable in Louisville. Six young volunteers, none of whom were over eighteen years of age, met him by appointment at the stable, and late in the night carried the articles in coffee sacks through the door into a back alley. Here wagons were ready to receive them, and when all were loaded we started out on the Elizabethtown turnpike.[5]

The rendezvous of new recruits and equipment took place in Meade County near Brandenburg. The first company mustered into Forrest's cavalry was Capt. Frank Overton's Boone Rangers, some ninety strong. A large crowd of the Rangers' family members gathered to see them off to war as they left Brandenburg for Nolin's Station, the rendezvous point on the Louisville & Nashville Railroad. As the soldiers mingled with their well-wishers, Forrest was informed that two companies of Union soldiers known as "home guards" were stationed at Munfordville, a little farther down the rail line, and that they were prepared to dispute his passage. Bedford quickly formed a plan that demonstrated a tactical foresight indicative of his cunning and strategic mindset through the rest of the war.

To inflate his numbers, he requested that all the recruits as well as their families and friends fall into formation together. He then extended their ranks, broke out a Confederate banner, and marched them down the road past a southbound passenger train waiting to leave for Munfordville. Aboard the train were many Union sympathizers who could be expected to relay to the waiting Union home guards what they had witnessed. As the martial parade marched past the train, observers hopefully would not distinguish between recruits and cheerful temporary "volunteers" and would see only an inflated number of troops under Forrest's new command. This, Forrest hoped, would be reported in Munfordville as the train passed through, thus saving the Confederates a fight.[6]

The maneuver was just a foretaste of Forrest's imagination and his intuitive sense of the art of psychological warfare. He would masterfully employ similar strategies of misinformation and deception to confuse and alarm his adversaries throughout the war.

All the men, equipment, and arms that had been gathered in Kentucky arrived in the Memphis area during the first week of August, along with a company of recruits organized by Capt. Charles

May. Captain May named his outfit the Forrest Rangers and joined forces with the other volunteers at their new camp, situated on the old fair grounds near Memphis.

On August 29, Forrest ran another recruiting announcement in the *Memphis Appeal:*

### FOR ACTIVE SERVICE!

> A few more companies are needed to complete a mounted regiment now being formed here for active service. There is also room for a few more recruits in a company of Independent Rangers not to be attached to any regiment unless on the option of the members. . . . To those desiring to engage in the cavalry service an excellent opportunity is offered. Now, freemen, rally to the defense of your liberties, your homes, your firesides.
>
> N.B. Forrest

The *Appeal* added the following editorial comment:

> To Arms! We invite attention to the call of Col. N.B. Forrest in today's paper. There are still hundreds of young men in the country anxious to engage in the military service. Those whose fancy inclines them to the cavalry service will find no better opportunity to enlist under a bold, capable and efficient commander. Now is the time.

During these late summer months of 1861, Capt. D. C. Kelley, a young Methodist preacher out of Huntsville, Alabama, also joined Forrest. For the rest of the war, Captain Kelley, later promoted to major, would perform the ministerial duties for Forrest's command, often holding his services on the field of battle. Kelley later recalled a service he held soon after meeting Forrest. He described the meeting as taking place in a clearing in the woods near the fair grounds and noted that Bedford's mother was in attendance, sitting "side by side with her son at the service in the woods."[7] Later, while visiting the new lieutenant colonel in his tent, Kelley noticed a well-worn Bible bearing the name of Forrest's mother. She had left it for her son. After the war Forrest credited his mother's testament with bringing him home alive.

## Sacramento: Forrest's First Fight

Realizing that Kentucky's staying in the Union was dependent upon a number of issues, including whether the Federal government could win the loyalty of the many Kentuckians who harbored a natural empathy for the Southern cause, Lincoln spoke of "conditional Unionism" in that state. Lincoln's "conditional Unionism" was precarious at best. So much so that he temporarily ignored the steady stream of weapons and supplies that flowed southward through his native state. Despite the Confederate Congress's acceptance of Kentucky into the Confederacy, the Bluegrass State would remain loyal to the Union, thus rewarding Lincoln's patience. Yet, the people of Kentucky continued to display divided loyalties as both armies maneuvered and drilled their recruits within the state, a threat to the temporary truce both sides warily recognized.

On September 3, Maj. Gen. Leonidas Polk, who was also an Episcopal bishop, moved to seize the village of Columbus on the terminus of the Mobile & Ohio Railroad, in the northwest corner of Kentucky. The move on Columbus caused much turmoil in the Confederate command, prompting protests to Richmond from Brig. Gen. Simon Bolivar Buckner, Governor Harris, and Leroy P. Walker, Confederate secretary of war. But Jefferson Davis himself had ordered the move the day before, stating simply that it was "justified by necessity."[8]

Countering the Confederate initiative on September 5, just before midnight, Brig. Gen. Ulysses S. Grant pulled out from Cairo by boat and steamed fifty miles up the Ohio River with approximately two thousand men and sixteen cannon. Arriving at the mouth of the Tennessee River on the morning of the sixth, he occupied the town of Paducah, Kentucky.

Gen. Albert Sidney Johnston had been appointed on September 10 as the new commander for the Confederate forces in the west and quickly moved to establish a garrison of twenty thousand men to fortify the position at Columbus, with heavy guns to control the river. But his shortage of manpower and equipment weakened the rest of his long, thin defensive line, which extended eastward through Kentucky to Bowling Green and on to Cumberland Gap in the east.[9]

With the powerful Confederate position at Columbus blocking a thrust down the Mississippi, the Federal invasion was sure to focus on the Tennessee and Cumberland Rivers. These two rivers flow across Tennessee then almost converge and run parallel to one another for a hundred miles before pouring across the western tip of Kentucky and emptying into the Ohio River just above Paducah. Realizing the strategic value of the rivers, the Confederates had constructed two forts just inside Tennessee to guard against a river-borne invasion from the north. Fort Henry was hastily constructed of timber and earth on the Tennessee. A mere twelve miles to the east, Fort Donelson on the Cumberland was a work in progress. Should these two forts fall to Union forces, Nashville would lie open up the Cumberland, while the Tennessee could lead the Union into northeastern Mississippi and northern Alabama.

In October 1861, Forrest's battalion left Memphis with orders to report to Col. Adolphus Heiman, who was at that time engaged in constructing the defenses at Fort Henry on the Tennessee River and Fort Donelson near Dover, Tennessee, on the Cumberland. Experiencing difficulty in handling the defense of Fort Henry, Colonel Heiman had requested a "company of cavalry."[10] He got more than he asked for with the arrival of Forrest's advanced squadron, commanded by Major Kelley, in the last week of October.

Forrest's first cavalry command consisted of eight companies when he took the field. In addition to the company of Tennesseans, three were from northern Alabama, one from southern Alabama, two from Kentucky, and one from Texas, some 650 soldiers on horseback. This total did not include forty of Forrest's slaves, who drove the wagon train. The chain of command for Forrest's new cavalry was as follows: Capt. D. C. Kelley, later promoted to major, Lt. C. A. Schuyler, appointed as adjutant, Sgt. Maj. J. P. Strange, and S. M. Wick, the surgeon.

Although Forrest had taken pains to secure military weapons for his command, almost half of them were armed with double-barreled shotguns. To be effective those men armed with shotguns needed to be as close as twenty yards to their targets. So much the better as far as Forrest was concerned.

In Forrest's first recorded dispatch in the *Official Records of the War of the Rebellion,* his impatience to engage the enemy is easily recognized:

> I have been operating with my command of eight companies of cavalry near Fort Henry and Fort Donelson, by order of General Polk. Finding the country impracticable for cavalry, and with scant subsistence, I moved a part of my command to Canton, north side of Cumberland River, leaving two companies at Dover. I am of no use south of Cumberland; desire my command united and can do vast service with General [Lloyd] Tilghman.[11]

On November 20, Forrest received information that the Union timber-clad gunboat *Conestoga* had steamed up the Cumberland to seize the Confederate stores at Canton. After an eight-hour forced march in the dark, Forrest reached the Cumberland and set an ambush above and below the landing at Canton. Forrest would develop a dislike and contempt for gunboats, especially after the fall of Fort Donelson the next February. Lt. Jeremiah C. Sullivan and a small detachment of artillerists carrying a four-pounder gun had also joined his command. At daylight they laid in wait as the *Conestoga* approached their position. In an attempt to lure the Union vessel closer, Forrest had left a few men visible, but the Yankee pilot was too savvy to fall for the bait and anchored the *Conestoga* near the opposite bank.

The action opened with the Confederate four-pounder firing a few rounds that bounced harmlessly off the gunboat. When the *Conestoga* returned fire on Sullivan's position, he and the small brass gun were driven back in short order, but Forrest's other troops, hidden behind logs and trees, poured accurate small arms fire into the open gun holes. The battle continued for two or three hours, until the gunboat was forced to close its gun ports and steam off down the Cumberland amid the cheers and shouts of Forrest's men.

The new regiment had marched all night and fought all day, only to ride another twenty-five miles the night of the twentieth, arriving at Hopkinsville on the morning of the twenty-first. This first engagement was a harbinger of gunboat battles to come and also a taste of what his men could expect concerning the speed and mobility that Forrest would demand of them during his campaigns.

They remained in Hopkinsville for the rest of the month and were reinforced by two companies from Huntsville, Alabama, led by Capt. D. C. Davis and another, under Capt. Charles McDonald, known as the McDonald Dragoons. With these additions, Forrest now commanded ten companies, approximately eight hundred men.[12]

On November 24, Forrest was ordered to make a reconnaissance toward the Ohio River. Taking three hundred men he marched to Greenville and captured some Union arms and supplies that had been warehoused there. Moving in the direction of Marion, in Crittenden County, Forrest was informed that a prominent Southern citizen accused of being a Confederate sympathizer had been arrested and was being held hostage by Union extremists.[13] Forrest led the detachment tasked with confirming this situation. As was his style, Forrest was wearing a white duster, his gun belts worn on the outside. From a distance he did not appear to be a particularly important figure. In contrast, Dr. Wick, the battalion surgeon, rode by Forrest's side, wearing a magnificent butternut uniform and a plume in his hat. As they approached the house of Jonathan Bells, where the prisoner was being held, the crack of a rifle rang out. Dr. Wick was blown out of the saddle by a bullet through the heart. The sniper who fired the fatal shot escaped from the cabin and into the woods believing that he had killed the rebel commanding officer rather than his surgeon. When Forrest's men searched the area, they discovered that the hostage had already been relocated when the Confederate cavalry appeared in the area.

It is safe to say that had Dr. Wick not been so conspicuously clad that day, the sniper's choice of targets might easily have been different, and the war for Forrest would have come to an end. "It would not be far from the truth," wrote historian and Forrest biographer John Wyeth, "to say that [had Forrest been killed instead] it would have been to the cause of the Union the most valuable piece of metal fired from the Northern side."[14]

For the next few weeks Forrest's men went into winter camp at Hopkinsville, where his son, Willie, and his wife, Mary Ann, joined him. The family spent Christmas together bivouacked in the field. On December 28, he was back in the saddle to challenge a reported enemy advance across Green River.[15] They moved out from the small hamlet of Greenville, following along the south bank of Green River, headed west. Preceding the main body of troops, Forrest sent out scouts and an advance guard led by Captains C. E. Meriwether and W. S. McLemore.

The main body was within eight miles of Greenville when the scouts returned at a gallop, reporting that they had observed the "enemy 500 strong" south of Sacramento. As soon as he heard the news, Forrest decided to overtake them and attack. He immediately ordered his men to "move up."[16] While Forrest's column trotted across the Kentucky countryside, the pursuit seemed to turn into a race as the Confederate horsemen were gradually overcome with battle fever. Galloping at the lead of his quickly deteriorating formation, the commander was not exempt from the infectious enthusiasm. The weather was cold and as they neared Sacramento, a drizzling rain began to fall. To exacerbate the situation, a volunteer in the form of a handsome Kentucky belle suddenly joined the column. Molly Morehead came charging up alongside Forrest and as the two rode side by side, she cheered him and his men forward. Later, Forrest would say that she had so impressed him that "her untied tresses, floating in the breeze, infused into my arm and kindled knightly chivalry in my heart."[17] Young Miss Molly had the best of intentions, but Forrest and his men hardly needed any extra motivation as they rode pell-mell in search of the enemy.

A mile south of Sacramento, the Confederates came upon the rear elements of the Union column. The Yankees bringing up the rear had stopped to observe the approach of the rebels. They seemed unsure as to whether the approaching horsemen were friends or foes. Snatching a rifle away from the man nearest to him, Forrest solved their dilemma by firing the opening shot of the battle. In so doing, he sent the Union stragglers and rear guard in quick pursuit of their main column, which was at that moment deploying into a line of battle across the road among a heavy grove of trees.

Forrest gave the order to advance but hold fire until at close range. At two hundred yards the Confederates came under fire, and Forrest realized that the hard gallop had strung out his command and that he did not have sufficient support at hand to continue the assault on horseback. Next he executed a maneuver that he would repeat successfully on numerous battlefields. He dismounted a portion of his command and threw them forward to keep the enemy busy. When Lt. Col. James W. Starnes and Maj. D. C. Kelley arrived with their companies, Forrest put a tactic into motion that would come to bear his signature. Here at Sacramento, as on dozens of battlefields to come, Forrest led the cavalry assault personally. It was a microcosm of his future engagements. *Looking for the bulge or hole*

He ordered Starnes, with thirty men, to the left flank and Kelley, with another sixty riders, to the right. Forrest then drew his saber with his left hand and focused his attention on the enemy line like a hunting bird intent upon its prey. He was looking for the first hint of confusion or weakness in the Union position. All the while his dismounted troopers, concealed behind brush and fences, continued to press from the front. It was not long before the moment arrived. Private Grey remembered Forrest saying to him, "Blow the charge, Isham," and then shouting for his main column to "Charge, Charge!" With that harsh and brassy roar, "Into the fight he went, a giant of a man standing high in the stirrups, his skin dark with the congestion of blood beneath the surface, his eyes ablaze."[18]

Over the past couple of days the ground had begun to thaw, and with the rain the turf was saturated. The charging Confederates were soon covered from head to foot in mud thrown from the hooves of their mounts. On the receiving end of a classic double envelopment, the Union force broke and ran, leaving a handful of brave and determined men as a rear guard. As Forrest charged from the front, Starnes got there first, slamming into the Union left, and began a desperate hand-to-hand fight. In short order Starnes had emptied both of his Navy Colts and in wild frustration hurled his empty pistols at his adversaries. Moments later, Major Kelley struck and drove in their right flank. Simultaneously, Forrest, at the point of the frontal charge, engaged the center of the Northern line, crashing into them at breakneck speed. The Union detachment didn't know what had hit them as Forrest's men swept in from three sides.[19]

Pvt. Adam "Stovepipe" Johnson, one of Forrest's scouts, remembered the scene:

> Led by this impetuous chieftain, we swooped down upon our foes with such terrific yells and sturdy blows as might have them believe a whole army was on them; and turning tail, they fled in the wildest terror, a panic stricken mass of men and horses . . . cutting and shooting right and left, and Forrest himself in his fury ignoring all command and always in the thickest of the melee.[20]

Quite a contest it was. Pvt. James H. Hammer wrote,

> The Colonel was about 50 yards ahead of us fighting for his life. I believe there were at least 50 shots fired at him in five minutes. One shot took effect in his horse's head, but did not kill him. He killed nine of the enemy.[21]

Forrest's transformation and ardor for battle surprised even his own men. Major Kelley wrote,

> It was the first time I had seen the Colonel in the face of the enemy, and when he rode up to me in the thick of the action, I could scarcely believe him to be the man I had known for months. His face flushed till it bore a striking resemblance to a painted Indian warrior's, and his eyes, usually mild in their expression, were blazing with the intense glare of a panther springing upon his prey. In fact, he looked as little like the Forrest of our mess table as the storm of December resembles the quiet of June.[22]

Driving through the Federals, Forrest was met by a large and muscular Union cavalryman whom Private Johnson described as a "blacksmith." While fighting furiously with saber and pistol, Forrest was nearly cut down from the rear. An unnoticed Union cavalryman was about to run Forrest through the back when he was killed by a timely shot from Johnson. A split second after this assailant's death, Forrest unsaddled his opponent with a vicious stroke from his sword.[23]

The ground was churned into a quagmire, and many riders and their mounts became stuck in the deep mud as the bloody brawl raged. Forrest found himself engaged with three Union officers at practically the same moment. One he wounded with his revolver as the other two continued the attack with sabers slashing, which forced Forrest to bend and twist in the saddle to elude the deadly blows. The horsemanship developed from a life in the saddle allowed Forrest to outmaneuver his opponents. His saber burned the air as he blocked, parried, and countered. Gaining the angle on them, he savagely thrust his saber into Lieutenant Colonel Burges and withdrew the blade. Before Capt. Albert G. Bacon could react, he also was run through. Using his horse as a weapon, the Confederate commander charged Capt. A. N. Davis and rammed his mount into Davis's horse, knocking both rider and mount to the ground, dislocating the Union captain's shoulder. A split second after bulldozing Captain Davis, Forrest collided with two riderless horses and crashed to the ground amid a heap of terrified, injured, and kicking animals. Forrest's report, written on December 28, 1861, said that "at this point Captain Bacon, and but a little before Lieutenant Colonel Burges, were run through with saber thrusts, and, Captain Davis thrown from his horse and surrendered as my prisoner, his shoulder being dislocated by the fall."

Miraculously, he emerged from the carnage only bruised and stunned but immediately began bellowing for someone to bring him a new mount. His call was answered by Adam Johnson, who gave the colonel his horse. Forrest resumed the pursuit, which was called off after a few miles due to the exhaustion of the men and their mounts. Pvt. Adam Johnson would become a brigadier general by 1864, commanding the Department of Western Kentucky. Tragically, both of his eyes were shot out in August 1864 at an engagement at Grubb's Cross Roads in Kentucky.[24]

Major Kelley, who had been apprehensive about Forrest's behavior as the fight began, was left with a vivid and new impression after the fight ended.

> So fierce did his passion become that he was almost equally dangerous to friend or foe, and, as it seemed to some of us, he was too wildly excitable to be capable of judicious command. Later we became aware that excitement neither paralyzed nor mislead his magnificent military genius.[25]

Kelley may have been the first to use the term "genius" in describing Forrest's performance in the heat of battle. There was something about Forrest on the battlefield at Sacramento that was recognized at a gut level by all who witnessed it. Many who fought with him throughout the war would say his very countenance changed under the ordeal of battle. The effect electrified his men and impressed his superiors.

The Confederates lost Capt. C. E. Meriwether, shot twice in the head while riding beside Forrest, and Pvt. William H. Terry died when he was pierced through the heart by a Union saber. Three others were wounded. Union brigadier general T. L. Crittenden reported two officers lost (presumably Bacon and Davis), eight soldiers killed, and thirteen captured. Forrest listed the Union casualties at closer to a hundred, including thirty-five prisoners. Forrest's men knew that Crittenden's numbers were understated; they believed from the rumors of the battle circulating through the command that Forrest had personally killed more men than the total losses declared by General Crittenden.

Forrest filed his report on December 30, stating that he had attacked the enemy on the twenty-sixth near Sacramento with just over three hundred men of his own:

> As only the advance guard of my command was seen, we came up to their main column. We halted, and seeing that they outnumbered me I fell back a short distance. [Forrest apparently didn't seem to think that his commanding officers needed to know exactly how he had arrived so far ahead of the rest of his column.] The enemy at once attempted to flank our left and began to move towards us, and apparently greatly animated, supposing we were retreating. They had moved over one hundred yards and seemed to be forming for a charge, and began to move towards us, when the remainder of my men coming on the ground, I dismounted a number of them with long-range guns, directed a flank movement upon the part of Major Kelley and [Lieutenant] Colonel Starnes upon the right and left, and with the balance of my command, mounted, we charged into their ranks. The enemy broke in utter confusion, and in spite of the efforts of a few officers commenced a disorderly flight at fast speed, in which the officers soon joined. We followed them closely, getting in an occasional shot, until we reached the village, when we began to catch up with them, and there commenced a promiscuous saber slaughter in their rear, which was continued for two miles beyond the village, leaving their wounded strewn along the route.[26]

After the battle Pvt. J. C. Blanton wrote:

> This battle had a splendid effect in our regiment causing men
> and officers to confide in and respect each other. We were con-
> vinced that evening that Forrest and Kelley were wise selections
> for our leaders. And in all the battles that followed in which
> these two men were actors, they well sustained the reputation
> made on the field of Sacramento.

Farther up the chain of command, Brig. Gen. Charles Clark took
notice of Forrest. After reading Forrest's battle report, Clark added
a postscript:

> For the skill, energy, and courage displayed by Colonel Forrest
> he is entitled the highest praise, and I take great pleasure in
> calling the attention of the general commanding and of the
> Government to his service. I am assured by officers and men
> that throughout the entire engagement he was conspicuous for
> the most daring courage; always in advance of his command.
> He was at one time engaged in a hand-to-hand conflict with 4
> of the enemy, 3 of whom he killed, dismounting and making a
> prisoner of the fourth.[27]

The rest of January was spent foraging and scouting. On February
7, Forrest received orders to report to the commanding officer at
Fort Donelson.

## Fort Donelson, February 1862

Two Union armies had begun to move on Forts Henry and
Donelson as the new year began. Maj. Gen. Henry Halleck, whose
nom de guerre was Old Brains, was stationed at St. Louis, from
whence he commanded the western part of Kentucky. At Louisville
was Brig. Gen. Don Carlos Buell, commanding Union troops in the
state east of the lower Cumberland River. The two generals had been
corresponding since November concerning the strategic value of the
two Confederate forts, and preparations had proceeded since that
time. While the Union leaders corresponded and planned, the
Confederates were busy fortifying in preparation for a coming attack.
When heavy rains began early in January 1862, the rising rivers threatened the new fortifications and encouraged the Federal commanders.

The first action came at the eastern end of Gen. Albert Johnston's
line when Confederate major general George B. Crittenden crossed

the Cumberland and advanced into southeast Kentucky. Buell's left, commanded by Brig. Gen. George H. Thomas, attacked and mauled Crittenden's force at Mill Springs, Kentucky. This battle unhinged Johnston's defensive line in the east. Upon the heels of this victory, Halleck, who had a reputation for being tardy in decision making, ordered Grant to move on Fort Henry at the end of January.[28]

Grant took fifteen thousand men and a squadron of Flag Officer Andrew Foote's gunboats and by February 5 landed his men three miles below Fort Henry. The next day, with Foote's gunboats in the lead, he attacked Fort Henry, which was built on low ground, making it, at that time of year, a relatively weak position. The Tennessee was at flood stage and part of the fort was underwater, allowing the Union gunboats to pull within close range and pound the Confederates into submission.[29] Brig. Gen. Lloyd Tilghman, realizing almost from the beginning that the fort was lost, sent most of the garrison to Fort Donelson and stayed behind with a token force. By two o'clock in the afternoon the fight was over. The Union army now had control of the lower Tennessee River.

Upon the surrender of Fort Henry, Grant turned east and began a ten-mile march cross country to capture his second prize, Donelson, a feat that would earn him his nom de guerre, Unconditional Surrender Grant. While Grant's troops marched, Foote was sent back down the Tennessee to steam around and up the Cumberland River to rendezvous with the army. This took place on February 12, a week after Fort Henry had fallen.[30]

Johnston immediately countered the fall of Fort Henry by abandoning his position at Bowling Green and rushing the fifteen thousand men from there to reinforce Fort Donelson. The rest of the Confederate army in the west fell back to Nashville.

Fort Donelson was a fortified enclosure of a hundred acres, a hastily constructed garrison just south of the boundary between Kentucky and Tennessee. The Confederate stronghold crowned a one-hundred-foot plateau on the south side of the Cumberland, where the river takes a sharp bend eastward then back to the north. The fortress was built approximately a quarter mile north of a small hamlet called Dover, which was a scattering of ramshackle dwellings with a courthouse and a two-story tavern that doubled as a hotel. In early February 1862, the Confederates built a hospital within the township. By the second week of February, the entire compound, including Dover, was enclosed on three sides by several miles of rifle pits preceded by heavy wooden obstacles. Backwater from the river flooded Hickman Creek to the north of the fort and Lick Creek to the south, creating nearly impassable sloughs. The terrain to the west of the river, from which the Union army would advance, was terraced woodland interlaced with deep, jagged ravines. Beneath the bluff, river batteries challenged all passage on the river.

Forrest was moving toward Fort Donelson through bitter cold and periods of intermittent freezing rain. The roads and trails were alternately frozen hard or churned into knee-deep mud when they thawed. In January and February the Tennessee and the Cumberland rose more than ten feet, causing a general flooding of low-lying areas, which had included the works and trenches at Fort Henry.

The fortifications at Fort Donelson were frantically being reenforced as Grant's army approached by land and his navy by waterway. Forrest's command, victorious in their small conflict at Sacramento, which had involved only several hundred combatants, would soon be engaged in their first major battle. More than thirty-five thousand men were about to clash on the frozen bluffs of Dover.

By February 7, when Brig. Gen. Bushrod Johnson arrived and assumed command of Fort Donelson, the weather had cleared and become unseasonably mild, causing the roads to become soft and difficult to negotiate. Two days later, on February 9, Brig. Gen. Gideon Pillow arrived, with Brig. Gen. Simon Bolivar Buckner and Brig. Gen. John B. Floyd following on the twelfth and thirteenth respectively. This collection of generals created a cloudy command structure complicated by personal antagonisms, agendas, and uncertainty. Success in defending the fort under such conditions was highly unlikely.[31]

Forrest arrived with his men on February 12 and was immediately ordered to head west to scout out Grant's exact position, which was at that moment less than three miles away from Donelson. With thirteen hundred cavalrymen Forrest proceeded up two parallel roads that led west toward Fort Henry. Coming from the other direction were two divisions of Union troops under Generals John A. McClernand and Charles F. Smith. The combined strength of these divisions consisted of twenty-two regiments of infantry, two regiments of cavalry, and nine batteries of artillery, approximately fifteen thousand men.[32]

Less than five miles from Donelson, Forrest met the enemy and began the battle. He promptly dismounted his men and formed an oblique line of battle across the road, intending to contest every inch of ground from that point on. Indeed, he not only meant to hold his ground, but to take as much as possible. Whether his orders were to attack and hold or to report back to his commanding officers the strength and disposition of the enemy, he never hesitated.[33]

As McClernand's vanguard came around a bend in the road and started across a small clearing, Forrest's men opened up on them with a hot fusillade, which dropped the Union riflemen in the front ranks. When the stunned survivors began to fall back, Forrest ordered Major Kelley to charge the Union cavalry that had been sent forward to protect the infantry's retreat. Kelley's men soon met and drove the Union cavalry back upon their own infantry to begin a vicious fight that immobilized the Union advance in that quarter of the field. McClernand then attempted to reform and turn Forrest's left flank. Countering McClernand's flanking maneuver, Forrest remounted Capt. Charles May's and Lieutenant Hambrick's companies and led a charge down the road which engaged and drove back the Federal cavalry for a quarter mile. The contest continued for five hours, until about 3:00 P.M., when General Buckner sent a messenger to direct Forrest to return to the entrenchments.[34]

Back at the fortifications the Southerners remained extremely busy through that evening. Frantic and backbreaking work extending and reinforcing the trenches went on all night. Conspicuous examples for all to see were Colonel Forrest and Gen. Bushrod Johnson as they handled picks and shovels with their men in the hard night's labor.

By daylight on the thirteenth, McClernand and C. F. Smith's divisions had partially invested the Confederate position—McClernand on the right and Smith on the left—with several cannon placed at highly favorable points to shell the rebels. Smith also had placed Col. John. M. Burges' regiment of sharpshooters in an advanced position of cover from which their special long-range rifles could reach the Confederate lines.[35] And with Andrew H. Foote's flotilla approaching by river, the Confederates were in danger of becoming trapped if drastic measures were not taken.

That morning the Union troops pressed forward under cover of the gun batteries and sharpshooters. General Pillow ordered Forrest and a few hundred riflemen to the most forward trenches to retard the enemy's advance, which had not penetrated beyond the abatis in front of the rifle pits. Soon after arriving and deploying his detachment, Forrest spotted a Union sniper in a tree several hundred yards distant. He reacted as he had at Sacramento: he grabbed a Maynard rifle from the man closest to him, took aim, fired, and dropped the man, who fell headfirst from the top boughs. Biographers Jordan and Pryor estimate the distance of Forrest's shot at more than three hundred yards.[36]

For the rest of the morning, Forrest's men fought from the trenches while their colonel moved calmly up and down the line, encouraging them all the while. At one point on McClernand's front, the Federals pushed to within fifty yards of the Confederate breastworks. For the next couple of hours the battle was waged at nearly point-blank range. So close were their adversaries that Forrest's men had to mount the parapets, fire into the faces of the Yankees, and then quickly duck down to reload.

While the fight for the trenches raged, the navy finally got into the battle. The first gunboat to arrive was the *Carondelet,* which immediately began a fierce cannonade upon the Confederate water batteries. The rebels responded in kind. During the exchange, the *Carondelet* fired 150 shells but was forced to draw off after taking a cannon shot that penetrated her casemate. The first round of the water battle would go to the Confederate gunners on shore.[37]

As the morning of the thirteenth came to an end, so did the decent weather. A wind began to blow, driving dark winter storm clouds before it and quickly dropping the temperature to ten degrees below zero. The wounded who had not been carried from the field suffered the most. A few died horrible deaths when "random fires ignited the dead winter underbrush and wind swept the flames over them as they lay helpless to save themselves."[38]

Later that night, Federal reserves landed downstream on the Cumberland while Gen. Lew Wallace's brigade marched overland from Fort Henry on the Tennessee to shore up the middle of the Union line between Smith's and McClernand's divisions. By the morning of the fourteenth, Grant would have nearly twenty thousand men at his disposal and would begin planning his grand assault using the Federal flotilla.[39]

As confusing as a four-general command could inevitably be, a decision had been made by dawn that day to attempt to drive the Union forces back and open an escape route toward Charlotte. Forrest's men would act as sharpshooters to provide cover for General Pillow's division as it moved out of the trenches to attack the enemy positions across Indian Creek. In spite of General Pillow's effort, the advance stalled and by early afternoon Pillow had come to believe it was too late in the day to continue and called off the attack.

At approximately 3:00 P.M., the Federal navy finally arrived, intent on reducing the Confederate river batteries. At a range of one mile Foote fired the opening shot from the bow of the *St. Louis*, signaling the other gunboats to begin the attack. When the gunboats came within 450 yards, the Confederate thirty-two pounders began to return fire. The cannonade was horrendous and deafening, with each side giving a good account of themselves.[40]

The Federal attack force included the *St. Louis, Louisville, Pittsburg,* and *Carondelet,* all ironclads and mounting a total of thirteen guns of the largest caliber. The wooden vessels included the *Tyler* and *Lexington,* each with nine large guns.[41] For thirty minutes both sides pounded each other, and although the Confederates were seriously outgunned, their fire was more accurate. The *Carondelet* had its lifeboats blown off their davits and her smokestacks were riddled by shot. The *St. Louis* was disabled by a shot to her wheel and received a total of fifty-seven hits. So many of her crew had been killed or wounded that the decks were slippery with blood. Some of that blood belonged to Flag Officer Foote, who was also wounded. With tears in his eyes he begrudgingly disengaged and ordered the retreat. One by one the other gunboats began to shear off out of range.[42]

The Confederate gunners were having no easy time of it either. The heavy Union projectiles fell amid the Confederate artillerists like a rain of thunderbolts. The explosions ripped huge fissures in the earthen works, throwing dirt into the air that partially buried rebel guns and their gunners, requiring a constant detail of men with shovels to dig them out.[43]

During the barrage, Forrest mounted a horse and rode to the head of a ravine by the river and watched the artillery exchange. From Forrest's vantage point, it seemed that the Union shellfire was falling with devastating effect within the Confederate works. When former Methodist minister Maj. D. C. Kelley rode down the ravine to join his commander, Forrest said, "Parson! For God's sake, pray. Nothing but God almighty can save that fort."[44] This was the first time Forrest witnessed the kind of devastating firepower that gunboats could bring to bear, and he would never forget the lesson nor lose his animosity toward them.

As Forrest was calling for prayer, a huge cheer could be heard from the fort as the defenders realized that the Union fleet was disengaging. But despite the exultation of the Southern troops over their victory, and the distinct rise in morale, the four Confederate commanders remained pessimistic about their chances. The responsibility now passed back to Grant's infantry. It would be up to them to finish the job the navy had started.

Confederate general Floyd had received a dispatch on the thirteenth from Gen. Albert Sidney Johnston saying that if the fort were to be lost, he should bring his troops to Nashville if possible. In the growing miasma of defeatism among the Confederate generals, this message seemed to take the sting out of what they considered an impending defeat. On the night of the fourteenth Floyd called a meeting of his division commanders at Pillow's Rice House headquarters.[45]

The council of war decided that due to their inferior numbers, they should attempt to fight their way out and march toward Nashville. But it seems that was not General Pillow's understanding of the plan. Pillow believed the orders meant to attack and defeat the enemy, if possible, and then, whatever the outcome, the commanders would decide whether to march to Nashville or stay at Dover.

Supplies for the troops seemed to be a major point of controversy, which in turn revolved around the question of Pillow's interpretation of Johnston's orders. If they were to attack the enemy with the intention of defeating him, the men would only need their weapons and ammunition. On the other hand, if the plan was to attack and then march to Nashville, the troops would require haversacks, bedrolls, and extra food. This question had not been clarified by the time the brigade commanders were briefed about the situation. According to the brigade commanders, John McCausland, John C. Brown, Bushrod Johnson, Col. John Simonton, Gabriel Wharton, Adolphus Heiman, William Baldwin, T. J. Davidson, Joseph Drake, and Forrest, there was no mention in their briefing of supplies, rations, or marching equipment.[46]

General Pillow's interpretation of Johnston's orders differed from that of Floyd, who was in nominal command, and General Buckner, who believed that if the attack was successful they should then abandon the fort and march to Nashville. Who was at fault? The blame should not fall to Pillow for his misinterpretation of the vague strategy suggested by General Johnston's message. As commander, General Floyd should have made the call and then made his views crystal clear to the other generals. "Thus," as Forrest's biographers Jordan and Pryor suggest, "the former Secretary of War must bear full responsibility for the confusion that resulted on the afternoon of the 15th."[47]

Around 4:00 A.M. on Saturday, the fifteenth, Confederate troops began moving into position to attack McClernand, who commanded the right wing of the Federal army. General Pillow led the operation with Bushrod Johnson serving as his second in command. Forrest's cavalry unit assembled in front of McCausland's brigade on the extreme right of the Union line, southeast of Dover. Although the Confederates moved into position undetected, the Union army had awakened by the time the Southerners were ready to begin their assault. The shivering Union soldiers were still shaking off their slumber when they were ordered to brace themselves for imminent battle.

At 6:00 A.M., Pillow ordered his men out of the trenches. Forrest's cavalry, some eight hundred strong, was in the lead along with Baldwin, McCausland, Wharton, Simonton, and Drake's brigades of infantry, a total of fourteen regiments and two small battalions. Their numbers were about sixty-five hundred.[48]

Pillow committed brigade after brigade to the fray until the Union line began to waiver. Forrest, still somewhat in the lead, was covering the left flank but was experiencing difficulty maintaining cohesion within the cavalry due to the dense undergrowth and rugged terrain. The din of battle rose to a roar as the Yankees were slowly driven back from ridge to ridge toward their center, parallel with the Confederate entrenchments. While the rebel infantry pressed their advantage, Forrest swept around the enemy's right until he had turned it and then descended upon the Federal flank and rear. However, his men soon became bogged down in marshy ground. Unable to reach their flank, Forrest maneuvered to the front to join the infantry that was making a hard push at the Federal line, which was beginning to fall apart.[49]

Forrest believed that the critical moment of the fight had arrived and requested permission from Gen. Bushrod Johnson to charge upon the disordered mass of enemy troops, some of whom had begun to raise white flags. Johnson feared an ambush and demonstrating the universal unsteadiness of command that plagued the Confederate cause at Donelson, vacillated and denied Forrest permission to go for the kill. This inaction allowed Gen. Lew Wallace time to act. Without orders, Wallace rushed his troops forward to reinforce the wavering Union line and form a new line of resistance, thus preventing a general retreat.

For the Confederates, the moment was lost. Having missed an opportunity to turn the Union panic into a rout, Johnson ordered

Forrest back to the left flank around 9:00 A.M. Forrest had plenty of fight left in him and was anxious to engage the enemy again. The opportunity came around 10:30, while moving by the left flank.

Forrest spotted a Union battery comprised of four brass and two iron 24-pounder pieces, which had worked its way in behind Pillow's line. Without orders Forrest ordered a charge, his men cutting lose a volley as they went. Riding down upon them at full speed, Forrest's men closed with the enemy in a narrow ravine hidden by timber and thick brush. Most of the artillerists abandoned their guns and ran. Forrest's cavalrymen made short work of those men who bravely held their ground.

It was an auspicious début for Forrest. These six guns were the first of more than one hundred that he would capture from the enemy during the course of the war. During the melee, Forrest had his horse shot out from under him. It would be the first of thirty mounts killed during the war while ridden by the Wizard of the Saddle.[50]

Forrest came under General Pillow's personal orders as the Confederate assault was renewed and was sent to the right to charge a position held by Lt. Col. T. E. G. Ransom's Eleventh Illinois. Augmented by the Second Kentucky Infantry from Buckner's division, he now commanded the full weight of cavalry and infantry. As he moved toward his objective, Forrest sighted another battery of enemy guns to the right that were "about to turn on us" and immediately attacked the gun emplacement across two hundred yards of open country.[51]

Galloping headlong into a hail of fire, they slammed into the enemy and began deadly work in earnest. Capt. Charles May, who had organized the Forrest Rangers in Memphis, was shot from the saddle. At the same time that Captain May went down, Forrest's second mount of the day was hit and died beneath him. As Forrest bounded to his feet, Cpl. Lansing Burrows, a young Baptist preacher, rode up and turned his horse over to his commander. Moments later an artillery round ripped the hind quarters off Burrows' horse, the shell striking just behind the saddle skirt and Forrest's leg. Blasted to the ground for the third time that day, Forrest arose stunned and covered in gore, but still game. "In that war, it would seem that nothing was quite so unsafe as a horse carrying Old Bedford."[52]

Forrest temporarily directed the action on foot as he ran across the battlefield in search of another mount. Back in the saddle, astride his fourth horse of the day, he was quickly on the move again with his cavalry and infantry. To this point in the battle Forrest's men had captured nine guns and taken more than a hundred prisoners.[53]

By now Forrest found himself to the rear of his original objective, the Eleventh Illinois of William H. L. Wallace's brigade, which was posted in a deeply recessed road. Without hesitation, he ordered his third charge of the day. The rebel horsemen swept in on the Illinois soldiers from their right flank, striking them hard and by surprise. Jeffrey Forrest's horse took a mortal shot and crashed to the ground, seriously bruising the shaken cavalryman. For a few moments the fight became a bloody hand-to-hand affair. Then the Union began to give way and was soon in flight. The Eleventh Illinois broke and ran back through the ranks of Col. Hugh B. Reed's Forty-fourth Indiana, creating panic in their ranks also. The Forty-fourth held off one more push by Forrest, then fell back in disorder along with the Eleventh Illinois, the latter regiment losing 70 killed, 181 wounded, and 88 taken prisoner.

With confusion manifesting along the Union line, elements of William H. L. Wallace's regiment fell back to Wynn's Ferry Road, where McAllister's battery held a redoubt. There they attempted to brace themselves for Forrest's arrival. The Confederate Cavalryman was tenacious in keeping up the pressure, forcing the enemy to give way on that section of the battlefield.

As Forrest continued to lead the attack, he crossed paths with General Pillow, who had been in another part of the battlefield. Pillow asked Forrest if he knew the whereabouts of General Buckner and added, in what Forrest may have taken as an accusatory manner, that he had heard no indications of battle from the quarter of the field from which Forrest had just come. Forrest answered that he had been a little too busy to keep track of the whereabouts of others. Perhaps less than satisfied with that answer, Pillow exclaimed, "Well, then, Colonel, what have you been doing since I saw you last?" Forrest fired back, "Obeying orders, General, by protecting your left flank." Then, as if on cue, Forrest looked over his shoulder at the scores of prisoners and captured guns that were just then coming into sight. Behind the prisoners came their captors, Forrest's men, marching them into the Confederate entrenchments.[54]

Pillow quickly changed his tone and commended Forrest, then ordered him to return to the left flank and attempt to take McAllister's guns, which were emplaced across the Wynn's Ferry Road. Forrest was already heading toward Wynn's Ferry Road, where W. H. L. Wallace and his men had reformed when he was stopped by Pillow. Now, augmented by Lt. Roger Hanson's Kentuckians, Gen.

John C. Brown's Tennessee Infantry Brigade, and two gun batteries, Forrest merely continued toward that objective with Pillow's consent.

McAllister's guns were supported by remnants of three Illinois regiments, the Eleventh, Forty-fourth, and Forty-third, along with the First Nebraska Infantry. The Confederate guns began the attack by laying down a barrage, which Forrest immediately followed with an infantry charge up the middle to engage the Union infantry. At the same time, he personally led his horsemen against an enemy cavalry detachment deployed to protect McAllister's batteries. It was 1:30 P.M.[55]

While Forrest's Kentuckians and Tennesseans were hotly engaged to the front, Confederate horsemen led by Forrest swept in and crushed the small detachment of Union cavalry. Moments later, he was upon McAllister's gun emplacement before the startled artillerymen could react and turn the cannon. The Confederates took the position in vicious hand-to-hand fighting. Forrest told his biographers, Gen. Thomas Jordan and J. P. Pryor, that during this struggle he was struck by the shocking contrast of the blood on the white, frozen ground. "As we charged, the feet of the horses splashed in the blood of the slain and wounded, flowing along the surface of the snow until it froze."[56]

As Roger Hanson's Second Kentucky Regiment and John C. Brown's Third Tennessee Infantry attacked, supported by Forrest's cavalry, the redoubt at Wynn's Ferry Road was carried. General Pillow observed the withdrawal of W. H. L. Wallace's troops and with his own division took part in driving the enemy another quarter mile before they were able to reform. This action brought the battle to a close, because Pillow believed that he had won a great victory.

Evidence supporting Pillow's assessment comes from a letter written on February 17 by Capt. L. D. Waddell of E Company, Eleventh Illinois Volunteers, who wrote to his father in New York that only sixteen men in his regiment had escaped being wounded, and of the eighty-five men in his company, only seven had survived. The young captain wrote that the battle on February 15 was "the most wholesale slaughter that was ever heard of."[57]

As the day's fighting came to an end, Forrest's men were given the duty of collecting arms from the battlefield before returning to the fort. Despite Pillow's belief that the battle had been won, Colonel Forrest's battle report reflected his opinion that the Confederates should have continued the attack.

> We had driven the enemy back without a reverse from the
> left of our entrenchments to the center, having opened

three different roads by which we might have retired if the generals had, as was deemed best in the council of the night before, ordered the retreat of the army.[58]

Forrest's assessment was partially correct. Wynn's Ferry Road was still blocked, but two others, the Forge and Charlotte Roads, lay open for escape. Most of the other Confederate commanders agreed with Forrest. Generals Buckner and Floyd also believed the fight should have been continued. Buckner was prepared to march as fast as possible to escape, but when he found Pillow, Pillow confirmed the order to return to the fort. At this point, the supply issue reemerged, because in Pillow's mind he had ordered his men out that day to fight and win the battle. Therefore, they were not carrying the necessary rations and other items required for a forced march. The command was now in a state of desperate confusion hearkening back to the previous day and Floyd's vague orders concerning the Confederate objective.

Buckner had gone into the battle sharing Floyd's interpretation of Gen. Albert Sidney Johnston's orders but had reluctantly bowed to General Pillow, who was field commander. As Buckner was returning to the Confederate entrenchments, he encountered General Floyd, who wanted to know why he was not either continuing the fight or preparing to escape toward Nashville to join Johnston's army. When Buckner explained that he was following Pillow's orders, Floyd immediately rode to find Pillow, who had already returned to the entrenchments. In the conversation that followed, General Pillow convinced Floyd that it was now too late to reverse the withdrawal. Floyd then sent orders to Buckner to return and reoccupy the trenches on the extreme right.[59] General Floyd's indecision and failure to make his plans understood, combined with his absence on the battlefield, where he immediately could have countermanded Pillow's order to withdraw, puts the responsibility for the resulting disaster at his feet.

Buckner still believed that there was a possibility they might fight their way out. At approximately 11:00 P.M., he ordered Bushrod Johnson, with Heiman's brigade, back to the same position they had occupied on Saturday morning, with the apparent intention of cutting their way out if necessary.[60]

All the while, unknown to the disorganized Confederate leaders, Grant was away from his command downriver, visiting the wounded Flag Officer Foote. Grant had learned that his army had been beaten back by the rebels and could not travel the distance back to the battlefield until midafternoon to organize a blocking action. So in hindsight, Forrest, Buckner, and Floyd were correct in believing that they might have been able to save the entire command before Grant returned.[61]

Meanwhile, as Forrest was busy on the battlefield bringing in the wounded and collecting the thousands of weapons that littered the ground, the sky darkened from gray to black, matching his mood as he and his men returned with several wounded, nine guns and more than 4,000 small arms. Forrest's men had been without sleep for nearly thirty-six hours and were ready for some well-deserved rest, though it would be short lived.[62]

Upon Grant's return Saturday afternoon, he sent Gen. C. F. Smith's division forward to seize a lodgment in Buckner's former position on the right before Buckner's troops returned in force. This maneuver placed the Union in an advantageous position for launching an attack on the morning of Sunday, February 16.[63] While the Confederate generals temporized, Grant was closing the door on the rebels at Fort Donelson. By dawn the door would be locked.

Meanwhile Forrest was catching a nap as a howling wind swept across the frozen, bloodied ground at Dover. Sometime between midnight and 1:00 A.M., Forrest was awakened and summoned to a meeting at Floyd's headquarters. A cloud of defeatism hung over the room where the commanders gathered. Upon his arrival, Forrest was informed by Pillow that eleven boatloads of enemy reinforcements had landed downriver and that the ground won by the Confederates on Saturday had been reoccupied by the Federals. Forrest was incredulous. He later wrote in his account of the meeting, "I told him I did not believe it as I had left that part of the field, on our left, late the evening before."[64]

The cavalryman had solid reason to doubt what he was being told. He had personally sent out two reliable scouts who had reported as late as 9:00 P.M. that the field was clear of hostile forces. However, Forrest suggested that they send out two more scouts to verify his earlier information. The other generals agreed. Adam Johnson and Bob Martin were dispatched to reexamine the ground in question. The assignment was hazardous and had to be executed in the most difficult of conditions. Adam and Martin were required to dismount and crawl on their stomachs and endure below-zero temperatures during their reconnaissance.

Within an hour they were back, shivering and hugging the old potbellied stove in the middle of the room, as they reported what they had seen. They said that they had observed numerous fires, but that there were only stragglers and wounded in the vicinity. Also, they had seen many fires in the distance, but on inspection these fires turned out to be started by the wind. This report suggests that the Confederate intelligence indicating that the Union lines had been reestablished on that part of the field was exaggerated.[65]

Forrest's report on the battle at Donelson reflected the same thoughts. "I am clearly of the opinion that two-thirds of our army could have marched out without loss, and that, had we continued the fight the next day, we should have gained a glorious victory, as our troops were in fine spirits, believing we had whipped them."[66]

Other scouts, however, had reported contrary information, which killed whatever enthusiasm there may have been to continue the fight, especially for Buckner. He continued to argue that any attempt to escape was sure to end in the destruction of the entire command and apparently made effective points among the other officers. Generals Pillow and Floyd emphatically stated that they would rather take any other course but surrender.

Forrest never wavered in his determination to fight it out. He put forth that he did not believe the Charlotte Road was blocked, but even if it were, he guaranteed that he could open it and hold it until the army had escaped. Buckner warned Forrest that he was not factoring in the Union cavalry, which would present a substantial problem for Forrest's plan. Forrest voiced disagreement, saying that he had faced Federal horsemen before and was not very impressed, nor worried. Floyd vacillated again and seemed to lean to Buckner's side of the argument. He warned Forrest of the inherent risk in trying to cut his way out and the inevitable casualties from frostbite and exposure that would occur trying to ride or march across swollen Lick Creek.

Sensing that the others were leaning toward surrender, Forrest grew angry and told the generals that he had promised the parents of many of his men that he would do everything in his power to protect their young sons. His agitation grew as he spoke. He would prefer, he said, that the bones of his men should bleach on the surrounding hills rather than his men be carried to the north and cooped up in open prison-pens during midwinter.[67]

No one responded, and it was clear that there was no confidence in his point of view. Forrest cursed and stalked out of the room but returned quickly. Upon his sudden reentry he said, "I think there is more fight in these men than you all suppose, and if you will let me, I will take out my command." Perhaps reaching the end of his patience, Pillow said, "Very well, Colonel. Cut your way out." No one in the room objected, and Forrest left to make preparations.[68]

With Forrest out of the room, a strange performance began as the generals discussed the transfer of command, which would seal the fate of more than thirteen thousand Confederate troops. Floyd's later report stated that because of Grant's overwhelming numbers it became the "universal opinion of the officers that we cannot maintain ourselves against these forces." His answer to this crisis was to toss command of Fort Donelson like a hot biscuit to his top subordinate "and to make an effort for my own extrication by any and every means that might present themselves to me."[69]

As a former governor of Virginia and secretary of war in Pres. James Buchanan's cabinet, Floyd perhaps had some concern that if he became a prisoner of the Union army, he might be treated more harshly than other prisoners of war. He agreed with General Buckner concerning the demoralization of their army but felt that the fort could be held for one more day, providing they could be resupplied. General Pillow was more adamant than the others about not surrendering, but just as determined as Floyd not to be taken prisoner. For whatever reason, Buckner seemed to get a grip on his courage and said that if he were placed in command he would surrender the post and allow Floyd to leave and take his brigade out with him.

Floyd capitulated to the noble gesture, turned to Pillow, the senior brigadier, and said, "I turn the command over, sir."

Pillow immediately responded, "I pass it."

"I assume it," Buckner replied. "Give me pen, ink and paper, and send for the bugler."[70]

Pillow and Floyd were already gone by sunup on February 16. General Pillow was ferried across the Cumberland. General Floyd commandeered two steamboats that had arrived around 4:00 A.M. and headed for Nashville with about thirteen hundred of his men. Floyd's departure nearly caused a riot on shore, as some of the men, feeling abandoned—and rightly so—demanded to be let on board. Before they could board and swamp the boats, which were already overloaded with Floyd's four Virginia regiments and personnel of his three Virginia batteries, the boat captains backed the transports away from the bank, leaving one Mississippi regiment cursing at their departing comrades. "It was the darkest hour of my life," one Confederate soldier said of his feelings of being left to the tender mercies of the enemy.[71]

Meanwhile, Forrest was preparing to take out as many men as would follow him. Five to seven hundred officers and men formed the column that followed Forrest and his brother Jeffrey out of Fort Donelson. They traveled along a route down the Charlotte Road, by the river where the scouts had gone out earlier.

The column halted briefly about a mile or so from Donelson when scouts reported that enemy troops had been seen ahead in a line of battle. Forrest and Jeffrey rode forward to check the situation. They discovered that through the low-lying fog and the dim predawn light, the scouts had mistaken a row of fence posts for enemy pickets. Soon the shivering column was on the move again preparing to cross an icy Lick Creek.[72] No one seemed prepared to test the depth of the water, so Forrest took the lead and rode into the freezing creek. Finding the water to be saddle-skirt deep, he ordered the column to follow. Major Kelley was ordered to take up a rear guard position to protect against any possible pursuit. "I ordered Major Kelley and Adjutant Schuyler," Forrest later wrote, "to remain at the point where we entered this road with one company, where the enemy's cavalry would attack if they attempted to follow us. They remained until day was dawning. . . . More than two hours had been occupied in passing. Not a gun had been fired at us. Not an enemy had been seen or heard."[73]

Forrest and his men camped some twenty miles from Donelson and about fifty miles short of Nashville on Sunday night, February 16. Making slower progress than usual because of the weather, they arrived at Nashville on Tuesday morning, February 18. No enemy soldiers had been observed during Forrest's escape.

"The Beginning of the End" read the *Harper's Weekly* headline for March 1, 1862. The article referred to the Union capture of Forts Henry and Donelson on the Tennessee and Cumberland Rivers. Many believe that the loss of the two Confederate forts near the mouth of these two major river highways was one of the critical events of the entire war. It was definitely the most critical event early in the war. The damage to the Confederacy is hard to estimate, and the ramifications are mostly guesswork.

The Confederate commanders surrendered more than thirteen thousand men at Donelson alone. Had this force remained intact might there have been two more divisions with the Confederates at Shiloh? Or perhaps the entire war strategy would have changed, and the Battle of Shiloh might never have taken place. However, one fact is indisputable. Several hundred more Confederate troops would have been lost to the Confederacy had it not been for an unlettered lieutenant colonel who refused to believe he was beaten. *Harper's Weekly* may have overlooked Lieutenant Colonel Nathan Bedford Forrest in its report, but the headline was prophetic in a sense because the loss of these two forts did lead to the carving up of the Confederacy into smaller and smaller pieces.

# Chapter Three

# ALL THE LANDSCAPE WAS RED

*—Bruce Catton*

## Shiloh
## April 1862

On Sunday morning, February 16, the church bells were tolling in Nashville, but not in celebration of the Sabbath. The Yankees had taken Fort Donelson, and on this morning the bells were ringing in alarm as desperation gripped the city. Less than a year into the war, the citizens of Nashville realized that their capital was about to fall into the hands of the enemy. The loss of Nashville was just one of the immediate repercussions that the Confederacy faced with the fall of Forts Henry and Donelson.

By February 14, Albert Sidney Johnston had already given up his position at Bowling Green to the north and was falling back toward Nashville. The heartland of the Confederacy now lay exposed, along with the left flank of their long, thin line stretching from Columbus, Kentucky, to the Cumberland Gap. Union general Don Carlos Buell was confident that Confederate troops would offer only nominal resistance, leaving him free to move his army overland to capture the capital of Tennessee.

On February 16, Confederate general William J. Hardee's army marched into Nashville from Bowling Green. Hardee's men spread the word that Buell's forces were not far behind, news that inflamed the quickly spreading sense of panic. Over the next week a state of chaos permeated the city, threatening to push its citizens to the verge of riot. The war had seemed far away, but now it "was brought home to them with the abruptness of a pistol shot in a theater."[1]

Many state officials, Gov. Isham Harris among them, quickly boarded southbound trains, leaving Mayor R. B. Cheatham to handle the pandemonium. That night the mayor spoke to a huge crowd

59

of Nashville citizens and attempted to quiet their fears. By word of General Johnston, Cheatham told the people, Nashville would not be defended and would be declared an open city. The capital city, therefore, would not be destroyed. He also informed the crowd that most of the provisions warehoused in the city would not be removed by the Confederate army and would be distributed among the people. This was not to be the case, however. Whatever Johnston told the mayor about the disposition of government provisions, it was not his real plan to turn over the contents of the warehouses to the people of Nashville.

The next day, February 17, General Floyd and his brigade of Virginians arrived and were immediately ordered by Johnston to take charge of procuring and loading the stored supplies on railroad cars to follow the retreating army. Johnston then continued his march toward Murfreesboro.

Floyd's actions angered the citizens and demonstrated that their mayor's promise to distribute the provisions among them was as empty as the warehouses soon would be. Amid protesting citizens, Floyd's soldiers did their best to carry out their orders. Tension was at the breaking point when, much to Floyd's relief, Forrest and his cavalry arrived on Tuesday, February 18. Floyd wasted little time putting Forrest in charge of finishing the unpleasant job, then marched his brigade out of Nashville on Thursday, the twentieth, to join Johnston at Murfreesboro.

With the situation building toward a full-blown revolt, Forrest set about the difficult assignment of restoring law and order and getting the supplies out of Nashville before the Yankees arrived. The quartermasters and the commissary people had all fled the city, and mobs were raiding the warehouses for food and ammunition. Before the chaos could spread further, Forrest took control with an iron hand. With several handpicked horsemen, Forrest rode into the crowds "beating down the ringleaders with the flat of his sword" and at one point resorted to turning a fire hose on them, using the cold water of the Cumberland River. This tactic seemed to have a "magic effect" on the mob and quickly dispersed it.[2]

Wednesday through Sunday morning, February 23, Forrest and his men worked with methodical desperation. Besides the trains that departed with tons of supplies, Forrest was able to salvage nearly one thousand wagonloads of ammunition, clothing, bales of osnaburgs, artillery, and food stores. The valuable materials were hauled to various rail depots for relay transport into the South. Although this operation was seemingly successful, Forrest stated that the remaining supplies he was unable to remove

> must be estimated by millions of dollars. . . . In my judgment, if
> the quartermaster and commissary had remained at their post
> and worked diligently with the means at their command, the
> Government stores might all have been saved between the time
> of the fall of Fort Donelson and the arrival of the enemy at
> Nashville.[3]

General Buell reached the north bank of the Cumberland twenty-four hours after Forrest pulled out. Mayor Cheatham kept his word and on February 24 met with General Buell and surrendered the city to the enemy. The fall of Nashville was a major boost to Northern morale and seemed to bear out the predictions of victory that had come with the fall of Forts Henry and Donelson. Widespread rejoicing followed when the news reached the North.[4]

Forrest's command reached Murfreesboro on Sunday night, February 23. The next day Johnston ordered Forrest's regiment to Huntsville, Alabama. Arriving there on the twenty-fifth, he immediately furloughed most of his men. Their orders required them to reassemble at Huntsville on March 10. It was reported that without exception the entire command returned as ordered. Bedford's brother Capt. Jesse Forrest, who commanded Company D, a cavalry detachment raised by the young captain himself, joined them at Huntsville, which brought the command to nearly full regimental strength. The Forrest brothers and their new regiment of cavalry were then ordered to Burnsville, Mississippi, in the vicinity of Corinth. There they would remain until Johnston began maneuvering his 44,000-man army into position to attack Grant, whose troops were reported gathering at and around Pittsburg Landing, Tennessee.

Since the loss of Nashville, the Southern press had been castigating Johnston, but Jefferson Davis stood by his man. In rebuttal to the critical abuse, Davis proclaimed, "If Sidney Johnston is not a general, we had better give up the war for we have no general."[5]

Grant had given Lincoln and the nation the most important victories of the war thus far, and the president's confidence in him and support for his leadership continued to grow throughout the war. Lincoln lionized him for his capture of Forts Henry and Donelson and had become his champion among the politicos in Washington. But, though Grant's rise to prominence had been swift, that ascent had been touched by controversy.

The commander of the department, Maj. Gen. Henry W. Halleck, had temporarily removed Grant from command. Rumor had it that Halleck dismissed Grant because of jealousy rather than for the vague recorded charges of having been absent from his command. Perhaps because of Lincoln's support, Grant was restored to command on March 12.

The army Grant now headed was formidable (nearly forty thousand by March 14) and, beginning in the first week of March, had been transported by steamboats up the Tennessee River to Savannah, Tennessee, and beyond. Expecting to be reinforced by Gen. Don Carlos Buell's Army of Ohio, which was marching overland from Nashville, Grant established his headquarters at Savannah, while on March 16, William Tecumseh Sherman led his most advanced division ashore farther upstream and made camp at Pittsburg Landing. Part of Sherman's division made their temporary home in an oblique line across the Corinth Road near a small, log church called Shiloh, a Hebrew word meaning place of peace. The irony in that word would soon be apparent, for with the coming battle it would resemble more a place of horror than a place of peace.[6]

Twenty miles to the southwest, at Corinth, Mississippi, Gen. Albert Sidney Johnston was assembling a Confederate army and intended to strike Grant as soon as possible. Though his troops were about equal in number to those in Grant's army, they were, in Braxton Bragg's words, a "mob, miscalled soldiers," and not yet ready for a major engagement. Though Johnston might have preferred more preparation, he could not spare that time. He knew that every day he delayed, Buell's army drew closer. Allow Buell to reach Grant before giving battle, and Johnston would be woefully outnumbered. He had to move.

Though Johnston had planned to have his army on the march on the morning of Thursday, April 3, numerous delays prevented the first elements from getting underway before the afternoon. As night fell, elements of the army were strung out across ten miles, reaching all the way back to Corinth. To add to Johnston's problems, that night a heavy rainfall muddied the already bad roads. Johnston had planned to open battle on Saturday, the fifth, but by that night his army found itself deploying only within a mile of Shiloh Church. Along the march from Corinth, the green, undisciplined Confederate troops often fired their weapons indiscriminately at squirrels and birds in the trees. Only recently living carefree lives on farms and in small towns, the Southern soldiers often acted as if this march were a country frolic. The grim truth was that somewhere up ahead Grant's 40,000 troops were camped and, though unsuspecting, were quite capable of introducing them to the realities of war.

Still ignorant of the imminent, momentous struggle, the two armies were so close to each other that it seems inconceivable that on that quiet Saturday, Grant could have been oblivious to the possibility of the impending clash. But earlier that day he had written to General Halleck that he expected no attack from the Confederates.

Serving as Johnston's second in command was Gen. Pierre G. T. Beauregard, whose gunners had opened the war by firing on Fort Sumter nearly a year earlier. Maj. Gen. Leonidas Polk, until recently an Episcopal bishop, was given the responsibility for the first four brigades, consisting of 9,136 men. Gen. Braxton Bragg led the second corps of six brigades, nearly 13,600 troops. Maj. Gen. William Hardee and another 6,789 men made up the third corps. In reserve were the 6,439 men of the fourth corps, commanded by the former vice president of the United States, Brig. Gen. John C. Breckinridge. Augmenting the Confederate attack force were 4,500 cavalrymen.[7]

Part of that cavalry command had been on a scouting mission earlier in the day, screening the Confederate advance and searching for the enemy. In the vicinity of Hamburg Landing, Forrest led a twenty-man scouting party that skirmished with and drove back a small Union cavalry force. This detachment was reported to have been the escort for Col. James B. McPherson, who was examining the area for possible bivouac sites for General Buell's army, which was expected to arrive in a couple of days. Forrest now knew that Buell was heading for Savannah and Pittsburg Landing, information he immediately reported to Johnston.

That evening Forrest, then a lieutenant colonel of cavalry, deployed his men to guard the crossing at Lick Creek, a short distance south of Pittsburg Landing on the road to Hamburg Landing. There they camped for the night and would remain during the opening hours of the battle that would commence the next morning, April 6. They were so near to the enemy camp that throughout the evening Forrest and his troops enjoyed the music being played by Union bands.[8]

Not far behind Forrest, General Johnston, whom many considered to be the best general on the Confederate side in that spring of 1862, weighed the possibilities. He was anxious to engage and defeat Grant. Based on the intelligence received from his scouts, Johnston decided that he must attack before Grant could be reinforced by Buell. This meant that he could not wait for Gen. Earl Van Dorn, who was en route from Arkansas with an additional 20,000 troops, but still too far away to be of any immediate help. Johnston believed that if he hit Grant suddenly and by surprise, he could defeat him then cross the Tennessee and whip Buell in a separate action.

Johnston's immediate subordinate, General Beauregard, fretted over the unknown strength of the enemy and the possibility of premature contact with the Union force. Beauregard was worried that Grant had been made aware of their approach due to the sporadic skirmishing and indiscriminate firing that had taken place throughout the afternoon. His principal concern was that the element of surprise had been lost. Beauregard urged Johnston to delay the possibility of a battle, even to prudently retire southward toward Corinth until the strength and position of the Union force were better known.

Johnston, however, was not disposed to caution. Since the Union victory at Fort Donelson, Grant had moved south. The Confederates had been falling back at the same time, causing many Tennessee civilians in their path to wonder if there was any fight left in the Confederate army. Johnston was determined to change that opinion and to bring Grant to decisive battle, thus restoring Southern confidence in their army by driving Grant back in defeat. His answer to Beauregard silenced his subordinate. "I would attack the enemy if he were a million," Johnston said with conviction.

On Sunday morning, April 6, Johnston's resolve bore fruit. His attack at first light caught the complacent, unprepared Federal troops completely by surprise. In a series of actions, the Union troops were driven back from one position after another, and by ten o'clock the division of Illinois and Iowa troops commanded by Brig. Gen. Benjamin M. Prentiss found itself facing the brunt of repeated Confederate attacks. A trail known as the Sunken Road and a rough rail fence that ran along most of its length provided a measure of cover for Prentiss's division of iron-willed soldiers who stood their ground throughout the morning against numerous Confederate attacks. Near the center of this line the withering fire laid down by Prentiss's boys assured that this spot would forever be know as the "Hornet's Nest." Precious hours were lost to the Confederates due to their inability to break this mile-long line.

Along that mile, and not far from the Hornet's Nest, was what had been, until that morning, a peaceful peach orchard, its trees covered with new blossoms. Just beyond, and near the end of the Sunken Road, was a large natural pool of water that would soon be known as Bloody Pond. As the Confederate hammer continued to fall upon Prentiss's anvil at the Hornet's Nest, another series of engagements were taking place on the left of the Union line in the orchard. General Johnston, leading the last attack through the orchard around 2:30 in the afternoon, had his uniform riddled by bullets and the sole of his boot shot away. A stray bullet struck him in the back of the leg, nicking the femoral artery and filling his boot with blood. An officer noticed Johnston weaving in the saddle. He rode to the general and asked if he were hurt. Johnston replied, "Yes, and seriously, I fear."[9]

Earlier, Johnston had sent his surgeon to another part of the field to care for Union wounded, depriving himself of the critical medical attention he now required. The officer who had come to the rebel commander's aid helped Johnston to the cover of a nearby tree and helplessly watched the general bleed to death. As Johnston's blood drained away, so ebbed the Confederate advantage of that first day at Shiloh. Confusion replaced the resolve of leadership with which Johnston had begun the battle.

Yet, at least one Confederate officer shared Johnston's persistent desire to strike and defeat the enemy. As would be proven in coming battles, relegating Lt. Col. Nathan Bedford Forrest to a rear-guard holding action at Lick Creek was an incredible misuse of valuable, though still raw, military talent. But Forrest was an unknown quantity at that moment in the war and was only an unlettered lieutenant colonel at that.

Forrest's assignment that first morning of the battle was to watch for an attack coming from Hamburg Landing, a few miles upriver from Pittsburg Landing. The sound of the raging battle at the Sunken Road hung heavy in the air and had been drawing Forrest's attention all morning. His blood was up. Guarding a creek crossing behind the battle was not his idea of military good judgment. When it became obvious that no attack was forthcoming from the south and that the excitement was elsewhere, he decided to move his command forward to where the action had been occurring since sunup. With his patience running thin, Forrest called to his troops, "Boys do you hear that musketry and that artillery? It means that our friends are falling by the hundreds at the hands of the enemy, and here we are guarding a damned creek! Let's go and help them. What do you say?"[10]

His boys thundered their support as they galloped toward the sound of the guns.

At about eleven o'clock they met the bloody remnants of Brig. Gen. Benjamin Franklin Cheatham's division, which had just returned from another failed attack on Prentiss's position. Almost at the same moment the Union began an artillery barrage. As the shells began to fall indiscriminately among the Confederates, four of Forrest's men went down with their horses under the exploding shells. Though he had just arrived, Forrest quickly surmised the situation and decided, as he would on countless future battlefields, that it was better to be a moving target than a sitting duck. Deferring to Cheatham as the senior officer, he asked permission to lead his men in a charge against the enemy line, but was refused.[11] The muzzle velocity of Civil War cannon was so slow that the Union cannonballs could be seen with the naked eye as they arced toward their targets. Forrest's cavalrymen watched the lethal projectiles coming toward them and took evasive action by waltzing their horses back and forth in a deadly game of dodge ball.

From behind the rail fence the Illinois and Iowa men fighting at the Sunken Road had stung the Confederates all morning with their fire as they listened to the relentless buzzing of rebel bullets through the leaves of spring growth all around them. Thirty years later visitors to the site could still make out the damage caused by the thousands of bullets that flew through the trees and undergrowth of the Hornet's Nest that day.

Around the time Forrest was calling upon Cheatham for permission to attack the Union line, the Confederate artillery, under the command of Brig. Gen. Daniel Ruggles, wearied of the stalemate and lined up sixty-two cannons about two hundred yards from the embattled Hornet's Nest and prepared to fire in an effort to dislodge the Yankees. The barrage fired against the Union line later that afternoon was, to that point in the war, the largest cannonade ever mounted in North America.[12]

As the ground around Forrest's cavalrymen continued to heave from the explosions of the Union barrage, Forrest once again appealed to Cheatham for permission to charge. Cheatham, reluctant to lose more men in another attack, which he probably considered at that point to be futile, told Forrest that he would not give such an order. "If you want to charge, you must do it on your own authority," Cheatham said.[13] That was the kind of order Forrest relished. He formed up his men and prepared to charge. The enthusiasm with which he gave the order infected his troops, and their fiery charge carried to within fifty yards of Prentiss's wall of bayonets, the deepest advance of the morning.

At that point the cavalrymen struck soft, marshy ground, which slowed the charge and caused it to waver. Nevertheless, there seemed to be some unsteady movement in the Federal ranks for the first time since the battle had begun nearly six hours earlier. Cheatham, seeing that Forrest's charge had gravely altered the steadfastness of the Union line, decided that one more attack might do the job. Adding to the unexpected, though slight change of luck, the line of Confederate guns began to focus their fire on the Hornet's Nest. Cheatham ordered his battered division now racing across the field to support the temporarily stalled cavalry. This rejuvenated assault finally reached the implacable defenders; some of them beginning to break and run under the combined pressure of the attack and the crash of cannon fire. At the same time Forrest directed his cavalry around the marsh and fell upon the retreating Federals from the flank and rear, causing them to scatter like a disorganized mob as they fell back in the direction of the riverboat landing. He continued his pursuit while Union colonel Webster, chief of the Federal staff, watched the scene with mounting concern.

On a slight ridge near Pittsburg Landing, Webster placed all the available Union guns in the path of the Confederate advance and began a well-directed fire over all the approaches to the river port. This bold action stopped the Confederates and prevented the Union rout from becoming a disaster. However, a more coordinated attack from the Confederate right might have revived the spirit of the assault.

Perceiving the opportunity, Beauregard urged his remaining force to press steadily forward upon the disorganized remnants of the Union retreat. This order was never fully implemented, however, because the hungry Southern soldiers paused to take advantage of the abundant spoils in the abandoned Federal encampments as they passed through. Others became lost or separated from their units by the thick woods through which they were advancing.

Exhaustion was taking its toll among the soldiers of both armies by five o'clock, when the first of Buell's reinforcements began to arrive on the east side of the river following a forced march of several miles. The first of these to arrive on the field, a brigade under Col. Jacob Ammen, was ferried across the river about 5:00 P.M. A larger body of Buell's command did not arrive until 9:00 P.M. but was slowed in landing by "6,000 to 10,000 entirely demoralized soldiery" seeking shelter under the river bank from Confederate gunfire.[14]

In the last major action of the day, which the Confederates had launched between four and five o'clock, elements of Hardee's and

Breckinridge's corps attempted to drive through the woods and neutralize Webster's batteries on the ridge beyond. Forrest and his men joined this action taking place on the Confederate right after having participated in the final push against the Hornet's Nest and the pursuit of the fleeing Union troops. The enemy in front of the ridge mounting Webster's cannon slowly began to give way, leaving behind supplies and about 2,500 survivors of the earlier fight at the Hornet's Nest. These troops were captured, along with their commander, General Prentiss.[15] But Webster's guns continued to batter the Confederates, especially the Louisianians under Colonel Mouton, who made the last charge of the day. The commanders on the Confederate right, sensing victory, began to disengage.

Meanwhile, Forrest sent word to Maj. Gen. Leonidas Polk, who was farther to the left of this fight, expressing his assessment of the situation. He still believed the Union position could be taken and the panic-tinged Federal soldiers driven into the river by one more vigorous charge.[16]

By this time, Union gunboats had appeared on the river below Pittsburg Landing and had joined in the cannonade, mingling their shells with those of Webster's batteries in a punishing fire upon the massed Confederates. Polk, comprehending the blistering effect of the shelling, ordered his cavalry, including Forrest, to fall back to a wooded area near a cluster of ancient Indian burial mounds south of the landing.

Shortly afterward, night began to fall, reducing the artillery barrage to sporadic and ineffective shooting intended to harass the Confederates through the night. The dead and wounded lay everywhere, making it possible, Grant later said, to walk in any direction without stepping on the ground.

Adding to the misery of both armies, a storm arose during the evening. The night had been filled with the screams of the wounded crying out for water, and one reporter suggested that perhaps God heard those prayers, because the heavens opened up and the rain began to fall. Lightning and artillery shells streaked white and red through the black sky. Occasional lightning flashes illuminated glimpses of a terrible wasteland strewn with human wreckage. The Confederate commanders, sensing victory, were oblivious to the portent of the flashes and crashing thunder and wind of the storm. But their victory was more precarious than they could have imagined.

It was not only the storm and the shelling that prevented Forrest from getting any rest that night. He had received two pieces of information that troubled his mind. The first concerned his only son,

William, who had enlisted with his father and had accompanied him to Shiloh. Early in the evening, Forrest had learned that William was unaccounted for and had been missing for some time. Fearing the worst, Forrest's parental instincts drove him into the dark in search of his missing son. His quest proved fruitless, however, and he returned to camp later in the evening to find that William and a friend had been off on their own unauthorized foray and had captured fifteen Yankee prisoners.

Undoubtedly relieved that Willie was alive and unharmed, Forrest then received news that assured he would get little sleep that night. Sometime after eleven o'clock, he learned that the main body of Buell's troops was at that time disembarking from their transports in the river below the landing to reinforce Grant. The scouts bringing this information had earlier been sent to reconnoiter the field toward Pittsburg Landing wearing confiscated Union overcoats to confuse the enemy pickets. There has been some dispute as to whether Forrest had personally witnessed this alarming development. However, given the proximity of his camp to the river and the landing, it only makes sense that he would have confirmed this story firsthand. This became his trademark in the years of fighting to come.

Nevertheless, whether he acted on the reports of his scouts or on his own eyewitness verification, Forrest spent the next several hours racing through the Southern camps in search of a commanding officer to warn of the impending danger. So, while the Confederate army slept, Nathan Bedford Forrest rode. Pushing himself through the intermittent rain, past the grotesque horror that had descended upon the battlefield, he probably passed by Bloody Pond, where hundreds of wounded from both sides had dragged themselves and now lay along its edge, their blood turning its waters red. Poe's imagination could hardly have fathomed a more nightmarish scene.

The first commanding officer Forrest found, around midnight, was Gen. James Chalmers, a lawyer from Mississippi who commanded a brigade. Chalmers did not invite Forrest into his tent, but rather met him outside. After impatiently listening to Forrest's information, he brushed him off by sending him in search of General Beauregard, who had become the ranking commander upon General Johnston's death.[17] Though Chalmers omitted from his official report any mention of this nocturnal meeting, he did recall the encounter in an account written after the war in which he quoted Forrest as having said, "If this army does not move and attack between now and daylight, it will be whipped like hell before ten o'clock tomorrow."[18]

After leaving Chalmers, Forrest rode on until he happened across the headquarters of corps commander Gen. John C. Breckinridge, the Southern Democratic presidential nominee in the recent election. Breckinridge also declined to give Forrest the order to attack. He, too, referred him to Beauregard, though neither Breckinridge nor any other commander seemed to know where to find him.

In the course of his desperate ride, Forrest eventually came across Gen. William Hardee, who was no more willing to authorize an attack than were the other commanders.[19]

Unable to locate Beauregard's headquarters, Forrest returned to his own camp. From there he sent out scouts to gather additional intelligence regarding the Union troop landings. When the scouts returned around two o'clock in the morning with news of continued Union reinforcements arriving at Pittsburg Landing, Forrest mounted up again and galloped into the night in a final effort to find Beauregard before it was too late. Given his lack of tolerance for inaction, Forrest must have been past agitation by this time.

Shortly after leaving his own camp, Forrest again met General Hardee and with renewed anxiety once again informed the general of the Union's increasing numbers. Hardee, perhaps impatient and dead tired, ordered Forrest to return to his troops and keep up a strong picket.

Though Chalmers, Breckinridge, and Hardee did not give much credence to Forrest or the information he had brought them, an important confirmation of this intelligence had already been obtained by Beauregard late that afternoon. Following his surrender, General Prentiss had revealed that Buell was nearby with an entire army of fresh troops, which would soon arrive to reinforce Grant.[20] Unfortunately for the Confederates, this information went unheeded by Beauregard, who had earlier received a message from a colonel in Alabama stating that Buell was headed in an entirely different direction. It is uncertain whether Beauregard allowed the misinformation from Alabama to overshadow Prentiss's revelations or simply distrusted the word of a Union prisoner of war. Perhaps, however, the commanders contacted by Forrest during his night ride might have reacted differently had they been aware of Prentiss's story.

Whatever the reasons for the rejection of Forrest's admonitions, his warning proved to be prophetic. The failure to destroy Buell's reinforcements and drive the remnants of Grant's army from the field would cost the Confederacy dearly in the Union counterattack of April 7.

Might the outcome of the battle been decidedly different had

Forrest been given even a thousand men to launch a surprise attack through the rainy darkness against the confused Union troops huddled along the river? Perhaps. Yet, the suggestion alone is brilliant in its audacity, and for that, if for nothing else, Forrest's name deserves mention in the annals of the battle.

As Forrest had warned every commander he could find, the battle resumed at dawn the next day, Monday, April 7, when the Federals counterattacked with renewed strength. The vision of defeat that Forrest had spun for his commanders now broke over the battlefield in bloody reality. Facing General Buell's fresh troops, the exhausted Confederate soldiers fought stubbornly to hold on to the victory they had won at such great cost the day before. The bodies of their dead comrades, as well as those of Union soldiers, from the first day of battle still littered the ground over which they were forced to retreat.

By early afternoon, Beauregard had determined to save the remainder of his army by retreating south to Corinth. Likely Johnston's resolve in attacking Grant at Shiloh, over the objections of his subordinate, rang hollow in Beauregard's ears as he ordered his command to fall back in as orderly a fashion as possible.

On Tuesday, April 8, Gen. William Tecumseh Sherman led the Federal pursuit. He deployed Col. T. Lyle Dickey's Fourth Illinois Cavalry in the van as pickets, followed by two infantry brigades commanded by Brig. Gen. T. J. Wood. Near Monterey, at a fork in the road leading to Corinth, Sherman paused to look across a marshy, log-covered field where a civilian logging crew had recently felled hundreds of trees. He could see the camps of the retreating Confederates less than a mile ahead.

Beyond the clearing and parallel to the road along which Sherman's troops were advancing, Forrest, who had been ordered to form a rear guard, lay in wait behind a wooded ridge with some 350 men. He had hastily assembled his rear guard from among his own command and men from Texas, Kentucky, and Mississippi. With the pursuing Federals so close to the main Confederate army, Forrest was unwilling to yield slowly to the approaching enemy troops. The crucial situation called for the kind of unorthodox action for which Forrest would become legendary in scores of battles and skirmishes during the next three years. The one thing the confident Yankees would not expect was a determined attack, but Forrest knew that any such charge at this moment must be made fearfully believable or it would be no better than suicide.

As Forrest watched the oncoming Federals, he saw his opening when Dickey's cavalry became momentarily confused in crossing a small stream. Instinctively seizing the moment, Forrest's small command struck the enemy like a thunderbolt. Leading the charge, he set a spectacular example for his men to emulate.[21] The pickup force of Confederates swept down the ridge with unexpected and startling fury. Colonel Dickey's cavalry reeled as Forrest crashed into them at full gallop, driving a wedge through the blue line. Taken fully by surprise, the Union cavalry broke apart. Such was the panic created by this onslaught that Dickey's horsemen stampeded over the top of their own infantry directly behind them. The horrified foot soldiers stood momentarily transfixed and dazed by the chaos sweeping over them.

Forrest's concentration, soon to become famous, led him blindly onward. Before he realized it, he had outdistanced his own men and found himself cut off and surrounded by the temporarily stunned Union infantry, who seemed to hesitate briefly. When the melee resumed, one reanimated enemy soldier thrust his musket toward the mounted Confederate colonel and fired point-blank. The ball plowed through Bedford's hip and lodged against his spine, causing a temporary paralysis in his right leg.

With his benumbed leg dangling from the stirrup, Forrest wheeled his warhorse and charged back across the ground he had just covered. Racing ahead of the storm of lead aimed at his back, Bedford snatched a bluecoat by the collar, jerking the hapless soldier off his feet and pulling the trooper up behind him for protection. When safely out of range, Forrest dropped his human shield and galloped into the ranks of his cheering men, who had been watching the whole affair with great concern for the safety of their commander. Characteristically, Forrest disregarded the pain from his own wound as he dismounted and went looking for the surgeon, whom he later found under his own power.

The ball, the surgeon determined, was resting against Forrest's lower spine and after a painful probing of the area around the wound, he decided it was best to leave it alone for the time being. Rather than take an ambulance to Corinth, because the jostling would be too painful, Forrest insisted on riding his horse. The brave animal died from his own wounds after faithfully carrying his master more than fifteen miles and once again to safety.

Though his escape at Shiloh is one of the most oft-quoted stories in Forrest lore, he apparently never mentioned the human shield incident to his biographers, Gen. Thomas Jordan and J. P. Pryor, who personally consulted with the general while writing their book. Their account of Forrest's rear-guard action does not include this incident, which might indicate that it either never happened, or that Forrest simply did not think it relevant at the time.

Maj. Gilbert V. Rambaut, who participated in the charge down the ridge, saw Bedford when he was trapped and thought his commander was finished. After the war Rambaut wrote his own eyewitness account of Forrest's miraculous escape. His story is similar to that of Jordan and Pryor's in the critical details and also omits the human shield exploit.[22]

Albert Castel, who wrote the new introduction for the 1992 republication of Jordan and Pryor's book, *The Campaigns of General Nathan Bedford Forrest*, says that it would have been physically impossible to execute the maneuver as described by later Forrest biographers. Since Forrest became famous for doing the impossible, who really knows? However, even given the confusion and desperation of the moment, one wonders how it could be possible that the massed fire from the Yankee riflemen could fail to hit their target. It was a disappearing act worthy of Merlin.

One indisputable fact, however, was that Forrest's escape was the closing act in the delaying action that possibly allowed Beauregard's army precious time to escape to Corinth and fight another day. Sherman reported,

> The check sustained by us at the fallen timbers delayed our advance so that night came upon us before the wounded were provided for and the dead buried, and our troops being fagged out by three hard days' fighting, exposure and privation, I ordered them back to camp.[23]

At Shiloh, and in the retreat to Corinth, Forrest had, by his dauntless actions, begun to define the persona that would be feared and heralded for as long as he lived. Forrest's performance during the heat of battle indicated that he was no ordinary guerrilla raider. Pleading for a night attack at Shiloh and charging under his own orders at Fallen Timbers provides early proof that he was unlike other Southern commanders. Although he harassed the enemy with numerous raids behind their lines, his true inclination was to battle the enemy whenever he met them in the field. This was not in the tradition of guerilla raiders. However, there was little of tradition in Nathan Bedford Forrest, who was a hard-fighting soldier first and a cavalryman second.

Although his wound at Fallen Timbers might well have proved

fatal, Forrest, even before he had completely healed, was busy enlarg-
ing the mythology that would fascinate his comrades and enemies
throughout the war. Ordered to Memphis for convalescent leave,
Forrest was back in Corinth on April 31, just twenty-one days after he
had been wounded and with the bullet still lodged painfully against
his spine. Shortly after Forrest's arrival, Dr. J. B. Cowan, a cousin of
Forrest's wife, finally removed the ball without benefit of anesthetic.[24]

Returning again to Memphis in the second week of June, Bedford
was drawn back to the bloody business of war. He decided to raise a
body of new volunteers since his command had been decimated
during the fighting at Shiloh. In June his call to arms ran in *The
Memphis Appeal:*

### 200 RECRUITS WANTED

I will receive 200 able-bodied men if they will present themselves at my headquarters by the first of June with good horses
and gun. I wish none but those who desire to be actively
engaged. My headquarters for the present is at Corinth, Miss.
COME ON BOYS, IF YOU WANT A HEAP OF FUN AND TO
KILL SOME YANKEES.

N.B. Forrest Colonel,
Commanding Forrest's Regiment[25]

"Obviously this was a man who either wanted to deceive his
prospective recruits into thinking 'kill[ing] some Yankees' was going
to be a 'heap of fun,'" Forrest biographer Jack Hurst wrote, "or a
man who actually felt it was."[26]

Though the battle at Shiloh had shocked both armies and their
governments into a new sense of reality concerning the gravity of
the war they had begun, neither side wavered in their resolve to
fight it out. The earth near Shiloh Church that had been so earnestly fought over now held the bodies of some four thousand men
slain, with almost twenty thousand more wounded in the most costly battle of the war thus far. The clash was comparable to the great
battle of Waterloo that brought Napoleon down in 1815. Before the
American Civil War ended, another twenty Waterloos would be
fought and a generation of young American men from both North
and South would be devastated.

# Chapter Four

# ON FIERY-FOOTED STEEDS

*—William Shakespeare*

## Murfreesboro
## June-July 1862

This most recent of Forrest's newspaper ads is interesting in the sense that it displays a discernable change in journalistic style and attitude. It lacks the literary technique contained in his other published articles, which most likely had been dictated by Forrest to one of his more academically trained friends. Instead it adopts a dark humor and verbiage more in character with the author.

Taking into consideration that the author was recovering from a large-caliber bullet wound near his spine, which very well could have paralyzed him, the article displays his obvious joy for the sting of battle and a certain disregard for his own mortality. He had already seen more personal combat than most officers ever would. Yet, his appetite for war was far from sated. He had found his true calling.

The same attitude is reflected in a letter he wrote to the Independent Order of Odd Fellows during the days surrounding the battle at Shiloh. Forrest's difficulty with grammar and spelling are obvious:

> I had a small brush with the Enamy on yesterday I Suceded in gaining thir rear and hot in to thir entrenchments . . . and Burned a portion of thir camp. . . . they wair not looking for me I taken them by Surprise they run like Suns of Biches. . . . this army is at this time in front of our Entrenchments I look for a fite soon and a big one. . . . Cant you come up and take a hand this fite wil do to hand down to your children.[1]

After Shiloh he began to apply the lessons he had learned while growing up on the frontier and during his rise to wealthy landowner.

Henceforth he would wage war on his own terms and trust his own instincts. Unschooled in military doctrines and tactics though he was, he needed no such training to be able to recognize incompetence and poor leadership. He could not have been much impressed by the example of military leadership set by Generals Floyd and Pillow at Fort Donelson, nor by what he had seen of Cheatham, Hardee, and Chalmers at Shiloh. Perhaps he now felt that he must take things into his own hands. He had no patience or time for unwritten codes of military conduct, nor antiquated rules of war. To him, everything depended on total destruction of the enemy by any means necessary. His personal survival and the survival of his newly founded nation depended on it.

With his mind set and his direction decided, Forrest learned that his own intuition and instincts were going to be more important than he might ever have thought. When the wounded cavalryman returned to his command in June, after only a short convalescence, he found that it had been taken away from him.

Forrest's future, fortunately, would not always be so bereft of providential interference. Beauregard had not forgotten the reports concerning a certain "unlettered colonel" who had tried so desperately to find him that night at Shiloh, a soldier who was such a fighter that he wanted to renew the attack in the dark. Beauregard needed a man who had the persistence to handle the difficult job of organizing the scattered cavalry units in southeastern Tennessee and welding them into an effective force to challenge the Union army in that area. With Buell moving at that very time across northern Alabama toward the Confederacy's important rail junction at Chattanooga, Beauregard decided that Forrest was the man for the job.

Beauregard's "man" was not exactly thrilled to learn that he would have to leave his old regiment, which he had led for more than a year. Beauregard's authorized biographer wrote that Forrest

> hesitated at first, modestly alleging his inability to assume such a responsibility; but yielded, finally, when again urged . . . and after receiving the promise that his old regiment should be sent to him as soon as it could be spared from the Army of the Mississippi.[2]

Undoubtedly, he was also motivated by a promise of promotion to brigadier general, and with his acceptance of the assignment, a request for a brigadier's star, an advancement that would elevate him to senior cavalry officer in the Chattanooga department, was forwarded to the War Department.

On June 11, 1862, Forrest left Major Kelley in charge of the old regiment and departed for Chattanooga with a small detachment of handpicked men, including his brother William. Arriving in Chattanooga a week later, he assumed command of two cavalry units consisting of Terry's Rangers, led by Col. John A. Wharton, and Col. J. K. Lawton's Second Georgia. Thomas Jordan, one of Forrest's biographers, remembered that some of Bedford's men were not enthused by their new leader or his immediate battle plans. The rumor was that Forrest's idea to disrupt Buell's drive against Chattanooga was "rash, inconsiderate, and likely to lead to disaster."[3] The doubters would be proven wrong on all accounts.

Forrest had never been particularly interested in drilling maneuvers or parade ground activities, but one day while observing his new troops he saw something that sparked his tactical imagination. Noticing that the horsemen were maneuvering themselves according to a variety of bugle calls, Forrest approached the officer in charge of the exercise and inquired if they could be made to circle a specific area on a battle-field in the manner he had just witnessed. When the officer answered in the affirmative, Forrest replied, "I will often have need of this maneuver, as it will be necessary from time to time for me to show more men than I actually have on the field."[4] In time, Forrest would perfect the art of deceiving the enemy into believing that he always possessed two or three times his actual numbers, and on numerous occasions over the course of the war, he would be able to bluff enemy commanders into surrendering their men to his own numerically infe-rior force. At Murfreesboro he would test out his new tactics of decep-tion on the Union commander, Gen. Thomas T. Crittenden.

On July 9, he crossed the Tennessee heading toward McMinnville, and after a forced march of nearly fifty miles, he and his men camped at Altamont, Tennessee, on the tenth. At Altamont, Forrest was reinforced by the First Georgia Cavalry, two companies of Kentuckians, and Lt. Col. C. C. Spiller's Tennessee Battalion. These additions brought his combined strength to 1,400 men.[5]

After another fifty-mile ride, Forrest arrived after dark on July 12 at the village of Woodbury, Tennessee, where he reported that both his men and his horses were on the verge of exhaustion after having traveled so far. The womenfolk of Woodbury were exceedingly happy to see the Confederates and were also in a high state of agita-tion. They soon sought the counsel of the rebel chieftain and explained that a Yankee army bivouacked in and around Murfreesboro had rounded up all their men and placed them in the jail at Murfreesboro. They further reported that some of these men were to be executed as Confederate sympathizers. Forrest assured the ladies of Woodbury that he would rescue their husbands and sons, but first his men required food and rest after their long march, and they needed to feed and tend to their animals. Forrest promised the distraught women that his command would move out at daybreak. Upon hearing his promises, the ladies gratefully supplied his troopers with food and their animals with fodder.

The next day, June 13, was Forrest's forty-first birthday. What he had in store for the Yankees at Murfreesboro was one hell of a surprise party, and he planned to deliver the invitations personally.

The Confederate cavalry moved out about 1:00 A.M. and covered the eighteen miles from Woodbury to Murfreesboro in a little over four hours. By 4:30 A.M., Forrest's vanguard had slipped in undetected and captured more than a dozen Union pickets without firing a shot. With information from these prisoners and intelligence he had received in earlier scouting reports, Forrest had a pretty clear picture of the Union dispositions at Murfreesboro. Gen. Thomas T. Crittenden of Indiana, who commanded the Union troops, had divided them into three different areas in and around the town. The Ninth Michigan Infantry and two companies of the Seventh Pennsylvania Cavalry were camped on the eastern edge of Murfreesboro. The Third Minnesota and Capt. John N. Hewett's battery of guns was a mile and a half beyond the town. In the center of the town, guarding Crittenden's headquarters and the prisoners in the courthouse jail, were the Eighth Kentucky Cavalry and one company of the Ninth Michigan.

What Forrest did not know as he made his preparations to attack was that John Hunt Morgan had seriously jeopardized his battle plans. Morgan and Forrest had a mutual interest in Murfreesboro and in June had discussed their operations in Kentucky and Tennessee. Though General Morgan did not know of Forrest's decision to attack Murfreesboro, he was aware of his intended operations in the region. Morgan's fiancée, his second wife-to-be, lived in Murfreesboro, and he was no doubt thinking of her safety. The week after Morgan's first raid into Kentucky, he cut the telegraph wires near the town of Horse Cave and had his own telegrapher, "Lightning" George A. Ellsworth, tap into the lines and send the following bogus message to the provost marshal at Louisville in the name of the Union provost marshal at Nashville:

> General Forrest, commanding a brigade, attacked Murfreesboro, routing our forces, and is now moving on Nashville. Morgan is reported to be between Scottsville and

Gallatin, and will act in concert with Forrest, it is believed. Inform general commanding.[6]

Though the message was sent innocently and was intended to further Morgan's own operations, one wonders how Forrest might have reacted had he known a fellow Confederate cavalry leader had jeopardized his move against Murfreesboro by attempting such a ruse. Nevertheless, the first part of the message was about to come true: the Union forces at Murfreesboro were attacked and routed, and ten days later Forrest moved his command within site of the capitol dome at Nashville.

Acting without knowledge of Morgan's message, Forrest decided to split his force into three parts and attempt to attack all three enemy encampments simultaneously. Col. John A. Wharton's Texas Rangers were to assail the Seventh Pennsylvania Cavalry and Ninth Michigan Infantry, camped just to the right of the turnpike that led into the town. Wharton's orders were to either capture them or hold them in place until the other Union detachments were defeated. Forrest would lead Col. A. J. Morrison's battalion straight into the center of town and then break into three different squadrons, which would attack the courthouse, the jail, and the Murfreesboro Hotel, the site of General Crittinden's headquarters. The men of Colonel Lawton's First Georgia Cavalry were to charge completely through the town and throw themselves between the Third Minnesota and Hewett's batteries to prevent them from reinforcing their comrades.[7]

Dawn was breaking as Forrest formed his assault force into columns of fours. They advanced at a slow gait until the white peaks of the enemy tents became visible. Suddenly, Forrest bellowed the command to charge, and fourteen hundred riders spurred their mounts ahead as they shattered the morning silence with a chorus of rebel yells. As they surged forward, the sound of the horses' hoofs upon the macadamized turnpike sounded like the rumble of distant thunder.

The Texas Rangers were upon the Union men as most of them were stumbling into wakefulness. Col. John G. Parkhurst later wrote, "The enemy, mounted and some 1,200 strong, with terrific yells, dashed upon us from three directions, armed with double-barreled shot-guns and Colt's navy revolvers." Acting Brigadier General W. W. Duffield ran out of his tent just in time to be shot in the groin and thigh by the rebels stampeding through the camp. Duffield was able to rally his boys to repel the attack but soon passed out from loss of blood and was carried from the field of battle. The Union command fell to Colonel Parkhurst, who began to organize an effective resistance by overturning hay-filled wagons to be used for cover.[8]

Most of the Pennsylvania cavalrymen were captured before they could reach their horses. The rest fell back to the nearby position of the Ninth Michigan and took cover behind the hastily constructed works. Soon they were pouring a severe return fire into the oncoming Confederates, successfully stalling their advance. During the early moments of the struggle, Colonel Wharton, leading the Texas Rangers, was shot from the saddle, seriously wounded. Col. John G. Walker assumed command of the Texans and ordered his men to hold their positions and keep up a continuous fire.

While all this was transpiring, Forrest, leading the charge of the second wave, rushed past the combat occurring on the outskirts of Murfreesboro and swept into the center of the town.

One of the prisoners in the nearby jail was Capt. William Richardson, who had been captured at Shiloh and later paroled in Indiana. A few days before Forrest's attack on Murfreesboro, he had been attempting to work his way through enemy lines with a guide named James Paul. Reaching Murfreesboro, they had been captured and sentenced to hang when it was learned that Paul was a Confederate spy. Their execution was scheduled for the very morning of the attack. Captain Richardson described what he heard and saw:

> Just about daylight on the morning of the 13th, I was aroused from sleep by my companion, who had caught me by the arm and was shaking me, saying, "Listen! Listen!" I started up, hearing a strange noise like the roar of an approaching storm. We both leaped to our feet and stood upon an empty box . . . and looked out through the small grating of our prison window. The roar grew louder and came nearer, and in a very few seconds we were sure we could discern the clatter of horses' feet upon the hard turnpike. In a moment more there could be no doubt as to the riders of these horses, for on the morning air there came to our ears with heartfelt welcome the famous rebel yell, the battle-cry of the Confederate soldiers. Almost before we could speak the advance-guard of the charging troopers came into sight and rushed by us on the street, some halting in front of the jail.[9]

As the heated combat continued around the jail, General Crittenden's hotel headquarters and the men in the courthouse also came under attack. Before anyone knew what was happening, the jail burst into flames. One of the Union troopers defending the jail had set fire to the building with the intention of burning the prisoners he believed were about to be rescued by attacking Confederates.

The fire had barely caught hold when Confederate troopers stormed the building and were able to rescue the trapped prisoners, including those civilians rounded up at Woodbury, from a horrible death. Captain Richardson wrote that Forrest himself "dashed up and inquired of the officer in charge if he had rescued the prisoners. He said that they were safe, but added that the jail had been set on fire in order to burn them up, and the guard had taken refuge in the courthouse." Forrest said, "Never mind, we'll get them." Richardson also stated that he would never forget Forrest's eyes "flashing like fire" when he was told about the Yankee arsonist.[10]

Forrest now turned his attention to the town courthouse, where a company of Michigan infantry was making a stubborn defense. Forrest formed an assault force to attack the courthouse from all sides. As they rushed forward, another group of rebel troopers used a battering ram to take down the front door to gain entrance, whereupon a vicious hand-to-hand fight began. Soon, the Confederates had control of the first floor but were unable to move up the stairs to finish the job. Forrest, believing that perhaps the Union troopers holding out on the second floor, one of whom was the soldier who had set the fire at the jail, deserved a taste of their own medicine, ordered the courthouse set ablaze to smoke them out. In his report Forrest said that after two hours of hard fighting the courthouse was fired, and in short order the defenders were rushing out of the building to surrender. General Crittenden and his staff were captured during the roundup of prisoners.[11]

Forrest then sent reinforcements to the Texans, who still had Parkhurst's men pinned down. With the remainder of his troops he rode to assist Colonel Lawton's First Georgia along with his Tennessee and Kentucky men, who had engaged the Third Minnesota and Hewett's gun batteries outside the town. Lawton's men had not made much progress due the position of Hewett's guns on top of a nearby hill, which gave their gunners an excellent command of the field. When Forrest arrived, he immediately led a flanking detachment, sweeping around the Union position, and hit them from their rear. The original campsite of Col. H. C. Lester's Third Minnesota Regiment was nearby and also overrun. Within minutes the Confederates had taken one hundred prisoners.

On the hill the Union troops still held a strong position. Forrest's instincts told him that it would take more time to defeat such a strong position than he had at the moment. He left a strong force to augment Colonel Lawton and quickly returned to aid the Texans in finishing off Parkhurst and his Michigan troops. Forrest was determined not to quit the battle until he had gained complete victory.

This intention was clear to some of his junior officers who, as yet unacquainted with their commander's unorthodox tactics, voiced their concern about the prudence of attempting to destroy all three enemy camps without reinforcements. They "urged Colonel Forrest to rest content with what had been accomplished and quit the field without further, as they were satisfied, fruitless yet costly efforts to carry the Federal position." They apparently had not been infected with the battle fever that burned within Forrest, nor had he fully caught hold in their imaginations and spirit. Disregarding their concerns, Forrest said, "I did not come here to make half a job of it. I mean to have them all," and he began making preparations to do just that.

He ordered a portion of his command to dismount in front of the Michigan and Pennsylvania regiments, then repeated that order to another group on their right flank and prepared to charge Parkhurst's position. First, however, he sent to the Union commander an order for surrender that would be repeated on numerous future battlefields:

> Colonel: I must demand unconditional surrender of your force as prisoners of war or I will have every man put to the sword. You are aware of the overwhelming force I have at my command, and this demand is made to prevent the effusion of blood.
> I am, colonel, very respectfully, your obedient servant,
> N.B. FORREST, Brigadier General of Cavalry, C.S. Army[12]

The language of the demand was of a chivalrous nature, common in those times, but to future students of the Civil War, Forrest's choice of words would not sound particularly respectful, nor were they words one would expect to hear from one's "obedient servant." He was learning to apply his own instincts to such confrontations, and if such terms did indeed prevent the effusion of blood, they were preferable to further fighting, and certainly more so to carrying out such threats. Further, in signing the note as he did, it mattered little to him that he had not yet officially received his promotion to brigadier general. Forrest had his own timetable to follow; the Confederate command had theirs.

By this point in the battle, Parkhurst had been fighting hard for nearly seven hours. He also had been wounded in the leg and apparently believed that Forrest would carry out the threat contained in his ultimatum. Receiving Forrest's note at 11:30, he forwarded it to Colonel Duffield with an attached message:

> [I] had ascertained that General Forrest had concentrated his entire force, save one squadron . . . in the immediate vicinity of my camp, hemming us in on all sides, and . . . preparing to make a charge upon us with his entire command . . . evidently intending, with his overwhelming force, to execute the threat contained in his demand for a surrender.[13]

Of course, this was the exact effect Forrest hoped his words would have on Parkhurst.

Colonel Duffield sent a return message to Parkhurst telling him that the situation was left to his discretion. At noon, Parkhurst surrendered his remaining 134 men to Forrest. As soon as this surrender was accomplished, Forrest raced back toward the west side of town to deal with Colonel Lester and his Minnesotans. The rebel leader sent in a duplicate of the terms he had sent to Parkhurst. Colonel Lester asked permission to confer with Col. W. W. Duffield before giving Forrest his decision. Permission was granted, but Forrest had another ace up his sleeve as he escorted Lester back to speak with Colonel Duffield, who was already his prisoner.

As they rode back through Murfreesboro together, Forrest's troops were ready to put on a show. Before Lester could reach Duffield's position, he would see the same Confederates several times, as Forrest's men marched around the buildings, mounted up out of sight, and then rode back into view as cavalry units. By the time Colonel Lester arrived at his destination, he had been thoroughly hoodwinked. He would later report Forrest's strength at 2,600, which was double his actual numbers.

Colonel Lester need not have felt embarrassed at believing Forrest's numbers to be larger than they were, for he was merely one of the first of many Union officers to fall victim to Forrest's cunning. Lester's surrender came around 3:00 P.M., giving Bedford a very happy birthday present of total victory. In his official battle report, sent to his superiors in Chattanooga, Forrest said that he had taken 1,200 prisoners and reported,

> [We] burnt $200,000 worth of stores; captured sufficient stores with those burned to amount to $500,000, and brigade of 60 wagons, 300 mules, 150 or 200 horses, and field battery of four

pieces; destroyed the railroad and depot at Murfreesboro. Had
to retreat to McMinnville, owing to the large number of prisoners to be guarded.[14]

Federal reports indicate that the Union losses were 20 killed and
170 wounded. Forrest reported that he lost "about 20 killed and 40-
60 wounded."[15]

Forrest's command arrived on the night of June 14 at McMinnville,
where he paroled all of his prisoners except the commissioned officers. The officers were taken on to Knoxville under a small detachment of guards. But before they had departed, Forrest apparently
took an interest in Colonel Parkhurst's choice in horses. Parkhurst
wrote in his battle report: "I was ordered to dismount and surrender
my horse, which General Forrest instantly appropriated."[16] Parkhurst
was understandably upset to lose his horse. Could he have foreseen
Forrest's future reputation for having horses shot from under him in
battle, Parkhurst might have been depressed as well that his horse had
become an endangered species. Forrest never mentioned the incident in his battle report, nor to his postwar biographers.

There were a few other more ominous incidents that were also
omitted from the official record. During the quick strike into the
rear of the Third Minnesota's camp, Forrest was reported to have
killed at least one black man. This incident, like others to come, is
aswirl in controversy. It occurred as Forrest led the charge into
Colonel Lester's base camp:

> While traversing the camp, he was fired at by a Negro camp-fol-
> lower, one of whose balls cut his hatband; but, just as the Negro
> was about to fire his fifth time, Forrest killed him with his pistol
> at the distance of thirty paces. The Negro displayed no common
> deliberation in his purpose to slay the Confederate leader.[17]

This version is the best documented of several that surfaced after
the battle.

Following the Fort Pillow incident later in the war, and while that
controversy was raging, Maj. Gen. David S. Stanley was quoted in a
*New York Times* article that Forrest had committed cold-blooded murder at Murfreesboro. Stanley's evidence, however, was thirdhand
and ultimately hearsay. He attributed the account to "a rebel citizen
of Middle Tennessee, a man of high standing in his community, who
had it from his nephew, an officer serving under Forrest." The
Stanley story went on to say:

A mulatto man, who was the servant to one of the officers in the Union forces, was brought to FORREST on horseback. The latter inquired of him, with many oaths, what he was doing there. The mulatto answered that he was a free man, and came out as a servant to an officer, naming the man. FORREST, who was on horseback, deliberately put his hand to his holster, drew a pistol, and blew the man's brains out.

The Confederate officer stated that the mulatto man came from Pennsylvania; and the same officer denounced the act as one of cold-blooded murder, and declared that he would never again serve under FORREST.[18]

Another anonymous participant in the Murfreesboro battle said that he had taken prisoner a black man dressed in Federal uniform and personally delivered his prize to the general himself.

> I took him and started to hunt up General Forrest. I soon found him Sitting on his horse his eyes blazing fire and I called his attention to my capture and instead of complimenting me he gave me a cussing that still amuses me when I think of it. I tried to reason that that was a Very Valuable n—— but the general reasoned that a Dead n—— in federal uniform was more valuable to the Confederacy than a live one but finally he ordered me to turn him over to Col. Morrison who had charge of the prisoners and he finally Sent the Negro home to his owner Dr. Rucker of Rutherford Co. Tenn.[19]

Later that summer, a Southern civilian wrote in his diary,

> The Negroes are rather afraid of familiarity with the Yankees since they heard that Forrest hung quite a number of them that were taken in arms at Murfreesboro & also at Gallatin. . . . This policy seems severe but the Southern people can never consent to treat negroes as prisoners of war & exchange for them with white prisoners.[20]

Rumors ran rampant after his brilliant victory, but Forrest said nothing. He never denied, qualified, or apologized for any of the many charges or rumors that were levied against him, especially during the war. More likely than not, it was by design. If he was truly feared, he would maintain a psychological advantage that could be exploited in combat. He had no thoughts of how history would view him, nor had he any plans for a political future. There was only now, and this was war. "War to the knife, knife to the hilt," Forrest had been quoted as saying, and at Murfreesboro, he sent a message to the enemy as well as to his own men. From this point forward, he would fight the war on his own terms, and by his own rulebook.

The last controversial incident worthy of mention, which also went unreported at the time, was the fate of the Union arsonist who had attempted to incinerate the Southern prisoners at the Murfreesboro jail. Captain Richardson, who had been one of the prisoners awaiting execution, remembered Forrest approaching him after the Union prisoners had been rounded up and placed in line for a head count. The general said, "They tell me these men . . . treated you inhumanly while in jail. Point them out to me." Richardson recalled,

> I told him there was but one man I wished to call his attention to, and that was the one who had set fire to the jail in order to burn us up. Forrest asked me to go along the line with him and point that man out. I did so. A few hours later, when the list of private soldiers was being called, the name of this man was heard and no one answered; Forrest said, "Pass on it's alright."[21]

It's fairly obvious that Forrest had knowledge of the soldier's fate, and one could easily divine the implications of Forrest's comment. If he did not personally execute this man, it was probably done on his orders.

The Murfreesboro raid whipped the Union command into a frenzy of activity. All the Federal garrisons in the area were immediately called back to protect Nashville. Buell, along with George H. Thomas's command, at Tuscumbia, Alabama, was ordered to move quickly on Murfreesboro. Forrest's raid also virtually stopped Buell's drive on Chattanooga and forced him to divert much of his command up and down the rail lines by which the Union supplied its army in the Nashville area.

With so many enemy troops converging on his position, it would not seem prudent for Forrest to stay in the immediate area, let alone attack Nashville, which was exactly what the enemy feared he would do. Forrest's command was not nearly large enough to actually threaten the occupied Tennessee capital, but with the inflated rumors of that commander's numbers, the Federals really did not know what to expect. Forrest was not about to let the confusion and chaos he had created go to waste. He decided to gamble and really shake the enemy's confidence by moving his small command toward Nashville. That his instincts were correct is borne out by a message of warning to the Federal command at the capital city:

Nashville, Tennessee, July 10, 1862: To Henry Dent, Provost Marshal, Louisville, Kentucky—General Forrest attacked Murfreesboro, routing our forces, and is now moving on Nashville with 7,000 men. Inform general commanding.[22]

Braxton Bragg, who had succeeded P. G. T. Beauregard as the Confederate commander in the West, called Forrest's victory at Murfreesboro a "gallant, brilliant operation . . . This added to his gallantry at Shiloh, where he was severely wounded, mark him as a valuable soldier."[23] Viscount Joseph Garnet Wolseley, field marshal and commander-in-chief of Her Majesty's armed forces, traveled to America during the Civil War to study the Confederate army, particularly the Army of Virginia, and became one of the first military historians to recognize Forrest's untutored military genius. He wrote of the Murfreesboro raid:

It was one of the most remarkable achievements of his life. . . . His operations that day showed a rare mixture of military skill and what is known by our American cousins as "bluff," and led to the surrender of the three camps attacked. . . . It was a brilliant success, and as it was his first great foray, it at once established his reputation as a partisan and as a daring cavalry leader to be dreaded by all commanders of Federal posts and stations within his sphere of action.[24]

# Chapter Five

# THE WIZARD OF THE SADDLE

*—Unknown*

## First West Tennessee Campaign
## July-December 1862

The military situation shifted drastically in the wake of Forrest's and Morgan's operations in Kentucky and Tennessee. On July 21, 1862, Bragg decided to move his army from the base of operations at Tupelo, Mississippi, to Chattanooga, Tennessee, leaving Gen. Earl Van Dorn and Maj. Gen. Sterling Price to protect Vicksburg and also to watch carefully for any advance by Grant from the Memphis-Corinth line. General Hardee was ordered to move his thirty-four thousand men up from Mobile and Montgomery, Alabama, by rail and join Bragg at Chattanooga.[1]

It was a vast and difficult operation. It was also a first in military history. This coordinated rail movement of Confederate armies that summer from one theater of operations to another was the inauguration of massive military movement by rail. Having discovered that such operations were feasible, armies in future wars would rely on rail to move large bodies of troops and maintain their armies logistically in the field. The American spirit of innovation was never displayed in a more dramatic manner than through the years of 1861-65. The American Civil War is often considered the first modern war, not only for the growing importance of railroads, but also for innovations such as the first combat submarine and use of armored war ships.

Operating in western Tennessee as a part of this major troop reassignment, Forrest would find himself in the cross hairs of several Federal columns. Converging upon the Confederate cavalry leader from different directions, the Union generals sent out to destroy him were about to witness the making of a military legend. Over the next few weeks Forrest would become known as the Wizard of the Saddle, but no one definitively knows the source.

Though Forrest is best known for his fiery temper, he could also display remarkable patience in tight situations. In July, he calmly waited for his scouts to return with their reports on the Federals' progress. Receiving the required intelligence satisfied him for the moment that he could maneuver his cavalry in relative safety. On July 18, he put his column on the road at McMinnville and headed toward Lebanon, Tennessee, which he reached at about one o'clock the next afternoon at the end of a hard, fifty-mile march. Forrest believed there was an encampment of five hundred enemy troops at Lebanon, and he prepared to attack them immediately. Such an attack proved to be unnecessary, however. The Union detachment at Lebanon had been forewarned of Forrest's approach and had been led to believe, erroneously, that Forrest had a force of nearly seven thousand men. Believing that they were outnumbered, they fled back toward Nashville. Part of the report had been true, of course. Forrest was heading their way, but with nothing near seven thousand men. The brigade he led at that moment was one-tenth that size.[2]

Forrest's troops spent the night at Lebanon and enjoyed the hospitality of the local people, who treated the rebels to a feast in the field of roasted pig, ham, and fried chicken. What they did not consume was packed away into a three-day supply of tasty rations. On July 19, Forrest and his seven hundred cavalrymen moved to within sight of the steepled skyline of downtown Nashville.

On July 21, Forrest received his promotion to brigadier general. At about the same time, Bragg had organized his army at Chattanooga into two wings and crossed the Tennessee River. Gen. Leonidas Polk commanded the right wing; Gen. William J. Hardee led the left. Forrest found himself on the far left with instructions to harass and "hold in close observation the rear of Buell's army," which was marching on Nashville. Now began a deadly game of hide-and-seek with the majority of the Union commanders in central and eastern Tennessee.

Four miles from Nashville, Forrest took several prisoners in an attack on a Union stockade, posted troops to guard the bridge over Mill Creek, and burned the railroad trestle. A half-mile farther up Mill Creek, another bridge was destroyed and forty more prisoners were captured. Continuing onward and around Nashville, Forrest's advance guard, the Eighth Texas, attacked a small Union garrison at Antioch Station. The Federals there were quickly routed and an additional forty prisoners were taken, along with a railroad depot filled with supplies. The Confederates also burned several railroad cars and another train trestle.[3]

The entire region around Nashville was in an uproar by the time Union general William Nelson, at Murfreesboro, received the news that Forrest was on a rampage and intended to attack the capital city. Nelson immediately started part of his division toward Nashville. By 10:00 P.M. on July 21, Nelson arrived with thirty-five hundred troops at Stones River, seven miles from his destination, but by that time Forrest had moved away from Nashville along the Murfreesboro-Nashville Turnpike and was causing alarm down the rail line toward Chattanooga.

Learning that Forrest somehow had doubled back on him, General Nelson immediately countermarched in pursuit back toward Murfreesboro. After dark on July 23, near a place called Chicken Road and approximately six miles from Murfreesboro, Nelson marched unawares right by Forrest's campsite. For several hours, the Confederates could distinctly hear the Union column passing along the main turnpike toward Murfreesboro.[4]

The next morning, after paroling prisoners and then riding in the direction of McMinnville, Forrest's command struck a detachment of Gen. W. Sooy Smith's Federals near Manchester, killing three and capturing fifteen. Then the elusive cavalryman vanished.

Over the next few weeks, Gen. Don Carlos Buell continuously prodded Nelson to keep up the hunt for Forrest, but by the last part of August, Nelson had reached the end of his wits. He sent a dispatch to Buell on August 30 expressing his frustration. "To chase Morgan and Forrest," he wrote, "they mounted on race horses, with infantry in this hot weather is a hopeless task."[5] Nevertheless, Buell ordered Nelson to hunt down and destroy Forrest and also asked General Halleck for help in the endeavor.

Under pressure from Washington concerning his lack of progress toward Chattanooga, Halleck sent a reply suggesting that his priorities should not be challenged. Buell was perturbed by the message and tried to soothe Halleck's concern by explaining in his reply that Forrest's cavalry had twice destroyed the rail lines between Nashville and Chattanooga and had disrupted his lines of communication. "The army," Buell stated, "could not be sustained in its present position, much less advance, until they were made secure. We have therefore found it necessary to fortify every bridge over more than 300 miles of road."[6]

As several thousand enemy troops from four different Federal units attempted to corner him during the last two weeks of August, Forrest seemed to be everywhere. The gray riders struck at Sparta, McMinnville, Smithville, Woodbury, and Murfreesboro, then disappeared again, leaving the railroad tracks in ruins and burning bridges in their wake. All the hell-raising by Forrest's command had whipped the Union forces in and around Nashville into a high state of agitation and had delayed Buell's move on Chattanooga.

While Forrest attempted to extract himself from the web being spun around him by the Union columns, Gen. Kirby Smith left Knoxville on August 14, heading northwest in an attempt to flank the enemy's position. At Richmond, Kentucky, he ran into 6,000 Yankees commanded by Nelson and won a great victory, killing 206 of Nelson's men, wounding 844, and taking more than 4,000 prisoners. On the very day of Smith's victory in the west, Robert E. Lee defeated John Pope's army in the second battle of Bull Run and would soon cross the Potomac into Maryland.

Kirby Smith moved on, easily taking Lexington in the first week of September. He then sent his cavalry to occupy the capital of Frankfort. Panic spread before the Confederate armies as the rebels began to drive the Union forces back on two fronts. Citizens of Cincinnati, on the north bank of the Ohio River, prepared to evacuate when they heard the news that Federal general George W. Morgan had given up Cumberland Gap and retreated across the Ohio River, a short distance above Cincinnati.

Forrest had contacted Bragg a few days earlier to notify him that he believed the Federals were beginning to retreat from Nashville, and he expected Bragg to react to his dispatch by attacking the city. Instead, he received his first reproach from this commanding officer, the first slight in a list that would eventually cause him to despise Bragg. At that moment, Bragg wanted Forrest somewhere else and assumed him incapable of operating in the face of the overwhelming Federal forces in that area. On August 22, Bragg ordered Forrest to "return and act according to instructions you have previously received." Those orders were to move into the Sequatchie Valley, where "the enemy is reported advancing" and then to meet up with Bragg near Sparta.[7]

As it turned out, Forrest was wrong about the Federals evacuating Nashville, but there soon would be action aplenty to occupy him. The original Confederate plan, of which Forrest may not have been fully apprised, was decided upon in Richmond on August 1 and called for Bragg to join forces with Kirby Smith for a combined thrust into Kentucky. According to the plan, General Smith was to move against Cumberland Gap and hold that position if possible.

Bragg and Smith would then join forces and drive into middle Tennessee and capture Nashville.

In the meantime Forrest led his weary troops into the mountain passes near Altamont. Concealing his command in a hidden cove at the foot of the Cumberland Mountains, he paused briefly.

On August 29, Forrest again moved out to join Bragg. Early the next morning his scouts returned with news that Union general Alexander M. McCook had control of Altamont and all the passes in the immediate area. Soon after, other scouts reported that heavy enemy columns were marching on their position along the roads from Manchester, Winchester, and McMinnville, and that all three roads converged into one that led over the mountain toward Altamont. The situation was critical. So sure were the pursuing Federals of Forrest's imminent capture, they prematurely telegraphed General Buell on August 30 that they had taken the Southern cavalryman prisoner along with eight hundred of his men.[8]

Forrest was indeed in a perilous situation and went out to observe the state of affairs for himself. He rode up a high mountain trail to a prominent point commanding a view of the landscape. What he saw confirmed his scouting reports. He now realized that McCook's had become the fourth column moving down upon him from Altamont. Forrest was a gambler at heart. With no thought of surrender and nowhere left to run, he made a swift decision characteristic of his coolness under fire. A short distance away he had observed a heavily wooded ravine with a dry creek bed running through it. It was the best chance available, and though the ravine would place his men within rifle range of the passing enemy armies, Forrest decided to conceal his entire command below its overhang of foliage.

Driven by desperation, the Confederates galloped into this opportune shelter:

> Scarcely had he [Forrest] done so, when the enemy came up the road, and, halting in a piece of woods, began to form line not six hundred yards from where the Confederates were quietly passing, completely hidden by the high overhanging banks of the water-course just mentioned.[9]

Moving silently along the serpentine creek bed, Forrest's seven hundred cavalrymen slipped past the thousands of enemy troopers who were confident they had him trapped and were about to finish the audacious rebel leader. Several miles farther on, the Wizard and his men emerged from concealment behind the pursuing Yankees and moved at a fast gait northward toward McMinnville. Within a few miles, Forrest veered off in the direction of Sparta to rendezvous with Bragg. He reported to his commanding officer on September 3 and was ordered by Bragg to protect the left flank of the army in the territory he had just been ordered out of.[10]

Setting off on September 6 to cover Bragg's advance and impede Buell's progress northward, Forrest was reinforced by Capt. W. C. Bacot's four Alabama companies and two gun batteries. Riding back into the same territory he had been terrorizing over the past few weeks, Forrest led his command from Sparta to Lebanon and then into Murfreesboro on September 7. As Forrest's brigade entered the town, they encountered some soldiers from the rear guard of McCook's division, who, upon seeing the approaching Confederates, tried to cover their retreat by setting fire to the same unfortunate courthouse that Forrest had fired during his earlier victory there. The Confederates saved the Murfreesboro Courthouse once again before Forrest put his command back on the road, heading toward the Cumberland River.

Crossing the Cumberland on September 8 near Hermitage, Kentucky, some twenty miles south of Franklin, Forrest encountered Federal cavalry and after a short skirmish had them in retreat. Tenaciously hounding the enemy's rear guard, Forrest caught up with them again at Tyree Springs on September 11. From Tyree Springs, Forrest was able to see the end of Buell's wagon train as the Union column moved toward Franklin. His first decision was to unlimber his artillery and throw his small force forward in an attempt to convince Buell that his rear was being seriously threatened. The demonstration worked.

When the Confederate guns cut loose and Forrest's troops charged forward, word was quickly sent to Buell of an impending Confederate attack. Buell immediately began to draw up his men in battle formation, thus halting his column's progress. Forrest's artillery continued to shell Buell's position for several hours, then quietly slipped away into the woods to begin a wide, ten-mile sweep to the north in an attempt to get around and strike the enemy in the front before they reached Franklin. "I have halted their whole command," Forrest later reported, "and they still remain where we left them. . . . I shall continue to annoy them as far as Franklin."[11]

It now became a race for Louisville, Kentucky, and Forrest would have a great deal to do with the Confederates winning that race. Bragg was bivouacked at Glasgow, Kentucky, on September 14 when he placed Forrest in command of all the cavalry units in the army's right wing, led by Leonidas Polk. The left wing of the cavalry attached to Hardee's command was under Gen. Joseph Wheeler.[12]

That same day Bragg also ordered Gen. James Chalmers, who was commanding the most advanced Confederate position at Bowling Green, to move rapidly toward Munfordville. Chalmers reached his objective later in the day and attacked the Munfordville garrison but was repulsed following a stiff engagement. Forrest was then ordered to "dispose of his baggage trains and everything else that may be in the way of his rapid movement via the Louisville turnpike" and attack Munfordville in support of Chalmers' men.[13]

When Forrest arrived the next day, he caught the Union command attempting to evacuate the fort and drove them back within their fortifications. Bragg's arrival with the main Confederate force on the sixteenth completed the encirclement of the Union works.

The Union commander, Col. John T. Wilder, was trapped and out of options. He engaged in surrender negotiations with Confederate general Simon Bolivar Buckner and gave up the fort on September 17, along with four thousand Union troops, five thousand small arms, and ten pieces of artillery. Bragg had thus won the race and now had his army in a blocking position across Buell's line of march.[14]

Only in one crucial detail were the Confederates lacking. Bragg was the wrong man for the job. On the night of September 17, Bragg held a council of war, and for reasons that will forever remain a mystery, he decided to give up his strong position in front of Buell and begin a march for Nashville. The next morning he suddenly changed his plans again and headed instead for Bardstown, leaving the door wide open for Buell to stroll unmolested into Louisville, where he began to receive reinforcements.

Many of Bragg's commanders were critical of his decision to avoid a battle. Bragg later defended his actions, stating that he was low on food and supplies and did not think it prudent to start a battle. Many historians believe Bragg had Buell in the palm of his hand and let him go. Others believe that Bragg's biggest mistake was in going to Munfordville to begin with, a maneuver that cost three valuable days he could have used to march farther north to join Kirby Smith for a combined attack on Louisville before Buell could get there. Almost everyone, including Forrest, who was especially and openly critical of his commanding officer, agreed that Bragg threw away the chance for a great Confederate victory in Kentucky.

Forrest's opinion of Bragg declined further when, on September 25, for the second time in three months, Bragg ordered Forrest to give up the troops he had personally recruited and seasoned in battle. This time his men were to go to Wheeler, the twenty-six-year-old

West Point graduate who commanded the cavalry's left wing.

Forrest was relieved of duty in Kentucky and given charge of operations in middle Tennessee, where he was to do all he could to cut off supplies, capture trains, and generally harass the enemy around Nashville and Clarksville and the surrounding area. He was allowed to keep his personal escort company, along with Captain Bacot's four Alabama companies. After turning his command over to Col. John A. Wharton of the Texas Rangers, Forrest rode off for his next theater of operations, no doubt harboring more than mild resentment toward Bragg. In only five days Forrest covered 165 miles and arrived back in central Tennessee on October 1.

## October-December 1862

At Murfreesboro, Forrest found only a small force consisting of the Thirty-second Alabama and Capt. S. L. Freeman's battery of two six-pounders and two twelve-pounders. Nearby, at La Vergne, Brig. Gen. S. R. Anderson commanded approximately 1,700 newly recruited militia-cavalrymen. With the enemy a mere fifteen miles away at Nashville, Forrest was justifiably anxious about the situation. He began to send requests for equipment and men to his new superior, Maj. Gen. Samuel Jones, who was in Knoxville. Forrest and his raw recruits did not have long to wait. On October 4, Union general William J. Palmer decided to move on La Vergne from Nashville, and on October 7, he attacked with 400 cavalry and 2,600 infantry, augmented by four pieces of artillery.[15]

Though expected, this sudden assault broke and demoralized most of Forrest's new command at La Vergne. His inexperienced troops began to run helter-skelter, falling back toward Murfreesboro. The Thirty-second Alabama, however, held their ground but were eventually overwhelmed, losing 175 men taken prisoner. When some of the Confederate cavalry escaping from La Vergne galloped into Murfreesboro with news of the disaster, Forrest immediately mounted up to counterattack. He urged his men on as he rode hard through a flood of retreating soldiers, many of them unarmed and barefoot. Deploying Bacot's battalion and Freeman's four guns across the Murfreesboro Turnpike, Forrest pushed forward into La Vergne, intending to check the enemy's advance.

Upon entering La Vergne the Confederates found that General Palmer had already pulled back toward Nashville. Forrest followed to within four miles of the Tennessee capital, then returned to start rebuilding his shattered force. For the next four weeks Forrest scoured the country and was able to recruit another thousand men, building his regiment to nearly 3,500. Then, in late October, Maj. Gen. John C. Breckinridge arrived at Murfreesboro with another 3,000 infantry and assumed command.[16]

Forrest's new, hand-built corps consisted of four regiments when he took up new headquarters at La Vergne:

> Along with his escort company and brother, Captain William Forrest's company of scouts, there was the Fourth Tennessee Cavalry commanded by Colonel George G. Dibrell, the Ninth Tennessee Cavalry under Colonel J.B. Biffle (with Major Jeffery E. Forrest), the Fourth Alabama Cavalry led by A.A. Russell and one battery of guns operated by Captain S.L. Freeman and Lieutenant John W. Morton.[17]

Young John W. Morton, who would become Forrest's chief of artillery, was only nineteen years old in 1862 and had an innocent look that perhaps matched his age but belied his experience. Morton and Forrest would eventually form a bond on the battlefield, much like a father and son, which would last beyond Forrest's death in 1877. Years later, when the ardor of battle had long since passed and old soldiers had begun to settle into reflection, Morton became one of Forrest's first biographers with the publication in 1900 of *The Artillery of Nathan Bedford Forrest's Cavalry*. It was also a less than innocent John Morton, a future Grand Cyclops of the Louisiana Ku Klux Klan, who would initiate his former commanding officer into the Invisible Empire in 1868.

But in November 1862, it was a very inauspicious beginning for Lieutenant Morton and General Forrest. Morton had been one of the thousands of Confederates taken prisoner at Fort Donelson in February 1862 and wrote in his book that he had always admired Forrest for his daring escape from Donelson and purposely made an effort to be assigned as an artillerist in Forrest's cavalry. He had been educated at a military academy and was the son of a wealthy physician from Nashville. That alone was probably enough to evoke disdain from the Tennessee frontiersman, but the fact that Bragg had, without conferring with Forrest beforehand, ordered Morton to report to Forrest as his new chief of artillery lit a fire under Bedford.

When Morton reported to his new commanding officer and presented his orders, he was probably unprepared for the reaction he got. He had unwittingly landed in the middle of a building storm between Forrest and Bragg, a storm he would be in a position to observe as it reached its height months later at Chickamauga.

Without warning, Forrest cut loose with a barrage of profanity that stunned the red-cheeked Morton. "I have a fine battery of six guns under Captain Freeman, and I don't propose to be interfered with by Bragg," Forrest raged.

After sharply dismissing the heartbroken youngster, Forrest looked to Maj. Charles W. Anderson and proceeded to turn the air blue, impressing any bystanders with his mastery of fine cuss words. "I'd like to know," Forrest bellowed, "why in the hell Bragg sent that tallow-faced boy here to take charge of my artillery? I'll not stand for it. Captain Freeman shan't be interfered with."

Forrest was still angry when he fired off the following dispatch to General Wheeler on December 3:

> I have no objections to receiving Lieutenant Morton into my command, provided he is willing to come under the command of Captain Freeman; but I am unwilling to exchange Captain Freeman (who has made a reputation at Shiloh and before Nashville, and proven a gallant and efficient officer) for any other officer."[18]

Forrest continued by stating that Morton's appointment had been "made without your knowledge or consent, and that you will . . . allow my command to go on as organized. You are well aware of the trouble and dissatisfaction caused by these types of changes and I hope none will be made."[19]

The next day Forrest relented and told Morton that he would accept him into his command only if Wheeler ordered it. To obtain that order, Morton rode from Columbia, Tennessee, to La Vergne, where Wheeler was camped, then back to Columbia, a total of 102 miles in less than twenty-four hours. Perhaps impressed with the youngster's tenacity, Forrest decided to give him an opportunity to prove himself.

On October 8, Bragg lost thirty-four hundred men out of fifteen thousand in a battle with Union forces at Perryville, Kentucky. Soon after, he withdrew altogether from that state and pulled back to the vicinity of Murfreesboro, Tennessee. By November, he was planning a move against Rosecrans at Nashville. Bragg's situation was indicative of what was happening to the Confederacy on many fronts. At about the same time that Bragg was stumbling out of Kentucky, Generals Van Dorn and Price were repulsed at Corinth, Mississippi. Two weeks later, Robert E. Lee limped back into Virginia after a bloody and indecisive battle at a place called Antietam in Maryland.

In the meantime, Grant was on the move east of the Mississippi, and Sherman was moving downriver with troop transports and gunboats. The objective of both Union generals was obviously the river port bastion of Vicksburg, the so-called Gibraltar of the Confederacy. Vicksburg's defenses controlled a two-hundred-mile stretch of the Mississippi, thus denying the Union free movement on the river. To capture Vicksburg would effectively cut the Confederacy in two. Clearly understanding the significance of holding Vicksburg, Richmond urged Bragg to reinforce Gen. John Pemberton, who commanded the defenses there. Eventually Bragg sent Gen. Carter L. Stevenson's division of ten thousand men to Vicksburg.

The next move was a result of one of the few good decisions Bragg would make over the next few months, and it would aid both himself in Tennessee and Pemberton at Vicksburg. Bragg realized that Gen. William Rosecrans' army in Nashville and Grant's in Mississippi were both dependent on the railroads for supply. From Louisville to Nashville and from Columbus, Kentucky, passing through Jackson, Tennessee, and on to Corinth, Mississippi, the Union armies in the west were supplied by a constant flow of railroad cars. A major problem for the Union in keeping these supplies moving was that there were only a few garrisons along the rail lines and not nearly enough troops to protect the hundreds of miles of track. It was to exploit this weakness that Bragg sent Brig. Gen. John Hunt Morgan to strike northward and destroy those tracks along the Louisville and Nashville Railroad. Bragg especially wanted Morgan to wreck the two train trestles south of Louisville. They were a hundred feet high and five hundred feet long and could not be repaired quickly. Morgan's "Christmas Raid" would result in a resounding success.[20]

At the same time, Bragg ordered Forrest to get into west Tennessee and slow Grant's approach on Vicksburg. Leading up to his departure on December 10, Forrest repeatedly asked Bragg and Wheeler for more and better supplies and equipment. Almost half his men were armed with squirrel rifles, shotguns, or flintlocks brought from home. Some had no weapons at all. The dearth of percussion caps was alarming as well. Forrest's entire command was depleted of the critical firing caps.

Bragg had declared a surplus of supplies yet refused to send Forrest the provisions he requested because, perhaps, he was unwilling to supply what he considered a partisan guerilla command. Regardless, on December 10, Forrest was ordered to get underway without delay. As it would be throughout his military career, he would have to supply himself out of his own pocket or from behind enemy lines by capturing from Yankee forces he met in the field the materiel and arms his men needed. He was becoming expert at this sort of provisioning and only got better as the war wore on. Forrest's fighting ability was matched by a calculating, strategic thought process and unorthodox organizational skills. Though he often used these skills unscrupulously, he was always ingenious and effective in their application.

The mission would have been hard enough for a well-trained, well-armed fighting unit, but many of Forrest's poorly equipped men had never been in combat before. Winter was closing in, and the weather would be a huge obstacle. The Tennessee River, one of the largest in America, would have to be crossed in terrible, freezing rain. The dirt roads in the area would be nearly impassable this time of year, and his meager, twenty-one-hundred-man brigade would be exposed to the river gunboats that heavily patrolled the river. They would also have to contend with attacks from the local Federal garrisons and mobile forces out of Columbus, Kentucky, and Corinth, Mississippi, and the Tennessee bases at Jackson and Fort Henry. Each of these Union forces was stronger than Forrest's command. Then, when the mission was accomplished, Forrest would have to recross the Tennessee River, chased by an aroused Union army of overwhelming strength, all focused on cutting off and destroying him. "With his [Forrest's] first independent operation in West Tennessee," wrote historian Robert S. Henry, "most of the famed raids around other armies, on both sides, or even longer raids into enemy territory, appear as something in the nature of military picnics."[21]

Days before setting off, Forrest had sent men ahead to build flatboats for the river crossing he knew was coming. A shrewd businessman and millionaire before the war, he also had taken steps to alleviate some of the shortages his men were facing and made a deal with "an unidentified citizen" who had procured fifty thousand percussion caps from behind enemy lines. This person was to meet Forrest on the opposite shore of the Tennessee once the crossing was completed.

On December 13, Forrest and his men arrived at the Tennessee River crossing near Clinton. A cold rainstorm drenched both men and animals, and there were no tents for refuge. One of Forrest's cavalrymen, Dan W. Beard, later spoke of that day and the added misery caused not only by the lack of shelter, but also by the fact that fires could not be built for fear of attracting unfriendly attention to the crossing. "We stood there in a cold drizzling rain," he wrote, "until we were wet to the skin all over, and so numbed with cold we could hardly stand."[22]

As the crossing continued Forrest sent sentries downriver to watch for enemy gunboats. The handful of small, wooden flatboats could carry only twenty-five men across the river at a time. Consequently, it took two days to complete the crossing. On the sixteenth, Forrest moved his command eighteen miles in the direction of Lexington and then camped for the night. Although he had taken precautions, the crossing did not go undetected. Soon the word was spreading from Union commander to Union commander, and with each successive dispatch, the reported size of Forrest's strength grew exponentially.

On the sixteenth of December, Rosecrans wired Grant in Oxford, Mississippi, that Forrest had invaded west Tennessee. The next day General Sherman reported the same information and added, "I rather suspect it is the design to draw us back from our purpose of going to Vicksburg." The following Union commands were notified of Forrest's movements immediately: Brig. Gen. Jeremiah C. Sullivan's at Jackson, Gen. Thomas A. Davies' at Columbus, Kentucky, and the garrisons at Forts Henry and Donelson. On the eighteenth, Sullivan wired Grant that Forrest was seven miles west of Clifton and moving on his position with ten thousand men.[23]

General Sullivan had missed the mark by only eight thousand men, as Forrest had barely two thousand troops. However, there was a good reason for his miscalculation. On the night of the seventeenth, Forrest's men had been busy demonstrating one of the ruses their leader used repeatedly throughout the war to confuse the enemy and trick them into inflating estimates of his strength. Realizing that the enemy was very likely close enough for their spies to observe his camps, Forrest ordered dozens of campfires built over a large area to simulate a huge force in bivouac. Small groups of troopers beat upon drums and barked commands to phantom companies, details of mounted troopers rode back and forth across the bridges, sometimes pulling the same pieces of artillery. The cavalrymen would then dismount, hide their horses, and become infantry, marching over the same bridges. He also had several Union sympathizers held prisoner who were allowed to see some of the demonstrations. Then, out of "the kindness of his heart," Forrest allowed them to escape and report whatever they believed their eyes to have beheld in the Confederate camps. Such deception was just another weapon to Forrest, and his men learned such tactics well, often using in their commander's absence the same tricks that made him so successful.

Before moving out on the morning of December 18, Forrest met with the stranger who had delivered the fifty thousand percussion caps and paid the man with his own money. Now a little more fit for duty, the Southerners moved on Lexington.

Eight miles out of Lexington, Forrest's scouts and advance pickets ran head-on into a Federal force coming down the same road to check the Confederate expedition. Forrest immediately sent Col. James W. Starnes to the front to engage and remove the approaching enemy from the road. Next, he took four companies of A. A. Russell's Alabamians, under Capt. Frank B. Gurley, down another road to the right. His intention was to swing around behind the enemy to cut off their retreat. About five miles from Lexington and moving at a gallop, they soon collided with the Third Battalion of the Fifth Ohio Cavalry, some three hundred strong.[24]

After a brief, hard fight, the Union cavalry battalion was on the run. Turning to the left, Forrest encountered a regiment of Federal Tennessee cavalry led by Col. Isaac A. Hawkins of Huntington, Tennessee, who also scattered and fled to the rear. The retreating Federal units, now under the overall command of Col. Robert G. Ingersoll, took up a position on an elevated ridge some distance farther. Among the Union troops deployed under Ingersoll were Hawkins' Second Federal Tennessee Cavalry and the regrouped Fifth Ohio Cavalry. The Eleventh Regiment of Illinois Volunteers was with them, along with their two guns, commanded by Lt. John W. H. McGuire. The force numbered over a thousand men.[25]

At this juncture, Forrest ordered a frontal demonstration by Captain Gurley, while he led his escort and Col. J. B. Biffle's regiment around to the left. This movement completed, Forrest ordered a charge on the Federal left, which was held by the unsteady Colonel Hawkins. Forrest's boys swept down upon Hawkins' position, filling the air with the rebel yell. At this moment, Gurley ordered his men forward. Colonel Ingersoll and the dismounted Eleventh Illinois suddenly found their position flanked and simultaneously enfiladed. Ingersoll attempted to save his men by fighting his way out, but he was surrounded and was soon forced to surrender. Hawkins was on the left with the Second Tennessee Cavalry. For the second time in two hours, they had broken and run.

The one Federal pocket that offered stiff resistance was the two-gun battery of artillerists commanded by Lieutenant McGuire, who refused to abandon their posts and continued to blast away with canister and grapeshot.[26] Most of McGuire's missiles went screaming over the heads of Gurley's Alabamians as they rushed in on foot. As the hail of deadly projectiles filled the air, a Private Kelly of Russell's Alabama regiment was the first Confederate to reach the guns. He put his hands on one of the guns, attempting in that brief instant to turn the piece back upon his enemies. In a flash, the cannon discharged its horrendous load, cutting him completely in two.[27]

The Yankee gunners continued to stand their ground as the rest of Gurley's men overran the battery. A vicious hand-to-hand brawl raged for a few moments, until the game artillerists were finally beaten down and taken prisoner. The way the Union gunners fought, one would think they somehow knew the kind of damage those two steel Rodmans might do if they fell into Forrest's hands.

In addition to the two artillery pieces, Forrest captured approximately 150 prisoners, 500 small arms, 200 horses, and more than 50 wagons. Captain Gurley personally captured Colonel Ingersoll, and as the Confederate captain held him at gunpoint, Ingersoll asked, "Is this your Southern Confederacy for which I have so diligently searched?" Gurley assured him that it was. Ingersoll, displaying wit in the face of great tragedy, replied "Then I am your guest until the wheels of the great Cartel are put in motion. Here are the Illinoisans [*sic*]; the Tennesseans have ingloriously fled."[28]

As Ingersoll's surrender played out, Colonel Starnes was in hot pursuit of the "ingloriously" fleeing majority of the Union command. Before the slower men could reach the town of Jackson, Starnes overtook them and captured another fifty to seventy-five prisoners, along with more ammunition and arms.

Forrest was well on his way to fully equipping his men as he pushed on toward Jackson. From the time he received his orders on December 10, it had taken him all of eight days. In that time he had transformed a poorly armed and vulnerable force into a formidable fighting machine while crossing a major river in the dead of winter and driving into enemy territory.

At about 4:00 P.M. on the eighteenth, Forrest's brigade pushed to within four miles of Jackson. Union general Jeremiah Cutler Sullivan held Jackson and had nearly fifteen thousand troops in the immediate vicinity. Outnumbered again, Forrest had not the strength to attack Sullivan. However, the Union commander was unaware of that fact, which was to Forrest's advantage. Bringing his six guns to bear, Forrest pushed the Federal pickets and skirmishers back within their outer works at Jackson. He had received word from local citizens that Union reinforcements were heading in his direction by rail from both the north and the south. Judging from the aggressive Confederate attack, Sullivan believed Forrest had between ten thousand and twenty thousand men. Sullivan's erroneous judgment kept him off balance and on the defensive while Forrest sent out several detachments to destroy the train stations, telegraph, train trestles, bridges, and tracks north and south of Jackson. All the while the Confederate artillery pounded away at Sullivan's entrenchments around Jackson, keeping his men busy.[29] The main objective of this strategy was to give Forrest time to destroy the Union's main line of supply that ran from that city to Bolivar, Tennessee, and then on to Corinth, Mississippi.

Simultaneously, he sent his brother Maj. Jeffrey Forrest and Col. George Dibrell toward Humboldt, north of Jackson, to seize the rail station, destroy tracks, and capture any trains approaching on the Mobile and Ohio Railroad. Colonel Biffle was sent to do the same thing on the rail line heading toward Bolivar. Maj. N. N. Cox headed south of Jackson on the Mobile and Ohio and captured the closest station, taking seventy-five prisoners, tearing up eight miles of track, and cutting the telegraph wires. The rest of the raiding parties were as successful as Major Cox. Dibrell seized Carroll Station, eight miles north of Jackson, where he took more than one hundred prisoners, one hundred rifles, and thousands of rounds of ammunition. Jesse Forrest took Web Station, along with approximately one hundred prisoners, and then burned the station and stockade before hauling away what supplies his men could carry. Biffle had similar success on the line toward Bolivar, capturing over fifty enemy troopers.[30] Each of these detachments tore up miles of track on all the approaches to Jackson, obstructing any trains bearing reinforcements to General Sullivan. They then returned with their captures to rendezvous with Forrest before daylight on the nineteenth.

Armed with the enemy's own weapons, Forrest made one more feint at Jackson to hold Sullivan's forces in check, then, late in the afternoon, quietly withdrew his force in the direction of Spring Creek and Trenton, Tennessee. Colonel Russell's regiment was left behind to cover the move.

As Forrest pulled back he had more than five hundred prisoners under his care, and while they were useless to the Union army for the moment, they could be very valuable to him. After pitching camp for the night, he arranged another demonstration to help him propagate the false notion that he possessed a larger army than the enemy might suspect. Throughout the night, Forrest put his men on show with several drummers dispersed in all directions, conspicuously banging away in marching rhythms. His intent was to give the impression that he was continually receiving reinforcements. Fires were built and the constant movement of horses, men, and guns went on until dawn.[31]

At five o'clock the next morning, well munitioned and supplied with twenty-five wagons full of provisions, Forrest ordered Colonel Dibrell to burn the Mobile and Ohio Railroad trestle spanning Spring Creek, then moved out toward Trenton. Dibrell accomplished his task, taking another 100 prisoners in the process, while another force of about 750 men was sent to attack and capture Humboldt. This detachment, consisting of a squadron of Biffle's regiment, Colonel Starnes' regiment, and Capt. William Forrest's independent company of scouts, arrived at Humboldt around 11:00 A.M. and after a short, hard fight, had the town under their control. The capture of Humboldt netted another 200 prisoners and three hundred thousand rounds of ammunition and also resulted in the burning of the train depot and trestle leading from town.[32]

While he closed on the Union garrison at Trenton, Forrest left four hundred men of the Fourth Alabama Cavalry with Colonel Russell at Forked Deer Creek, near Humboldt, to hold back any Union troops that might attack from that direction. Before Forrest had reached Trenton, two thousand Union infantry attacked Russell and his Alabamians, who counterattacked and drove the Yankee infantry back across Spring Creek and held them there until eight o'clock that night.

In the early afternoon of the twentieth, Forrest arrived at Trenton with Capt. S. L. Freeman's battery and made dispositions for an assault on the Union positions. Maj. Jacob D. Cox was ordered to take his battalion and secure a position at the train depot east of town. Captain Biffle's Ninth Tennessee Cavalry was sent to ride around the town and come in from the north. Finally, Forrest was to lead his personal escort in a charge straight through the center of town.

Forrest and his elite company thundered down Trenton's main street, blasting away with their Navy Colts and driving the Union troopers back into their breastworks of cotton and tobacco bales. Their return fire from behind this formidable barricade became so heavy that Forrest was forced to pull back some two hundred yards southeast of the train depot, where enemy riflemen had occupied the roofs of some two-story brick buildings nearby. Forrest dismounted part of his command and sent them into adjacent houses as sharpshooters. A hot firefight ensued for a few minutes, with the Confederates getting the better of it.

John P. Strange, Forrest's adjutant general, was ordered to bring up a battery of artillery to a position behind the residence of Monroe Elder, north of the cemetery. From three hundred yards out, Forrest's guns opened fire on the Union position.[33] After receiving a few exploding rounds that blew apart one of their sheltering buildings, the enemy hoisted several white flags from numerous windows. Major Strange was given the duty of arranging and receiving the surrender from the Union commander, Col. Jacob Fry. When Fry asked about the type of terms he could expect, Forrest replied, "Unconditional." That word convinced Fry that he had no other choice but to surrender. He unbuckled his sword and reluctantly handed it to Forrest with the explanation that the weapon was a relic and had been in his family for forty years. "Take back your sword, Colonel, as it is a family relic," Forrest told him, "but I hope, sir, when next worn it will be in a better cause than that of attempting the subjugation of your countrymen."[34]

While the surrender was underway, some of Fry's troops thought to deprive the Confederates of their spoils by setting fire to a nearby building containing ammunition and other supplies. Forrest became enraged when he spotted the fire through a window and rushed outside with sword drawn to stop the perpetrators. Major Strange saw what was happening, drew his pistols, and followed his commander. Forrest shouted after the men to stop or they would be unceremoniously shot, a threat they apparently took seriously for they immediately threw up their hands and re-surrendered. They were smart to do so, for though they had no way of knowing at the time, Forrest was not a man who made idle threats, nor did he brook interference from prisoners of war. Forrest's anger was still smoldering when he returned to Colonel Fry and told him to explain to his men that any more such stunts would result in the summary execution of the offending prisoners.

As events soon proved, this was not an empty warning issued merely to keep Fry's men under control. A 1903 article in the local newspaper, the *Herald Democrat*, described an incident that took place after the surrender in which two ex-slaves were shot on Forrest's order. Charles B. Harwood, who was thirteen at the time of the battle at Trenton, remembered how things were that day after the Confederate victory when many of the townspeople had run into the streets "cheering the soldiers and taking them by the hand, many of them shedding tears":

> There were quite a number of us boys out front of the depot and General Forrest placed his hand on our heads and said, "the Yankees may kill us but these boys will take our places," I cherish the memory of that touch today.

That Harwood obviously admired Forrest lends credibility to the next part of his story, although the incident goes unmentioned in official reports and in most of the other accounts covering this particular battle. Forrest already had taken nearly thirteen hundred prisoners, three hundred of them African-American. Harwood tells of a black man named John Davis, whether slave or free, the article does not say, who as a local blacksmith had established himself a dubious reputation among the citizens of Trenton. Now among the prisoners, Davis somehow came to the attention of Forrest, who advised him that he was a prisoner and would be coming with the Confederates when they resumed their march the next day. Davis defiantly told the Confederate general, "I'd rather go to hell than go with you." With that, Harwood reported, Forrest turned to the nearest troopers and ordered them "to start him on his way." Harwood stated that Davis and another man, referred to as a "Negro barber," whose offense is not revealed, were taken down to a gum thicket by the side of Eaton Road and shot to death. They were buried where they fell.[35]

If Harwood's account is true, he had unintentionally delivered a damning testimony regarding Forrest's dark side. Seldom was Forrest involved in a battle that did not include incriminating rumors and hearsay accounts concerning his personal behavior. Such charges circulated throughout the war based primarily upon circumstantial and undocumented evidence. Harwood's story could well be true. Rumors of Forrest hanging and shooting blacks had followed him since Murfreesboro but are difficult to substantiate. Sometimes, where there's smoke, there's fire. Other times there's just smoke.

Forrest now had almost as many prisoners in his cavalry command as he had soldiers. Among the prisoners taken at Trenton was Col. Isaac Hawkins, who had earlier escaped capture at Lexington. In terms of materiel captured, the monetary value placed on the arms and equipment amounted to nearly half a million dollars.

One of the weapons taken in the haul was an imported sword of Damascus steel that Forrest claimed and would carry for the rest of the war. Though no one knows exactly why, Forrest had the blade sharpened on both edges, with the usually dull edge of the blade sharpened back from the point for about eight to ten inches. This transformed the traditional saber into a veritable four-foot-long bowie knife. This sword became a part of Forrest lore and drew the attention of his future chief of artillery, John Morton, who wrote in his memoirs,

> It has been stated that he drew his sword with his left hand, but the writer has seen him draw it hundreds of times and always with the right. Instead of being left handed, the dauntless cavalryman was, in reality, ambidextrous, with a preference ordinarily for the left hand.[36]

The large numbers of prisoners Forrest had taken were unaware that they were being prepared to circulate inflated reports of Forrest's military strength. He had demonstrated troop movements designed to convince the prisoners that his command was three to four times its actual numbers, but he wanted to make certain his "guests" believed the ruse. On the night of December 20, he put on one final show. With the parole process set to begin the next morning, Forrest wanted to hammer the point home. Consequently, from dusk till dawn fires burned, bugles blew, and phantom companies arrived, bringing "reinforcements."[37]

The paroling of prisoners was completed before dawn, and Forrest left Colonel Dibrell in Trenton to cover the rear while he moved northward along the Mobile and Ohio Railroad toward Rutherford Station, some seven miles away. Along the way his men destroyed large sections of the railroad. Colonel Ingersoll and Colonel Hawkins were allowed to return to their homes while the other prisoners were to be marched to Columbus, Kentucky, and turned over to the Federal commander there. Those prisoners, under guard and escorted by Lt. Col. N. D. Collins, would shortly find themselves involved in a controversy concerning the surrender of the Union garrison at Union City.

When Forrest reached Rutherford Station he found the train trestle garrisoned by two companies of Federals who surrendered with little resistance. The Confederates then burned the trestle and proceeded to wreak havoc on the railroad for another twenty-five miles, ripping up track and burning the other bridges and trestles as they went. At Kenton the small Union garrison of some 250 soldiers surrendered to Forrest following a few salvos from Morton's six-gun battery.

Up to this point, Forrest had been marching with only his escort company and Morton's battery and wagon train. At Kenton his main command caught up with him. They crossed the Obion River before dark and soon after they encamped for the night.[38]

Because of all the hell being raised by Forrest in northwest Tennessee, the Union forces were mobilizing with their focus on the Confederates' movements. Forrest's scouts reported on the morning of December 23 that ten thousand enemy troops had left Jackson, moving northward. Their intention seemed to be to intercept the Confederates before they could recross the Tennessee River. Nevertheless, Forrest decided to continue his march north as far as Union City before making a run for the river.

The Confederates reached Union City, Tennessee, around 4:00 P.M. on the twenty-second and quickly drove in the enemy pickets a few miles from the stockade. At this point Forrest's command consisted of Biffle's regiment, Major Cox's squadron, William Forrest's independent company, Captain Morton's section of artillery, and Forrest's escort company. Having caught the enemy at Union City by surprise, they quickly surrounded the garrison and sent in a demand for surrender.

Surrender negotiations were in progress when Lieutenant Colonel Collins, en route to Columbus with the 1,000 prisoners taken at Trenton, came into view about a half-mile south of the Union earthworks. Capt. Samuel B. Logan of the Fifty-fourth Illinois, who was in command of the fortifications, believed the formidable-looking force to be the main body of Forrest's troops coming to reinforce the Confederates who were attacking him. Acting on that belief, Logan surrendered his 250 men and officers, as the situation seemed to him to be hopeless. His official report, however, would tell a distinctly different story.[39]

Logan's report indicated that Colonel Collins' prisoner column arrived twenty minutes before Forrest's main force. While Logan negotiated the situation with Colonel Collins under a flag of truce, Forrest's real command rushed in behind the first flag of truce, took up an investing position, and sent in a second flag of truce. Logan said he believed that Forrest had used the first flag as a ruse to gain an illegal advantage over him. Therefore, he sent a messenger to Forrest to protest this irregular tactic and advise Forrest of what Logan believed to be a breach of military protocol. According to Logan's report Forrest brushed aside the grievance, seeing no such fine distinctions during war, and demanded Logan's "immediate and unconditional surrender." Since, under the circumstances there was no other realistic choice, Logan surrendered under protest, noting,

"I would do Lieutenant Colonel Collins and General Forrest whatever justice there may be in their emphatic denial of collusion in the two flags of truce."[40] Forrest never mentioned anything about the two-flag incident in his official reports.

The next night, December 23, Forrest sent a detachment across the Kentucky border toward Columbus to attack and capture the garrison at Moscow. Upon the approach of the small rebel column, the Union defenders at Moscow fled their works, leaving Forrest's men in possession of their stockade, which they immediately burned before returning to the main Confederate force.

On Christmas Eve, 1862, Forrest reported to General Bragg:

> We have made a clean sweep of the Federals and the roads north of Jackson. . . . Reports that are reliable show that the Federals are rapidly sending up troops from Memphis. One hundred and twenty-five transports passed us loaded with troops. General Grant must either be in a very critical condition or else affairs in Kentucky require the movement.[41]

Forrest's presence was alarming to the Union commanders west of the Tennessee River because the Confederates were systematically destroying Grant's main line of supply. The entire line of track was wrecked and not one bridge or train trestle had been left standing from Jackson, Tennessee, to Moscow, Kentucky. Consequently, as Brig. Gen. Jeremiah Sullivan's army moved on Forrest out of Jackson, Gen. Thomas Davies, commanding at Columbus, Kentucky, also was being urged to move southward against Forrest with his five-thousand-man garrison.

Davies, however, was concerned that Forrest had destroyed the railroad bridge at Moscow, only ten miles south of his position at Columbus. Reacting to what he believed was an immediate threat and remembering General Halleck's admonitions to take care not to lose his command at Columbus, Davies began spiking his big guns at Island No. 10 and New Madrid and throwing his gunpowder into the river. He also began loading supplies and ammunition aboard steamboats to make sure it did not fall into Forrest's hands.[42]

Though his Union counterparts were scrambling to prepare, Forrest, with the main objectives of his mission accomplished, gave his men a day of rest on Christmas. They were joined the next day by Col. J. B. Napier's four-hundred-man battalion and two mountain howitzers commanded by Lt. A. Wills Gould.[43] Thus reinforced, Forrest's men destroyed the bridge over the north fork of the Obion

River and under a cold winter rain, commenced a twenty-six-mile march to Dresden, where they camped for the night. After a needed rest it was time to make their run for the Tennessee River.

Although Davies received 2,000 reinforcements, bringing his numbers to over 7,000 men, he never ventured from his fortifications to challenge the Confederates. Davies' apprehension was summed up by one of his subordinate officers, Brig. Gen. Clinton B. Fisk, who wrote on December 27 that "Cairo, Paducah, Columbus and vicinity are in danger of falling prey to the marauding chieftains, Forrest and Cheatham . . . with a force of about 15,000 very near us."[44]

In reality, neither Davies nor Fisk was in real danger. It was Forrest who was in peril. To extricate his command from behind enemy lines and escape back across the Tennessee would take a great deal of ingenuity and luck. Both were with him as he traveled south through the swampy bottoms of the south fork of the Obion River.

Camping near McKenzie Station on the twenty-seventh, Forrest received word from his scouts that the Federals were advancing on the road from Trenton to Union City and up the Obion River in the direction of McLemoresville and Huntingdon. They intended to cut the Confederates off and intercept them before they could cross the Tennessee. Their scouts also reported that the enemy had destroyed the bridges over the Obion from Jackson to Paris, Tennessee; all, that is, but one. Between McKenzie and McLemoresville there was a small, rickety, little-known bridge that partially spanned the Obion. Apparently the Union forces had either deemed the structure impassable or had missed it all together. It was toward this one and only possible escape route that Forrest now directed his column. The harried outfit reached the decaying structure at 11:00 P.M. on December 27.[45]

At least four thousand Federal troops were converging on them as Forrest and his men set to work cutting trees to shore up the bridge. The reconstruction went on all night, with Forrest personally leading the men in the hard physical labor, motivating them in the torchlight by his example, just as he did in combat. The axe-wielding, heavy-lifting work was carried out under the worst of conditions. Freezing temperatures and a drizzling rain harassed the men as they worked in knee-deep mud. Forrest was as weary as his men, and the strain led him to indulge his inclination to cut loose with bursts of profanity that simultaneously belittled and encouraged.

Once the shaky structure was made as solid as possible, Forrest drove the first wagon team across the narrow, slippery planks as an example of confidence for the others. Inspiring example not withstanding, the next two teams slipped off the bridge and crashed into the deep stream and mud below. For a few moments things looked grim for the Confederates; however, Forrest refused to accept defeat. He ordered up some five hundred men to finish the job by manhandling the rest of the wagons and artillery across the Obion—twenty men to a wagon, fifty for each gun.

When they reached the opposite shore, they found the road in such terrible condition that logs had to be used to fill the larger mudholes. Having no sandbags for filler, the Southerners used sacks of flour and coffee instead.[46]

The crossing was completed at about 3:00 A.M. on December 28. Forrest moved his muddy, shivering command another four miles to the vicinity of McLemoresville and there rested and fed his men and animals. Later that day, scouts reported a large enemy force only twelve miles distant at Huntingdon and closing rapidly. They broke camp early in the morning of the twenty-ninth and were quickly on the move toward Lexington, traveling over rough, hilly, and nearly impassable roads.

Also, on December 29, Brigadier General Sullivan wired General Grant,

> I have Forrest in a tight place, but he may escape by my not having cavalry. The gunboats are up the river as far as Clifton, and have destroyed all the boats and ferries. . . . My troops are moving on him in three directions, and I hope for success.[47]

That same morning, General Fisk, at Columbus, wrote that "the brigand Forrest" and his band were on the run and scattering. "I am fully convinced," he continued, "we can defeat or skedaddle the entire rebel horde."[48]

Forrest's situation was dismal indeed. The seven thousand Federals at Columbus were no immediate threat, but from all over west Tennessee and southern Kentucky enemy columns were swarming in to prevent his escape. At that moment, between Forrest and the Tennessee River were two of Sullivan's brigades, both larger in strength than Forrest's. East of Forrest and closer to the river was Col. W. W. Lowe, out of Fort Henry. Moving up from Corinth was another Union force led by Gen. Grenville M. Dodge, who was closer to Clifton than was Forrest's brigade. Heading north out of Jackson was another brigade led by Col. M. K. Lawler, who was likewise closer to the crossing at Clifton than the Confederates. To make the odds against Forrest even longer, the Tennessee was rising and Union gunboats were already patrolling up and down the river at Clifton.[49]

The Confederates camped at Flake's Store on the twenty-ninth, approximately ten miles from Lexington and three miles from Parker's Cross Roads. Earlier in the afternoon, Forrest had kept his command hidden while Col. John W. Fuller's Third Brigade passed by on their way to Huntingdon. Simultaneously, Sullivan's Second Brigade, under Col. Cyrus L. Dunham, already at Huntingdon, was on its way to intercept Forrest, who was reported, and accurately so, to be moving from McLemoresville toward Lexington. The roads upon which both Union commands traveled converged at Parker's Cross Roads.

Chances were growing short that Forrest would be able to make it to the Tennessee River, let alone cross it. Even using the flatboats they had used to cross the river several days before, a crossing now would take at least a day and a half. With the enemy already awaiting him at the Tennessee River, and Sullivan in hot pursuit, Forrest decided it was time to stop running.

The Confederate chieftain framed his next move in a gamble that he might be able to defeat both Union brigades by getting between them and engaging each separately before either one could reinforce the other. On December 30, Forrest sent his brother William and his company of scouts toward Huntingdon to observe enemy movements and to keep him closely informed. After dark on the thirtieth, Captain Forrest's scouting command came in contact with Col. Cyrus L. Dunham's troops near Clarksburg, setting off a skirmish with losses on both sides. Notified immediately, Forrest decided to give his men and animals a few more hours' rest. At daybreak, he would attack.

## Parker's Cross Roads
## December 31, 1862

William Forrest's detachment drove the Union troops out of Clarksburg, where he began a holding action, attempting to give the main body of the Confederate column a few more precious hours of rest. Twenty-four hours earlier, Forrest had sent Colonel Biffle, with four companies of Alabamians, in the direction of Trenton to retard the enemy's progress should he be advancing in that quarter. He did the same thing with Colonel Starnes, sending a second detachment up the road toward Huntingdon to support his younger brother at Clarksburg. Both detachments collided with enemy forces and were engaged in short, bloody skirmishes that prevented them from rejoining Forrest until after the battle at the crossroads had begun.[50]

At about 2:00 A.M. on the thirty-first, Col. C. L. Dunham received information about the clash between William Forrest's men and Union troops at Clarksburg. He also was advised of the location of Forrest's main camp, which was about four miles west of Clarksburg. Dunham sent a message to General Sullivan concerning the developing situation and requested Sullivan to hurry to Parker's Cross Roads, where he intended to attack Forrest that morning. Dunham, in the van for Sullivan's regiment, was approximately five miles north of Parker's Cross Roads when he decided to engage Forrest. He began preparations to march at daylight. Ten miles to the north, near Huntingdon, Col. John W. Fuller's brigade also moved out at sunup, heading south toward the crossroads.[51]

Parker's Cross Roads, also known as Red Mound, lies approximately thirty-five miles west of the Tennessee River and about twelve miles north of Lexington. At that point on the map, the road coming south out of Huntingdon intersects with the one coming north from Lexington. The ground at the crossroads was an open, undulating field interspersed with peach orchards. Heavy woods surrounded the entire area.

On the morning of the thirty-first, before moving out, Forrest sent Captain McLemore and three companies of the Fourth Tennessee Cavalry toward Clarksburg to join William Forrest's command. The written orders McLemore received were vague and did not specify with any clarity exactly what he was supposed to do other than back up William Forrest.

When McLemore's command arrived near Clarksburg, he found that William Forrest had been forced to fall back. Although there were ample signs that a large body of troops had recently traveled through the area, McLemore failed to take any action or precaution with respect to enemy troops in the vicinity. He and William Forrest could hear the booming of the guns opening the battle back at the crossroads and moved to the right at a quick gait to reach the site of the battle so they could support the main body of Bedford's troops. In their rush to the crossroads, they left one of the roads out of Huntingdon wide open, allowing Fuller's brigade to slip through the gap undetected and unreported. This mistake would allow Fuller, arriving as his comrades were losing the battle at the crossroads, to suddenly strike Forrest in the rear and turn the tide.[52]

In the meantime Dunham's brigade reached the crossroads about 9:00 A.M. and drove in Forrest's advance pickets. He then threw his men into a line of battle on a ridge overlooking Hick's Field, facing to the north, the direction from which Forrest would come. Dunham's command consisted of the Thirty-ninth Iowa Infantry, the Fiftieth Indiana Volunteer Infantry, the 122nd Illinois Volunteer Infantry, the Eighteenth Illinois Mounted Infantry, and six guns operated by the Seventh Wisconsin artillery battery.[53]

Forrest had decided by the time he reached Parker's Cross Roads that he would attempt to defeat Dunham using his artillery and "unless absolutely necessary was not pressing them with my cavalry."[54] Within sight of the Union line, Forrest immediately dismounted Dibrell's Eighth Tennessee and Russell's Fourth Alabama and threw them forward. His next move was unorthodox, dangerous, and effective. He ordered Morton's and Freeman's batteries to lead the advance of the dismounted troops.

Those schooled in the constant military tactics of the day would not have thought of such a maneuver—artillery in the front lines with infantry supplying covering fire for the cannoneers. But Forrest owed nothing to orthodoxy, so his mind was free to be innovative, shattering old rules and setting new precedents. His artillery batteries were employing the theory that armored tanks would emulate on future battlefields as they led infantry into battle.

Morton's battery took the center, near a peach orchard, with two of Freeman's batteries on each flank. While the gunners were maneuvering into their respective positions, Forrest personally ordered one of the artillerists, Sgt. Nat Baxter of Freeman's battery, to an advantageous position on a ridge within rifle range of the Union line. Baxter placed his gun and then began to drive his team of horses toward the safety of a clump of nearby trees. Forrest misperceived the maneuver and assumed that Baxter was "running away." Forrest galloped over and unceremoniously cracked Baxter across the back of the head with the flat of his sword, shouting, "Turn those horses around and get back to where you belong, or by God I'll kill you."[55] Baxter, undoubtedly stunned, humiliated, and confused, quickly explained to Forrest that he was following standard procedure. After unlimbering his gun, he shouted back, he was moving his team to a place of safety to the rear of the emplacement. When the logic of the maneuver was explained, Forrest relented and told Baxter to proceed.

Perhaps motivated by the encounter with Forrest to prove his prowess in handling artillery, Baxter's guns opened fire with startling accuracy. Baxter's first few rounds struck direct hits upon the Wisconsin battery, blasting their guns and killing several men and horses. In front of an assembly of the troops following the battle, Forrest commended his artillerymen, with specific mention of Sergeant Baxter's performance. This apology of sorts may have soothed Sergeant Baxter's wounded ego but probably did little to ease his bruised head.

Though Forrest is often referred to as an untutored military genius, it is doubtful that Baxter would have used those words to describe the man who had ambushed him. Baxter and other artillerymen on the field that day can be forgiven if they failed to follow their commander's orders to the letter. Only Forrest understood what was in his mind, and at times his vision outdistanced the traditional execution of military techniques. At Parker's Cross Roads he wanted to advance his guns along with the front line as it moved forward, and in order to accomplish that he would need the horse teams and caissons kept closer by the gun emplacements than was the standard practice.

The artillery of Forrest's cavalry performed brilliantly during the early stages of the fight, advancing with the infantry and blasting the enemy out of their first line of resistance, back to where they reformed, east of the Huntingdon-Lexington Road near the crossroads. A portion of the Union line took cover behind a split-rail fence, a shelter that provided only an illusory protection. Constantly advancing his battery, Morton quickly and accurately pinpointed Dunham's new position behind the fence. Soon, the exploding shells from Morton's guns ripped the fence apart, filling the air with deadly slivers of splintered wood. The unfortunate soldiers behind the fence were shredded by the wicked missiles, forcing them to seek new cover. Forrest's battle report stated, "Their position in the fence corners proved . . . a source of great loss, as our shot and shell scattered them to the winds, and many were killed by rails that were untouched by balls."[56]

Between the salvos from Morton's and Freeman's batteries, Col. T. Alonzo Napier, new to Forrest's command, decided to launch an ill-advised charge upon the Union line. Colonel Napier and several of his men were cut down as they reached the rail fence.[57]

By noon Dunham's eighteen hundred troops had retreated into a clump of woods bordered on three sides by open fields. His men had been driven back but were still full of fight. Twice they charged from behind their cover, once coming to within "sixty paces of our pieces and their supports, though only to be repulsed with slaughter."[58]

Around this time Colonel Biffle's Ninth Tennessee returned from their earlier reconnaissance. Soon after, Colonel Starnes and Russell arrived on the scene, bringing Forrest's command to full strength.

He now had all twelve hundred of his cavalrymen at his disposal and immediately began to maneuver his troops with the intention of trapping Dunham's men in a classic double envelopment. Dividing his command, he sent Starnes around the left flank of the wooded area in which Dunham had taken cover. Forrest sent Russell's brigade along with Col. Thomas G. Woodward's battalion around the right flank to strike the enemy's rear and cut off his only escape route. He then repositioned his gun batteries by shifting N. N. Cox's battery to the right, where it would have a greater effect upon the Union left flank. This deployment would bring down upon Dunham's men the horror of enfilading cannon fire on both flanks while simultaneously pressing them from the front with the infantry advancing with Morton's battery.

As the noose was tightening around Dunham's position, and Forrest unleashed all the firepower he could bring to bear upon them, Col. H. J. B Cummings, commanding the Thirty-ninth Iowa Infantry, reported the following:

> Exposed to a murderous fire from two pieces of the enemy's artillery in front and a battery of about six guns upon our right, which enfiladed my entire line; we were also exposed to a heavy musketry fire from the enemy's dismounted cavalry. . . . We were opened upon by a heavy fire of dismounted men, who had advanced under cover of the thick underbrush to within fifty feet of my men. They then in more confusion fell back.[59]

The "advancing" men were Russell's and Woodward's troops, who had been sent around the right flank and had "found a covered hollow or gentle ravine which led north and south into the rear of the Union line." From there they suddenly sprang from concealment, firing their weapons as they charged. Russell's men soon captured Dunham's three guns along with his wagon trains and three hundred prisoners. Dunham's situation was becoming desperate, as unofficial white flags began to break out up and down his line. Forrest later reported, "We drove them through the woods with great slaughter and several white flags were raised in various positions in the woods and the killed and wounded were strewn upon the ground."[60]

It was now about 1:00 P.M. Dunham was finished, and Forrest knew it. As the terms of surrender were being negotiated, there was a sudden explosion of rifle and cannon fire coming from the Confederates' rear. At the same moment Col. Charles Carroll of Forrest's staff galloped up and informed the general that they had been attacked in the rear by two enemy brigades. They were Fuller's two brigades, which would lay claim to being the only men who ever took the Wizard of the Saddle by surprise on a battlefield.

Fuller's brigades were at Clarksburg when Fuller heard the opening guns of the battle at the crossroads some three miles distant. General Sullivan had ordered Fuller to wait for Sullivan's command to join him at Clarksburg before moving out. Soon after receiving this message, Fuller's scouts returned and informed him that Dunham's command was in desperate straits and if not immediately reinforced would be annihilated. Fuller decided to act without orders and rushed ahead to Dunham's aid. This unauthorized move by Fuller saved more than one thousand Union soldiers from death or certain capture.

Colonel Fuller quickly moved his troops on either side of the Lexington-Huntingdon Road. His infantry was moving through a peach orchard behind the Parker house when they caught Dibrell and Cox by surprise and took their three-gun battery, which had been placed in the front yard of the Parker home. It was in this orchard that Forrest nearly became a prisoner of war.

Also surprised by Fuller's arrival were the Iowans, who according to John Morton, had begun to mingle with the Confederates. "All firing had ceased; and when the leaders met to arrange terms, the soldiers in both armies mingled freely, as was their custom."[61] It was quite common at such times during the Civil War for the opposing troops to exchange goods, tobacco, and food and even to serenade each other during lulls in the combat. It was often a strangely intimate war.

Forrest immediately rode to the scene, incredulous that Fuller had slipped through his earlier reconnaissance detachments. As he reached the peach orchard near the crossroads, he realized that the momentum of battle had shifted. "I rode myself into their [the enemy] lines," he later reported. Before he could react he was nearly surrounded in the peach orchard by Union soldiers who demanded his surrender. Surprised, but calm and confident, Forrest replied, "I've already surrendered, I'll go back and get what few men I have left." Then, as if still in command, Forrest wheeled his mount and rode off. The Union soldiers were apparently stunned and confused by what had just happened. This time, the roll of the dice was with Forrest, and the gamble allowed the Wizard to escape once again.[62]

It may have seemed that Forrest had nine lives, but some of his men that day were not as lucky. Over three hundred of his horsemen from Dibrell's and Cox's brigades were caught off guard and on foot. Before they could reach their horses, the Union soldiers swarmed over them, taking them prisoner. Forrest began to rally what troops were available before it was too late. He was still caught in a vise between two enemy armies, both numerically stronger than his.

At this juncture in the battle Forrest uttered another of his legendary declarations. Although the documentation supporting his words is thin, one of Forrest's staff officers supposedly approached him and cried in desperation, "General, what shall we do?" Forrest unflinchingly, and characteristically, replied, "Charge them both ways." Charging them both ways was an oversimplification, but it was essentially what happened.[63]

Russell and Starnes, on the opposite end of the battlefield and farthest from the attack, immediately understood what had happened and reacted like the battle-toughened veterans they were. Comprehending the gravity of the situation and the threat still posed by what remained of Dunham's demoralized command, they charged in to engage Dunham's troops and keep them out of the fight. Although Forrest had not personally communicated his order to Russell and Starnes to "charge both ways," they performed as though he had.

Gathering some 125 cavalrymen from Dibrell's regiment and his own personal escort, Forrest, on the other end of the field from Russell and Starnes, prepared to make a charge into Fuller's left flank. This charge would decide the day. Though he was outnumbered by ten to one on that section of the field, Forrest was determined to break Fuller's line. Had he failed, his military career would have come to an end. Such were the stakes as Forrest and his small force maneuvered their warhorses into attack formation.

Fuller must have been surprised to see that Forrest had turned on him and was leading the charge. At a full gallop the rebel horseman slammed into the advancing enemy. The attack was carried with such vicious spirit that Fuller's infantry and artillerists broke and ran, allowing Forrest to retake Dibrell's three guns. Forrest's charge shocked the Federals and threw them into disarray long enough for him to extract his command from the field and escape. Although he did lose six guns and three hundred men, Forrest inflicted similar casualties on the enemy and took the major portion of Fuller's wagons away with him.

In certain pockets of fighting that day there was a great slaughter of men and, especially, of horses. The opposing armies left a horrific mess on Reverend Parker's farm.

> Several hundred horses were killed in the orchard behind the Parker house by the initial Union volleys and [as eyewitness

reported, it was literally possible] "that one could walk on dead horses all over the orchard without touching the ground."[64]

Forrest captured 300 prisoners at Parker's Cross Roads, the approximate number he had lost, including 60 men killed in the action. The enemy reported a total of 237 casualties.

The Union dispatches and reports concerning the battle were fairly outrageous considering the actual size of the command that Forrest led at Parker's Cross Roads. To Grant, Sullivan reported, "We have achieved a glorious victory. We met Forrest, 7,000 strong. After a contest of four hours, completely routed him with great slaughter." On the second of January, Sullivan wired Grant:

> Colonel Lawler with 3000 troops and eight pieces of artillery were to follow the retreating enemy to the river. Forrest's army is completely broken up. They are scattered over the country without ammunition. We need a good cavalry regiment to go through the country and pick them up.

Everything that Sullivan was reporting to Grant was an exaggeration, as William K. M. Breckinridge would discover when General Dodge sent him at the head of a cavalry regiment to follow Forrest's "completely broken up" army.[65] It was not the first time Union commanders had mistaken Forrest's strength, and it would not be the last.

The night of the thirty-first, Forrest's men camped in good order at Lexington, some twelve miles south of the battlefield. The next morning, New Year's Day, 1863, Forrest again turned back upon the enemy detachment pursuing him and attacked. Breckinridge's reaction to such an onslaught by an army supposedly "scattered over the country without ammunition" is not recorded. Perhaps he subconsciously rehearsed what he would say to Sullivan if the two ever again met. But whatever his thoughts, it was Breckinridge's regiment that within hours was "scattered" and "broken up."

After this last fight, Forrest and his men moved to a spot on the Tennessee River near Clifton, where he had originally crossed to begin this campaign. They arrived around noon and lost little time making preparations.[66] Within twelve hours the crossing was complete, in part because Sullivan appeared to have been in no real hurry to catch up with Forrest.

The campaign had been a marked success. Forrest had proved to commanders on both sides that he was no ordinary cavalry leader, but a man of great resourcefulness and natural military talent. He would only get better as the war continued.

# Chapter Six

# THE HAUNTED BLUFFS OF DOVER

*—Unknown Rebel Soldier*

## Return to Fort Donelson and Thompson's Station
## February-April 1863

The day before Forrest recrossed the Tennessee River on December 31, a battle had begun at Stones River, some fifteen miles northwest of Murfreesboro. Bragg's Confederates attacked at dawn and pushed the Union line back about three miles before Rosecrans was able to rally his troops and form a battle line. In a conspicuous display of bravery under fire, Rosecrans rode up and down the line, steadying his men. Seemingly oblivious to the danger, he continued to inspire his troops even after his aide's head was blown away by cannon fire as he rode beside his commander. The cannonade was so thunderous that soldiers from both sides picked cotton from the field in which they were fighting and stuffed it in their ears to deaden the horrific din. At the end of the day, neither commander could tell who had won. So exhausted were the two armies that for the next thirty hours there were no hostilities.

The battle resumed on January 2 with Breckinridge advancing on the Union left flank at approximately 4:00 P.M. The rebels took the hill near Stones River and drove the enemy back across the river. Their enthusiasm, however, impelled them to pursue the Yankees beyond a point of control, and they ran straight into a massed artillery barrage of fifty-eight Union guns, which decimated the oncoming Confederates, inflicting nearly two thousand casualties.[1]

The battle at Stones River was basically a draw, with both sides losing nearly one-third of their strength. Bragg settled the issue by falling back thirty miles to the Duck River, where he established his headquarters at Tullahoma. The district commander, Joseph E.

Johnston, who renamed his army the Army of the Tennessee, commanded the line that ran from Shelbyville, on the left, to Wartrace, on the right. Both sites were in Bedford County. This Confederate line was approximately eighty miles long and anchored on both ends at McMinnville and Columbia by cavalry detachments.

Rosecrans' gunboats roamed freely on the Cumberland River, however, and were a constant threat to Confederate operations. Near the end of January, the Confederate commanders decided to disrupt their freedom of movement on the river. Gen. Joseph Wheeler was to be in charge of the expedition that was to accomplish this.

Forrest had spent the majority of January refitting and resting his worn-out troops and animals at Columbia, only a few miles from where he was born. On the twenty-sixth he was ordered to the left wing of the crescent-shaped line to join Wheeler's command, overtaking him on January 28 near Palmyra, about twenty miles up the Cumberland from Fort Donelson.[2]

General Wheeler had taken several of Forrest's regiments along with him when he moved out to begin operations along the Cumberland River. When Forrest caught up with him at Palmyra, he began a meticulous inspection of those of his troops who had arrived with Wheeler. As was Forrest's style he included every minute detail of men, animals, arms, ammunition, and equipment. He was disturbed to find that his men were dangerously low on ammunition and that the artillery was little better off. Considering that Wheeler planned to use these brigades in the coming assault on Fort Donelson, Forrest was particularly anxious about their readiness for such an enterprise.[3]

Forrest brought his concerns to Wheeler's attention, along with his general misgivings about the coming operation. The intrepid Forrest always avoided assaulting a fortified position unless all other tactical approaches had been exhausted. In this case, operating a hundred miles behind enemy lines, he did not believe the outcome would justify the risk to the command. Even if the Confederates should be successful, he believed, the rewards would be meager indeed. In reality, if the Confederates took Fort Donelson, they would be in no better position to block the river than they already were at Palmyra. The enemy knew this and had suspended further boat traffic up and down the river at that point for as long as the Confederates should hold that position. An attack on Donelson and its strong point at Dover would accomplish no more, even if successful. But Wheeler had his orders and intended to carry them out. He overruled Forrest's objections and moved on Donelson despite his subordinate's concerns. The Confederates arrived below Donelson on the afternoon of February 3 and found the Union position strongly fortified. Col. Abner C. Harding commanded the fort and upon hearing of the Confederates approach, recalled the steamboat *Wild Cat* to help support his post. This vessel carried two field guns and a company of infantry protected by bales of hay stacked on the deck. By late morning Harding had all the garrison troops ready and well prepared to receive the Confederate assault.

Forrest once again voiced his aversion to Wheeler's planned attack. This time he told two of his staff officers, Maj. Charles Anderson and Dr. Ben Wood, that he wanted it on the record that he was going to do his duty, but if he should be killed, he wanted these two confidants to know that he was against the attack and that he had told his commanding officer, General Wheeler, as much.[4]

Wheeler planned an assault on foot against Dover, the little town adjacent to Fort Donelson. His plan called for Forrest to attack from the south and southeast, while Colonel Wharton's force would attack from the south and southwest. Before the hostilities began, Wheeler sent in terms of immediate and unconditional surrender, which Colonel Harding rejected out of hand. Wheeler then decided to join Wharton on the other side of Dover.

Shortly after Wheeler left, Forrest noticed movement within the enemy fortifications that he thought indicated a withdrawal. Forrest mounted his men and charged across the hollow between them and the rise upon which Dover's defenders were entrenched. The Yankees, however, were not pulling back but were preparing to receive an attack. They opened a withering fire of rifles and cannon, which caught the charging Confederates completely by surprise. Forrest attempted to continue the charge but had his horse shot dead under him. Locating another mount, Forrest rallied his men and made another charge, this time with his men on foot. Forrest lost his second mount of the day within a few paces of the enemy guns but managed to gain a foothold in some of the houses on the south side of Dover, where he and his men were fighting.[5]

Whether he could have held is unclear, because he once again perceived a movement among the enemy. Thinking they were about to attack the men he had left behind as horse holders, Forrest pulled back and rushed to defend his troops across the hollow, where he found the situation just as he had left it. The two charges had nearly depleted their ammunition, and consequently Forrest's men were rendered effectively *hors de combat*. "I have no fault with my men," Forrest wrote later. "In both charges they did their duty as they always have."[6]

In the meantime, Wharton had been able to take some houses on the southwest side of the town but had to withdraw after dark because his men were also virtually out of ammunition. They did manage, however, to burn a boatload of provisions in the river and to return with a captured brass twelve-pounder. In the bungled operation Forrest and Wharton lost almost 25 percent of their force, some two hundred men.[7]

That night, with the Union troops celebrating their victory within their fortifications, the Confederates pulled out from Donelson, ragged, frozen, and demoralized. Leaving a party behind to search for the wounded and dead, they fell back to Yellow Creek Furnace, about three miles from the river. Forrest, Wharton, and Wheeler sought relief in a farmhouse, while the Union gunboats, which had come upriver, shelled the woods roundabout. Forrest rested on the floor, his head and shoulders against an overturned chair. He was sore and bruised from the fall he had suffered when his horse had been shot out from under him during the second charge at Dover. Wheeler sat by the fire dictating his report. Wharton sat at his side.

When Wheeler came to the part of his report concerning Forrest's premature action, Forrest jumped to his feet to protest. He was in a foul mood or he might have tempered his words, but he was known to express himself forcefully, sometimes to be chagrined later at his intemperate outbursts. He reminded Wheeler that he had warned against the attack and that whatever Wheeler might think, his men had done their duty as expected. His reproachful tone left no doubt that he blamed Wheeler for the failed attack that had cost him so many of his men. In that spirit he vowed that he would never again fight under Wheeler's command.[8]

Wheeler must have been stunned. He had openly expressed his admiration of Forrest and would continue to prove himself a friend to the insubordinate general. Before the coming summer was out, he would fight a desperate and bloody battle against overwhelming odds to hold a bridge he thought Forrest would need in order to escape from pursuing enemy troops. On this disappointing night Wheeler calmly ignored the charges and would not accept Forrest's resignation. Without rancor he arranged to make certain that for the rest of the war Forrest would not again be ordered to serve under his immediate command.

By the time the traumatized Confederates began their march away from the Donelson area the next morning, February 4, Union troops were already gathering for the pursuit. Union brigadier general Jeff C. Davis was hastening westward from Franklin to cut off their retreat, but the Confederates beat him to the Duck River and crossed at Centerville, on the way to Columbia. Davis did manage to capture some thirty Confederates who were on a scouting and foraging detail. Among these was Maj. Gilbert V. Rambaut, who had been with Forrest since Shiloh. It would be several months before Rambaut was exchanged and returned to Forrest's command.[9]

Forrest used the downtime at Columbia to reoutfit and drill his men so that they would be ready to take to the field again upon a moment's notice. It was good that Forrest kept his men in a state of readiness, for a general order was soon issued for all cavalry commanders to go on the hunt for deserters, "the great number of [which had] joined [other] cavalry commands, and avail themselves of that peculiar service to roam over the country as marauders, avoiding all duty."[10] Forrest was also aggressively scouting his current theater of operations. One of his scouting parties reported that there were about six thousand Federals around the Franklin area and that they had repaired the telegraph and the trestle over the Harpeth River.

Too, Forrest was expecting the arrival of Maj. Gen. Earl Van Dorn, the newly named commander of cavalry. Van Dorn carried an impressive reputation that went back to the war with Mexico. A graduate of West Point, he had served earlier under Robert E. Lee in the Army of Virginia.[11] When Van Dorn arrived on February 25, he had two divisions consisting of Generals William T. Martin's and William H. Jackson's cavalry. Combined with Forrest's command, the Confederate strength was brought to about sixty-three hundred, and when added to Wheeler's, their combined strength numbered nearly eighteen thousand.[12] Forrest now suggested a three-pronged attack on Franklin, using his and Wheeler's troops, and sent the plan to Wheeler for consideration.

## Thompson's Station

Urged by General Halleck to act, Rosecrans decided on March 3, 1863, to send out a reconnaissance in force from Franklin toward Spring Hill. Rosecrans gave the assignment to Col. John Coburn, who commanded the Thirty-third Indiana Infantry. In support, Coburn took the Eighty-fifth Indiana Infantry, Twenty-second Wisconsin Infantry, and Nineteenth Michigan Infantry, accompanied by Capt. Charles C. Aleshire's Eighteenth Ohio artillery battery. Coburn left Brentwood on the third and arrived at Franklin at 10:00 P.M. that same night. Before moving out again at 11:00 P.M. on the fourth, Coburn's force was augmented by the Ninth Tennessee Cavalry (Union), Second Michigan Cavalry, and Fourth Kentucky Cavalry, 600 horsemen in all. Coburn's column marched into the dark Tennessee night with a total of 2,837 men and pulling a supply train with over eighty wagons. Simultaneously, Gen. Philip H. Sheridan was moving out from Murfreesboro in command of another Union column. Both commands were to rendezvous at Spring Hill.[13]

At the same time the Union troops were getting underway, Confederate general W. H. "Red" Jackson's division of cavalry was ordered northward into the hills surrounding the small train depot of Thompson's Station, nine miles south of Franklin. The place was named for the Thompson family, who owned and lived on the land. This area of Tennessee was rich farm- and pastureland and not well suited for cotton. The land immediately around Thompson's Station was broken and rugged, with ridges and swells that rose to two hundred feet in some areas. Hidden in those ridges and swells were Jackson's three cavalry brigades along with Capt. Houston King's Second Missouri battery.

On the morning of March 5, the advance elements of Coburn's column approached the Confederate force near Thompson's Station and came under fire from King's concealed battery around 10:00 A.M. The Missouri gunners subjected the Union soldiers to the horrific experience of seeing twelve- and twenty-pound shells bouncing through their ranks with fuses hissing.[14] Coburn immediately brought up Captain Aleshire's section of Rodman guns to the Franklin road and began returning fire. For the next few hours the air was filled with screaming missiles and exploding shells as an artillery duel ensued. Eventually, Captain King's battery was forced out of its position and fell back through the woods. The chess match had begun.

At approximately 5:00 P.M., Coburn put out a strong, picked force for security and went into bivouac. That night the Union commander sent several scouting detachments to check on any enemy dispositions or movements that would indicate he might be moving into a trap. Coburn was expecting trouble and wanted to be able to move quickly. He asked and was given permission by his commanding officer, Gen. C. C. Gilbert, to send a portion of his forage-carrying wagon train back to Franklin.

The next morning Coburn sallied toward Spring Hill to rendezvous with General Sheridan. Coburn was serious about not being taken by surprise. He moved his column at a very cautious pace, placing one Rodman gun just behind his advance cavalry units, three-quarters of a mile to his front. His skirmish line stretched out for more than a mile. Coburn escaped ambush not solely because of his precautions as he moved through the Tennessee hills, but also because Van Dorn wanted it that way.

Later that morning Coburn's cavalry units encountered and attacked a small, obstinate Southern force posted across the Franklin Turnpike and drove the Confederate infantrymen back across an open field and over a hill northward, toward Thompson's Station. In his official report Coburn described the geography of the country he was now entering:

> Before reaching Thompson's Station, the road passes a wooded hill to the left, with a field in the valley on the right, and, still beyond it, is bounded by a range of hills. This field extends to the range of hills just north of Thompson's Station, and covers both sides of the road north of this range. The field becomes narrower on the east side of the road as it extends to the southeast, where it ends in a gap through the ridge. This ridge, or range of hills, traverses the road at nearly right angles, running east and west and is broken into knobs, some of which, on the left, are covered with a thick growth of Cedar. . . . The ground ascends as you approach it, and continues to ascend as you enter it, broken into irregular knolls.[15]

Coburn was encouraged by the small group's flight. He moved his troops into a line of battle and continued to press the retreating Confederates. The Federal right was made up of Lt. Col. James M. Henderson's Thirty-third Indiana Infantry and Col. J. P. Baird's Eighty-fifth Indiana Infantry, augmented by two guns from Aleshire's battery. On the Federal right were the Twenty-second Wisconsin and the Nineteenth Michigan, also carrying the added firepower of a two-gun battery. The 124th Ohio was in reserve and guarding the wagon train.[16] Coburn advanced with two wings of Indiana cavalry thrown out to his front. He also directed several companies of dismounted cavalry to the top of a cedar-covered hill to the left of the Franklin road.

The Union column had just entered the jaws of the Confederate trap. Lying in wait in the hills that overlooked the Franklin road were Jackson's dismounted regiments. Brig. Gen. Frank C. Armstrong's brigade was on the right side of the road with Col. J. W. Whitfield's brigade on the left side. Forrest was stationed, somewhat by himself, on the extreme right, along with Freeman's batteries. Captain King's battery was also on the extreme right, in a position that commanded a view of the entire valley and enabled the Missouri gunners to sweep a large section of the field with shell and shot.[17] Though Van Dorn's successes until now had been sporadic, at Thompson's Station he had maneuvered his command into an advantageous position, and thanks to Forrest's innovative and unauthorized tactical moves, he would achieve a great victory later that day.

At approximately 10:00 A.M. the Confederate gun batteries cut loose with the opening salvos of the battle. The Union batteries were soon replying in concert. The battle now raged very near the Thompsons' residence, and the concussive booming of the artillery barrage shook the windows of their small farmhouse.

King's battery was wreaking such havoc on the Union line that Coburn ordered a charge upon the Missourians' position from five hundred yards out. Across the open field came the Hoosier, Michigan, and Wisconsin regiments, receiving heavy small-arms fire and the pounding of King's guns. The Confederate gun emplacement was well protected by Whitfield's Texans and Col. S. G. Earle's Arkansas regiment, who held strong positions behind a four-foot stone wall. After firing a couple of volleys, the Texans and Arkansans leaped over the stone wall and countercharged the oncoming Yanks, driving them back over the field they had just crossed.[18]

On the extreme Confederate right, Forrest was already ahead of the game. Anticipating the Federal charge, Forrest had sent James W. Starnes' Fourth Tennessee and Capt. James H. Edmondson's regiments to take the cedar-covered hill and drive the dismounted Union cavalry from their strategic position there. He also ordered the remainder of his force, along with Freeman's guns, to attack the position held by the Twenty-second Wisconsin and Nineteenth Michigan cavalry. With memories of the recent calamity at Fort Donelson still fresh in his mind, Forrest must have relished the opportunity to fight in the open field again and engage in the tactics to which he was most accustomed.

Riding his favorite war-horse, Roderick, Forrest led the frontal assault on the cedar ridge at the head of Starnes' and Edmondson's dismounted troops. Roderick had a reputation among Forrest's men for his loyalty and used to follow Forrest around camp like a pet dog. As he carried his master through the cedar trees, Roderick was hit three times by enemy fire. Forrest rode him to the rear and turned the wounded animal over to his son, Willie, returning to the front on a fresh mount.

After Willie removed Roderick's bridle and tack and was attempting to tie him off, the horse, attracted by the sounds of the continuing battle, broke away from Forrest's sixteen-year-old son and returned to the battlefield in search of his master. The brave old warhorse leapt two fences on his way, and just before reaching Forrest, he received his fourth and fatal wound. He died at Forrest's side.[19]

Back on the cedar-covered knoll, Forrest's men quickly dislodged the Union cavalry and unceremoniously hammered them back to where they took cover behind their own infantry. He then ordered Captain Freeman to wheel his batteries about and open fire upon the rear of Coburn's advancing line of infantry. The shelling effectively eliminated the Federal cavalry and half of their gun batteries. Unaware that the enemy's rear guard had been shattered, Forrest, on his own initiative, had slammed the back door on Coburn's command, closing the jaws of Van Dorn's trap.

Whitfield's Texans, facing the front of the Union line, were ordered to charge the two Indiana regiments that had charged them earlier. With Cpl. John McCaffery's artillery in support, they had taken a defensive position on the top of a hill very near the Thompson farmhouse. The rebel yell echoed above the clamor of the battle as the Texans came forward, charging hard. When they had crossed half of the five-hundred-yard distance, McCaffery's battery began to fire canister. When the Texans closed to one hundred fifty yards, McCaffery ordered the canister double-shotted. Then, as the Confederates broke into a dead run, he depressed the barrels of his guns to zero degrees and began blasting bloody, gaping holes in the onrushing Confederate line. The implacable Texans reached the summit but were driven back down the hill by the points of the Hoosier bayonets.[20]

When Van Dorn saw the Texans being repulsed he ordered the charge again, but this time he reinforced them with Armstrong's brigade. Once again, colors flying, the Confederates charged back across the field and up the hill. "Up the summit the Rebels charged, heads bent low, chins on chests, plowing into the thin blue line."[21]

Cresting the top of the hill, leading the Third Arkansas, Colonel Earle died instantly as half his head was blown away. The regimental colorbearer went down at the same time. The Confederate attack wavered; then, suddenly they were rallied and inspired by a new participant in the battle. Seventeen-year-old Alice Thompson, who had been watching the Confederates charge past her home, saw the colorbearer go down. She then bravely, and foolishly, rushed from her house, picked up the fallen flag, and ran forward toward the Federal line, screaming for the Texans to follow her example. Despite Alice's courageous rush to battle, the Texans were still unable to take the hill and were bloodily repulsed for the second time, losing nearly two hundred men during both assaults.[22]

Forrest, still acting on his own, had driven the Federal cavalry back over a half a mile. While Freeman's guns continued to hammer at the Union rear, Forrest joined his artillery and prepared to make another charge, this time on the rear of Coburn's line. Coburn's battle report mentioned his concerns for the whereabouts of his cavalry and the rest of Aleshire's batteries: "The cavalry went off. I saw them no more." Forrest was the reason Coburn saw his cavalry "no more."[23]

Meanwhile, as the Texans and Alabamians prepared to charge the Hoosier position on the hill for the third time, events were rapidly unfolding on the far left and rear as Forrest's cavalry, with Freeman's batteries in tow, thundered toward the enemy's exposed flank. Forrest's horsemen burst upon Coburn's rear with his artillery pushed in to an extremely close range, adding a devastating and shocking impact to the sudden attack. Many sections of the Union line were thrown into a panic, causing some of the Federal companies to flee into the trees like a disorganized mob.

Moments after Forrest hit the Union line's rear, Van Dorn ordered the third charge of the day upon the Indianans atop the battle-ravaged hill. Charging over the bodies of their fallen comrades and through a haze of black powder smoke, the tenacious Confederates came forward across the field. This time the stubborn Federals fought with desperation to hold their weakened position. The Indianans were weakened not only from the two previous assaults, but also because they had sent the Eighty-fifth Indianan regiment to the rear in a futile attempt to stop the stampede created by Forrest. On the peak of the hill, the fighting turned hand-to-hand as the Union soldiers fought in desperation, but soon they were overwhelmed and many were forced to surrender. The rest joined the scattered cavalry detachments and infantry that were retreating up the Franklin Turnpike.

Coburn attempted to gather up his deteriorating command and reorganize them for an orderly and respectable withdrawal. While that was happening, Forrest was one move ahead of Coburn and his own commanding officer. Again anticipating the turn of events on the field of battle before other commanders seemed to recognize them, Forrest and two regiments rode hard in a wide-sweeping arc around to the right, across the rail line, and in front of the Eighty-fifth Indiana and Nineteenth Michigan, cutting off the enemy's escape route.[24]

Coburn's greatly reduced column moved up the pike and rounded a sharp bend in the road, where they were surprised to find Forrest's cavalry deployed across the Franklin highway, blocking their way. Coburn realized that his options were spare. He could attack and try to cut his way out or surrender and sit out the rest of the war in some hellhole like Andersonville. Surrender was not an attractive option, so the stubborn Union colonel ordered his men to charge.

Forrest anticipated Coburn's attack and ordered his fourth charge of the day. It was approximately four in the afternoon as the final fight was taking shape. Colonel Biffle's Ninth Tennessee and Cox's Tenth Cavalry regiment, led by Lieutenant Colonel Trezevant, would spearhead the charge. The Confederate horsemen, some with sabers unsheathed, supported by dismounted troopers, rode forward toward the enemy position. Breaking into a gallop as they closed upon the Federals, the Confederates projected their yells above the thundering hooves and small-arms fire.

Coburn's troops abandoned their own charge and deployed into a short line of battle. As they approached the Union line, Lieutenant Colonel Trezevant and Capt. Montgomery Little, who had organized Forrest's scouting company back in Memphis in 1861, were both shot from the saddle and killed. Seeing their officers go down, the outraged rebel cavalrymen raised the decibel level of their battle cry and increased the speed of the charge to a full gallop.[25]

At twenty paces the willpower of the tough Indianans broke. They threw down their rifles and surrendered. This final charge decided "the fate of the day," Van Dorn later reported. He also reported that he had taken 1,300 prisoners, including 78 officers. Among the officers captured were Colonel Coburn and Maj. William R. Shafter, who, thirty-five years later, commanded the American expeditionary force in Cuba during the Spanish-American War.[26] Van Dorn estimated Coburn's casualties at 500 though Coburn himself reported 378 killed and wounded. The Confederates lost approximately 357 men at Thompson's Station. However, Maj. Thomas Jefferson Jordan's cavalry, Aleshire's batteries, James Pickand's 124th Ohio Cavalry guarding the wagon train, and the Twenty-second Wisconsin were able to make their escape before Forrest could get to them.

Coburn's battle report reflected the disgust he felt for his subordinates' flight:

> That a colonel of cavalry [Jordan] and a captain of artillery [Aleshire] should without orders, and against orders, leave the field with their entire commands, in haste, and without notice to me, at the very moment when they should have put fourth greatest exertions to repel the enemy rushing upon us, and carry with them also [the 124th Ohio], on duty as a reserve, with the train, and with it all our ammunition, was a contingency against which human foresight could not provide, and left the surrounded and unflinching men, who withstood the storm, no alternative but a disgraceful and fatal flight, or to do as they did—fight till further resistance was in vain.[27]

## Brentwood and Franklin

Coburn's defeat at Thompson's Station was only one part of a long struggle for possession of the grain-rich farmland that constitutes the part of middle Tennessee between Franklin and Columbia. At the time he surrendered, Colonel Coburn had been only five miles from Spring Hill and Sheridan's support.

In Spring Hill, Sheridan could hear the booming of the cannon and the spattering of rifle fire coming from the direction of Thompson's Station. The Union general surmised what had happened and dispatched Col. Robert H. G. Minty to investigate. He also prepared an alternative approach for his planned assault on Columbia, joining his forces with those of Maj. Gen. Gordon Granger, who commanded Union troops at Franklin.

On the morning of March 11, they moved out and crossed Rutherford Creek. Minty's cavalry arrived at the Duck River that same morning, finding the Confederates nowhere in sight. He had barely missed them. Just hours earlier Forrest had been at Rutherford Creek in a rear-guard position while Van Dorn's main body of troops had crossed the flooded Duck River on a pontoon bridge.

Van Dorn's crossing had been a precarious operation, staged during a hard, driving rainstorm. Barely did the Confederates make it over the fast-moving current when the pontoon bridge was swept away. In order to rendezvous with Van Dorn, Forrest was forced to march twenty-five miles upstream to the next available crossing at White's Bridge.[28]

After the Confederates escaped, Sheridan returned to Franklin, and Forrest returned to Columbia. By March 15, the pontoon bridge had been repaired and Van Dorn recrossed the Duck River and set up camp at Spring Hill. Forrest was assigned independent outpost duty near College Grove, on the Harpeth River.

Halfway between Franklin and Nashville was Brentwood, where Van Dorn's next action would take place. At Brentwood and nearby at the Little Harpeth River was a large force of some eight hundred Union troops from the Twenty-second Wisconsin and the Nineteenth Michigan Infantries. The troops were divided basically in half. One group was at Brentwood guarding the town and the supply stockpiles. The other was a mile and a half away in a stockade at the river. Forrest planned on taking each one separately before either could reinforce the other. Van Dorn put his stamp of approval on the operation.[29]

On the night of March 24, Forrest's command moved northward from College Grove. He ordered Starnes, now in charge of Forrest's old brigade, to cross the Big Harpeth at Half-Acre Mill, approximately six miles east of Franklin, and move on the enemy at Brentwood. He was to be joined by Armstrong and Forrest by the time the assault would begin. Coming in from the east, Starnes cut the telegraph wires north of Franklin, then held his command behind a range of hills and awaited Forrest and Armstrong, who were supposed to be coming in from the west.[30] Starnes waited until 7:00 A.M. on the twenty-fifth. Then figuring something had held Forrest up, he marched to the Hillsborough Turnpike, where he believed Armstrong's brigade was moving. But Forrest and Armstrong were delayed when Armstrong's artillery had run into trouble crossing the Harpeth south of Franklin. When Starnes arrived at the road he believed Armstrong to be traveling upon, he discovered that Armstrong had already passed by on another road just north of the Hillsborough highway. Consequently, Forrest and Armstrong arrived at Brentwood ahead of Starnes and would have to adjust their plan of attack without the benefit of Starnes' brigade.[31]

Had Forrest been in command on the field at Thompson's Station, it is probable that he would have mounted a ruthless pursuit of the retreating enemy in the style later used against Union forces at Brice's Cross Roads. It turned out, however, that the men who had escaped Forrest at Thompson's Station were inside the works at Brentwood. As Forrest approached the Union position at Brentwood, scouts reported that a quarter mile of felled trees had been sharpened and placed around the entrenchments of the

Union garrison. Inside were approximately five hundred Wisconsin troops, commanded by Lt. Col. E. Bloodgood, who had led part of the Wisconsin and Michigan regiments in retreat from Thompson's Station. A mile and a half south, on the Little Harpeth, three hundred Michigan troops guarded the railroad bridge.

Before he attacked, Forrest ordered Col. J. H. Lewis's Sixth Tennessee Cavalry to make a feint on Nashville, drive in the Union pickets, and put the scare into the city's enemy commanders in hopes of convincing them that they were under attack. This move would also prevent any reinforcements being sent from that direction. There would be no repeat of the surprise Forrest had experienced at Parker's Cross Roads.[32] Two additional companies were also ordered to the rear of Bloodgood's position to cut off any possible retreat.

With these detachments on the move, Forrest proceeded to invest the enemy position with his remaining six companies of the Tenth Tennessee Cavalry, Forrest's personal escort company, and Captain Freeman's battery of two guns. Within a few minutes, terms of unconditional surrender were delivered to the Union commander. Bloodgood, feigning courage he did not possess, replied, "Come take us."[33] These were bold words indeed for a man who, upon seeing Forrest moving his cannon into position to begin the shelling, quickly reversed himself and surrendered his five hundred troops without a shot fired. Gen. Gordon Granger later described the men who had surrendered at Brentwood as the "milk and water variety" of troops.[34]

Meanwhile, the troops Forrest had sent to harass the enemy at Nashville were having a good time doing just that by convincing the occupying army that the city was under attack. The daredevil horsemen rode completely around Nashville, coming to within two or three miles of the city and within site of the capitol tower.

Forrest knew that time was of the essence. His command was far behind enemy lines and in between two hostile armies, one at Franklin and the other at Nashville. Five hundred prisoners in tow, Forrest sent Armstrong's brigade to march the prisoners to the Hillsborough Pike with orders to destroy the Union stockade and all supplies that could not be carried away. Then, riding southward hard with the Fourth Mississippi Cavalry, the Tenth Tennessee Cavalry, his personal escort company, and the artillery, Forrest moved on the Union stockade at the Little Harpeth River trestle.

When Forrest arrived at the river crossing stockade, he wasted no time and ordered Freeman's guns forward. Without ceremony he fired a round into the enemy's works. Turning to Charles Anderson,

Forrest said, "Major, take in a flag of truce, and tell them I have them completely surrounded, and if they don't surrender I'll blow hell out of them in five minutes and won't take one of them alive if I have to sacrifice my men in storming their stockade."[35]

Major Anderson began searching his person and gear for something to use as a flag of truce. Eventually pulling out a handkerchief, Anderson was attempting to stick the small piece of cloth on the tip of his saber when Forrest's patience ran thin. "Strip off your shirt, Major!" Forrest bellowed. Off came Anderson's uniform top and slightly stained undershirt, which quickly replaced the handkerchief. Charging off, Anderson delivered the terms.[36]

Captain Basset, the Union commander within the works, took little time in considering his situation and surrendered approximately 230 men of the Twenty-second Michigan Infantry. The railroad bridge was burned and the supplies carried off along with eleven wagons and three ambulances.

On the morning of the March 25, Gen. Gordon Granger, at Franklin, had been alerted of the Confederate attacks at Brentwood. He immediately dispatched four regiments of cavalry under Brig. Gen. Green Clay Smith, who would become a United States congressman and governor of the Montana Territory (1866-69), to reinforce Bloodgood's command. When Smith arrived at Brentwood, he found the remains of the stockades and bridge in smoldering ruins. Smith's scouts then reported good news. The rear of the rebel wagon train was only two miles distant.

Forrest had left the Fourth Mississippi Cavalry in charge of destroying the garrison and carrying away the supplies and train. Some of the men from the Tenth Tennessee and the Fourth Mississippi were straggling in the rear, enjoying some of the enemy's food and goods when Smith's Sixth Kentucky and Second Michigan Cavalry swept down upon them. In columns of fours the Union cavalry slammed into the stunned Confederates, throwing Armstrong's troopers into full flight and creating panic.[37]

Caught completely by surprise, the teamsters whipped their horses and attempted to outrun the enemy horsemen. Smith attacked and reported later that his men, armed with five-shot Burnside repeating carbines, "shot with wonderful and fearful aim" and "drove more than twice their number, with two pieces of artillery, over six miles, perfectly dismayed and whipped." Then Smith reported that "but for overwhelming forces, numbering not less than 5,000, [we] would have gained an unquestionable success."[38]

It was not Smith's gross overestimation of enemy numbers that prevented him from gaining an "unquestionable success." It was the quick thinking and determination for which Forrest had become famous that denied Smith's success. Riding at the head of his column, Forrest received word of the attack upon his rear. Immediately, he wheeled his escort company, along with his artillery, and rode hard to take charge of the chaotic situation threatening to reverse the day's events.

Almost at that same moment scouts notified Starnes, who had missed the action at Brentwood because of the earlier misconnection with Armstrong, that the Confederates south of Brentwood "were falling back rapidly and the enemy following them with great vigor." He then turned his brigade off the Hillsborough Turnpike and galloped toward the renewed fight. Trumping Smith's surprise attack on the Confederate rear, Starnes suddenly appeared on the scene. He charged into the Union right flank and rear, driving them back "with great precipitation" to the top of a hill. Here Smith began to deploy his cavalry units into formations indicating he intended to again charge the Southern column.[39]

Meanwhile, Forrest was coming from that direction, gathering as many retreating troopers as possible. Realizing that the situation had deteriorated more than he had imagined, Forrest took matters into his own hands and began to do what he did best: scare the hell out of people. This time it just happened to be his own people, as Sgt. J. G. Witherspoon and Dr. John Wyeth would later testify. Witherspoon had taken cover behind a stone wall from where he could see "Forrest . . . charging up the pike, cursing a blue streak as he came."

> He had a considerable force, seven or eight hundred men. (I learned afterward that in coming up the pike he had gathered a conglomerated medley of men of different commands that had been stampeded.) He had a flag in his hand, which he waved over his head. As he came up I heard him say, "Fall in! Every damned one of you!" I presume that he thought we had stampeded too. We fell in, of course. We couldn't have stayed out if we had wanted to. I dropped in immediately in his rear, and we charged up the pike like Old Scratch was after us. When we got within good long rifle range of their muskets, which we could see glistening from behind the stone fences, two or three to one of us, and I began to think, Old man, I wonder if you are going to charge those fences in the shape we are in—for we were going then in columns of fours—he reined up his horse

and commanded "Halt!" Turning his horse he looked back down the line, then coolly as if he were simply on his way to church, "Boys, I'll be damned if it will do to charge like that." Then I thought again: "Old man, you have certainly said something." In an instant he gave the command: "March to the left flank! —double quick!" and when we had cleared their right he threw us into line on their right flank, dismounted us, and in less time than it takes to tell it we had them whipped, chased them back about two miles toward the railroad and were bothered with them no more that day.[40]

Dr. Wyeth's account includes some dramatic scenes that Witherspoon apparently did not witness. In his book, Wyeth stated that Lt. Nat Baxter of Freeman's battery personally told him of the following incident:

> Forrest who with his escort and the guns had reached the head of the retiring column, having heard of the disaster at the rear, now hastily retraced his steps and took charge of affairs. With the escort he threw himself in front of the frightened, panic-stricken men and ordered them to halt and fall in line. Seeing that some of these paid no attention to his command, he seized a double-barrel shotgun from one of his men and emptied both barrels into a squad of the dismayed troopers who refused to halt. This radical measure was immediately effective, and he was soon able to make a very respectable showing with the troops he had rallied.[41]

Forrest's counterattack recaptured the majority of the wagons, animals, and supplies that Smith's men had recently taken and drove them all the way back to Brentwood. Forrest then ordered the wagon train and the prisoners moved to Columbia while he and the rest of his command returned to Spring Hill to set up his headquarters. The Confederate casualties totaled fifty-nine during the Brentwood-Franklin engagements. The Union suffered much worse, losing approximately 760 troopers killed, wounded, missing, or taken prisoner, which was the case with the majority.[42]

Safely at his new headquarters, Forrest, taking advantage of his store of seized supplies, was able to upgrade the weaponry of his men by exchanging their muskets and shotguns for the Federals' state-of-the-art rifles. Some of the lucky ones received the five-shot breech-loaders. General Forrest had long since established the practice of distributing captured weapons to the men he felt deserved the spoils of war. This would get Bedford in hot water with his superiors on more than one occasion.[43]

On March 31, Bragg made an official report of congratulations to Van Dorn and Forrest for the brilliant operations at Thompson's Station and Brentwood, which had bagged approximately two thousand prisoners, including ninety commissioned officers. The raids carried out by the rebel cavalry also forced General Rosecrans to supply his army with provisions brought in by rail from afar, rather than allowing him to use local forage. In addition, the raids further dimmed Rosecrans' marginal victory at Stones River. After the Union defeats at Thompson's Station and Brentwood, their methods of waging war also backfired on them.

Brig. Gen. James B. Steedman, commanding a Federal division in and around the Franklin and Murfreesboro area, commented on the destruction of civilian property and crops that he had observed that spring. When Steedman's command searched for forage, they found nothing but smoking ruins.

> In the destruction of property under the order of Major General Stanley to his command to burn the houses of all citizens who have sons or near relatives in the Confederate service, a large amount of forage was burned also. I do not suppose [Steedman continued] that General [Sheridan] would have permitted it had he known that it was being done.[44]

However, there was no time for the Confederates to rest on their achievements. The shifting strategic situation in the uncontrolled area between the two armies would require the Confederate cavalry very soon to go on the offensive once again. From March 25 to April 9, Forrest performed picket duty in the Spring Hill and Franklin neighborhood. Then, on April 10, Van Dorn's command was ordered to move on and attack Gordon Granger's stronghold at Franklin, Tennessee. On the morning of the tenth, Van Dorn sent Gen. Red Jackson's cavalry on the road from Spring Hill. Forrest was ordered to move on Franklin via the road from Lewisburg. These two roads roughly parallel one another and converge at the south end of Franklin, one coming into the town from the south and the other from the southeast.[45]

Pushing in the enemy pickets, Forrest and Jackson had advanced nearly to the city limits of Franklin by 2:00 P.M. Things were going well for the Confederate cavalry as Forrest and Jackson converged on Granger's camp. But within half an hour, the rebels would suffer a sudden reversal of fortune due to an unexpected attack and their own negligence.

The Confederates moved on Franklin with Armstrong's brigade and two of Captain Freeman's guns in the van, hammering away at the opposition. Forrest's and Starnes' brigades were two miles to the rear of Armstrong with Biffle's regiment leading. The problem was that Armstrong and Freeman had not thrown out skirmishers or any protection for their flanks. This oversight would soon be brutally exploited.

Maj. Gen. David S. Stanley, commanding Rosecrans' cavalry, was four miles from Franklin, coming from the direction of Murfreesboro, when he heard the sounds of battle coming from General Granger's position. At approximately 2:30 P.M., he crossed the Harpeth and rode hard toward Granger's position at Franklin. Captain Freeman was just moving his battery forward past Wilson's Mill using part of Armstrong's cavalry for protection when, near the fork in the road, Stanley's Fourth Regular Cavalry burst from a tree line only one hundred yards to the right and swept down upon Freeman's guns. Freeman saw them coming and attempted to unlimber his guns and go into battery, but it was too late. Armstrong's cavalry was forced to withdraw, and approximately thirty men from Freeman's artillery team were overrun and captured before they could get off a round.

Forrest and Starnes received the bad news and came rushing forward. Someone reported to Forrest, "General Stanley has cut in behind you, has captured the rear guard battery and many prisoners, and has now got into General Armstrong's rear!" Forrest, wearing his best poker face, said,

> You say he's in Armstrong's rear! That's where I've been trying to get him all day, damn him! I'll be in his rear in about five minutes! Face your line of battle about, Armstrong; push forward your skirmish line; crowd 'em both ways! I'll go to the rear brigade and you'll hear from me there directly![46]

Though the name of the officer who informed Forrest of Stanley's maneuver is unknown, he might well have been Armstrong himself.

Charging to the rescue, Starnes arrived first and overtook the Union cavalry as it attempted to haul Freeman's guns away. Forrest's subsequent arrival so thoroughly reversed the situation that "there was not a private soldier who was then present who does not to this day believe that General Stanley fell into a trap that Forrest had deliberately laid for him." Though the Confederate counterattack forced the fourth Regulars to abandon their newly won prizes and to fall back or be captured, "Forrest afterwards admitted that at the moment [of receiving news of the attack] he thought his whole command was 'gone up.'"[47]

Put to the run, the Federals, however, did not relinquish their prisoners and forced Captain Freeman and his men to run at gunpoint in front of their horses. Though their lives were at stake, Captain Freeman and Dr. Skelton were not in good enough condition to keep up the pace. When they lagged they were accused of feigning exhaustion and executed on the spot. At least those who did the shooting thought they had killed them both, but Dr. Skelton survived by falling as though he had been killed, suffering only a gunshot wound to the hand. Captain Freeman wasn't so lucky. He was shot directly in the face and died almost instantly.[48]

When Forrest reached Captain Freeman's body, he dismounted and approached his old friend. Several witnesses said that Forrest was as emotional as they had ever seen him. Standing over Freeman's body, Forrest was heard to say, "Brave man, none braver." A few days later when on April 11 Captain Freeman's funeral service was held near Forrest's headquarters at Spring Hill, Bedford was moved to tears over the loss of his favorite cannoneer.[49]

Forrest was able to break Stanley's sudden attack, but the assault on Franklin faltered, and the Confederates eventually pulled back and returned to their respective camps. During the previous several months Forrest's command had performed brilliantly, other than the three surprise attacks they had endured. Forrest was still an inexperienced leader, but he was a quick learner and had the ability to adapt with the speed of light on the battlefield.

Perhaps Bragg did not appreciate the transformation taking place in his fiery subordinate and continued to look upon Forrest as an excellent partisan raider and nothing more. The reported disagreements with both Wheeler and Van Dorn did not enhance his reputation with the brass either. Around that same time Forrest and Van Dorn had a nearly violent confrontation in which sabers were drawn. Both officers were known for their huge egos, volatile dispositions, and penchant for risky behavior. In Forrest's case, he was a gambler; Van Dorn's risky behavior tended toward womanizing.

After the victories at Thompson's Station and Brentwood, the disputes between Forrest and Van Dorn erupted due to a quarrel with the quartermaster, who had a disagreement over the property captured during that series of conflicts. Forrest had listed a quantity of captured weapons as spoils of war but many were unaccounted for. When Van

Dorn's quartermaster wanted to know their whereabouts, Forrest informed the officer that he had given them to his men, who had been poorly armed before the battle. The quartermaster apparently intended to "go by the book" in an effort to account for the missing property. One can imagine what Forrest told him he could do with his book on military protocol.

Consequently, the situation was reported to Van Dorn, who later brought it to Forrest's attention at a staff meeting. The missing guns and ammunition, however, were apparently not the real issue on Van Dorn's mind when he confronted Forrest at the meeting; it was glory. Van Dorn felt Forrest was getting too much attention for the victory at Thompson's Station, and he, as Forrest's commanding officer, was not getting enough. Maj. J. Minnick Williams of Van Dorn's staff was one of the witnesses to the scene during which their face-off nearly spun out of control.

The crux of the matter was a series of articles that had appeared in the *Chattanooga Rebel*, supposedly written by one of Forrest's officers, heralding Forrest as the champion of Thompson's Station.[50] Van Dorn demanded to know the identity of the author and if Forrest had commissioned the publications. Forrest did not accept or tolerate demands to defend his actions, even from his commanding officer, and he reciprocated by introducing profanity into the conversation as he denied any knowledge of the existence of the articles. Van Dorn escalated the dispute when he refused to believe Forrest's explanation, implying that Forrest was a liar.

It is unclear which of the generals took the next step, but either Forrest or Van Dorn suggested that the matter be permanently settled then and there. Van Dorn later reported that he then "stepped to where my sword was hanging against the wall, snatched it down and turned to face him." Forrest was already on the move, advancing toward Van Dorn with his saber half drawn from its scabbard. Their eyes were locked on each other like two gladiators when inexplicably there was a momentary hesitation on the part of the combatants. Brief though it was, it was just long enough to allow their ardor to cool and a saber duel was averted.

Still leaning aggressively toward each other, Forrest broke the deadlock.

General Van Dorn you know I'm not afraid of you—but I will not fight you—and leave you to reconcile with yourself the gross wrongs you have done me. It would never do for two officers of our rank to set such an example to the troops, and I remember, if you forget, what we both owe to the cause.

Van Dorn then told his staff officer, who later reported the incident to the Confederate Veterans Association,

I never felt so ashamed of myself in my life and recalled by Forrest's manly attitude and words to our true position, I immediately replied that he was right, and apologized for having used such expressions to him. And so we parted to be somewhat better friends, I believe, than we have been before. Whatever else he may be, the man certainly is no coward.[51]

As it turned out Forrest and Van Dorn would never see each other again. On the morning of May 7, 1863, Dr. George B. Peters, the jealous husband of a woman with whom Van Dorn was rumored to be having relations, gunned Van Dorn down in his headquarters at Spring Hill. While both men seem to have succumbed to their particular weaknesses from time to time, Forrest's penchant for betting on card games and horse races was not as dangerous in the long run as Van Dorn's betting he would not be caught trifling with a married woman.[52]

# Chapter Seven

# ALL IS FAIR IN LOVE AND WAR

*—Napoleon Bonaparte*

## Streight's Raid
## April-May 1863

Forrest's raids in the vicinity of Columbia and Franklin had taken the luster off Rosecrans' victory at Stones River. Consequently, General Rosecrans was in the mood to listen when Col. Abel Streight came to him with a bold proposition. Streight proposed a drive deep into Confederate territory to strike at the enemy's supply line as Forrest and Morgan had been doing to the Union. Chief of Staff James A. Garfield was for the plan, believing that the Army of Tennessee must be split in two. With endorsements from the highest levels, Rosecrans issued the orders on April 7, directing Streight to start out by steamboat from Nashville on the first leg of a one-thousand-mile campaign that would take him across Alabama and into Georgia. Along the way he was to hamper and destroy railroads supplying the Confederates around Chattanooga, specifically the Western and Pacific.

Though Streight's departure was normal enough, he soon ran into serious delays caused by bad weather, bad mules, and bad rations. The first delay came when Streight discovered that many of the five hundred mules his men were to use as mounts were wild and unbroken. Untamed as they were, the mules would be of no use to Streight's men. It took two days of hard and dangerous work resembling an impromptu rodeo for the infantrymen to break the mules and learn to control them. In the process many of the men "were at first easily dismounted, frequently in a most undignified and unceremonious manner."[1]

Gen. Grenville Dodge was ordered out from Corinth, Mississippi, to provide a screen to protect Streight's preparations and movements. The original plan called for the two to meet at Eastport, just inside Mississippi, on April 16, but Streight did not arrive until April 19 because of further complications caused by miscommunication and weather. Upon reaching Eastport, Streight learned that Dodge had moved on several miles ahead and was bivouacked on Bear Creek. Anxious to overcome the three-day delay as soon as possible and get back on schedule, Streight went ahead to meet General Dodge while the mules were being unloaded and corralled.

With travel and the time it took to conclude his business with Dodge, Streight returned to his command at Eastport later that night only to find that the mules had stampeded, and some four hundred of them were roaming loose around the countryside. Another two days were lost rounding up the errant mules.[2] A superstitious man might have begun to question the wisdom of the enterprise after such an inauspicious beginning.

Forrest must have harbored some very special thoughts about the Tennessee River. It had barred his way time after time as he campaigned back and forth across the west. On April 26, he approached the obstructing river once again. By the end of the day, his command was safely across the river near Decatur, about seventy miles from the scene of Streight's roundup. By the twenty-eighth, Forrest had joined Col. P. D. Roddey, who had withdrawn from Tuscumbia following a sharp, all-day fight with Dodge's troops in an attempt to prevent them from crossing Town Creek.

At this point the Confederates did not yet fully realize the Union strategy of using Dodge to cover Streight's movements. Despite the unfortunate delays encountered by Streight thus far, the plan seemed to be working. As he struggled to get into position to begin his march toward his first objective at Rome, Georgia, the Confederate command was unaware that Streight was taking a page from Forrest's own book. However, every delay gave the Confederate cavalryman more time to figure out what was happening and where Streight was headed.

Streight spent April 25 and 26 in Tuscumbia making last-minute preparations to move out across northern Alabama. His men had received medical checkups, and those unfit for the coming campaign had been placed on the inactive roster and left behind. Streight recorded that he now had fifteen hundred handpicked men. On the night of April 26, as Forrest was completing his crossing of the Tennessee, Streight's raiders marched out of Tuscumbia, following the road south to Russellville. From there they turned eastward toward Moulton.[3] Throughout the next day the Federal raiders made slow progress through rain and mud, and only the advance elements of the command had reached the outskirts of Mount Hope by nightfall, where they stopped for the night. The rest of the troops caught up about midmorning on April 28. Word reached Streight that same morning that Dodge had turned back the Confederates to the north of Mount Hope. The raiders, all together again, then prepared to move on toward Moulton.

However, the Union column had not been unobserved. Earlier that day James Moon, one of Roddey's scouts, had spotted the Union command and near dusk reported back to Forrest that he had seen a Union force of about two thousand moving through Mount Hope. Though the information was sketchy at best, Forrest surmised that the earlier fighting with Dodge was but a feint to cover Streight's movements and that Moon's report revealed the real threat. He immediately made arrangements to put Roddey's men between Streight and Dodge to prevent either from reinforcing the other. It appears that he had determined to pursue Streight if the Northern commander continued his march into the lightly defended region south of Forrest's position.[4]

Forrest then turned his attention to preparing his own troops for the pursuit. Throughout the night the meticulous preparations continued; horses were selected, food prepared, and caissons double-teamed. Bedford might not yet have had a clear picture of the situation, but he instinctively sensed a coming clash, and his formidable skills as a commissary and strategist were working together perfectly.[5]

At dawn on April 29, Forrest marched toward Moulton, arriving only six hours after Streight had departed the area. The Union column made thirty-five miles that day and camped atop the Sand Mountain plateau to the northeast of present-day Birmingham. The next morning the raiders prepared to break camp. Lt. A. C. Roach, aide to Colonel Streight, later wrote,

> The sun shone out bright and beautiful, as spring day's sun ever beamed; and from the smoldering camp fires of the previous night the mild blue smoke ascended in graceful curves, and mingled with the gray mist slumbering on the mountain tops above. The scene was well calculated to inspire and refresh the minds of our weary soldiers.[6]

And it was a beautiful spring day, an inspiration for poets and writers of letters home.

Streight had reason to be optimistic. After all, he was moving through a part of Alabama that was home to many strong Union sympathizers. Further emphasizing that not all Southerners were rebels was the fact that most of Capt. D. D. Smith's cavalrymen were recruited from Tennessee. Streight also knew that Dodge's force was behind him to engage and hold off any attack in his rear, and as far as he knew there was nothing insurmountable between him and his objective at Rome, Georgia.

However, Streight did not know that Forrest was only four miles behind him and that he had sent Starnes and Biffle ahead to flank the Union column. He only became aware of the Confederate presence when his scouts reported this flanking maneuver to him as it was happening. Surprised though he might have been at the nearness of Forrest's flankers, Streight was nevertheless a capable and resourceful officer and immediately made preparations to receive an attack. Selecting a good position near Day's Gap, about three miles from Sand Mountain on a high, sandy ridge with a steep ravine protecting his right and a swampy marsh to his left, Streight laid his trap.[7] Carefully choosing his ground for advantage, Streight concealed his main force on the ridge and threw out skirmishers to the front. These riflemen were to fire on the advancing Confederates then fall back toward the main line, thus drawing them into an ambush.

Capt. William Forrest and his scouts led the attack, charging ahead into the ambush, just as Streight had planned. When the Confederates were within range, Streight ordered his men to rise from the underbrush and fire point-blank. The withering fire, supported by cannonading from two twelve-pounders, cut down several riders, including Bill Forrest, who suffered a shattered thighbone. Reinforcements quickly arrived, with Capt. John Morton's and Lt. Wills Gould's batteries opening fire at three hundred yards. At this time Streight ordered a countercharge, which drove the Confederates back in great confusion. During the countercharge Lieutenant Gould's guns were overrun and captured, a loss that "put Forrest into a towering, thunderous rage and which would indirectly cost" Gould his life within the month.[8]

As the battle of Day's Gap began, Forrest had only one thousand men with him, but soon more reinforcements arrived, and he quickly formed a new battle line. He was anxious to recapture the guns lost by Gould and to retake the initiative after having been checked by Streight's ambush. Raging up and down the line, Forrest threw his newly reinforced command against the Yankee raiders. The attack lasted until Streight skillfully withdrew his column from Sand Mountain around 11:00 A.M. and resumed his march. Round one had gone to Streight, but this was to be a distance fight, and Forrest was just getting warmed up.

At Crooked Creek, six miles from the first fight, Streight was compelled to form another line of battle, because Forrest was again hot on his heels. Near dark, Streight drew up on a ridge called Hog Mountain. The Confederates reached this defensive position some-time after nightfall, and aided by the light of a full moon, Forrest immediately attacked.[9]

Both sides fought stubbornly amid flashes of gunfire and exploding shells, and at one point Biffle's regiment overran an enemy battery and recaptured Gould's guns. However, when the guns were inspect-ed it was learned that before the raiders fell back they had spiked and ruined them, information that drove Forrest to new heights of anger. "Shoot at everything blue and keep up the scare," he bellowed.[10]

Forrest's pursuit was so swift that Streight was forced to turn and fight once more around midnight. Laying another ambush, Streight left Lt. Col. Gilbert Hathaway's Indiana brigade and two guns hidden in a dense thicket to slow the Confederates. This time Forrest sensed the trap and ordered Capt. C. B. Ferrell's battery "pushed forward by hand without noise, along the road of soft sand shimmering in the moonlight." Ferrell's gunners spotted the hidden Union troopers and delivered a devastating and accurate barrage that quickly drove the Indianans off to catch up with their main column.[11]

With Forrest breathing down his neck, Streight had no time to rest his men or mounts. For the rest of the night and into the morning of May 1, the raiders continued their march another forty-three miles, arriving at the village of Blountsville about 10:00 A.M. For the first time in hours he felt he might have time to at least feed his men and ani-mals, but before noon Forrest was driving in the Union pickets. To lighten his load, Streight transferred as much of his supplies as possi-ble from the wagons to pack mules and then set fire to the wagons. But so closely did Forrest's men pursue, they were able to put out some of the wagon fires and retrieve much of the abandoned supplies.[12]

Forrest's men were also saddle weary, but they were being pushed by a man whose physical constitution seemed to have no limits. From Blountsvile toward Gadsden, a running fight ensued until late in the afternoon. Throughout the chase Forrest rested his main body of troops while smaller detachments kept up the "skeer" with relentless pressure. In this rotating fashion, Forrest was able to rest part of his command while others continued to chase and fight the retreating enemy column. Streight, on the other hand, could not rest his men and animals because he was never sure at any given moment of the strength of the enemy chasing him.[13]

On May 2, about nine in the morning, Streight's exhausted and ragged column came upon a wooden bridge over the Black Warrior

River, and he put his men across, burning the bridge behind him. Believing this would seriously slow Forrest's pursuit, he left sharp-shooters behind to cover the crossing and proceeded toward Gadsden with high hopes of reaching Rome with his command intact.[14]

Coming up fast Forrest reached the bridge while it was still burn-ing and immediately began receiving fire from the Union skirmish-ers on the east side of the stream. It seemed for the moment that Streight had finally foiled Forrest, but he had not counted on his enemy's resourcefulness and the help of a teenaged Alabama girl.

While the bridge burned, Forrest spotted a nearby farmhouse that was the home of the widow Sanson and her two daughters. He reined in his horse in the front yard and shouted into the farmhouse, "Can you tell me where I can get across this damn creek?"[15] Emma, Mrs. Sanson's sixteen-year-old daughter, ran out to Forrest and advised him that there was a shallow spot about two hundred yards up the creek where the Confederates might cross. There was no time to sad-dle up a horse for Emma so Forrest took the young lady's hand and pulled her up behind him. Unlike the incident at Shiloh, this rear passenger was much more willing to ride a spell with the general.

Riding down the bank on the west side of the creek, Forrest and young Emma came under fire from Streight's rear guard. Spurring his horse into nearby trees, Forrest avoided their fire as he moved serpentine through the partial cover. Finally dismounting, Forrest and Emma made their way to the spot she had spoken of, but as they emerged from the foliage they came under fire once again.

According to Jordan and Pryor, Emma placed herself in front of the general, saying, "General, stand behind me. They will not dare to shoot me." Unlettered though he was, Forrest instinctively had the gallant manner of all Southern cavalrymen. "I'm glad to have you for a pilot," he said to Emma, "but I'm not going to make breastworks of you."[16] Forrest placed Emma safely in the shelter of the roots of a fall-en tree while he proceeded on hands and knees toward the creek to reconnoiter. He had crawled barely fifty yards when he looked back to find Emma right behind him. Concerned for her safety, he demand-ed with some consternation to know why she had not stayed under cover as he had told her. She replied, "Yes, General, but I was fearful that you might be wounded; and it's my purpose to be near you."[17]

Emma pointed out the exact spot where she had seen cattle cross-ing the creek. Forrest looked the area over carefully for landmarks so he could find the place again. With Emma at his side they started back the way they had come, but they again came under heavy fire from the Union rear guard. A later examination of Emma's clothing showed that several bullets had passed through her skirt. Her reaction to such a close brush with death was the calm reply, "They have only wounded my crinoline."

With bullets buzzing and whizzing through the trees, Emma faced the enemy riflemen and waved her bonnet defiantly. When the Union soldiers realized that they had been shooting at a female, they ceased firing and gave three cheers. Forrest's immediate reaction to Emma's display of courage is not recorded.[18]

Taking advantage of the lull in the fighting, Forrest mounted up and returned Emma to her anxious mother and sister. He directed the ladies to find shelter from the firing and rode off to supervise his troops in crossing the Black Warrior.

All the while Streight was racing toward Rome believing he had put an impassable barrier between himself and the gray wolves stalking him. His rear guard shared that same belief, ceased fire, and marched off to join their main force.

After the shooting had subsided, the Sansons started walking back toward their home and met Forrest on the way. He explained that he had gone by the house to leave a note for Emma and had also left inside their home the body of one of his men, Robert Turner, who had been killed in the fighting at the bridge. Forrest asked that Mrs. Sanson kindly see that trooper Turner receive a proper burial in a nearby cemetery. He then asked Emma to send him a lock of her hair.

Thirty years later, as Dr. John Allen Wyeth was preparing to write his biography of Forrest, he received an account of the incident at the stream crossing from the adult Emma Sanson. With her remembrance was a facsimile copy of the note she received from General Forrest that day:

> Hed Quarters in Sadle
> May 2, 1863
> My highest regardes to Miss Ema Sanson for hir gallant conduct while my forse was Skirmishing with the Federals across Black Creek near Gadisden, Allabama
> > N.B. Forrest
> > Brig Genl Comding N. Ala

The state of Alabama also held Emma Sanson in high regard and following the war presented her with a gold medal commemorating her exploit and awarded her a section of public land "as a testimony of the high appreciation of her services by the people of Alabama."[19]

Taking advantage of the cattle crossing Emma had pointed out to Forrest, the Confederates were completing their crossing of the Black

Warrior when Mrs. Sanson and "several ladies" approached Forrest with a request. Mrs. Sanson's brother, who had been fighting with the Confederate army in Virginia, was home on furlough and had been captured that morning as Streight's raiders passed through the area. Mrs. Sanson begged the general to rescue her brother and return him to her. "It shall be done before ten o'clock tomorrow," said Forrest. Considering the events of the next several hours, it would appear that the promise was fulfilled, though perhaps not to the hour.[20]

While Forrest was getting his troops across the creek, Streight passed through Gadsden, pausing long enough to destroy the Confederate supplies stored there. Eight miles east of Gadsden, Streight reached Turkeytown, where he sent two hundred men under Capt. Milton Russell to ride as hard as possible to Rome and once there to seize the bridge over the Oostanaula River and to hold it at all costs until the main column arrived.

Meanwhile, after making the crossing of the Black Warrior, Forrest sent part of his men ahead to "devil them all night" while the majority of his men took a short, but much needed rest. That night and through the next day, Forrest chased and harassed the exhausted Union rear guard toward Rome.

The race for Rome, Georgia, was on. Forrest had sent messengers ahead to warn of the Yankee approach. John Hunt Wisdom, a mail carrier, got the word and drove his mail buggy wildly toward town to warn the citizens of Rome. Like the Pony Express, Wisdom changed teams at various farms, eventually abandoning his buggy and borrowing a horse. Sixty miles later, and after changing horses several times, Wisdom arrived at Rome just before midnight. Riding through the streets of Rome and sounding like Paul Revere a hundred years before, he aroused the citizens shouting, "The Yankees are coming."[21]

Rome began to mobilize immediately. Virtually every citizen turned out to lend a hand. Convalescent soldiers came from the military hospitals. People arrived from surrounding towns to help construct works from bales of cotton and overturned wagons.

Around six o'clock on Sunday morning, May 3, Captain Russell approached Rome. Through his field glasses he could see the barricades thrown up during the night by the locals and the bustling activity in the town beyond. An old black woman told him that the town was full of soldiers, and a local mail carrier passing by unwittingly gave him much information, most of which was inaccurate, but nevertheless underscored the size of the reception the citizens of Rome had prepared for the Yankees. Continuing his reconnaissance, Russell concluded that the fortifications were formidable and that he had not the strength to take the bridge. He sent a messenger to inform Streight of the situation, and after watching conditions around Rome grow even more animated with activity, he and his men started back in the early afternoon to join Streight. At this point in the running fight, Streight's raiders were doomed. The Union commander was trapped between Forrest from behind and several hundred fortified civilians at Rome.[22]

That same morning, Streight, unaware that Captain Russell had not been able to secure the bridge, was forced to stop and rest his men. He chose the plantation of a Mrs. Lawrence in Cherokee County, Alabama. He was only about twenty miles from his objective, but his men were falling asleep in the saddle, and the animals were as worn out as the soldiers.

Even though Streight's men had stopped to rest, Forrest, with some six hundred men, continued his tenacious pursuit and made contact with Streight's pickets that Sunday morning. By 8:00 A.M., the pickets had been driven in, and Streight's command was forced to abandon their breakfast and form a battle line. Streight found it almost impossible to keep his men from falling asleep. He reported later that "the command was immediately ordered into line and every effort was made to rally the men into action, but nature was exhausted and a large number of my best troops actually fell asleep while lying in line of battle under a severe skirmish fire."[23]

Streight's men had run as far as they could, and there was no place to hide. Sending Capt. W. S. McLemore around the Union right flank with what was left of the Fourth Tennessee and Biffle to the right with the Ninth Tennessee, Forrest began his demonstration against the center. What he had begun with boots and saddles he would finish like a magician using smoke and mirrors.

Desperation and exhaustion were epidemic throughout Streight's remaining command. Forrest's pursuit tactic had so thoroughly confused and demoralized the Yankees that Streight now believed he was outnumbered at least three-to-one. Actually, the exact opposite was true. Adding to Streight's distress was the recent news that Captain Russell had been unable to secure the bridge at Rome. Streight was now convinced that his position was untenable and felt that the only way to salvage anything positive from the situation was to call for an audience with Forrest.

First, however, Forrest sent Capt. Henry Pointer under a flag of truce to demand the Union surrender. At that time, Streight requested his audience with the rebel commander. When they met a short time later in a small wooded area, Forrest immediately demanded his surrender.[24] Momentarily Streight held tight, telling Forrest that he would not surrender until Forrest proved to him the advantage in numbers he suspected the Confederates of having. At that very moment, as if on cue, the only Southern battery that could keep up with Forrest moved into sight. Streight began to protest this movement of troops under a flag of truce.

Forrest played the game to the hilt. He sent Captain Pointer to order the artillery back, a confident gesture to Streight, who had to decide for himself if these were the only Confederate guns on the field. Captain Pointer, familiar with Forrest's style and propensity for sub-terfuge, understood his commander's nod and wink to mean that it was time to begin the show in earnest.[25] Within minutes the same two guns began to appear and reappear within Streight's line of sight, first in one place, then in another, giving the impression that Forrest had a great number of cannon at his disposal. This display prompted Streight to demand, "In the name of God, how many guns have you got? That's fifteen I've counted already." Forrest later reported, "Turning my head that way, I said, 'I reckon that's all that has kept up.'"

As the negotiations continued, Forrest would occasionally stop his conversation with the Yankee colonel and snap off some bogus order for nonexistent Confederate companies. McLemore and Biffle picked up on Forrest's deception and began marching their men around the hillside, having them appear here and there, then reform and mount up to transform themselves back into cavalry detachments.[26]

By the time Streight excused himself to confer with his officers, he must have felt that he had much in common with a rabbit caught in a snare. As Streight returned to his men, Forrest's boys were scur-rying all around the hilly terrain, beating drums and blowing bugle calls. It was a tremendous effort for the Confederates, who were nearly as exhausted as their prey.[27]

About noon, Streight resigned himself to what appeared to him to be inevitable and surrendered his command to Forrest. The Union soldiers stacked their surrendered weapons, and their offi-cers were methodically separated from the men. Only then did Forrest call forth all the men he actually had on the field, and about four hundred tattered Confederates appeared in the open. Streight stared in disbelief. He couldn't believe that he had just surrendered his fifteen hundred men to a force less than a third his own.

Streight can be forgiven his indignation and humiliation when he realized that he had been tricked. He flew into a rage and demanded that his arms be returned. Forrest went to his side, patted Streight on the shoulder, and said, "Ah, hell, Colonel. All's fair in love and war."[28]

Moving on toward Rome with his prisoners, Forrest met Captain Russell and his detachment returning from the critical bridge he had failed to secure. Forrest gathered up Russell's men and added them to his column of prisoners of war, now numbering in excess of seventeen hundred. Forrest found the citizens of Rome excited and in a festive mood when he and his column of prisoners appeared on the outskirts of town. When they saw their conquering hero approaching, a few exuberant citizens rushed to the cannon that had been placed near the barricades. Those guns had been emplaced to cover the road when the Union troopers first appeared, but their plan now was to fire a two-gun salute to welcome Forrest. The problem was that no one thought to remove the shot from the cannon. Bad aim, perhaps aided by some home brew, saved the day, as the projectiles of "friendly fire" flew harmlessly wide.[29]

Avoiding this last obstacle, Forrest was met by the relieved mob of citizens as he rode into town. For the next forty-eight hours Forrest's men were able to enjoy a much needed rest. The grateful townsfolk planned a great celebration of feasting and thanksgiving to be held on May 6. In the meanwhile Confederate troops were sent up from Atlanta by rail to take custody of the prisoners. On Tuesday, May 5, they were transported via the Little Rome Railroad toward detention camps.[30]

Unfortunately for the Confederates, their rest was cut short when Forrest received word the same night they arrived that a new party of Yankees had left Tuscumbia, headed toward the present-day site of Birmingham. By sunup the next morning, the sixth of May, the Confederates had left to meet this new threat, leaving the locals to celebrate their deliverance alone.

The humiliation of surrender was only the beginning for Abel Streight. Southern politicians, who interpreted the affair differently, would shortly overturn the terms under which he assumed he had surrendered. Alabama governor John G. Shorter and Pres. Jefferson Davis decided to renege on the deal that Forrest had negotiated and that would have allowed Streight and all his raiders to be treated normally as prisoners of war, with the possibility of repatriation. Instead, the politicians charged Streight with "negro stealing." Their justification for this charge was based on appearances as much as anything else. As Streight's raiders had moved through Alabama, a small group of black runaways had attached themselves to the column and had been captured along with the worn-out Yankees. One wonders how they were able to keep up with the hard-driven Union troops.[31]

At first Streight believed he would be transported back to the Union lines under a truce, but he was surprised when he and his officers were separated from their men. The troops were sent on to be returned to Union control, but Streight and the officers were detained for possible trial in the Alabama Superior Court on the charge arising from the captured camp followers. Military theorist Carl Von Clausewitz wrote, "War is simply a continuation of political intercourse, with the addition of other means."[32] This was never truer than in Streight's case. Hauling him into court on such a charge would send a message to the Northerners about setting slaves free as they passed through Confederate territory. Conviction could lead to hard labor in a penitentiary, a possibility that did not set well with Streight.

Perhaps the idea of trying a high-ranking Union prisoner of war held little appeal for the state of Alabama as well; nevertheless, the terms of surrender had been contravened. Streight and his officers were sent on to Richmond to be held until an exchange of prisoners could be arranged. This took until November, when the U.S. commissioner on prisoner exchange, Col. James Ludlow, arrived at City Point, near Richmond, with one hundred Confederate prisoners to be exchanged for Streight and his officers.

Confederate officials refused the exchange, however, and the prisoners were sent back into captivity, heartbroken. Streight remained in Richmond's Libby Prison for nearly three more months, until on February 9, 1864, one hundred nine Union prisoners of war escaped from Libby in the largest prison escape of the war. Col. Abel Streight was one of those men. It had taken the escapees months to dig a tunnel fifteen feet deep under the kitchen fireplace and then out another fifty feet under the perimeter wall to an outside warehouse. In the escape attempt two men drowned trying to swim the James River and another forty-nine were recaptured.[33]

Streight not only made good his escape, but also returned to active duty and by the spring of 1865 was leading one of the Union commands chasing Forrest and the Army of Tennessee toward Selma, Alabama.

Forrest's victory over Streight was celebrated throughout the western theater of operations. Since General Van Dorn had been assassinated at Spring Hill, and General Bragg found himself in a tough spot, he ordered the now-renowned Forrest to report to him for a new assignment. Leaving his command in the able hands of Colonel

Biffle, Forrest departed for Huntsville, where he met Bragg on May 11. Bragg greeted Forrest with a promise of a promotion to major general, which Forrest surprisingly declined. Instead he recommended Gen. Gideon Pillow, whom he said was more suited for the rank. Pillow mentioned Forrest's statement in a letter he later wrote to Tennessee governor Isham Harris.[34]  *Why?*

Having declined the promotion, Forrest was sent back to Spring Hill to take over the vacant leadership of Van Dorn's command, which composed the left wing of the army. Now near division strength, Forrest roamed throughout the Harpeth Valley through the months of May and June, scouting all along the front.

On June 3 he was conducting a reconnaissance in force against the Federal positions at Franklin, Tennessee, when he found himself in a potentially catastrophic situation. Mistaking a Union signal flag for a flag of truce, he sent in a truce flag of his own. Anxious to get the business over with immediately, he followed the flag to within firing distance of the Federal fortifications. Grasping the significance of Forrest's error, a chivalrous Union officer rose from hiding and shouted a warning to the Confederate general, "General Forrest, that isn't a flag of truce. It's a signal flag. Go back, Sir! Go back!" Forrest waved his hat in reply and quickly returned to his own troops. No doubt there were some Union commanders who would have paid money for such an opportunity to permanently retire Forrest from the Confederate service, but as to the gallant Union officer who allowed Forrest to escape, the record is silent.[35]

Forrest and his men had made their way to Columbia, Tennessee, for a short bivouac after the surrender of Streight's raiders and the incident at Franklin, but his irritation over an incident on the battlefield at Sand Mountain followed him there. Forrest was a man who angered easily and found it hard to forgive.

Lt. A. Wills Gould had commanded a section of Morton's artillery battery during the pursuit of Streight's raiders. While engaged at Day's Gap, Gould's two guns had briefly fallen into the hands of the Union troops. Though they were recaptured later the same day, they had been spiked and ruined by the retreating raiders, but Forrest's rage over the initial loss of the guns had continued to smolder. In his fury he had reportedly called Gould a coward and had even begun the process of having Gould transferred out of his command.

If Forrest indeed had called Gould a coward, Capt. John Morton did not share that assessment. Morton wrote in his memoir, published in 1900, that he had personally commended Gould to the general for his courage and competence in the same action.[36]

Lieutenant Gould shared with many Southern males a heightened sense of honor and subscribed to a code of conduct that required a response when one's honor had been impugned. No one knows how long Gould had been brooding about the incident, nor whether he knew the entire truth concerning General Forrest's actions, but on June 14, he decided to act in the only honorable way he felt left open to him.

Maj. John Rawle, another officer in Forrest's command, knew of his general's order to transfer Gould and that the young lieutenant was rumored to be looking for Forrest for the purpose of demanding an apology and satisfaction for his bruised honor. Captain Morton learned of this from Rawle and, having known Forrest for some time, instantly realized what this could lead to. Though he was several miles from Columbia at the time, he immediately mounted up and rushed toward town to try to head off what might easily have become a deadly encounter. Forty years later Morton was still convinced that if he had reached Forrest before Gould had, he could have averted the tragedy that ensued.[37]

Early on the afternoon of June 14, Forrest was passing the time at Columbia's Masonic building, which was also his headquarters for the time being. After the news of the Streight campaign began to circulate, Forrest was the object of the hero-worship of the young boys in town, four of whom followed him around, basking in his heroic presence. These four boys were on the scene when Gould reached the Masonic hall that afternoon and confronted Forrest. One of the boys was Frank A. Smith, who later became a teacher at the Columbia Athenaeum as well as secretary of the Maury County Historical Society. Years later he would recount the events of that day with great detail in a newspaper article that recorded his story for the enlightenment of its future readers.[38]

From the start neither man was willing to be the first to give peace a chance. Gould, the scion of a respected family, would not accept the general's assessment that he had acted cowardly or ignobly. And Forrest would not relent in his assessment, nor was his mind changed after Gould's attempted explanations and justifications. Within a flash of seconds the two men were beyond reason.

Dueling for personal and family honor had not been entirely abandoned in the South, though this ancient practice often took some strange turns when Southern men attempted to settle serious differences. Perhaps intending to resort to whatever force was necessary to exact his apology, Gould had come to the meeting with

Forrest carrying a pistol in the pocket of his linen duster.

Here, the account varies somewhat. In a blaze of temper, Gould moved toward Forrest. As Gould attempted to draw the pistol from his duster, it snagged on the pocket, allowing Forrest a fraction of a second to react and stop Gould from firing. As they struggled briefly, the pistol discharged, driving the ball into Forrest's lower abdomen, where it lodged in his hip, near the spine. Forrest's strength and will probably saved his life. Instead of recoiling in pain as one might expect of a man who had just been shot, he went on the offensive. Before Gould could bring the pistol to bear for a second shot, Forrest seized the gun hand and forced it high above Gould's head.

When the confrontation began, Forrest had been holding a folding pocket penknife in his hand, which he had just used to cut a piece of fruit, and he immediately brought it into play. Continuing to force Gould's hand toward the ceiling, he opened the knife blade with his teeth and thrust it into his assailant's abdomen. The blade had run truer than Gould's pistol ball, and the young officer seemed to realize that he had been seriously injured. He tore loose from Forrest's grip, stumbling away and through the door leading to the street beyond in an effort to save his life.

Outside the Masonic Hall, Gould met two civilian surgeons, James H. Wilkes and Luke Ridley. Dr. Ridley recognized the wounded lieutenant and cried out, "My God, it's Wills Gould." At the same moment, Maj. C. S. Severson, Forrest's quartermaster, shouted, "Stop that man! Stop that man! He shot General Forrest!"[39] The two doctors rushed after him and took him into the first available building, a tailor shop, so they could stabilize Gould and administer medical treatment. They placed him on a table and began to examine the wound.

The four boys who had been hanging around the Masonic Hall had seen Gould rush into the street and followed him and the doctors to the tailor shop. The tumult had attracted a sizeable crowd, which now gathered around the door of the shop. The onlookers were all attempting to get a glimpse of what was going on inside.

In the meantime Forrest had walked to the office of Dr. L. P. Yandell to seek treatment for his injury. Dr. Yandell hurriedly examined the pistol wound and related his prognosis to his patient. The wound, he told Forrest, could possibly be fatal, and that because of the summer heat and the proximity of the bullet to the intestines, sepsis was almost certain to develop. Upon hearing the ominous prognosis, Forrest became more angry than worried. He shouted to the doctor, "By God, he has mortally wounded me, and no damned man shall kill me before I kill him dead first."[40] He stormed out of Dr. Yandell's office, determined to find Gould and kill him. Just outside the office he met a passing Confederate officer and ripped two pistols out of his gun belt, then set out on a search and destroy mission to find and kill the man he now believed had inflicted a fatal wound upon him.

The crowd gathered in front of the tailor shop drew Forrest like a beacon. He pushed through the onlookers and burst into the makeshift operating room, startling the doctors and frightening Gould, who, covered in blood and holding his stomach wound with both hands, rolled from the table with great effort and fled from the shop through the back door. Forrest quickly followed, firing as he went. One of his reckless shots ricocheted and wounded a nearby soldier in the leg.

Weakened from loss of blood, Gould could only stumble a few yards before he collapsed in a patch of weeds behind the tailor shop. Not realizing that Gould was down, Forrest went back through the front door of the tailor shop and into the street, thinking to cut off Gould's escape. When he entered the alley he saw Gould lying in the weeds and approached to determine if he was alive. Though he might not have realized that Gould was dying, he could at least see that he was no longer a threat. Some of the anger seemed to go out of him.

He reentered the tailor shop and asked Dr. Wilkes to treat his wound. Dr. Wilkes replied that his first duty was to the young lieutenant whom he had been treating. Forrest ordered him to accompany him outside to a carriage and thence to a private home where he could be more properly attended to. Just outside the shop they met Dr. Ridley, who, having gone to get medical instruments with which to treat Gould, was returning with the equipment in hand. Forrest ordered him too to get into the carriage, and as they proceeded to the nearby home of a Confederate officer, they picked up yet another physician, Dr. Sam Frierson.

The four boys who had been watching the drama unfold tagged along, holding on to the back of the carriage. The boys went into the house with the men and saw the doctors attempt to assist Forrest up the stairs to a bedroom. Swearing, Forrest declined their help. "His rage was terrible."[41] When Dr. Wilkes had Forrest more comfortably reclining on the bed, he probed the wound and found that the bullet had missed the vital organs and had lodged in the large muscles of the hip. His prognosis was less dire than the last one delivered by Dr. Yandell. The bullet had only inflicted a flesh wound in the muscle of the hip and could be readily removed. Forrest would live. With this news, Forrest's rage finally subsided. "It's nothing but a damned little pistol ball—let it alone," he said.

Trusting in Dr. Wilkes' assessment, Forrest now believed that he would live, and for the first time he expressed concern for Gould. He ordered Dr. Ridley to take Lieutenant Gould to the Nelson House and give him every comfort and aid. "And by God, Ridley, when I give such an order, I mean it." Forrest may have meant it, but this was the first indication that he gave a damn about Lieutenant Gould's condition, and the order came too late.[42]

Later that night, as the story goes, Forrest, following a lifelong propensity of losing control of his temper then upon reflection, sincerely apologizing for his behavior, went to the bedside of Lieutenant Gould and the two made amends before Gould passed away.[43] Nevertheless, the bedside apology and pardon may never have occurred, as there is no record that Forrest himself perpetuated that version. However, despite Forrest's remorse, Gould was beyond help. He died two days later, leaving behind a young lady of Columbia to whom he had become engaged when his battery was first stationed there in February.

The following campaign and battle maps depict the movements of Nathan Bedford Forrest during his career in the army of the Confederate States of America, from his enlistment in June 1861 to his final drive for the defense of Selma, Alabama, in April 1865.

On 6·14·1861, Nathan Bedford Forrest enlisted as a private at age 40. In early October, he was elected Lt. Col. and organized and led his 1st command on its 1st campaign as depicted on this map.

JTT  2002

ILL.

Ohio River

Mario

Cairo

Paducah

Columbus

FT. DONELSON

Ft. Henry

Union City

Paris

Mississippi River

Obion River

Forked Deer Creek

Trenton

McLemoresville

So. Fork

Humboldt

Ft. Pillow

Sharron's Ferry

Browns-ville

Jackson

Hatchie

River

Tennessee River

Memphis

START

Somerville

Shiloh Church

Pittsbur SHIL(

Wolf

Moscow

Grand Jct.

To Memphis by

and back rail

River

Corinth

MSS.

Scale in Miles

0   3.5   7   10.5   14   17.5   21   24.5   28

Coseyville

Marion

Madisonville

Princeton

Cadiz
Canton

SON
2-11/15-62
enry

SACRAMENTO 12-28-61
Sacramento

Greenville

KY

River
Munfordville

Bowling Green

Green

Hopkinsville

Memphis Jct.

Dover

Clarksville

Gallatin

Cumberland City

Cumberland Furnace
Charlotte

Edgefield

Cumberland River

Johnsonville

Kingston Springs

Nashville

Stones River

sville River

Tennessee River

Duck River

Murfrees boro

Wartrace

Columbia

TEN.

Shelbyville
Tullahoma

Clifton Ferry

Mulberry

Pittsburg Landing
SHILOH 4-6/8-62

Fayetteville

FURLOUGH
2-25/3-10-62

Shoal Creek

AL

Elk River

Iuka
Florence

Athens

Tuscumbia

Huntsville

Decatur

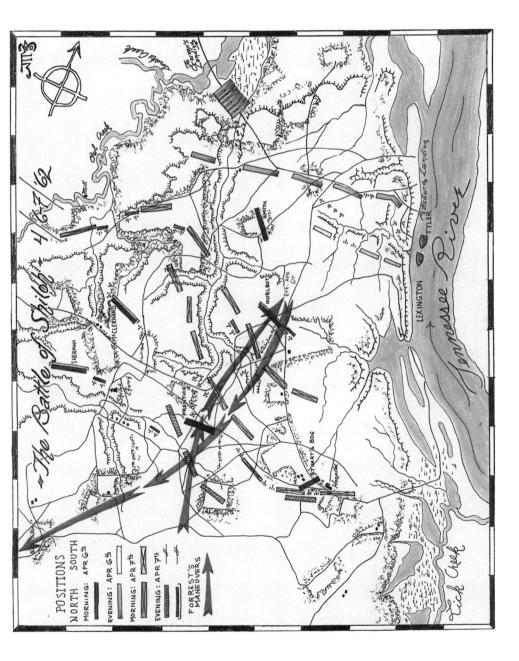

The Battle of Shiloh

4 & 7/62

POSITIONS
NORTH    SOUTH
MORNING: APR 6th
EVENING: APR 6th
MORNING: APR 7th
EVENING: APR 7th
FORREST'S MANEUVERS

SHERMAN
McCLERNAND
SHILOH
PRENTISS
HURLBUT
EVE APR 6th
SMITH
STUART'S BDE

Owl Creek
Snake Creek
Lick Creek

Tennessee River
LEXINGTON
TYLER
Pittsburg Landing

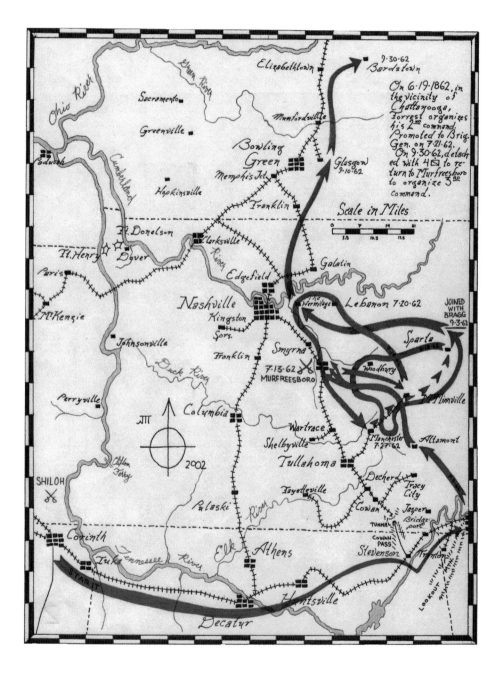

Ohio River

Green River

Elizabethtown

9.30.62
Bardstown

Sacramento

Greenville

Munfordville

Paducah

Cumberland

Bowling
Green

Glasgow
9.10.62

On 6·19·1862, in
the vicinity of
Chattanooga,
Forrest organizes
his 2ⁿᵈ command.
Promoted to Brig.
Gen. on 7·21·62.
On 9·30·62, detach-
ed with 4□ to re-
turn to Murfreesboro
to organize 3ʳᵈ
command.

Memphis Jct.

Hopkinsville

Franklin

Scale in Miles

Ft. Donelson

Clarksville

0      7      14      21
1.5        10.5     17.5

Ft. Henry    Dover

Paris

River

Edgefield

Gallatin

The
Hermitage

Lebanon 7·20·62

JOINED
WITH
BRAGG
9·3·62

McKenzie

Nashville

Kingston

Sprs.

Sparta

Johnsonville

Duck River

Franklin

Smyrna

7·13·62

MURFREESBORO

Woodbury

McMinnville

Perryville

Columbia

Wartrace

Manchester
7·27·62

Altamont

Clifton
Ferry

Shelbyville

Tullahoma

Decherd

Tracy
City

SHILOH

Pulaski

Fayetteville

Cowan

Jasper

Bridge-
port

TUNNEL

COWAN
PASS

Corinth

Iuka    Tennessee    River

Elk River

Athens

Stevenson

Trenton

STAR IT

Huntsville

Decatur

⫫
2002

LOOKOUT MT. RR

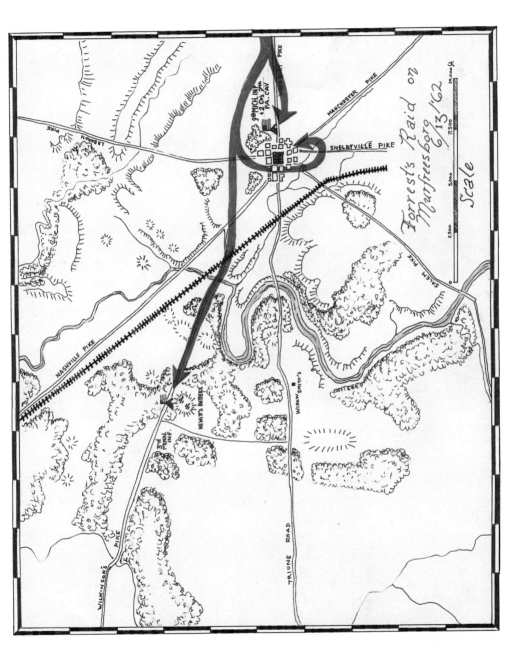

Forrest's Raid on Murfreesboro 6/13/62

Scale

MANCHESTER PIKE

SHELBYVILLE PIKE

SALEM PIKE

9TH MICH. INF. +2 COS. 7TH PA. CAV.

LEBANON PIKE

PIKE

NASHVILLE PIKE

HEWIT'S BATTERY

3RD MINN. INF.

WIDOW SMITH'S

WILKINSON'S PIKE

TRIUNE ROAD

Moscow
Hickman
Fulton
KENTUCKY
Ft. Heiman
Ft. Henry
FT. 2·3·63
DONELSON
Dove

Union City
Gibbs
N. Fork
Lick Cr.

Obion R.
Kenton
Dresden
Paris
Paris Landing

S. Fork
McKenzie
Big. Sandy R.
Johnsonville

Rutherford
N. Forked
Trenton

McLemoresville
Huntingdon

Humboldt
G.
Lavinia
Clarksburg
PARKER'S CROSS ROADS
12·31·62
Duck

Spring Creek
River

S. Forked
Lexington
Beech Cr.
Perryville
Forr
3ʳᵈ com
Ma

Jackson
12·15·62 ⟶ 1·1·63
1ˢᵗ West
Tennessee
Raid
Tifflin
Jacks Creek
Henderson
G.
Tennessee
= ya
bso
hous
Way

Clifton Ferry
W. 12·15·62
C. 1·1·63
3/4 mi. wide

1·26·63 ~ 2·17·63 With
Wheeler, 2nd Ft.
Donelson
Campaign

Clarksville

Gallatin

Dover

Palmyra

Cumberland City

Cumberland River

Edgefield

The Hermitage

Cumberland Furnace

Nashville

Charlotte

Antioch

Stones River

Yellow Cr.

LaVergne

Landing

Kingston Springs

Harpeth R.

Smyrna

Pinewood

Penny Cr.

Franklin

Murfreesboro

Duck River

Centerville

START

Forrest's
3ʳᵈ command
Map #1

1·26·63

Columbia

Wartrace

✠ = yankee
block
house

1·10·62

Mt. Pleasant

Shelbyville

Scale in Miles

0  2  4  6  8  10  12  14

Waynesboro

JTT  2002

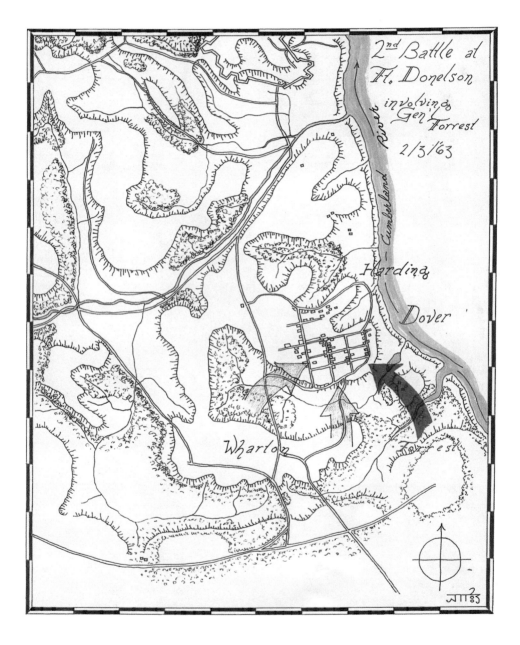

2nd Battle at
Ft. Donelson
involving
Gen'l Forrest
2/3/'63

Cumberland River

Harding

Dover

Wharton

Forrest

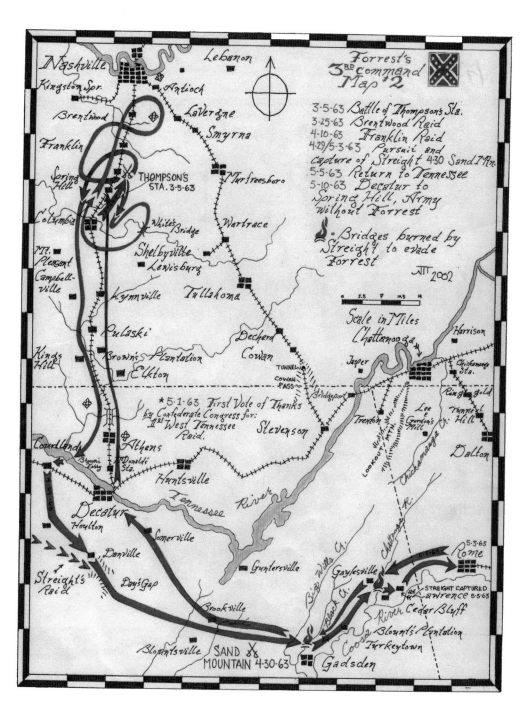

Forrest's
3RD command
Map #2

Nashville
Kingston Spr.
Lebanon
Antioch
Brentwood
LaVergne
Franklin
Smyrna
Spring Hill
THOMPSON'S STA. 3-5-63
Murfreesboro
Columbia
White's Bridge
Wartrace
Mt. Pleasant
Shelbyville
Campbell-ville
Lewisburg
Wynnville
Tallahoma
Pulaski
Decherd
Brown's Plantation
Cowan
Kings Hill
Elkton
TUNNEL
COWAN PASS
Chattanooga
Harrison
Jasper
Chickamauga Sta.
Bridgeport
Ring-gold
*5-1-63 First Vote of Thanks
by Confederate Congress for:
1st West Tennessee
Raid.
Stevenson
Trenton
Lee & Gordon's Mill
Tunnel Hill
Ch. Hill
Courtland
Athens
McDonald's Sta.
Dalton
Brown's Ferry
Huntsville
Tennessee River
Decatur
Houlton
Somerville
Danville
Guntersville
Streight's Raid
Day's Gap
Brookville
Rome
Gaylesville
STREIGHT CAPTURED Lawrence 5-3-63
River Cedar Bluff
Bloutsville
SAND MOUNTAIN 4-30-63
Coosa Turkeytown
Blount's Plantation
Gadsden

3-5-63 Battle of Thompson's Sta.
3-25-63 Brentwood Raid
4-10-63 Franklin Raid
4-29/5-3-63 Pursuit and
capture of Streight 4-30 Sand Mtn.
5-5-63 Return to Tennessee
5-10-63 Decatur to
Spring Hill, Army
without Forrest

= Bridges burned by
Streight to evade
Forrest

JTT 2002

0   3.5   7   14.5   14
Scale in Miles

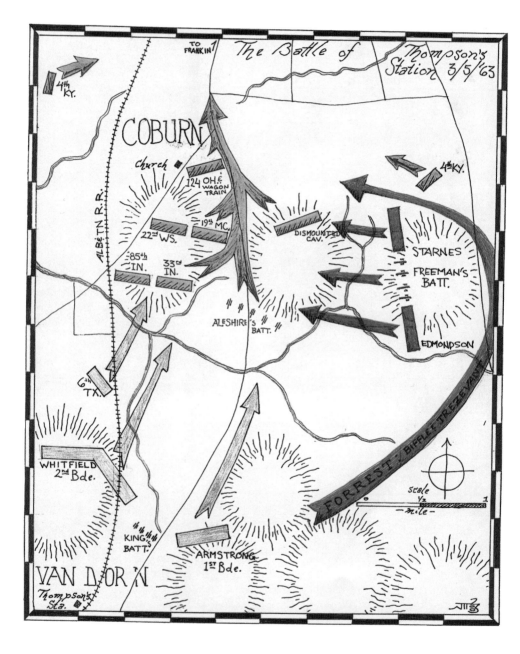

The Battle of Thompson's Station 3/5/'63

TO FRANKLIN

4th KY.

COBURN

Church

124 OH. & WAGON TRAIN

19th MC.

22nd WS.

85th IN.

33rd IN.

DISMOUNTED CAV.

4th KY.

STARNES

FREEMAN'S BATT.

EDMONDSON

ALESHIRE'S BATT.

A.& TN. R.R.

6th TX.

WHITFIELD 2nd Bde.

KING'S BATT.

ARMSTRONG 1st Bde.

VAN DORN

Thompson's Sta.

FORREST: BIFFLE: TREZEVANT

scale
0     ½     1
— mile —

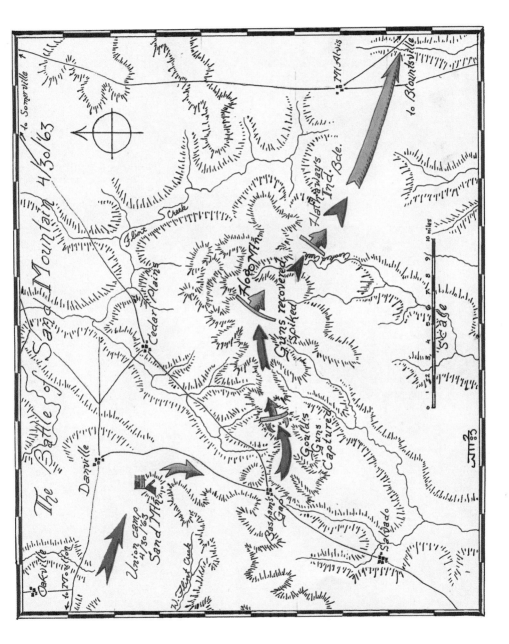

The Battle of Sand Mountain 4/30/'63

to Somerville

to Brownsville

7th Arvis

Flathaway's Ind. Bde.

Flint Creek

Sand Mtn.

Guns recovered & spiked

Crooked Creek

Cedar Plains

Gould's Guns Spiked

Gould's Guns Captured

Darville

Union Camp 4/30/'63 Sand Mtn.

W. Flint Creek

Bastian's Gap

Salvado

to Oakville

to Houston

Scale

10 miles

Franklin
M.St.
St. 6·4·63
Triune
College Grove
Murfreesboro
Woodbury
6·4·63
6·10·63
6·27·63
McMinnville
6·27·63
Wartrace
Manchester
Shelbyville
Lewisville
Hillsboro
Tullahoma
Pelham
Mulberry
Decherd
Tracy City
Fayetteville
Cowan
Jasper
RR TUNNEL
1 mi. long
COWAN
PASS
10 mi. long
Elkton
Bridgeport
0 2 4 6 8 10 12 14
Scale in Miles
Stevenson
Athens
McDonald's St.
Huntsville
Somerville

Forrest's 3rd Command
◦ Map 3 ◦

-4·63  Raid on Triune
-10·63  2nd Triune Raid
-27·63  Rear Guard
ullahoma Campaign
-30/7·6·63  Cowan Pass
· Chattanooga
-18/20·63  Battle of
  Chickamauga
-30·63  Battle of
  Philadelphia

ЈЛ  2002

10-5-63 Relieved of
Command. Went by
rail to Montgomery
and Atlanta.
11-7-63 Left to
Organize 4th Command.
11-16-63 Reassembled at
Okolona Mississippi.

Kingston
PHILADELPHIA
9-30-63
Athens
Charleston
Cleveland
Harrison
Chattanooga
Jasper
Birds Mill
Chickamauga St.
Rossville
Ringgold
Tunnel Hill
Dalton
Reed's Br.
Trenton
E&G Mill
LOOKOUT MTN.
CHICKAMAUGA 9-19/20-63
LaFayette
Summerville
Alpine

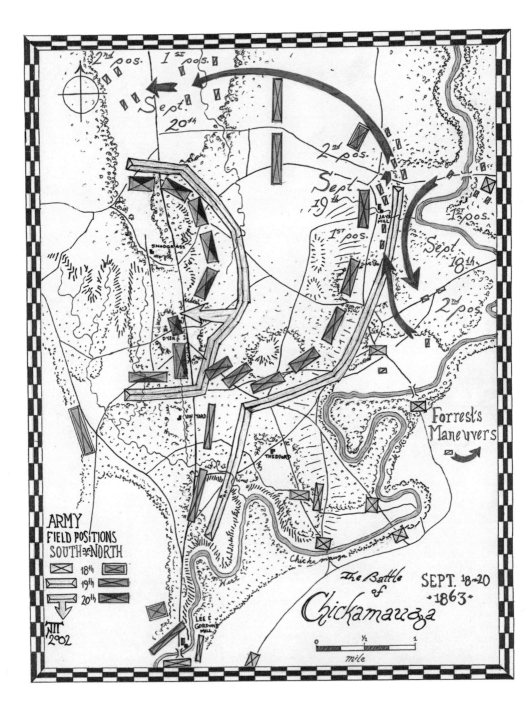

The Battle of
Chickamauga
SEPT. 18–20
1863

Forrest's 4th Command Map #1

Hatchie River
Jackson
Mifflin
Estenaula
Whiteville
Jack's Cr.
Somerville
New Castle
Henderson
Bethel Spr.
Bolivar
Purdy Cr. Rds.
LaFayette Sta.
Moscow
Grand Jct.
Shiloh Church
Collierville
LaGrange
Mt. Pleasant
Wolf River
Corinth
Monterey
Salem
Ruckersville
12-29-63 → 2-15-64
Holly Springs
Ripley
Rienzi
Wyatte
Tallahatchie River
Abbeville
Booneville
Hurricane Cr.
Stubb's Farm
Baldwyn
Oxford
Ellistown
Guntown
12-1/29-63 2nd West Tennessee Raid
New Albany
Pontotoc
Harrisburg
Tupelo
Verona
2-15-64 → 2-26-64
1st Defence of Mississippi
Tupelo Road
Ivey's Hill
2-21-64 Battle of West Point
Okolona
OKOLONA 2-22-64
2-22-64 Battle of Okolona
Houston
** 12-4-63 Promoted to Major General
Prarie Sta.
WEST PT. 2-21-64
Grenada
2-17-64 Second Vote of Thanks by Confederate Congress, for: Capture of Streight, and Valiant Conduct at Chickamauga
Sakatonchee Creek
Tombigbee River
Ellis Br.
West Pt.
Colum.
2-10-64
bus 2-26-64
Scale in Miles
0 1 2 3 4 5 6 7
Starkville
Artesia
2002

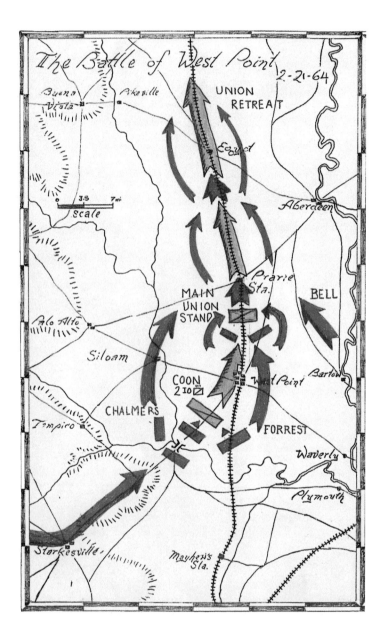

The Battle of West Point 2-21-64

UNION RETREAT

Buena Vista

Pikeville

Egypt

Aberdeen

scale 3.5 7mi

Prarie Sta.

BELL

MAIN UNION STAND

Palo Alto

Siloam

West Point

Barton

COON 2 10

CHALMERS

FORREST

Tempico

Waverly

Plymouth

Starkesville

Mayhews Sta.

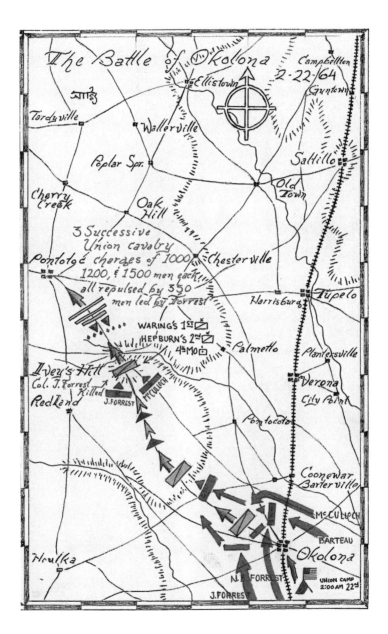

The Battle of Okolona 2-22-64

Ellistown · Campbelltown · Guntown

Tardyville · Wallerville · Saltillo

Poplar Spr. · Old Town

Cherry Creek · Oak Hill · Chesterville · Tupelo

3 Successive Union cavalry Pontotoc charges of 1000, 1200, & 1500 men each, all repulsed by 350 men led by Forrest

Harrisburg

WARING'S 1ST

HEPBURN'S 2ND

4TH MO.

Palmetto · Plantersville

Ivey's Hill · Col. J. Forrest Killed · Verona

Redland · J. FORREST · McCULLOCH · City Point

Pontotoc

Coonewar Barterville

McCULLOCH

BARTEAU

Houlka · Okolona

N. B. FORREST · UNION CAMP 2:00 AM 22ND

J. FORREST

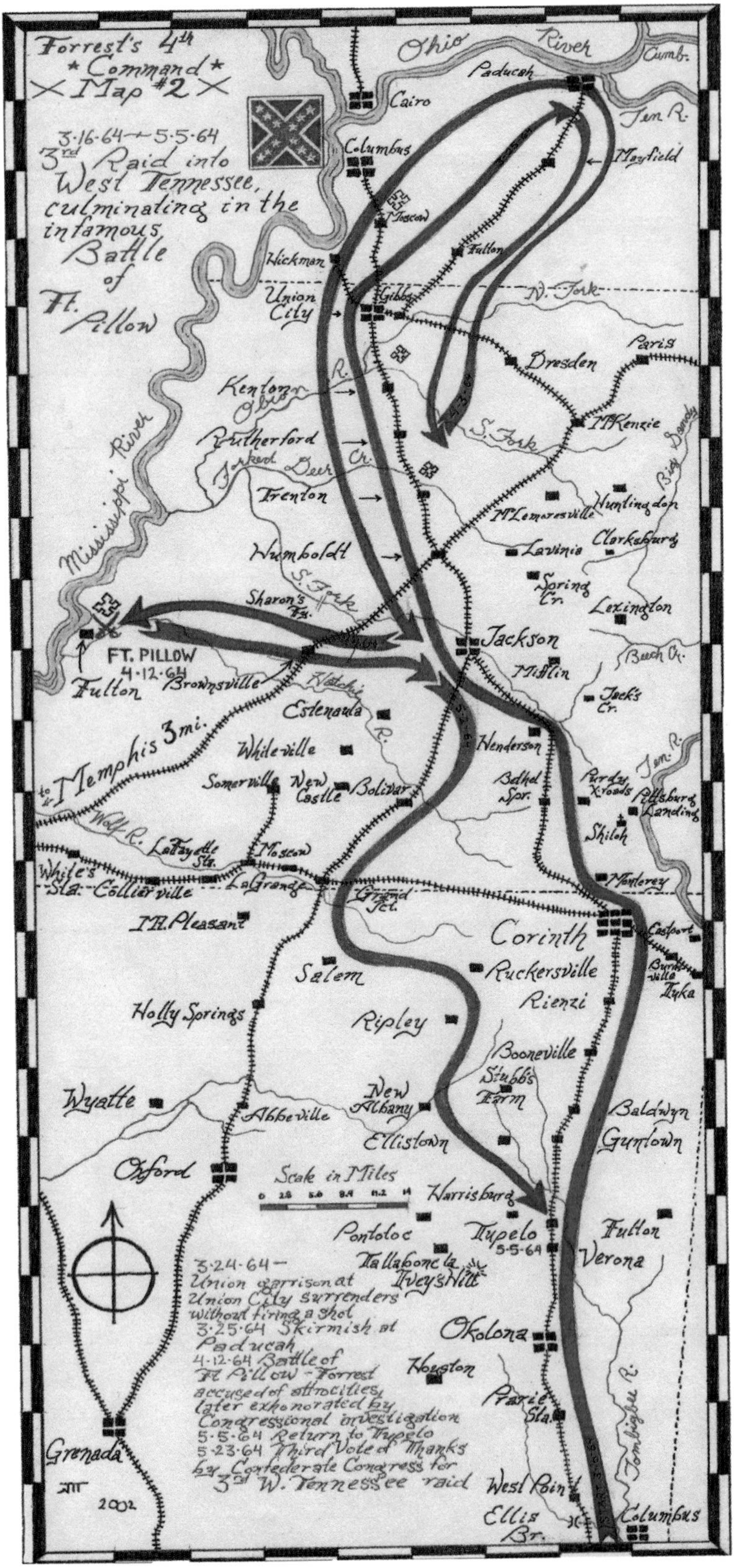

Forrest's 4th
Command
Map #2
3.16.64 – 5.5.64
3rd Raid into
West Tennessee,
culminating in the
infamous
Battle
of
Ft.
Pillow
Ohio River
Paducah
Cumb.
Cairo
Ten. R.
Columbus
Mayfield
Moscow
Hickman
Fulton
Union
City
N. Fork
Dresden
Paris
Kenton
Obion R.
McKenzie
S. Fork
Rutherford
Forked Deer Cr.
Trenton
Huntingdon
Mt. Lemoresville
Big Sandy
Mississippi River
Humboldt
Lavinia
Clarksburg
Spring Cr.
Sharon's Fy.
Lexington
Jackson
FT. PILLOW
4-12-64
Fulton
Brownsville
Mifflin
Beech Cr.
Estenaula
Jack's Cr.
Henderson
Memphis 3 mi.
Whiteville
Somerville
New Castle
Bolivar
Bethel Spr.
Purdy X-roads
Pittsburg Landing
Ten. R.
Shiloh
Wolf R.
Lafayette Sta.
Moscow
White's Sta.
Collierville
LaGrange
Grand Jct.
Monterey
Mt. Pleasant
Corinth
Eastport
Burnsville
Iuka
Salem
Ruckersville
Rienzi
Holly Springs
Ripley
Booneville
Stubb's Farm
Wyatte
New Albany
Abbeville
Baldwyn
Guntown
Ellistown
Oxford
Scale in Miles
0 2.8 5.6 8.4 11.2 14
Harrisburg
Pontoloc
Tupelo
5-5-64
Fulton
Verona
Tallaboncla
Ivey's Hill
3.24.64 –
Union garrison at
Union City surrenders
without firing a shot
3.25.64 Skirmish at
Paducah
4-12-64 Battle of
Ft. Pillow – Forrest
accused of atrocities,
later exhonorated by
Congressional investigation
5.5.64 Return to Tupelo
5.23.64 Third Voted Thanks
by Confederate Congress for
3rd W. Tennessee raid
Okolona
Houston
Prarie Sta.
Tombigbee R.
Grenada
West Point
Ellis Br.
Columbus
2002

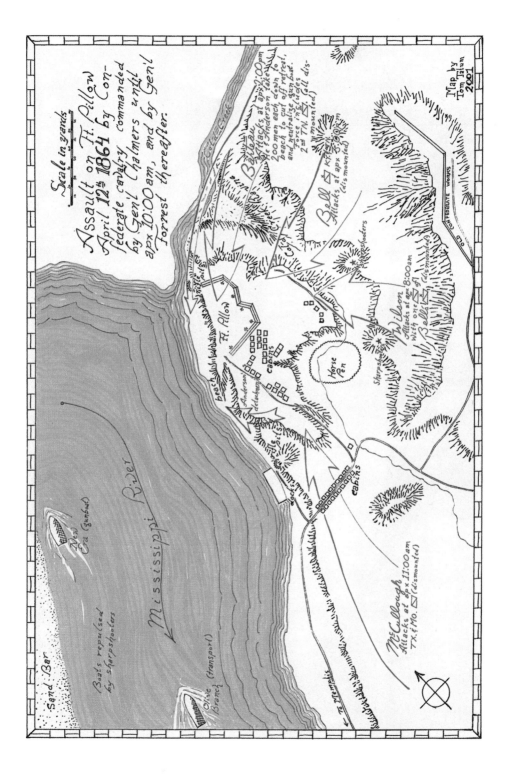

Scale in yards

Assault on Ft. Pillow
April 12th 1864 by Confederate cavalry commanded
by Gen'l Chalmers until
apx 10:00 am, and by Gen'l
Forrest thereafter.

Map by
Tom Blum
2001

Sand Bar

New Era (gunboat)

Boats repulsed
by sharpshooters

Mississippi River

Olive Branch (Transport)

tree roots

Coal Creek

Bell at apx 2:00pm
(Lt. J. Anderson takes
200 men each down to
beach to cut off retreat,
and neutralize gunboat.
Force includes
2nd TN (all dismounted)

Bell 4 KIA (dismounted)
Attacks at apx 3:00am

McCoy

Bell
Attacks at apx 1:00pm

ravine

Coal Cr.

Ft. Pillow

sharpshooters

Anderson (dismounted)

cabins

beach

Wilson
Attacks at apx 8:00am
with one gun
(dismounted)

Bell's

Horse Pen

sharpshooters

OLD CONFEDERATE WORKS

cabins

McCullough
Attacks at apx 11:00am
TX. & MO. (dismounted)

Memphis

Somerville

Bolivar

Wolf River

LaFayette Sta.

White's Sta.

Moscow

Grand Jct.

Collierville

LaGrange

Mt. Pleasant

Salem

Hernando

8-12-64

Holly Springs

Coldwater

Senatobia

Wyatte Tallahatchie

Como

Abbeville

New River

Albany

Ellisto

Panola

8-18-64

Oxford
8-10-64

HARRIS
7-13/1

Pontotoc

Tallaboncla

Iver

Forrest's 4th
Command-Map #3
6-1-64 ⚹ 7-17-64  2nd
Defense of Mississippi
6-10/11-64 Battle of Brice's X-roa
7-13/15-64 Battle of Harrisburg
7-17-64 Command dis-
bands, reassembles 8-10-64
at Oxford.
8-18-64 ⚹ 8-23-64  3rd
Defence of Mississippi
8-21/22-64 Memphis Raid

Hous

Grenada
8-23-64

Forrest alone
by train via
Jackson & Meridian
to Verona.

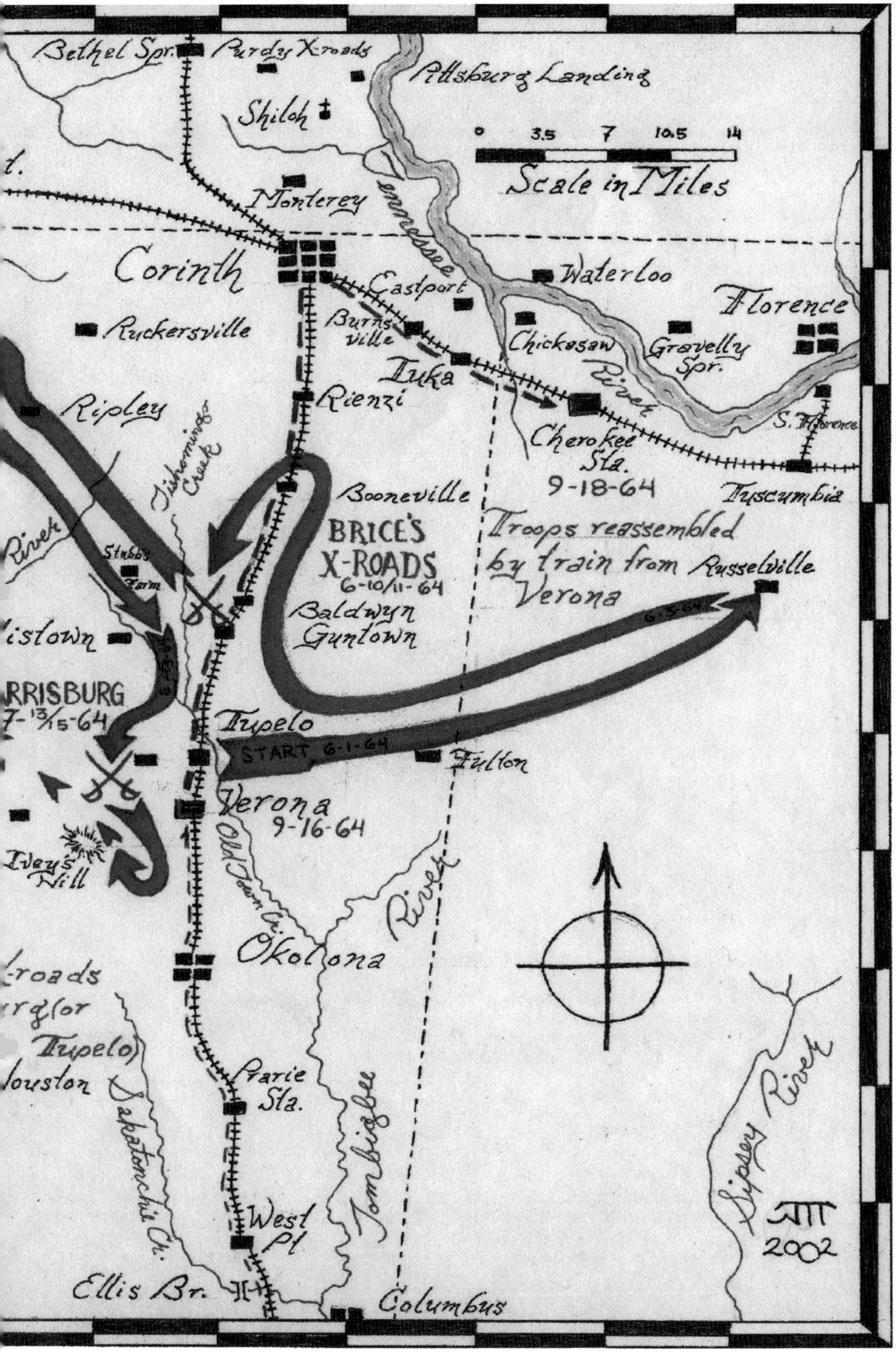

Bethel Spr.
Purdy X-roads
Pittsburg Landing
Shiloh
0 3.5 7 10.5 14
Scale in Miles
Monterey
Tennessee
Corinth
Eastport
Waterloo
Florence
Ruckersville
Burnsville
Chickasaw
Gravelly Spr.
Iuka
River
Rienzi
Ripley
S. Florence
Cherokee Sta.
9-18-64
Tishomingo Creek
Booneville
Tuscumbia
BRICE'S X-ROADS
6-10/11-64
Troops reassembled by train from Russelville
Verona
River
Stubbs Farm
Baldwyn
Guntown
RRISBURG
7-13/15-64
Tupelo
START 6-1-64
Fulton
Verona
9-16-64
Old Town Cr.
Ivey's Hill
River
Okolona
Tupelo)
Prarie Sta.
Sakatonchie Cr.
Tombigbee
Sipsey River
West Pt
JTT
2002
Ellis Br.
Columbus

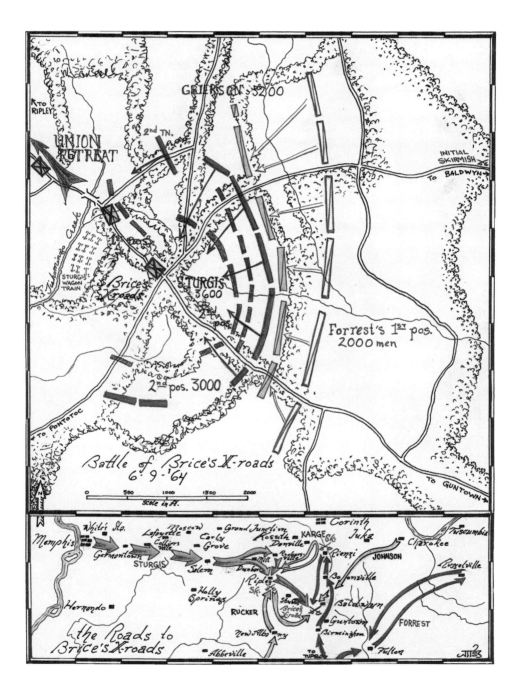

GRIERSON 3200

R. TO
RIPLEY

UNION
RETREAT

2nd TN.

INITIAL
SKIRMISH

TO BALDWYN

Tishamingo Creek

STURGIS
WAGON
TRAIN

Brice's
X-roads

STURGIS
3600

1st pos.

Forrest's 1st pos.
2000 men

2nd pos. 3000

TO PONTOTOC

Battle of Brice's X-roads
6·9·'64

0    500    1000    1500    2000
Scale in ft.

TO GUNTOWN

N

Memphis

White's Sta.

Germantown

Lafayette

Moscow

Collierville

STURGIS

Salem

Corly
Grove

Grand Junction
Roseuth
Danville

KARGE

Corinth
Juka

Tuscumbia

Chaxokee

Pienzi

JOHNSON

Russelville

Hernondo

Holly
Springs

RUCKER

Dunbar

Mill

Ruckers
ville

Ripley
Sk.

South
Brice's
X-roads

Bollonville

Baldwyn

Guntown
Birmingham

FORREST

New Albony

Abbeville

TO TUPELO

Fulton

the Roads to
Brice's X-roads

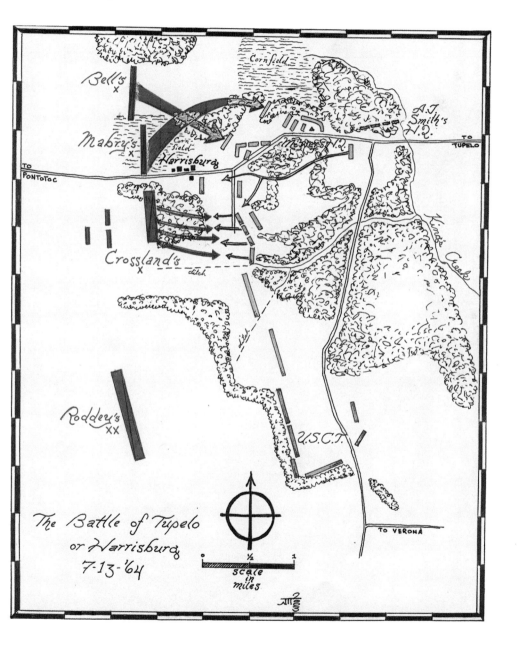

Cornfield

Bell's
X

Mabry's
X

A.J.
Smith's
H.Q.

TO
TUPELO

Corn-
field

Harrisburg

Moreland?

TO
PONTOTOC

King's Creek

Crossland's
X

ditch

Roddey's
XX

U.S.C.T.

The Battle of Tupelo
or Harrisburg
7-13-'64

TO VERONA

0        ½        1
scale
in
miles

Paris
Dresden

Cumberland
City

Pal

M'Kenzie

Cumb

Huntingdon

JOHNSONVILLE
11-4-64

Pinew

M'Lemores-
ville

Clarksburg

Duck

Lavinia

Spring
Creek

Forrest's
4ᵗʰ Command
X Map #4 X

Cente

Lexington

9-21-64 ~ 10-6-64 North
Alabama-Mid-Tennessee

Jackson

Perryville

10-16-64 ~ 11-16-64
4ᵗʰ West Tennessee
raid

M'Ti

Mifflin

Jack's Cr.

Clifton
Fy.

Touche Sp

Henryville

Henderson

Waynesboro

Purdy
Xroads

Bethd
Spr.

Pittsburg
Landing

11-4-64 Battle of
Johnsonville

Shiloh ✝

0 1 2 3 4 5 6 7
Scale in
Miles

Monterey

Shoal Ch

Corinth

Cast
port

Waterloo

Chickasaw

2002

Burn
sville

Florence

Iuka

Bainbri
S. Flore
Town

Rienzi

Cherokee
Sta.

Booneville

Tuscum

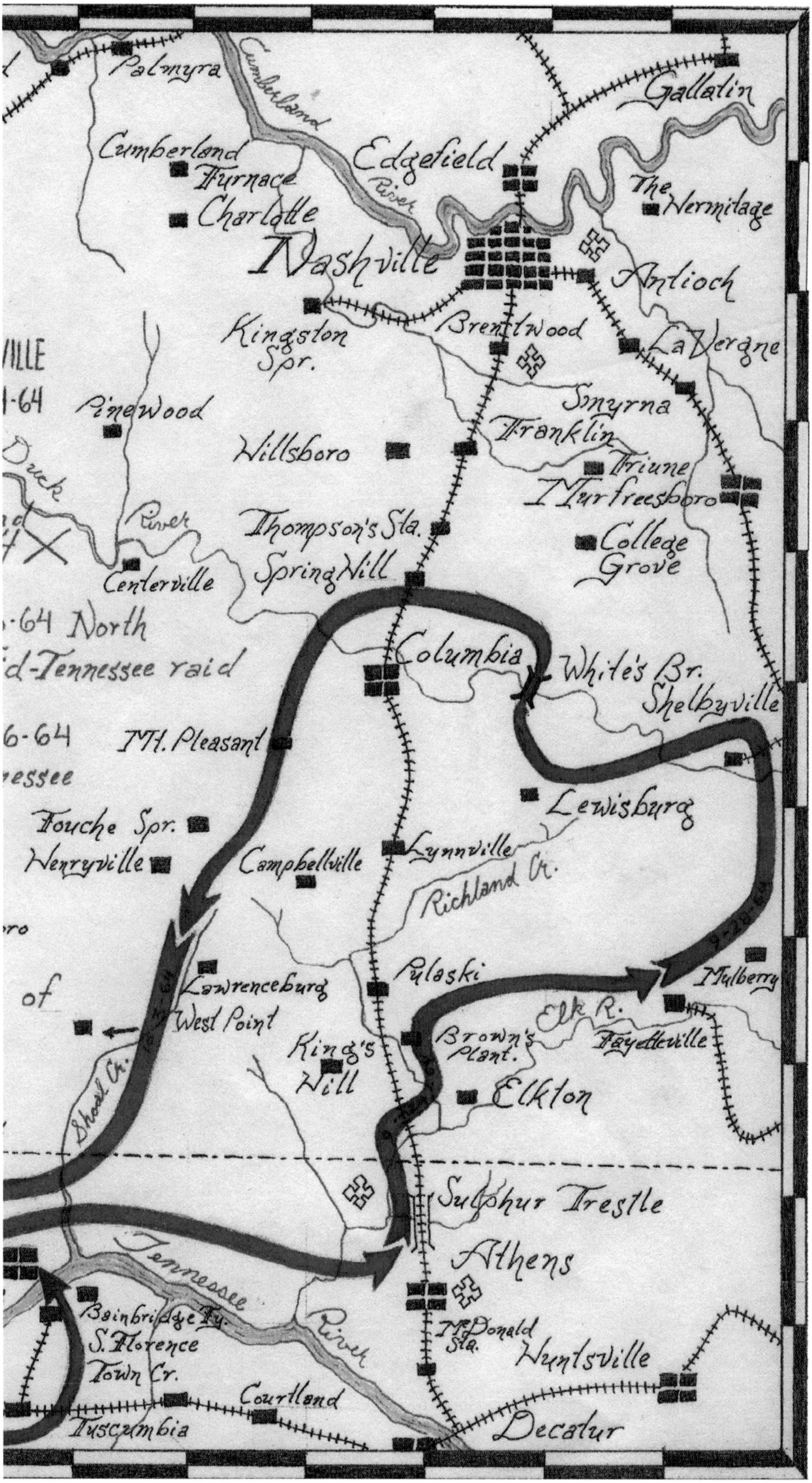
Palmyra
Cumberland
Gallatin
Cumberland Furnace
Charlotte
Edgefield
River
The Hermitage
Nashville
Antioch
Kingston Spr.
Brentwood
LaVergne
Pinewood
Smyrna
Franklin
Hillsboro
Triune
Murfreesboro
Duck
River
Thompson's Sta.
College Grove
Spring Hill
Centerville
Columbia
White's Br.
Shelbyville
Mt. Pleasant
Lewisburg
Fouche Spr.
Henryville
Lynnville
Campbellville
Richland Cr.
9-28-64
Pulaski
Mulberry
Lawrenceburg
West Point
Elk R.
Brown's Plant.
Fayetteville
King's Hill
Elkton
Shoal Cr.
Sulphur Trestle
Athens
Tennessee
River
Bainbridge Fy.
S. Florence
Town Cr.
McDonald Sta.
Huntsville
Courtland
Tuscumbia
Decatur

# '64 Nashville Campaign

11-19-64 ~ 12-27-64

## Gen'l Hood in Command

11-19-64 Army of Tennessee marches north from Florence, Alabama
11-27-64 Inconclusive engagement at Columbia ◊ 11-29-64 Missed opportunity to rout Federal army at Spring Hill ◊ 11-30-64 Battle of Franklin – Pyhrric Victory ◊ 12-6-64 – Forrest awarded 4th Vote of Thanks by Confederate Congress for 4th W. Tennessee raid ◊ 12-15/16-64 Battle of Nashville total rout ◊ 12-25-64 Rear-guard action at King's Hill & Sugar Creek ◊ 12-27-64 Army of Tennessee recrosses the Tennessee River.

12-15/16-6

Kin

11-3

N

Foche Spr.

Henryville

Waynesboro

Cam

Lawrence

West Point

START 11-19-64

Monterey

Corinth

Scale in Miles

0 2 4 6 8 10 12 14

Waterloo

Eastport

1-1-65
40
1-20-65

FURLOUGH

Iuka

Florence

Tennes

S. Florence

Co

Rienzi

Cherokee Sta.

Tuscumbia

Booneville

Baldwin

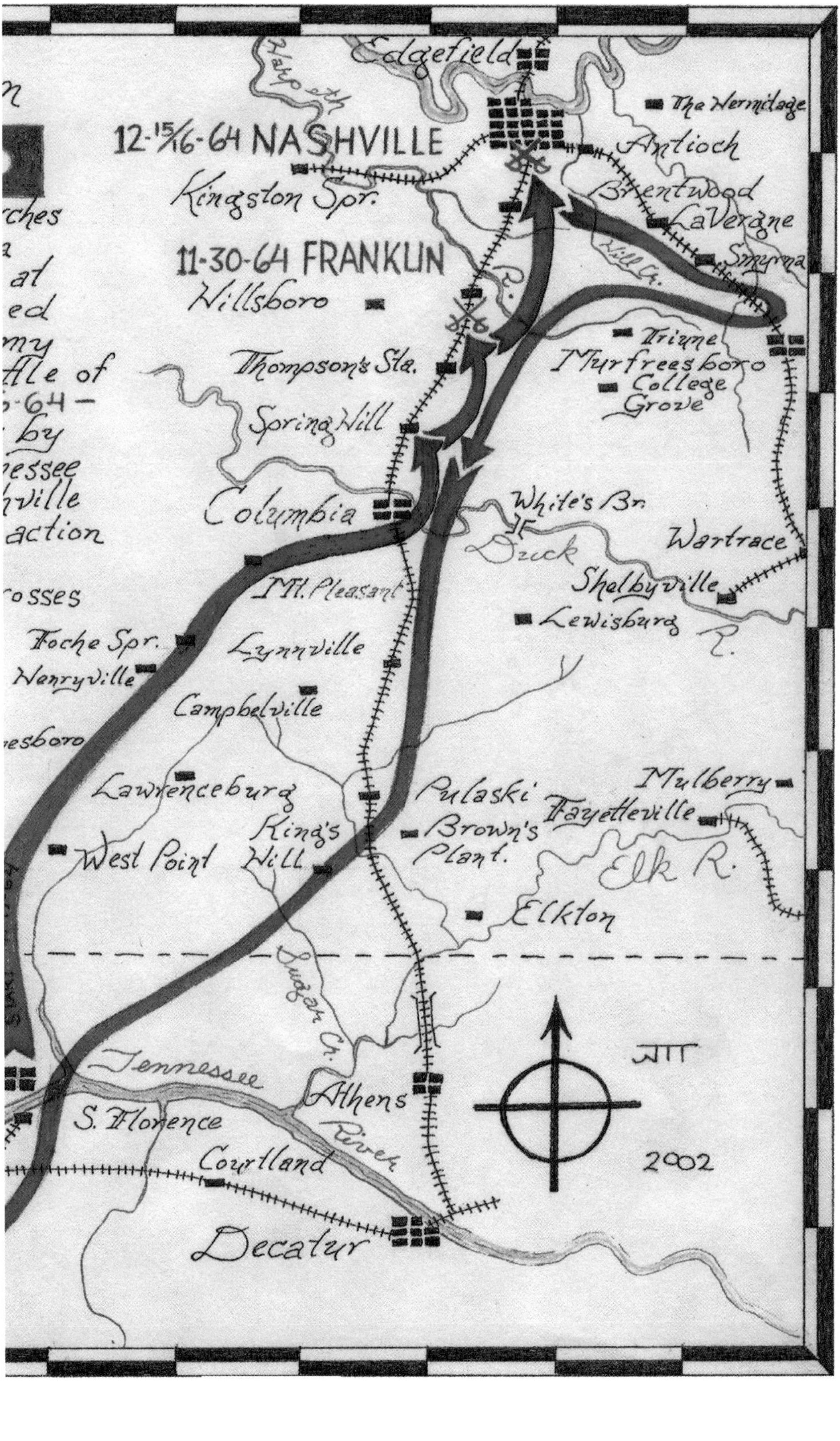
Edgefield
Harpeth
The Hermitage
12-15/16-64 NASHVILLE
Antioch
Kingston Spr.
Brentwood
LaVergne
11-30-64 FRANKLIN
Mill Cr.
Smyrna
Hillsboro
Triune
Murfreesboro
Thompson's Sta.
College Grove
Spring Hill
Columbia
White's Br.
Duck
Wartrace
Mt. Pleasant
Shelbyville
Lewisburg
R.
Foche Spr.
Lynnville
Henryville
Campbelville
Lawrenceburg
Pulaski
Mulberry
Fayetteville
King's Hill
Brown's Plant.
West Point
Elk R.
Elkton
Sugar Cr.
Tennessee
Athens
S. Florence
River
Courtland
Decatur
JTT
2002

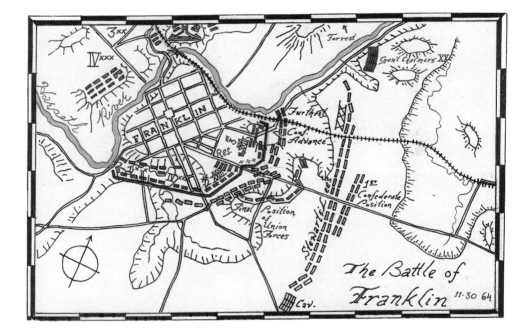

The Battle of Franklin 11-30 64

3 xx
IV xxx
Nashville River
FRANKLIN
Res.
Furthest Conf. Advance
Final Position of Union Forces
Stewart
1st Confederate Position
Cav.
Forrest
Gen'l Chalmers XV

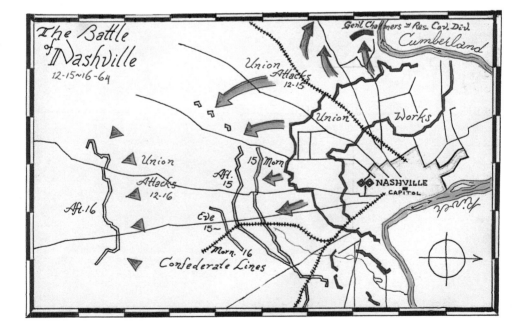

The Battle of Nashville 12-15~16-64

Gen'l Chalmers Z Res. Cav. Div.
Cumberland
Union Attacks 12-15
Union Works
Union Attacks 12-16
Aft. 16
Aft. 15
15 Morn
NASHVILLE CAPITOL
Eve 15~
Morn. 16
Confederate Lines
River

Decatur

■ Russelville

**• Forrest's Final Campaign •**

1·20·65 Left Corinth    ◆ 2·28·65 Promoted to Lt. Gen'l.
camped at Verona till 3·1·65
camped at West Point till 3·27·65

✕ Battle of Selma 4·2·65 ✕

4·15·65 Arrives at Gainesville

5·9·65 Exactly 1 month after Lee,
Forrest surrenders his command

Scale in Miles          2002

Stubb's Farm
Baldwyn
Guntown
from Corinth 1·20·65
Old
down
Tripelo    Fulton
Narris-burg
Verona camped till 3·1·65
Okolona
Jasper
Mulberry Fork
Locust Fork
Prarie Sta
Warrior
River
Elyton (Birmingham)
Johnson's Fy.
West Point
camped till 3·27·65
Columbus
Moore's Br.
Stark-ville
Reform
Alternate Route
Carrolton
Warrior River
Artesia
Fy.
Trion
River
Montevello
Macon
Pickensville
Dipsey
Tuscaloosa
Will's Plant.
Scottville
6 Mile Cr.
Randolph
Centerville
Tombigbee
Black
Forrest crosses bridge before Federals burn it
Maplesville
Ebenezer Church
Plantersville
Finch's Fy.
Eutaw
Cahaba
Gainesville Surrendered 5·9·65
Greensboro
Marion
Burnsville
Gainesville Jct.
River
Demopolis
SELMA
4·2·65

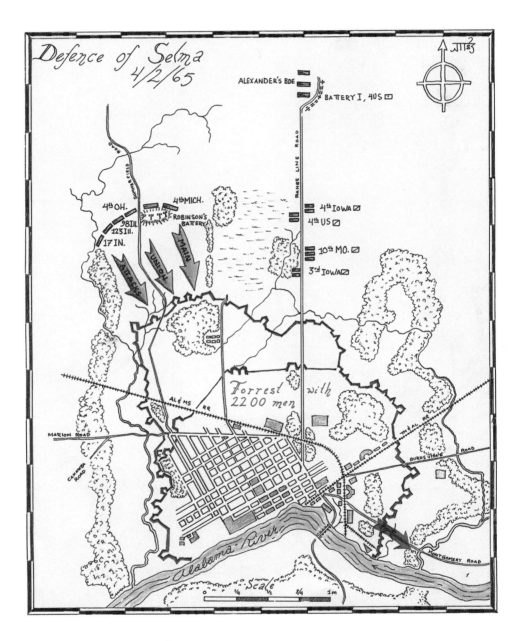

Defence of Selma
4/2/65

ALEXANDER'S BDE

BATTERY I, 4US

RANGE LINE ROAD

4th OH.

4th MICH.

98 Ill.
123 Ill.

ROBINSON'S BATTERY

17 IN.

ATTACKS

UNION

MAIN

4th IOWA

4th US

10th MO.

3rd IOWA

Forrest with 2200 men

ALEMS RR

MARION ROAD

CAHABA ROAD

TN AL RR

BURNSVILLE ROAD

MONTGOMERY ROAD

Alabama River

Scale
¼        ¾        1m

# Chapter Eight

# ACROSS THE TERRIBLE FIELD

*—Ambrose Bierce*

## Chickamauga
## June-September 1863

The summer of 1863 waned slowly for the Southern soldiers while the appalling defeats at Gettysburg and Vicksburg were being touted in the North as the death knell of the Confederacy. Though these losses had been devastating, the fighting spirit of the Confederate armies remained high. Robert E. Lee had withdrawn to Virginia following Gettysburg and there set about reorganizing and preparing his forces to continue the fight. The Confederate army in the trans-Mississippi, cut off by the closing of the Mississippi River with Pemberton's surrender of Vicksburg, continued to fight on under the command of Gen. Kirby Smith. The conflict west of the Appalachian Mountain barrier was heating up, and the focus of the war was shifting to that theater. More than a year and a half of war still lay ahead.

Forrest had ranged across central Tennessee in May and June, reorganizing his forces while the Federals outmaneuvered Gen. Braxton Bragg, pushing him out of the grain-rich portion of west Tennessee and southward into the mountains around Chattanooga. After Murfreesboro, Forrest had received his promotion to brigadier general, but his activities had been hampered by circumstances beyond his control. The constant rebuilding of his command and the time spent recovering from wounds had hamstrung him on occasion over the last year and a half and had consumed most of his time for the past two or three months.

On June 3, 1863, General Rosecrans began his march southward from his defensive lines, which were in and around Murfreesboro. Now began a series of maneuvers that would bewilder General Bragg and undermine his confidence. Rosecrans sent Gordon Granger in a feint toward the Confederate left center, between Forrest's wing and the main body of the rebel army. Simultaneously he sent the Union right wing from Franklin and Triune to close on the Confederate center. All the while the Union main advance was swinging wide around the Confederate right wing commanded by Hardee. Rosecrans' plan promised to work perfectly.

On June 25, less than two weeks after suffering his second serious war wound, Forrest was back in the saddle and moving eastward toward Shelbyville to join up with Gen. Leonidas Polk. Both armies were hindered by torrential rains, mud-clogged roads, and swollen rivers.

Fully aware of Forrest's ability to imperil their army, the Union commanders in the west made every effort from that point forward to know of Forrest's whereabouts at all times. That would prove to be more difficult than any of them imagined. "No news from Forrest yet," wrote Union cavalry commander David S. Stanley on the night of June 26. Twenty-four hours later, Gordon Granger, commanding the Union move on Shelbyville, telegraphed Rosecrans that he was "keeping a portion of the cavalry watching for the movements of Forrest whose whereabouts I am unable to ascertain. He will turn up yet in some unexpected place."[1]

Still, the Union feint was working. Rosecrans' cavalry and Gen. John T. Wilder's mounted infantry flanked Hardee's position on the extreme right and drove the Confederates out of both Liberty and Hoover's Gaps. Bragg fell for Rosecrans' carefully crafted strategy when he received this news on the twenty-seventh. The Confederate retreat began. Polk was ordered to leave Shelbyville and fall back to Tullahoma across the Duck River to keep from being outflanked and cut off. Meanwhile, Forrest was slugging his way over muddy terrain by way of Riggs Road near Eagleville. Flooded creeks slowed him, and before he could reach Shelbyville, the Confederate army was in retreat.

By late in the morning of the twenty-seventh, Polk had most of his army across the Duck River. His wagon train had just crossed when Gordon Granger suddenly attacked Polk's rear guard. Granger had broken through the Confederate outer lines at Guy's Gap and galloped virtually uncontested down the turnpike from Murfreesboro with Gen. D. S. Stanley's cavalry in the lead. It was now time for "Fightin'" Joe Wheeler to live up to his nickname. Wheeler was in charge of Polk's rear guard, consisting of approximately six hundred cavalrymen. It was his job to remain in Shelbyville and hold off the Union advance, should it come. It definitely was coming and bringing with it overwhelming odds.

Throughout the afternoon, Wheeler's small force held off Stanley's cavalry with repeated charges and countercharges. The Confederate general was expecting Forrest to march through Shelbyville and either join in the fight or divert to the Skull Camp Bridge and attempt to cross there, so Wheeler did his best to hold the bridge for his fellow Confederates' crossing. Wheeler finally decided that Forrest was not coming and began to fall back across Skull Camp Bridge, which spanned the surging Duck River. The bridge was to be fired as the last of Wheeler's command was crossing. At that moment Major Rambaut, of Forrest's command, rode up and informed Wheeler that Forrest was approaching.

Upon receiving that message, Wheeler called for volunteers to hold the bridge for Forrest. With a roar from the ranks, Wheeler and his second in command, Gen. Will T. Martin, and some four hundred volunteers rushed back across the bridge. Most of that volunteer force was made up of Russell's Fourth Alabama, who had previously served under Forrest. One of these men who survived to tell the tale was Dr. John Wyeth. And it was quite a story he told. In 1900, Wyeth wrote *That Devil Forrest*, which is still considered one of the best accounts on Forrest's military career written by a contemporary.[2]

Wheeler's small command was giving a good account of itself, but they were being driven back toward the river. The fight turned hand-to-hand as Stanley's cavalry rode over the top of the thin gray line, driving a part of Wheeler's splintering command into the river and across the bridge. During the melee a caisson was overturned on the bridge, effectively blocking all traffic. Wheeler and his boys were trapped. Hell's fury seemed to swirl around them as it became every man for himself. In a wild cinematic scene, Wheeler was able to form up some sixty riders for a desperate charge to freedom. With sabers slashing, they collided headlong with Union cavalrymen, hacking and shooting a path to momentary safety. Once able to break loose, Wheeler and his men began a daring race for the river.

The riverbank was some twenty feet above the surface of the water at the point the Confederates approached. But there was nowhere else to go. With the Union cavalry stampeding in hot pursuit, Wheeler and about forty of his riders never hesitated. At full speed they all rode straight off the cliff, launching themselves into the arms of fate.

The Confederates and their mounts hit the fast-moving current of Duck River with a tremendous impact. The stunned Union pursuers had no intention of duplicating the incredible stunt they had just witnessed. Instead they reined in, dismounted, and opened fire from the bank. Many of the cavalrymen and their mounts were

killed as they swam for the opposite shore or were washed downstream and drowned. Luckily for the Confederacy, Wheeler and
Martin were among the survivors.[3]

Forrest, who was a few miles away, heard the sounds of the battle
at the bridge and assumed that this route was closed to him. He
diverted his command to a ford some four miles below the bridge
that Wheeler had so gallantly defended and there crossed the Duck
River, bivouacking five miles to the west of the river.

All things considered, the situation turned out to be fortuitous for
Polk's retreating wagon train. By the time Granger realized that
Forrest had slipped past him it was too late. Forrest had already
interposed his small force between Granger and Stanley's Union
troops and the Confederate retreat. On the morning of the twenty-
eighth, Granger reported,

> Forrest pressed around our rear last night, moving eastward.
> Had I known he was doing so, I could have thrown my force
> between the retreating Rebel army and his forces, but even then
> our men and horses were too badly used up to insure any
> prospect of success.[4]

Polk and his wagon train pulled into Tullahoma at approximately
4:00 P.M. on the twenty-eighth, but by that time Tullahoma itself was
endangered, as the Union forces had already occupied Manchester,
only twelve miles to the northeast. The columns of Brig. Gen. Philip
H. Sheridan and Gen. John T. Wilder were pushing on around the
Confederate right flank, threatening the bridge and railroad leading
south toward Chattanooga. Bragg was dependant upon that railroad.

Rain was falling heavily and continued to drench both armies.
Moving up the Cumberland Plateau, Forrest reached Tullahoma on
June 30. That afternoon Bragg gave up Tullahoma and fell back
once more in the face of Rosecrans' aggressive moves. He was uncertain as to whether he should fight at the Elk River crossing or continue to fall back some twenty more miles to the foot of the
Cumberland Plateau and there make a final stand.

By the end of the day on the thirtieth, Bragg decided he could
neither hold nor fight at either location. Bragg reviewed the situation for the next several hours before making up his mind about
1:30 on the morning of July 2 to order the Confederate army to
cross the Cumberland Plateau and the Tennessee River beyond.

As Bragg fell back toward Chattanooga, Forrest was ordered to protect the rear of the main column. Fighting small, delaying skirmishes,

Forrest passed through his wife's hometown of Cowan, Tennessee. As he rode through Cowan, a local woman shouted at him angrily, "You great big coward, you, why don't you turn and fight, instead of running like a cur? If old Bedford Forrest was here, he'd make you fight."[5]

On July 6, Forrest, following behind Bragg's army, crossed the Tennessee at Bridgeport, Alabama, and burned the bridge behind him. This was the same bridge the Confederates had burned after the evacuation of Corinth. Bragg was now back in the same position he had been a year earlier, when he had sent Forrest on his Kentucky campaign.

On August 9, Forrest was sent to Kingston, Tennessee, seventy-five miles northeast of Chattanooga, where he dictated two letters, one to the Confederate adjutant general, Samuel Cooper, in Richmond, and the other to President Davis. The letters were sent to Richmond because Forrest neither respected nor trusted Bragg and was sure that Bragg would be unwilling to allow Forrest to leave his command otherwise. The subject of the letters was to request that he (Forrest) be allowed to operate on his own where he felt he could do the most good: patrolling his old familiar home turf. "I believe I can serve my country best along the banks of the Mississippi River where I have resided for over 20 years," he dictated.[6] He went on to note that he knew the country perfectly, as he had bought and sold slaves up and down the Mississippi from Memphis to Vicksburg.

Forrest's proposal suggested that he be placed in command of all forces in that area. He went on to say that he would organize all those who may join his force from southern Kentucky, Arkansas, Tennessee, and Missouri. Forrest thought he could

> raise between 5,000 and 10,000 men and would seriously, if not [entirely] obstruct the navigation of the Mississippi. . . . I am confident that we could move and harass and destroy boats on the river, that only flat [boats] heavily protected by armored gun boats would be able to make passage.[7]

Most likely, his true motivation was to break free of Bragg and Wheeler and to operate alone, and in retrospect, it would appear perhaps that the Confederate command should have cut him loose. As it turned out, however, Forrest was premature in assuming that Bragg would thwart any attempt Forrest might make to leave his command. Bragg not only forwarded the letter but did so with a glowing recommendation and endorsement.

Jefferson Davis, for reasons that are unclear, did not act on the recommendation, thus missing what might have been one of the greatest opportunities of the war. Had he acted immediately on Bragg's recommendation and Forrest's plan, the course of the war in the western theater might well have been altered. While Davis procrastinated, Rosecrans continued to move. Forrest's request and Bragg's endorsement soon became irrelevant. The priority for the Confederate Army of Tennessee now became Rosecrans' threat to Chattanooga and northern Georgia.

By late summer Rosecrans' army was pouring through the gaps and passes of the Cumberland Mountains. Bragg seemed confused as to the enemy's intent although he had access to ample professional opinions on exactly what the Union might have been up to. On September 4, 1863, Lt. Gen. D. H. Hill, a brother-in-law of Stonewall Jackson, wrote of the situation in and around Chattanooga and the mountainous region south of there. Hill predicted of the Union troops:

> [They will] work their way up Will's Valley until they get in a position to drive us from Chattanooga. They will then be in position to hold the country, bring in their supplies, [and] operate among the disloyal portions of East Tennessee and Western North Carolina. If we wait until meshes be thrown up around us, we may find it hard to break out.[8]

Bragg continued to hesitate and eventually did just what Rosecrans hoped he would. He evacuated Chattanooga and moved his command to Lafayette, Georgia, a few miles away from the city. The evacuation fell directly into Rosecrans' plan.

The Union army marched through the mountains almost as if they had no concern for Bragg's troops, who were believed to be somewhere ahead of them. Had a more decisive and combative commander led Bragg's army at that moment, Rosecrans would have had a lot to worry about, for so moving, the Federal troops presented an amazing opportunity to a Confederate commander. The three Federal army corps moved south in three separate columns, with each column less than twenty miles from one another. Thomas's corps was in the center, coming past Lookout Mountain by way of Steven's Gap. On the right, near Alpine, was McCook's corps. Rosecrans' third corps, under General Crittenden, was marching through and around the evacuated city of Chattanooga. Unknown to all three Union corps was that Bragg's army was closer to each of the Union commands than the Federals were to each other.

The Confederate commander, with his force in hand in the Chickamauga Valley, had but to fall upon the scattered Union Corps singly and in detail, and to crush them one by one—such an opportunity as came to no other commander during the whole four years of the war.[9]

Committing what was arguably the greatest blunder of the war, Bragg failed to act. In so doing he lost a chance for the Confederacy to turn the tide of the war or at the least, to shift the momentum.

The rain that had fallen indiscriminately through midsummer would eventually let up, but the weather would go from one extreme to the other. It turned from wet and chilly to hot and dry, straining and weakening the immune systems of all those men exposed to such severe conditions.

An additional predicament resulting partly from their success hampered the Yankees. Wherever the Northern armies moved, slavery went out of existence. In Virginia this meant little, for the Federal armies had failed to extend their control over very much of that state, and the slave owners of threatened areas of Virginia had already managed to move their slaves to safety. But in Tennessee, northern Mississippi, and Alabama, the Union armies ranged far, burning, destroying, and liberating as they went. The Union armies in the western theater were followed wherever they moved by hordes of recently freed slaves who had no means of support other than what they could solicit from their liberators.

By 1863, the numbers of these throngs had diminished only slightly as many free blacks enlisted in the Union army. Since the Emancipation Proclamation was announced in the autumn of 1862, thousands of freedmen had put on the uniform of the United States Army. Their presence in the army was like a shot of adrenaline for the Union cause, but it renewed a sense of rage throughout the South. It was probably more than a sense of racism that caused the Southerners to react the way they did to the arming of their former slaves. There was also a sense of betrayal. At the height of command in Richmond, reprehensible steps were being considered that would lead to some of the darkest episodes of the war.

By summer's end the armies were on the move across a sun-baked landscape, raising clouds of choking dust as they converged in the southeastern foothills of the Cumberland Plateau. The commanders of neither army knew exactly where their foe was concentrated, but the Cumberland Plateau proved to be more of a shield for

Rosecrans' maneuvers than a protective barrier for General Bragg.

Some thirty miles south of Chattanooga, in the steep, wooded hills near Pigeon Mountain, runs the west fork of a stream called Chickamauga. This Indian word, it is said, means "river of death." If so, the meaning is ominous, for the area drained by the Chickamauga was about to be the setting for one of the bloodiest battles of the war.

About August 10, Forrest sent Dibrell's Eighth Tennessee Regiment back over the Cumberland Plateau to round up horses and recruits, and to keep an eye on Rosecrans' movements. Contact with the enemy came quickly. On August 18, thirty days before the showdown battle at Chickamauga would begin, Dibrell ran into Minty's cavalry near Wild Cat Creek. Fighting and falling back along the banks of the Wild Cat and Little Calf Killer River, Dibrell inflicted some one hundred casualties upon Minty's force. These were the only losses Rosecrans' army suffered during the entire crossing of the Cumberland Plateau.[10] Dibrell fought a hit-and-run action as he retreated to the western edge of the Cumberlands near the town of Bon Air, where Forrest had sent reinforcements to meet him. The colonel forwarded a report that Minty's cavalry was the lead in a great general advance by Rosecrans.

As players move their pieces on a chessboard, fate was beginning to shift the parts of the opposing armies into their places for the costliest conflict fought in the west during the war. On August 21, Rosecrans' troops arrived on the west side of the Tennessee River, directly across from Chattanooga, and began shelling the city. General Rosecrans had so far managed a well-planned and executed march of his army, but the attack, including the Chattanooga artillery barrage, was a feint. The real move was to be made forty miles farther south of Chattanooga, along the railroad line from Nashville that drops into Alabama near Bridgeport. The towns of Stevenson and Bridgeport, Alabama, were the real objective, and Rosecrans had three divisions poised to strike. At the same time he kept up an effective demonstration from Chattanooga to the mouth of the Hiwassee River with a division under command of General Crittenden.[11]

The Union deception was effective. Up and down the Tennessee River, fires were lighted to give the impression of a vast bivouac of troops. Artillery was constantly in motion. Men were set to work cutting trees and hammering planks to suggest the construction of large pontoon bridges for crossing the river. These efforts worked perfectly. Chattanooga was evacuated on September 8. The Confederate Army of the Tennessee meanwhile marched south in four columns as

Crittenden's troops occupied Chattanooga the next day.

On September 10, lead elements of Crittenden's force had pushed southward from Chattanooga toward Ringgold, Georgia. When John Pegram's brigade engaged them just beyond the town, Forrest and his escort and 240 men from Morgan's command rushed to the scene of the fighting. Forrest at once surveyed the situation and visualized a larger opportunity in this seemingly small clash on the Ringgold Road. He sent an immediate dispatch to Polk, whose infantry was six miles away at Lee and Gordon's Mill. Crittenden's troops were isolated, his message said, and reinforcements from Polk could possibly disrupt the Union battle plan.[12]

As the night wore on, no word came from Polk, nor from Bragg, who was headquartered at nearby Lee and Gordon's Mill. About midnight Forrest rode over to Lee and Gordon's Mill to deliver his request personally but found that both generals had recently abandoned their headquarters and moved on. He returned to Brigadier General Pegram's position and continued his preparations for the resumption of the battle at first light. He placed Scott's brigade of nine hundred men and four pieces of artillery across Crittenden's line of march. These preparations were complete just before the enemy began to advance at sunrise.[13]

Dibrell's and Pegram's people joined Forrest as the battle began. At the beginning Crittenden's men pushed Forrest and Pegram back about a half-mile before a rally stopped Crittenden's advance and forced him back toward Ringgold. During this engagement Forrest was slightly wounded. The wound was serious enough that Forrest was forced to take a drink of whiskey to dull the pain. However, Jordan and Pryor, Forrest's biographers, never mention the actual nature or location of the wound.[14]

Crittenden turned west from Ringgold and occupied Bragg's and Polk's abandoned headquarters at Lee and Gordon's Mill. Even in his new position, Crittenden's force was isolated and would remain so for several more days. Bragg had half his army and Polk's corps within easy marching distance but allowed the opportunity to destroy Crittenden to slip away.

Finally, Rosecrans realized that with his army divided as it was, he was in potential danger. And he realized that Bragg was through running and was attempting to concentrate his own army for a clash. Rosecrans began to shift his army to the east, toward Chickamauga Creek.

Not certain of each others' strength, the two armies sparred with each other in isolated pockets from the eleventh through the fourteenth of September, and by the seventeenth, they practically faced each other along the River of Death, the Union on the west, the Confederates on the east.

Forrest, in the meantime, had become more agitated by the inaction of the previous few days. When he finally fell in with the main Confederate force, he found himself positioned on the Confederate right flank. Here Forrest's command would again be one of the first engaged and would be seriously tested. The battle of Chickamauga would prove that there was little of the orthodox in cavalry troops led by Nathan Bedford Forrest.[15]

With reinforcements under Gen. James Longstreet just arriving by train from Virginia, Bragg ordered all his forces to cross Chickamauga Creek. Although at this point the Confederates numbered about sixty-six thousand, the Union had a slight numerical advantage as the battle began.

At about 11:00 A.M. on Friday, September 18, four miles west of Ringgold, Forrest and his escort, along with a detachment of John Hunt Morgan's men under the command of Lt. Col. Robert M. Martin, a total of approximately three hundred men, proceeded to the front of the line on the Confederate right and engaged the enemy near Reed's Bridge, spanning Pea Vine Creek. Forrest's skirmish at Reed's Bridge opened the greatest battle of the war in the west. As Forrest was moving forward, Bushrod Johnson, who was within one mile of Pea Vine Creek, threw his men into line of battle. "While forming the line, Brigadier General Forrest joined with his escort, proceeded to the front to develop the position of the enemy, and was soon skirmishing with them."[16]

When Johnson's men joined with Forrest's escort, the Federals were driven back across Reed's Bridge. The Confederates crowded the Yankees with artillery and continued to press them with charges from both their cavalry and infantry. Minty's cavalry was forced to retreat in such a hurry that they were unable to burn the bridge after they had crossed. By 3:00 P.M. Brig. Gen. John Pegram's division joined Forrest and Johnson. Shortly thereafter, the Confederates forced the crossing of Chickamauga Creek.

At 4:00 P.M. Maj. Gen. John Bell Hood arrived and took command on this part of the field as the battle was drawing to a close. Forrest spent the night scouting the enemy's position and went into bivouac near Alexander's Bridge in the rear of Hood's main line.

Before dawn on Saturday the nineteenth, Forrest was ordered to move his cavalry to the extreme right of the Confederate line, in the direction of Chattanooga and Reed's Bridge. Upon arrival, Forrest was to develop the enemy's position. About 7:30 A.M. Forrest's cavalry met Gen. John Croxton's brigade of Brig. Gen. John Milton Brannan's division at Jay's Saw Mill. However, Forrest soon realized that while the Confederates had been moving upstream, the Federals had been moving downstream and had outflanked their opponents. Forrest immediately dispatched a messenger to call up Bragg's infantry and quickly dismounted his and Pegram's horse soldiers. Forrest now "prepared to fight the infantry way." As the situation developed, it became evident that Rosecrans had outwitted General Bragg. General Pegram later wrote,

> It became apparent that we were fighting overpowering numbers. General Forrest having sent several messengers for the infantry to come up, finally went for them himself, ordering me to hold the position until their arrival. In obeying this order our loss was about one-fourth of the command.[17]

The only reinforcements to arrive were escorted to the front by Forrest himself. With Col. Claudius Wilson and his brigade of Walker's division in tow, Forrest ordered Wilson's infantry to the left, where his dismounted men were barely hanging on. "Forrest, conspicuous in the long linen duster he wore that day, with his sword and pistol belted over it" drove the enemy back a quarter mile and captured a battery of enemy artillery.[18]

The opposing armies tested each other's mettle from 11:00 A.M. until 1:00 P.M. Charges and countercharges pushed the lines back and forth. Many commands became disoriented and separated from their units, fighting fierce independent battles without officers to guide them, and as the first day ended the rebels made one last thrust. Gen. Henry Vanness Boynton, who commanded the Thirty-fifth Ohio regiment, on the extreme left of the line opposite Forrest, later wrote of the charge:

> On came these men in gray in magnificent lines, bending their faces before the sleet of the storm and firing hotly as they advanced to within forty yards of the goal, where the artillery poured a nearly enfilading fire of canister down these long lines, standing bravely there and fighting almost under the mouths of our guns. After the smoke cleared from the third round of this fire, however, the front was cleared of everything but the heaps of dead and wounded.[19]

On the second day of battle, Forrest's command fought more as infantry than as cavalry. They pushed the enemy back, turning his flank, only to be pushed back themselves. Ordering a portion of his men to mount up, Forrest led a charge that partially broke the Union resolve and returned the momentum to the Confederates.

During the night of the nineteenth, the sound of axes echoed through the dense woods, and trees crashed to the ground as soldiers prepared breastworks for their protection in the fighting that would resume the next day. In some places men of the two armies were so close that they could hear the heavy breathing of the enemy caused by the exertion of felling, chopping, and stacking hundreds of fallen trees.

The third day's fighting, on September 20, began with the rising of the sun. As the battle raged on through that day, Forrest once again proved what he could do during large-scale battle conditions. He was much more than the leader of a guerilla band, as he is often accused of being, and his men proved to be much more than ruffians in uniforms. In toe-to-toe engagements the first day, Forrest had nearly swept the enemy before him at every juncture. Still fighting on the extreme Confederate right, Forrest's men once again validated their reputation won on other hard-fought fields of battle.

Gen. D. H. Hill, who had come fresh from the titanic confrontations in Virginia and Maryland, rode with his staff past the Confederate right later that day. He was attracted by the precision and steadiness of movement of a certain body of men on the field and inquired as to whose infantry he was observing. When he was told that the infantry in question was actually Forrest's cavalry, he asked to be taken to Forrest to congratulate him personally. Upon finding Forrest, he greeted the general:

> I wish to congratulate you and these brave men moving across that field like veteran infantry upon their magnificent behavior. In Virginia I made myself extremely unpopular with the cavalry because I said that, so far, I had not seen a dead man with spurs on. No one can speak disparagingly of such troops as yours.[20]

On the Union left Gen. George Thomas had been under heavy assault by Breckinridge and Forrest and had received reinforcements from Rosecrans when a new attack by Gen. Patrick Cleburne's division of D. H. Hill's corps sorely strained his ability to resist. Thomas continued to call for help as the determined Confederate assault grew in intensity. One of Thomas's staff officers, sent to Rosecrans to ask for additional help, passed by the right, where Gen. John M. Brannan's men were posted in the dense woods. Unable to see Brannan's unit, the officer reported to Rosecrans that there was a gap in the line. Rosecrans accepted this information as reported, did not investigate the report, and ordered Gen. Thomas J. Wood to move his division to the left to support Gen. Joseph J. Reynolds. In obeying his orders Wood's division pulled back from the line and began moving to the left, behind Brannan's division. In attempting to plug a hole in the line that, in reality, did not exist, Rosecrans unwittingly opened a dangerous rift that would lead to the general collapse of the entire Union right.[21]

Longstreet, with Bushrod Johnson's division leading, now began to move his troops out of the woods that had screened his position from Union eyes. As they came into the open, the troops under Gen. Thomas Hindman and Brig. Gen. E. McIver Law immediately came under intense fire from the left and the right. Bushrod Johnson's division, advancing between these two divisions, was receiving fire from the left and the right, but not from its immediate front. Not until they reached the Union breastworks did they understand the reason why: they were marching into the gap created by Wood's withdrawal.

Longstreet recognized the opportunity and rushed his men through the gap. It was the beginning of a rout that could have become the annihilation of Rosecrans' army. Caught up in the rapidly developing flight were Rosecrans himself, his staff, the division commanders (including the renowned Phil Sheridan), two corps commanders, and Charles A. Dana, assistant secretary of war, who was there as an observer sent by Secretary of War Stanton. According to Dana's later report published in *McClure's Magazine,* the fleeing men all believed that their army was being destroyed.[22]

The only portion of the Union line that did not dissolve was on the left, where Thomas continued to fight and fall back in good order on Snodgrass Hill, directly behind his original position. However, the Confederates managed by late afternoon to capture a large number of Thomas's troops and to bend both ends of his line into a horseshoe.

As Thomas battled for his life, Gordon Granger, who commanded the Union reserve corps near Rossville, heard the firing and correctly surmised that Thomas was taking a beating. Without orders he marched his men toward the sound of the guns at the double-quick to give whatever help he could.

Forrest's scouts immediately noted Granger's movement and reported to their commander, who, though badly outnumbered, borrowed some artillery from Breckinridge and massed those guns across the road in Granger's path. Granger's superior numbers pushed Forrest back, but the Union general's troops were forced off the road by the continued fire from the Confederate artillery batteries. With Granger's men detouring through the dense woods, Forrest took possession of the Yankees' former position, thus putting him in control of the Lafayette road, the Federal camps and hospitals, and a number of prisoners.[23]

Forrest's disposition forced a two-hour delay in Granger's march to reach Thomas on Snodgrass Hill. Even without support and in the face of such extreme Confederate fire, Thomas held out until dark. The coming of night brought an end to the second day's fighting, and Thomas began his withdrawal toward Chattanooga under cover of darkness.

Forrest and his men slept on the field near the Confederate hospital that night. It was cold, especially cold after the fever of combat, and there was little water. Across the battlefield, men in blue and men in gray clumped together and built fires in an attempt to hold off the numbing chill. For thousands of lifetimes, survivors of both sides would recall the suffering of that night. For whatever cheer there might have been, some sang songs. The songs became ballads of death for others as they moaned or screamed for their mothers and awaited their passing into the great mystery. Some wounded men simply crawled off seeking private places to pray and die.

It seemed that hell had ascended and come to rest in this tiny place in the foothills of the Cumberland Mountains. By flickering lamplight in field hospitals on both sides, the wild night's work of mending and amputating went on until dawn. In a nightmare filled with shrieks of pain and frightening dreams of death and battle, could these men, as exhausted as they were, have gotten any sleep?

On Monday morning, September 21, Forrest's men were greeted with a horrific sight. As they rode out from their chilly bivouac near the hospital, they passed a small mountain of human limbs. A young soldier in Forrest's command was haunted by what he saw. He reported the pile to be twenty feet wide at the base and over ten feet high.[24]

As the third day of the battle began, redemption was within Bragg's grasp. How many commanders receive a second chance to crush the enemy during the same conflict? Once again victory was presented to Bragg on a veritable silver platter, albeit one bent and bloodied by the desperate clash of the past two days. Unfortunately Bragg was a commander who could recognize the wrapping, but not the gift inside.

Not so with Forrest. The instinct that had left so many Union leaders bent on his destruction now asserted itself. On September 21, Monday morning, Forrest saw clearly, as he had at the crucial moment at Shiloh, an opportunity developing to finish Rosecrans and sweep the enemy back across the Tennessee, through Chattanooga, and beyond. While most of the Confederate force abandoned the pursuit or awaited further orders, Forrest moved to seize the moment. He would use the same technique on a smaller scale in other battles. Once the enemy had broken and run, they must be kept running, never allowing them time to reform. Hill and Longstreet's breakthrough had given the Confederates the bulge on Rosecrans; now was the time to "keep up the skeer."

It was obvious to Forrest that the Union troops were defeated and on the run and that a determined pursuit would finish them. Perhaps he did not envision a decisive victory that would win the war, but he understood the immediate opportunity, and he was resolute in his determination to make the most of it. He probably did not even consider waiting for orders. Orders were for those who could not see the obvious.

Charging up the LaFayette road, which ultimately led to Chattanooga, Forrest approached Rossville, where he ran into Col. Robert H. G. Minty's cavalry. Minty's small force, which was acting as a rear guard for the retreating Federals, put up a minor resistance, firing only a few shots before joining the stampede making for the perceived safety of Chattanooga.

In the exchange, a bullet punched a fifty-caliber hole in the neck of Forrest's mount. A fountain of blood spurted from a severed artery and sprayed Bedford with a crimson mist. He quickly jammed his index finger into the wound to stem the flow of blood and galloped on. He finally reined in under a large tree on a high knoll overlooking the Tennessee River. When he removed his finger from the wound in his horse's neck and dismounted, the faithful steed slumped and without ceremony, dropped dead.[25]

Forrest glanced upward into the boughs of the tree and saw four startled Yankee signalmen on a platform high above him in the branches. After ordering the discomfited officers down, he commandeered a pair of field glasses from one of them and climbed up to the observation nest to study the situation. Though it was early in the morning, the sun having barely risen, what he saw elated him and confirmed what he already knew.

Back on the ground, he dictated a message to General Polk with the request that it be forwarded to General Bragg:

> Can see Chattanooga and everything around. The enemy's trains are leaving, going around the point of Lookout

Mountain. The prisoners captured report two pontoons thrown across for the purpose of retreating. I think they are evacuating as hard as they can go. . . . I think we ought to press forward as rapidly as possible.[26]

Longstreet felt, even long after the war, that this dispatch gave Bragg a false impression of the situation on that morning following such a great Confederate battlefield victory. Bragg, according to Longstreet, felt that he could take his time moving on Chattanooga, as the city would be abandoned within a few hours and would then fall easily into his hands. This thinking caused Bragg to reject Longstreet's suggestion that the Confederate army march northward and around Chattanooga to cut Rosecrans off from his bases of supply.[27]

Actually, Forrest, in his excitement, had not accurately interpreted what he saw and in a later dispatch would correct his error. About 11:30 on the twenty-first, Forrest sent a second message to Polk that the enemy were apparently "fortifying, as I can distinctly hear the sound of axes in great numbers." Rosecrans was not preparing to give up Chattanooga but was indeed felling trees and preparing to defend the city.

Regardless of the correction in Forrest's later dispatch, his attitude was still the same as in every other battle. He saw a demoralized enemy in retreat, a result of having gotten "the bulge" on them, and his only thought was to exploit their panic. Even though he later observed that the Yankees were fortifying and preparing for a fight, his last statement was as applicable as ever: "press forward as rapidly as possible." That Rosecrans was preparing to defend Chattanooga did not mean in Forrest's thinking that he could hold it against an immediate and determined attack. His second dispatch said as much. "The appearance is still as in the last dispatch, that he is hurrying on toward Chattanooga."[28]

It should have been clear from earlier dealings with Bragg that Forrest held very different military viewpoints from those of his commanding general. Whether or not Bragg acted as he did because he believed Forrest's first report, he should have been informed of the next message, which made it clear that Forrest still believed the Confederates should attack. Forrest could not understand Bragg's reluctance to pursue a retreating enemy; neither could he forgive him for it. But as it turned out, Bragg's indecision left both Forrest and Longstreet disappointed and Chattanooga firmly in the hands of the enemy.

Forrest had only enough men with him to harass the enemy's retreat. He expected reinforcements, and when he had waited for a reply to his message for as long as he felt necessary, he threw his men against the Union force that blocked the gap at Rossville. Once there, he found the enemy too strong, and though he fought with them for several hours, he finally called off the attack.

Later that night Forrest galloped back to Bragg's headquarters to make one more argument to his commander's face for an all-out pursuit. Accounts of Forrest's physical appearance in the heat of battle are legend. The spectacle he presented before Bragg must have been impressive: a subordinate demanding action, not requesting it. Yet Bragg had his reasons for delaying pursuit. The number of casualties sustained by his army during the battle, 18,450, was higher than the enemy's losses of 16,170. His surviving soldiers were exhausted, and he was concerned about the general condition of his army. He would remain inactive until the men were rested.[29]

The actual condition of Bragg's army stood before him in the person of Nathan Bedford Forrest: defiant, expecting superhuman performance from his men, incredulous that his commander could not see the opportunity of his career awaiting only the order to attack. All the supplies Bragg's army needed were at that moment being destroyed by the Yankees in Chattanooga, Forrest told him. Still, Bragg vacillated and refused to give Forrest the reinforcements he wanted.

In disgust, Forrest rode away to rejoin his men, and with a sense of acute dread reminiscent of Shiloh, he watched the continuing desperate retreat of the Federals. Forrest had always known that the Confederacy was at a disadvantage in manpower and that their salvation, if there were to be one, was in the fighting spirit of its soldiers. Any faith he had had in his commanders was evaporating in the steam of his anger. He was later heard to mutter, perhaps to himself, "What does he fight his battles for?"[30]

But Forrest was not the only one asking that question. Private soldiers throughout Bragg's command exchanged variations of the same inquiry throughout that fateful Monday. Bragg's indecision knew no bounds, and he seemed willing to allow the previous weekend's sacrifice of so many lives to go unredeemed as the Confederacy's "last great opportunity" slipped away.[31]

Forrest continued to act in the belief that his commander would come to his senses and order an attack against Rosecrans' defeated army. The next morning, Tuesday, September 22, found Forrest's command in line of battle along Missionary Ridge, awaiting the order to begin the assault. As the morning wore away, Forrest became more impatient and finally gave the order to move down from the heights to do what had to be done. By early afternoon he had not only driven the Yankees back through the valley toward the growing fortifications of Chattanooga, but he also had his troops in a position to threaten Rosecrans' railroad supply line along the Tennessee River to the west of town. In addition he had two brigades closing in on the fortifications east of the city. Forrest himself held the middle of the valley, from whence he could strengthen either flank. "Forrest's small cavalry force" spent that night spread thinly from the base of Lookout Mountain on the west to the east of Chattanooga.[32]

Not until noon on Wednesday the twenty-third, the third day following the Confederate victory at Chickamauga, did Bragg begin to move infantry into position to relieve Forrest's exhausted cavalrymen, who were pulled back and sent into camp east of Chattanooga. Stopping only long enough to take care of some repairs and make some adjustments, Forrest's command was off again, and for the next several days, they pursued detached Union units nearly as far as Knoxville and halfway back to Chattanooga. All this time Bragg was moving his main force erratically, frittering away the Confederate advantage as Rosecrans completed his fortifications at Chattanooga.

On September 28, Forrest was in the vicinity of Athens, Tennessee, when he received a terse dispatch from Bragg, completely lacking in any spirit of appreciation for what Forrest had accomplished. It said simply and abruptly, "The general commanding desires that you will without delay turn over the troops of your command previously ordered to Major-General Wheeler."[33]

The reason for Bragg's order was apparently a weak attempt to have Wheeler, now appointed commander of all cavalry in Tennessee, sweep into middle Tennessee to disrupt Rosecrans' lines of supply and communications. Though Forrest would withhold some of his brigades, those sent to Wheeler were barely effective. The men and horses were completely worn out and would be of little use to Wheeler.

Forrest was troubled over this turn of orders, and he sought to assuage the pain of losing his army by requesting leave to visit his wife at La Grange. On October 5, while in La Grange, he received another order that drove him over the edge. He and the rest of his troops were thereby placed under Wheeler's command. Bragg was pushing all of Forrest's buttons at once, and the last one was his being assigned to serve under Wheeler, which he had vowed never again to do. This was more than Forrest could tolerate, and it ripped away the last vestige of respect and sense of duty or subordination he felt he owed to Bragg.[34]

What happened next has been reported in accounts at some variance with each other. Jordan and Pryor, in their Forrest-sanctioned telling, say simply that he resigned. The second and most colorful account was related by Dr. J. B. Cowan, Forrest's surgeon and kinsman, who accompanied Forrest to Bragg's headquarters sometime after receipt of the order transferring him to Wheeler's command. According to Cowan's version, arriving at Bragg's command tent, Forrest brushed past the sentry without even acknowledging his salute and accosted the commanding general. Cowan relates that when Bragg arose and extended his hand, Forrest began a tirade covering what he considered a catalog of past grievances by his commander, all the while stabbing with his index finger in Bragg's direction to emphasize each point. Bragg could not possibly have been ready for the Tennessee twister that blew into his tent that day. In a confrontation like no other in military history, Forrest expressed his disdain for Bragg and his sense of betrayal:

> I am not here to pass civilities or compliments with you but on other business. You commenced your cowardly and contemptible persecution of me soon after the battle of Shiloh, and you have kept it up ever since. You did it because I reported to Richmond facts, while you reported damned lies. You robbed me of my command in Kentucky, and gave it to one of your favorites—men that I armed and equipped from the enemies of our country. In a spirit of revenge and spite, because I would not fawn upon you as others did, you drove me into west Tennessee in the winter of 1862, with a second brigade I had organized, and with improper arms and without sufficient ammunition, although I had made repeated applications for the same. You did it to ruin me and my career. When in spite of all this I returned with my command, well equipped by captures, you began again your work of spite and persecution, and have kept it up; and now this second brigade, organized and equipped without thanks to you or the government, a brigade which has won a reputation for successful fighting second to none in the army, taking advantage of your position as the commanding general in order to further humiliate me, you have taken these brave men from me.
>
> I have stood your meanness as long as I intend to. You have played the part of a damned scoundrel, and are a coward, and if you were any part of a man I would slap your jaws and force you to resent it. You may as well not issue any more orders to me, for I

will not obey them, and I will hold you personally responsible for any further indignities you endeavor to inflict upon me. You have threatened to arrest me for not obeying your orders promptly. I dare you to do it, and I say to you that if you ever again try to interfere with me or cross my path it will be at the peril of your life.[35]

This was possibly the greatest speech of insubordination ever pronounced by an American military officer. When he had finished his outburst, Forrest turned on his heel and stalked out of the tent. Considering the desperation of the day and Forrest's propensity for violence, General Bragg was lucky. Forrest might as easily have left a corpse in his wake as a stunned, yet still breathing, army commander.

Dr. Cowan was more concerned about retribution than Forrest as they rode away to the west and suggested that Forrest had finally gone too far. But Forrest knew human nature, perhaps even better, he knew Bragg's nature. "He'll never say a word about it," he answered. Bragg, he said, would "be the last man to mention it . . . and . . . he'll take no action in the matter. I will ask to be relieved and transferred to a different field, and he will not oppose it."[36]

Forrest was apparently correct. The incident, and its language, do not appear in the Official Records and showed up in print for the first time years later. Forrest got his reassignment and would continue to scourge Union forces throughout west Tennessee and northern Mississippi until war's end.

With the crisis in Bragg's army, President Davis arrived in October and spent five days interviewing commanders and various generals in an effort to settle the near rebellion against Bragg. Disputes, well told in oft-repeated stories and many memoirs, are steady testament to the anger and disappointment many officers and men felt toward their commander.[37] If he tired of receiving such reports, President Davis made no protest. Finally, on October 14, after addressing the troops, Davis and his entourage left for Mississippi.

Two weeks later the Confederate president was in Montgomery, Alabama, where he invited Forrest to meet with him. They traveled together by train to Atlanta, discussing Forrest's plans and hopes as they went. It appears that Forrest put a good case before President Davis for remaining in the west, well out of Bragg's territory. On October 29, Davis wrote Bragg approving Forrest's transfer to Mississippi and his request for troops. The requested number of troops was not fully met, leaving Forrest to mount yet another recruiting campaign.[38]

# Chapter Nine

# MY VOICE IS IN MY SWORD

*—William Shakespeare*

## Okolona
## October 1863-February 1864

Jefferson Davis had a crisis on his hands within the Army of Tennessee. The infighting and dissension among the officers under General Bragg threatened to cripple the war effort in the western theater of operations. His visit to the west was an attempt to bring things into hand. During their two-day journey to Atlanta, Forrest laid out his plans for a transfer from Bragg's command and for his next campaign. At some point during the train ride Davis agreed with Forrest, probably out of concern for losing one of his most "distinguished soldiers," who was an integral part of the cause, and whose service was "necessary to this army."[1]

Their conference ended with Davis's granting most of Forrest's requests. On October 29, Davis wrote to Bragg from Atlanta to advise him that Forrest would be transferred to northern Mississippi. Considering his near-violent confrontation with Forrest, Bragg was probably just fine with this transfer. The order allowed Forrest to keep the nucleus of his old command, but he had to leave Woodward's battalion of the Second Kentucky Cavalry with the Army of Tennessee.

The core of Forrest's new command was a mere three hundred men made up of Charles McDonald's battalion from Forrest's old regiment, his personal escort company, and the men and four guns of Jacob Huggins' and John Morton's batteries. Once again Forrest was beginning a new campaign with a recruiting effort. He would have to expand that core of three hundred horsemen by raising his own army deep within enemy territory, without any resources from the government, and with no line of supply upon which he could rely.

Forrest was in Meridian, Mississippi, on November 4, 1863, when he received orders from Gen. Joseph E. Johnston assigning him and his small force to western Tennessee. Maj. Gen. Stephen D. Lee had recently been appointed commander of the mounted forces in Mississippi and was hoping to bring Forrest under his command. He wrote Bragg on November 6 that "there is a good field for his [Forrest's] labors in West Tennessee," where his popularity would enable him to raise at least four thousand men.[2]

On November 7, Forrest received a cordial dispatch from Gen. Stephen Lee warmly welcoming the cavalry leader to his new command:

> I take this occasion to state, general, that whether you are under my command or not, we shall not disagree, and you shall have All the assistance and support I can render you. I would feel proud either in commanding or co-operating with so gallant an officer as yourself and one who has such an established reputation in cavalry service.

General Lee understood the logistical problems of the western area and more importantly, how valuable a well-supplied Forrest would be to his operations in that region. He commented in closing that he had ordered his staff to fill Forrest's "requisition as far as practicable and afford you every facility in your new assignment."[3]

Moving northward, into the teeth of a potential meat grinder, Forrest's small band of horsemen reached the vicinity of Okolona on November 15. There he was joined by his younger brother Jeffrey's regiment, which brought his numbers to 450 cavalrymen.

Even with the help proffered by General Lee, Forrest's march into western Tennessee would be a precarious undertaking at best. Union garrisons had been established all along the railroad from Memphis to Corinth. Gunboats patrolled the Mississippi, Ohio, and Tennessee Rivers, offering protection for Federal garrisons at Paducah, Fort Heinman, Union City, and Fort Pillow. Besides, there were Union cavalry patrols sweeping across Tennessee and northern Mississippi.

General Lee delivered the first installment of his promised cooperation by making a feinting demonstration toward LaGrange and Saulsbury, Tennessee, attacking the enemy forces at Pocahontas and Lafayette Station. This maneuver allowed Forrest to swing over behind Lee and cross the Memphis-Charleston Railroad near Bolivar and from there to cross the Tallahatchie River on December 2.

The force arrived at Jackson, Tennessee, on December 5. However, even with Lee's diversion, which entailed destroying several miles of track on the Memphis-Charleston line and burning all the bridges he could find, Forrest's movements did not go unobserved.[4] Dispatches flew back and forth between the Union commanders based along the Tennessee and Ohio Rivers when their scouts reported that Forrest had crossed into west Tennessee.

On December 5, Gen. Stephen A. Hurlbut, headquartered in Memphis, wired Gen. Henry W. Halleck, who passed the word on to U. S. Grant that Forrest was in west Tennessee. His message confidently stated that he was "organizing as rapidly as possible for a strong cavalry movement" to counter the interlopers. Gen. A. J. Smith was at Columbus, Kentucky, when he got the word on December 7. His reaction also exuded confidence as he replied that he "desired to make thorough work of these trespassers."

In contrast to the tone of the messages of his comrades, Gen. J. G. Stevenson, a post commander on the Tennessee, wrote to General Halleck at Memphis that Forrest was conscripting all the men in the area that could bear arms. Then, revealing the panic that Forrest's appearance was creating, Stevenson ended his dispatch by adding that Forrest was also recruiting or subverting into military duty "all the Negroes fit to be soldiers."[5]

The only Union commander who seemed unruffled by Forrest's arrival was William Tecumseh Sherman. Though the general had had ample reason in the past to take such news seriously, this particular dispatch seemed to be but a temporary bother to Sherman. "I have made the junction at which I was aiming, and am rather indifferent to Forrest's reported expedition. Forrest may cavort about that country as much as he pleases," he wrote with disdain. "Every conscript they now catch will cost a good man to watch."[6]

The tension permeating the Union camps was the exact opposite of what was occurring in Jackson upon Forrest's arrival. During the first week of December the word spread quickly that Forrest was raising a new army, and soon the immediate countryside was bursting with fresh recruits. On December 5, the citizens of Jackson, Tennessee, and the surrounding area were throwing a homecoming party in honor of one of their favorite sons. One of the observers of the celebratory mood in Jackson was Pvt. John Johnston of General Chalmers' regiment. In a letter home, Private Johnston wrote that Forrest's arrival "carried joy and hope and enthusiasm everywhere. The country now seemed thick with Confederate soldiers—and within the 18 days which he spent at Jackson, he had gathered an army of not less than 3,000 men—and this in mid-winter!"[7]

While Forrest was frantically, and successfully, recruiting and building his new command behind enemy lines, he was aware that the enemy would soon be swarming down upon him. He desperately needed the supplies, arms, and reinforcements that had been promised him and sent messages to both Gen. Joseph E. Johnston, the departmental commander, and Gen. Stephen D. Lee, his immediate commanding officer, informing them of his situation. When the material he requested did not arrive, Forrest, with small chance of ever being reimbursed, once again was forced to dip into his own personal funds to keep his men fed and supplied.

Whatever Sherman might have thought of Forrest's activities, Bedford was as serious about this task as any other, even though he was undertaking it in the bitter cold of winter and mostly at his own expense. Forrest wrote on December 6 to General Johnston, "[I] have had to advance to my quartermaster and commissary $20,000 of my private funds to subsist the command thus far."[8] He continued:

> I am exceedingly anxious to get the arms promised me by the President, and earnestly ask that General Lee, with all the cavalry that can be spared, be brought up to west Tennessee at this juncture, bringing with him the arms and ammunition needed for the new troops. If this were done, we could effectually destroy the Memphis and Charleston railroad, and drive out from her between four and six thousand head of good beef cattle for the use of the army. If I hear that he is coming to help me, I will build a pontoon bridge across the Hatchie, and will have the cattle gathered up by the time he can reach me. I am in great need of money.[9]

Though he would go on to request $100,000 for supplies, very little came of it, and he was continually called upon to drain his own wealth as the war wore on. Before the war was over, Bedford would deplete his entire fortune in this same manner.

If he could receive the requested supplies and Lee's cooperation in blocking the enemy advance from Memphis, Forrest, realizing that he was in an advantageous position, knew he could "take care of any force that came at me from the North." Regardless of the overwhelming numbers of enemy troops initially in the area, he would then have time to completely destroy the Memphis and Charleston Railroad and block the passage of the Tennessee River, "which . . . gives us west Tennessee." Forrest's plan was ambitious and risky, but he was correct in believing that the possession of the grain-producing farmland in west Tennessee was crucial to the Confederacy's war effort.[10]

The size of the force he had raised and the short time it had taken him to do it did not look so much like "cavorting" to Sherman after all. Sherman and the other Union commanders were no longer amused by Forrest's presence, and immediate plans were undertaken to drive him out of west Tennessee, or better yet, to kill him. Hurlbut ordered five columns of cavalry totaling some fifteen thousand troops under Brigadier Generals Joseph A. Mower, Benjamin H. Grierson, Andrew J. Smith, William Sooy Smith, and George Crook to converge on Forrest at Jackson. The plan was to hunt down and destroy this rebel commander who had the audacity to raise an army right under their noses. This may have seemed bold of the Union command, who believed they held the territory, but it was also Forrest's own backyard, where he was well acquainted with the people and the terrain.

The recruiting campaign carried out by Forrest and his officers was a dangerous game of hide and seek. West Tennessee was swarming with Union patrols. The Federals had established recruiting bureaus of their own in all the major towns and were aggressively pursuing all males in the area, both black and white, who were of age for military service. Consequently, the Confederates carried out their mission in meetings held in the dense cane breaks, river bottoms, and at midnight rendezvous deep in the woods. Simultaneously, other detachments rounded up hundreds of head of livestock needed for provisions in the coming weeks. At that moment, Forrest's cavalry was approximately thirty-four hundred strong, but more than a third of his men were untrained and unarmed, and on top of that, his entire command had the added burden of herding five hundred head of cattle and hogs.[11]

For two weeks, Forrest was able to avoid a serious fight, but the intelligence reports coming in from his network of scouts and spies confirmed what he had already suspected: his time was quickly running out.

On December 18, the order was given to begin the concerted move against Forrest's cavalry. Coming at the isolated Confederate commander from the east was Gen. W. Sooy Smith, who marched out of Nashville toward Columbia. Closing in from the southeast was Gen. Joseph A. Mower, based in Corinth, Mississippi. A third column, under Gen. B. H. Grierson, was on the march from the southwest, coming out of La Grange. The fourth, commanded by Gen. A. J. Smith, was descending from the north out of Columbus, Kentucky. A fifth column, from Huntsville Alabama, under the leadership of

Gen. George Crook, cut off any escape to the south. This force seemed more than sufficient for the task as hand.

In Memphis, Hurlbut exclaimed, "I think we shall cure Forrest of his ambition to command West Tennessee." Sherman confirmed the enthusiasm with an emphatic recommendation to "get on his heels and chase him to the wall."[12]

Forrest had come to recruit and resupply, not necessarily to fight. He would need time to prepare his new recruits, for raw and untrained as they were, they were no match for the overwhelming force driving toward them . . . yet.

Scouts reported the Union movements to Forrest, who wrote to both Johnston and Lee that he needed help in order to maintain his present position. He wrote that he was "gathering up as rapidly as possible all the absentees and deserters" in the area and planning to "use them until they can be returned to their proper commands." Forrest believed that he could handle any one of the advancing columns, but against more than that he would "have more than I can manage with the raw and unarmed troops I have." He suggested that if Lee could move his troops into west Tennessee, "we can whip anything they may send against us." He also realized that alone his position would be untenable and that with his force of "undrilled and undisciplined troops it will not do for me to risk a general engagement with superior force."[13]

Staying one move ahead of the enemy, but slowed by a large supply train of forty wagons and a herd of three hundred hogs and two hundred cattle, Forrest started his command south on December 23. At dawn he sent Gen. Dick V. Richardson's brigade from Brownsville to the crossing of the rain-swollen Hatchie River near Estenaula, eighteen miles west of Jackson. Once there, Richardson was to guard the stream and secure a landing for the ferryboat that had been scuttled earlier to conceal it from the enemy so that it could be refloated in case all other available bridged crossings had been destroyed.[14]

Forrest divided his command further. Col. Tyree Bell was sent out first with the main column of some twenty-five hundred men, including the unarmed recruits, the wagon train, and herd of cattle. Bell's orders were to push toward the river as fast as was negotiable. Soon after Bell had departed, Forrest sent Lt. Col. D. M. Wisdom with five hundred troops, including part of Forrest's escort company, southeast out of Jackson to challenge the advance of the enemy from that direction. Forrest and the remainder of his escort company stayed in Jackson organizing and facilitating the rapid evacuation of the final elements in the area before pulling out late that evening.

General Grierson guessed Forrest's line of march and realized that if he could beat Forrest to the Hatchie River, the rebel chieftain would be forced to take a long detour around the headwaters of the Hatchie and the Wolf Rivers north of Bolivar, where he could be easily trapped and eliminated. To that effect, on the twenty-third, Grierson sent Col. Edward Prince and the Seventh Illinois Cavalry ahead to destroy all remaining structures on the Hatchie and to block and hold Forrest on the north bank of the river.[15]

Making the situation nearly insurmountable, a cold December rain had been pounding both armies as they attempted to negotiate the muddy roads and swollen streams that spiderweb their way across the heavily wooded landscape. If Colonel Prince could have beat Forrest to the river, things would have looked very bad for the Confederates. However, Forrest got their "first with the most."

On the morning of December 24, the weather finally broke, revealing a crystal-clear and frosty countryside. Colonel Prince arrived at Estenaula at approximately 4:00 P.M. on Christmas Eve only to discover Colonel Richardson's brigade, which had arrived earlier to secure a landing for the ferry, blocking their way. After a hot exchange of gunfire, Richardson's men fell back to Slough's Bridge, where the Confederates formed up once again and held firm for the next several hours, eventually forcing Prince to withdraw.

Earlier that morning, Lt. Col. D. M. Wisdom's detachment, sent southeast of Jackson to check the enemy from that direction, struck the approaching Federal column near Jack's Creek. It was an all-day fight that ended with the second Federal column also withdrawing. This bought Forrest's main body of troops moving toward the river valuable time to start the crossing.[16]

The fight at Jack's Creek was a toe-to-toe affair that ended in memorable fashion. Nearing the end of the daylong battle, Wisdom, seeing that he was about to be flanked, quickly selected eighty men to counter the Union's move with a bold charge. He placed Lieutenants H. A. Tyler and John O. Morris in charge of the striking force that was mainly comprised of men from Forrest's famous escort company, who were all remarkable horsemen and fighters. Lieutenant Tyler, the senior officer of the two, was placed in command. In a style that Forrest would have appreciated, the Confederates charged headlong into the Union cavalry with reckless abandon. The fight was severe, as men fired away at each other at point-blank range. The fiery muzzle discharges from the Navy Colts and shotguns set men's uniforms on fire as they blasted away at one another from a wickedly close and shockingly intimate distance. The ground was littered with the dead and wounded, their clothing smoldering from the burning powder. Some of the wounded died beneath the hoofs of rampaging horses, trampled before they could crawl away.

Several of the mounted troopers were locked in individual combat with Yankees. Young Lieutenant Morris, "while grappling with a Union trooper, their horses dashing at full speed along the highway, was mortally wounded." As they fought,

> he and his antagonist, thrusting the muzzles of their pistols against each other, fired almost simultaneously, and both fell to the ground mortally hurt. It was brief but bloody work, and, as the Federals gave way, the column under Forrest was not molested by further pursuit from this direction.[17]

Forrest, who had been bringing up the rear, arrived at the river at around 10:00 P.M. and immediately began to harangue the men to set to work getting the wagons and animals across the Hatchie. The work was brutal, as the river was freezing cold and swollen to capacity. Infecting the column with his manic energy, Forrest demanded the entire operation be accelerated at once. He ordered all the remaining cattle that had not already crossed be driven into the icy water and forced to swim to the opposite bank. Capt. Mike Pirtle remembered the sound of Forrest's voice as he cursed at his men and barked out orders: "It penetrated you through and through and made you move."[18]

Forrest had not been at this work long when Col. J. J. Neely of the Fourteenth Tennessee Cavalry reported to Forrest that Colonel Prince and the Seventh Illinois regiment, with approximately six hundred men, were camped only five miles away. Colonel Neely had been with Colonel Richardson in the fight with Prince's column near Estenaula earlier in the day. Confident that the crossing was progressing at a rapid rate, Forrest decided to attack and drive Prince's command back to where he was sure they would no longer pose a threat to the final stages of his river crossing. Joining the Fourteenth Tennessee, Forrest gathered his escort company and mounted up to engage the Illinois regiment. The temperature had plunged to the freezing mark. It was Christmas Eve, and beneath a pale December moon that shimmered off the ice-covered trees and grass, Forrest's force moved toward the enemy camp.

Halting the brigade a short distance from the enemy campfires, Forrest decided to dip into his bag of tricks. Rather than executing an orthodox attack, he advised his company commanders to spread their troops out into a long, thin line that would stretch over a quarter mile in length. The men were to advance through a cornfield, making as much noise as possible. When the order to move forward came, Lt. Nathan Boone, commanding the escort, bellowed, "Brigade, charge!" The junior officers were instructed to repeat all command orders as though they also were commanding companies of their own. Riding and stomping their way through the dried and frozen cornstalks, Forrest and some sixty men kept up the tremendous racket as they came forward, hoping to create the impression that they were a much larger force. The still and frosty night air carried the rebels' explosion of noise across the field and into the Union camp where a startled Colonel Prince fell for Forrest's deception.

Convinced that he was facing a superior force and about to be overrun, the Federal commander fell back to a position near Somerville, more than ten miles to the west. Effectively eliminating Prince's column without losing a man, Forrest turned back toward the Hatchie River and returned to the main body of troops, who continued to cross the river.[19]

The crossing was progressing, but not without setbacks. Colonel Bell and his troops had just ferried Morton's two guns across the swollen stream when on their next trip a wagon and team of mules got out of control and capsized the boat, drowning the teamster in the process. Forrest arrived on the scene during the chaos created by the capsized boat and immediately dismounted and rushed into the icy water, "armpit deep," to lend a hand. Forrest was able to save the drowning mules by cutting them out of their harnesses and then continued to work with the rest of the men in the rushing current of the river.

During the emergency one particular conscript on the shore was raising hell, loudly stating that he was not about to jump into the stream and he did not give a damn who told him that he must. His noisy comments were overheard by his commanding officer, who once finished with the task at hand, scrambled up the muddy bank and quickly approached the malcontent. Grabbing him by the scruff of his neck and by the seat of his pants, Forrest picked the large man up off the ground and heaved him over the bank and into the water. "After that," Pvt. Mack Watson, one of the escort company troopers remembered, "that fellow made a pretty good hand."[20]

Welcome to Forrest's cavalry.

Soon the process of crossing the river resumed its organization and calm. The elements of Forrest's force slipped in and out of the darkness, for other than the few campfires lit alongside the banks of the stream, the only available light was the trembling threads of moonbeams that filtered through the bare branches of the giant hard-woods along the Hatchie bottoms. The men and animals crossing the river presented an "eerie sight for the night before Christmas."[21]

Christmas Day was bright and clear, which helped Forrest complete the crossing by late afternoon. However, the Southerners were not home free just yet. There was still one more river to cross. Also on Christmas, Forrest received his promotion to major general, officially dated December 4, 1863.[22]

Having completed their initial river crossing, the Confederates' situation was perhaps even more precarious now that they were in between the Hatchie and Wolf Rivers, where their maneuverability would be reduced. Also, between the two streams were strong detachments of Union troops at Bolivar and Grand Junction. All along the Memphis-Charleston rail line were additional troops with orders to keep a sharp eye out for the Confederate cavalry. At Grand Junction and Collierville large bodies of Federal cavalry stood by, on, or near trains whose locomotives were kept steamed up for an immediate departure to any point that Forrest appeared. It did seem as though Brigadier General W. H. L. Tuttle, garrisoned at La Grange, had every right to believe, as he wrote in a dispatch to Hurlbut in Memphis, "it looks to me like we will get them sure this time."[23]

Increasing Forrest's difficulties was that the Wolf River, which flows due west into the Mississippi near Memphis, was overflowing its banks. The high water had flooded the entire area, creating a complex situation for any attempting to cross it. The Confederates added to the situation by having already destroyed all the bridges that spanned the Wolf in that vicinity.

On December 26, Forrest once again turned on his pursuers and attacked the enemy in an effort to buy more time. But the wily Confederate general was running out of moves. He was going to have to fight his way out of west Tennessee during terrible winter conditions with a ragtag, half-armed command of raw recruits.

The weather held out on the twenty-sixth; it was another cold but clear day. Early that morning, Forrest's scouts reported two enemy columns approaching. One was from the south; the other was the pesky Colonel Prince and the Seventh Illinois Regiment, coming in from the north between Bolivar and Somerville. Being closer to Prince's column than the other, Forrest rode in the direction from which the Seventh Illinois had been sighted. Dividing his force, Forrest sent General Richardson's command ahead by another route while he and Captain McDonald's battalion, along with his escort company, found Prince's trail and fell in behind the Federal troops, who were unaware that their roles had just been reversed. The hunters had become the hunted.[24]

At about 4: 00 P.M. Forrest and Brig. Gen. Dick Richardson converged upon Prince's position, approximately four miles from New Castle. Forrest deployed McDonald's battalion into line of battle. Though they carried only sticks to simulate weapons, the unarmed troops were included in this deployment in hopes of creating a more formidable appearance. With no more than a ghost battalion of men, half of whom were weaponless, and his escort company, Forrest ordered the advance toward the Yankee position.

The enemy did not give way at first, and a hot engagement broke out that lasted for the next couple of hours, causing severe losses on both sides. Among the Confederate killed and wounded were Lt. Nathan Boone, who was seriously wounded, and his brother, who was shot dead during the struggle. Forrest continued to maneuver his men and press the enemy up the middle until almost 6:00 P.M., when he and his escort separated from the main body of troops and slipped out the back of the column to execute a flanking move so that they could gain Prince's rear. In another half-hour, Forrest suddenly burst in upon the enemy's rear and flank, throwing them into a panic and starting a chaotic stampede that Prince, in his battle report, understated when he wrote that the Federals "were compelled to retire, and, owing to the broken character of the ground, in considerable disorder."[25] After driving Prince's six hundred men some ten miles to the southeast, Forrest suddenly stopped the pursuit and turned due west, heading toward Somerville, where he rendezvoused with Colonel Bell and the wagon train.

When the news of Prince's route reached Union general Tuttle at La Grange, his tone suddenly rose to a shrill pitch. Wiring all the Union commanders farther east toward Corinth, Tuttle warned, "Later information makes it sure that Forrest and Richardson are coming like hell." At the same time the warnings were going out over the wires that he was heading east toward Corinth, Forrest was actually marching in the opposite direction.[26] Forrest was doing some incredible broken field running as he moved toward the Wolf River, the one direction that the enemy did not think he could go because they believed that all the bridges had been destroyed.

The night of December 26, Forrest made camp just north of New Castle. That same night, he received some incredibly important information. Col. Thomas Logwood, of Forrest's old regiment, had been on a recruiting mission north of Memphis, in the vicinity of the Wolf River, when he received word that Forrest was at Jackson and on the run. During a recent reconnaissance, Logwood's company had come across a bridge at Lafayette Station that had not been burned, only partially dismantled. The flooring planks had been removed and stacked on the south bank for easy replacement should the Federals need to recross the Wolf. Nevertheless, this deviation from their orders to completely destroy all the crossings over the river was just the break Forrest needed.

The bridge at Lafayette was only a few miles southeast of Memphis, where General Hurlbut had a huge occupying force garrisoned around the city. This force easily could have been mobilized and dispatched to swarm down upon Forrest had they known he was less than twenty minutes away at a hard riding pace.[27]

From his camp near New Castle, Forrest detached Col. W. W. Falkner and seven hundred men to ride along the north side of the Wolf, find a crossing, and then move into Mississippi by way of Hernando. The diversionary tactic seemed a suicide mission for Falkner, who had only fifty armed men out of the seven hundred he led. Falkner's orders were to create the impression that Forrest's command was marching on the Mississippi capital and intending to cross the Wolf River between Moscow and La Grange.

After snatching less than four hours' sleep, the rebels awoke to a freezing drizzle that would become a downpour as the day progressed. As bad as the weather conditions were for both armies, the rain, shortness of daylight during late December, and poor visibility may have benefited Forrest's small force in concealing its movements. In the dim, overcast, early-morning light of the twenty-seventh, Forrest sent Col. Tyree Bell and two hundred men toward Lafayette Station with the vital mission of driving away the Federal force garrisoned at the bridge then to seize and hold it until Forrest and the wagon train could arrive.[28]

At approximately noon, Bell's men arrived at Lafayette Station and immediately attacked the garrison, held by some seventy-five Union troops. As they saw the Confederates boldly charging, and unaware that only the first line of Southerners actually held weapons, the Federals unceremoniously abandoned their post and fled. In short order Bell's boys had relain the planks and taken up positions on both sides of the river to await Forrest and the rest of the command.

Meanwhile, at about 1:30 P.M., General Grierson, at La Grange, received a telegraph just before the lines were cut, informing him that Forrest was not marching toward Corinth but was only a few miles away, near Lafayette Station. Grierson immediately ordered Col. William H. Morgan of the Twenty-fifth Indiana Infantry, commanding the Third Brigade at Grand Junction, to board the waiting train and go under full steam to Lafayette. Unfortunately for Grierson and the Union cause, Morgan did not get underway, nor mobilize with the urgency needed, and did not steam out of Grand Junction until 3:30 P.M.[29]

By approximately 4:00 P.M., Forrest had his entire command across the Wolf, including the five hundred head of cattle and hogs he had been herding. Leaving the last bridge over the river burning in their wake, Forrest's motley crew marched toward Collierville through a driving rain that came down so hard the men were barely able to see two or three hundred feet ahead.[30] As darkness set in, Morgan's Third Brigade detrained a half-mile from Lafayette Station and deployed into a battle formation to challenge Forrest's passage over the river. But the gray riders had already disappeared into the mist like spirits in the night.

On the way to Collierville, where Forrest intended to make a demonstration to hold the enemy in check and hopefully further confuse the Federal commanders about his true escape route, he sent the unarmed men, livestock, and wagon train southward with orders to march as quickly as possible for Holly Springs, Mississippi.

At 10:00 P.M., in a continuing downpour that aided the Confederates in disguising their actual numbers, Forrest attacked the Federal camp at Collierville from the west. The rest of his command deployed east of Collierville, facing toward Grand Junction in order to stop any advance by Grierson's troops stationed there. Putting on a convincing show, Forrest's men drove the Union troops camped two miles west of Collierville back through the town and into their fortifications. Then, just as suddenly as they had appeared, the Confederates vanished, heading southward to catch up with the wagon train. This tactic left the Federal officers thoroughly confused about where Forrest was and what he was really up to.[31]

The impression this series of maneuvers imposed upon the Federal commander at Collierville was just what Forrest had hoped to create. At approximately midnight, Collierville's commander was on the telegraph wiring for help, stating that they expected an attack at dawn from Forrest's cavalry, numbering at least forty-five hundred. In reaction to the news from Collierville, at 3:00 A.M., Benjamin H. Grierson again ordered Colonel Morgan at Lafayette Station to march west and attack Forrest's rear while the Confederates supposedly were assaulting the works at Collierville.[32]

Early on the morning of the twenty-eighth, Grierson realized that he had been tricked again and in desperation sent out a wire for all the Federal columns in the area to converge on Cold Creek, just south of the Wolf. This was the next stream of considerable size the Confederates would have to cross, for "Forrest has gone south like hell."[33] It was all in vain for the Union pursuers, however, because the elusive rebel horsemen already had crossed the Mississippi state line at Mount Pleasant. They eventually arrived near Holly Springs, where they rendezvoused with the wagon train and made camp early that same morning.

Forrest had left the Yankee generals mesmerized and confused as they ordered their freezing men to march and countermarch, train and detrain, back and forth across western Tennessee, only to find that Forrest was somewhere else. To his commanding officer, Stephen D. Lee, Forrest wrote that he could have almost doubled the number of conscripts brought out if he could have stayed ten days longer. He suggested that he be allowed to withdraw to the Tallahatchie River to rest his men and mounts because they "were much jaded and require rest." To Gen. James Chalmers, who had been on a diversionary attack in the area of Germantown, he requested a meeting in Holly Springs, "as I am unwell and much fatigued."[34]

The last statement was out of character for a man known for his iron will and physical strength. Of course, his fatigue was justified considering the demands, both physical and mental, put upon him and his men during their harrowing escape out of Tennessee and into Mississippi. However, the Confederates were not the only ones saddle weary and worn down. The Federal columns that had been chasing him helter-skelter over southwestern Tennessee for the past week were also cold, exhausted, and demoralized. Their officers fared little better and were soon fighting among themselves over who was at fault in letting Forrest get away.

Col. William H. Morgan had already resigned himself to Forrest's escape. Almost immediately an inspector characterized Morgan's report as "inefficient." General Grierson apparently shared the views of Morgan's critic and wrote in his own battle report, "If Colonel Morgan had evinced as much enterprise in pursuing and attacking the enemy as he has in making excuses for his tardy movements, success would undoubtedly have attended our efforts."[35]

Forrest had a knack for driving many of the Federal commanders he faced to turn on one another in attempting to understand, justify, and rationalize what had just happened to them. On January 12,

1864, a war correspondent writing for a Northern newspaper in Memphis declared,

> Forrest, with less than four thousand men, has moved right through the Sixteenth Army Corps, has passed within nine miles of Memphis, carried off a hundred beef cattle, three thousand conscripts, and innumerable stores; torn up railroad-tracks, destroyed telegraph-wires, burned and sacked towns, ran over pickets with a single derringer pistol, and all in the face of ten thousand men.[36]

## The Battles of West Point and Okolona

On January 1, 1864, Forrest moved his command thirty-four miles south of Memphis to Como Station. There he began to build his new army into a cohesive fighting machine. This was going to be a difficult task considering that these men came from dozens of different units. Many were deserters and others were raw conscripts with little discipline or loyalty.

On the thirteenth, Forrest was called to department headquarters at Meridian, Mississippi to meet with the new district commander, General Polk, and Stephen D. Lee. At this meeting a new cavalry command was created. The order designated the new organization as "Forrest's Cavalry Department," and it included "all cavalry commands in West Tennessee and North Mississippi."[37] Forrest also received the equipment, arms, and ammunition that his men had desperately needed. The enemy would now find out just what kind of hell Forrest could raise with a fully equipped and supplied command.

Returning to Como, Forrest lost no time organizing his men into four small brigades. Brig. Gen. Dick Richardson was assigned command of the First Brigade, Col. Robert McCulloch was given the Second Brigade, Col. Tyree Bell would lead the Third Brigade, and Col. Jeffrey Forrest was named to lead the Fourth Brigade, which included the famous Seventh Tennessee Cavalry that Bedford, Jeffrey, and Willie had joined as privates in 1861. Brig. Gen. James R. Chalmers now commanded the First Division, which would include Jeffrey Forrest's and Robert McCulloch's brigades.[38]

By mid-January, Sherman was back in Memphis and planning his winter campaign in middle Tennessee and northern Mississippi. He did not intend to ease the pressure on the Confederate forces in west Tennessee. Sherman immediately developed an aggressive and, as it turned out, overly confident plan to cut and burn a path directly through Forrest's new jurisdiction and on to Selma and Mobile, Alabama.

Sherman's fame would be forever associated with his march through Georgia and the Carolinas, but he developed his methods in northern Mississippi and southern Tennessee in 1864. It was there that he began to direct his operations not only against enemy soldiers, but also against the civilian population, which produced the food, material, and support for those soldiers. This practice would be called total warfare in future wars.

The campaign Sherman planned for early 1864 would send a large infantry force up from Vicksburg toward Meridian, Mississippi, and a cooperating cavalry force southeastward from Memphis to follow and destroy the Mobile and Ohio Railroad. Sherman would lead the infantry, made up of McPherson's Seventeenth and Hurlbut's Sixteenth Army Corps. Brig. Gen. William Sooy Smith, Grant's chief of cavalry, commanded the horsemen. If things went as planned, Sherman hoped to join the two forces at Meridian then move on to Selma, destroying trestles, bridges, arsenals, and the grain-rich agricultural area of the Black Prairie region as he went, thus crippling the Confederacy's war-making capability in the western theater.

General Smith intended to follow closely on Forrest's trail. "I have been anxious to attack him [Forrest] at once . . . but General Sherman thinks I had better await his movement, and in the meantime collect, organize and supply my command."[39] That was not all that Sherman was thinking concerning Sooy Smith. Back on November 11, 1863, Grant had chosen Smith as his chief of cavalry over Sherman's objections. Although Smith was a West Point graduate and had commanded an infantry brigade at Shiloh and Perryville besides commanding a full division during the Vicksburg campaign, Sherman did not think Smith was the man for the job. On December 19, 1863, Sherman had bluntly stated to Grant, "I deem General William Sooy Smith too mistrustful of himself for a leader against Forrest. Mower is a better man for the duty."[40] In retrospect, it seems that Sherman may have been a better judge of men than was General Grant.

Smith's cavalry command to this point in the war was the largest and best-equipped cavalry force ever put into the field in the western theater. The Union column consisted of five regiments led by Gen. Benjamin Grierson at Collierville and Col. George Waring out of Columbus, Kentucky. Each of the seventy-five hundred cavalrymen was to be armed with revolvers and the new Colt repeating carbines. Twenty pieces of double-teamed artillery and a large train of supplies supported the march. In addition to this assemblage, Sherman started a third expedition of troops aboard gunboats to move up the Yazoo River into Mississippi to draw attention from his true objective. As Sherman's force was preparing to leave Vicksburg on February 3, he believed that Sooy Smith had been given charge of "the best and most experienced troops in the service" and added that this command was "superior and better in all respects than the combined cavalry which the enemy has in all the State of Mississippi."[41]

Though the Union expedition was impressive in its size, it could not move unobserved by Confederate scouts. Forrest, therefore, realized that something significant was taking shape and began to put the pieces together. On the fourth Forrest halted his southern movement at the request of Gen. Leonidas Polk and awaited developments. Responding to reports about the gunboats, Forrest sent one regiment to challenge the flotilla coming up the Yazoo. Two days later, he received reports from his scouts and from headquarters about Smith's advance out of Memphis and the enemy's concentration of cavalry at Collierville. To stay in front of Smith's force and to put himself closer to the support of Lee's troops in central Mississippi, Forrest fell back below the Tallahatchie River between Abbeville and Oxford.[42]

Sooy Smith was supposed to have departed on February 3, in concert with the other Union columns, but he was delayed while waiting for Col. George Waring's brigade of two thousand troops to reach him. On his way to Collierville, Waring had run into trouble coming across the flooded river bottoms and creeks that flow westward toward the Mississippi. He did not arrive until February 9, which in turn delayed Smith's departure until February 11, the day the general was to have rendezvoused, according to the plan, with Sherman in Meridian.

The stress of the delay affected Smith to such a degree that he wrote to Sherman an apology of sorts. General Smith stated that his ordeal had been "so long and vexatious that I have worried myself into a state of morbid anxiety and fear that I will be entirely too late to perform my part of the work."[43] Sherman was infuriated by the delay and wired the commanding officer at Columbus, Kentucky, the post from whence Waring had departed, that it was "a disgrace to the cavalry arm of the service that they cannot cross a creek. . . . Of course the use of that cavalry is lost to us in this movement."[44]

While Smith was bogged down in Memphis with logistical details, Sherman had already reached Jackson, Mississippi, on February 5 and crossed the Pearl River. He reached Morton on the seventh. General Polk, at Meridian, was braced for a battle but then had second thoughts and evacuated the city, falling back to Demopolis, across the Tombigbee River and into Alabama. But before evacuating Meridian, Polk removed nearly all the rails and manufacturing material and sent it on to the safety of Selma and Mobile.

Meanwhile, near Oxford, Mississippi, Forrest continued to mold his new band of misfits into a disciplined army. The month of February was extremely cold that year and warm clothing, arms, and equipment were hard to come by. Consequently, desertion temporarily infected Forrest's command. In the Confederate service, "Absence without leave might almost be called a custom . . . and its close relationship to desertion was not apparent to many a soldier."[45]

In the second week of February, nineteen men from Bell's brigade went over the hill and headed home. They were soon captured and returned to camp to face trial for desertion. All nineteen were found guilty and summarily sentenced to die before a firing squad on Friday morning, February 12. The next day Colonel Bell's brigade was ordered to fall out and witness the execution. The ladies and other citizens of Oxford came forward with petitions for clemency, but Forrest was adamant. Even appeals from fellow officers had no effect. General Forrest intended for the execution to go ahead as ordered.

The appointed time arrived, and the condemned men were marched out to an open field where they were greeted by freshly dug graves with new coffins placed by each one. The column was marched by the line of graves and ordered to halt so that each man stood in front of a coffin. The riflemen of the firing squad somberly took their places. An officer raised his sword, and the ritual began. "Ready!" he called. "Aim . . ." But before the order to fire could be given, a messenger from Forrest's staff charged up on horseback shouting, "Stand down!" General Forrest had decided at the last moment to cancel the executions and pardon each of the condemned men.

The suddenly lucky men fell to their knees in disbelief and gratitude. A huge cheer burst from Bell's brigade. When the cheering subsided Forrest's messenger relayed his commander's final point: this was the last and only time their general would fail to apply the prescribed punishment for desertion. It was said that the desertion rate in Forrest's cavalry dropped off dramatically after that display.[46]

In the meantime Sherman was waiting anxiously in Meridian for Colonel Smith's arrival. His comments during this period made it clear that what little confidence he had in Smith was slowly eroding. In fairness to Smith, he was a hundred miles farther from Meridian than Sherman when the march began. Even in the absence of delays beyond his control, Smith could not have arrived at the same time as his commander. But Sherman was not interested in hearing about any difficulties Smith faced. His confidence in Smith was already low and Sherman seriously doubted Smith's ability to successfully lead the cavalry against Forrest's fierce and unorthodox horsemen.

Though Smith had made an effort to appear enthusiastic and capable, his own self-confidence might well have been weakened by Sherman's constant warnings and admonitions concerning Forrest. In one message he told Smith "that in his route he was sure to encounter Forrest, who always attacked with a vehemence for which he [Smith] must be prepared."[47] In another dispatch Sherman warned of "the nature of Forrest as a man, and of his peculiar force," and that now they were in Forrest's country, where he maintained a pipeline of information concerning the Union movements.

Indeed, Forrest was being apprised of the situation. He had been informed in early February that a heavy Federal column was advancing from Friars Point, very near Forrest's own three-thousand-acre plantation. By February 9, he had already read Sherman's mind. He wrote to General Chalmers on that day, "I am of the opinion the real move is in the direction of Meridian."[48]

Forrest's intelligence regarding Smith's strength and disposition was uncanny. In a letter to General Polk, written on the thirteenth, Forrest said, "General Smith, with 10,000 mounted infantry and cavalry and 31 pieces artillery, passed Holly Springs on the evening of the 12th, going toward Beck's Spring and New Albany."[49]

All along the way from Vicksburg, Sherman had fretted that Sooy Smith's column had fallen further and further behind schedule. Waiting now in Meridian for Smith to join him, Sherman's patience ran out on February 14, and he ordered the systematic destruction of the city. Between then and the twentieth, his troops reduced Meridian to rubble. They worked vigorously with crowbars, sledgehammers, claw hammers, and teams of horses to raze every structure to the ground, and when they had finished they put the ruins to the torch. With Meridian reduced to little more than ashes, Sherman wrote:

> For five days 10,000 [men] worked hard and with a will in that work of destruction . . . and I have no hesitation in pronouncing the work well done. Meridian, with its depots, storehouses, arsenals, hospitals, offices, hotels and cantonments, no longer exists.[50]

By the seventeenth, the weather had cleared and the roads were becoming more passable. On that day, Smith's command crossed the Tallahatchie River. At the Tallahatchie, Smith sent out two brigades of infantry, one to Panola, Mississippi, and the other to Wyatte. This division of his force was merely a feint and made to confuse Forrest as to his true route, which took him out of Collierville heading southeastwardly toward Pontotoc along the rail line that led into the Black Prairie region near Okolona.

On February 18, Secretary of War James Seddon sent orders directly to Forrest instructing him to "leave General Chalmers with his cavalry to check the enemy in North Mississippi and proceed with dispatch to aid General Lee in operations against the enemy in East Mississippi."[51] Around that same time, Gen. Stephen D. Lee, in charge of all cavalry units in Alabama, wrote to Forrest, telling him essentially the same thing. Lee also concurred that Forrest was to use his "discretion as to all movements against the enemy."[52] Forrest was already ahead of the game and on the move to place his cavalry between Smith and his intended junction with Sherman at Meridian.

Smith had moved from New Albany on the eighteenth, heading toward Pontotoc. On that same day Forrest ordered his brother Jeffrey's brigade toward Okolona to determine the enemy's exact location and strength. From Pontotoc southward, Sooy Smith's troubles increased tenfold due to the thousands of contrabands (slaves) who had fallen in with his column for safety, bringing with them their wagons, horses, mules, possessions, and booty that had been looted from the surrounding plantations.

As he drove his men south that day, Smith described the country through which he passed as the "rough, hopeless, God-forsaken land of Tippah County Mississippi. . . . Its hills were steep," his lament continued, "mud was deep, its houses and farms were poor, its streams, torrents of bottomless muddy water, fast swelling from the thaw." Perhaps his sense of dread, exacerbated by Sherman's warnings about Forrest, was reflected in his description of the landscape through which he passed.

Col. George E. Waring was covering the same ground as was his commanding officer, but he wrote about the countryside in a much more positive manner. On February 19, Waring used other words to describe the same landscape Smith had found "God-forsaken." To Waring the landscape was the "marvelous prairie region of Northeastern Mississippi, an interminable, fertile, rolling prairie before us in every direction."[53]

While Smith and Waring gauged the countryside and dealt with the unexpected increase to the size of their column, Forrest continued to move his command to the southeast, ahead of Sooy Smith's troops. He arrived at Starkville, Mississippi, on February 18 and made temporary camp. There he awaited developments and word from General Chalmers and his brother Jeffrey, who were in the vicinity southwest of West Point, reconnoitering near Ellis's Bridge over the Sakatonchee River. General Forrest had purposely left this one bridge intact should his own command need it in a sudden move northward. It was also an enticing crossing for Smith's column, standing as bait for the trap that Chalmers and Col. Jeffrey Forrest were preparing for him.

Though traveling slower than Sherman wanted, the Federal wrecking crews under Smith had not only destroyed fifty-five miles of the Mobile and Ohio Railroad, but anything else in their path. Sherman's orders to Smith were to "destroy [Confederate] communication from Okolona to Meridian and thence eastward to Selma" and to take the "abundance for forage collected along the railroad, and the . . . standing corn in the fields . . . as well as horses, mules, cattle, etc. As a rule," Sherman reminded him, "respect dwellings and families . . . but mills, barns, sheds, stables and such like things use for the benefit and convenience of your command."[54]

Had these orders been carried out to the limits requested there would have been very little left standing, yet Smith's passing left in his wake a scene of devastation far exceeding his orders. The runaway slaves following the column lost control and began a rampage of arson and pillaging that quickly drew in a large number of the Union troopers. Smith's efforts to regain control generally went unheeded, as did Sherman's call for the respect of homes and private property of Confederate families along the way. Colonel Waring's report of the carnage painted a colorful but terrible picture of the scene. "For two days," wrote Waring, "the sky was red with the flame of the burning corn and cotton, all the way down to West Point." The contrabands, "driven wild with the infection, set the torch to mansion houses, stables, cotton gin and quarters. . . . They came en masse to join our column, leaving only fire and absolute destruction behind them."

Smith eventually had to take drastic action. On the eighteenth he issued orders to shoot any man caught participating in this "incendiarism of the most shocking kind." A shaken Smith wrote to Grierson, "I have ordered the first man shot, and I have offered a $500 reward for his detection."[55] Even so, the riotous behavior increased.

Smith perhaps regretted what had happened, but he continued

to move. There had been so much burning that as his troops proceeded, the Federal line of march was marked by smoke in the daylight and by the glow of fire at night.[56]

On the next day, February 19, Smith met light resistance as he approached the Houlka River at Pontotoc. The opposition came from Brig. Gen. Samuel J. Gholson's state guard of six hundred men "whom we met," Smith reported, "and drove pell-mell across the swamp."[57]

Proceeding deeper into Forrest territory, Smith became more and more anxious about when and where he would finally meet the famous Confederate cavalryman. His anxiety was reinforced by the alarming and exaggerated reports he was receiving concerning Forrest's strength. The Union general had heard a report from a trooper of the Seventh Indiana Cavalry who had been briefly held prisoner of war by General Chalmers' command that Forrest was concentrated at West Point with almost nine thousand men. Believing the report to be true, Smith veered off toward Prairie Station and the night of the nineteenth made camp approximately fifteen miles north of West Point.[58]

By this time, Sherman had not been informed of Smith's whereabouts for several days and was growing more agitated. On February 20, he abandoned his plan to march on toward Selma and Mobile. "It will be a novel thing in warfare," he wrote, "if infantry must wait on the motions of cavalry." Chagrined, Sherman began to march his troops back to Vicksburg. The return to Vicksburg presaged his later march across Georgia, as his army "made a swath of desolation fifty miles broad across the state of Mississippi which the current generation will not forget."[59]

Without firing a shot, Forrest had accomplished the first part of his objective. Sherman was withdrawing and Smith was unwittingly being drawn farther and farther from his home base and closer to the meeting with Forrest that he dreaded. Forrest's allies in defeating the enemy's grand strategy were the weather and the nearly impassable roads that slowed Smith and sapped the strength of his men.

Smith's troops had broken camp in the early-morning darkness of Sunday, February 20, and were moving cautiously toward West Point. The Yankees were unaware that Jeffrey Forrest's brigade had made a hard forty-five-mile ride and arrived at West Point ahead of them. Around 2:00 A.M. Smith's and Forrest's men collided a mile or so north of West Point. A two-hour firefight ensued, with Colonel Forrest's brigade slowly falling back through West Point and toward Ellis's Bridge over the Sakatonchee River, held by General Chalmers' division. When Jeffrey's brigade reached the bridge, he drew into line of battle on the north side of the Sakatonchee, with McCulloch's brigade in place on the south bank. The trap was now set.[60]

Approaching the river, Smith recognized the geographic advantage the Confederates held and realized that he was moving into a three-sided box. To his front (south) was the Oktibbeha Creek, to his left (east) was Aberdeen Creek, to his right (west) was the Sakatonchee River. In between was a pocket of swampy bottoms that left little room for maneuvering a cumbersome command of seventy-five hundred troops, not to mention the three thousand camp followers and over ten thousand animals he was burdened by. He was more than ten days late for his rendezvous with Sherman and calculated, correctly as it turned out, that his commanding officer had already departed Meridian. Smith was alone.

To put the best face on it, Smith reported that he had driven Jeffrey Forrest's men back several miles after a "short, sharp fight." Rationalizing that he had done all the damage he could under the circumstances, Smith chose the better part of valor and decided that he had better extricate his army while he still could, rather than keep up the pursuit.

In a subsequent report he continued to make his case by pointing out that he had been receiving constant reports of Forrest's strength and that Lee was about to reinforce him. Furthermore, he wrote,

> All the state troops that could be assembled from every quarter were drawn together at my front to hold the Oktibbeha against me, while a heavy force was seen moving to my rear. . . . Under the circumstances, I determined not to move my encumbered command into the trap set for me by the rebels."[61]

Smith then retired to his tent, telling his adjutant that he was very sick and not to be disturbed.

Late that night of the twentieth, Bedford Forrest was closing on the crossing at Ellis's Bridge. He knew his forces were still scattered across a wide area and that he would probably have to engage the enemy with a force less than half the size of Smith's. The prospect was a daunting one, but for Forrest it was routine.

On Sunday morning, the twenty-first, Smith prepared to pull his force back. He ordered Maj. Datus E. Coon and the Second Iowa Cavalry southward to engage and hold the Southernes at the Sakatonchee River while the main body of the column, including the freed slaves, wagons, and animals, pulled out and headed back the way they had come.

General Chalmers had prepared for the Union attack by redeploying his troops along the southern bank of the Sakatonchee. Jeffrey Forrest was on the north side of the creek, bracing for the enemy assault by throwing up breastworks of logs and railroad ties. At 7:30 A.M., Major Coon made his move and the battle began.[62]

A few miles east of Ellis's Bridge, Bedford engaged and captured a Federal raiding party of around thirty men. He could hear the sound of the gunfire coming from the river where the battle had begun. At around 8:00 A.M., Forrest arrived on the scene in what General Chalmers described as "a cloud of dust." Chalmers was sitting on his horse when Forrest charged up and demanded to know the situation. Chalmers had never been with Forrest in combat and was not prepared for the transformation about to come over him.

To Chalmers it seemed that Forrest was "very much more excited than I thought was necessary under the circumstances," and he asked in "rather a harsh, quick tone . . . what the condition of affairs was at the front." Chalmers "replied that Colonel Forrest had reported nothing to me beyond the fact that there was some skirmishing." Bedford appeared "nervous, impatient and imperious," and said, "Is that all you know? Then I'll go there and find out for myself."[63]

With Chalmers following, Forrest galloped off over the bridge and through what Chalmers referred to as "pretty thick" gunfire. At that moment a terrified Confederate trooper, minus hat, gun, and anything else that might slow down his full sprint for the rear, came tearing by. Chalmers later wrote,

> As he [the trooper] approached General Forrest, the latter checked up his horse, dismounted quickly, threw the bridle reins to the orderly . . . and rushing at the demoralized soldier, seized him by the collar, threw him down, dragged him to the side of the road and, picking up a piece of brush that was convenient, proceeded to give him one of the worst thrashings I have ever seen a human being get.

When the beating ceased, Forrest turned the unfortunate man loose and shouted, "Now, God damn you, go back to the front and fight, you might as well be killed there as here, for if you ever run away again you will not get off so easy." Chalmers added, "The poor fellow marched back and took his place in line, a wiser if not braver soldier."[64]

In the months to come this incident took on a life of its own, told with great humor throughout Forrest's command. Eventually it reached the ears of a Northern newspaperman who produced a woodcut illustration to accompany the *Harper's Weekly* article titled "Forrest Breaking in a Conscript."[65]

The person who inspired that illustration was, for good and bad, a man of excess. Many knew of Forrest by his reputation alone. However, Chalmers and hundreds of men new to Forrest's army were about to learn it from personal experience. J. P. Young, the Seventh Tennessee Cavalry's historian, wrote of the positive aspect of Forrest's battle fever. "This was the first fighting under their new commander, Forrest," he wrote, "and his immediate presence seemed to inspire every one with his terrible energy, more like that of a piece of powerful steam machinery than of a human being."[66]

His anger over the escaping trooper now diminished, Forrest turned his attention to the larger battle. A dangerous and detailed reconnaissance of the front convinced Forrest that he was facing a rear-guard action meant to allow Smith's main column to escape. Near midmorning, Forrest ordered Chalmers to send forward two thousand of his best cavalrymen and James L. Hoole's battery of mountain howitzers for, he said, "I think they are badly scared."

For the pursuit, Forrest himself rapidly gathered W. W. Falkner's regiment of Kentuckians, John Morton's flying battery, and one regiment from "Black Bob" McCulloch's brigade. "It was not my intention to attack them or bring on a general engagement, but to develop their strength, position and movements," Forrest later wrote. But when he "found the enemy had begun a systematic retreat . . . being unwilling they should leave the country without a fight, [I] ordered the advance of my column."[67]

Three different Confederate columns shadowed Smith's retreat. Col. Tyree Bell's brigade had jut crossed the Tombigbee and was on the east, moving parallel to Smith's main force. Chalmers was on the west and blocked any attempt by Smith to cross the Sakatonchee. Forrest's group was right behind the fleeing opponent and the only force close enough to actually close and engage the Federals. Col. George E. Waring commanded one of the Union brigades and was beginning to feel the pressure. When "Forrest saw that his time had come," he later wrote, "he pressed us sorely all day and until nightfall."[68]

By the time darkness fell, Forrest had already forced his adversaries to turn several times to put up a brief fight. The Confederate commander later reported, "They made several stands, but . . . we continued to charge and drive them on, killing and wounding fifteen or twenty of them and capturing a number of prisoners."[69]

Four miles north of West Point the Federals made their strongest stand of the day, taking up a position in a clump of oak trees located strategically across a narrow pathway. Forrest ordered a portion of his much smaller force to dismount and attack from the front as infantry, while two other flying detachments swept around to hit the enemy "on the end." In this fashion he dislodged the Federals and chased them to within fourteen miles of Okolona, where near tragedy struck. In the confusion of a night attack, the rebels fired on one another, almost killing their general in the same way that Stonewall Jackson had been mortally wounded at Chancellorsville the year before. In this case the bullet ripped through Bedford's clothing, nearly ending the history of Forrest's cavalry.[70]

Some time after midnight the Confederates gratefully made camp in one of the Union's abandoned campsites, where the fires still burned, some with coffee brewing over the flames. By 4:00 A.M. on the twenty-second, after less than three and half hours' sleep, Forrest had his men back on their horses, and the pursuit resumed. Though he had had only two hours' sleep in the prior forty-eight hours, Bedford was alert and energetic, every bit the "piece of powerful steam machinery" J. P. Young called him. As on numerous other battlefields he could not rest until the fight was finished and the enemy destroyed or driven out of northern Mississippi.

Smith had marched on until 2:00 A.M. that morning and had camped a few miles south of Okolona. His men barely had time to close their eyes before Forrest was upon them, forcing them again to pull back. Two hours before first light Forrest's men were closing, following the trail of the retreating Yankees northward by the debris and equipment strewn in their wake.

In the gray early-morning light of February 22, Forrest sent his brother's brigade to the left on a route parallel to his own and leading to Okolona. Colonel Forrest was to follow his route to where it intersected with the Pontotoc road and deploy his brigade across the road to block Smith should he veer off in that direction.

A short time later, just after Smith's main force had retreated through Okolona and out the north side of the town, contact was made with the Union's rear guard. Col. C. R. Barteau's Second Tennessee Cavalrymen had been camped farther north when the pursuit began that day, allowing them to reach the Union line about forty-five minutes before Forrest arrived. Barteau's men, along with a brigade from Bell's regiment, began preparations to engage Smith's main force. Although Colonel Barteau was ridiculously outnumbered, he boldly deployed his twelve hundred men into a line of battle. General Grierson, commanding the Federals' rear guard, seemed to be bluffed by the audacity of Barteau's demonstration and momentarily hesitated. That moment of hesitation was just enough to allow the initiative to slip away.

As the two sides faced each other, Forrest suddenly burst upon the scene with his escort company. A rousing cheer rang out up and down the line when the troops saw Forrest gallop to the front of their formation, his hat raised in recognition of their cheers. Bedford realized that he was isolated on an open plain, facing an enemy of overwhelming numbers. Should Greirson have chosen that moment to throw an all-out attack at the Confederates, the thin rebel line might have been overrun easily.

Living by the maxim "He who hesitates is lost," Forrest rode up alongside Colonel Barteau and asked, "Where is the enemy's whole position?" Barteau replied, "You see it, General, and they are preparing to charge." Forrest's answer was characteristic. "Then we will charge them."[71]

Forrest instinctively sensed the value of the offensive, even when the situation seemed to dictate otherwise. This instinct had been nurtured while growing up in the backwoods of Tennessee and honed to a razor's edge in dozens of battles since the war began. Gen. Gideon Pillow, speaking at Forrest's funeral in 1877, spoke of a similar incident at Fort Donelson early in the war. When threatened by a heavy force of enemy cavalry, Forrest had asked permission to charge them first. "We can't hold them," he had said, "but we can run over them."[72]

Forrest now looked across the open field at the superior force preparing to attack him. He placed himself at the front of the Second Tennessee Cavalry, stood in his stirrups, and bellowed, "Charge!" His men immediately responded and the line of Confederates thundered across the black prairie toward the Federals, who sought cover behind a rail fence. Behind the fence, Grierson's boys opened a deadly volley from their breech-loading rifles, momentarily checking the Confederate assault. In response, Forrest ordered Russell, Wilson, and Newsome to dismount their men and threw them forward up the middle. At the same time, shouting, "Come on boys!", he led the Second Tennessee in a galloping sweep around Grierson's left flank to "hit 'em on the end."

Black Bob McCulloch's brigade of Texans and Missourians arrived at this moment and joined in the push. When the Confederate Second Tennessee Cavalry reached Grierson's flank, they were met there by the Union Second Tennessee Cavalry. The two like-named regiments slammed into one another, and the Second Tennessee dressed in blue soon gave way and began to fall back. This started a chain reaction of panic that quickly spread into pandemonium.

The Fourth Regulars began to give way as the Second Tennessee Cavalry began its retreat. Grierson's after-action report explained that the two regiments, "being about to be outflanked, were forced to retire in haste upon the column." The retreating Federals then ran through the position held by the Third Tennessee Cavalry, who joined the flood northward. Grierson reported that all three regiments became "entirely disorganized by being mixed up."

The fleeing Northern soldiers found their escape hampered by more cavalry. Lt. I. W. Curtis of the First Illinois Artillery Battery later wrote, "We had not proceeded very far when we were unexpectedly surprised by the presence of flying cavalry on both sides of us. They [the Union troops] were in perfect confusion; some hallooing, 'Go ahead, or we will be killed.'"[73]

The Southern cavalry came on quickly, forcing the Federals to give up several cannon before they were overrun. In an attempt to salvage something from the humiliating rout, the Union gunners hurriedly spiked some of the cannon—which Forrest disdainfully referred to as "Smith's pop guns" in his report—and "cut out the horses and abandoned five pieces of artillery and gaining the hilly country on the Pontotoc road their resistance became more stubborn."[74]

That resistance took place some five miles northwest of Okolona, high up on a ridge of scrub oak and heavy brushwood. Colonel Waring reported that he had "immediately formed my brigade in line and remained in this position until the 3rd Brigade passed through, portions of it in such confusion as to endanger the morale of my whole command." To maintain the last vestige of cohesion among his men, Waring also began to fall back to a ridge about a mile away on a plantation called Ivey's Hill.

From atop Ivey's Hill, Colonel Waring witnessed an appalling sight as the horde of soldiers and contrabands, or liberated slaves, flooded his way. Waring reported that he watched "other brigades retiring." He could also see that "the immense train of pack-mules and mounted contrabands, which had been corralled in a field near the road, swarmed up with such force as to carry past the line of the 2nd New Jersey and the 2nd Illinois Cavalry, which were then marching to this position."[75]

When the wave of retreating soldiers and contrabands had passed through, several other partial brigades came up with the Second New Jersey and the Second Illinois Cavalry and formed up with Smith and Waring. Once in place, those of Smith's command still rallying to their officers took up a position adjacent to an old gin house and other empty farm buildings. They immediately threw out flankers, unlimbered the gun batteries, and double-timed skirmishers forward to form two lines of defense. Colonel Waring reported that no sooner had these troop movements been completed than the "Confederates soon attacked us with heavy musketry fire, which was replied to with good effect by the battery of the 4th Missouri Cavalry."[76]

A force of Union troops made up primarily of Waring's First Brigade, Maj. Francis Hepburn's Second Brigade, and a battery of artillery from the Fourth Missouri held Ivey's Hill. In order to effectively contest the control of the hill, Robert McCulloch and Jeffrey Forrest had been ordered to bring their brigades up the Pontotoc road and relieve the Second Tennessee, which had been fighting hard, both mounted and on foot, for nearly ten hours. There was also exhaustion among McCulloch's and Colonel Forrest's men, and though their mounts were "somewhat broken down" from their own exertions, they were itching to get into the fight. General Forrest ordered his brother's regiment to the left and McCulloch's boys to the right of the Pontotoc road and once in position, to charge the Federals. It was the last order the general would ever give his younger brother.

Charging forward, up the rising ground toward Ivey's Hill, came Colonel Forrest's and McCulloch's men. Artillery explosions heaved the ground and heavy musketry fire emptied many saddles as the Confederate charge broke through the first line of resistance. Unrelenting, the rebels spurred their horses to within fifty yards of the second Federal line, which suddenly crackled with the flame of a deadly volley from Waring's riflemen. Several horses and riders came crashing to the ground. One of them was Jeffrey Forrest.

Riding at the head of his brigade, Colonel Forrest was shot through the throat and died moments later. Colonel McCulloch was hit in the hand. Bedford saw his younger and, some said, favorite brother go down and rushed to the scene. Dismounting, he ran to his brother's side, calling out his name over and over. Experiencing new and rare emotions, General Forrest dropped to his knees and held Jeffrey's head in his arms, unable to hold death back as it overtook his brother.

The entire forward movement hesitated and then came to a halt. The Confederate troopers, shaken by the loss of their colonel and the pathetic sight of his brother's obvious grief, momentarily stopped fighting. The lull in the battle continued for almost ten minutes. Finally, as Colonel Russell later remembered the scene, Forrest slowly "rose up" from his kneeling position with tears in his eyes and his brother's blood on his hands. Somehow, Russell said, the general was able to push "aside those reflections which had unmanned him for a few moments, [and] by a strong mental effort," signaled for Maj. J. P. Strange "to take charge of the body."[77]

Bedford bent down and placed "the dead man's hat over his face." Casting a wild eye on the enemy position, he "called out in a ringing, passionate voice to the bugler to sound the charge once more."[78] As the bugle sounded, General Forrest ordered Col. W. L. Duckworth to take command of Jeffrey's brigade and to sweep around the enemy's left flank. Forrest would lead his escort up the gut in a frontal assault. Before the last note from Sgt. Jacob Gaus's bullet-marked bugle had died away, Forrest and his escort brigade were gone.

Major Strange, standing next to Colonel Forrest's body, was extremely worried about Bedford's mental state. He was concerned that Forrest was hell-bent on a suicide mission and called out to J. B. Cowan, "Doctor, hurry after the general; I am afraid he will be killed."[79] Doctor Cowan immediately responded. Putting spurs to horse he raced off after the escort to provide whatever assistance he could.

At that moment Sooy Smith attempted a countercharge with the Fourth Missouri Cavalry, but they were no match for what was coming at them. Forrest was single minded in his grief and anger, and the three hundred men charging with him were set on vengeance. On this day Forrest truly was the devil, and demons rode with him. They ripped into the Fourth Missouri, riding right over and through them. The Union charge was shattered and swept aside.

About a mile farther west the Federals attempted to reform. Only a hundred or so Confederates had been able to keep up with Forrest; still they drove a wedge in the partially formed Federal line where a vicious hand-to-hand fight raged. Sabers rang as steel clashed against steel. In a cloud of gun smoke and dust, muzzle flashes erupted, blinking like countless fireflies at dusk.

Riding hard to catch up with Forrest, Doctor Cowan reached the new battleground shortly after the melee had begun. He later recalled the shocking sight that met him:

In about a mile, as I rounded a short turn in the road, I came upon a scene that made my blood run cold. There in the middle of the road was General Forrest with his escort, and a few of the advanced-guard of the Forrest Brigade, in a hand-to-hand fight . . . with Federals close enough . . . to have pulled them form their horses.[80]

Forrest and about one hundred of his men were surrounded by more than five hundred Federal cavalry and infantrymen, and fighting for their lives.

Suddenly, McCulloch's brigade reached the site of the desperate battle. Stunned by the fierce scene before them and the large number of enemy troops in the road, they hesitated. Black Bob McCulloch realized the danger to their comrades and rode his horse to the front of his formation, waving the bloody bandage over his head that had covered the wound he received earlier. "My God men," he shouted above the tumult of battle, "will you see them kill your general? I will go to the rescue if not a man follows me!"

McCulloch's Missourians and Texans split the air with the rebel battle cry and surged forward to save their general. Duckworth's dismounted brigade, advancing by the right of the road, also came up about this time and helped to drive the Federals back. By the time these soldiers crashed against the Sixth and Ninth Illinois, Forrest had already killed at least three Yankee troopers with his saber and pistols.[81] Also killed during the attack was Col. James A. Barksdale. Leading the Fifth Mississippi, he was cut down as he crested the hill, but he continued to urge his men forward until his last breath.

As the sun was setting on that terrible day of battle, Smith's men retreated to their fifth and final line of defense, about ten miles from Pontotoc. Smith still hoped he could save his wagon train and the liberated slaves. He had already lost five cannons and an undetermined number of men and horses, and though he didn't realize it, his army was still more than twice the size of the command that Forrest led. In a last effort, Smith threw out a heavy battle formation three lines deep and waited for the Confederates to arrive. He did not have long to wait.

The Confederates approached the new Federal position, where Forrest found Smith "formed up in three lines across a large field on the left of the road, but which a turn in the road made . . . directly in our front. Their lines were at intervals of several hundred paces, and the rear and second lines longer than the first."[82] As soon as the horsemen came within range, the Union gunners opened up. Forrest reported that "ammunition was nearly exhausted, and I knew that if we faltered they would in turn become the attacking party, and that disaster might follow."[83] Forrest understood by the enemy's disposition that the artillery barrage was only a softening-up tactic for the massive cavalry charge that was coming. However, at that moment, there was little he could do about it. He had with him only the troops of the Seventh Tennessee Cavalry and his escort brigade, too few to attempt a preemptive strike. Besides, they were in an exposed position.

Dr. Cowan, riding alongside Forrest, urged his commander to take cover from the exploding shells and reminded him that they were within range of the enemy's carbines. Forrest replied contemptuously, "Doctor, if you are alarmed, you may get out of the way; I am as safe here as there."[84] No sooner had he spoken those words to Major Cowan than fate seemed to give him a nudge. Forrest's horse was quickly riddled with five minie balls. On the way down three more rounds struck the poor animal, shattering Bedford's saddle rig. Amazingly uninjured, Forrest pulled himself from under the dead horse and called for a new mount, supplied by Pvt. J. B. Long from Forrest's escort company.

Forrest realized the extreme danger of his exposed position and quickly ordered his command into a shallow ravine at the edge of the field, where he threw his men into a thin line of battle and prepared for the Union assault. As he sat his second horse of the day, giving orders, this animal was killed under him. He then called for King Phillip, his twelve-year-old gelding. A few moments later, King Phillip took a bullet in the neck, but the wound was not fatal. The old warhorse not only survived this wound, but the war as well.

While his men deployed in front of the huge Federal cavalry corps, Forrest and Cowan spotted a woman and her small children attempting to hide from the carnage behind a log cabin. Noticing a deep hole nearby that had been dug in the clay to build a chimney, Forrest hollered for Cowan to get the woman and children into the depression, where there was better refuge. "In there," Forrest told Dr. Cowan, "they will be perfectly safe."[85]

Forrest rode fast to return to his men and arrived just as Smith's cavalry prepared to charge forward in what Bedford would later describe as the "grandest cavalry charge I have ever witnessed." It must have been an amazing sight from a distance. There, exposed in an open meadow, stood Forrest's 350 men before the approaching blue wave of approximately 2,000 mounted horsemen. William Witherspoon remembered of the charge:

We opened ranks to extend across the field. As the line was formed, Forrest rode into the field, in our rear, saying to us, "I think they are going to charge you, boys, hold this line for me." He passed on down the line, repeating it. . . . Now, when you charged that line, it was not one Forrest you were contending with, but every man in that line was a Forrest.[86]

After the war, in 1910, Witherspoon, a sergeant in the Seventh Tennessee Cavalry, published several accounts of his experiences with the Second Tennessee under Forrest's command. At a meeting of the Confederate Veterans in Louisville, Kentucky, in the lobby of the Galt House, Witherspoon recounted a conversation he had with General Lyon and an unnamed Union lieutenant colonel from the Seventh Illinois Cavalry. This officer had specific knowledge concerning the Federal charges at Okolona on February 22, because he had been a participant.

As Witherspoon and Lyon discussed that day, the ex-Federal lieutenant colonel joined the conversation:

> I was in those charges. You did resist and more than repulse, you came near annihilating us and night, blessed night, too, the only thing that saved us. Your version gives the strength of the 7th Tennessee about 350 men. Now, what perplexes me is how 350 men in an open field, dismounted, could do what they did. We brought against you in the first charge, mounted, 1000 men, you drove us back. We then reinforced to 1,200, charged the second time, with the same result, driven back, after getting as we did in the first charge in about seventy-five yards of your line. We reinforced to 1500 strong, and at the sound of the bugle charge we went at you, with a full determination to win, but met with the same repulse. Not only a repulse, but an almost annihilation.[87]

It was a brave band of men who withstood three separate and successively larger charges, but at this point in the war the Union cavalry had not learned an important lesson: using the saber as a primary weapon in the cavalry charge was traditional, but not effective. Witherspoon then explained to the ex-Union officer why he believed Forrest's small force was able to withstand and drive back Sooy Smith's massive cavalry assault.

"You said, Colonel, you had fought Forrest frequently, and I suppose a good many of the men in that charge had done so. Now did you ever whip Forrest in any of those engagements?"

He replied, "No."

"Was it not that Forrest decidedly got the best of you?"

"I think so," he admitted.

Witherspoon's explanation was beginning to sound like a lecture. He continued:

> You were forming your line in the edge of the woods bordering the field. You made a formidable appearance, mounted, with your charges well reined and sabers drawn, you looked fearful and to raw troops would have been so, but it had no effect on the seasoned veterans before you, we had "seen the monkey before." At the sound of the bugle you dashed forward, holding your horse with the left hand and saber grasped by the right. . . . When you were near enough for our rifles to do good work we commenced pumping lead, some of you were firing occasionally, but the greater part of you were intent on holding that rein and saber. As you got within seventy-five yards we dropped our carbines (which were strung by a strap across the shoulder) drew the navy sixes one in each hand, then we fed you on lead so furious and fast you whirled with your backs to us. Then it was again with the carbine until you got back into the woods and we saw you were forming again. "Well boys, we whipped the first charge, and we can whip the next," was the universal remark with us.[88]

Witherspoon said that they all knew a heavier charge was coming, but every soldier in that line was intent on "making good the pledge we gave Forrest."

> You came on us the second time as you did the first. At one time we had sabers, but had discarded them as a fighting weapon, useless, except in the hands of the officers. In your second charge you got within the same distance as the first (seventy-five yards). When the navy sixes began their music you whirled.[89]

Then the Federals formed up fifteen hundred men for their third and largest assault. This time the Union horsemen would breech the Confederate line, and the combat would become a brutal hand-to-hand affair in which Forrest accounted for several confirmed kills. During the brawl, Maj. Thomas S. Tate of Forrest's staff ran out of ammunition and in desperation threw his carbine at a Federal officer who was about to shoot him. At that moment, Forrest charged up "and with a sweep of his saber, nearly severed the Federal officer's head from his shoulders. The man toppled to the ground, and as he did so, Tate, taking the revolver from his hand, swung himself into the vacated saddle."[90]

Witherspoon's remembrance of the third and last assault continued:

> Just before you charged the third time we had crossed a deep gully,
> a wash through the field. As you rode upon us, you cried out,
> "Surrender! Surrender!" Now, Colonel, how many of us paid any
> attention to that demand. Not one. It was a word not in Forrest's
> vocabulary or in his manual of arms. . . . As you rode through us
> the firing with no let up, but more furious and terrible, than ever
> before, and espying that gully in your front, you were forced to
> come back through our line or yourselves to do the surrendering.[91]

At this moment in the battle, Lieutenant Colonel McCulloch's
Second Missouri arrived and poured on flanking fire "coupled with
our volleys in your backs. That, as you say was not only a repulse but
an annihilation, and night, good night, is all that saved you."

Witherspoon, the old Confederate veteran, could not keep his
Southern pride from surfacing and twisted the knife a bit in closing the
conversation. "Reverse the forces," he said to his former Union friend,
"with 1000 of Forrest's riders mounted charging 350 dismounted men
on open ground. It would have been like a cyclone ridding a farmer's
field of his wheat shocks." Witherspoon added, "Forrest would have
whipped Smith the next day anyhow if he failed in holding that line.
At the time Smith was on the run and badly discomfited."[92]

Forrest's stand at Pontotoc was as gallant and tenacious as any ever
made by an inferior force in the face of seemingly suicidal odds, and it
broke the back of Smith's resistance. Smith's army retreated over the
horizon with the setting sun. It was as Witherspoon said all those years
later: the coming of night saved Smith's army from annihilation. That
and the fact that Forrest's command was almost out of ammunition.

Sometime after dark, Gholson's Mississippi brigade arrived and
was ordered to "keep up the 'skeer'" and pursue Smith's column the
rest of the night. Smith's scattered and demoralized troops
recrossed the Tallahatchie River on the twenty-third and stumbled
back into Memphis on February 26.

The speed at which they abandoned the field is illustrated by an
incident following the battle. Before making camp that night,
Forrest and some men from his escort company happened upon
a group of log cabins. A hospital flag fluttered above one particular cabin, which had been a Union field hospital. From within
came the horrific wailing of a man in agony. Forrest went inside
and discovered a poor soldier abandoned by the Union surgeons.
They had fled in such haste and confusion that they had left a sur-
gical saw embedded in the bone of the man's leg, the amputation

half-finished. The nightmarish scene matched the fury of the battle.

The bloodlust of battle had drained away and compassion now filled Forrest. He called for Dr. Cowan to come forward and complete the surgery. Acting as surgeon's assistant, Bedford "saturated a cloth with chloroform and applied it to the nostrils of the sufferer."[93]

As might be expected, Smith, now safely away from Forrest's terrorizing horsemen, submitted a somewhat whitewashed report to his superiors. In his version of the battle, he wrote that his command retired, "fighting for over 60 miles day and night, and had the fighting all our way except for Okolona."[94]

Colonel Waring was closer to the mark when he stated, "The retreat to Memphis was a weary, disheartened, almost panic-stricken flight, in the greatest disorder and confusion, through a most difficult country. . . . The expedition filled every man connected with it with burning shame. It gave Forrest the most glorious achievement of his career."[95]

In Memphis, General Hurlbut was pained to admit that Smith's defeat and subsequent ragged withdrawal had "demoralized the cavalry very seriously." Grant was more sympathetic, but mistaken, when he noted that Smith was most definitely badly beaten, but "Forrest's command possessed twice as many men as did Smith's [and were] not equal man to man, for the lack of a successful experience such as Forrest's men have had."[96] Of course, the exact opposite was true. Sooy Smith's expeditionary force numbered seventy-five hundred troops. Forrest never had more than three thousand men at Okolona, and the Confederates, all but a few hundred veterans, were raw recruits or seeing combat for the first time. Sherman believed he very well understood why his planned campaign launched from Meridian deep into Alabama had been wrecked. Sherman could not excuse Smith's allowing Forrest's inferior force to whip him and was blunt and unforgiving concerning the general's failure.

The stunning victory at Okolona notwithstanding, Forrest was not satisfied with his accomplishments between December 1863 and February 1864. He knew that had he received any support from his superiors, he could have brought twice as many men out of west Tennessee. To his mind there was still plenty of unfinished business left in that theater of operations. For the next three weeks, Forrest would rest and reorganize his command. Amazingly he was ready to march again in March 1864. Recruiting and outfitting as he went, he would make another savage thrust into western Kentucky and Tennessee, terrorizing or capturing nearly all the Union fortifications on the Tennessee River above Memphis.

# Chapter Ten

# NO BEAST SO FIERCE

*—William Shakespeare*

## Fort Pillow
## February-April 1864

Some forty miles north of Memphis, near the summit of the bluffs above the Mississippi River, stands Fort Pillow, the object of the most controversial military action Forrest and his men ever undertook. The Fort Pillow "incident," as it has become known, was a confusing riot of incompetence and arrogance, revenge and loyalty, stupidity and military acumen. The infamy of Fort Pillow has been seared into the subconscious memory of generations of Americans and continues to blight Forrest's standing as a military genius to this day. The search for the enigma that is Nathan Bedford Forrest inevitably leads to those same haunted bluffs upon which stood Fort Pillow.

The easy question: was there needless killing at Fort Pillow? There was. The difficult questions may never be put to rest. The one constant in such an investigation of controversial behavior on the battlefield is that armed conflict clouds judgment and loosens, even makes useless, the rules of civilized society.

When all the pieces of the Fort Pillow incident are separated and examined, it seems in retrospect that the tragic outcome could virtually have been predicted. Circumstances, personalities, and the fortunes of war all combined to create an explosive combination that ignited along that short stretch of the Mississippi River on April 12, 1864. However, on that particular day, the vicissitudes of fate had combined to set the fuse so precariously that a dreadful conflagration was inevitable. More than enough volatile elements were present in the situation at Fort Pillow, and each was added like kindling wood as the minutes of that day ticked away. Could Forrest, or anyone, have seen the ultimate outcome ahead of time?

As the campaign got underway days before the battle at Fort Pillow, certainly such a tragic conclusion would not have been foreseen.

In less than three years of war, Forrest had accomplished feats unparalleled in American military history. In 1864 he would surpass his earlier achievements and burn his name into its pages as one of the best cavalry commanders who ever lived. As the year began, however, Forrest found himself in a familiar position: commanding a small, lightly supplied, under-equipped, and poorly armed force in dire need of weapons, ammunition, fresh, reliable mounts, and as many recruits as he could raise. Once again he was practically on his own.

With less than three hundred men and only two pieces of artillery, he set off to raise his new command from behind enemy lines. Forrest's small force began to move from Jackson toward western Tennessee and northward into Kentucky to obtain the men and supplies he needed, and by March he had raised two thousand volunteers who were operating in several separate groups along the Kentucky border, scouring the countryside for more recruits and supplies as they moved toward Paducah.

The first major contact between Forrest's men and the enemy came on March 24 at Union City, in the northwest corner of Tennessee. Colonel Duckworth, leading a force of less than three hundred men, came upon a larger force of five hundred Union troops commanded by Col. Isaac Hawkins. This was the same Hawkins who had surrendered to Forrest on another occasion fifteen months earlier.[1] It is unclear whether Duckworth specifically recalled the earlier surrender and expected lightning to strike twice. Nevertheless he concocted a ruse worthy of the Wizard, and using the spell of Forrest's name, Duckworth, whose own command was about half the enemy's size, called upon the Yankees to surrender or be put to the sword if they forced him to prove his superiority. Hawkins showed a touch of suspicion and asked to meet personally with Forrest, whom he knew from the earlier incident, to discuss the matter. In Forrest's name, Duckworth carried his own message in reply, saying that Forrest would not treat with an officer of inferior rank to his own. Duckworth's message authorized him, a colonel, to treat for Forrest and "arrange terms and conditions with you under instructions."[2]

Hawkins, having apparently learned little in his earlier encounter with Forrest, rejected the counsel of his junior officers to the contrary and surrendered his entire garrison without firing a shot, a decision that might have seemed to Hawkins somewhat mitigated by a seemingly impossible pledge of help sent just hours earlier from

Brig. Gen. Mason Brayman. Brayman's message promised that reinforcements were being sent by train from Columbus, but the railway bridge between Columbus and Union City had been burned by Duckworth as a precautionary measure, and Hawkins was persuaded that since the relief train could not reach his garrison, resistance would cost many lives. The troop-carrying train was just six miles away when at 11:00 A.M., Hawkins gave the order to surrender, turning over five hundred prisoners and around three hundred horses to Duckworth.[3]

Word of Duckworth's economical victory spread quickly, and soon Hawkins' infamy was common knowledge among other Union officers and men. There were those, no doubt, who resolved not to be so easily hoodwinked should they meet Forrest under similar circumstances.

Farther north, Forrest led part of his command against Paducah, Kentucky, on the Ohio River, arriving there in the early afternoon of March 25. Paducah held a garrison of some 675 Union troops, 274 of whom were African-American soldiers, commanded by Col. Stephen G. Hicks. As the Confederates attacked, the Union defenders held their ground within the earthworks of Fort Anderson, on the western edge of Paducah, near the river. This was the first time Forrest's men had faced black troops.[4]

Expecting reinforcements within a short time from nearby gunboats and transports on the river, Colonel Hicks refused to give up when Forrest issued his customary demand for surrender. Hicks continued to fight, and his black troops reportedly gave a good account of themselves in the process. Forrest's tactic of calling for surrender and threatening no quarter if denied had worked in the past, but in spurning the surrender terms this time, Hicks may have created a future backlash that, taken together with Hawkins' surrender to Duckworth, would require Forrest to prove his words when rejected again.

Several days later Hicks reported another incident that would be repeated in the growing Forrest lore and foreshadow events surrounding the coming fall of Fort Pillow. During the surrender negotiations, Hicks said, Forrest raised a flag of truce; but before a message of refusal had been transmitted to the Confederate commander, and while the truce flag was still flying, Forrest moved troops into a strategic location and began preparing an artillery battery for action.[5] Hicks retold this part of the battle on several occasions in the coming months, suggesting that Forrest's resituating his troops while a flag of truce was flying was something less than honorable.

Though Colonel Hicks held firm at Fort Anderson, the town of Paducah fell temporarily into Confederate hands and was subsequently shelled mercilessly by guns from the fort and from the Union gunboats on the Ohio. Forrest later said he could have held the town against the shelling, "but when he found small-pox raging throughout Paducah he evacuated the area."[6] Reports of the battle for Paducah that appeared in pro-Union newspapers naturally presented a slanted account of what happened. Such reports made it appear, to the chagrin of the Confederates involved, that they had been ignominiously driven from the town. Forrest's battle report and the soldiers' own version describe the events differently, portraying an orderly withdrawal with large amounts of what they had come for: horses and supplies.

From Paducah, Forrest's men pushed southward toward Memphis, devastating the railway as they proceeded. As he and his various units marched and rode from the northwest corner of Tennessee southward, they would twice experience refusals to surrender similar to that of Hicks at Fort Anderson. Forrest was unaccustomed to such rebuffs, having become an expert in the use of psychological warfare. He may have been coming to the realization that sooner or later he would be forced to deliver the "consequences" he threatened if his surrender demands continued to be refused.

Forrest was also quickly coming to the conclusion that Sherman's and Grant's movements indicated some major Union strategy. Across western Tennessee, Forrest could rely on a network of scouts, spies, and citizens to make him aware of Union movements. From the reports he was receiving, it is clear that he was not entirely unaware that Grant and Sherman were attempting to keep him busy. He had sensed since perhaps as early as mid-March that something significant seemed to be afoot and that the Union commanders had major plans in the works. Sherman, in fact, seems to have concluded that Forrest had indeed presaged the wider implications of their strategy. "The whole object of Forrest's movements," Sherman wrote from Nashville, "is to prevent the concentration going on here as against Georgia."

> Except for a few posts on the rivers, Forrest held the interior of western Tennessee and Kentucky, which gave him the opportunity to observe everything passing up and down the waterways. He soon sensed the nature and purpose of what he saw. Almost a month before Grant and Sherman began to put forward their grand strategy of a coordinated Union advance in both East and West, Forrest perceived that such a plan was afoot. Though he was far removed from the focus of the war that both Southern

and Northern leaders seemed to believe was in the East, Forrest intuitively suggested what historian Robert Henry called the "one plan" that could have halted and defeated the new Northern grand design.[7]

Having surmised the Union plan, Forrest wrote to Joseph E. Johnston, who was commanding the Confederate force at Chattanooga and awaiting Sherman's march into Georgia:

> Everything available is being concentrated against General [Robert E.] Lee [in Virginia] and yourself. Am also of the opinion that if the cavalry of this and your own department would be moved against Nashville that the enemy's communications could be utterly broken up.[8]

Johnston's reaction to this communication is unknown. For whatever reason he disregarded Forrest's suggestion; the requested reinforcements were not sent, leaving Forrest to continue his campaign as an isolated, regional commander. Johnston was also left to face the gathering might of Sherman's army, which shortly would be unleashed against him.

Not only had Forrest's vision of the meaning of Union activity in Tennessee been accurate, but Sherman had correctly surmised the danger Forrest posed to his grand design against Johnston and Georgia. He ordered that Forrest be hunted down and brought to ground. Ordering Brig. Gen. B. H. Grierson of Illinois to "follow and attack Forrest, no matter what the odds," makes it clear that Sherman considered Forrest an immediate threat and intended to have him eliminated. At the same time he instructed Gen. James Veatch to "hurry up the Tennessee [River] and strike inland to intercept Forrest" near Purdy, Tennessee.[9] Sherman continued issuing orders to various commanders, all of whom had the intention of harassing and putting Forrest out of action in western Tennessee. By steamboat he even sent downriver from Nashville an envoy led by Brig. Gen. John M. Crouse to deliver special instructions to each Union commander along the way as to what his part would be in the planned operation against Forrest.

In the days to come, Sherman alternated between glee and frustration as each plan came to naught. The primary source of those frustrations was Forrest himself. While Sherman, Grierson, and the other Union commanders focused on their strategy, Forrest and his commanders concentrated on the tactics that continued to make them so successful.

On April 5, recognizing that Hurlbut's estimated ten thousand men posed a serious threat from Memphis, Forrest ordered Chalmers to send Colonel Neely's brigade to "demonstrate" toward Memphis in an effort to convince Hurlbut that an attack there was imminent, thus holding Hurlbut's command in place while Forrest continued his own campaign. The move had the desired effect. The one significant attempt by the Yankees to move against the Confederates on April 7 succumbed faintheartedly to erroneous reports that Forrest was advancing in force. Hurlbut fell back to Memphis and prepared to burn his stores and public buildings as his troops retreated "concentrically" from the Confederate assault he expected.[10]

In another action, a unit of Grierson's cavalry led by Col. George E. Waring was halted by about 150 Confederates under the command of Lt. Col. J. M. Crews. Crews prudently fell back in the face of Waring's superior force, but using typical Forrest tactics, he deployed his men in such a manner as to convince Waring that he was being led into a trap by a Confederate force vastly greater in numbers than his own. When Grierson joined Waring, he accepted his subordinate's assessment and continued the retreat, reporting that they had been "repulsed and driven back." There is truth in this report, for Grierson's 2,200 men had been repulsed and driven back, but by only 60 of Crews' men.[11]

Thus did Forrest manage to hold the Union troops in place as he developed his own plan to harass Sherman's troops and keep the pressure from building against Johnston in Chattanooga. And by April 10, Forrest was ready to move on a Union outpost on the Mississippi River that had been on his mind for some time. He had written to Gen. Leonidas Polk on April 4, "There is a Federal force of five or six hundred at Fort Pillow, which I shall attend to in a day or so."[12]

Not only was Fort Pillow strategically located as a military objective, but also there is reason to believe that there was a broader dimension to Forrest's intentions to attend to the garrison there. Fort Pillow had been reoccupied some weeks earlier by troops of the Thirteenth Tennessee Cavalry (Union), made up of Unionist volunteers from Tennessee. These Tennessee Yankees were commanded by Maj. William F. Bradford, a lawyer from Forrest's own home county of Bedford. General Hurlbut, at Memphis, had operational command of the troops at Fort Pillow and expressed some doubt about Bradford's leadership qualities, describing Bradford as "a very young officer, entirely inexperienced in these matters."[13]

In addition to being "inexperienced," Bradford had built for himself an ignoble reputation among the folk of Bedford County, and his joining the Union army only magnified his negative prewar standing. That he led a battalion of Tennesseans was bad enough, but many of his men were reputed to be deserters from the Confederate army as well. The others were considered malcontents who harbored a hatred for Confederate soldiers and their civilian families and friends.

There was ample reason for Forrest to be interested in Fort Pillow and its garrison—part of it, at least. Ever since arriving in the Jackson area, he had been hearing reports of depredations committed by the Union troops at Fort Pillow upon the civilian population in that vicinity of west Tennessee.

> Under the pretense of scouring the country for arms and "rebel soldiers," Bradford and his subalterns had traversed the surrounding country with detachments, robbing the people of their horses, mules, beef cattle, beds, plate, wearing apparel, money, and every possible movable article of value, besides venting upon the wives and daughters of Southern soldiers the most opprobrious and obscene epithets, with more than one extreme outrage upon the persons of these victims of their hate and lust.[14]

Many of the victims of Bradford's men were family members of the soldiers under Forrest's command. These relatives joined a delegation of civilians from Jackson and the area round about who were so concerned for their safety that they asked Forrest to leave a brigade of his troops to protect them from Fort Pillow's soldiers, whom they considered no better than outlaws.

To loyal Southerners, their neighbors in Federal uniform were considered traitors and were often referred to as "homemade Yankees." The fact that a battalion of these troops held Fort Pillow was enough to engender deep-seated feelings of hostility, but Hurlbut's next move rendered the situation practically incendiary.

On March 28, General Hurlbut acted on his concern for Bradford's inexperience by sending reinforcements, all of them black troops, except for their officers, who were white. The Confederate leaders at Richmond had railed against the recruiting of former slaves by the Union army, and individual Southerners had no love at all for those who dared leave their labors to take up arms against their former masters.

Commanding these new arrivals was Maj. L. F. Booth, who, with time in grade over Bradford, would assume command of the fort. Bradford's failings would be tempered by the firm hand of a senior officer of greater experience, or so it seemed. Hurlbut must have breathed easier to entrust the fort to "an old soldier who had served in the regular army."

The reinforcements brought into Fort Pillow by Major Booth consisted of the First Battalion, Sixth U.S. Heavy Artillery, with eight commissioned officers and 213 men, and one section of Company D, Second U.S. Light Artillery, which consisted of one commissioned officer and 40 men. Added to Bradford's 295 white troops of the First Battalion, Thirteenth Tennessee Cavalry, the total number of troops at Fort Pillow came to 557. According to reports, there were at least ten additional white civilians who would join in the defense of the Union positions.[15] Major Booth probably thought that his force was sufficient for the assigned task, as he had told Hurlbut that he could hold the post "against any force for forty-eight hours."

In addition to the force of nearly six hundred men, Booth had a substantial backup in the form of several gunboats moving up and down the Mississippi just below his position. On some of these boats were several hundred Union troops who could be landed to reinforce Booth should he need help. Later testimony in hearings concerning the battle for Fort Pillow suggests that this was part of a plan agreed upon in advance by Major Booth and Capt. James Marshall, of the gunboat *New Era*. Another part of the plan called for the gunboats to mount a rescue in the event the fort could not be held.

Never one to be content with half measures, Forrest determined to move against the offending Federal garrison at Fort Pillow rather than post a brigade to protect the civilians of the area. His soldiers would be only too willing to support their commander's determination and, no doubt, resolutely looked forward to participating in the coming attack on the fort.

On April 10, Forrest sent orders from his headquarters at Jackson for Tyree Bell and Robert McCulloch to march their brigades toward Fort Pillow. Watson's artillery battery was also assigned as part of the operation. This combined force of about fifteen hundred men was to be under the direct command of General Chalmers.

Bell and McCulloch began their march almost immediately. A drizzling rain fell during most of their march, requiring the men to deal with muddy roads that made their movements all the more exhausting. Though they proceeded by different routes, Bell being some twenty miles farther from Fort Pillow than McCulloch's brigade, they arrived about the same time before sunrise on the morning of Tuesday, April 12.[16]

Southern troops had constructed Fort Pillow some forty miles north of Memphis on strategic bluffs overlooking the Mississippi River. The original area of the fort covered about three hundred acres, with a distended crescent of outer earthen works, each end of which was anchored at the bluffs. Two shorter lines of works stood farther inside the outer fortification along with corrals, storage shacks, and cabins used as barracks for the garrison. The last, and smaller of these earthen works, was built with the open side of its semicircle facing the Mississippi from the bluff upon which it stood. This position, standing several hundred yards beyond the outer works, was most easily defended by a small force, such as that commanded by Major Booth.

The entire fort had been designed as an important link in the Confederate river defense system, but it had been abandoned in June 1862 under bombardment of a Union gunboat flotilla moving down the Mississippi following the fall of Forts Donelson and Henry to the northeast. Union troops occupied the site and held it for about eighteen months before temporarily abandoning it themselves. It was the oversight of leaving the fort undefended that the Union had sought to correct by sending in Bradford and Booth to reoccupy its sturdy earthworks.[17]

By first light on April 12, Chalmers' force was well inside the first and second lines of outer works and had killed or captured most of the pickets. At least one of them, however, managed to escape in order to warn the garrison within the last line of earthworks that Confederate troops were nearby.

Intending to strike before the warning led to an effective defense, Chalmers quickly moved his men forward to take advantage of the terrain leading to the Union redoubt. He placed sharpshooters upon several knolls about four hundred yards from the works. This high ground overlooked a deep ravine that ran in front of the Union position and curved back toward the river on the north side of the fort. From their positions the sharpshooters had a clear field of fire into the fort, which would prove critical during the maneuvers leading to and including the storming of the Union ramparts.

For now, the sharpshooters sent an unerring hail of bullets into the fort every time a target presented itself. During this stage of the battle, at about 9:00 A.M., Major Booth was shot dead along with his adjutant, who was standing beside him, leaving the unsteady Major Bradford in command.[18]

A short distance in front of the last line of earthworks was a group of rough cabins that were used for storage and as barracks by some of the defenders. As Chalmers' men quickly occupied the first line of trenches, Bradford sent a Union detail out to burn the cabins in order to prevent their use as cover by the attacking Confederates. What happened at this point is the subject of some disagreement. Observers from both sides reported that the Union detachment came under heavy fire and was forced to withdraw. Lt. Mack J. Leaming, the fort's adjutant who wrote the primary Union account of the battle, verifies this.

> The barracks had previously been ordered to be destroyed, but after severe loss on our part in the attempt to execute the order our men were compelled to retire without accomplishing the desired end, save only to the row nearest to the fort. From these barracks the enemy kept up a murderous fire on our men despite all our efforts to dislodge him. Owing to the close proximity of these buildings to the fort, and to the fact that they were on considerably lower ground, our artillery could not be sufficiently depressed to destroy them or even render them untenable for the enemy.[19]

Other reports state, as did Leaming's, that the first line of barracks were set afire by this detail of defenders, with some dead and wounded Union troops perhaps still inside.

Forrest arrived with his troops about 10:00 A.M. and assumed command from Chalmers. He immediately began his customary personal reconnaissance of the battlefield, which took about an hour and took him completely around the horseshoe-shaped parapets. For most of the ride he was under fire from Union soldiers who, rising to aim their weapons from the protection of the earthen walls, risked being shot themselves by the Confederate riflemen on the knolls across the ravine.

Near the end of his reconnaissance, Forrest's horse reared as it was hit by a Yankee bullet and crashed to the ground with Forrest aboard. Although injured, he ignored the pain and immediately mounted a second horse, which was also shot and killed, taking its rider to the ground again. Within minutes he had mounted a third horse; it too was shot, but unlike its predecessors, it survived. Forrest was more seriously injured than he let on, though he did not seek aid until the preliminary work for the assault on the fort was completed.[20]

His examination of the ground finished, Forrest detached three hundred additional sharpshooters to join those Chalmers had already placed on the strategic knolls in front of the fort. Noting the ravine that ran across the front of the earthworks, Forrest recognized it as an additional and critical asset in assaulting the fort. If the ravine could be taken, it would provide shelter for his force as they prepared to attack the ramparts. Under fire from the sharpshooters on the knolls beyond the fort, the defenders would not be able to depress their guns to fire into the ravine without risking certain death, nor would the defending riflemen dare to rise above the parapets to fire down upon the Confederate soldiers below.

Forrest planned to send eight hundred men under McCulloch to invest the ravine from the south, while another eight hundred under Colonel Bell were to attack simultaneously and take the ravine to the north end of the fort. When the order was given, they moved rapidly in short rushes. In the process, McCulloch's men drove the Union defenders from the rifle pits in the immediate vicinity and took the remaining barracks before they could be burned.[21]

Once the ravine was taken, it provided relative safety from the guns of the fort just above the Southern soldiers, and a brief lull set in. Forrest took advantage of this respite and went to the rear to receive treatment for the injuries he earlier had sustained when his horses had been shot from under him. This absence from the field at the critical moments of the battle might have affected the outcome, though once the final assault began and his men had gone over the walls, Forrest took only twenty minutes to reach the scene.

The gunboats in the river did not play a significant role until late in the morning, when *New Era* began shelling the Confederates in an attempt to drive them out of the ravine. The bombardment continued until about 1:00 P.M., when the gunboat commander decided his cannonade was ineffective and ceased firing.[22] From this point, Fort Pillow was doomed. The steamboats on the river, whose smoke could be seen for miles, provided only a false sense of hope for the Union defenders. The Union troops were now isolated and even *New Era*, which of all the gunboats had offered any support, would be of no further assistance. Booth, had he still been alive, might have recognized this fact and taken actions that would have prevented the tragedy that would shortly occur.

Forrest's adjutant, Maj. Charles W. Anderson, was in a position to see the truth of the matter. In his report of the battle he wrote,

> As far as safety was concerned, we were as well fortified as they were; the only difference was that they were on one side and we were on the other of the same fortification. They had no sharp-shooters with which to annoy our main force, while ours sent a score of bullets at every head that appeared above the walls. . . .
> It was perfectly apparent to any man endowed with the smallest

amount of common sense that to all intents and purposes the fort was ours.[23]

Not only did the Union gunboat stop firing, but the Confederates' shooting also died down as their ammunition began to run low. The ordnance wagons carrying additional ammunition and other supplies had been slowed by the muddy roads and did not reach Fort Pillow until about 3:00 P.M. With their arrival, Forrest was ready to launch the final assault with every confidence of success.

In spite of the reputation, whether deserved or not, that preceded Forrest, his custom before attacking was to call for the unconditional surrender of the enemy "to prevent a further effusion of blood." Sometime after the supply wagons reached his lines, Forrest sent Capt. Walter A. Goodman, Chalmers' adjutant general, under a flag of truce to deliver his written terms of unconditional surrender. He addressed this communication to Major Booth, not knowing that the Union officer had been killed earlier in the day.

Major Bradford, now in command, chose to keep this information from Forrest for reasons that are not entirely clear and signed his messages to Forrest in Major Booth's name. Perhaps he believed that this information might prove advantageous to Forrest in some way, or he might have been concerned that the Confederates, already angry because of the depredations of Bradford's troops in the vicinity of Fort Pillow, might be further enraged to learn that he was now in command. Jordan and Pryor, writing as partisans for the Southern cause, refer to Bradford as the "feeble handed" commander of the "odious" Tennessee Tennessee Battalion.

Forrest's call for the surrender of the garrison featured familiar language. To Major Booth he wrote:

Major L.F. Booth
Commanding U.S. Forces at Fort Pillow

Major: your gallant defense of Fort Pillow has entitled you to the treatment of brave men. I now demand the unconditional surrender of your forces, at the same time assuring you that you will be treated as prisoners of war. I have received a new supply of ammunition and can take your works by assault, and if compelled to do so you must take the consequences.

N.B. Forrest
Major General
Commanding Confederate Cavalry[24]

Major Bradford, in Booth's name, responded to the demand and ordered Lt. Mack J. Leaming to deliver the reply to Goodman.

> Major General N.B. Forrest
> Commanding Confederate Cavalry
>
> General: Yours of this instant received, and in reply I have to ask for one hour for consultations with my officers and the officers of the gunboat.
>
> L.F. Booth Major, Commanding U.S. Forces

Forrest apparently read this to mean that the Union commander had misunderstood his original communication and thought that he was also calling on the gunboat to surrender. At the same time Forrest could no doubt see the gunboat maneuvering in the river below the fort and suspected that the fort's commander was stalling for time in order to receive reinforcements. Thus, Forrest's reply to Bradford read:

> I do not demand the surrender of the gunboats; twenty minutes will be given you to take your men outside the fort and surrender. If in that time this demand is not complied with I will immediately proceed to assault your works, and you must take the consequences.[25]

Upon consultation with his officers Bradford made a very foolhardy decision. In his reply to Forrest's last message he said, "General; I will not surrender."

The temporary cease-fire provided by the surrender negotiations gave the Union soldiers their first opportunity to safely raise their heads above the parapets since the Confederate sharpshooters had begun raking their positions early in the morning. Many of the Yankees began to taunt the rebels who were awaiting orders to assault the fort. Perhaps the Confederates wondered what had so emboldened men who, in their view, were about to be caught in the full fury of an assault by such overwhelming numbers that they would be unable to withstand it.

The method the Union commanders had used to encourage such bravery in their men was, for the moment, unknown to the Confederates, but no matter. It was fools' courage at best. Though disputed in other accounts, Major Bradford was said to have placed open barrels of beer and ale (some reports say the barrels were filled with whiskey) at strategic locations around the inside of the walls, with several dippers for drinking hanging from each barrel. In this manner it was hoped that the Union troops would become too inebriated to feel fear. Unfortunately, they might also have become so inebriated that they could not summon up a supply of good judgment as well. Colonels Tyree Bell and Robert McCulloch mention this circumstance in their reports.[26]

During the exchange of messages in the surrender negotiations, Forrest was informed of the movements of the Union gunboats, particularly those of *New Era*. Forrest was convinced that the Yankees were stalling for time so that the gunboats could come to their aid, and with an anxious eye on the river, he ordered two detachments of men to the foot of the bluff to repel any attempted landing of reinforcements from the gunboats. Major Anderson was to take two hundred men from McCulloch's brigade, move down the ravine on the south side, and occupy the rifle pits on the beach by the river, while Col. C. R. Barteau took two hundred men from the north side for the same purpose. This left some twelve hundred troops waiting in the ravine to make up the assaulting force.[27]

As Anderson and his men arrived at the river, they saw the troop-laden Union gunboat *Olive Branch* nosing toward the east bank near where they were taking up positions. Understandably surmising that the purpose was to land reinforcements while a flag of truce flew within site of both the fort and the river, Anderson opened a warning fire on the pilothouse of the boat. *Olive Branch* immediately sheered off toward the opposite bank and proceeded upriver.

The controversy that has continued to haunt Forrest's actions at Fort Pillow began with this movement of men to the beach while surrender negotiations proceeded atop the bluff. Time and again the accusation has been made that Forrest unchivalrously and illegally moved troops to a "more advantageous" position while holding the Union defenders idle in peace talks. But the question has also been asked: since the flag of truce was flying in plain sight, should not the actions of the gunboats be considered both illegal and provocative as well?

It appears that the movement of Anderson's and Barteau's men was not only legal under the circumstances of the troop-carrying boats maneuvering in the river, but also prudent in the deliberations of any competent military commander. The maneuver was made in plain view of both armies, yet it was said that these detachments were moved into a more advantageous position in order to attack the fort once a signal was given. In reality, they moved themselves away from the fort some two to three hundred yards down to the beach. These two detachments did not participate in the storming of the fort. In fact, they did not come into action until after the fort fell and the defenders retreated between the enfilading fire of the two groups of Confederate riflemen.

Lieutenant Leaming complained after the battle of several breaches of protocol and civilized warfare that he says Forrest committed at Fort Pillow. He seemed to read hidden malice in Forrest's words to surrender or "take the consequences." In a letter to the *New York Times* in 1867, Leaming expressed his interpretation of Forrest's terms. He seemed to believe that the words "take the consequences" carried an additional, unexpressed threat to expect no quarter, regardless of the actions of the Union commander of the fort.

If Bradford refused to surrender, what would be the obvious consequences should the rebels be forced to storm the works? People were going to die. Forrest called on the defenders to avoid that by surrendering. Those surrendering would be "treated as prisoners of war" with every ensuing privilege and consideration being guaranteed. It seems simple enough, but it was known to Bradford and others that Forrest had often bluffed commanders into surrendering to his smaller forces on other occasions. Though, as Anderson wrote, "any man endowed with . . . common sense" would have realized that the fort was lost, Bradford either did not believe Forrest, or he was not "endowed with common sense" and chose not to submit to the Confederates.

The smoke from the stacks of the Union transports on the river may also have bolstered Bradford's misplaced bravado and perhaps he believed that he could hold the fort in spite of visual evidence to the contrary. In any case, Bradford said that he did not want to be remembered as another Isaac Hawkins, a reference to the Colonel Hawkins who had just days before surrendered at Union City to a bluff dramatically carried out by Colonel Duckworth.

Forrest now may have believed he had little choice but to order the assault. The stage was set. After the rebuffs at Paducah and on the recent march to Jackson, Forrest could not have his bluff called once again; otherwise, all such subsequent demands could be ineffective. Forrest obviously preferred the fruits of psychological warfare, but he was a realist and understood that one must carry out a threat from time to time.[28]

Sgt. William Hancock heard him say, "We must take them."

Chalmers rode with Forrest to a rise some four hundred yards beyond the fort from which they had a clear view of the terrain leading to the fort's walls. The time limit had expired, and having received

Bradford's reply that he would not surrender, Forrest sent runners to the commanders who would lead the assault. The messages encouraged a spirit of competition among the Missourians, Mississippians, Texans, and Tennesseans who surrounded the fort and informed them that Forrest would "watch with interest the conduct of the troops . . . and I desire to see who would first scale the fort."[29]

Giving the order for the sharpshooters to lay down a suppressing fire across the parapets, Forrest told Sgt. Jacob Gaus to blow the charge. At the sound of the bugle, twelve hundred men charged forward and into the ditch at the base of the fort. The first men to hit the ditch offered their bodies as footholds to boost the following wave up and over the parapets. At this point the rebels were receiving virtually no casualties due to the supporting fire from the sharpshooters, who now resumed raking the ramparts with a storm of lead.

Some one thousand men crested the earthworks "as if rising from the very earth," wrote Leaming, and fired their pistols and carbines point-blank into the defenders. The fighting became brutal as the two sides closed almost immediately with each other. A frenzied hand-to-hand fight ensued that turned the small enclosure inside the walls into an abattoir as the Union losses quickly mounted. The struggle was so close that men who were shot often collapsed upon the soldier who shot them. Both sides harbored a hatred for each other that made this fight more than just two enemy armies engaged in combat. This was personal, and one can only guess how many defenders lost their lives in the first minutes of the assault.[30]

As the fierce fighting continued inside the fort, several Confederate officers and men noticed the large barrels of spirituous drink strategically placed around the fort, with dippers for drinking still attached to their rims. These were kicked over by prudent Confederate officers who did not want the spirits to fall into the hands of their own men.

Bradford, whose judgment had been so impaired as to think he could hold the fort against a force three times the size of his own, now seemed to be touched with a sense of panic. Within minutes of the assault, Pvt. John Kennedy, a member of the Second U.S. Colored Light Artillery, heard Major Bradford shout, "Boys, save your lives." This invitation to a rout was not shared by all the Union defenders. According to Private Kennedy, Lt. Peter Bischoff of the Sixth Heavy Artillery replied to Bradford, "Do not let the men leave their pieces; let us fight yet." Bradford now saw the futility of trying to save the fort and answered, "It is of no use any more."[31]

Black troops gave a good account of themselves in the initial clash, though they were accused in Leaming's later writings of being the first to retreat. Other accounts said that the white troops were the first to flee. Whether initiated by black or white, or whether at Bradford's command or in response to the awful rush of the attackers, the defenders broke and ran in all directions. They were funneled into the only exit available. Down the bluff and toward the riverbank they stampeded. The rebels who had breeched the walls were fast upon them, shooting them down at every step. The defenders were being driven straight into a waiting crossfire on the beach.

There seemed to be no thought of surrender among them as the retreating Union soldiers ran down the bluff to the south, where they came under heavy, close-range fire from Anderson's detachment. The survivors turned north, firing as they ran, but were stopped by a withering volley from Barteau's men, waiting at the mouth of the Coal Creek ravine. A nightmarish scene ensued as the doomed defenders sought refuge from the sixteen hundred or so small arms firing into them from both flanks and from the force pursuing them from behind, which had minutes before swept over the walls of the fort.

There was one chance: to make their way to the river in the hope of being rescued by the gunboats. Captain Marshall, *New Era*'s commander, said later, "We had agreed on a signal that if he [Booth] had to leave the fort, they would drop down under the bank, and I was to give the rebels canister."[32] Whether or not the fleeing bluecoats had all been given to understand this arrangement, it seems clear that they expected help from one or more of the Union vessels in the river and were determined to reach the water, where they could be reinforced or evacuated.

Apparently, surrender was not their intent, nor did the Confederates seem to believe that what was happening signified surrender. The Federal flag still flew above the fort and could be plainly seen by Captain Marshall from the pilothouse of his gunboat and by the Confederates on the beach. The presence of the flag, still waving from its tall staff, should have been a clear signal to all that the fight was still on.

Though this must have been apparent to Captain Marshall as well, he probably also recognized the peril presented to his boat by the desperate struggle going on along the river's edge. He had reason to choose the better part of valor and turned his boat upriver without giving "the rebels canister" as previously agreed. With him went the final hope of rescue for the Union defenders of Fort Pillow.

No single account can accurately portray the confusion that

reigned in the final desperate minutes of the struggle. Caches of ammunition had been laid down earlier under the bluff by the Union commanders so that they could be readily used if needed in a last-ditch fight for survival. Several boxes of ammunition, the tops removed, were found below the bluff following the battle. Some of the Union soldiers made for these hidden caches, obviously intending to continue the fight. In the midst of this chaos, some Federal soldiers tossed their weapons aside and tried to surrender. Within minutes some of these took up arms again and continued to fight.[33]

Bradford had lost control. He was no longer capable of calling upon his men to surrender, and he did not. There was no controlling Union authority that could, or would, put an end to the slaughter. In the absence of such command, it was every man for himself.

Frustrated, angered, driven in some cases by hate, the Confederates perhaps felt themselves in the same situation. Where one Union soldier was surrendering, the man next to him was not. Many, mostly black soldiers, were shot in the act of surrendering or after having thrown down their arms. However, these actions of capitulation were spontaneous and individual, and were not in themselves an indication that a general surrender was being offered. Both sides only knew that the battle still raged.

The fighting was often vicious, hand-to-hand, with men on both sides using their weapons as clubs. Scores of men locked in individual combat were in scattered pockets up and down the beach, while others attempted to surrender and were shown no mercy. Several accounts told of Federals surrendering and then running off, finding a weapon, and resuming the fight. This did not help the fate of those who were legitimately laying down their arms. In some cases black and white Union soldiers were chased off into the woods by small groups of rebels. One can only guess what may have happened to them.

Twenty minutes into the battle the Federal flag came down. Forrest and Chalmers rushed into the melee, ordering their men to cease firing. Bringing an end to the carnage probably took several minutes more since the fighting was widespread and was most likely still in progress on the beach below when the cease-fire order was given. It has been suggested that Forrest was personally responsible for the large numbers of Union killed and wounded, but his and Chalmers' actions undoubtedly reduced the number of casualties. A Confederate soldier, Sgt. Samuel H. Caldwell, wrote his wife from Brownsville a few days later that Forrest had charged between the two sides, his sword and pistol drawn, and forced an end to the shooting. It was Caldwell's belief that this action not only ended the fighting, but also left little doubt that Forrest was trying to save lives, not encourage further bloodshed.[34]

Having stopped the fighting, Forrest seemed intent on securing the prisoners, gathering the captured arms, and realigning the cannon on the river to be used against any Union gunboats that might try to reenter the contest. Several witnesses on both sides attest to his actions during this period of activity. Only one incident was reported in which Forrest was personally aware of a Union soldier being shot after the cease-fire order, and the offending Confederate was immediately disarmed and put under arrest. It appears evident that the fighting ended on the orders of Forrest and Chalmers, and other Confederate officers carrying out their orders, but there never was a formal surrender of the fort by Major Bradford or any of his subordinates.

In the closing moments of the battle the fort surgeon, Dr. Charles Fitch, a Massachusetts native who had made his way to Iowa before the war, joined a Confederate soldier who was leading a horse back up the bluff toward the fort. Anxious for his safety, the doctor noticed a tall Confederate officer nearby sighting a captured artillery piece. When he inquired who the officer was, he was told that it was General Forrest himself. The doctor immediately approached Forrest for protection and identified himself as a surgeon and, therefore, a noncombatant. Forrest replied, "You are Surgeon of a Damn N—— Regiment." Dr Fitch, perhaps more than a little concerned for his life, answered that he was not. You are a Damn Tenn. Yankee then," said Forrest. When Dr. Fitch protested that he was from Iowa, as if Iowa were devoid of any offense, Forrest said to him, "What in hell are you down here for? I have a great mind to have you killed for being down here. . . . If the North west had staid [*sic*] home the war would have been over long ago." These words to Fitch seemed to have been intended as a lecture and not a direct threat on his life. The general then turned to a soldier and told him to take charge of Fitch and see that the surgeon was not harmed, for which Dr. Fitch thanked Forrest.[35]

A short time after Forrest passed on, some Confederate soldiers noticed Dr. Fitch and his fine riding boots. They were harassing Fitch as they tried to appropriate his boots when General Chalmers saw what was happening and rode to the rescue. He cursed the unruly soldiers and repeated Forrest's order to guard the doctor. Fitch stated that Chalmers told the guard to "shoot the first one that molested me."[36] The surgeon was having a difficult afternoon, as were others, but he survived under the approbation of the two Confederate commanders, who would be vilified by their detractors ever after as murderers.

Later in the afternoon, between 5:00 and 6:00 P.M., Dr. Fitch encountered Major Bradford near the river, as they were both being held with other prisoners taken during the day's fighting. When they met they shook hands, and having seen the high cost paid by the Union defenders in a fight that had been allowed to go on too long, Dr. Fitch asked Bradford why he had not surrendered earlier. Bradford, who seemed to have by then regained his composure, answered with some bravado, "I am no Hawkins." One wonders how this misplaced pride struck Dr. Fitch, especially considering the circumstances in which he and Bradford now found themselves. This brief conversation would be the last time the two would ever see each other. Fitch was released the next day after two Confederate surgeons who came to Fort Pillow to attend the wounded prisoners took Fitch with them to General Chalmers' headquarters and interceded on his behalf.[37]

Though charges were made that the killing of prisoners went on throughout the night and into the next day, there is testimony from both sides that the cease-fire ordered by Forrest and Chalmers held up. Within an hour of the cease-fire, unwounded Union prisoners were set to work under the supervision of their own officers, removing the wounded to the hospital, tents, and other buildings and burying the dead. As this was going on Maj. Anderson and a Union prisoner, Capt. John T. Young, went up and down the riverbank attempting to attract the attention of Captain Marshall aboard *New Era* by waving a white flag, by which they hoped to bring him ashore to take off the wounded.[38]

Marshall testified later that he ignored their pleas because he was fearful that "they might hail in a steamboat from below, capture her, put on 400 or 500 men, and come after me." Since the river traffic throughout the day had been dominated by Union vessels, it is unclear why he seriously considered such a possibility. Had Marshall come in, he could have ferried the wounded to Memphis within a short period of time so that they could have received proper medical attention. Since the gunboat captain seemed determined not to have anything to do with what was going on along the beach, the injured Federals were left to whatever assistance might be available on shore.

Forrest by now was suffering pain and discomfort from the injuries he had sustained when his wounded horses had crashed to the ground with him, and he prepared to leave the field and head back toward Jackson. Chalmers was to stay behind and clear the battlefield of arms and burn the remaining buildings except for the hospital and such other tents and buildings as might be needed to shelter the Union wounded. Forrest seemed to be especially mindful of these wounded enemy soldiers. In ordering that the hospital be spared he also reminded Chalmers to "leave with the wounded . . . slightly wounded men sufficient to wait on them . . . [and] five or six days' supply of provisions and any medicine they may need."[39]

Sometime before 6:00 P.M., Forrest headed toward Jackson, leaving Chalmers in charge of the field, but his injuries got the better of him, and he and his escort stopped and made camp for the night about three miles from the fort. But before Forrest departed the field Chalmers had already begun the burying process and the dispensing of medical supplies. It was during this time period, 5:00 to 7:00 P.M., that one of the later allegations arose suggesting that Union wounded had been buried alive. Though the Confederates oversaw the process, the burial details were made up of the Union prisoners. Some of the wounded who were unconscious (or playing dead, as in Lieutenant Leaming's case) may have been mistaken for dead. In any case, a few Union men miraculously resurrected from the dead as dirt was thrown upon them in their shallow graves. From this incident, perhaps, arose the rumors that the rebels had buried the living wounded along with the dead.[40]

Shortly after Forrest departed, and with darkness approaching, Chalmers gathered his command and also left the battlefield, camping for the night about two miles away. If, as Lieutenant Leaming later claimed, there was an all-night orgy of killing and bayoneting of the wounded and captured, it must have been done by "stragglers and prowlers" since the organized Confederate forces had withdrawn.[41] As for the stories of Union wounded and prisoners being killed by bayonet, it has been widely reported that Forrest's men rarely, if ever, carried or used bayonets.

About 6:00 A.M. the next morning Chalmers and his men returned on Forrest's orders to finish the job of seeing to the wounded, gathering arms, and destroying the remaining buildings. During this task, at approximately 8:00 A.M., the gunboats *Silver Cloud* and *Platt River* began to shell Chalmers' men. Expecting the gunboats to come ashore with reinforcements, Chalmers, in response, ordered the burning of buildings and tents and began to pull back. Soon after the bombardment began, and while some fires still burned,

Chalmers sent a flag of truce to the shore to signal for a cease-fire, intending to allow a small landing party to reconnoiter the battlefield under his supervision. According to testimony given later at the Congressional hearings in Cairo, Illinois, some Confederate officers were also invited aboard the *Platt River*, where they had drinks with Union officers.[42]

During the temporary truce, General Chalmers met Capt. John G. Woodruff of the 113th Illinois Infantry and several other Northern officers who had come ashore to inspect the field. As the group proceeded up the bluff and into the fort, Chalmers was asked about the condition of some of the bodies they observed, some of which Woodruff later reported were partially burned inside tents and buildings. He also described tattoo-like gunpowder burns around the head wounds of several corpses, indicating that they were shot at extremely close range. Perhaps noting the concerned suspicion displayed by the Union officers, Chalmers made a statement that included words later interpreted to damning effect in support of the massacre argument. Woodruff quoted Chalmers as saying, "They were not killed by Gen. Forrest or his orders. . . . Both Gen. Forrest and I stopped the *massacre* [emphasis added] as soon as we were able to do so." He added, "It was nothing better than we [the Union] could expect *as long as we persisted in arming the Negro* [emphasis added].[43]

After conducting the Union guests around Fort Pillow and turning over the wounded to them, Chalmers attended to his orders and began to remove the captured arms from the area. Had he known how the infamy of the battle would grow, he might have felt disposed to be more circumspect in his meeting with the Union officers, and in the comments he made to them.

In unhesitatingly offering to lead a tour of the battlefield, Chalmers would not seem to have had anything to hide. However, his own use of the word "massacre" would not help the Confederate position that no such event had taken place at Fort Pillow. Did Chalmers use the word deliberately, and was he thereby attempting to describe what he had observed during the battle? Whether this is what he intended or whether he had misspoken, there is no reason to believe Chalmers deliberately suggested that Fort Pillow had been a massacre site, as would later be charged in the Northern press and among military and political leaders.

"Massacre" is a word that conjures up wild visions of cold-blooded murder and deliberate atrocities against unresisting and unarmed individuals, and there is evidence that some soldiers did behave in that manner at Fort Pillow. Newspaper reports from both the North and the South carried reports throughout the war, most unfounded, of terrible acts and atrocities being committed by the other side. Yet, there were proven acts of barbarity committed on battlefields by soldiers of both the North and the South.

War, by its very nature, is a crime against humanity. On the battlefield savage deeds can be considered heroic or heinous, depending on the circumstances. Wearing its best face, war is a bloody, inhumane affair. Warfare inevitably produces events and actions that can, when reason is applied, be described as atrocities or even massacres. The battle at Fort Pillow has the dubious distinction of being labeled as both. A combat soldier's view of a battle is only a few feet wide. Commanders may see the sweep of battle, but the individual soldier knows and can testify only to what is happening immediately around him.

Word of the Fort Pillow "incident" spread like wildfire. The words "atrocity" and "massacre" immediately became synonymous with the battle and with the name of Forrest. Union leaders, from generals to the president of the United States, understandably demanded an investigation. Though Federal efforts to eliminate Forrest were renewed, in western Tennessee, Forrest was no stranger to Union forces, whom the Wizard had out-thought and outfought for months. The mention of his name had sent Union commanders into panic attacks as they took the psychological bait Forrest threw out, believing and reporting time and again that he had thousands more men than he actually commanded. There is a suspicion that part of this immediate rush to judgment was based in part on that reputation and that many Union leaders were quick to characterize Forrest as a man of whom such outrageous deeds could be expected.[44]

On April 22, 1864, with angry passions generated by the recent events at Fort Pillow running high, a Congressional committee convened at Cairo, Illinois. For several days investigators traveled down the Mississippi visiting sites connected with the battle and conducting interviews with as many as sixty-six persons. Seventeen of those were black soldiers and twenty-one were white soldiers. In addition one black and one white civilian, one white officer, and one surgeon were questioned. The rest of the witnesses interviewed consisted of six surgeons of the Mound City, Illinois, hospital and five army and navy officers of rank. Additional testimony was taken from five white soldiers and four civilians who were in the fort during the battle and four others who had been there the next day.[45]

After hearing the lengthy and often conflicting testimony of the witnesses, the committee concluded that a massacre did occur at

Fort Pillow. Many historians agree with that conclusion. Was Fort Pillow a massacre of defenseless individuals who were unresisting? The evidence indicates that in individual and widespread cases, some Union men who had ceased fighting were shot. But the battle below the bluffs of the fort resembled a riot more than it did a classic military operation.

Colonel Barteau's report, written before the incident became politicized, expanded on the same theme:

> They [the Union defenders] made a wild, crazy, scattering fight. They acted like a crowd of drunken men. They would at one moment yield and throw down their guns, and then would rush again to arms, seize their guns and renew the fire. If one squad was left as prisoners . . . it was soon discovered that they could not be trusted as having surrendered, for taking the first opportunity they would break loose again and engage in the contest. Some of our men were killed by negroes who had once surrendered.[46]

From this mass of evidence the Congressional committee produced five conclusions:

1. The Confederates, under a flag of truce, advanced their positions for the storming of the fort.

The reports and evidence on this count clearly demonstrate that the Confederates under Barteau and Anderson were dispatched to the river to repel any attempt by the Union transports to land. The Confederate detachments that were sent to the river did not position themselves in a more advantageous spot to assault the fort. On the contrary, they took themselves completely out of that action.

2. After the fall of the fort, the Confederates "commenced an indiscriminate slaughter of soldiers, civilians, women and children."

The testimony on this particular charge is voluminous, controversial, and contradictory. So much so, that any firm stance or definite opinion concerning the real truth is a stance taken on with only thin support. It is difficult to find testimony, interviews, newspaper articles, or opinions that are not tainted by partisan animosities. Much is condemnatory concerning the rebels' conduct, but there is an equal quantity of reports that were exonerating as well.

There were very few actions or battles involving Nathan Bedford Forrest that did not have controversy attached to them, but in the case of Fort Pillow, the evidence that a massacre was deliberately planned and carried out is inconclusive. After assimilating the reports, letters, articles, books, and memos written since 1864, it is possible to come to some conclusions that fly in the face of the massacre theory, though the myth lives on.

Northern newspapers reported conflicting numbers of Union soldiers killed at Fort Pillow. Some articles fanned the flames by claiming that all the African-American soldiers had been singled out for execution by the Confederate attackers and that even women and children had been slaughtered without distinction. Yet, taking more reliable reports at their word, it appears that there were well over three hundred Union survivors, and no bodies of women or children were ever officially reported being found among the fallen at Fort Pillow.[47]

The explanation for the absence of women and children among the dead is found in battle reports from before the investigation. Early in the morning, before the fort was almost entirely surrounded except for the river route, *New Era* took what was thought to be all the women and children upriver and put them ashore on an island. For some reason they left approximately forty black women and children behind, and these were taken prisoner after the battle and released.

As to the number of soldiers killed in the battle, both black and white, a true total is impossible because of the many varying accounts. For example, witnesses said that the Union troops surrendered but were shot down or bayoneted as rapidly as they gave up and that the slaughter went on past dark and into the morning. Union survivors said that most of the 262 African-American soldiers in the Sixth Heavy Artillery were killed, many of them as they were begging for mercy after surrendering. Three-quarters of the 557-man force, including white troops of the Thirteenth Tennessee Union Cavalry, were reportedly wiped out. Upon these kinds of numbers was the massacre charge built.

However, an exhaustive study of the reports and of the work of later scholars makes it possible to at least estimate more accurate figures. Approximately ten white male civilians chose to stay and defend the fort rather than depart with the women and children. Of those ten, eight survived. There were 557 defenders inside the fort at 3:30 P.M. when Bradford made the decision not to surrender. With all available statistics, at least 336, and as many as 350, men survived the failed Union defense of Fort Pillow. The mortality figures range from a low of 180 dead to a high of 225. These numbers reflect a 31 to 42 percent casualty rate. Such losses, and higher, were not uncommon in many other Civil War battles.[48]

Many of the battle reports as well as testimony given by those who were there concentrate on the havoc wreaked upon the defenders once they reached the beach at the edge of the Mississippi. Often not referred to, but certainly important in coming to a fair assessment of the charges, is the fact that many fleeing Union soldiers lost their lives in the panic-driven retreat from the earthen ramparts to the beach.

From nine o'clock in the morning until the fort fell at about four in the afternoon, the rebel sharpshooters killed several defenders, including Major Booth, the original Union commander. No one knows how many fell in this early stage of the assault, but the deadly accuracy of these sharpshooters is attested to in the reports of witnesses from both sides of the battle.

At 3:30 in the afternoon, when twelve hundred Confederate soldiers crested the parapets and fired their weapons at point-blank range into the defenders, logic dictates that the loss of life at this point must have been significant. The battle at that position was, by all accounts, a close and vicious hand-to-hand affair that, although lasting but minutes, accounted for significant numbers of dead and wounded.

Almost immediately the Union defenders began a wild stampede down the bank toward the river. Their escape route took them directly between the four hundred rifles of Anderson and Barteau, who had taken up positions in the rifle pits on the beach at the water's edge. The crossfire from these positions undoubtedly took an additional heavy toll. According to some reports, a considerable number who survived this gauntlet chose the muddy currents of the Mississippi over the carnage that was occurring on land. Many of these men were shot as they swam or else drowned attempting to swim out of harm's way. In a later speech to his troops Forrest stated, "The Mississippi was dyed red with the blood of the slaughtered for 200 yards." On more than one occasion during interviews after the war, Forrest used these same words to describe the scene at the beach.[49]

Some twenty minutes had passed since the sounding of the charge that commenced the final stage of the battle. The Union flag still flew over the fort, signifying to onlookers that those within the fort responsible for doing so had not formally surrendered. Once again, logic dictates that a high percentage of the casualties occurred before four o'clock, at which time the U.S. flag came down and Forrest ordered a cease-fire.

Finally, there was the ill-conceived emergency plan that called for a retreat and regrouping at the beach if the fort was lost. Caches of ammunition, and possibly weapons, had been placed in certain areas for such a contingency, along with the expectation of backup from *New Era*. Many Union men were killed who had surrendered and then rearmed themselves as they resumed the fight. The fight was chaotic, with pockets of men still engaged while others attempted to surrender. "Considering all the outrageous circumstances of this battle it would have been a strange and wonderful thing had there been no cases of individual crime in the closing positions of a fight which came to such a ragged, scattered and indefinite end."[50] Of course, the alcohol situation also may have aggravated the erratic resistance on the beach. However, the majority of historians who have commented on the Pillow situation believe the alcohol story was fabricated by the Confederates and played no significant role in the battle. Nevertheless, no serious historian can deny nor play down the fact that many men were killed after they had surrendered. The difficult question to answer is, how many and did Forrest order those killings?[51]

   3. The committee charged that not only was there a massacre, but
      it also had been deliberately planned by Forrest and unhesitat-
      ingly carried out by his men.

It seems incredible that Forrest would have planned a massacre in light of the fact that he called for the surrender of the garrison with the promise of their humane treatment as prisoners of war. A charge of deliberately ordering a massacre can only be considered if indeed a massacre had taken place; otherwise it is a moot point.

In considering the charges that he ordered a massacre of the Fort Pillow garrison, "one must look at Forrest's previous conduct and character in military matters. Known to be a man of integrity" there is no evidence that anything vaguely resembling the massacre of surrendering troops had ever been perpetrated upon Forrest's orders.[52] No evidence exists that Forrest planned to kill everyone in the Fort Pillow garrison. There is no record that he gave such orders or made any plans to exterminate these troops. He probably didn't have to. The circumstances surrounding the event seem to presage an inevitable disaster. Had a massacre been his desire, he would not have needed to issue any orders whatsoever; the nature of the beast would have taken care of the rest.

What was in Forrest's mind at the time will probably never be known. It seems pretty clear, however, that after the battle he wasn't feeling particularly remorseful about the losses on the Union side. In his battle report, filed three days after the fight, Forrest said, "This will demonstrate to the Northern people that Negro soldiers cannot cope with Southerners."[53] Despite the sensitive situation, Forrest may have been using psychological warfare again when he made that statement. He knew this would not be the last time he would meet black troops. The war was not over, and he possibly desired to "keep up the skeer" with respect to the threat of an army of former slaves. He most assuredly was not worried about a future political career.

If the psychological gambit was Forrest's plan, it temporarily backfired because Fort Pillow galvanized the black troops into vowing a war of no quarter should they ever again meet Forrest's men in battle. So bent on vengeance for their losses were the African-American troops in the Memphis area that they took an oath "on their knees" to pay the rebels back, and they validated that oath by sewing patches on their uniforms that carried the words, "Remember Fort Pillow."

4. It was alleged in the early charges that the Confederates had intentionally burned Union wounded in their tents and barracks.

The primary source of this charge seems to have arisen from the accounts offered in testimony that some Union soldiers had been found burned to death, and at least one corpse had been nailed, through his clothing, to the floor of a tent before being set ablaze.

The Confederate after-action reports offer a possible explanation. Early in the battle Union soldiers had been sent to defend a row of buildings that lay a few hundred yards outside the fort and to burn them and retreat if they could not hold them against the rebels. A few Union soldiers were killed and wounded in this fight and were left behind when the buildings were fired. Some Union men who had been killed might have been burned in this action, and others, wounded and unable to escape, perhaps perished in the flames.

Later in the evening, after the battle had ended, a second incident occurred that might account for the presence of burned bodies in some of the tents and buildings. Late in the afternoon the gunboat *Silver Cloud* pulled in to shore to rescue some twenty survivors who had gathered on the beach. As she came in, *Silver Cloud* began firing a barrage of shells into Fort Pillow. Believing that the Union was coming ashore in force from the boats in the river, the Confederates started burning the tents and buildings in and around Fort Pillow before they pulled back for the night.

It is possible that bodies may have burned at this time. There is the testimony, however, of one fort civilian who said that the Confederates pulled him and other wounded men out of the burning structures before they left the area. Lieutenant Leaming's report verifies this. Might some seriously wounded men have died accidentally in the flames? Possibly; but were any of these incidents intentional on the part of the Confederate soldiers? Other than an account of a burned Union corpse nailed through his cartridge belt to the floorboards of a tent, the only thing the landing party could attest to was that they had found several partially burned bodies in some tents and buildings. This testimony alone does not confirm that the alarming sight of partially burned bodies constitutes deliberately committed atrocities by the Confederates. It was impossible to have known whether they were dead or alive before they were burned.[54]

Many other bodies of both black and white Union soldiers were found with bullet wounds to the head. There were gunpowder burns around the bullet holes that suggest the men were shot at very close range. To some Union investigators this was proof that they had been executed, either after surrender or in the act of surrender. Another possibility is that they were shot at close range as they fought in the confined space of the fort.

5. The final charge alleged that the Confederates buried the living wounded along with the dead.

If this charge is accurate, then Union soldiers buried their own men alive, for it was Union prisoners, under the supervision of Confederate soldiers, who composed the burial details. Forrest himself was probably not in the vicinity during this incident, nor at any subsequent time after about five o'clock. He had left earlier for Brownsville, leaving Chalmers in charge of mopping up.

On May 3, 1864, Abraham Lincoln said of the Fort Pillow affair, "a massacre is now quite certain" and asked his cabinet for recommendations as to what actions should be taken. Lincoln's own counsel was to wait and take no action until Grant's battle in the wilderness had yielded victory.[55] It could be concluded that since no action was taken, Lincoln and Sherman came to believe that no massacre occurred. However, the president was at that time approaching a difficult campaign for reelection, a campaign in which his opponents were beginning to favor a negotiated settlement that would end the war and leave the nation divided. As for Sherman, he was notoriously insensitive toward African-Americans, as he demonstrated on his march through Georgia. This attitude was shared by many of the voters Lincoln hoped to win to his cause in November.

On whichever side of the fence one finds oneself, the most agreed upon aspect of Fort Pillow is that it has continued to be misrepresented as the worst case of butchery in the Civil War. Many other battles of that war produced higher casualty percentages, some approaching double, than those that resulted at Fort Pillow. Added to the casualty rates in those battles was the savagery with which they were fought. All this suggests that to single out Fort Pillow for infamy solely on the percentage rate of casualties contradicts the use of words like "massacre" to describe it.

Fort Pillow, a relatively minor battle in the sweep of Civil War engagements, continues to inflame emotions. This is true, in part, because of the immediacy with which rumor and innuendo spread along with reports of the battle and its aftermath. The fact that Forrest led the Confederate troops, no doubt, is another reason. His reputation had become legend long before Fort Pillow, and his post-war activities seemed to aggravate the public perception of the man.

The five conclusions above were based on the detailed testimony of the sworn witnesses at hearings following the battle. Their statements, though taken in total are not as conclusive as the final disposition of the committee indicates, still leave much room for controversy. When taken together with other accounts written within days of the battle by several Confederate soldiers in letters to relatives, and of Union officer Lt. Col. Thomas J. Jackson, the conclusions are even less convincing. Much of the testimony taken by members of the committee said the same thing and supported the committee's conclusions; however, the letters written by the Confederate soldiers and by Jackson have the veracity of having been written without the influence of the political pressures that followed the incident.

In a letter written to his sisters within days of the battle, Sgt. Achilles V. Clark of the Confederate Twentieth Tennessee gave an account that presented the most damning testimony of the Confederate position:

> The slaughter was awful. Words cannot describe the scene. The poor, deluded Negroes would run up to our men, fall upon their knees, and with uplifted hands scream for mercy but they were ordered to their feet and shot down. The white men fared but little better. . . . I with several others tried to stop the butchery and at one time had partially succeeded but Gen. Forrest ordered them shot down like dogs and the carnage continued.[56]

This account clashes with others that show a more compassionate Forrest who ordered the firing to stop and actually "ran between our men and the Yanks with his pistol and saber drawn," even, in one account, shooting one of his own men. Is it possible the same man was capable of such opposite behavior? One Forrest biographer wrote,

His temper may have undergone one of its characteristic wax-
ings and wanings. Angered by the taunts of the black soldiers
and especially by the Union refusal to surrender, necessitating
the paying of more precious Confederate lives for this victory he
had to have, he may have ragingly ordered a massacre and even
intended to carry it out—until he rode inside the fort and
viewed the horrifying result. Then, begged for his protection,
he was probably both vain enough to be flattered and sensitive
enough to respond.[57]

Captain Woodruff, who, at Chalmers' invitation, had come ashore
on April 13 with the Union party that inspected the area, said that
he witnessed evidence that several black soldiers had been shot
through the head at close range.

> Some of them were burned as if by powder around the holes in
> their heads, which led me to conclude that they were shot at
> very close range. One of the gunboat officers who accompanied
> us asked General Chalmers if most of the negroes were not
> killed after they [the enemy] had taken possession. Chalmers
> replied that he thought they had been, and that the men of
> General Forrest's Command had such hatred for the armed
> Negro that they could not be restrained from killing the
> Negroes after they had captured them. He said they were not
> killed by General Forrest's or his orders . . . that both Forrest
> and he [Chalmers] stopped the massacre as soon as they were
> able to do so. He said it was nothing better than we could expect
> as long as we persisted in arming the Negro.[58]

Before the final assault, Pvt. Daniel Stamps of the Thirteenth
Tennessee's Company E (Union), was sent as a sharpshooter to a
position under the bluff to oppose the Confederate drive down Coal
Creek. His eyewitness testimony confirms the charges that the
Confederates committed atrocities. "When the negroes had given
way on the left," he said, "I saw them run out of the fort down the
bluff close to my vicinity." He continued:

> Then I saw the white soldiers coming down after them, saying
> the rebels were showing no quarter. I then threw down my gun
> and ran down with them, closely pursued by the enemy shoot-
> ing down every man black and white. They said they had
> orders from Forrest to "kill the last god damn one of them."
> While I was standing at the bottom of the hill I heard a rebel
> officer shout out an order of some kind to the men who had

taken us. And saw a rebel soldier standing by me. I asked him what the officer had said. He repeated it to me again. It was, "kill the last damn one of them." The soldier replied to his officer that we had surrendered; that we were prisoners. . . . The officer replied, seeming crazy with rage that he had not been obeyed, "I tell you to kill the last god damned one of them." He then turned and galloped off. . . . I saw 2 men shot while I was under the bluff. They had their hands up; had surrendered, and were begging for mercy. I also . . . saw at least 25 negroes shot down, within 10 or 20 paces from the place where I stood. They had also surrendered, and were begging for mercy.[59]

The majority of the testimony considered by the Congressional committee came from the Union landing party that went ashore the day following the battle and was concerned chiefly with the charred bodies found inside tents and buildings. Testimony given by Ransom Anderson, a black soldier, gave the impression that Confederate troops had deliberately, and with some effort, driven Union soldiers into those same tents and buildings, then set fire to them. Anderson stated, "They [the Confederates] put some in the houses and shut them up, and burned the houses." He went on to say he could hear the men screaming from inside the buildings as they burned.[60]

Lieutenant Leaming, on the other hand, who had been shot during the battle, said that he was rescued from one of the burning buildings by the rebels. His story, while not conclusive evidence that soldiers were not burned in the building and tent fires, does suggest something short of a deliberate attempt to corral and burn Union soldiers alive. Such point and counterpoint in the testimony gathered by the committee offers contradicting evidence in every major circumstance that occurred at Fort Pillow.

In addition to Ransom Anderson's account, there is one other piece of testimony concerning the burning of Union soldiers. Eli A. Bangs, a ship's mate aboard the New Era who was with the landing party, said he saw the body of one Union soldier, among three found in the same tent, whose clothing and cartridge belt had been nailed down to the tent's floorboards.[61] No one else in the landing party corroborated Bangs' story, but there are accounts throughout the pages of testimony, from both sides, that allude to such general atrocity stories in varying detail and language. Throughout the reports individuals claim to have seen this or done that, but the significant detail necessary to corroborate the testimony beyond a doubt is lacking. It appears that in many instances individual witnesses may have reported on situations or incidents that they had only heard about from others and, perhaps unwittingly, wove such accounts into their own.

Lieutenant Leaming's report was especially incriminating, but inconsistent at the least. He related the death of Major Booth by rifle fire from the Confederate sharpshooters, which had occurred at nine o'clock in the morning. In discussing Booth's death, Leaming contradicted the Union commander's decision to refuse the opportunity to surrender when Forrest offered it. The Confederate marksmen, he went on to say, were in such an advantageous position that, for all intents and purposes, the fort was doomed from that point on. "We suffered pretty severely in the loss of commissioned officers by the unerring aim of the rebel sharpshooters."[62]

Leaming's report further states that he was shot down after he had surrendered, then played dead until the next morning. He also says that he was spared because he was a Mason and was taken prisoner by a Confederate trooper who also belonged to the Masonic order.[63]

Between the time Leaming was wounded after surrendering at about 4:00 P.M. (notwithstanding his reported rescue by a fellow Mason) and his playing dead until daybreak the next morning to avoid being murdered in the orgy of killing carried out by the Confederates, he claims to have observed the "butchery" of other Union wounded throughout the night. Since Forrest had left with his men late in the afternoon of the battle and Chalmers had pulled his men back around 6:30 P.M. to a position about two miles from the fort to camp for the night, who was Lieutenant Leaming trying to avoid by pretending to be dead? This part of his testimony is not fraught with credibility and does not square with other accounts from both Union and Confederate sources that suggest the fighting and killing was well over by 5:00 P.M.

Another troublesome omission from Leaming's report concerns the Union prisoners who had begun burying the dead around 5:30 P.M. on the afternoon of the battle. During this same time frame, and in response to Forrest and Chalmers' orders, the wounded were moved into buildings and medical supplies were being dispersed. It will be remembered that at about 5:00 P.M., Confederate major Anderson was on the beach with a flag of truce, attempting to hail in the *New Era* to get the seriously wounded aboard for transport to a hospital upriver, a signal that Captain Marshall, commanding the Union boat, ignored. All of these actions on the part of the Confederates appear to be well within the expectations of civilized behavior, even during wartime. But not according to Leaming, who fails to emphasize that there was never any formal surrender of the fort, an action that might have been a clear signal to both sides that the fighting should stop. Second Lieutenant Daniel Van Horn of the black artillery regiment, however, did state unequivocally that "there never was a surrender of the fort."[64]

Following the Congressional committee investigation of the Fort Pillow incident, a second investigation was convened a few weeks later, coordinated by Gen. William Tecumseh Sherman. This investigation went over much of the same ground reviewed by the Congressional committee, but its conclusions were much less certain. Sherman had gone into his investigation determined to find out the truth and to exact revenge if the massacre reports were proven true and could be laid at the feet of Nathan Bedford Forrest.

Sherman had little reason to be gentle with Forrest's reputation. After all, it was he who had seen Forrest as his most competent and dangerous opponent in the last several months of fighting in Tennessee. For these reasons one could expect Sherman to be remorseless in ferreting out every detail. If the findings proved to be condemnatory of Forrest, Sherman would surely have called for unerring justice upon him. Yet, Sherman apparently considered the evidence to be lacking and at the end of the hearings, let the matter rest there.

Those two official inquiries were by no means the last to go over every slip of evidence in the attempt to understand this event. Scholars ever since have crossed and recrossed the terrain of evidence and memory. In the past forty years several studies have been done, and from this massive amount of information, striking differences in opinions arise.

The latest sources supporting the massacre theorists are John Cimprich and Robert C. Mainfort's two articles concerning Fort Pillow. The first was titled "Fort Pillow Revisited," published in 1982; the other, "Dr. Fitch's Report on the Fort Pillow Massacre," published in 1985 in *The Tennessee Historical Quarterly*. In the more recent article, Dr. C. Fitch's testimony is used to back up the authors' first conclusion that a massacre did occur at Fort Pillow. Dr. Fitch, of Chariton, Iowa, was the surgeon attached to the Fort Pillow command and, some time after the incident, he wrote a report that was virtually ignored by the investigators in 1864. Subsequently his report was misplaced for more than a hundred years and had only recently come to light when it was used by Cimprich and Mainfort in their articles. Cimprich and Mainfort had already concurred with

Albert Castel's 1958 study on Fort Pillow. All these historians base their conclusions on six documents written immediately after the battle. They conclude that these reflect, above all others, the truest perspective untainted by politics and propaganda. Their position seems to indicate that the massive amount of testimony and sworn statements taken from Confederates at a later date should be viewed with suspicion.

Dr. Fitch wrote nothing about the battle at Fort Pillow until April 30, two weeks after the clash, when he submitted his report. Fitch also refused to testify at the Congressional hearings that had been called to investigate the Fort Pillow controversy. Why, as an eyewitness, did he take so long to speak up? Was he not encouraged by his commanders to do so? We can only speculate. However, Dr. Fitch did refuse to put the blame on the Confederate commanders for any excesses committed at Fort Pillow. His report gives credit to Forrest and Chalmers for saving his life and for attempting to enforce a cease-fire.

It should be remembered that at the time Dr. Fitch and Major Bradford were shaking hands in a group of Union prisoners, Lieutenant Leaming, according to his report, was observing the carnage, which he says was still occurring up and down the beach. The Fitch report also describes the killing in graphic detail, but the Union command did not particularly feel that Fitch's account was very reliable. This could be one reason why his report was mysteriously lost after it had been forwarded up the chain of command.

The charges and countercharges over what happened at Fort Pillow and the intentions of the Confederate commander before, during, and after the battle continue to rage. However, Forrest and Chalmers seemed to be concerned chiefly about cleaning up the field and marching prisoners off either to internment or to be exchanged.

Later, Forrest did have to explain the death of one of these prisoners, Major Bradford, the last Union officer in command of the fort. Reports of the circumstances surrounding Bradford's death are contradictory; however, the one aspect upon which all seem to be in agreement is that Forrest was not present when Bradford died.[65] The central version of Bradford's death is based upon the testimony of W. R. McLagan, who stated that Major Bradford, who tried to hide his identity by "putting on citizen's clothes," was taken apart from the other prisoners and deliberately executed. The other main version, which Forrest argues, is that Bradford had been given permission to attend the burial of his brother, Theodorick, who had been killed at Fort Pillow. Bradford gave his word that he would return to the group of prisoners after the funeral, but instead he changed into civilian clothes and started out for Memphis. He was subsequently apprehended and was shot attempting to escape.

The version inspired by McLagan's testimony was circulated in the North and became the most often repeated. It was this version that provoked Union general Cadwallader C. Washburn to confront Forrest by letter in which the allegations raised in McLagan's statement were recited. One particular charge seemed to directly implicate Forrest: that as the prisoners were being marched toward Brownsville, five Confederate soldiers "seemed to have received special instructions about something" (at Colonel Duckworth's headquarters) and "took Major Bradford about fifty yards from the road" and shot him dead.[66]

In his reply to Washburn, Forrest recounted the version of events in which Bradford was shot during an escape attempt and explained that he knew nothing of the affair until "eight or ten days after it is said to have occurred." He wanted Washburn to know that such an act as reported in the Union version was not acceptable in civilized warfare and that he would not tolerate it in his command. "If he [Bradford] was improperly killed," Forrest wrote, "nothing would afford me more pleasure than to punish the perpetrators to the full extent of the law, and to show you how I regard such transactions I can refer you to my demand upon Major-General Hurlbut (no doubt upon file in your office)." This was a reference to Union colonel Fielding Hurst who had been charged with cruel and barbaric acts, including the murder and mutilation of five of Forrest's men near Jackson, Tennessee.[67]

The fate of Major Bradford would continue to swirl around the Fort Pillow controversy as another example of Forrest's brutality and culpability, but for Forrest, personally, Fort Pillow was the end of his successful expedition into west Tennessee and Kentucky. Beginning in March with twenty-eight hundred men and ending in May with five thousand, this campaign was evidence of Forrest's ability to recruit and lead. It also attests to his ability to "transfer" from the Union army most of the arms, ammunition, and other supplies needed to support a military force such as his.

The campaign that culminated in the battle for Fort Pillow was seen as a success among leaders of the Confederacy. While Northern officials were conducting inquiries and newspapers were trumpeting extreme versions of the battle's outcome, Fort Pillow was considered by the Confederates, if at all, a minor part of a much larger triumph. A joint resolution of the Confederate Congress was issued on May 23 to extend their gratitude to Forrest and his men for their "brilliant and successful campaign in Mississippi, West Tennessee and Kentucky—a campaign which has conferred upon its authors fame as enduring as the records of the struggle which they have so brilliantly illustrated."[68]

Whatever place in history the Confederate Congress intended Forrest to occupy, the Northern press was preparing quite another. The taint of Fort Pillow in the public view in the North would make Forrest the preeminent war criminal and overshadow all his other stunning accomplishments on the battlefield. A *New York Tribune* article reprinted in the *Chicago Tribune* illustrates the growing resentment of Forrest in light of the Fort Pillow tragedy:

### THE BUTCHER FORREST AND HIS FAMILY
All of them Slave Drivers and Woman Whippers.

Knoxville, E[ast]. T[enn]., April 18, 1864

The news of the capture of Fort Pillow by Forrest, and the cowardly butchery which followed of blacks and whites alike, has produced a profound sensation here. The universal sentiment is "Let no quarter be shown to these dastardly butchers of Forrest's command while the war lasts." These Forrests, the oldest of whom, Gen. Bedford Forrest, has by this and other atrocities obtained such a record of infamy, were all negro traders. There were four brothers—Bedford, who kept a negro pen for five years before the war on Adams Street, in rear of the Episcopal Church, Memphis; John, a cripple and a gambler, who was jailor and clerk for Bedford; Bill Forrest, an extensive negro trader at Vicksburg; and Aaron Forrest, general agent and soul driver to scour the country for his older brothers. They accumulated large sums of money in their nefarious trade, and Bedford won by that and other influences a natural promotion to a Brigadier in the women-whipping, baby-stealing Rebel Confederacy. He is about 50 years of age, tall, gaunt and sallow-visaged, with a long nose, deep-set black, snaky eyes, full black beard without a mustache, and hair worn long. He usually wore, while in the "nigger" trade in Memphis, a stovepipe hat set on the back of his head at an angle of forty-five degrees. He was accounted mean, vindictive, cruel and unscrupulous. He had two wifes [*sic*]—one white, the other colored [Catharine], by each of which he had two children. His "patriarchal" wife, Catharine, and his wife had frequent quarrels or domestic jars. The slave pen of old Bedford Forrest, on Adams Street, was a perfect horror to all negroes far and near. His mode of punishing refractory slaves was to compel four of his fellow slaves to stand and hold the victim stretched out in the air, and then Bedford and his brother John would stand, one on each side, with long, heavy bull whips, and cut up their victims until the blood trickled to the ground. Women were often stripped naked, and with a bucket of salt water standing by, in which to dip the instrument of torture, a heavy leather thong, their backs were cut up until the blisters covered the whole surface, the blood of their wounds mingling with the briny mixture to add torment to the infliction. One slave man was whipped to death by Bedford, who used a trace-chain doubled for the purpose of punishment. The slave was secretly buried, and the circumstance was known only to the slaves of the prison, who only dared to refer to the situation in whispers. Such are the appropriate antecedents in the character of the monster who murdered in cold blood the gallant defenders of Fort Pillow.[69]

This disparaging account surrounding Fort Pillow makes Forrest appear to be a monster beyond redemption in the eyes of many, even to this day. Perhaps the exaggeration and hyperbole were so great that Forrest, the aggressive man of action that he was on the battlefield, saw little reason to defend his actions in his own lifetime. So let it be in trying to sort out his enigma today. Fort Pillow will undoubtedly remain a contest of fact and interpretation, charge and countercharge; and Forrest's intentions, whatever they may have been, will never be fully known.

# Chapter Eleven

# THEN FALL LIKE A THUNDERBOLT

*—Sun Tzu*

## Brice's Cross Roads
## April-June 1864

Forrest had been a plague to Federal forces in the west during the first half of 1864. Since January he had won battles as far north as Kentucky, in Mississippi at West Point and Okolona, and across west Tennessee from Fort Pillow to Johnsonville. These successes had been costly, not only in the numbers of his men he had buried, but also on a more personal scale. Forrest learned shortly after the battle at Fort Pillow that his brother Aaron had died of pneumonia. Aaron Forrest was a lieutenant colonel with a Mississippi cavalry regiment on an expedition to Paducah, Kentucky, when he became ill. He died in Dresden, Tennessee. Aaron was the second brother Bedford had lost in the war.[1] The news must have been a heavy blow, but the pace of events was moving too quickly to allow Forrest time to indulge his grief.

In each battle, though usually outnumbered, Forrest seemed invincible, yet commanders from Sherman down were determined to stop him. A vengeful Union army under Gen. Samuel Sturgis marched from Memphis in the heat of early June 1864 to do just that, but at a place called Brice's Cross Roads, Forrest made believers of everyone.

In mid-April, Sherman was headquartered in Nashville, Tennessee, where he worked on the plans for his spring campaign. He had to keep his army of one hundred thousand men and thirty-five thousand animals supplied over 475 miles of single track leading south from Nashville to Chattanooga. To do this he would have to deal with the threat of Confederate horse soldiers. The only one who truly worried Sherman—and Grant—was Maj. Gen. Nathan

Bedford Forrest, "whose men worked hard and could wreck a railroad as effectively as Sherman's infantry."[2]

The success of Forrest's campaign had made him one of General Sherman's top priorities, and Sherman reacted by shaking up the Union command structure. On April 18, he replaced General Hurlbut with Gen. Cadwallader Washburn, and almost immediately he sent a new general officer, Samuel D. Sturgis, to command Washburn's cavalry. After dispatching Sturgis, a West Point man with considerable experience, Sherman wrote to Washburn, "I have sent Sturgis down to take command of that cavalry and whip Forrest. I know there are troops enough at Memphis to whale Forrest if you can reach him."[3]

Sherman had plenty of issues to worry about besides one Southern cavalryman, but Forrest was always a thorn in his side, and it had become clear to Sherman that as long as Forrest could move at will across Tennessee and northern Mississippi, the planned invasion of Georgia was in peril. Sherman asked Adm. David Porter to "keep a bright lookout up the Tennessee that Forrest doesn't cross and cut my [rail]roads when I am in Georgia." Sherman also wrote to warn Washburn once again. "We are all in motion for Georgia," he said. "We want you to hold Forrest . . . until we strike Johnston. This is quite as important as to whip him."[4]

Gen. James McPherson hammered home the same point to Washburn. He made it clear that if Forrest were allowed to roam at will, he would be able to get into their rear where he would be in a position to break up their railroad communications.[5]

During the period from the end of April to late August, the Union undertook a total of four expeditions in west Tennessee and northern Mississippi with the goal of tying down or destroying Forrest's command. They would meet the first goal of keeping Forrest busy but would fail to destroy him.

Sturgis moved out of Memphis on April 30, 1864, on his first expedition to find Forrest. The strength of Sturgis's command was more than eight thousand men, with twenty-two pieces of artillery. Excellent scouting had consistently given Forrest the edge through three years of war. It was no different now as Forrest's scouts kept him advised of Sturgis's movements from the time he left Memphis. Thus apprised, Forrest pulled out of Jackson and fell back to Tupelo in northeast Mississippi as a precaution.

Sturgis and his men pursued Forrest as far as Ripley, Mississippi, but he found the countryside so devastated and devoid of food and forage from two years of war that he returned to Memphis without engaging

Forrest. Upon his return, Sturgis somehow fantasized that he had driven Forrest from west Tennessee and broken up his command:

> My Little campaign is over, and, I regret to say, Forrest is still at large. He did not come to West Tennessee for the purpose of fighting, unless it might so happen that he could fall upon some little party or defenseless place. . . . It is idle to follow him except with an equal force of cavalry, which we have not in this part of the country. I say except with an equal force of cavalry but even then he has so many advantages, and so disposed to run that I feel that all that could be done in any case would be to drive him out unless, indeed he might be trapped. . . . I regret very much that I could not have the pleasure of bringing you his hair, but he is too great a plunderer to fight anything like an equal force, and we have to be satisfied with driving him from the State. He may turn on your communications and I rather think he will, but see no way to prevent it from this point and with this force.[6]

While Sturgis congratulated himself on avoiding Forrest, Sherman advanced on General Johnston's position at Dalton, Georgia, outmaneuvering the Confederates there and forcing them to abandon Dalton after a flanking march through Snake Creek Gap. The two forces then resumed maneuvering as if to gain the advantage, and therefore the victory, by outflanking each other. As Sherman moved crablike back and forth across the Confederate front, the two forces fell into battle positions and clashed again at the rail center of Resaca. By May 15, Johnston's position became untenable when Sherman outflanked him again by crossing the Oostanaula River at Lay's Ferry. In consecutive battles the two armies fought at New Hope Church on May 25, Picket's Mill on May 27, and at Dallas on May 28. Johnston's strategy was to hold and delay, hoping Sherman would make a fatal mistake that would deny him Atlanta and thus a major victory that might turn Lincoln's downward political slide into a great political victory for anti-Lincoln forces in the November elections.

Meanwhile Sherman's supply line became longer and longer, and he worried what might happen if Forrest should cross the Tennessee River and strike the Nashville, Chattanooga and Decatur Railroad along which Sherman's provender traveled. To prevent this, Washburn and Sherman sent out their second force to find and destroy Forrest.

In addition, Washburn had received information that the Confederates had repaired the Southern railroad of Mississippi as well as the Mobile and Ohio, which Sherman had destroyed on his Meridian expedition in February 1864. The locomotives were again running north on the Mobile and Ohio rail line up to Okolona. Washburn was to send cavalry to strike out and destroy the Mobile and Ohio trestle at Tupelo and then proceed south to Meridian, Mississippi, burning all the bridges as they went. Maj. Gen. James B. McPherson also admonished Washburn, "It is of the utmost importance, however, to inflict as much damage to the enemy as you can—keep his forces occupied, and prevent him from forming plans and combinations to cross the Tennessee River and break up the railroad communications in our rear."[7]

On June 2, Sturgis set out once again, but this time with a larger force than he had had on his first expedition in May. His army consisted of thirty-five hundred cavalry commanded by Gen. Benjamin H. Grierson, forty-eight hundred infantry, twenty-two cannons, four hundred cannoneers, and over two hundred wagons—close to nine thousand men in all. With such manpower, Sturgis was to march for Corinth, Mississippi, via the Salem and Ruckersville route. After capturing Corinth he was to destroy all the public property that he could not carry with him. He was then to move on Tupelo and destroy the railroads as he advanced.

While Sturgis moved out in search of fame and glory, Forrest was once again in Tupelo. With urging from General Johnston, Forrest was sent into middle Tennessee to wreck the Nashville and Chattanooga and Decatur Railroads. At the same time Sturgis was moving south, Forrest, with twenty-four hundred men and six pieces of artillery, was riding northeast into the hill country of northwest Alabama. On the morning of June 3, Forrest was notified that a powerful enemy column was advancing on Corinth and the fertile Black Prairie region.

The urgent dispatch had come from Forrest's commanding officer, Gen. Stephen D. Lee, who urged Forrest to return immediately to the Tupelo area. Thus, without firing a shot, Sherman had temporarily gained a key strategic imperative for his Georgia campaign. Sturgis's column had forced Forrest's recall from the one mission that potentially could have thwarted Sherman's march. On June 5, Forrest ordered Col. P. D. Roddey to send Col. William A. Johnson with his brigade ahead to Corinth. This proved to be a smart move on Forrest's part. From the sixth to the ninth, Sturgis and Forrest were once again moving toward each other.

When Gen. S. D. Lee joined Forrest at Tupelo on June 6, Forrest informed Lee that his scouts estimated Sturgis's column at ten thousand strong. The scouts were fairly accurate in their appraisal of the enemy column. They had reported enemy strength at twenty-five hundred cavalry and seventy-five hundred infantry, which included three thousand black troops, though actually there were nearer thirty-five hundred cavalry and five thousand infantry, including twelve hundred black soldiers.

After Fort Pillow, less than two months earlier, the black Union troops with Sturgis's command had more than victory on their minds; they had vengeance in their hearts. Forrest had received information that, to a man, they had fallen upon their knees vowing to show no quarter to the butcher Forrest and his men. They also displayed their resolve with "Remember Fort Pillow" patches sewn on the breasts of their uniform tunics. Soldiers from both sides later testified that neither Forrest's men nor the black troops expected mercy to be shown by the other. This understanding would lead to vicious fighting, as both sides seemed to have believed that surrender was tantamount to suicide.[8]

The rain pounded both armies as they sought each other over mud-clogged roads and flooded meadows. As was usually the case, Forrest's scouts and information network were better than the enemy's. He would know where Sturgis was and his strength before Sturgis had reliable information on Forrest's dispositions.

Strike one against Sturgis.

The Union column dragged itself through the muddy quagmire created by the heavy rain and arrived at Ripley on June 7. Sturgis contemplated turning back, but now that Sherman had selected him personally, turning back without facing Forrest on this second expedition would be detrimental to his career. Col. William L. McMillen said to Sturgis, when hearing of his plans to possibly turn back, "I would rather go on and meet the enemy, even if we should be whipped, than go back to Memphis without having met them."[9]

On June 9, Forrest and Lee learned of the Union column at Ripley and realized that Sturgis was heading straight toward the breadbasket of Mississippi to destroy the crops and huge stores of grain and corn in the Black Prairie. Lee left Forrest with complete discretion in dealing with the Union threat, but he departed for Okolona hoping that Forrest would lure Sturgis even farther south, away from his supply base in Memphis. However, Forrest had other plans for Sturgis, and the Union advance would never reach the main Confederate force around Okolona.

Forrest knew that Sturgis was encamped at the Stubbs' farm,

approximately ten miles northwest of Brice's Cross Roads. At sunset on June 9, Forrest's command was dispersed as follows: Johnson's five-hundred-man brigade was bivouacked at Baldwyn, six miles east of Brice's Cross Roads; Lyon's and Rucker's brigades of sixteen hundred men along with Morton's artillery batteries consisting of eight guns were at Booneville, eighteen miles away; and Bell's brigade of twenty-eight hundred troops was twenty-five miles from the crossroads, at Rienzi. The next morning Forrest would make one of the boldest moves in military history.

At 5:00 A.M. on June 10, Sturgis began to move southeast toward Brice's Cross Roads. Col. George Waring's brigade was in the van as the Union command rode slowly toward the crossroads. Sturgis was about to make another mistake although the weather and terrain could be considered mitigating circumstances in the coming events. Sturgis's cavalry detachment, led by General Grierson, had moved dangerously forward of the infantry and wagon train. From head to tail the Union command was stretched out eight to ten miles.

Strike two against Sturgis.

Sturgis planned to start his infantry moving two hours after the cavalry departed Stubbs' farm, but the appointed hour of 7:00 A.M. came and went as trivial delays held up their departure. About 10:00 A.M. the infantry finally began to move, but at little more than the pace of a cattle drive. As the delay caused the infantry to fall farther behind Grierson's cavalry, Forrest saw a golden opportunity developing.

While Grierson's division, led by Waring's brigade, rode toward the Brice farm, Sturgis and McMillen shared an eyeopener in the form of a strong belt of whiskey. Sturgis then ordered his infantry forward into the muddy wake left by the cavalry. That morning Sturgis rode at the head of the infantry column along with McMillen. Behind them was a company of pioneers from Colonel Hoges' brigade. Col. Edward Bouton's brigade of black troops guarded the 250 wagons bringing up the rear of the column.

The sun was out for the first time in several days and with it came the heat and debilitating Mississippi humidity. Where the infantry descended into the Hatchie bottoms, the road became a ribbon of mud. The pioneer company was called forward to "corduroy" the road, which delayed the infantry even longer. All the while the cavalry pulled farther and farther ahead of the infantry. George E. Waring's cavalry detachment arrived at Brice's Cross Roads at approximately 9:45 A.M. At that moment most of Forrest's men were farther from the crossroads than was the entire Union force.

Early that morning Forrest rode side by side with Edmund Rucker at the head of Rucker's brigade. As they rode along Forrest said to Colonel Rucker,

> I know they greatly outnumber the troops I have at hand, but the road along which they will march is country and is densely wooded and the undergrowth so heavy that when we strike them they will not know how few men we have. Their cavalry will move out ahead of the infantry, and should reach the crossroads three hours in advance. We can whip their cavalry in that time. As soon as the fight opens they will send back to have the infantry hurried up. It is going to be hot as hell, and coming on a run for five or six miles over such roads, their infantry will be so tired out we will ride right over them. I want everything to move up as fast as possible. I will go ahead with Lyon and the escort and open the fight.[10]

As Rucker and Forrest were riding through Old Carrollville, Lt. Robert Black of the Seventh Tennessee rode up and hurriedly reported that about fifteen hundred Yankee cavalry directed by General Grierson had already arrived at Brice's Cross Roads. Forrest had only thirteen hundred men to put on the field at the beginning of the battle. The other thirty-two hundred would come up later.

Moments after receiving Lieutenant Black's report, Forrest spotted the bluecoats moving in the distance. He ordered Capt. L. Randle of the Seventh Kentucky to charge the enemy. He also ordered Gen. Hylan B. Lyon to dismount the Third, Seventh, and Eighth Kentucky Regiments. The small Confederate force was deployed across the Wire Road near the edge of the woods. Across an open field of blackjack oak, Colonel Waring's force came to a halt. The two enemy forces faced each other with less than a quarter mile between them.[11]

Suddenly, three of Lyon's Kentucky regiments burst from the tree line and brush, natural obstacles that Forrest knew would hide his numbers. Although the forces at this time were almost evenly matched in manpower, they were not in weaponry.[12] Waring's men were armed as follows: The Second New Jersey Cavalry was armed with Spencer repeating carbines. The Third and Ninth Illinois Cavalries carried Colt revolving rifles. The rest of Waring's command was armed with single-shot carbines.[13] By contrast, many of Lyon's Kentuckians carried long-range rifle-muskets. Although outgunned, the Confederates held an advantage in distance, as their rifles had much greater range than the Union carbines.

The newly arrived Grierson was so shaken by the news of the Confederate onset that he immediately sent urgent dispatches to the rear that the enemy had been engaged in force. Grierson's message said that he believed he was facing four thousand enemy troops and needed Sturgis's infantry immediately. Sturgis and McMillen reacted to the news by calling up Col. George B. Hoges' brigade and ordered them to make a forced march to the crossroads. That forced march would leave exhausted men strewn by the wayside all along the road. At least two Union soldiers died from exhaustion and dehydration struggling to the front to relieve the cavalry. Forrest's prophetic statement to Rucker several hours earlier was becoming reality.

While the infantry was rushing forward, General Grierson deployed his men for a fight. Six to seven hundred horsemen blocked the Old Carrolville Road near the crossroads. Col. Edward Winslow's brigade crossed Tishomingo Creek Bridge and took position on Waring's right, while the remaining twenty-eight hundred Union horsemen prepared to give battle and drive the rebels toward Baldwyn. The Union cavalry dismounted and their artillerymen unlimbered four mountain howitzers and prepared to defend the approach to Brice's Cross Roads and Tishomingo Creek Bridge.

Four hundred yards to the Union front, partially concealed by scrub oak and brush, were Lyon's eight hundred Kentuckians, eighty-five men from Forrest's escort company, and Capt. Henry Gartrell's fifty Georgia horsemen. Grierson was still unsure how large a force he faced, but knowing that McMillen and the infantry were coming up, he acted without conviction. Perhaps his unconvincing attack also reflected the shock of the first Confederate charge.

At approximately 10:45 A.M., with no Confederate artillery batteries closer than ten miles, Forrest rolled the dice.[14] Once again he sent the eight hundred Kentuckians charging across the field to buy more time until the rest of his force arrived. Though the three Kentucky regiments were driven back under a withering fire from the Spencer carbines, Forrest's gamble was working. He was keeping the Union cavalry commanders on their heels until reinforcements could come up.

At 11:00 A.M., Colonel Rucker's brigade arrived, providing some support. Forrest ordered Rucker to dismount two of his three units and join Lyon's brigade. The Eighth Mississippi Cavalry, led by Col. William L. Duff, were sent around to the left to watch for a flanking move on the Guntown Road. The new arrivals had doubled Forrest's strength although Grierson still maintained an edge in the number of men he had on the field.

Abruptly, and for the third time, the Kentucky brigade charged, joined by the Seventh Tennessee and the Eighteenth Mississippi Battalion. Forrest was keeping the bulge on the enemy along with the psychological edge he had gained. At that moment, however, it was a precarious edge he held over Grierson, but hold it he did while he waited for his dispersed units to show up a piece at a time.

Pvt. John H. Hubbard of the Seventh Tennessee Cavalry later recalled the scene:

> Will I ever forget it? The enemy was posted in a dense wood and behind a heavy fence pouring a galling fire into our ranks. It looked like death to go to the fence, but many reached it. Four men of Company E were killed in the charge. Chalmers' Mississippians advanced too far and being unsupported on the left found their ranks swept by deadly enfilade fire delivered by a battalion of the 3rd Iowa Cavalry. The Mississippi troops withdrew into the woods, where they rallied. Its flank uncovered by the Mississippians' repulse, the 7th Tennessee Cavalry also began to withdraw.[15]

As the Confederates fell back, Colonel Johnson arrived from Baldwyn with his Alabama brigade and took up a position north of the Old Carollville road on the right of Lyon's Kentuckians. Forrest now had two thousand men on the field. The Union's advantage in numbers was slowly narrowing. The moment of truth had arrived. Grierson was still convinced that he was outnumbered and facing Confederate infantry as well as cavalry. He sent couriers to the rear with desperate messages for McMillen to get to the crossroads with reinforcements soon or he would be overwhelmed.

From left to right Forrest had three brigades in action: Rucker's, Lyon's, and Johnson's. Forrest knew that Morton's eight cannons were coming, but he still had no cannon on the field. He now moved to the immediate front to lead the attack and personally motivate his men. It was "high noon" at the crossroads. As the artillery shells exploded and the ground heaved, Forrest rode up and down the line exhorting his men and filling them with his terrible energy and confidence.

Forrest's trusty bugler, Sgt. Jacob Gaus, was told to sound the charge. The Confederates surged forward like howling demons with Edmund Rucker in the lead. Under a blistering barrage from

cannon, Spencer carbines, Colt revolving rifles, and single-shot carbines, Rucker's men pressed Waring's right, and the Seventh
Indiana began to waver. During the charge Rucker's horse was shot
five times and finally went down, so the colonel continued to lead
the charge dismounted. As he rallied his men, a minie ball struck
Rucker in the stomach, but with sheer toughness he forced himself
to continue. North of the Old Carrolville road, the Second New
Jersey also gave way. The Third and Fourth Iowans of Winslow's command were on the right and holding, but it was all soon about to go
to hell. There was no wind on this day, and a heavy, dense smoke
soon covered the battlefield.

At 1:00 P.M., Rucker's command punched a hole through the
Seventh Indiana and began forcing them to fall back. Now, as
though it had been planned, Bell's brigade, led by Gen. Abraham
Buford, arrived along with Morton's flying artillery, which unlimbered and immediately went into battery. The battle was vicious in
many pockets on the field. J. P. Young, historian for the Seventh
Tennessee Cavalry, noted,

> Never did men fight more gallantly for their position than the
> determined men . . . for the blackjack thick. Sergeant John D.
> Huhn, of Company B, being a few feet ahead . . . came face to
> face with a Federal soldier, and having only an empty gun, he pre-
> sented it at the bluejacket and ordered him to throw down his
> gun. This he promptly did; but several of his companions sprang
> to his rescue, and the sergeant avoided a bullet in the brain by
> wrenching aside the muzzle as the gun exploded. They then
> struck his extended carbine from his hand, breaking a finger and
> his arm in two places, and then laid him out by a terrible blow to
> the crown. Privates Lauderdale and Maclin, of Company B, then
> came to his assistance, shooting two of his stouthearted assailants
> and driving the others off [using rifles as clubs].

During the brawl, Pvt. Henry J. Fox shot the Yankee dead who had
clubbed down his friend Sergeant Huhn.[16]

By this point in the fight the Union cavalry was beaten. Forrest had
accomplished the first step of his battle plan by having the cavalry
whipped before the infantry arrived. But Sturgis's infantry was close.
The sun beat down on the Union infantry as it huffed and puffed its
way toward the fighting. Behind them was Sturgis's wagon train, which
had just emerged on the high ground from the Hatchie bottoms.

Maj. Charles Anderson earlier had been sent up the Wire Road to

Carrolville to watch for Buford. Upon meeting Buford's brigade, Anderson relayed Forrest's plan of attack. Buford immediately detached Col. Clark R. Barteau and the Second Tennessee Cavalry to head south and flank the Union, hitting them at Tishomingo Creek Bridge. The other regiments pushed on to reinforce Forrest.

The Union cavalry was on the verge of breaking when the infantry arrived. Sturgis and his staff along with the Nineteenth Pennsylvania Cavalry reached the crossroads just before Hoges' infantry brigade. Sturgis was greeted by a sight that must have made his blood run cold. The situation was deteriorating rapidly and the smell of panic was in the air. A crisis was at hand. Sturgis ordered Hoges' infantry to relieve Grierson's cavalry, which was beginning to fall apart after two hours of desperate fighting.

Soon the 113th Illinois infantry arrived and were ordered into the battle, but the man-killing pace had rendered many men completely ineffective. Soaked in sweat from their rapid march, their blue uniforms appeared black. Some men were so weak that they were unable to load their weapons. Ambulances and horses jammed the road. When McMillen's infantry arrived at 1:00 P.M., McMillen noted the confusion on the battlefield and recognized that everything "was going to the devil as fast as possible."[17]

It was shortly after 1:00 P.M., when Sturgis arrived on the field and sent Hoges' and Wilkins' infantry to relieve the Union cavalry, that Forrest began his first all-out attack of the day. As the Union infantry drew into an ever-tightening semicircle about the crossroads, Morton's guns came into action with deadly effect. Not allowing the Union soldiers time to catch their wind, Forrest again resumed the attack. Buford was to assault the left and center with Lyon's Kentuckians and Rucker's and Johnson's brigades. Simultaneously Forrest dismounted Bell's Tennesseans and hurled them against the Union right. Forrest rode with Bell's brigade as the push began.

At that hour, the Guntown Road was held by the 114th Illinois on the left and the Ninety-third Indiana on the right. In this area the fighting was vicious and at times hand-to-hand. During the close-quartered combat in the dense blackjack, the Confederates had excellent success using their Navy Colts. Forrest's men carried extra-capped cylinders in their pockets and were far more effective in this type of fight than the Union boys with their cumbersome muskets.

The fighting ebbed and flowed for the next hour, but the Union lines were constricting ever tighter and beginning to deteriorate. After a determined Union counterattack, there was a distinct lull all along the front, as though both sides held their breath, awaiting the renewal of the carnage. Forrest's instincts told him that now the battle must be won or lost.

It is a safe bet that Nathan Bedford Forrest never studied the military tactics of Hannibal at Cannae, where in 216 B.C., he annihilated a numerically superior Roman army, or of Alexander the Great's masterpiece in 326 B.C., at the Battle of the Hydaspes River in India. However, with his West Point education, Sturgis certainly had. Nevertheless, like Hannibal and Alexander's enemies, the Union commander was about to fall victim to a classic double envelopment.

Strike three against Sturgis.

Before the final assault could be launched, Colonel Wilkins, on the right of the Guntown Road, committed his reserve of the Ninth Minnesota to reinforce the Ninety-third Indiana on Tyree H. Bell's left. When this occurred, Duff's Eighth Mississippi and the Nineteenth Mississippi, on the right of Duff's men, began to fall back. Capt. H. A. Tyler later recalled that he heard men shouting, "Look out Captain, the damned Mississippians are running." Tyler kept cool and redeployed his squadron behind a fence and opened fire into the flank of the Ninth Minnesota.

When Forrest received the news about the crisis, he sent an urgent dispatch to Buford on the Confederate right to immediately attack with Hylan B. Lyon's Kentuckians and William A. Johnson's Alabamians. Forrest then placed himself at the head of his escort company of elite fighters and prepared to lead them forward into the gap created by the retreating Mississippi regiments. These were the men whom Forrest always kept close by in case of an emergency such as this. They were his fiercest fighters and would be used on many battlefields to counterattack if the enemy was about to breach a critical position on the field. Or if the enemy was about to give way, the men of Forrest's escort were vital to exploiting a success.

Forrest's escort company slammed into the Ninth Minnesota, checking the advance of the enemy on that section of the field. The battle continued as both sides fought desperately to hold their positions. Astride his big sorrel, King Phillip, Forrest was riding from left to right, encouraging his men along the line. He had stripped off his general's jacket and laid it across the pommel of his saddle. His shirtsleeves were rolled up, and he carried his saber in his hand as he arrived in the vicinity of the Wire Road.

As Forrest prepared his final sledgehammer blow, he encountered John Morton a short distance to the rear. He told Morton that in about ten minutes he was going to attack. As Forrest explained what he wanted Morton to do, Morton's mouth fell open in disbelief. Forrest told the young Captain Morton to have his guns double shotted with canister, and at the sound of the bugle he was to charge the enemy—with his guns. Pointing to a spot beyond the Union line, Forrest said, "Give 'em hell right over yonder where I'm going to double 'em up."[18] Forrest wanted Morton to get as close as humanly possible before unlimbering and opening fire. It is generally believed that this was the first time a commander ordered his guns forward in a charge without immediate support.

After the battle, Morton confessed to Forrest that the plan seemed exceedingly dangerous and that he "was afraid they might take my guns." Forrest jokingly replied, "Well, artillery is made to be captured, and I wanted to see them take yours."

Forrest rode behind Bell's brigade, crossed the Guntown Road, and met with Captain Tyler. He ordered Tyler's men to charge across the Pontotoc Road, sweep around the flank of the Ninth Minnesota, and move into the Tishomingo Creek bottoms south of the bridge. Col. Clark R. Barteau and the Second Tennessee had received orders from Forrest to storm the knoll held by the Seventy-second Ohio and the guns of the Sixth Indiana, which were guarding the northeastern approaches to the bridge. All was ready as Morton stood by his guns, waiting. A savage silence lingered before Sergeant Gaus's shrill bugle call split the air. The Confederates charged, and Morton's batteries put spurs and whips to their horses. Forrest's command stormed forward. The Confederates, along with Morton's exposed guns, were moving out in a cloud of dust before the first note died away.

At the Confederate charge, the Union line constricted even further. Within a few minutes the line contracted from eight hundred yards in length to a jammed-up three hundred yards.

At 2:00 P.M., Barteau and the Second Tennessee, approximately 250 men, closed on the Union position at the bridge from the rear. That same moment Captain Tyler and Forrest's escort company swept around the Union right to turn the Ninth Minnesota as they continued down the Pontotoc Road into the Tishomingo Creek bottoms south of the bridge. The Confederates drove on with single-minded determination over and through fields of blackjack and brushwood that clawed at their clothing like something alive.

A member of the Seventh Tennessee Cavalry later recalled the desperate fighting that day as Forrest kept up the scare on the surprised Yankees: "When our movement was too slow to suit Forrest, he would curse, then praise and then threaten to shoot us himself, if we were so afraid the Yanks might hit us. . . . He would praise in one breath, then in the next would curse us and finally said, 'I will lead you.'" The fighting was wicked and fierce as "guns once fired were used as clubs and pistols were brought into play, while the two lines struggled with the ferocity of wild beasts." The Union troopers quickly learned that the bayonet was no match for a Navy Colt at close quarters.

Forrest's tactics, perfected in so many battles since the war began, had been embraced by his men. The Second Tennessee was widely deployed to exaggerate their numbers, and their bugler, Jimmy Bradford, galloped back and forth through the fields and woods sounding charge after charge for imaginary regiments. "So many bugle calls, blown so loudly and so far apart, made the skeleton regiment scattered through the woods seem a veritable host."[19] For McMillen's infantry, on the west side of Tishomingo Creek Bridge amidst the thunder and chaos of battle, it probably did seem as though the Second Tennessee Cavalry were many times larger than its 250 men.

While the fighting at the bridge intensified, Morton's guns pounded the Yankee position with uncanny accuracy. Each time Morton's gun crews fired, they would push their guns a little closer to the enemy. In his book, *The Artillery of Nathan Bedford Forrest's Cavalry*, John Morton wrote, "Halting within 60 yards of the enemy's position on the hill, the guns were ordered into action. . . . The Federals made a gallant defense of their position, but no mortal could withstand the incessant terrible fire of the artillery at short range."[20] Morton's "bull pups," as he called his pair of steel Rodmans, were indeed wreaking havoc across the field, blowing bloody, gaping holes in the Union line at powder-burn range. "There was not a moment's faltering anywhere on the field in the Confederate ranks," Morton recalled. "The Federals made desperate efforts to countercharge, but with no more affect than to meet the Confederates in a hand-to-hand struggle when too close for the guns."[21]

By 2:30 P.M., six Union guns had been captured and another battery was attacked some three hundred yards west of Ripley Road. The Federals fell back to the protection of this battery, and Captain Morton urged his and Rice's batteries forward, pouring a blazing hail of canister into their lines as the enemy retreated. The destruction wrought by Morton's guns was ghastly, and the Union gunners soon abandoned their battery and joined the Union troops crowding back along the Ripley Road. Not only were these soldiers abandoning their positions under Morton's guns, McMillen was also being hammered back, step by step. The entire Union line was disintegrating.

Dr. Agnew's house, farther down Ripley Road, was now enveloped in the battle. Thirty-five wagons, with ten days' rations, were abandoned on the doctor's property.

At this time Col. Edward Bouton's black troops reached the Agnew house, northwest of the crossroads. Sturgis lost no time in ordering him to corral the wagons and then ordered two companies of his black soldiers at the double time over the last half-mile to the bridge. Along the way to the bridge Bouton and his men passed hordes of men from McMillen's command who had retreated on a dead run. As he neared the crossroads, the colonel became convinced that the Union army was about to be routed, so even before he reached his objective, Bouton called up Capt. Franklin M. Ewing and two companies of the Fifty-fifth U.S. Colored Infantry. Bouton crossed Tishomingo Creek Bridge with the Seventy-second Ohio and two guns of the Sixth Indiana and took up a position on the knoll. The fate of the Union campaign now depended on these men. The black troops reacted with cool professionalism as they made way through the remnants of Grierson's cavalry and McMillen's infantry, who were retreating from Forrest's attack, then closed ranks and prepared to hold the bridge.[22]

When McMillen crossed the bridge to the west side of the creek, he realized that the entire command was in danger of annihilation. He approached Colonel Bouton and issued chilling orders: Bouton was to hold the bridge at all costs. Bouton pressed McMillen for clarification and asked if he was to fight to the last man. "That's right," McMillen replied. "If you can hold this position until I can go to the rear and form on the next ridge, you can save this entire command. It all depends on you now." Before McMillen rode away he ordered two battalions of the Fourth Iowa Cavalry and eight more companies of the Fifty-fifth and Fifty-ninth Colored Troops to reinforce Bouton by taking up a position on the ridge separating Dry Creek and the Tishomingo Creek bottoms. Within ten minutes of receiving these orders all the white officers leading the Fifty-fifth U.S. Colored Troops were dead.

The Confederates were closing on the bridge when Gen. Abraham Buford joined the Kentucky brigade. Buford was an imposing figure of a man at three hundred pounds, and his booming voice could be heard above the crash of battle. Sensing the fright among the Federal troops, he began to issue orders intended to further confuse the enemy. "Fix bayonets!" Buford shouted for the benefit of the anxious Yankees. To them, Buford knew, the order portended a fierce and determined charge by the Confederates. But Forrest's men carried carbines and had no bayonets. They had long since discarded bayonets in favor of Navy Colts that were much more effective in close combat. "Forward guides center march!" Buford roared, and the Confederate lines started forward. After a few paces Buford ordered the charge.[23]

Some of the Union soldiers at the bridge began to give way, but many stood tall as the Confederates crashed into their lines. A vicious hand-to-hand affair ensued. The fight became even more merciless because the men on each side believed they would be shown no quarter in surrender. For a short period of time the melee resembled Fort Pillow. Ewing's black troops, the Seventy-second Infantry, fell back with the Fourth Iowa Cavalry and the Hoosier cannoneers but found the bridge blocked by overturned caissons and horses tangled in their harnesses. The bridge offered no escape. Luckily for the retreating Yankees, the Tishomingo had fallen a few feet, making the stream appear more fordable. Rather than face the firestorm exploding on the banks of the creek, many chose to jump into the water on both sides of the bridge. Numbers of them were killed as they swam or ran for their lives.

For a time, Bouton's black troops held fast and fought ferociously in a pitched toe-to-toe battle that resembled the physical, individual combat of an ancient battlefield. However, they could not withstand the savage Confederate attack for long and soon joined the stampede heading back up the Ripley Road.

Forrest's pursuit was unrelenting as he pushed them toward the ridge upon which stood the Agnew House. There, McMillen and Grierson intended to make another stand. Soon Bouton and his remaining troops joined the newly formed line.

All the while John Morton continued to rake the retreating ranks of the enemy with a devastating fire. Several accounts attest to Morton's unerring accuracy and tenacity on this field as he pushed his guns forward, at times by hand.

As dusk approached on Ames Ridge, Sturgis could rally only fifteen hundred of the more than eight thousand men with whom he had begun the battle earlier that day. Forrest now brought his horse holders into action. Every fourth man had been designated to that duty. This meant Forrest never had more than three thousand men engaged against Sturgis's eight thousand at any one time. As these fresh reinforcements joined Forrest, it was clear that he intended to keep the bulge on the enemy and chase them until they dropped, surrendered, or died.[24]

The sun was setting when Morton joined Forrest and his escort in confronting Bouton and McMillen's troops on Agnew Ridge. These African-American troops had possibly saved a good portion of Sturgis's command earlier in the day. Now they would pay a terrible price. Using rifles and pistols as clubs, Forrest's men drove into the Union line.

Nightfall brought an end to the fighting, marking the end of the first day, but more significantly it was the last attempt to stop the Confederate juggernaut. The surviving defenders of Agnew Ridge fled, littering the ground with Remember Fort Pillow patches as they ran. In the next few hours Sturgis made a few hopeless attempts to stop the flood of men running to the rear, "but before I could do so troops from all directions came crowding in like an avalanche from the battlefield and I lost all possible control over them."[25]

By this time the Union wagon train was virtually lost. Many teamsters had already cut their horses loose and abandoned the wagons, while ambulances full of wounded men were sunk to the axle in deep mud. The mob of troops fleeing up the Ripley Road passed wounded men begging for water, but nothing could or would be done for them. Sturgis ordered the remaining wagons to halt. In the meantime they were to "issue rations and ammunition to the troops, after which he would burn the god-damned train and the remaining supplies."[26]

At one point during the rout, Bouton found Sturgis and said to him, "General for God's sake, don't let us give up so." The demoralized Sturgis replied, "What can we do?" The colonel answered, "If you will give my blacks the ammunition the whites are throwing in the mud, my men will hold the enemy in check and allow the wagons and ambulances to get across the bottom." Bouton added that he believed he could save the entire column with one white regiment. On this he would stake his life, a questionable exchange since it was his black troops who had given the best account of themselves that day. The fight had gone out of Sturgis, who had days earlier promised to bring Forrest's hair to Sherman. His last comment to Bouton was heavy with resignation, "For god's sake, if Mr. Forrest will let me alone, I will let him alone. You have done all you could do and more than was expected of you, and now all you can do is save yourselves." At the moment Sturgis seemed most concerned with saving his own hide.[27]

Though the order was unnecessary because most of his men had already fled the battlefield, Sturgis called for a full retreat. But if he thought retreat would end his nightmare, he was wrong. Forrest would not relent. Col. Abel Streight, now residing in Richmond's Libby Prison, could have told Sturgis a thing or two from his own experience. Forrest would not stop until he had ridden Sturgis into the ground.

The pursuing Second and Seventh Tennessee Cavalries followed a trail of abandoned knapsacks, weapons, clothing, wagons, and cannon. Occasionally Winslow's Iowans attempted to form a defensive line, but Forrest, personally leading the pursuit, flanked them each time and drove them back toward Ripley.

Generals Sturgis and Grierson and Colonel McMillen arrived in Ripley at 5:00 A.M. and planned to make another stand. But Sturgis lost his nerve when he caught sight of the cloud of dust raised by the approaching enemy and once again resumed the retreat. Some of the remaining wagons were set afire; the rest were left behind at Ripley to be claimed as Confederate property.

Though Forrest and his men were also terribly exhausted, they somehow continued the chase. Along the way they passed several Union soldiers who had passed out or fallen asleep. Approaching Ripley, Forrest spotted the burning wagons and anxiously rode into town, where he found several rebel troopers and one lieutenant standing around, mesmerized by the fires. Forrest immediately dismounted and began cussing at the men, "Don't you see the damn yanks are burning 'my' wagons? Get off your horses and throw the burning beds off!" Every man jumped to the task except for the lieutenant, who felt that as an officer such duty was not in his job description. Forrest drew his saber and advanced toward his lieutenant, shouting, "I'll officer you." The lieutenant quickly scrambled down from his horse and joined in the work.[28]

As the night wore on, the weary retreat continued with Forrest's fresher troops "keeping up the skeer." As the Confederates crowded the rear of Sturgis's command, they occasionally pushed up among the stragglers. One Union fugitive, walking alone in the dark, was unaware that he was walking with rebels, whose mud-covered uniforms were indistinguishable from his own. "Old Forrest gave us hell today," he said. "Yes, we sure were fooled about ol' Forrest's strength. He certainly had 50,000 men in that fight. The woods were full of them, they were everywhere." The amused Confederates then informed their erstwhile marching companion that he too was now a prisoner of ol' Forrest.[29]

This unfortunate soldier's overestimation of Forrest's strength differed only slightly from that of his commanders. Forrest and his officers had surely helped to give that impression in the way they had maneuvered their troops to appear more numerous on the field, but the local inhabitants had also helped to create overestimations in the size of the Confederate force.

A few days earlier, on the eighth, as the Union column headed along Ripley Road toward the battle site, Col. Dewitt Thomas of the Ninety-third Indiana was informed of Forrest's strength and location. Passing the home of Mrs. William W. Falkner, wife of a Confederate colonel, Thomas was invited in for a cup of coffee. The Falkners were the grandparents of renowned twentieth-century Southern writer William Faulkner, who later added the "u" to the family name. Thomas asked Mrs. Falkner for information about Forrest and was told that he had been sent to northeast Mississippi to reinforce General Johnson, but that he had been recalled. Mrs. Falkner assured Thomas that the Yankees "would have plenty to do in a few days." When asked how many troops Forrest had, Mrs. Falkner exaggerated and told Thomas that there were twenty-eight thousand men with him. Forrest never had twenty-eight thousand men under his command. If he had, there is a good chance the Union forces would have paid a much dearer price for northern Mississippi and west Tennessee.[30]

While Forrest slashed away at Sturgis's rear guard, the enemy was never able to offer any kind of organized resistance. All that was left for the haggard Yankees was to get off the road and seek safety in the woods or to "break to the bush," as it was called. It was every man for himself. All that night and into the next day the Union army marched, stumbled, and ran toward the sanctuary of Memphis. It had taken a week to march the ninety miles or so from Collinsville to Brice's Cross Roads. It took the same starved and exhausted remnants of that command just two nights and one day to return.

Chasing is much more exhilarating than being chased, and though Forrest's command was equally exhausted, they had that advantage. Between 4:00 A.M. on June 10 and 8:00 P.M. on the June 11, Tyree Bell's brigade marched twenty-five miles over difficult terrain, nearly impassable roads, and through inhospitable weather and pursued the enemy for fifty-five more miles. Morton's artillery brigade had marched eighteen miles to reach the fight, fought from 1:00 P.M. to nightfall on the tenth, and continued to push the enemy for another forty-three miles.[31]

Over the same time period Forrest drove himself harder than any of his men, but even his iron constitution had limits. While part of his men took short rests, Forrest was constantly on the move, and the lack of sleep began to wear on him. Mack Watson, a private in Forrest's escort company, was riding close to Forrest as they passed near Salem, Forrest's boyhood home. Looking over at the general he realized that Forrest had fallen asleep in the saddle.

Watson reported this to Captain Jackson, commanding the escort. "Go wake him up, Mack," Jackson said. "No sir, you wake him up," answered Watson. Jackson then suggested that Watson tell Colonel Bell to wake him up, but Bell did not want the dubious task either and passed the buck back to Watson.

While this discussion was taking place the situation took care of itself. Forrest's horse was apparently also exhausted and slowly, with Forrest aboard, veered off the road and into a shallow ditch where the worn-out animal ran into a tree. Lacking documentation to the contrary and considering the reluctance among Forrest's men to wake him, it is safe to assume that no one laughed when this happened.

At the time Forrest rode his horse into the tree he was attempting to reach Salem ahead of the fleeing Federals in order to cut off and completely destroy Sturgis's command. Meanwhile, what was left of Sturgis's column was already straggling through Salem, where Sturgis wired Washburn at Memphis that Forrest, with ten thousand to twenty thousand men, had driven him back toward Memphis. Only Sturgis knew whether he truly believed that he had been badly outnumbered at the crossroads or whether he was attempting to cover his failure to accomplish his mission. But Washburn knew the truth of the matter, and so did Sherman.

From Salem the Federal column dragged itself north to LaGrange, where the exhausted survivors could be put aboard a train to continue the retreat to Memphis. It was said that some of the men were literally crawling when they reached the railroad.

Forrest's losses at Brice's Cross Roads were estimated at 96 killed and 396 wounded. Though proportionally these losses represented a heavy blow to Forrest's command, the overwhelming victory he had achieved would stand as his military masterpiece. The booty captured was welcome succor to the Confederates, but more notably, Forrest had inflicted a devastating psychological defeat upon the enemy, the effects of which would be permanent upon the Union cavalry in the western theater.

Colonel Waring, whose boys had been the first to break and retreat during the battle, reported that "the expedition sent out by Sherman was a tub to the Forrest Whale." He further reported that McMillen's infantry had come on the field at the crossroads a regiment at a time, "only so fast as the Forrest mill could grind them up in detail."

Long after the war, an unnamed trooper summed up the devastating loss from the viewpoint of the common soldier: "It is the fate of war that one or the other side should suffer defeat, but there was more. The men were cowed, and there pressed upon them a sense of bitter humiliation, which rankles after nearly a quarter century has passed."[32]

The Confederate captures at Brice's Cross Roads also included 60 officers and approximately 1,600 hundred Union troopers, 16 cannon, hundreds of artillery shells, 300,000 small-arms rounds, and 176 wagons, not to mention the medical supplies and other vast amounts of equipment gathered from the field.[33]

Back in Memphis, Sturgis reported losses of 2,240 men, of which 223 were known dead, 394 wounded, and 1,623 missing. He had lost all 22 pieces of artillery and 200 wagons and, as historian Robert Henry wrote, "brought back not one single strand of Forrest's hair."[34]

Seen from the viewpoint of either side, Brice's Cross Roads was a crushing and humiliating defeat for the Union forces in the west. Many of the participants believed superior numbers had overwhelmed them, but most blamed Sturgis and McMillen, who were rumored to be drunk during the battle. Though not averse to having a drink, Sturgis was not intoxicated the day of the battle. Nevertheless, his wartime military career was basically over. After a board of investigation "chaired by Brigadier General Mason Brayman," Sturgis was relieved of command and returned to his home in Covington, Kentucky, "where he remained until 1865, when he was ordered to Austin, Texas, to assume command of the 6th U.S. Cavalry."[35]

Forrest's victory at Brice's Cross Roads was not without controversy. There were very few battles in which Forrest fought that his actions did not stir up some type of dispute. When General Washburn was told of the loss of life among the black troops, he suggested that the battle at Brice's Cross Roads was a repeat of the "massacre at Fort Pillow." Supporting his allegation was the fact that almost as many black troops had been killed and wounded as in all five of Sturgis's other brigades. It was reported that the wearing of Remember Fort Pillow patches and the rumored vows taken by black soldiers to show no mercy to Forrest's command had incensed the Southern soldiers and motivated them to relentlessly shoot down the blacks. Another soldier stated that Forrest's men were eager to "confront the damned Negroes."[36]

Taken from Washburn's point of view, the disproportionate losses among the black troops might suggest that the Confederates at Brice's Cross Roads levied special retribution upon them. Another answer could lie in the nature of the battle. It was Bouton's African-American units who faced the fiercest combat that day as they bravely bore the brunt of the action, and by many accounts, saved Sturgis's force from annihilation. Specifically selecting certain soldiers, particularly more vulnerable ones, as targets is one thing. Charging against an unwavering wall of enemy soldiers is quite another.

To Washburn's charges that the Confederates at Brice's Cross Roads deliberately and specifically targeted black soldiers, charges similar to those following Fort Pillow, Forrest had a ready answer. His men knew of the reports, he said, that the black troops had taken oaths before Major General Hurlburt himself to avenge the deaths of black troops at Fort Pillow. He told Washburn that he also knew that this oath included a pledge to show no quarter to Forrest's troops. The Confederate leader and his men believed the accusations regarding Fort Pillow were misrepresented and untrue. Forrest was blunt in telling Washburn that he believed this perception and the reaction to it by the black troops who fought at Brice's Cross Roads had led to the high degree of bloodshed during the battle at the cross roads. It was clear to Forrest that these perceptions caused men on both sides to believe that they were unsafe in surrendering even when logic would dictate that further resistance was useless. In short, he was laying a large share of the blame at the feet of the Union soldiers and General Hurlbut.

A short time later Washburn accepted Forrest's offer to exchange wounded prisoners. In his communication to Forrest, Washburn wrote that he believed "that it is true that the colored soldiers did take such an oath but not in the presence of General Hurlbut." To Washburn's inquiry concerning the status of colored prisoners Forrest replied, "My prisoners, both black and white, are turned over to my government to be dealt with as it may direct." Forrest also suggested that Washburn contact authorities in Richmond for further information concerning how such prisoners were "regarded by my government, and the disposition which has been and will hereafter be made of them."[37]

Before Brice's Cross Roads, Sherman had expressed concern about the most serious threats to his proposed invasion of Georgia. One of these threats was Gen. John Hunt Morgan. The other was Gen. Nathan Bedford Forrest. Sherman wrote to Grant that he was not worried abut Morgan, who was in Kentucky. He considered Forrest to be a far more dangerous adversary and hoped that an expedition would be sent against Old Bedford around the first of June, which would keep Forrest too busy to interfere with Sherman's plans.

Morgan was defeated in Kentucky on the day the letter was written, thus confirming Sherman's assessment that Morgan was the lesser of the threats. However, the expedition that was to give Forrest "full employment" would shortly be running for their lives back toward Memphis having suffered a complete rout at the hands of the man Sherman considered the most dangerous of the two.

The force sent against Forrest with such high hopes of neutralizing him had fallen far short of its intended goal, but it had at least succeeded in keeping him busy for a short time. The full employment Sturgis was expected to cause had been fearfully short lived, however, and Forrest now loomed as an even greater danger. The stunning Confederate victory at Brice's Cross Roads required Sherman to divert forces from his projected Georgia campaign to deal with Forrest yet again. A. J. Smith's

> formidable command was diverted to Memphis and given the task of destroying Forrest and his corps—a mission that was to engross its energy until after the capture of Atlanta. A Union brigade led by Colonel John H. Howe, then stationed at Decatur, Alabama, and Brigadier General John E. Smith's 15th Corps, camped at Huntsville, and both under orders to reinforce Sherman in Georgia, were held where they were "in consequence of the repulse of Sturgis by Forrest."

As events would demonstrate, the Confederate command's inability to fully appreciate Forrest's value in the west would nullify his effectiveness far more than Sherman and all the Union forces he would send against him. Though Forrest had become more widely regarded by Sherman as the most dangerous obstacle for the Union army in that region, the Confederate leadership failed to grasp the significance of what both Sherman and Grant knew regarding the peril Forrest posed.

The summer of 1864 was critical for both sides, and the last chance for the Confederacy was slipping away. The rhetoric of the 1864 presidential campaign made it clear that there was a great war-weariness among the people of the North. Lincoln badly needed a victory at the polls, and the Confederacy could not afford another major loss on the battlefield. The desperation of the moment was almost palpable.

Sherman understood the far-reaching ramifications of Sturgis's defeat at Brice's Cross Roads and intended to do what he could to lessen the effect on his army. He wrote to Union secretary of war Edwin M. Stanton on June 15:

> I will have the matter of Sturgis critically examined, and if he should be at fault he shall have no mercy at my hands. I cannot but believe he had troops enough. I know I would have been willing to attempt the same task with that force; but Forrest is the devil and I think he has our troops under cower. I have two officers at Memphis who will fight all the time A.J. Smith and Mower. The latter is a young Brigadier of fine promise and I commend him to your notice. I will order them to make up a Force and go out to follow Forrest to the death, if it costs ten thousand Lives and breaks the treasury. There never will be peace in Tennessee Until Forrest is dead.[38]

The next day, June 16, Sherman wrote to Stanton again concerning Forrest:

> I have made necessary orders through General McPherson to inquire well into the Sturgis matter; also to send a large force again as he can get on Forrest's trail, and harass him and the country through which he passes. We must destroy him if possible.[39]

Sherman obviously believed that Forrest must be eliminated before the march to the sea could continue. He considered Forrest such a serious threat that he was willing to escalate the war in that area to include retribution against all civilians who supported him. His comments to Secretary Stanton continued:

> We will not attempt the Mobile trip now, but I wish to organize as large a force as possible at Memphis, with General A.J. Smith or Mower in command, to pursue Forrest, devastating the Land over which he has passed, or may pass, and to make people Of Mississippi and Tennessee feel although a bold, daring and Successful leader, he will bring ruin and misery on any country Where he may pass or tarry. If we do not punish Forrest and the People now, the whole effect of our vast conquest will be lost.[40]

It seems clear what Sherman and Grant thought about Forrest and his military actions and that they perceived him as a personal threat to their grand plan of cutting the Confederacy in two east of the Mississippi. However, Sherman's call for punishing the people along with Forrest was something new in war. He seemed to believe that punitive measures aimed not only at the Confederate army but at civilians as well would break their will to support the war effort. Sherman introduced these tactics to stop Forrest in the west and continued to lay waste to the countryside in his later march through Georgia and South Carolina.

For now, Forrest's impact on Sherman's operations in the western theater was seen as one of the primary threats to Union victory, and he Forres) was considered a central figure in the war. The failure of Sherman's "Forrest hunters" to eliminate him had culminated in the most humiliating defeat of all. The battle at Brice's Cross Roads apparently convinced Sherman that Forrest had the ability to seriously endanger the all-important march through Georgia. Though later historians minimize Forrest's potential in this regard, it is clear that Sherman, as the one man responsible for the campaign's success, saw Forrest's threat at the time as real and immediate.

Sherman rescheduled his invasion of Georgia for July 6 and once again wrote Grant and the secretary of war:

> I had previously written to General Washburn in Memphis that he should employ A.J. Smith's troops, and any other that he could reach, to pursue and destroy Forrest. This will give Smith an effective force of 12,000 or 15,000 men and leave 5,000 for other operations. . . . A cavalry expedition will start the same time from Vicksburg for the purpose of distracting the attention of the enemy from Smith's operations.[41]

Sherman continued to urge upon General Mower the importance of destroying Forrest's command and killing its leader. Sherman's urgency was demonstrated by his promise that should either Smith or Mower kill Forrest, they would receive immediate promotions to major general. To impress his sincerity upon Smith and Mower, Sherman wrote to Abraham Lincoln on June 24, 1864:

> Sir I have ordered General A.J. Smith and General Mower from Memphis to pursue and kill Forrest. I have promised a promotion to major general should they succeed. Should accident befall me, I ask you to favor Mower if he succeeds in disposing of Forrest.
>
> William T Sherman
> Major General[42]

By this request, Sherman had put a formal bounty on the head of a Confederate general. However, his focus on Forrest was not an idle fixation. Others also realized the hazard Forrest posed to Sherman's plans. When the invasion of Georgia finally began and Johnston's troops were relentlessly driven back, several prominent Georgians called for attacks on Sherman's rear echelons and suggested that

Forrest was the man for the job. Gov. Joseph E. Brown and former Georgia congressman, now Confederate general, Howell Cobb wrote to Johnston requesting that Forrest be given command of a cavalry detachment for the express purpose of destroying Sherman's vital lines of supply. Johnston and his cavalry commander, Joseph Wheeler, were of the same mind and urged Jefferson Davis and Braxton Bragg in Richmond to briefly relieve Forrest from his task of protecting the crops in Mississippi. They both believed Forrest should be immediately turned loose to wreak havoc on Sherman's three-hundred-mile supply line through northern Georgia and east Tennessee.

A hundred years later Civil War historian and Pulitzer Prize-winning author Bruce Catton shared these views and believed that had the Confederate high command ordered Forrest to attack Sherman's supply line before he ever reached Atlanta, the course of the war might have been altered. Catton went on to explain why he believed Forrest was up to the assignment.

> When Forrest struck the Federal rear, [Catton wrote] it took a real fight to keep him off; not just skirmish-line firing between galloping patrols, but a grinding, man-killing battle in which everybody played for keeps. . . . When Forrest hit a railroad line with evil intent, that line was obliterated with as much care and effort devoted to its destruction as had gone into its original building.[43]

In another observation concerning Forrest's effectiveness Catton wrote, "This man [Forrest], who better than anyone else in the Confederacy could create chaos in the rear of an invading army, had not been used for that purpose when an invasion was threatening the Confederacy's very life." In conclusion, Catton believed that had "Forrest ever got on Sherman's railroad line, Sherman [would have been] in serious trouble."[44]

On four separate occasions between June 13 and July 16, Gen. Joseph E. Johnston wrote to Davis expressing his views on just such a plan. In one communiqué he suggested that

> an adequate force under the most competent officer in America for such service, General N.B. Forrest, be sent to operate against Sherman's communications. This Cavalry will serve the Confederacy far better by insuring the defeat of a great invasion than by Repelling mere raids.[45]

# Chapter Twelve

# ONCE MORE UNTO THE BREACH

*—William Shakespeare*

## Tupelo and the Memphis Raid
## July-September 1864

In the midsummer months of 1864, the North and South were at a critical juncture of the war, and both sides were hoping for a miracle. Atlanta was under siege but had not yet fallen to Sherman. Abraham Lincoln's reelection was hanging in the balance and the president felt that emotionally he had hit bottom. Barring a great victory, he realized that the possibility of winning reelection was slight. The Democrats offered an end to the war by compromise, and Lincoln feared that all he had fought for so hard was slipping away and the country would be left permanently divided.

While Lincoln hoped for a decisive victory that would bring the voters back, Richmond hoped for European intervention and a miracle of their own while continuing the policy of a dispersed defensive to the bloody end. Regardless of all the suggestions and protests from military advisors and civilians alike, the Confederate war authorities would not change and order a campaign in Tennessee to cut Sherman's line of supply to his army pressing into Georgia. Consequently, Forrest, "the greatest soldier in the West[,] was not to be used to ensure the defeat of a great invasion, but to repel a mere raid."[1]

With Jefferson Davis unwilling to relinquish Mississippi, his home state, and "unleash" Forrest on Sherman's supply line, "Stephen D. Lee continued to demonstrate that he did not comprehend the strategic thinking behind the advance of Sherman's 'Army Group' toward Atlanta and the activities of the Union forces based at Memphis and Vicksburg." Echoing the same lack of tactical forethought as his commanders in Richmond, Lee stated on June 18 that "as long as the Federals held Memphis in force . . . a raid on the foe's

281

Middle Tennessee supply lines and depots would be impracticable."[2]

While the controversy continued over how he should be used, Forrest was making ready to meet the next formidable expedition sent out against him from Memphis. In June, Sherman was relentlessly pushing Joe Johnston farther into Georgia to the slopes of Kennesaw Mountain. With a hundred thousand men and thirty-five thousand animals to feed and provide for, Sherman was becoming more and more reliant on his line of supply. From Nashville to Stevenson, Alabama, Sherman had two rail lines in operation. The first was a direct line southeast from Nashville to Chattanooga, and the alternate line ran south from Nashville to Decatur, Alabama, and on to Stevenson. From Stevenson there was only a single line running forty miles across the Tennessee River and over the mountains to Chattanooga. From there the supplies were transported another hundred miles by wagon to Sherman's front.

Though Confederate policymakers would not threaten Sherman's supply lines, the Union commanders obviously believed that Forrest could and would. This new threat would be the fourth expedition sent out specifically to destroy Forrest's command, and true to Sherman's orders, Smith and Mower would lay waste to the countryside, burning Hernando and Oxford on their way toward Ripley and Tupelo. Sherman wrote to Grant, "I have now fulfilled the first part of my grand plan. Our lines are up to the Chattahoochee. Morgan failed in his Kentucky raid, and we have kept Forrest away from us, and now A. J. Smith is out with a force amply sufficient to whip him."[3]

When Smith and Mower took the field they left nothing to chance. The main column would be preceded by a line of battle that stretched a mile and a half in length. Grierson's cavalry, nearly four thousand strong, flanked the heavy column in the front and rear. A regiment of infantry also protected the rear, and the wagons were judiciously supervised to keep them closed up. This was wise on the part of the Union commanders, for they were going deep into Forrest territory, and visions of Sturgis, Smith, and Streight danced in their heads. Each successive expedition sent out to engage Forrest was larger than the last: approximately thirty-five hundred with Streight in April 1863, seventy-five hundred under Sooy Smith in February 1864, ninety-five hundred with Sturgis in June 1864. Now, in July of 1864, A. J. Smith was bringing nineteen thousand troops with him into the Black Prairie, a region rapidly gaining a reputation among the Federal cavalry commanders as something akin to the Bermuda Triangle.

While Smith and Mower prepared to move out, Forrest was

preparing to greet them. Earlier in the month his scouts had observed ominous developments. Several steamboats carrying A. J. Smith's division from Vicksburg moved up the Mississippi. On June 12, five trains steamed through Forest Hill, heading east with box-cars jammed so full of infantry that hundreds of troops rode on top of the cars. Forrest received this information on June 15. In response he concentrated Roddey's division at Corinth, Mississippi. On the twentieth, Forrest became aware of the troop buildup in Memphis. It came as no surprise.

On June 21, Chalmers was ordered to take the Twenty-first and Second Missouri Cavalry Divisions, including McCulloch's brigade and Pettus's flying battery, to Abbeville and once there "to observe the movements of the enemy in that quarter." From Guntown, Rucker's brigade joined Chalmers at Abbeville.[4]

While events began to accelerate, on the twenty-third Stephen D. Lee warned Richmond that he had learned that the Federals in Vicksburg had been reinforced by five white regiments and two thousand black troops. These men moving up from the south toward Jackson, Tennessee, constituted a second column in support of Smith. This maneuver was designed to require Stephen Lee to contemplate dividing his command.

On Tuesday, June 28, Lee advised his superiors that Forrest had informed him that Smith's expedition would leave Saulsbury within the week. He also let them know that Sherman was intending to support Smith and Mower's thrust from Memphis with a second column from Vicksburg. That same day, Forrest reported his strength at approximately six thousand and related that he had ordered Chalmers, at Verona, to be ready to take the field on Thursday at 6:00 A.M. with two days' forage for the animals and five days' rations for the men. Each man was to be outfitted with forty rounds for their carbines and thirty rounds for their pistols.[5]

That evening Forrest boarded a train at Tupelo and steamed toward Corinth to inspect Roddey's division. He also sent off a letter of congratulations to Lee on his recent promotion to lieutenant general:

> Allow me to congratulate you on your promotion. I am suffering from boils. If the enemy should move out I desire you to take command of the forces. Our force is insufficient to meet this command. Can't you procure some assistance?[6]

The strain on Forrest's system after the constant exertions of three and half years of war was taking its toll on him as he approached his forty-third birthday. He had driven himself like a demon. Three times he had been seriously wounded—twice at point-blank range—and it must have seemed to Bedford like he had been born in the saddle. And right now the saddle was the last place he really wanted to be. He had been plagued by boils on his buttocks for some time and was worn razor thin. His cheekbones were pronounced, and dark circles hooded his feverish-looking eyes.

However, under Sherman's relentless pressure, there was no chance for any rest. Arriving back in Tupelo on June 30, Forrest established a camp for the five or six hundred troops who had been recruited without mounts or whose horses were "unserviceable."[7] Anticipating the enemy's departure, which would take them south following the Mobile and Ohio Railroad in early July, Forrest reinforced his outpost at Ripley with Hyman's Mississippi regiment from McCulloch's brigade. Colonel Hyman's boys had barely joined their comrades near Orizaba when the massive Union column converged upon their position and forced them to fall back.

On July 6, the Federals broke camp at LaGrange and at Saulsbury, and both Union columns moved southward on parallel routes. A. J. Smith was in overall command of the force that sallied out of LaGrange, some fourteen thousand strong. General Grierson commanded the cavalry detachment out of Saulsbury, with Col. Edward Winslow's Tenth Missouri in the van.

On the seventh, Stephen D. Lee arrived at Tupelo to find Forrest's command had increased to approximately seventy-five hundred troops, twenty-one hundred of whom were dismounted. Augmenting his force were twenty guns. Lee and Forrest decided to lure Smith farther south to the Okolona area before engaging the enemy. Lee hoped that he could pull Smith into a position that would allow the Confederate commander to quickly shuttle troops to Mobile should Gen. E. R. S. Canby's army assault that city. Blacks were immediately put to work building rifle pits and artillery redoubts covering all the approaches to Okolona.

Moving ever so cautiously Smith, with "a line of battle and skirmishers about one mile in length," ran into Hyman's small force at Orizaba and drove them back through Ripley. Before moving on, Smith ordered the town burned. The ensuing inferno consumed the courthouse, the Masonic hall, the Methodist and Presbyterian churches, and the majority of the remaining buildings.

On July 8 at 5:00 A.M., Bell's Tennesseans moved out from their camp near Tupelo and rode to Ellistown where Bell deployed the

Second, Sixteenth, Nineteenth, and Twentieth Tennessee Cavalry brigades across the New Albany-Pontotoc road, effecting a blocking action.

On July 9, Colonel Datus Coon spearheaded Smith's advance, which crossed the Tallahatchie unopposed at Williamson's Mill and bivouacked that night at New Albany. When Smith did not move farther down the New Albany-Pontotoc road, Gen. Abraham Buford was ordered to follow the Union column to determine its strength but not to bring on a general engagement. Forrest also ordered General Chalmers to place a brigade at Pontotoc ahead of the enemy's progress.

Buford was in the saddle all night, arriving at Pontotoc with his nearly exhausted men at daybreak on the tenth. Chalmers took command of his and Buford's men and prepared to offer Smith his first real resistance. Having learned of the enemy's position the previous day, Forrest also had dispatched McCulloch's brigade to Pontotoc to reinforce Chalmers. Black Bob McCulloch reported to General Buford at 9:00 A.M. on July 10.[8]

Following Forrest's orders of the ninth, Buford mounted up at 1:00 P.M. and rode about six miles down the Okolona road and posted Col. Hinchie P. Mabry's and Lyon's brigades at Chiwapa Creek. Chalmers did not find Buford again until after dark on the tenth. Meanwhile, Bell's brigade had exhausted its forage and moved down to Okolona to replenish the men and animals at the Confederate stores of grain and corn. There had been so many movements by the numerous rebel units that confusion began to infect the cohesion of the operation. Chalmers was worried about Bell's brigade, which had left the field with a section of artillery. These cannon were necessary to effectively engage the opposing troops, for "unless the rebels were authorized to employ artillery it would be impossible to compel the Federals to show their strength." Since Chalmers had received no such authorization on the tenth, he felt there was no way he could engage the enemy.[9]

Smith knew the Confederates were massing to his front early on the morning of July 10, so he decided to divide his command again and move on parallel roads as far south as Cherry Creek. Smith's infantry traveled on the Plentyude road, while Grierson's horse soldiers rode down the Pontotoc road. Both columns moved out at 9:00 A.M. with Winslow's brigade in the lead. Lt. John H. Peter and the Fourth Iowa Cavalry were in the van.

Just south of Cherry Creek the two Federal corps converged upon one road and ran into Barteau's Second Tennessee. Barteau held a strong position on a high ridge, which required Smith's Iowans to flank them out of their foothold. The day was hot and humid, sapping the strength of the troops and soaking the uniforms on both sides with sweat. Barteau reformed his men farther down the road and threw out firing lines on both sides of the Pontotoc turnpike at staggered intervals. As the Fourth Iowa advanced, the first Confederate line fired away and fell back behind the next line, which then repeated the maneuver. In this manner Barteau's boys seriously slowed the Federals and sapped the strength of the Fourth Iowa to the point that Colonel Winslow relieved them with the Third Iowa Cavalry and continued the forward push.

At the same time, Smith's infantry drove the Sixth Mississippi Cavalry off the Plentyude Road, which also forced Barteau to withdraw toward Okolona to keep from being outflanked and cut off. Smith's troops continued their persistent progress to the banks of Cherry Creek, where they deployed into battle lines and made camp for the night.

Early on the eleventh, Smith had his column mustered and on the move across Cherry Creek, marching down the Pontotoc road. Colonel Coon's Seventh Kansas Cavalry took the point. The fierce heat hammered the Yankees as they moved closer to Pontotoc. Soon they ran into McCulloch's brigade, which was deployed around the town with a reserve posted on a hill just south of Pontotoc. McCulloch had no choice but to call up his horse holders and fall back down the Okolona stage road.

When he reported to Chalmers, south of Pontotoc, McCulloch was relieved by Lyon's Kentucky brigade, which was posted behind a rail fence atop Pinson's Hill. Chalmers then sent Barteau's Second Tennessee to block the Tupelo road, with Rucker's brigade on the Cotton Gin road. Black Bob's men were placed astride the Houston road. Forrest, concerned with Chalmers' deployment of the troops, asked him to hold the enemy for forty-eight hours while he and General Lee completed the preparations to engage Smith near Okolona. The problem was that A. J. Smith was not going to cooperate with Forrest's plan.

While the enemy approached Chalmers' position, Forrest sent Captain Tyler and a hundred handpicked men riding around to the rear of Smith's column, north of Cherry Creek, to create a diversion between Smith and his base of supplies and to harass the enemy's rear and flanks. Late in the afternoon, Tyler's men struck Smith's rear in several locations, continuing their attacks until coming upon the

Tupelo road, where they pitched camp that night next to the road. Smith and Grierson camped that night in the hills south of Pontotoc.

On the morning of July 12, Smith decided to seriously probe the Confederates' defenses. With the Ninth Illinois Cavalry in the lead, the Federals pushed forward to a ridge that overlooked Chiwapa Creek. Through his field glasses, Smith observed Lyon's strong position on top of Pinson's Hill. He also saw that his men would be forced to approach the rebels across a marshy swamp bottom that was some mile and a half across. It was a well-chosen site for a defensive action.

Smith sent in Capt. Henry M. Buel's battalion first, armed with their seven-shot Spencers. Lyon's Kentuckians watched them come and held their fire until the bluecoats were virtually upon them. Then, the Confederates cut loose a deadly fusillade directly into the faces of Buel's men. The volley took a devastating toll. In the midst of the of the hail of bullets, "Pvt. Jesse Hawes of Company I, 9th Illinois, was within an arm's length of the barricade when he heard a dozen voices shout, 'Don't shoot him!' A big, burly Kentuckian reached over the breastworks and dragged him in" to safety, sparing his life. Such was the character of the men and the strange nature of this war fought between brothers and fellow countrymen.[10] The lucky Private Hawes told the Confederates that Buel's men were about to make an infantry charge, information that caused Lyon to hold his position rather than ordering a countercharge of his own. This, in turn, allowed Buel to withdraw following his bitter repulse.

At the same time, Grierson's Third Iowa Cavalry was testing the rebels' strength on the Houston road. There they encountered Col. Leonidas Willis's Texans posted atop a hill beside the road. After a stubborn resistance, Grierson pushed the Texans off the hill and occupied it with a battalion of his own.

About 2:00 P.M., the Eighth Mississippi Cavalry of Rucker's brigade attacked Bouton's Fifty-ninth U.S. Colored Troops, who were caught off guard while they were picking berries five miles from Tupelo on the Tupelo road. Colonel Bouton immediately called up Company C of the Fifty-ninth U.S.C.T. and was able to drive the Southerners back and hold their position.

Notified of the new developments later that afternoon, Forrest sent a message to General Chalmers "to let the enemy come if he would, as everything is ready to receive him."[11] At 6:00 P.M. that afternoon, July 12, the Confederate retrograde movements around Pontotoc were called off, as Generals Lee and Forrest would be arriving that night to take command. These new orders from Lee and Forrest caused some confusion among the separated Confederate units on the battle front, and somehow the Tupelo road was left unguarded, providing Smith an opportunity "to steal a march" on Forrest.[12]

Around 4:00 P.M. on July 13, Smith decided not to come as Forrest had predicted, which would have accommodated Forrest and Lee. Rather, he suddenly turned east and headed for the Mobile and Ohio Railroad at Tupelo, some ten miles distant. Smith also deployed a small force to continue his original line of march to distract the rebels. Forrest and Lee did not arrive at Pinson's Hill until well after dark, when they discovered that the situation had completely changed. Angered at Rucker's and Barteau's uncoordinated movements that had left the Tupelo road wide open, Forrest immediately sent Mabry's brigade, Jesse Forrest's Alabama cavalry regiment, Bedford's escort company, and Pettus's Flying Battery to follow and attack Smith's rear guard.

He also dispatched General Buford to march for Verona on the Pontotoc and Camargo Ferry road to assail the enemy's right flank and rear. Col. Edward Crossland was to join his brigade of Kentuckians with Buford's. These assorted units hit the Union rear guard hard at various points during Smith's run for Tupelo. Rucker's brigade, spearheaded by the Eighth Mississippi, overtook Smith's wagon train at Chiwapa Creek, broke through the Fourteenth Wisconsin, "and got possession of his train at first, and killed the mules, so he [the enemy] was forced to abandon and burn 7 wagons, 1 caisson, and 2 ambulances."[13]

However, Lt. Col. James W. Polley's Wisconsin boys did not panic and quickly reformed. They were also reinforced by Colonel Ward's Thirty-third Wisconsin. The two commands staged a rallying charge that scattered Rucker's horse holders and most of his brigade. In their panicked retreat, the Eighth Mississippi were forced to leave their seriously wounded and dead on the field. The Mississippians also suffered the humiliation of abandoning their regimental colors to the swarming Wisconsin infantrymen.

Colonel Bouton's Fifty-ninth, Sixty-first, and Sixty-eighth U.S.C.T. fell in behind the Wisconsin troops and began a hard-nosed delaying action near a small hamlet called Burrow's Shop. Forrest arrived on the scene at about this time and joined his force with that of Chalmers and continued to hammer away at the black troops who were giving as good as they got. Meanwhile, General Buford was engaged in a bloody fight at Coonewah Creek in which he was unable to cut off the enemy's wagon train and was driven back after suffering heavy losses. Forrest continued to harass Bouton's stubborn regiments eastward toward Tupelo as darkness approached.

Smith refused to allow the slashing attacks on his rear to slow his progress and pushed on to a small hamlet two miles west of Tupelo called Harrisburg. There he stopped his train, drawing battle lines around it. Smith's line was nearly two miles long, facing west, with Grierson's cavalry posted on the flanks and rear. His troopers worked all night reinforcing their barricades with timbers and cotton bales. By 3:00 A.M. the next morning they were well prepared to receive any Confederate attack that would be coming with the daylight.

The night of the thirteenth, after the Confederates had settled down about two miles from the Union campsite, Forrest rode to Lee's headquarters. Lee and Forrest walked out of earshot of their men to discuss the disturbing developments of the day. Forrest laid his coat on the ground and stretched out, "greatly exhausted from the heavy work and intense heat." Lee was sitting on the ground with his back against a tree. Not long after they had begun their conversation, Forrest suddenly jumped up, whipped his coat back on and called to his aide, Lt. Samuel Donelson, to mount up. Forrest could never rest in the face of the enemy nor completely rely upon the reports of scouts and other officers. He needed to see their actions with his own eyes regardless of the exposed risk that a perilous night reconnaissance behind enemy lines presented.[14]

Riding through dark, wooded terrain and cloaked in jackets that were indistinguishable from those worn by Union cavalrymen, Forrest and Donelson penetrated the enemy camp. For half an hour they brazenly rode among the Federal troopers, weaving their way around campfires, wagons, and Yankee patrols. Finally, Forrest figured he had tempted fate long enough and slipped away into the night. Almost.

Just as it appeared that he and Donelson had gotten away clean, two sentries appeared and challenged the two horsemen. Forrest, who could bluff a man holding an inside straight flush, reined in and in a booming voice demanded, "How dare you halt your Commanding officer." The two Yankees hesitated and lowered their rifles. At that moment, Forrest put the spurs to his mount, and he and Donelson, hunched over their saddles, raced off expecting hot lead. The pickets quickly recovered and fired after the fleeing horsemen as they disappeared into the shadows.

Forrest often showed an interesting sense of humor in some of the most dire situations. After making it safely back into camp, he jokingly said to Lieutenant Donelson that it might have "been a great relief" if one of the Yankee bullets had "opened up" some of the boils on his derriere, though he probably didn't use that word to describe his buttocks.[15]

Forrest's battle report on the day's activities reads as follows:

> I had now driven the enemy 10 miles, and as his flanks had not been attacked, I was fearful he was being driven too rapidly. I therefore halted my command and waited on the attack on his flanks. In about an hour our guns [Morton's] opened upon him three miles ahead. I resumed the march and hurriedly pressed forward, and on reaching the ground I found General Chalmers had dashed into the road, surprised the enemy, and had taken possession of his wagon train. He, however, threw back a large force upon Chalmers, and forced him to retire, although not until he had killed and wounded many men and horses which forced the enemy to abandon and burn several wagons, caissons, and ambulances. About this time heavy firing was heard still farther up in the direction of Tupelo, which admonished me that General Buford was also attacking the enemy's flank. As night approached, the enemy became more obstinate in his resistance, but I attacked his rear with renewed energy until nine o'clock, when I reached a point two miles form Harrisburg, where I was joined by my entire command, which halted for the night. Being anxious to learn the exact position of the enemy I moved Mabry's brigade forward, and opened with four pieces of artillery. At a late hour in the night, accompanied by one of my Staff officers, I approached Harrisburg, and discovered the enemy strongly posted and prepared to give battle the next day.[16]

Strongly posted was an understatement. At daylight on the morning of July 14, Forrest and Lee squinted into the morning sun toward the heights to their front. Smith's battle line, two miles long, was facing west with interior firing lines fortified by fallen timbers and cotton bales. Grierson's huge cavalry force was supporting the flank and rear.

From this moment forward in the battle the typical Forrest operation failed to materialize, and according to numerous sources, Forrest admitted that he did not feel that this was the place to make an assault in force. To others he as much as admitted that he felt it was practically suicidal. Yet, because of his physical condition, reported to Lee in a dispatch before the campaign began, he requested that Lee take the command of what was essentially his own hand-built army. Others have suggested that Forrest's heart was not in the coming battle because of alleged feelings of jealousy toward Lee for his promotion to lieutenant general. This theory is based on the possibility that the Tennessee general believed that Lee had been receiving credit for victories that Forrest had actually won.[17]

Whatever the reality of the situation, Lee and Forrest did not coordinate and execute the attack as they should have, either because of unfortunate circumstances that arose or from a basic lack of communication and poor tactical battlefield execution. The pressure of time and Lee's promise to send two thousand men to help reinforce Mobile cannot be overlooked as a significant factor in the decision to proceed with the assault on July 14. Anyway one looks at the evidence, neither Lee nor Forrest gave their best performance, and the coming attack was disastrous for the Confederates.

As the years passed, the controversy lived on, with many of Forrest's associates firmly maintaining that Forrest earnestly objected to making a fight against A. J. Smith that day because of Smith's advantageous position and his overwhelming numbers.[18] Forrest's assistant adjutant, Major Anderson, who was thought to have been very close to Bedford, stated that on the morning of the fourteenth, he heard Forrest say in Lee's presence:

> The enemy have a strong position—have thrown up defensive works and are vastly our superior in numbers and it will not do for us to attack them under such conditions. One thing is sure; the enemy cannot remain long where he is. He must come out, and when he does, all I ask or wish is to be turned loose with my command. I will throw Chalmers' Division on the Ellistown Road, and if Smith undertakes to cross the country to Sherman, turn south to devastate the prairies, or return to Memphis, I will be on all sides of him, attacking day and night. He shall not cook a meal or have a night's sleep and I will wear his army to a frazzle before he gets out of the country.[19]

Colonel Rucker's later statement was in accord with Forrest's thoughts. He later argued that had Forrest alone commanded the Confederate force at Harrisburg, the enemy would have been forced into a disastrous withdrawal, though even so it was a dishonorable retreat.

Chalmers, however, while addressing the Southern Historical Society in 1879, two years after Forrest's death, said the following:

> Lee, Forrest, Buford and I were riding to the front, when the battle was about to begin. Buford said to Lee and Forrest, who had spent the night and morning together in consultation:

"Gentlemen, you have not asked my opinion about this fight, but I tell you, we are going to be badly whipped." Forrest replied sharply: "You don't know what you are talking about; we'll whip 'em in five minutes." Buford replied: "I hope you may be right, but I don't believe it."[20]

Most historians agree that this does not clear up the matter. Forrest was quite possibly supporting Lee in the presence of other officers rather than undermining his superior officer's authority once the attack had been decided upon. However, it does seem that in light of his later actions during the blistering hot day of the battle, Forrest's support was superficial and his spirit was not in the fight. Perhaps he knew the shape of things to come, because after July 14, 1864, the Forrest Cavalry Department would never again be the same fighting machine it once had been.

There is one indisputable fact: Stephen D. Lee decided upon the battle strategy and the time of the attack. That attack would begin at approximately 7:30 A.M. on July 14. Buford's cavalry division held the middle of the field with Mabry's brigade on the left facing east. Roddey's division was on the right facing north and Chalmers' division was held in reserve.

The Confederates were in a timberline that opened up onto a perfect killing field that stretched several hundred yards up a sloping rise to the crest of a ridge where some nineteen thousand Union troops waited behind a heavily fortified position. From these angles the Yankees would be shooting with their backs to the sun and the rebels would be moving up hill with the sun directly in their eyes.

Lee took command of the left and center; Forrest was given charge of the right with Roddey's small division. Lee gave the order to begin the attack, and Forrest charged off toward his designated section of the field.

> Lieutenant-General Lee gave the order to advance . . . and directed me to swing the right around upon the enemy's left [he reported]. I immediately repaired to General Roddey's right with all possible speed, which was nearly a mile distant, and after giving him the necessary orders in person I dashed across the field in a gallop for the purpose of selecting a position in which to place his troops.[21]

After the battle questions would arise over how the signal to begin the attack was to have been delivered. Some Confederate officers were under the impression that a cannon would be fired to begin the attack rather than waiting for a courier to relay verbal orders. Others did personally receive orders from their commanding officers to go forward at a specified time, but there was some kind of breakdown in communicating the exact moment of demarcation to all the effectives. Consequently, the attack was uncoordinated from the very beginning.

With the number of horse holders required, the Confederates could only place about six thousand rifles in their battle formation. The long roll of the drums was heard across the field as battle flags unfurled and final preparations began. As the morning sun fell upon the soldiers' faces, "there now precipitated a battle tragedy for a parallel the historians will in vain search the records."[22]

Forrest was on his way to the left when he noticed that Mabry and Crossland had already begun to move in oblique lines toward the enemy position. However, their move opened a gap that forced General Buford to rush Bell's brigade and his guns forward to plug the hole. This movement had to be made so quickly that the guns had to be pushed into position by hand. But before Buford could straighten out his lines, Colonel Crossland's Kentuckians, unable to restrain themselves, raised the rebel battle cry and broke into a full sprint toward the Yankee barricades. The time required to coordinate such an attack was rapidly evaporating.

In reserve on the Confederate right were Capt. Daniel Beltzhoover's infantry battalion and twenty-one hundred dismounted cavalry under Lyon. Lyon's Kentucky brigade, however, would find itself in the thick of the fighting. Colonel Crossland, leading Lyon's brigade of Kentuckians, stated that although he attempted to move his men steadily,

> it was impossible to restrain the ardor of my men. Believing that they were strongly supported both on the right and left, raising a shout, they charged forward on the enemy's line, which was keeping up a constant, destructive fire. Arriving within two hundred yards of the enemy, exposed during the whole time in an open field and under a most terrific fire of artillery and small arms from a force greatly superior to their own and strongly entrenched, the enemy suddenly opened up an enfilading fire from both flanks.[23]

Realizing that retreat would now be disastrous, Crossland and Colonel Falkner, both mounted, began shouting, "Forward men." Falkner was wounded twice and his horse was killed under him. All across the field, scores of men fell under the merciless enfilade fire from two different Union batteries blasting away with grape and canister. Crossland later reported that the "failure of Roddey's division to advance, and thus draw the fire of the enemy on my right flank, was fatal to my me. . . . The ranks were decimated; they were literally mowed down."[24] Mistake compounded upon mistake as the attack began to fall apart.

Under the circumstances, the first mistake was to have begun the attack at all. The second was Crossland's unauthorized charge. It could also be said that Forrest made the third mistake of the day by reversing his orders. Forrest later reported,

> Upon reaching the front, I found the Kentucky brigade had been rashly precipitated forward, and were retiring under a murderous fire concentrated upon them. I seized their colors and after a short appeal ordered them to form a new line, when they held their position.[25]

Forrest then changed his mind, deciding it was insane to send more of his men into the jaws of a meat grinder, for it had already been amply demonstrated "that the enemy were in overwhelming numbers in an impregnable position." Forrest wrote,

> Wishing to save my troops from the unprofitable slaughter I knew would follow any attempt to charge his works, I did not push forward [as were his orders] General Roddey's command when it arrived, knowing it would receive the same concentrated fire which repulsed the Kentucky brigade.[26]

Forrest's change in the plan left Crossland's boys to suffer extreme casualties from a deadly crossfire. General Buford also was still engaged, pushing his cannon forward by hand and driving the men and his brigades up the middle into a hailstorm of lead. But due to the actions of Forrest and Crossland, Buford's brigades were now isolated and began to take the concentrated fire from thousands of Yankee weapons, forcing Buford to retreat, leaving a staggering number of casualties on the field behind him.

Young Captain Morton, who was in command of all the Confederate artillery batteries that day, wanted to mass his artillery and move forward with the Kentuckians to blast a hole through the Federal line for his onrushing comrades. General Lee, who had led an artillery battalion in the Army of Northern Virginia, where such tactics were virtually unknown, had denied Morton's request before the battle. Instead, Lee dispersed Morton's guns throughout various brigades and positions, which prevented Morton from implementing the tactic he and Forrest had used on many other battlefields with shocking effect. Who knows if Morton's suggestion would have changed the outcome, but it does suggest that virtually all the officers on the field that day had their own ideas about improving on General Lee's battle plan.[27]

Meanwhile, Chalmers began to move his division to the front but received three separate, conflicting orders on the way. One order from Forrest told Chalmers to bear right and support Roddey. A second order came to him at the same time from General Lee instructing him to go to the left to support Mabry. And a third came from Buford requesting Chalmers to bring his division to the middle and support him. Obviously Chalmers was in a quandary. He decided to follow Forrest's order, but just as he was about to move, he received a fourth order from Lee that divided his command, sending Rucker's men to the left and leaving McCulloch's brigade in reserve. Chalmers later reported that the last order from General Lee divided his command, and although the troops "behaved with as much gallantry as men could . . . they were unable to accomplish anything."

The entire Confederate attack seemed uncoordinated and the officers executing it, negligent. John Wyeth wrote in 1900, "One brigade after another as wave after wave of the ocean is scattered in spray against the unyielding cliffs, were dashed to pieces."[28]

From the Union perspective, Gen. A. J. Smith said,

> [The attack] seemed to be a footrace to see who could reach us first . . . yelling and howling like Comanches . . . gallantly made, but without order, organization, or skill. They would come forward and fall back, rally and forward again, with the same result. Their determination may be seen by the fact that their dead were found within thirty yards of our batteries.[29]

The battle effectively ended when Smith saw that the Confederates could not bring enough weight against him and he ordered his men to advance within a half-mile of their breastworks, driving the remaining rebel forces from the field and "covering their dead and wounded."

That night Smith began burning Harrisburg, which angered the Confederates to the point that they launched a night attack and drove the outer lines back upon the main body of the Federal line. The night attack was made under "the heaviest small arms fire heard during the engagement." However, the main idea behind the audacious night maneuver was to harass Smith's army and probe his defenses.

Forrest led Rucker's brigade to the southeast, beneath the eerie glow cast from the burning buildings in Harrisburg, and continued to harass the enemy by lobbing artillery rounds into his lines throughout the night. The close-range barrage forced Smith to have the long roll beaten calling out Colonel Bouton's and Gen. C. C. Gilbert's brigades on the double with bayonets fixed to reinforce Wolfe's brigade, which had remained on the line. Bouton's U.S.C.T. and the 117th Illinois "sent volley after volley crashing into the darkness."

Forrest later reported that when the three Yankee brigades opened up on him it was "one of the heaviest . . . I have heard during the war. There was [an] unceasing roar of small-arms, and his whole line was lighted up by a continuous stream of fire." Luckily, Forrest had placed his men in the hollows of the field so that the enemy continued to fire over the heads of the Confederate troops. "Since he had stirred up the Yankees and made sure there would be little sleep in their camps," Forrest withdrew his force under the cover of darkness and returned to the Confederate campsite.[30]

The Confederates braced themselves for the counterattack that should have come, but didn't. Smith was not convinced that the mauling he'd given the rebels had weakened them enough to chance an attempt to finish them. It was a mistake on Smith's part and an indication of Forrest's reputation among the Federal cavalry commanders. Had Sherman known about this wasted opportunity, he might have reconsidered any promised promotions to Smith or Mower.

Sherman already feared that the majority of his cavalry officers were intimidated by Forrest, but he did not think that a grizzled veteran like Smith would blink during the crucial point of his campaign. Nevertheless, Smith and Mower, somehow forgetting the main objective of their mission, which was to kill Forrest, and using the excuse of spoiled bread stores, prepared to claim laurels for what they had already accomplished and return to Memphis in one piece. They had, after all, done more than the other expeditions sent against Forrest. A. J. Smith may have failed to destroy Forrest's command, but he most certainly crippled it.

During the battle on July 14, the Confederates had seven mounted and dismounted brigades on the field. Their reported losses were approximately 1,249 killed and wounded and 49 missing. This amounted to losses of 34 percent, perhaps the worst defeat for a cavalry command during the war. Buford's division alone lost 22 officers killed and another 104 men wounded. Nearly all the commanders, from every shattered regiment, had been shot down, if not killed. These included Col. R. M. Russell, Col. C. R. Barteau, A. N.

Wilson, Col. John F. Newsome, Lt. Col. D. M. Wisdom, and Maj. W. T. Parnum. In Barteau's Second Tennessee, only one commissioned officer remained. "Never again would these units be capable of mounting an effective assault on a Union position. Their combat effectiveness had been destroyed."[31]

Late that night Forrest attempted to avoid an officers' staff meeting, claiming that his physical condition and illness prevented him, but Lee summoned him anyway. After arriving at Lee's tent headquarters, Forrest found the conversation between him and General Lee to be less than cordial. When Lee asked Forrest if he had any "ideas about how things had broken down on the battlefield," Forrest angrily fired back at Lee, "Yes, sir, I've always got ideas, and I'll tell you one thing, General Lee. If I knew as much about West Point tactics as you, the Yankees would whip hell out of me every day."[32]

The battle at Tupelo was shades of the second fight at Fort Donelson and several other battles during the Civil War where frontal assaults on fortified positions failed miserably. Necessity seemed to dictate the use of such tactics on many occasions, but in the end, the cost in blood always outweighed any military or political advantage gained in the doing. Unfortunately, the men who fought the battles did not have a crystal ball nor did they have the advantage of historical hindsight. However, Forrest did seem to possess a strategic insight and understanding of contemporary weaponry and tactics. This understanding allowed him to see beyond the Napoleonic thinking of the officers trained at the military academies of the nineteenth century. Nevertheless, on July 14, 1864, it seemed that Forrest did not want command and refused to take complete control in a situation in which he felt the battle strategy was flawed from the beginning. Perhaps there was no choice due to the circumstances except to back up his commanding officer even if he did not agree with his decision to attack. In the end, it was neither Lee's nor Forrest's best performance during the war.

The conflict at Tupelo also seems to add weight to the theories concerning Bedford's alleged inability to share the command on a battlefield and acquiesce to another man's judgment. Of course, in the opinion of Forrest and the surviving grizzled veterans of his cavalry corps; Forrest should have been in complete command on every battlefield that they had ever fought upon together.

Those same grizzled veterans stood up for Forrest after his death in response to Lee's published account of the events at Tupelo. Stephen D. Lee, who made no report at the time of the battle, wrote his remembrances in the third person, as had John Morton in his personal account of the war. Thirty-seven years after the war Lee wrote that Forrest had changed the battle plan by not sending in Roddey's division from the right:

> Gen. Lee moved to the right. . . . He soon met Gen. Forrest, and said to him: "Why did you not carry out the plan of attack?" Forrest replied: "Buford's right had been rashly thrown forward and repulsed. In the exercise of my discretion I did not move Roddey forward but I have moved him to the left, and formed a new line." Gen. Lee said, "In doing as you did, you failed to carry out the plan of battle agreed on." Gen. Lee then replied that it was too late to remedy the matter.[33]

In a fashion similar to filing a class-action suit, nine of Forrest's surviving officers, three of whom (Bell, Rucker, and Lyon) were educated at West Point at the same time Stephen Lee was attending the academy, submitted a statement rebutting the facts of Lee's report. In it they stated that there was no official signal gun fired to start the battle and that Lee was mistaken about many other facts that seemed to elude his memory, "which after a lapse of thirty-seven years is not always reliable."[34]

However, it seems that Forrest and Lee maintained a good relationship until Forrest's death in 1877. On the day that Forrest died Lee was heard commenting on the battle at Tupelo. The old veteran sadly stated, "I am sure he did his best as he saw it. I am sure I did my best as I saw it."[35]

## Smith Retreats and the Fight at Owl Creek

Having borne only a fraction of the losses suffered by the Confederates, and with an army twice as large as the enemy's still intact, Smith decided to retreat. Smith's reported reason for this action was that he had received news that his hardtack and bread supplies had spoiled, leaving him only one day's rations. Historian Robert S. Henry wrote that Smith made this decision "right at the edge of the greatest granary of breadstuffs in the Confederacy."[36]

However, the Yankees had little time to bake bread. Smith seemed to be more concerned with getting the hell out of the Black Prairie and becoming the first commander to engage Forrest and escape with his hair. He was in such a hurry to disengage and return to Memphis that he left his seriously wounded behind in order to facilitate his withdrawal.

On the morning of July 15, Lee and Forrest were in the saddle probing the enemy's defense. As soon as it was apparent that Smith was withdrawing, Lee ordered Forrest in pursuit. Approximately five miles north of Tupelo, Forrest caught up with the enemy's rear guard. A heated exchange of gunfire and artillery exploded up and down the line as the Federals fought a desperate and spirited holding action to give Smith's main column, which was on the Ellistown road, time to cross Owl Creek.

The heat was oppressive and General Buford reported that at least eighty of his troops had to be carried to the rear due to heat stroke. As Forrest rode through the smoking ruins of Harrisburg, he discovered the makeshift Union field hospital filled with Smith's wounded. He was horrified to find many of the men had wounds that were "fly-blown and filled with maggots." Detailing some of his men to take control of the sad situation, Forrest rode forward to continue the harassment of the retreating Yanks.[37]

The vicious fighting continued as the Union rear guard fell back toward Owl Creek. Grierson's cavalry countercharged the Confederates, only to be driven back again through a large cornfield. The "Rebel line . . . with its battle-flags waving in the sunlight, was boldly and firmly advancing" only one hundred yards behind them.[38] As the Confederates emerged from the tree line and started across the cornfield, Brig. Gen. C. C. Gilbert's brigade quickly deployed in front of Owl Creek. On the west side of the road the Thirty-second, Fourteenth, and Twenty-seventh Iowans braced themselves for another assault.

Colonel Crossland and Colonel Bell had only about one thousand men in their front units. Rice's battery opened up on the Iowans as Bell's and Crossland's troops charged forward. Buford, observing the action through his field glasses, was optimistic at first as he watched the rebels begin to push the Iowans' cavalry brigade back to the banks of Owl Creek. Then suddenly McMillen's and Gilbert's infantry recrossed the creek and joined the fray. The tide began to turn as the troops of the Third and Fourth Iowa and the Ninth Illinois Cavalry (dismounted) also reinforced Grierson's troops. Colonel Crossland was hit and forced to relinquish command of his Kentuckians as the Confederates began to give ground. General Buford was contemplating the possibility of abandoning the Confederate position when General Chalmers arrived on the scene. Forrest galloped up a few minutes later.

Forrest lost no time in sending McCulloch's brigade to support

Rice's battery as Chalmers took command of Forrest's Alabama regiment and moved to check Gilbert's advance. While this movement was in progress Forrest suffered his fourth wound of the war. A bullet struck him on the ball of his foot and exited through his arch. Forrest said that this was the most painful wound he had ever received and it was so disabling that he was forced to turn command over to General Chalmers.[39] Soon after Forrest was hit, Colonel McCulloch was shot in the shoulder and carried from the field. At this point, Forrest called off the attack and sent a courier to report the situation to General Lee.

Before Chalmers received word of Forrest's wound, he was attempting to rally the troops. At this point in the fight, considering their massive losses at Harrisburg, the rebels' ranks had been drastically reduced. Nevertheless, Chalmers called for Buford to reform his division. When he received no immediate response, Chalmers again demanded, "General Buford, move your division." Buford replied, "I have no division general. . . . They are dead and wounded."[40]

It was the same in nearly every other Confederate brigade. Chalmers had no choice but to withdraw and recall Rice's battery from the ridge that it had held throughout the fight at Owl Creek. Soon the Federals took possession of the ridge but made no further attempts to chase the Confederates as they fell back approximately four hundred yards and formed a new line. With darkness approaching, the Federals crossed back over Owl Creek and bivouacked for the night.

That evening, with Forrest uncharacteristically absent, the rumor began to spread through and beyond the Confederate camp that he was dead. Forrest was in the field hospital where the doctors were working to stop the bleeding from his wounded foot when he received the news that his men believed that he had been killed. He understood that the loss of a commanding officer in the face of the enemy could be catastrophic to the morale of an army and ordered the surgeons to quickly bandage his foot. Then, not even taking time to put on his riding coat, he hobbled out to his horse in his shirt-sleeves and mounted up. With only one foot in the stirrups, Forrest rode up and down the ranks of his troops speaking words of encouragement to quell their fears and so they could see for themselves that he was certainly not dead. "The effect produced upon the men by the appearance of General Forrest [was] indescribable. They seemed wild with joy at seeing their great leader still with them."[41]

In late July, General Washburn, in Memphis, jubilantly wired Sherman that Forrest had died of lockjaw. Sherman was skeptical that the old Confederate cat had used up the last of his nine lives.

"Is Forrest surely dead?" he asked. A few days later when Washburn learned the truth, he had to dash Sherman's hopes. "General Forrest is not dead but was in Pontotoc four days ago," he wrote.[42]

Smith had his column on the road by sunup on July 16. Due to the terrible condition of Forrest and Lee's army, any pursuit in force was called off. Chalmers was ordered to pursue with Roddey's division and Rucker's brigade and harass the enemy. Chalmers caught up with Smith's Seventh Kansas Cavalry at Ellistown, and a long-range fight ensued. The firefight continued until Grierson called up Wolfe's brigade and Company G's gun battery. Soon after the Redlegs of Company G opened fire with their cannon, Chalmers realized he was extremely outnumbered. He fell back and went into camp for the night.

The next day Chalmers renewed the chase and continued until Smith's column arrived at New Albany that evening. From New Albany, Smith began to break up his command. The infantry was "given another free ride on box cars into Memphis" while his cavalry marched toward Memphis via the State Line Road. They arrived back at their home base seventeen days after they had left.

Smith's campaign had failed to achieve total success, but it had kept Forrest from wrecking the single track railroad that Sherman so desperately relied upon to supply his army marching through northwest Georgia. It also had destroyed the combat effectiveness of Forrest's cavalry. However, Sherman was not satisfied and on July 23, wired Washburn:

> It was by General Grant's special order that Smith was required to pursue and continue to follow Forrest. He must keep after him until recalled by me or General Grant and if Forrest goes to Tennessee, General Smith must follow him. . . . It is of critical importance that Forrest does not go to Tennessee.[43]

The Tupelo campaign was a success in that regard and kept Forrest fully employed at a critical point in the war. Smith had not killed Forrest, but he had wounded him and pounded his command. Nevertheless, Sherman wanted Forrest dead, not wounded. For now, he would have to get by without the icing on his cake. Sherman honored his promise and followed through on the promotions of Smith and Mower to brigadier general. "Mower's task was to kill Forrest but only crippled him, nevertheless, he was a young and game officer deserving of the promotion."[44]

The week after Tupelo, Stephen D. Lee was sent to become a corps commander under John Bell Hood, who had been sent to assume the defense of Atlanta after President Davis had removed Gen. Joseph E. Johnston from command. Lee was not to be succeeded by Forrest but by Maj. Gen. Dabney H. Maury from Virginia. Forrest was passed over once again by Richmond; the power of tradition chose yet another West Point officer rather than the man whom many believed all along should have commanded in west Tennessee and northern Mississippi.

That Maury was a West Pointer takes nothing from his military talent, or his ability to command. Maury was a highly cultured Virginian and personal friend of Stephen Lee. He had graduated from West Point in 1846, in the same class as George McClellan, Joe Johnston, and Stonewall Jackson. To Forrest, Maury wrote,

> I intrust you the operations against the enemy threatening an invasion of North Mississippi. I would not, if I could, interfere with your plans for conducting these operations, but must confine myself to that duty of sending you the means, as far as I can, of accomplishing the successful results it has been your good fortune so constantly to achieve. . . . You know as well as I the insufficiency of my means. . . . But we must do the best we can with what little we have and it is not small satisfaction I reflect that all of the commanders of the Confederacy you are accustomed to accomplish the very greatest results with small means when left to your own untrammeled judgment. Upon that judgment I now rely.[45]

At the moment about all Forrest could do was suffer. He was unable to ride a horse, so a modified farm buggy was rigged up to "get the general around for a few days." Seeing Forrest bumping along in a buggy with his bandaged foot elevated on a specially rigged rack over the dashboard must have been a humorous sight to some, but it is doubtful that anyone laughed, at least not in his presence. John Allen Wyeth thought Forrest presented quite a "novel sight" seated in a ragged buggy, guiding a spiritless nag among the trees and along the highways of Mississippi, carefully dodging stumps and roots and stones, or anything that might jolt the crippled foot, not to mention the boils that still plagued him.[46]

## The Memphis Raid
## August-September 1864

Sherman was as relentless as Forrest was tenacious during their strategic duel in 1864. Late on the night of July 22, General Washburn notified Smith that he had received a dispatch from General Grant ordering him to begin immediate preparations to return to north Mississippi and resume the hunt for Forrest. Smith knew his men would not be thrilled to return on such short notice to the Black Prairie region. The best he could do to prepare them was to give them a night's rest before breaking the news to them the next morning.

This time around Washburn and Smith intended to be better equipped and more prepared to go after Forrest. Some of the field pieces that had been lost at Brice's Cross Roads had not yet been replaced. Washburn located the needed equipment and guns in St. Louis and had them shipped to Memphis. This expedition was to proceed down the Mississippi Central Railroad, which had been abandoned since the winter of 1862 because all the bridges and trestles had been burned and much of the track torn up. Washburn and Smith planned to move Smith's army to Grand Junction and establish an advanced operating base. From there Smith would move his corps southward, repairing the line as they went. Smith also intended to establish supply magazines at Holly Springs, Abbeville, and Oxford. From Oxford, Smith planned to move into the Black Prairie via the Pontotoc Ridge.

The trains carrying Smith's troops steamed out of Memphis on July 29 and arrived at Grand Junction late that afternoon. The repair work on the Mississippi Central began with the arrival of construction crews on August 1. That same day Col. Joseph J. Woods and the Twelfth Iowa Cavalry rode the twenty-five miles from Grand Junction southward to Holly Springs, occupying the town when they arrived there about 11:00 A.M. the next morning.[47] By the third, Mower's Eagle Brigade along with McClure's brigade had also marched into Holly Springs. The Union presence there was firmly established with the arrival on August 5 of Bouton's U.S.C.T., in charge of the artillery and wagon train.

On August 7, the 178th New York, Forty-ninth Illinois, and the Fifty-second Indiana detrained at Grand Junction. Col. Edward Winslow rode into Grand Junction on the eighth with one more division made up of the Third and Fourth Iowa Cavalries and the Tenth Missouri Cavalry. This brought Smith's over all strength to ten thousand troops divided into two large divisions. Smith's troop concentration at Grand Junction and the lead elements occupying Holly Springs were nearly complete by August 8.

Though still suffering from his wound, Forrest was back in the saddle again by late July, albeit it with only one foot in the stirrups. His headquarters was established at Okolona, where his intelligence network of spies and scouts soon informed him of Smith's exact position and troop displacements at Grand Junction and Holly Springs.[48]

Still unsure about Smith's intentions, Forrest began to redeploy his troops. His command had been so decimated at Tupelo that the horses belonging to the dead and wounded men and officers would be enough to remount more than two thousand of his troops who had been traveling and fighting on foot. By July 18, his various units were on the move to their staging areas, and on the twentieth, the Confederate brass established several magazine stockpiles along the Mobile and Ohio Railroad to facilitate the rebuilding of Forrest's command.

Attempting to determine Smith's strength and destination, Forrest sent Colonel Chalmers' Eighteenth Mississippi Cavalry Battalion to Abbeville on July 22 to ascertain the Federal disposition in that area. Chalmers reported back on the twenty-fifth that the enemy's strength was nearly fourteen thousand and that he had observed huge Union construction crews working hard to repair the Mississippi Central. From his headquarters at Okolona on August 1, Forrest canceled all furloughs, and two days later he ordered General Chalmers, along with his own escort company, staff, and Thrall's Arkansas battery to proceed to Oxford and establish a base. Realizing that Chalmers would be exposed at Oxford, Forrest sent Col. J. J. Neely's brigade to Pontotoc to be within easy supporting distance of Chalmers.[49]

While Chalmers was en route to Oxford, he received a dispatch from Forrest to conscript five hundred black workers to begin felling trees on the north side of the Tallahatchie River and to start throwing up earthworks at Oxford. On August 5, as Chalmers began the work of fortifying a position at the Tallahatchie near Oxford, Forrest discerned Smith's true line of march. Smith was not going to move into the Black Prairie but rather, as the construction indicated, was going to come straight down the Mississippi Central. On August 7, while the Confederates were digging in at the river, Smith was preparing to assault Chalmers at the Tallahatchie.[50]

Chalmers was on the south side of the Tallahatchie with Col. William B. Wade's brigade of the Fifth and Eighth Mississippi Cavalries, augmented by Willis's Texas battalion, held in reserve at Hurricane Creek, six miles north of Oxford. At 2:00 P.M. on August 7, Smith's Task Force Hill followed the railroad south and came into contact with the Confederates a half-mile north of the river. The

Eighteenth Mississippi Cavalry had established a roadblock at that point to slow Smith's approach, but the Third and Fourth Iowa Cavalries quickly drove the small detachment of Mississippians back across the river and moved to the bank of the Tallahatchie to force a bridgehead.

Before falling back the Confederates were unable to scuttle a flatboat at the river, which the Iowans quickly commandeered and used to begin ferrying men across. By nightfall, two companies of the Thirty-fifth Iowa, the Seventh Minnesota, and the Twelfth Missouri Cavalry were on the south side of the Tallahatchie. Having received the disappointing news that the enemy had gotten across the river, Chalmers decided upon a night attack to attempt to dislodge the Yankees' foothold. At about 11:00 P.M. Thrall's Arkansas battery and the troopers of the First Mississippi Partisan Regiment moved silently into position.

Cutting loose a barrage with their guns, and in the pitch-blackness, the rebels rushed the Federal position on the riverbank. Fire exploded in return from the Union emplacement and drove the Mississippians back under the cover of Lt. James C. Thrall's guns. Quickly reforming, the Confederates surged forward again only to be hammered back as the Federal line crackled with flame, lighting up the night. Although he had beaten the Confederates back twice, Colonel Hill lost his nerve, and "just as the first streaks of dawn appeared on the eastern horizon," Hill decided to give up his bridgehead and cross back over the Tallahatchie.[51]

On the morning of August 8, Colonel Hill was still intimidated by the apparent strength of the Confederates on the opposite side of the river and made no attempt to recross. Instead, he waited upon the arrival of Gen. Edward Hatch's cavalry coming up from Holly Springs.

Under oppressive humidity the Confederates watched the Federal force grow in strength to the point that Colonel Wade ordered his men to fall back from the river to avoid being flanked. At approximately 5:00 P.M. on the eighth, General Hatch had reached the scene. He immediately put the Third Iowa Cavalry back across the river and began the construction of a floating bridge large enough to get his division of horsemen, guns, and small supply train over the Tallahatchie.

When Chalmers got word that the Union cavalry had recrossed the river he immediately dispatched to Forrest for help. Forrest was still unsure whether the enemy's thrust at the Tallahatchie was a feint or whether it was Smith's true line of march. Forrest replied ordering Chalmers to fall back to Oxford if absolutely necessary but to make a fight of it every inch of the way. Perhaps to cheer his fighting commander somewhat in the face of such dire instructions, Forrest advised Chalmers that reinforcements would soon be on the way should developments indicate Hatch's attack was the vanguard for Smith's column.[52]

That night Chalmers fell back to Hurricane Creek, considering it prudent to reestablish his line on the heights north of Abbeville. At 2:00 A.M. on August 9, General Hatch started his cavalry across the river. The Union cavalry moved toward Chalmers' position two miles south of the river, where an artillery exchange began between Thrall's Arkansas battery and the Union Redlegs. Seeing that his lines were about to be overlapped, Chalmers withdrew his small unit across Hurricane Creek to avoid being flanked, burning a bridge and trestle as they fell back. However, the Union advance and strength were too much for Chalmers' men to hold back. Soon, Chalmers was forced to retreat to his recently built earthworks on the northern outskirts of Oxford.

But there would be no refuge for the Confederates at Oxford. Within a few hours not only had Hatch advanced on the town, but he also had sent Col. William S. Jenkins and two of Herrick's regiments of cavalry around Oxford to take Chalmers on the flank and rear. About to be surrounded and trapped again, Chalmers and his men were forced out of Oxford at a dead run. The Confederates then crossed to the south side of the swollen Yacona River, an operation that might have proven disastrous had Hatch pressed them in force.

During the short occupation of Oxford by the Union troops, General Hatch allowed his men free rein to prowl the streets in search of booty. When the Federals pulled out of Oxford, General Hatch had his headquarters wagons loaded with "pictures, china, glassware, and other items from the houses that attracted his fancy."[53]

Hatch also had received word that a Confederate column was approaching from the east. This would be Forrest, riding hard from Pontotoc to support Chalmers. At about that same time Chalmers was recrossing the Yacona and moving back toward Oxford. Late on the afternoon of August 10, Hatch, feeling he had completed his mission of driving the Confederates out of Oxford, rode north and stopped at the Tallahatchie to await support. Forrest and Chalmers converged upon Oxford under a downpour and entered the city at 11:00 P.M.

The citizens of Oxford, who had gone to bed the night of the tenth in an occupied city, awoke to a liberated one with Confederate soldiers scattered throughout the town square. The exhausted and muddy cavalrymen lay on the ground, holding the reins of their horses as they caught a few winks of sleep following the hard, rain-drenched ride from Pontotoc. The rain would not let up for nearly two weeks. The humidity can be suffocating during the dog days of summer in the heavily wooded areas of northern Mississippi, and with the rain, it becomes nearly tropical, wilting both man and animal. The short rest was a godsend for the exhausted Confederates.

The first thing Forrest attended to the next morning was arranging his command into two parts. Chalmers would lead one, Forrest the other. He quickly established his line of resistance at Hurricane Creek, where both armies sat and suffered the rain and attacking insects through the remainder of that day and the next.

At noon on August 13, Mower's column, which had arrived earlier at Abbeville, moved out toward Hurricane Creek with Hatch's cavalry in the lead. When the two antagonists met on the north bank of the creek, it was apparent that Forrest could not hold Mower and Hatch's overwhelming force, so he employed what has been called an elastic defense: stubbornly giving ground, then suddenly falling back, reforming and repeating the maneuver. The tactic forced the Federals to take several hours to painstakingly drive a relatively small Confederated unit back across Hurricane Creek. Finally, when the left end of his line threatened to collapse, leaving Forrest's men in danger of being flanked and possibly routed, Bedford ordered his troops to fall back across Hurricane Creek. The Fifty-second Indiana, Twelfth Iowa, and Eighth Wisconsin bluecoats chased Forrest's command southward until darkness ended the pursuit.[54]

For the next five days neither army moved on one another than a few skirmishes in the no man's land between Abbeville and Hurricane Creek. A. J. Smith, Mower, and Hatch gathered their supplies and additional strength during the same period as they prepared to move on Oxford. With the Mississippi Central repaired, a great cause for relief among the Federals, and the trains running as far south as the Tallahatchie, Smith felt ready to attack the rebels and on August 17 marched south, though the weather still showed no sign of clearing any time soon.

With Smith and Mower poised to drive Forrest out of Oxford and, they hoped, out of existence, the situation was rapidly becoming desperate for the Confederates. Lt. Tully Brown of Forrest's command expressed the concern among the men. "We knew we couldn't fight General Smith's big fine army," he later wrote, "and we knew that we couldn't get any reinforcements anywhere, and we boys speculated about what Old Bedford was going to do."[55]

What Old Bedford was going to do was attempt to execute one of the most audacious cavalry raids in history. His target was Memphis, the bastion the Yankees had created in Forrest's old business district. On August 18 at 5:00 P.M., Colonels Bell, Wade, and Neely hand-picked the best men and mounts from their brigades for the coming operation. Lt. T. Sanders Sale was ordered to prepare a battery of four guns from Morton's artillery command to accompany the combat team. Altogether, they numbered two thousand troops.

General Chalmers' job was to stay at Oxford with General Buford and Colonel Falkner's brigade as well as Capt. Thomas W. Rice's battery and convince the enemy, when he came, that Forrest's command was not divided, but still intact. What Forrest was going to ask of these troops would require a superhuman effort, not to mention a little luck.

Forrest's plan was to pass around and through the right flank of Smith's fourteen-thousand-man army as it advanced on the current Confederate position at Oxford. His small attack force would have to move at night through torrential rain, build bridges over three flooded streams, travel sixty miles, attack a heavily fortified city, capture Generals Washburn and Halleck, escape, recross the same three creeks, and avoid Smith's army as it hopefully was recalled back to Memphis.

No one could ever say that Forrest lacked strategic imagination when it came to analyzing a difficult military situation. Regardless of the difficulty, his tough and game horse soldiers never blinked when the plan was revealed, nor did they seem to think in any negative sense about being led by a man whose wound required that he still ride with one foot in the stirrups. They mounted up shortly after 5:00 P.M. and followed their leader out of town.

After laboring through nearly forty miles of mud and rain the Confederates arrived at Panola around 7:00 A.M. on the nineteenth. The hellacious conditions required Forrest to assign ten horses to each field piece in order to pull the guns through mud that occasionally became waist deep. Within three hours they had crossed the Panola utilizing a pontoon bridge. The skies began to clear as they moved northward, but the roads were still rivers of mud. The hard-driving rebels arrived at Senatobia, Mississippi, at dusk on August 19 and camped for the night.[56]

On Saturday morning, August 20, Forrest's men moved out from

Senatobia, stripping the flooring planks from gin houses and abandoned buildings to use at the next crossing, at Hickahala Creek. Meanwhile, General Chalmers, back at Oxford, was preparing to do his best to bluff the overwhelming enemy force descending upon his position.

Having slogged their way forward for about a mile from Senatobia, the drenched, mud-splattered gray riders arrived at the Hickahala and found it flooded over its banks, as much as sixty feet wide in places. A light pontoon bridge would not suffice in the Hickahala's fast-moving current, so Forrest's men went to work building a bridge using telegraph poles lashed together with muscadine vines. Working like men possessed, the Confederates had the huge structure completed in just over an hour and made the crossing.[57]

Huffing and puffing under their exertions, the raiding party moved six miles farther north to the Coldwater River. Things were not getting any easier for the Confederates. The Coldwater River was also flooded and twice as wide as the Hickahala. Transforming themselves once again into carpenters and engineers, they built another telegraph-pole bridge, and the Coldwater was crossed by the high-spirited, albeit exhausted, Southerners in a little more than three hours. Considering the horrible conditions, Forrest later said, "I had to continually caution the men to keep quiet. They were making a regular corn shucking out of it. Wet and muddy, but full of life and ready for anything. . . . Those were great soldiers."[58]

Forrest's men entered his old hometown of Hernando at nightfall on Saturday evening. After conferring with friends and spies, the column moved out again and within a few hours crossed the Tennessee state line ten miles south of Memphis. Four miles south of Memphis, the Confederate combat team moved silently to the banks of the Nonconnah Creek. Once across, Forrest gleaned more information from local citizens on the exact locations of Hurlbut and Washburn's quarters in the city.

Evaluating these reports, Forrest came to the conclusion that Memphis was not as securely fortified as he had been led to believe. Upon closer examination the very fortifications at Memphis seemed lacking. Fort Pickering and its garrison was the only earthworks protecting the city, and although it commanded a strategic position, there were many gaps in the ten miles of picket lines surrounding Memphis through which a well-trained detachment of horsemen could slip on a dimly lit and foggy morning.

When Forrest called his subordinates together to discuss the final

aspects of the raid, he was informed that only fifteen hundred horses remained in good enough condition for another foray against the
Yankees. Over five hundred had broken down during the arduous
trip and would be of little use for the plan Forrest had in mind.
Several hundred disappointed men were sent back with the hapless
mounts to rejoin Chalmers at Oxford. Though this reduced
Forrest's number of raiders, it had at least one advantage as well.
Should the rejected men and horses be seen by Union scouts or
spies they would probably assume they were retreating, not part of a
force preparing to attack Memphis.

Capt. William Forrest and his "company of reckless scouts" were
briefed about their specific mission to capture the Union outposts
and then gallop directly through the city to the Gayoso Hotel, where
General Hurlbut was known to be living, and take him prisoner
along with any other Union brass there present. Lt. Col. Jesse
Forrest and the Fifteenth Tennessee Cavalry got the juicy assignment of capturing General Washburn, the other high-ranking
Union officer in Memphis. Jesse and his men were to proceed down
De Soto Street, then wheel onto Union Street, where Washburn was
quartered, and hopefully take him prisoner as well.

Lt. Col. Thomas H. Logwood would follow Jesse Forrest's team
into the city with the rest of the Fifteenth Cavalry and what was left
of the Twelfth Tennessee. Once in town they would throw up roadblocks at the intersections of Main and Beal as well as at Shelby and
Beal. In addition, Logwood was ordered to take the steamboat landing at the end of Union Street.[59] Col. J. J. Neely and the Second
Missouri from McCulloch's brigade, the Fourteenth Tennessee
under the command of Lt. Col. Raleigh White, and Lt. Col. Alex
Chalmers' Eighteenth Mississippi were to attack the troops quartered on Hernando Street. Tyree Bell and the Second, Sixteenth,
and Twentieth Tennessee, supported by the guns of Sales battery,
would be held in reserve.[60]

An article had appeared the day before in the pages of the
*Memphis Review,* heralding that Smith had defeated Forrest at
Oxford and had the rebels on the run. "The Rout Complete—Our
Cavalry Pursuing," trumpeted the headline. With that news fresh in
the minds of readers on Sunday morning, the rebels were "on the
run" in a manner of speaking. They were running straight up Union
Street into the heart of downtown Memphis.[61]

Stealth was considered of the utmost importance as William
Forrest's band of scouts moved out at 3:15 A.M. on Sunday morning,

August 21, through a soupy fog. Two miles from the court square of Memphis they came upon the first Union outpost. Suddenly came the universal challenge, "Who goes there?"

Captain Forrest replied coolly, "A detachment of the 12th Missouri with Rebel prisoners."

"Dismount and come forward on foot."

Other than from his oldest brother, Nathan Bedford, Bill Forrest did not take orders well from anyone. Using the poor visibility to his advantage, he moved his horse slowly forward until he was nearly on top of the Union sentry. Then suddenly his horse leapt forward as he applied the spurs. In a blur Forrest knocked the man unconscious with a sharp blow to the head with his Navy Colt as his men rushed in upon the outpost, capturing twelve men of the 137th Illinois—but not before one trooper managed to fire off a single warning shot, which may have alerted the sentries ahead.[62]

The Confederates came to the next outpost about a quarter mile farther on. The guards at the second outpost, perhaps having been alerted by the gunshot fired a few moments before, opened fire when Forrest's patrol appeared, and a short firefight broke out. The Federal troopers were soon overpowered, but during the short melee Forrest's men forgot their orders to remain as silent as possible. In the excitement of the skirmish several of them burst forth with the rebel battle cry before they recalled their orders of silence. Many of the Confederates were anxious to get on with the raid, as Memphis was their hometown.

The piercing "rebel yell" could carry a long distance and sounded especially eerie dampened by the heavy fog. Realizing that their cover had been blown, Forrest's scouts put their spurs to their mounts and charged hooting and hollering headlong down the Hernando road, the noise be damned. Thundering straight through the enemy encampments, the Confederates surprised the gunners of the Seventh Battery, Wisconsin Light Artillery, and killed two and scattered the rest before they could man their six guns. Forrest's boys rode over the top of the Union artillery emplacement and raced toward their objective like heat-seeking missiles.

When they reached the old Gayoso Hotel, the men quickly dismounted and rushed into the lobby, but Bill Forrest, in grand, cinematic style, crashed his horse through the front doors of the hotel and rode directly into the lobby. He spurred his horse up the wide staircase to the second floor where he took several astonished Union officers by surprise. The shocked Union officers made the mistake of opening fire when they confronted a mounted Confederate trooper, pistols drawn, in the hallway just outside their rooms. Several more Southern soldiers rushing up the stairs quickly shot several of the Union officers as the others threw themselves back into their rooms for cover.[63]

Fortunately for the astonished Union officers, the rebels were not on a search and destroy mission, but had come expressly to capture their general. Lucky Hurlbut! He had spent the night at the personal quarters of Col. Asher R. Eddy and escaped capture.

Meanwhile, throughout the city, on what would otherwise have been a quiet Sunday morning, the streets were turning into the devil's playground. Jesse Forrest's men reached General Washburn's quarters on Union Street to find that Washburn had escaped just in the nick of time, having being warned by Col. Matthew H. Starr. In his haste, General Washburn fled out his back door wearing only his nightclothes and made his way down the alleys and streets until he reached the relative safety of Fort Pickering. Lieutenant Colonel Forrest, chagrined that Washburn had gotten away, and not wanting to leave empty handed, took some satisfaction in capturing the Union general's uniform.

Washburn was criticized for fleeing and not leaving any orders for how to deal with the chaotic situation. Lt. Col. William H. Thurston was quoted as saying that the general "could much more easily have retired to [the] headquarters of [the] provost guard than have gone to the fort." As it turns out the provost guard headquarters was only three blocks from Washburn's location on Union Street, whereas the fort was over a half-mile away.[64]

Washburn himself later said that he had "barely a moment to escape." General Hurlbut, apparently still feeling the sting of his demotion, made an unsympathetic and memorable statement when hearing the news of Washburn's adventure: "They removed me from command because I couldn't keep Forrest out of West Tennessee, and now Washburn can't keep him out of his own bedroom."[65]

In another part of the city, Col. Thomas H. Logwood's men were using their carbines as clubs to smash through a detachment of Yankees while their officers slashed their way with their sabers. On they charged into the heart of the city to establish the roadblocks Bedford had ordered, while Forrest himself became heavily engaged supporting Neely's brigade in the Southern outskirts of the city. Seeing that Neely was being driven back, Forrest gathered his escort company and men from Bell's brigade, some sixty horsemen in all. Mounted on his favorite war-horse, King Philip, Forrest led his men through the gardens and yards of private dwellings, swooping down upon the Federals "like a scythe over a wheat field," checking the enemy and driving them into the State Female College to seek refuge.[66]

There was never any serious thought about whipping the enemy at these various sites around town. The real intention was to create havoc and confusion and to take high-ranking prisoners. The ultimate goal, of course, was to force the recall of Smith's army. The real challenge for Forrest's men was in making the raid appear as though it was an all-out assault on the city. The plan worked.

Down at the river wharf, the Union ironclad *Essex* sat undergoing repairs. Fearing that the Confederates might destroy her, the gunboat *Red Rover* had gotten up a head of steam to tow *Essex* out into the Mississippi, safe from the reach of the marauding rebels.

Across the city alarm bells rang out, adding to the confusion and panic of the Union defenders. Two thousand militia soldiers poured into the street to assist the reeling Federal troops. Partisan Southern citizens also began to fill the windows of their homes and front yards, cheering the Confederates as they charged up and down the streets. The ladies of Memphis filled balconies and doorways dressed in all sorts of evening wear and undergarments, waving handkerchiefs and shouting encouragement to the wild, gray horsemen.

The city was in an uproar. Pandemonium reigned in the streets. Cannons boomed and crashed. Some people were screaming in fear while others cheered with jubilation. It was exactly the kind of chaos that the mastermind of this riot had intended, and many of Forrest's men were having a grand ol' time in the process.

Many of the rebels broke away from their units and went on their own unauthorized missions. Some sought out the homes of their parents, charging by and waving their hats and shouting greetings. Others went in search of replacements for their worn-out horses. At the Eclipse Stable, a Confederate raiding party showed up and appropriated several horses. It was going to be difficult to get the entire Southern command out of the city intact.[67]

Meanwhile, Colonel Logwood was attacking Gen. Ralph Buckland's headquarters and the Block Prison on Second Street where many Confederate prisoners were confined. However, the Confederates were driven back without being able to free the prisoners or capture General Buckland.

With the city still in chaos, Logwood and the other officers began the task of rounding up all the men who were running helter-skelter through town. Around 9:00 A.M., the commanders received word from Forrest to abandon the city and rendezvous with him at the southern end of Memphis near the Hernando road. On their way, Logwood's column was forced to crash their way through a road-block the Yankees had thrown up near the Province House on the Hernando road. Just beyond, they joined up with General Forrest near the State Female College.[68]

The Confederates were by no means clear of peril once they left Memphis. The Union commanders would not placidly suffer such a humiliating raid. Col. Matthew H. Starr of the Sixth Illinois Cavalry led the first organized pursuit and was soon chasing in the Confederate stragglers and closing on the rear of Forrest's command. Forrest saw them coming and called for the Second Missouri to meet the Union detachment. When Colonel Starr saw Forrest and his men preparing for a fight, he ordered the charge.

The clash of the two forces sounded like a train wreck. A vicious, close-quarter fight immediately ensued. Colonel Starr spotted Forrest astride King Philip and in the old tradition of cavalrymen, singled Forrest out and engaged him in personal combat. Starr gave an excellent account of himself, slashing and parrying savagely in a deadly saber duel with one of the best hand-to-hand fighters of the war. Steel crashed against steel as both men cursed and hacked away at one another. Sensing an opening, Forrest used the point of his saber and ran the game Colonel Starr through.[69] When the rest of the Federal troopers saw their leader go down, they lost heart and disengaged, leaving the Confederates free to fall back down the Hernando road. Forrest moved his column a few miles farther and stopped near Nonconnah Creek at about 2:00 P.M.

Meanwhile, back in Memphis, Col. Edward Winslow had organized a pursuit party of 650 men and was approximately two and a half hours behind the Confederates. He caught up with them at Nonconnah Creek, where he was met by Major Anderson carrying a flag of truce and offering terms for paroling the Union prisoners taken at Memphis. Forrest had taken more than 600 prisoners in Memphis. Most of them were only partially dressed and barefoot. At first Winslow declined, stating that he would have to get permission, but he soon capitulated due to the poor conditions of the bootless, and, in many cases, trouser-less prisoners.

While terms were being renegotiated, Forrest sent Washburn's uniform back to him. A few days later, Washburn contacted

Forrest's personal tailor in Memphis, who had Bedford's exact size and specifications on file in his shop, and ordered a fine new dress gray uniform to be delivered to the Confederate general. It was a gesture typical of enemies on both sides during the American Civil War.

With the prisoner-exchange terms complete, the hostilities were once again resumed. Forrest moved his command to Hernando and camped there the night of August 21. Colonel Winslow was ordered to continue the pursuit at 5:00 P.M. but was halted near dusk due to a shortage of forage and rations and awaited supplies to come from Memphis. This delay prevented the Union pursuers from catching up to the Confederates again. The rebels were back in the saddle early the next morning and, riding all that day and into the night, entered Panola at 10:00 P.M.

Col. William Duffield's command, part of Winslow's brigade, entered Hernando five hours after Forrest had departed. Realizing that the Confederates were by then across the Tallahatchie, Duffield turned back to Memphis, thus ending any further pursuit. On August 23, Forrest, accompanied by his escort and Sale's battery, boarded a train at Panola and proceeded by rail to Grenada, leaving Col. Tyree Bell and rest of the column at Panola.

On his way to Memphis, Forrest had left the telegraph wires uncut between there and LaGrange. He knew, or hoped, that General Washburn would wire Smith's command of the situation in Memphis and order him to turn his army around and return to home base. Of course, Forrest also knew that meant he would have to evade Smith's column again on his way back to Oxford, and he managed to do so.[70]

Meantime, back in the Oxford area, Chalmers had his hands full attempting to convince the enemy there that they were facing Forrest's entire command. Chalmers performed admirably considering that at his front was an army four to five times the size of his own and at his rear was the rising water in Hurricane Creek. On August 19, General Chalmers attempted to bluff the enemy with an attack near Hurricane Creek. The attack was effective enough to prompt General Grierson to write Washburn that the "enemy was found in force" but was driven back.[71]

As Forrest had requested, Chalmers "was contesting every inch of ground," but he was forced to fall back through Oxford. On the twenty-first, Smith's army moved into Oxford once again. This time his men would nearly destroy the entire town before pulling out the next day. The destruction was such that the *Chicago Tribune* published an article stating, "Where once stood a handsome little country town . . . now only remained the blackened skeletons of the houses, and smoldering ruins."[72]

On August 22, as Chalmers awaited Smith's inevitable advance, something strange happened. Chalmers' scouts reported that the enemy had turned and was heading back toward the Tallahatchie crossing. Chalmers realized what the sudden change in the circumstances meant: Forrest had succeeded. When Chalmers' men rode back into Oxford, the shell-shocked citizens must have been afraid to look out their windows to see which side was entering their town this time.

When Smith, Mower, and Grierson received the news that Forrest had passed right through their lines and was fifty miles in their rear attacking Memphis, "they could not believe it." To add insult to injury, Chalmers fell upon the rear of Smith's column and harassed them all the way back toward Hernando, destroying the telegraph wires and rail line as they followed. This action on Chalmers' part quite possibly distracted Smith from executing his second set of orders, which was to cut off and capture Forrest on his return trip.

Disappointed that his troops had been unable to catch or kill Forrest, Washburn wrote:

> We had a big thing here on Sunday morning, and ran a very narrow escape, indeed it was almost a miracle that I was not either killed of captured. One main drive of the Expedition was to catch me. Forrest fooled A. J. Smith very badly, leaving his immediate front at Oxford and making a dash at Memphis without Smith knowing it, tho he had 4,500 Cavalry with him. Had not Smith disregarded my orders he would have caught Forrest on his retreat. The whole Expedition was barren of fruits. They were in so great a hurry to get away that they carried off hardly anything. I lost two fine horses, which is about the biggest loss of anybody.[73]

Washburn's self-serving report downplayed the visceral effect Forrest's attack had left upon the Federal authorities in Memphis and the rest of the country. For weeks after the raid, rumors of Forrest sightings would suddenly panic the commanders in Memphis into fortifying and refortifying the city, whose citizens and troops expected to see the rebels riding down Union Street at any moment. The repercussions of the raid can be seen in the recruiting advertisement run by the Union Eleventh Tennessee Infantry on September 3: "Tennessee Invaded! Memphis Threatened! Forrest Is Coming!"[74]

On the other hand, news of Forrest's bold raid on Memphis had a salutary effect on Southerners. On August 24, General Maury wrote Forrest from Alabama, "You have again saved Mississippi. Come and help Mobile."[75]

The pragmatic Sherman later said of Forrest's raid on Memphis, "I admire his dash but not his judgment . . . in running his head against Memphis."

However, the highest tribute paid to Forrest came from the Unionist politicians. During the meeting in Memphis in September 1864, the Grand Jury of the Circuit Court of the United States for the District of West Tennessee returned an indictment against Nathan Bedford Forrest for treason! Strange though it might seem that an indictment for treason should be issued at a time of war, and against a participant in that war, the powers that be in Memphis had apparently decided that Forrest's command was not a regular Confederate army unit and attempted to categorize Forrest as a Quantrill-like guerilla force. The charges stated that there was:

> An open and public rebellion, insurrection and war with force and arms . . . against the government and laws of the United States of America by divers persons . . . styling themselves "the Confederate States of America" . . . on the twenty-first day of August 1864 . . . not weighing the duty of his said allegiance but wickedly devising and intending the peace and tranquility of the said United States of America to disturb, and to stir, move, excite, aid and assist in said Rebellion, insurrection and war . . . with force and arms unlawfully, falsely, maliciously and traitorously did raise and levy war . . . with a great multitude of persons whose names to the grand jurors aforesaid are unknown . . . armed and arrayed in a warlike manner . . . with guns, swords, pistols and other warlike weapons as well offensive and defensive . . . did . . . in a hostile manner array and dispose themselves against the said United States of America . . . most wickedly, maliciously and traitorously did ordain, prepare and levy war against the United States of America, contrary to the duty of the allegiance and fidelity of the said Nathan B. Forrest . . . etc. etc. etc.

The arrest warrant fell onto the desk of the marshal of the United

States Court, who now held the responsibility of bringing the suspect to justice. The Federal marshal's remark about how this should be done was unintentionally humorous: "Defendant not to be found in my district."[76]

# Chapter Thirteen

# THAT DEVIL FORREST

*—William Tecumseh Sherman*

## Athens and Johnsonville
## September-October 1864

Atlanta finally succumbed to Sherman's siege on September 2. Although it was actually too late to make any significant difference, Stephen D. Lee and Jefferson Davis at long last decided to "concentrate all the cavalry in Mississippi and Tennessee on Sherman's communications." As Atlanta fell into the enemy's hands, Forrest was moving toward Mobile, Alabama, at the request of Maj. Gen. Dabney Maury. However, Maury's fear concerning Mobile turned out to be exaggerated, and Forrest was diverted to Meridian, Mississippi, to rendezvous on September 5 with Gen. Richard Taylor, the new commander for Alabama, Mississippi, and east Louisiana. General Taylor wasted no time following his meeting with Forrest.

> Regarding the campaign in Georgia of paramount importance, [he wrote] "I have ordered . . . the operation of Gen. Forrest's entire cavalry force on the line of Sherman's communications. This will be productive of more benefit than the detachment of a portion of it for the defense of Mobile. The former is of general, the latter, of local, interest.[1]

General Taylor was well connected. He was the son of Gen. Zachary Taylor, hero of the war with Mexico and former president of the United States. His brother-in-law was the president of the Confederacy, Jefferson Davis. He later authored a book, *Destruction and Reconstruction,* in which he described his first meeting with Forrest:

> A train from the north, bringing Forrest in advance of his troops, reached Meridian, and was stopped, and the General,

whom I had never seen, came to report. He was a tall, stalwart man, with grayish hair, mild countenance, and slow and homely speech. In a few words he was informed that I considered Mobile safe for the present, and that all of our energies must be directed to the relief of Hood's army then west of Atlanta. The only way to accomplish this was to worry Sherman's communications north of the Tennessee River, and he must move his cavalry in that direction at the earliest moment.

To my surprise, Forrest suggested many difficulties and asked numerous questions: how he was to get over the Tennessee; how he was to get back if pressed by the enemy; how he was to be supplied; what should be his line of retreat in certain contingencies; what he was to do with prisoners if any were taken, etc. I began to think he had no stomach for the work; but at last, having isolated the chances of success from causes of failure with the care of a chemist experimenting in his laboratory, he rose and . . . at once stated what he could do in the way of moving supplies on his line, which had been repaired up to the Tennessee boundary. Forrest's whole manner now changed. In a dozen sharp sentences he told his wants, said he would leave a staff officer to bring up his supplies, asked for an engine to take him back north twenty miles to meet his troops, informed me that he would march with the dawn, and hoped to give an account of himself in Tennessee.[2]

Taylor's words "march with the dawn" could have been a lapse of memory over the ten years that passed before he wrote his memoirs after the war, because realistically Forrest would not have had the time to prepare his command for such a perilous expedition. In fact, Forrest spent the next ten days at his headquarters near Verona, Mississippi, preparing to move out. Every contingency had been thought through. Forrest's attention to every detail was meticulous.

An event occurred during this planning stage for his campaign into middle Tennessee that demonstrated Forrest's fierce concentration and lack of patience. One evening Forrest was observed pacing deep in thought around a small railroad station. His hands were clasped behind his back and his head was down as he walked round and round the station. As Forrest made his rounds an unfortunate trooper located his commanding general and proceeded to air his grievances. The man attempted to get Forrest to listen to his problems as the general walked by. He was ignored as though he did not exist. On Forrest's next pass, the soldier once again demanded to be heard. Suddenly, with no advanced warning, nor indication of his agitated state, Forrest threw an explosive, short punch that knocked the man out cold. Then, as though nothing had happened, Forrest continued his rounds "calmly and unconsciously stepping over the prostrate body each time he came around again."[3]

Forrest's command moved out on September 16, this time by rail on the Mobile-Ohio line to Corinth, Mississippi, and then eastward on the Memphis-Charleston line to the Cherokee Station a few miles west of Tuscumbia, Alabama, arriving there on September 19. Shortly after arriving, Forrest and Gen. Joseph Wheeler met to combine their commands. Unfortunately, Wheeler's command was severely reduced in numbers from their futile raid behind Sherman's lines, and the men were badly demoralized.[4]

Forrest was disappointed when he found that the support he was to receive from the addition of Wheeler's men was virtually nonexistent. After conferring with Fightin' Joe, Forrest informed Gen. Dick Taylor, "when I left the brigade with him last November it then numbered over 2,300 men for duty. . . . Now they were barely sixty men left." Forrest continued by adding, "I hope to be instrumental in gathering them up."[5]

By September 21, when he began the crossing of the Tennessee River, Forrest had gathered nearly four thousand troopers, four hundred of whom were without mounts. Viscount Joseph Wolseley, retired commander of the armies of Great Britain and Forrest biographer, recounted an interesting comment made to him by an officer who was new to Forrest's command. He told the field marshal that as the Confederate troops passed by him on the way to the crossing it would have been easy to mistake them for a Yankee brigade because the U.S. Army emblem was stamped on virtually every piece of equipment the men, horses, and wagons carried on and with them. Thus did Forrest "requisition" for the needs of his troops.[6]

Forrest had always supplied his men at the expense of the enemy. During this campaign, however, Forrest would outdo himself. Before the operation was complete he would add a few Union gunboats and cargo vessels to the list of usurped Federal property.

The crossing of the Tennessee at Ross's Ford completed, Forrest's command camped approximately two miles from Florence, Alabama, the night of the twenty-first. The next morning, while moving over Shoal Creek, Gen. P. D. Roddey's brigade joined Forrest, bringing his total numbers to about forty-five hundred. Near Masonville, the rebels camped for the night.

Late in the evening Forrest sent Lt. Col. Jesse Forrest's and Lt. Col. Raleigh White's regiments on a night march toward Athens,

Alabama, to destroy the telegraph lines at McDonald's Station.[7] Forrest's command bypassed Brig. Gen. Robert S. Granger's post at Decatur to strike the more lucrative objective at Athens, where Col. Wallace Campbell commanded the town's formidable fortifications. The fort sat atop an embankment surrounded by a ditch eight feet deep and ten feet wide. Across the top of the earthen works were abatis constructed from the tops of trees lashed together using wire with sharpened wood spikes pointing outward.

By the afternoon of September 23, General Granger and Colonel Campbell had been caught completely off guard by the appearance of the Confederates. Before he knew what was happening Campbell's works were completely invested. They should have known something was coming when earlier in the afternoon Jesse Forrest's men had arrived four miles south of Athens and begun tearing up the track in preparation for the trap he intended to lay for the train. This tactic was meant to draw Campbell out of his fortifications and hopefully to capture the locomotive and cargo. Campbell was soon notified that a group of three hundred rebels were destroying the track and telegraph lines between Decatur and Athens. Colonel Campbell, who commanded the 110th U.S.C.T. at Athens, ordered a hundred men onto the train, which had just brought in supplies to the fort and was preparing to return to Nashville. The engineer was ordered to drive the Confederates off at full steam and repair any damage they may have done.[8]

After tearing up the track, Forrest's men mounted up and rode north to set the second half of the trap. Lieutenant Colonels Forrest and White waited with their small brigades, allowing Campbell's south-bound train to steam out of the fort at Athens. Two miles out the Federal train easily blew past a Confederate picket line. However, there was nowhere for the train to go because they soon ran out of track. Colonel Campbell began to realize that he had been lured into a trap when he was notified that the Confederates were constructing a barricade across the tracks to the rear, thus cutting off his escape.[9]

The only course open to them was to abandon the train. Campbell and his men scrambled out of the cars and ran for their lives northward toward the closest blockhouse. On the way they had to fight their way through Forrest's men, who closed in on them from the north and south. Incredibly, ninety of the one hundred men made it to the safety of the blockhouse.

Near dusk, Forrest's main column approached Athens. Barteau's

Second Tennessee and Forrest's escort company broke off and rode for the north side of town to cut the telegraph and destroy the tracks. Later in the evening Major Kelley's brigade was ordered to the southeast part of Athens. Buford's and Lyon's brigades were deployed on the west side of town. Lieutenant Colonels Forrest and White, just returned from their night mission, were posted between Brown's Ferry and the railroad.[10] That night Forrest completed his encirclement of the works at Athens as a hard rain fell.

Although Campbell had been reinforced around nine o'clock that night by five hundred cavalry under Lt. Col. William F. Prosser, he could see the writing on the wall. Since the telegraph wires were cut he had no way to inform Gen. Gordon Granger of his predicament in defending the fort against the attack he knew could come at any time. In spite of this, Prosser showed no stomach for the coming fight and refused to engage his cavalry, believing they would be wasted in the attempt to stop Forrest's overwhelming force.[11]

At 7:00 A.M. on September 24 the attack began. Captain Morton's guns opened up on the Union position from three different sides with pinpoint accuracy. The Union reports indicated that nearly every shot fired exploded within their fortifications. After thirty minutes of bombardment, Forrest called for a cease-fire and sent in his terms of surrender:

> Headquarters Forrest's Cavalry, In The Field, Sept. 24, 1864
> Officer Commanding U.S. Forces, Athens, Ala.
>
> I desire an absolute and unconditional surrender of the entire force and all government stores and property at this post. I have a sufficient force to take your works; and if I am forced to do so, the responsibility of the consequences must rest with you. Should you, however, accept the terms, all white soldiers shall be treated as prisoners of war and the Negroes returned to their masters. A reply is requested immediately.
>
> > Respectfully, N.B. Forrest, Major General C.S.A.

The circumstances were obviously similar to the tragic battle at Fort Pillow in April. Only five months after the nationally publicized incident, it is doubtful that this fact was lost on either side.

Campbell replied that he would not yield, so the cannonade resumed with a vengeance. After a short period Forrest sent a second message in to Campbell:

> Colonel: I desire an interview with you outside of the fort, at any

place you may designate, provided it meets with your views. My only object is to prevent the effusion of blood that must follow the storming of the place.

N. B. Forrest, Major General

This time Campbell relented, and though he likely had never heard of psychological warfare, he was about to receive a hard lesson in its application. During their conversation, Forrest earnestly explained that he had eight thousand troops and more reinforcements on the way. All Forrest wanted was to save lives in what would be a suicidal stand if Campbell refused to surrender. Campbell said, "Show me your troops."[12]

By this point in the war, Forrest's men were well rehearsed for the performance they were about to give. While Campbell and one of his officers rode along with Forrest across the lines of battle, the Confederate general began directing Campbell's attention to several bodies of his dismounted soldiers whom Forrest stated were infantry. He asked Campbell if he saw the cavalry posted in the distance, which were, in reality, the horse holders. All the while, Morton's batteries appeared everywhere, giving the impression Forrest possessed at least fifty guns.

Detachments of men moved about the field as if readying themselves for a general attack. Drum rolls, bugle calls, and numerous commanders barking out loud orders that carried across the battlefield accompanied all this grandstanding. At least three separate times Campbell observed Forrest's troops in various positions as the Confederates mounted and remounted, appearing now as infantrymen and again as cavalry. The maneuvers convinced the Union commander that he was greatly outnumbered. His confidence shattered, Colonel Campbell rode back to the fort and told his officers, "The jig is up, pull down the flag."[13]

Firing was heard down the Nashville-Decatur line while the flag was coming down. The only real fighting of the day was taking place south of Athens as Kelley's and Rucker's brigades engaged a relief column of seven hundred Michigan and Ohio troops coming up from Decatur. Campbell's officers and men, especially the black troops, pleaded and protested with their commander not to surrender and condemn them all to a prison camp or a return to slavery. Their objections fell on deaf ears. All Campbell could hear was the word "massacre" echoing inside his head. It was the word he would use in making the case to his subordinates for the surrender.

Campbell told his men that Forrest "was determined to take the place; that his force was sufficiently large, and have it he would, and if he was compelled to storm the works it would result in the massacre of the entire garrison."[14] Whether Forrest deliberately planted the thought that a potential massacre was pending when he induced Campbell to surrender is not known. Perhaps Campbell intoned the word himself to impress the gravity of the situation on his own officers. Whatever the circumstances, the shadow of Fort Pillow had definitely fallen across Athens.

Meanwhile, Col. Jonas Elliot, leading the 102nd Ohio and the Eighteenth Michigan from Decatur was trying to fight his way to Athens to save Campbell's command. During the hard-fought battle on the tracks of the Nashville-Decatur line, Jesse Forrest was seriously wounded in the thigh and taken out of the action. His wound would keep him out of the war for six months. Colonel Elliot was also shot from the saddle; however, his wound proved fatal. The Union troopers drove to within sight of the works at Athens at 11:00 A.M., "just in time to see the garrison march out and stack arms."[15]

The relief column was soon beaten back and retreated toward Decatur. Then, Forrest's one thousand or so prisoners were marched under guard to Cherokee Station. He was also able to supply three hundred new horses for his dismounted troops along with seven hundred small arms and two pieces of artillery. It should be noted that there was no massacre of any Union troops, including the black prisoners, who were all accounted for when they were placed on trains at Cherokee Station.

Once in captivity at Enterprise, Mississippi, thirty-one of Campbell's officers wrote a lengthy and scathing letter that basically denounced Campbell as a coward. Brig. Gen. R. S. Granger reported that Campbell's actions "were disapproved by everyone, and disgraceful in the extreme." Campbell requested a court of inquiry and later resigned with an honorable discharge. Colonel Campbell was neither the first nor the last Union commander Forrest would send into early retirement.[16]

Forrest's next objective was to move up the rail line destroying or capturing all the blockhouses and fortified positions between Athens, Georgia, and Pulaski, Tennessee. A few miles north of Athens, Forrest attacked blockhouse No. 5 (a fortified position on the rail line) commanded by Capt. A. Poe, a Dutchman, whose encounter with Forrest would be quite an adventure. A flag of truce was sent in, which Captain Poe curtly refused. The rebuff angered Forrest, who replied, "Does the damn fool want to be blown up?" After a burst of profanity, or as Morton put it, "Forrest made the atmosphere blue for awhile," Bedford said, "Well, I'll blow them up. Give him Hell Morton—hot as you've got it."[17]

Morton's first two rounds blew the blockhouse apart, killing several of the enemy within, but not Captain Poe, who began to wave a small white flag from the window of the smoking structure. As the blockhouse was being reduced to rubble, Forrest said to the young Morton, "Go on John. Go on. That was bully. Keep it up." Morton advised the general that he could see a flag of truce waving out a porthole in the blockhouse, to which Forrest replied, "Well, I don't see any, keep on firing. It'll take a bed sheet to attract my eye at this distance."[18]

Morton continued to hit the position with a few more shells and there soon appeared a much larger white cloth out the window, whereupon Forrest ordered the cease-fire. The Dutch captain, who at first had refused to surrender, was relieved to be alive and became very useful to Forrest as a mediator when Forrest's command captured the next few blockhouses on the way to Pulaski. Upon arrival at each successive fortification, the Dutchman was sent in to warn the defenders that their cause was hopeless.

The night of September 24, Forrest camped eight miles north of Athens. The next morning, the Confederates approached the blockhouse and trestle at Sulpher Springs, Alabama, one of the most important points on the rail line. The four-hundred-foot trestle spanned a seventy-five-foot ravine and was defended by three hundred black troops of the 111th U.S.C.T., augmented by two gun batteries. The heavily fortified position also held two hundred Indiana cavalrymen and four hundred (Union) cavalrymen from Tennessee. The blockhouse walls were forty inches thick and surrounded by earthen works.[19]

The Confederates soon had the works invested, with Morton's guns acquiring commanding positions from four different directions, allowing him perfect angles to lob shells directly into the enemy fortifications. During the artillery barrage an interesting duel took place. When the battle opened, the Federal guns "were handled with excellent style," and one particular battery on the north side of the fort was firing with accuracy into the rebel lines. This gun portal caught Morton's eye, and he directed Sergeant Zaring to train his piece upon the prescribed spot and hold his fire until given the signal. While the Confederate guns kept up their fire, Morton watched closely until he saw his chosen targets moving their guns into position. At that moment, Captain Morton gave Sergeant Zaring the order to fire. The first round from Sgt. Lemuel Zaring's gun, as Morton put it, "struck square into the face of the opposing gun, exploding it and killing five men, including the major of the fort."[20]

The next two rounds from Morton's battery killed six more troopers.

Early in the bombardment, the commanding officer, Col. William H. Lanthrop, was killed. The responsibility of command fell to Colonel J. B. Minnis, who was seriously wounded from shrapnel but survived. Calling a cease-fire, Forrest sent in the terms of surrender, which were refused.[21] Morton was ordered to open fire once again. Over the next two hours, eight hundred rounds were poured into the enemy's position. After Morton's guns ceased their thunderous fusillade and the clouds of smoke cleared, no more terms of surrender would be necessary. Piles of bodies could be seen, even from the Confederates' distant position.

The unconditional surrender garnered another thousand prisoners (approximately half of them African-Americans) and three hundred more horses, which finished mounting Forrest's entire command. The prisoner of war situation was becoming critical, as the number of prisoners began to outnumber the troops he led. Consequently, Forrest decided to use part of his command to escort the prisoners and captured guns back to Florence, Alabama. He was gambling that he could take the ammunition he would need in the immediate future from the enemy once he entered Tennessee.[22]

On September 26, at Brown's Plantation, Forrest's command captured a "Government Corral . . . of commissary stores and medical supplies." There were also two thousand black civilians inhabiting the location whom Forrest noted were "all ragged and dirty, and many seemed to be in absolute want. I ordered them to remove their clothing and bedclothes form the miserable hovels in which they lived and then burnt up this den of wretchedness. Nearly two hundred houses were consumed."[23] Forrest was not impressed by the conditions that liberation had brought the unfortunate blacks. He also realized they could become future Federal troop recruits and had them escorted to train depots for transport back to their owners.

That day, Forrest reported to General Taylor, "I succeeded yesterday in capturing three blockhouses and the fort at Elk River . . . without loss of a man, and have entirely destroyed the railroad from Decatur to Pulaski, and five large railroad bridges, which will require sixty days to replace."[25]

Forrest's rampage through Alabama and now into Tennessee "had waked-up the Yankees a little bit," as Forrest might have said. On the twenty-sixth, General Grant dispatched a memo to Sherman that underlined his concern regarding Forrest's current operation. "It will be better," he wrote, "to drive Forrest from Middle Tennessee as a first step, and do anything else that you may feel your force sufficient for."

Sherman fired back,

> Have already sent one division [Gen. John Newton's] to Chattanooga, and another [General Corse's] to Rome. Our armies are much reduced, and if I send back more I will not be able to threaten Georgia much. There are enough men to the rear to whip Forrest, but they are necessarily scattered to defend the road. Can't you expedite the sending to Nashville of the recruits that are in Indiana and Ohio? They could occupy the forts. Forrest is now Lt. General and commands the enemy's cavalry.[24]

These communications between the two most important Federal commanders add a noteworthy angle to the debate over Forrest's significance in the overall Union strategy in the west. While some historians believe that turning Forrest loose earlier would have had no affect on Sherman's Georgia campaign, Grant and Sherman most certainly believed—and feared—at that time and place that he could.

The next day, September 27, Forrest moved on Pulaski. Early in the day, the Confederate advance guard had run into a heavy Union force. The Federals resisted stubbornly but were steadily driven back into the town within their fortifications. At approximately 1:00 P.M. Forrest made a personal reconnaissance of the enemy position and decided it was too heavily defended to risk a general attack. He dispatched Gen. Dick Taylor:

> I have driven the enemy, after fighting all day, into his fortifications at this place, and find Maj. Gen. Lovell H. Rousseau with a heavy force well fortified. I will move to the Nashville and Chattanooga Railroad. My loss to date about 100; enemy's much heavier, having contested ground for several miles. Enemy concentrating heavily against me.[26]

Forrest was correct when he said the enemy was concentrating heavily against him. Nearly thirty thousand troops under Generals George Thomas, Lovell H. Rousseau, Daniel Webster, Gordon Granger, Cadwallader Washburn, and A. J. Smith were being diverted from their original missions concerning the Georgia campaign and were ordered to focus and converge upon Forrest in Tennessee. General Thomas stated that the various Federal corps were to hunt down and "press Forrest to the death, keeping your troops well in hand and holding them to their work. I do not think that we shall ever have a better chance than this."[27]

With heavy Union reinforcements arriving at Pulaski on the night of the twenty-seventh, Forrest ordered dozens of campfires built along his entire line "for the purpose of deceiving the enemy." He then threw out a strong picket line and slipped away in the darkness. The next morning found his command ten miles east of Pulaski, Forrest having canceled his immediate plans to wreck the Nashville-Chattanooga line.[28]

The rain had rendered the roads nearly impassable while Forrest's command made their way across mud-clogged trails on their march to Fayetteville. Driving his men through the dark, rough terrain, Forrest came across a caisson stuck in the mire and wanted to know "what in the hell was holding things up." He rode up alongside the struggling teamsters and demanded, "Who has charge here anyhow?"

"I have sir," answered Capt. Andrew McGregor.

"Then why in hell don't you do something?" Forrest continued, profanely raking the Scottish captain over the coals. McGregor, growing weary of the verbal attack, suddenly grabbed a lit torch and rammed it into the ammunition caisson, "exclaiming no man talks to me in such a manner"![29]

Forrest was momentarily stupefied by the suicidal move, then he "clapped spurs" to his horse, wheeled away, and charged up an embankment. Riding up alongside a few of his officers who had witnessed the incident, Forrest reined in and shouted, "What infernal lunatic is that just out of the asylum down there? He came near blowing himself and me up with a whole caisson full of powder!" Captain Morton and the other officers observing the encounter were aware that McGregor had earlier emptied that particular caisson to lighten its load, and the horsemen were unable to contain themselves at the sight of the master bluffer being out-bluffed and so burst into laughter. Forrest, seeing that he'd been had, joined in and had a good laugh along with the others.[30]

As Forrest moved into Fayetteville, Tennessee, on September 28, massive Union resources were being "turned against Forrest until he is disposed of," as Sherman put it. To General Halleck, Sherman wrote, "Forrest's Cavalry will travel 100 miles in less time than ours will. . . . I can whip the enemy's infantry, but his cavalry is to be feared."[31]

Sherman sent off urgent dispatches to Brig. Gen. W. L. Elliott, chief of the Cavalry Department of the Cumberland, two warnings to General Granger, another to General Ammen, commanding the district of east Tennessee, and other memos to Generals Rousseau and Jacob Dolson Cox. They all amounted to the same thing: find

Forrest and kill him. General Rousseau summed up the situation to Sherman as follows:

> Forrest struck the road at Athens, and destroyed it to within a few miles of Pulaski, where I had repulsed him on the 27th instant. He is here to stay, unless driven back and routed by a superior cavalry force. Infantry can cause him to change camp, but cannot drive him out of the State. Forrest's movements are much more cautious than formerly. He has attacked no place held by white men, but every post held by colored troops has been taken, and his destruction of railroad was most thorough. I have here about three thousand cavalry, not enough to fight him without support. This is much more than a raid; I regard it as a formidable invasion, the object of which is to destroy our lines, and he will surely do it unless met by a large cavalry force, and killed, captured, or routed. The cavalry, supported by infantry, can fight and defeat him, but he must be caught. He will not give battle unless he chooses to do so.[32]

The two thousand or so white Union troops and officers Forrest had captured might have begged to differ with General Rousseau's opinion that Bedford had "attacked no place held by white men."

On the twenty-ninth, Union secretary of war Edwin M. Stanton urged the governor of Michigan to send every enlisted man he could to guard Sherman's communications without delay. On that same day, Forrest was dividing his command into two parts. He sent Buford's brigade southward to attack Huntsville, Alabama, and to destroy the rail line from there to Decatur. Forrest would then lead Bell's and Lyon's brigades and the Seventh Tennessee Cavalry to the west to divert pursuit on Buford's assignment and to attempt to tear up the Nashville-Decatur line, which he had yet to significantly damage.

On the last day of September, Buford's brigade and Morton's artillery appeared at Huntsville and immediately demanded its surrender. General Granger was having a bad month, having lost nearly four thousand men and miles of the rail line he was assigned to guard. He had no intentions of surrendering and told Buford "to come and take it as soon as you get ready."[33] Having had his bluff called, Buford marched four miles westward and began tearing up the track that a pursuing Federal division was traveling upon. On October 1, Brig. Gen. John T. Morgan's division was forced to detrain and work all night in the rain to repair Buford's damage.

On the afternoon of October 1, Buford was at Athens, which had an entirely new garrison manned by two hundred Indiana and

Tennessee Federal troops and one gun battery. The rain was unrelenting on the first and second days of October. After a short artillery barrage and another attempt to bluff the enemy into surrendering, Buford pulled out on the night of October 2 and headed for the Tennessee River. The fifteen hundred rebels, along with Morton's guns, arrived at the river before dawn and camped, leaving Morgan's pursuit column more than a day behind.

Making his way to the right of Shelbyville, Forrest passed on to Lewisburg and arrived on October 1 at Spring Hill, tearing up the railroad and capturing the town. Moving southward, destroying the track as they went, Forrest's men captured four blockhouses and took another 120 prisoners twelve miles outside Columbia. On October 2, Forrest assaulted Columbia from the north as Lyon's brigade came in from the west and burned all the bridges and trestles around the town. Making no serious threat toward the Federal forces at Columbia, Forrest marched twelve miles southwest of Columbia and camped for the night at Mount Pleasant.

While the various Union columns converged and attempted to pick a fight with Forrest, battle was the last thing in which he intended to engage. His mission was to disrupt the enemy's communications and their equilibrium in the process, which he was doing quite effectively. On October 4, perhaps due to the fact that all the main roads were patrolled by Union forces, Forrest chose to travel on the old military road that Andrew Jackson's army had built between Tennessee and Natchez and on to New Orleans during the War of 1812. That night, Forrest's command camped in Alabama about twenty miles north of Florence. By the fifth he had arrived at the banks of the swollen Tennessee, where he rendezvoused with Buford.

The Union pincer action was closing in and time was running out. Coming hot on Forrest's heels was J. D. Morgan's infantry, marching toward the crossings at the Tennessee from Athens. Croxton's cavalry brigade was heading in from the west, in the direction of Wartrace. General Washburn and three thousand cavalry were soon to strike inland from the Tennessee and join in the chase. Gunboats were steaming from the lower and upper river regions bringing even more troops and patrolling the major waterways in search of the elusive rebel cavalryman.[34] Sherman, Grant, and Thomas all believed that this time they would finally catch and destroy Forrest's command. Thomas sent orders to the commanders of all the participating columns to "press Forrest to the death."[35]

For the next thirty hours, from October 5-6, the Confederates worked feverishly to complete the crossing of the Tennessee before being trapped against the river. By the afternoon of October 6, all but a thousand troops had made it across. At that same moment, J. D. Morgan's infantry was within a few miles and closing fast on the crossing. There was no time to get the last regiment across on the ferry, so Forrest ordered them to mount up and ride downstream to a narrower point on the river to an island seventy-five yards off shore. From there, they would have to swim their horses to the island, where they later could be ferried to safety. Forrest also ordered Col. Andrew N. Wilson's regiment to hold off Morgan as long as possible then make their escape and cross the river at an advantageous point and time. The strategy worked, because as one Confederate trooper said, "Forrest was pretty good at the git."[36]

Meanwhile, Forrest was actively engaged in the physical labor involved in the crossing and had little patience or pity on any slacker who was not pulling his weight. Every man in his command was expected to do what the situation called for, officers included. Forrest himself was handling one of the long poles used to propel the raft like a ferry when he observed a particular young lieutenant standing at the bow, giving a good impression of George Washington crossing the Delaware. Forrest was worn out and his patience for non-sense was razor thin. As Robert Henry wrote, his language was "showing considerable disregard for the third commandment."

"Why don't you take hold of an oar or pole and help get this boat across?" Forrest asked of the young officer. Apparently this lieutenant was new to Forrest's command or was just plain stupid, because he curtly responded to Forrest's demand by stating that there were plenty of privates to handle the job. Forrest flew into a rage and backhanded the man across the face, knocking him out of the boat and into the river. He was soon pulled back on board to face Forrest, who said, "Now, damn you, get hold of the oars and go to work! If I knock you out of the boat again I'll let you drown."[37]

While the Seventh and Sixteenth Tennessee and Fourth Alabama held off and harassed the oncoming Federals, Forrest made good his escape. The game rear guard continued their daredevil mission for nearly twenty-four hours, then dispersed and crossed the Tennessee at different points. When J. D. Morgan's men arrived at the river, all they could do was shake their fists in frustration at the enemy across the river. "Forrest has escaped us," said the report to Sherman received on October 7. The Union command was astounded to find they had not been able to even engage Forrest, let alone catch him. General Thomas was incredulous "Our force . . . ought to have crowded that damn rebel into the river."[38]

That "damn rebel" and his command reached their original jumping-off point at Cherokee Station on October 6. The last bit of fighting took place at Eastport, where Forrest correctly predicted the enemy would attempt to put troops across the river. After shelling the gunboats *Aurora* and *Kenton,* which were attempting to bring men across, the two partially disabled gunboats drifted down-river, out of range. In this short engagement, Colonel Kelley's brigade and a battery of Hudson's guns accounted for twelve casualties. Thirty more prisoners were taken, along with twenty horses and a few hundred small arms.

In the two weeks he was engaged in northern Alabama and central Tennessee, Forrest's expedition had wreaked havoc on the area, but the damage may have been more psychological than physical. Forrest's raid into northern Alabama and Tennessee had been a grand display of finesse and tactics. At every juncture during the campaign he had been "first with the most," then gone like a ghost. Unfortunately, Forrest's effort failed in its attempt to slow or divert Sherman, and he was not able to do serious, lasting damage to the main line between Nashville and Chattanooga. Nevertheless, he had taken approximately 4,000 prisoners, including 86 commissioned and 1,274 noncommissioned officers. He also had captured approximately five hundred horses, seven pieces of artillery, two thousand small arms, and large amounts of medical supplies, wagons, and ambulances. The greatest effect of the expedition was the destruction of the rail line from Decatur to Spring Hill. Forrest had overestimated the time it would take to make repairs, but it did take over thirty days to get the trains rolling again.[39]

Sherman now realized that he would not have to rely solely on his tenuous line of supply, as the crops in Georgia were coming to harvest and the trees were bearing fruit and nuts. Had Sherman's line been interrupted three months earlier in the summer rather than in the fall, it would have been quite a different scenario and he would not have been able to write Grant in mid-October that "with the crops ripe the men could subsist luxuriously on the bountiful fields and sweet potato patches. . . . Even now our poor mules laugh at the fine corn fields, and our soldiers riot on chestnuts, sweet potatoes, pigs, chickens etc." While Sherman's men were feasting simultaneously upon and wasting the countryside, Georgia was howling indeed.[40]

In October the Tennessee and Mississippi timberland burst forth into a kaleidoscope of Indian summer colors. However, with the wolves at the door, there was no time to take in the seasonal beauty. The Confederacy was in crisis. Lee was under siege by a hundred thousand of Grant's troops at Petersburg. Sherman had burned Atlanta and taken control of northern Georgia. General Hood had abandoned Georgia and moved into northern Alabama to regroup for a thrust into middle Tennessee.

Forrest was exhausted and wanted time to see his family. When he requested a furlough, General Taylor refused, believing that Forrest's presence was needed now more than ever. The day after Taylor refused Forrest's request for leave, Taylor wrote to Forrest that General Hood's move around Sherman's right flank would draw the Union forces out of western Tennessee and Forrest should move into the area to capture all the available supplies. Forrest's plans concerning the situation were a little more ambitious than a foraging expedition. He wrote back to Taylor explaining the mission he had in mind. He suggested that if he must stay in the front lines he might as well have something to say about how to best strike at the enemy in the current circumstances:

> The enemy derives much of his supplies from the Northwestern railroad, which are shipped up the Tennessee River and thence to Johnsonville and Nashville. It is my present design to take possession of Fort Heiman, on the west bank of the Tennessee River below Johnsonville, and thus prevent all communication with Johnsonville by transport. . . . It is highly important that his line be interrupted if not entirely destroyed, as I learned during my recent operations in Middle Tennessee that it was by this route that the enemy received most of his supplies at Atlanta.[41]

Forrest went on to say that he felt he could significantly increase his numbers by rounding up deserters and absentees in the process. Also, Johnsonville was a hotbed of activity and a huge supply depot where freight from steamboats was transferred to railcars by the use of "powerful machinery."[42] His letter to Dick Taylor also included mention of possible foul play committed by others against the African-Americans he had captured during his middle Tennessee campaign. "I have captured on the road upward of 1,000 negroes. I understand only about 800 have reached you. This matter should be investigated, and I shall endeavor to punish the delinquents."[43]

Forrest wasted no time waiting for permission and put his plan into motion, moving out toward Johnsonville, which lies about twenty miles west of Fort Henry and Fort Donelson. Johnsonville was the rail hub of the Nashville-Northwestern Railroads. Before the war the line extended out twenty-one miles west of Nashville and later was extended another fifty-one miles by the U.S. Army. The complete line ran from Kingston to the Tennessee River and offered Sherman an alternate line of supply as far as Nashville.

Marching orders were cut for the morning of October 16, and the column was under way early that morning. Five days later, on the twenty-first, they arrived at Jackson, Tennessee. Generals Chalmers and Buford joined Forrest there. The tough and resilient General Buford had just recently recovered enough from the wounds he suffered at Tupelo to return to action.

## Johnsonville and the Forrest Horse Marines

No man could have maintained the supercharged intensity level at which Forrest had performed for the past three and a half years, not to mention carrying a few ounces of Yankee lead from the four wounds he had suffered in combat along the way. His health was failing and his personal fortune and business were in ruins. He also had not seen his wife for eighteen months. In the second week of October he had written to Dick Taylor,

> As soon as you can do so relieve me of duty for 20 or 30 days, to rest and recruit. I have been constantly in the field since 1861, and have spent half the time in the saddle. I have never asked for a furlough for over 10 days in which to rest except when wounded and unable to leave my bed have had no respite from duty.[44]

Taylor could not spare such a valuable weapon as Forrest at this critical juncture in the war, no matter what his condition, and somewhat callously he denied Forrest's request. With the denial came orders to move on Johnsonville in northeast Tennessee near Fort Henry. What neither of them realized was that in six months the war would be over.

Before moving out, it became necessary to send out recruiting and foraging parties and to release nearly a thousand of his men to return home to acquire new mounts. This left Forrest with approximately three thousand effectives. All this movement of rebels traversing the countryside was causing a general panic in Memphis and the surrounding area. Brig. Gen. Solomon Meredith recalled all forces in west Kentucky to return to Columbus and Paducah and the protection of their fortifications. In late October and early November, Meredith and Washburn expected an imminent attack. Washburn was still spooked from the earlier raid on Memphis and exclaimed, "I have barely enough men here to defend this place from Forrest and his ten thousand men . . . and should not be surprised if he should plant batteries above here at Randolph and Ft. Pillow." One wonders if Washburn also hid his uniforms just in case.[45]

General Buford was sent ahead to take up strategic positions on the west bank of the Tennessee. With him were Morton's batteries, two twenty-pound rifled Parrott guns sent up from Mobile, and a brigade of Lyon's Kentuckians. Chalmers was a few hours behind Buford and within supporting distance. Dragging the heavy artillery over the mud-clogged roads was exhausting work, but Buford's column arrived on October 28 at the old Confederate works of Fort Heiman on the west side of Tennessee River.[46]

Buford placed Col. J. B. Walton's battery inside the works at Fort Heiman and a section of Morton's guns a few hundred yards farther downstream. Captain Morton's second section of artillery and Bell's Tennesseans were sent five miles upriver to Paris Landing, where the river narrowed for a short distance. Once the Union vessels passed through the narrow expanse of the Tennessee at this point in the river, they would fall into a trap. Buford's choice of ground to set his ambush was a "judicious disposition, which effectively blocked the river." When Forrest arrived the next day, he approved of the chosen position and dispersed his command to augment those posts already manned by Buford's men.[47]

The first vessel to enter the nautical gauntlet was the freight ship *Mazeppa* on the twenty-ninth. As she steamed around the bend, the Confederates let the ship pass the lower battery. Once the *Mazeppa* was between the two lower gun batteries, which were well hidden in the trees and brush on the shore, the Confederate guns cut loose. In short order the *Mazeppa* was being blown to splinters as it made for the opposite shore. Floating helplessly near the east bank of the Tennessee, the *Mazeppa*'s crew abandoned ship and hotfooted it into the woods. Since the Confederates had no boats or ferries, volunteers were called to swim across the river and take possession of the Union ship and her cargo then tow it back across the river.

When the rebels went through the cargo they discovered a rich and varied supply of clothes, blankets, shoes, hard tack, and a few bottles of whiskey that General Buford quickly appropriated for his personal use. While dispositions were being made to unload the cargo, three Federal gunboats rounded the bend and began shelling Buford's position, forcing the Confederates to temporarily pull back.

The Southerners were not going anywhere for long, however. On the next morning, the thirtieth, they were back in their original positions ready to contest the passage of the river. The steamer *Anna,* bound for Paducah, was the next ship to come through the passage. When the Confederates opened fire, the shrewd captain of the *Anna* quickly hoisted a white flag and turned in the direction of the Confederates on the west bank. Buford's men held their fire, as the *Anna* appeared to be pulling into dock and surrendering. Suddenly, the captain of the *Anna* fired up the steamer and veered off downriver attempting to escape. Buford's men ran back to their gun positions and opened fire as soon as they could, hitting the retreating vessel many times. Morton's guns and Bell's Tennesseans hammered the Federal ship at the other end of the gauntlet, inflicting several casualties. Nevertheless the *Anna* survived the barrage, and with a damaged engine, she floated downstream to safety.

At approximately 2:00 P.M., the transport steamer *Undine,* carrying eight 24-pound bronze howitzers, came under fire from two guns of Bell's position at Paris Landing. For approximately an hour the *Undine* traded fire with the Confederate batteries on shore. In the process, the *Undine* had its escape pipe shot off and took four rounds through her gun casements, which killed four men and wounded three more. Damaged but still able to limp away the *Undine* moved downriver between Paris Landing and Fort Heiman and pulled to shore out of range of both Confederate gun emplacements.[48]

A few minutes later, the transport ship *Venus* floated into sight and failed to see the warning signals from *Undine.* Coming under heavy small-arms fire, the captain of the *Venus* was shot dead, but the determined crew on board continued full steam ahead downriver. Within a few hundred yards the *Venus* had taken heavy damage but she reached the cover of the *Undine's* guns and came to anchor. Approximately twenty minutes after the *Venus* came to anchor, a third transport came into view towing a barge. This was the *J. W. Chesseman* returning from Johnsonville, which had its steam pipe blown off as she came through the Confederate shooting gallery. With Rice's and Hudson's batteries belching flame, Forrest ordered the troops he had hidden in the cane and reeds to rush the banks and open fire with small arms. The *Chesseman* was soon completely disabled and had to pull in to the west shore.[49]

The crews and supporting infantry aboard the gunboat *Undine* and the transport *Venus* attempted to hold out but were driven off their vessels, which were soon commandeered by the rebels. The *Chesseman* was too badly damaged to repair and was burned after it was unloaded. However, the *Venus* and the gunboat *Undine* were soon rendered seaworthy and moved to the west side of the Tennessee, where their cargoes were unloaded and the necessary repairs made.

On the morning of October 31, Forrest's men viewed an amazing sight as the Confederate banner was raised on the two newest additions to the Confederate navy. Most of the Southern troopers had not seen a Confederate battle flag afloat since watching their colors go down with the Confederate gunboats two years earlier at Memphis. Over twenty-five hundred rebels "made the air ring with cheer after cheer" at the christening of the "Forrest Horse Marines." It seemed somehow appropriate that this celebration was taking place on Halloween.[50]

As Forrest inspected the ships, he realized that his first problem was finding the men to pilot them. John Morton, in his postwar book, related an interesting idea that his general came up with. Captain Morton explained how Forrest approached him and asked if he would like to transfer his guns to one of the captured boats and become the commander of a gunboat fleet. Charging with his guns in the front lines was one thing; this was quite another. Morton was quick to say that he knew nothing about the water and preferred to keep his feet on dry land.

Thinking fast, lest he be ordered to become a naval gunner, Morton recommended that fellow artillerist Capt. Frank M. Gracey, a former steamboat captain, be considered for the honor. Gracey probably would not have thanked Captain Morton for volunteering his services for him, but shortly after Morton made his desperate recommendation, Captain Gracey was ordered to place his guns on the *Undine* and assume command of Forrest's new fleet.[51]

Lt. Col. William A. Dawson was named the captain of the *Venus,* which bore two 20-pound Parrots. Before embarking on their naval adventure, Dawson asked for a private audience with his commanding officer. Dawson wanted to let Forrest know that this ship was nothing like the steamboats he had piloted in private life and hoped for some assurance from the general that he would not curse at him and his men if they should lose their general's new fleet and have to rejoin the cavalry on foot. Forrest assured him that as long as he could keep his boat between the banks of the Tennessee he had nothing to worry about. However, Forrest gave his novice crews the rest of the day to practice maneuvers and become as accustomed to their vessels as best they could in a few hours.[52]

On November 1, 1864, Forrest's naval command moved up the

river toward Johnsonville, the main target of the mission. The day was cloudy and rainy and the banks of the river, where the cavalry and artillery labored to keep pace with their comrades in the ships, were semi-flooded and mud clogged. Although the day was dark, the spirits of the men were high as the boys on land swapped insults with their buddies having an easy time of it relaxing on a little boat trip up the Tennessee. As the troops sweated and struggled on shore, dragging the guns from mud hole to mud hole, they had to be satisfied with the age-old soldier's game of calling insults and threats to their comrades on the river, whom they felt were for the moment living a much easier life than themselves.[53] That night, Forrest's command pulled to shore and anchored their boats under the ruins of an old railroad trestle that had spanned the river near Danville, Tennessee.

On November 2, they moved out and by 3:00 P.M. the Confederates were six miles below Johnsonville. However, the *Venus* and the *Undine* had pulled too far ahead of their riverbank support, and as they rounded a bend at Davidson's Ferry, they ran into two Federal gunboats, *Key West* and *Tawah*. Within minutes the river battle was on. The cavalrymen aboard the *Venus* were no match for the trained crews of the Union gunboats, who soon blasted the tiller off the rebel vessel, which caused the *Venus* to lose all control. The crew had no choice but to ground her and make their escape into the woods. The *Undine* attempted to come to the rescue but was driven back downstream. She was not pursued because General Chalmers had placed a gun battery at Davidson's Ferry to provide covering fire.[54]

On the night of the third, Forrest made a personal reconnaissance of ground and river ways in and around Johnsonville. The rainy night provided cover for his troops as they made the herculean effort of dragging Morton's gun batteries into position across the river from Johnsonville in preparation for a surprise attack in the morning. Rice's and Walton's guns remained in place above and below Reynoldsburg Island to contest any reinforcements from the Federal navy once the attack on Johnsonville began.

The next morning, Lt. Cmdr. Leroy Fitch steamed into the river with six gunboats, unaware that the main portion of Forrest's command was only a half-mile away and directly across the river from Johnsonville. Fitch's six-vessel flotilla consisted of the gunboats *Moose, Brilliant, Victory, Paw Paw, Fairy,* and *Curfew,* which mounted seventy-nine guns among them. As Fitch moved on the Confederate position on the north end of Reynoldsburg Island, Lt. E. M. King, commanding the *Key West, Tawa,* and *Elfin* (No. 54), sporting twenty-five guns, moved below Pilot Knob to attack the *Undine* between Fort Heiman and Paris Landing. There were now over a hundred guns afloat on that narrow expanse of the Tennessee River.[55]

All that opposed this impressive display of naval power was the captured *Undine* with her eight guns, supported on land by Rice's two-gun battery at the head of Reynoldsburg Island. Down below, near the narrow channel between the island and the west shore of the Tennessee, was Col. Walton's two-gun battery. Captain Gracey of the *Undine* soon found himself trapped between the two gunboat fleets and was quickly forced to shore, where the *Undine* was torched. As the crew took to the woods, effectively ending the career of Forrest's navy, the *Undine* blew up in a fiery explosion.

Meanwhile, the incredibly accurate fire from Rice's battery was pounding the Union navy above Reynoldsburg Island. Lieutenant King of the *Key West* said of this engagement, "Out of 30 shots fired, 17 struck their mark." Ten shells penetrated the upper works of the *Key West* while seven shells tore open the deck and hull, forcing the entire three-boat fleet to draw off back toward Johnsonville.

Fitch's six-boat fleet attacking the Confederates on the north end of Reynoldsburg Island kept up a long-range barrage until 11:00 A.M., but they did not attempt to enter the narrow channel where they could put themselves in a better position to engage the Confederate batteries. Fitch stated that he did not enter that narrow channel due to the fact that the Federal gunboats would be forced to enter in single file and against the current. If one vessel were sunk it would block the channel, possibly trapping all the other ships. Consequently, all six gunboats, less than four miles away from Johnsonville, were completely blocked off from providing support when the battle began.

While Forrest's river batteries held off the Union vessels from below Johnsonville, Captain Morton was completing the strategic placement of the gun batteries across the river from the unsuspecting township. Commanding the Union facilities at Johnsonville was Col. Charles R. Thompson. He had been notified earlier that Forrest was nearby, but he never realized just how near until all hell broke loose.

As Morton made final preparations he observed that several gunboats

> with steam up were moored at the landing. Another piled
> almost directly beneath the bluff. The artillery captain
> [Morton] could almost have dropped a stone upon it. A

number of barges clustered around; negroes were loading them, officers and men were coming and going, and passengers could be seen strolling down to the wharf. . . . It was an animated scene, and one which wore an air of complete security.[56]

Through his field glasses, Forrest watched the beehive of activity across the river. At the docks were numerous ships being loaded by hundreds of workers. Forrest took in the sight of the three gunboats, eleven transports, and eighteen barges, all lined up like ducks in a shooting gallery. Upon the higher ground sat the stockade, which was surrounded by several large warehouses and vast stockpiles of supplies, ammunition, and goods of all descriptions that were covered by tarps and tents. Steam billowed from the locomotives awaiting their Georgia-bound cargoes.

Johnsonville had been named for Tennessee Unionist Andrew Johnson, Lincoln's running mate in the election that was only four days off. At 2:00 P.M. on November 4, all ten of Morton's guns were fired simultaneously with a huge report that sounded like a "clap of thunder out of a cloudless sky."[57] For nearly an hour Morton's guns focused on the gunboats and transports at the wharf until the majority of the boats were burning and exploding. In short order the entire fleet docked at Johnsonville was in flames and sinking into the Tennessee. The skeletal remains of these sunken vessels could still be seen as late as 1925 when the river ran low.[58]

Next, Morton trained his guns upon the warehouse district and stockade on the elevated ground. The guns in the fort and aboard a few of the serviceable ships attempted to return fire, but their aim was wild due to the heavy cloud of smoke that obscured Johnsonville. Besides the smokescreen, increasing the Union gunners' difficulties was the fact that the Confederate positions were lower than the ground at Johnsonville. The east bank of the river was more than twenty feet higher than the west. In some cases the Federal batteries were unable to depress the elevation of their guns low enough to do more than fire shells harmlessly over the heads of the Confederates.

By 3:30 P.M. the warehouses were aflame along with several acres of tents and stacked crates that were soon consumed by the spreading inferno. The Confederate gunners now began firing independently and chose to zero in on targets of their own fancy. One of the more spectacular direct hits was upon a large warehouse filled with barrels of whiskey. As the structure caught fire, the barrels of alcohol exploded and let loose a blazing river of blue flame that flowed like a lava stream down the hill and into the Tennessee.[59]

Even Forrest got caught up in the excitement and pandemonium being created across the river. Dismounting, Forrest took command of a piece of artillery and began directing its fire. As Capt. John Morton passed by, he observed Forrest helping with the loading and unloading of the gun. Morton was amused to hear Forrest singing a little tune as he blasted away. When a shot would go wide or long, Forrest would exclaim, "Rickety-shay! Rickety-shay! I'll hit her next time." As one cannon shot went long, Forrest then gave a curious command: "Elevate the breech of that gun lower." His men understood the humorous order nevertheless. Seeing the fun Forrest was having, General Buford and Colonel Bell joined in with their general manning the piece with the enthusiasm of boys shooting off fireworks on the Fourth of July.[60]

The smell of burning bourbon, which smoked and hissed as it ran into the river, mixed with the smells of burning coffee, beans, bacon, and cordite, wafted on the wind to the other side of the river. The delightful smells drove the graybacks wild, inspiring cheer after cheer. Not only was it a spectacular scene, it was also spectacularly expensive for the Yankees. Colonel Thompson would later estimate the Federal losses at $2,200,000. However, this did not include the naval losses. Forrest's estimation was closer to the mark. His figure on the damages inflicted on the enemy was $6,700,000.[61] Forrest lost two men and nine wounded during the entire raid. The Federals lost a hundred fifty men taken prisoner, but there was no report on their casualties.

The rebels pulled back southward some six or seven miles the night of the fourth, "traveling by the light of the enemy's burning property," and pitched camp the next morning. Forrest returned to the river on the morning of the fifth to facilitate the withdrawal of Lt. H. H. Brigg's battery and Rucker's brigade in support of the guns, left as rear guard when the Confederates pulled out.

As the Southerners were pulling back,

> a regiment of negroes, emerging from their cover, displayed themselves upon the opposite bank. . . . Throwing off their coats, and shaking their clenched fists at the hated Confederates who had wrought the desolation around them, they hurled across the stream upon the morning air their whole arsenal of explosive, offensive epithets, oaths and maledictions.

They were also well aware that this was not just the regular brand of "hated Confederates"; this was, in their minds, the butcher of Fort Pillow.

Forrest, however, had never been the most tolerant of men, nor was he immune to the verbal barrage launched at him and his men from the other side of the river. He called a halt to his withdrawal and commanded Brigg's gunners to unlimber their field pieces and Rucker's men to dismount. His surprised tormentors were dispersed by the first volley "in the wildest confusion; but a number were left dead or wounded upon the river bank."[62]

The campaign against Johnsonville would earn Forrest his second colorful nickname during the war. Sherman would never refer to his old antagonist as the Wizard of the Saddle. His newest reference to Forrest was personal, because to Sherman, Forrest had become a demon that he could not seem to exorcize. As he said, "That Devil Forrest was down about Johnsonville making havoc among the gunboats and transports."[63]

In his memoirs Grant wrote, "Forrest indeed performed the very remarkable feat of capturing, with cavalry, two gunboats and a number of transports, something the accomplishment of which is very hard to account for." Soon after Johnsonville and the recall of the Georgia state troops to gather in the crops, Grant and Sherman became convinced "that with the army he [Sherman] had with him it would be impossible to hold the line from Atlanta back and leave him any force whatever with which to take the offensive . . . or else Sherman would have been obliged to make a successful retreat." Sherman's army would now be required to live off the land to a great extent from this point forward in his march to the sea.[64]

On November 7, the rains came again, along with new orders to report to General Beauregard in northwest Alabama near Tuscumbia. General Hood had called for Forrest's help. Forrest began pushing hard for his rendezvous with Hood in Alabama, but the weather and mud became factors and seriously slowed Forrest's progress. At times, Forrest was required to use sixteen-horse teams to drag his guns over terrible roads that occasionally needed to be corduroyed with tree logs so that his forces could continue. It would be nearly a week and a half before Forrest would reach Hood, who was severely agitated at the delay. In a letter to Dick Taylor, the only commander, it seems, whom he completely respected, Forrest wrote that "he deplored" being sent off to Hood's command and leaving Taylor and Tennessee behind.

I know not how long we are to labor for that independence

for which we have thus far struggled in vain, but this I do know, that I will never weary in defending our cause, which must ultimately succeed. Faith is the duty of the hour. We will succeed. We have only to work and wait.[65]

# Chapter Fourteen

# INTO THE MOUTH OF HELL

*—Alfred, Lord Tennyson*

## Spring Hill, Franklin, Nashville
## November-December 1864

As Forrest was turning south at Perryville on November 7, the day before the presidential election of 1864, he could not possibly have known the turmoil and panic his attack on Johnsonville had created. On that day Maj. Gen. Joseph Hooker received a fantastic telegraph from Capt. W. Fithian, the provost marshal at Danville, Illinois. The dispatch read:

> Forrest has been in disguise alternately in Chicago, Michigan City and Canada for two months; has 14,000 men, mostly from draft, near Michigan City. On the 7th of November, midnight, will seize telegraph and rail at Chicago, release prisoners there, arm them, sack the city, shoot down all Federal soldiers, and urge concert of action with Southern sympathizers.[1]

General Hooker was understandably skeptical of the story, but nevertheless, he sent troops to Indianapolis, St. Louis, and Chicago to stand by at those cities until the national election was over. He eventually went there himself to check things out.[2]

Forrest was returning to service in the Army of Tennessee almost a year since he had left it. In that twelve-month span he had fought the enemy in almost fifty battles and smaller engagements. Forrest and his men had killed, captured, or put out of action three times their number of the enemy. He had taken forty-eight guns and destroyed as many or more. His commands had captured or destroyed five locomotives and seventy-five railroad cars, two thousand animals, three hundred fifty wagons, ten thousand small arms, four gunboats, and fourteen transports and torn up nearly one hundred miles of railroad track.[3]

After an arduous journey through the rain and mud, Forrest arrived at Hood's headquarters in Florence, Alabama (across the Tennessee from Tuscumbia) on November 14, and the next day he was placed in command of all the cavalry in the Army of Tennessee. Soon after his arrival he addressed his troops. The speech was reported in the *Montgomery Daily Mail* on November 26:

> Well, soldiers, I came here to jine you. I'm gwine to show you the way into Tennessee. My conscripts are going, and I know Hood's veterans can go. I came down here with 350 men. I got 3,500 conscripts. Since May I have fought in every county in West Tennessee. I fought in the streets of Memphis, and the women run out in their nightclothes to see us, and they will do it again in Nashville. I have fought a battle every 25 days. I have seen the Mississippi run with blood for 200 yards, and I'm gwine to see it again. I've captured 78 pieces of artillery and 16,000 Yankees, and buried 2,500 of them.[4]

No one can positively know if these were Forrest's exact words, but his use of slang and prideful statements on his accomplishments also seems to be in character. As for the veiled reference to Fort Pillow—"I have seen the Mississippi run red with blood for 200 yards, and I'm going to see it again"—one could easily draw the inference that he wasn't losing any sleep over his infamous reputation in the Northern states.

Not everyone was pleased with Forrest's appointment as cavalry commander of the Army of Tennessee. General Hood had felt Joe Wheeler was better suited for the job, and many of Hood's men were unhappy about serving under Forrest, having foreknowledge of his reputation and temper. Harry St. John of the Army of Tennessee wrote in his diary on November 18, "the dog's dead: we are under the command of N. Bedford Forrest." One particular trooper, John Dixon, had "dreaded" such a situation "since the death of the noble Van Dorn." He went on to express his

> distaste [at] being commanded by a man having no pretension to gentility—a Negro trader, gambler, an ambitious man, careless of the lives of his men. . . . Forrest may be & no doubt is, the best Cav[alry] officer in the West, but I object to a tyrannical, hot headed vulgarian's commanding me.[5]

In the meantime, while Hood had waited on Forrest, Gen. George

H. Thomas continued to build his army at Nashville to nearly triple the size of Hood's Army of Tennessee. During the same time period, the Union bands were playing as General Sherman sat on his horse on a hill east of Atlanta watching the "gleaming gun barrels" and "marching columns" of his sixty-thousand-man legion as they moved toward Savannah, Georgia, and the sea. They marched out of Atlanta underneath "the black smoke rising high in the air and hanging like a pall over a ruined city."[6] While Sherman marched to the Atlantic, his opposition became weaker and weaker. The Army of Tennessee would eventually face an enemy force that was becoming insurmountable.

Hood's immediate objective was to interpose his army between Brig. Gen. George H. Thomas at Nashville and Maj. Gen. John M. Schofield's corps, some eighty miles south at Pulaski. Thomas currently commanded approximately thirty-five thousand troops and Schofield had nearly the same. If the Army of Tennessee, some thirty-eight thousand, could drive a wedge between General Schofield and General Thomas and cut their communications, Hood might have a chance to destroy each army separately. However, his long-range plan was a fantasy. After defeating Thomas and Schofield, General Hood planned to drive the enemy back to the Ohio River, liberate Nashville, and then cross the Cumberland Mountain range and join Robert E. Lee in Virginia to aid in the defeat of Grant. In hindsight, it is hard to believe that anyone felt this was a feasible plan. Both Beauregard and Jefferson Davis denied authoring this strategy. It seems to have been Hood's own creation.

Sherman believed that part of Hood's strategy was to head into Tennessee in an effort to entice him to abandon the Georgia campaign and follow the Confederates northward. Sherman expressed his opinion of this idea, and of Hood, in a dispatch to Grant: "If he will keep going to the Ohio, I'll send him provisions."

The real question was who was responsible for placing Hood in command of the Army of Tennessee when he should have been in a hospital. John Bell Hood was only thirty-three years old and the youngest man to command a major army in the entire war. In June 1862, Hood earned his reputation by leading a bloody bayonet charge in the battle of Gainesville, Virginia, which transformed him into a celebrity in Richmond. In the summer of 1863, he received two horrific wounds. His left arm was shattered at Little Round Top during the battle of Gettysburg. The limb was rendered useless and was tied to his side. Three months later at Chickamauga he lost his leg, amputated at the hip. Eighty percent of the men who underwent this type of surgery died during the operation or shortly thereafter.

Hood's survival proves his toughness, but in November 1864, he was aged beyond his years and terribly disfigured.[7]

Lee had advised Jefferson Davis against placing Hood in command because he was "all lion and no fox." Lee was absolutely right. Hood's wounds should have disqualified him for command, not to mention his addiction to alcohol and laudanum. A special harness was required to strap and hold him in the saddle when on the march. On at least one occasion he fell from his horse in a very humiliating fashion and required the help of several men to return him to his saddle.

In 1885, Grant wrote in his memoirs,

> Mr. Davis was disappointed with General Johnston's policy. My own judgment is that Johnston acted very wisely: he husbanded his men and saved as much of his territory as he could, without fighting decisive battles in which all might be lost. . . . Sherman and I were rejoiced. Hood was unquestionably a brave, gallant soldier not destitute on ability, but, unfortunately his policy was to fight the enemy wherever he saw him without thinking much of the consequences of defeat. I think that his [Johnston's] policy was the best one that could have been pursued by the whole South—protract the war, which was all that was necessary to enable them to gain recognition in the end.

Grant continued that the North was growing weary and "the South was a military camp, controlled absolutely by the government with soldiers to back it, and the war could have been protracted."[8]

Others in the Union command knew Hood even more personally. General Thomas had been one of Hood's instructors at West Point, where Hood graduated forty-fourth in the class of 1852. Maj. Gen. John M. Schofield had actually tutored Hood at the academy. Neither of the Union officers was overly impressed by Hood's academic ability. If the Confederacy had a death wish, it had chosen the right man for the job.

The Army of Tennessee was blessed with an array of brilliant commanding officers dedicated to their duty and their cause. Any general in full possession of his senses could have written glorious pages of military history with such men, but, alas, Hood was all used up. He, among the least capable of leading in such a crisis, now led the Army of the Tennessee, and he would command it regardless of the advice of his subordinates.

Forrest had returned to the Army of Tennessee as Hood's second choice to command its cavalry. The reservations and fears of many who questioned Forrest's appointment were soon borne out. Not long after Forrest arrived at Florence, Alabama, he received a memorandum from Hood to reduce the number of mules that he had assigned to each team for the upcoming march and turn the extra mules over to Hood's quartermaster. Forrest ignored the memo as though it were more of a suggestion than an order. When he did not respond, the quartermaster sent Maj. A. L. Landis to contact Forrest and ask for an explanation. Landis found Forrest the next day and asked what was the holdup in delivering the requested mules to the quartermaster. For his trouble, Major Landis was blasted with a verbal barrage certain to be reported with great color and comment through the chain of command. Capt. John Morton happened to be present during the encounter and quoted Forrest's reply to the chagrined major. It seemed, wrote Morton, that

> the good Lord had been ousted and old Nick had taken full possession of the sanctuary. The atmosphere was blue for a while. Stripped of General Forrest's bad words, he said to Major Landis: "Go back to your quarters, and don't you come here again or send anybody here again about mules. The order will not be obeyed; and, moreover, if Major Ewing bothers me any further about this matter, I'll come down to his office, tie his long legs into a double bowknot around his neck, and choke him to death with his own shins. It's a fool order, anyway. General Hood had better send his inspectors to overhaul [his] wagons, rid them of all surplus baggage, tents, adjutant desks, and everything that can be spared. Reduce the number of his wagons instead of reducing the strength of the teams. Besides, I know what is before me; and if he knew the road from here to Pulaski, this order would be countermanded. I whipped the enemy and captured every mule, wagon and ambulance in my command: have not made a requisition on the government for anything of the kind for two years, and now that they are indispensable my teams will go as they are or not at all."[9]

As General Hood and his staff discovered, this was a different breed of soldier. Forrest's response was close to insubordination, but it was also good common sense. The mules stayed where they were.

Hood had chosen to go first after Schofield's command of the Fourth and Twenty-third Corps at Pulaski, Kentucky, which was seventy-five miles south of Nashville and thirty miles south of

Columbia. To that end Forrest was sent ahead on November 16. Five days later, Hood would follow with the rest of the army. Both groups would be forced to march through a severe snow and ice storm. On the morning of the sixteenth, Forrest crossed to the north bank of the Tennessee via a pontoon bridge and proceeded through Henryville and Mount Pleasant heading toward Columbia. On November 21, Hood moved out with three corps advancing on separate roads. Gen. Benjamin F. Cheatham was on the left moving toward Waynesboro. Gen. Stephen D. Lee marched in the middle, between the two roads, and Gen. Alexander P. Stewart marched on the right flank on the road leading to Lawrenceburg.[10]

Forrest's cavalry was clearing the way for Hood's infantry between the sixteenth and twenty-first and engaged in constant skirmishing with the Federal forces he met for the next several days. On Monday, November 21, Forrest was leading three slim divisions of approximately thirty-five hundred men when he ran into Union general Edward Hatch's cavalry, which was covering the movements of Schofield's infantry. From Monday through Wednesday the twenty-third, Forrest drove the enemy back to the vicinity of Henryville.[11]

Once there, Hatch's column drew up into a line of battle and prepared to receive Forrest's attack. Dividing his force, Forrest outflanked Hatch's position. Bedford personally led his escort in a charge, which produced a rout, a "perfect stampede," that drove the retreating Federals from their position toward Mount Pleasant. At about 2:00 A.M. on the twenty-fourth, as the Confederates pushed the Union troopers toward Mount Pleasant, Maj. Gen. Jacob D. Cox threw his infantry division across the road and effectively checked Forrest's progress. This action prevented Forrest from continuing on to Columbia and seizing the crossing at the Duck River, thus giving Major General Schofield's main column time to reach Columbia first. The blocking action by Cox allowed Schofield precious time to burn all but one of the bridges that spanned the river and to develop a defensive position while Hood's infantry was still making their way over the sloppy roads below Mt. Pleasant on the way to join Forrest.[12]

During the fighting on November 24, Lt. Col. William A. Dawson, the former captain of the *Venus* at Johnsonville, was killed charging the Union line, shot dead as he attempted to "wrench" the flag from the Federal colorbearer's hands.[13]

By nightfall on Thursday the twenty-fourth, Forrest had invested Schofield's position at Columbia, and he continued to harass the enemy until General Hood arrived late in the evening on Sunday. Hood did not intend to attack Schofield with a frontal assault.

Instead, he sent Forrest's cavalry a few miles north of Columbia to cross the Duck River and threaten the enemy's rear and hopefully draw Maj. Gen. James A. Wilson's cavalry northward to free up Hood's infantry.[14]

Wilson, however, was not fooled and sent a desperate dispatch to Schofield advising him that he had observed a large Confederate force moving north of Columbia. This force would have been Forrest's cavalry sweeping around in an attempt to cut off Schofield. Schofield was also informed that Forrest had laid a pontoon bridge across the Duck River for Hood's infantry to follow. Wilson told Schofield that he had better withdraw on the double and "get back to Franklin without delay." Schofield also telegraphed Thomas in Nashville of the situation and was on the march toward Spring Hill at 8:00 A.M. on Tuesday, November 29.

In the early afternoon of the twenty-ninth, after Forrest's command had crossed the Duck River (Chalmers at Carr's Mill, seven miles from Columbia; Gen. Wirt Jackson's command at Holland's Ford; and Biffle's regiment at Owens's Ford respectively), all three columns ran into heavy resistance. This resistance was from Wilson's cavalry, who were providing a rear-guard action while Schofield's main body of troops withdrew to Spring Hill. Hood, following behind Forrest, left Gen. Stephen D. Lee and most of his artillery behind to decoy the Federals.

Earlier that day, Hood's infantry had crossed the Duck River at Davis Ford, but not before Union general David Stanley had already secured a crossing at Rutherford Creek and established a defensive position at Spring Hill. A few hours later Forrest arrived and was able to capture the small Union garrison posted there and effectively cut Schofield off from Thomas's support in Nashville. However, Hood's plan began to unravel in the late afternoon hours on November 29, resulting in "lost Confederate opportunities and eyelash escapes for the Union forces which, with different fortune or better management" on General Hood's part, would have produced a decisive victory for the Confederates at Spring Hill.[15]

Two miles out from Spring Hill, near the Rally Hill Pike, Forrest called for Chalmers' command to do an exploratory sweep of a patch of woods just south of the tiny hamlet to see if they were occupied by Federal troops. As Chalmers and his horse soldiers moved into the timberline, a sudden burst of gunfire exploded from the brush, driving the rebels out of the trees at a gallop. When General Chalmers returned and rode up alongside his commander, Forrest cynically remarked, "They was in there sure enough, wasn't they, Chalmers."[16]

Maj. Gen. James A. Wilson commanded the Union soldiers hidden in the trees, and this was the first time he had met Forrest in battle. General Wilson was the new cavalry commander in the west and great things were expected of him. He had made his reputation as a cavalry commander under Grant in Virginia and with Sheridan in the Shenandoah Valley campaign. At twenty-seven years of age, Wilson was one of the youngest major generals in the cavalry service, or in the army, for that matter. He was determined to carry out Grant's orders to "not let Forrest get off without punishment." Wilson said that "the only power of cavalry is in a vigorous offensive; therefore I urge . . . hurling it into the bowels of the South in masses that the enemy cannot drive back as it did Sooy Smith and Sturgis." However, that plan was not yet complete until the spring of 1865. In the winter of 1864, Wilson did not consider his force ready to face the Wizard of the Saddle, and in his own words he described Forrest as "hitherto the most successful of the rebel cavalry leaders." Before the day was over, Wilson would prove the truth of that statement to himself. He wasn't quite ready for Forrest just yet.[17]

Early that morning, as soon as Buford's division was across the river, Forrest had driven the Federal cavalry out of Hurt's Cross Roads northward to Mount Carmel Church. Then, having accomplished his first task of taking Wilson out of the game, he left Wirt Jackson's brigade of Texans to continue pursuing and harassing the Federal cavalry while he wheeled the remainder of his command and turned west toward Spring Hill.[18]

By the time Forrest reached Spring Hill, Col. George D. Wagner, of Schofield's command, had already deployed his troops in a semicircle that extended from the road south of Spring Hill to the pike north of the town. By 3:00 P.M. the remainder of Schofield's army had double-timed it to Spring Hill and brought their artillery with them. The guns were placed on some high ground southwest of town, providing cover for the eight hundred wagons that continued to fall in behind their lines until 4:00 P.M.

The first of Forrest's men to arrive behind him were those of Brig. Gen. Frank Armstrong's brigade from Jackson's division and Buford's Tennesseans, who were immediately ordered to mount a cavalry charge that was quickly repulsed. Soon after this charge, Forrest received word from Hood to hold the enemy at all costs, for he was "rapidly advancing" on Spring Hill. Dismounting his men, Forrest began an attack on the enemy's left, where the wagon train was still pulling in. Forrest had now completed both aspects of his mission by taking the Federal cavalry out of the fight and holding

Schofield at Spring Hill. However, rather than ordering Forrest to hold Schofield in place, Hood should have ordered him to seize the road from Spring Hill to Franklin, which would have cut off the Union column completely. Nevertheless, Hood's flanking maneuver was a success. The Confederates were in an advantageous position to isolate Schofield's divisions and destroy them separately.[19]

Soon, the Confederates at Spring Hill had assembled on the field of battle one of the most potent combinations of infantry and cavalry commands imaginable. The combination of Nathan Bedford Forrest's cavalry with the infantry of Patrick R. Cleburne created something of a Confederate dream team.

At approximately 4:00 P.M., the spearhead elements of Hood's army arrived on the scene led by the fiery General Cleburne, whose infantry command was said to have been the best Confederate foot soldiers and fighters in the western theater. Close behind was General Cheatham's corps along with the divisions of Maj. Gen. William B. Bate and Maj. Gen. John C. Brown. Bringing up the rear were the divisions of General Stewart and Maj. Edward Johnson, whose division was from Lee's corps.[20]

This would be Hood's best chance. Gen. George D. Wagner's force was the only Union division on the field at this time, and although Wagner had most of Schofield's guns on site and held the high ground, the next closest Union support was at Rutherford Creek and the other was twelve miles away at Columbia, where the muffled booming of Stephen D. Lee's cannons could be heard. Lee's cannonade kept up a successful decoy action, holding a major part of Schofield's army at Columbia. Not since Gen. Braxton Bragg blundered at Chickamauga had there been such an opportunity presented to a commander to seriously maul the enemy as that which came to Hood on that November afternoon. His troops were positioned advantageously to stop Schofield and his divisions, who were tired, disoriented, and strung out along the road to Franklin. [21]

It was not to be. Why things turned out so badly for the Confederates is a story of contradictions with no clear recollections from the participating generals on the field. What happened next at Spring Hill was a mistake that would be compounded by another and another that caused a chain reaction leading to the virtual annihilation of the Army of Tennessee. The primary suspect in this debacle was Hood. The responsibility must be laid at his feet and, to some degree, upon his superiors for failing to realize that Hood was mentally and physically unfit for command.

Just after 4:00 P.M., acting on Hood's order, General Cleburne moved out with his infantry along with Bell's brigade of cavalry. Forrest and Cleburne, at the front of the formation, rode side by side with their sabers drawn. This deadly duo was the perfect picture of martial splendor, inspiring their men the way few commanders could. For the moment, Forrest and Cleburne maneuvered their commands with confidence and clarity in their mission. However, Bell's dismounted troopers were going into battle with only four rounds per man. Yet, as Forrest later reported, "they charged with promptness and energy and gallantry which I have never seen excelled."[22]

Forrest and Cleburne separated, with Cleburne's division taking position on the left of Bell's brigade. Simultaneously, from the front and left flank, the Confederates attacked General Stanley's troops, who had positioned themselves behind a breastwork of fence rails, and drove them in full retreat from behind their fortifications. Forrest and Cleburne's troops continued to chase the Yankees, hollering insults as they went. The pursuit was unceremoniously stopped when the Confederate surge ran into the Federals' massed gun emplacement on the southern end of Spring Hill. The Union batteries opened up with a terrible fire of grape and shrapnel that drove the Southerners back and forced them to reform for another charge.[23]

At approximately 4:30, with the sun beginning to set, Cleburne reformed his men for another assault on the pike held by Wagner's troops. Before the second attack could begin Cleburne received orders from his superior officer, Maj. Gen. Benjamin F. Cheatham, to stand down and hold his current position until he received further orders. Those further orders never arrived. Cleburne, without leaving his position, eventually went into bivouac for the night. This would not be the last instance of contradictory and confusing orders that would hamstring Hood's commanders in the field the night of November 29.

At approximately 6:00 P.M., General Cheatham ordered his Second Division, under Maj. Gen. William B. Bate, to move into the line of battle on Cleburne's left flank. As Bate was moving his division toward Cleburne's left, he ran into General Hood, who countermanded Cheatham's orders and told Bate to move to the turnpike and sweep southward toward Columbia.[24]

Darkness had set in as Bate's division marched across the Nat Cheairs farm, approximately a mile and a half south of Spring Hill. Near the Cheairs home General Bate's orders were countermanded for the third time when Lt. A. B. Schell, one of General Cheatham's aides, advised him to halt his progress and join his division to General Cleburne's left. Bate could not understand the logic of this last order. He was only a hundred yards from the Columbia-Spring Hill road and had already engaged an enemy division marching down the road. He later reported that he had checked their "movements in my front, and lines were being adjusted for a further forward movement" when the new order was issued. Reluctantly, Bate halted his forward push and fell back to the northeast to Cleburne's position, which left the road open. As he did so he watched the Federals continue on down the road. General Bate went into bivouac at 9:30 P.M. with both his and Cleburne's divisions facing Spring Hill awaiting the signal for the attack to resume.[25]

Meanwhile, General Brown, Cheatham's Third Division commander, was ordered to come up and position himself on Cleburne's right. Cheatham had planned a general attack on Spring Hill, and Brown's division was to launch the assault from the right flank once the signal was given. When Brown arrived at 5:00 P.M. and began to move into position, he found the enemy line, thrown out from Spring Hill, overlapping and extending past his own by several hundred yards and that "Forrest's Cavalry, which I had been assured would protect my right, had been ordered to another part of the field."[26]

Consequently, Brown's division, which was to begin the fight, held its current position and did not move up on Cleburne's right flank because, in General Brown's words, to do so would have invited "inevitable disaster." Brown reported the situation to Cheatham, who concurred with Brown's decision and advised Brown to stand by and await General Stewart's corps. Stewart's corps was supposed to be on the way to cover his exposed right flank. Cheatham also told Bate "to be ready to move at a moment's notice." But, as was the case with Cleburne and Bate, further orders never came.[27]

Cheatham then rode to make sure that Cleburne and General Bate understood that Brown's troops would begin the attack from right to left when the order to attack came. That order would be given when Stewart's corps arrived. However, Stewart was not going to arrive for several hours. Why? Because Hood had personally ordered him to move below Rutherford Creek and deploy his troops into line of battle "across the pike" beyond Spring Hill and to extend his line "down this way." A short while later Stewart had his orders changed by a courier from General Cheatham stating that General Hood wanted him to move as quickly as possible and place his division on Brown's right. By this time it was pitch dark, and Stewart's men were exhausted when they reached General Brown's position on the right flank of the rebel line at 11:00 P.M.[28]

While stumbling through the dark and attempting to find the correct position, Stewart ran into Forrest, who had just returned from resupplying his men and feeding his mounts. Forrest was able to provide Stewart with some bearing and information on the enemy's position; however, in the confusion and darkness, Stewart ended up with his line of troops facing away from "the all important pike instead of towards it." Forrest and Stewart knew that the situation was confused and soon rode to Hood's headquarters at the Thompson house to sort things out.

Meanwhile, Cheatham had been contacted by a messenger who advised him that General Hood had called a conference at headquarters. When Cheatham arrived, he found Forrest and Stewart already present. Hood was told of all the conflicting orders and misunderstandings but he seemed undisturbed. He told Forrest, Stewart, and Cheatham not to worry and that their current concerns "were not material, to let the men rest." Hood had "concluded to wait till morning . . . and be in readiness to attack at daylight."[29]

After General Cheatham departed, Hood turned to Forrest and asked if he could make sure that the Spring Hill road was blocked. Forrest advised Hood that most of his men were out of ammunition. Hood replied that Forrest could get the ammunition that he would need from the infantry commanders, but as it turned out Cheatham, Bate, and Brown could not provide Forrest with what he needed because any spare ammunition was in Columbia with the wagon train. Forrest was not confident about the situation but told Hood "he would do the best he could in the emergency."[30]

Before the meeting broke up, General Bate arrived for the same reason Forrest and Stewart were there: to find out exactly what he should be doing and where he should be doing it. Bate told Hood that as he approached the Spring Hill road south of the town, he had momentarily stopped the movements of wagons, equipment, and men passing down the pike. But because of his orders from Cheatham he had halted and realigned himself with Cleburne's left and did not continue to sweep toward Columbia as previously ordered. Bate also voiced concern about the continuing passage of Federal troops down the road.[31]

Forrest was dismissed from the meeting at that point and rode away with serious misgivings about the situation. All his instincts told him that the Confederates should be reforming and resupplying themselves immediately for an all-out attack before daylight. As the meeting concluded Hood was obviously weary and in pain. He was also confused about the reality of the situation, as his answer to

Bate's question on the movement of the enemy clearly reflects:

> It makes no difference now. . . . It is alright anyhow, for General Forrest, as you see has just left and informs me that he holds the turnpike with a portion of his forces north of Spring Hill, and will stop the enemy if he tries to pass toward Franklin, and so in the morning we will have a surrender without a fight. We can sleep quiet tonight.[32]

However, this was not what Forrest had told Hood about his combat readiness or his ability to block or hold the road. Bate was ordered to return to his position on the road south of Spring Hill, on the Confederate extreme right, and to get a good night's sleep! General Hood had placed a great deal of unrealistic responsibility on Forrest if he expected him to stop any attempted retreat or movement of Schofield's army in the dark while the rest of the Army of Tennessee slept quietly.

Around midnight, about the time Hood's meeting with his commanders was breaking up, Schofield began his precarious escape toward Thompson's Station through the Confederate lines. Schofield sent word to Cox's three divisions to follow his path, which would pass within site of the enemy campfires. Due to the pitch-blackness many Union troops accidentally wandered into Confederate campsites and were captured attempting to light their pipes on the enemy fires. If not for the coming catastrophe at Franklin, Schofield's escape would seem a comedy of errors on the part of the Confederates and an audacious stroke of luck and daring for the Union troops at Spring Hill. The famous author Ambrose Bierce was one of the soldiers with Schofield's rear units and later wrote, "We sneaked by the Confederate campfires with our hearts in our throats."[33]

The escape was nearly clean except for the brief intervention of Brig. Gen. Lawrence S. Ross's brigade of Texans, approximately six hundred strong, who had recently arrived in the area of Thompson's Station, returning from their pursuit of Wilson's cavalry earlier in the day. Ross's brigade had arrived on the scene as Schofield's column was passing and attacked the rear of the Federal train, stampeding the cattle and burning about forty wagons. However, Ross's force was too small to seriously impede the progress of Schofield's army. Nearing 1:00 A.M. Gen. Wirt Jackson gathered Ross's Texans and a brigade from Frank Armstrong's command and made a hopeless attempt to stop Schofield's progress by hitting his rear elements once again.[34]

The next morning, Wednesday, November 30, while Schofield's

army rushed up the road to Franklin and began fortifying the old existing trench works that ran from the neck of the loop of the Big Harpeth River into the little town, Hood's generals were being called to another meeting and breakfast at Rippavilla.

At approximately 5:00 A.M., the Confederate commanders rode to the nearby home where the breakfast meeting was to convene. Once everyone was present, Hood began throwing the blame at nearly each commander. As he dressed down this illustrious array of Confederate officers, Hood mainly accused Generals Cheatham and Cleburne. Hood blamed everyone but himself, and it was well known within the ranks of the Army of Tennessee that Hood had no great love for his new command. Hood felt that the Army of Tennessee had developed a defensive mind-set since its long retreat under Joseph E. Johnston and even "after a forward march of one hundred and eighty miles, [it] was still seemingly unwilling to accept battle unless under the protection of breastworks."[35]

Dawn was breaking as the Confederate staff meeting came to a close. Hood ordered Forrest to muster his command and retrieve the needed ammunition as quickly as possible and then to pursue and attack Schofield's rear. The rest of the Army of Tennessee would be coming behind him. Within an hour Forrest had secured his ammunition from Maj. Gen. Edward C. Walthall's infantry division. Moving to the front and flanks of the advancing rebel army, Forrest sent Chalmers west to the Carter's Creek Pike and General Buford's command down the Lewisburg Pike. Forrest and Wirt Jackson's division followed directly behind Schofield on the Spring Hill-Franklin road. Halfway between Franklin and Spring Hill, Forrest caught up with the rear elements of Schofield's column and drove them hard toward Winstead's Hill and then all the way into their entrenchments at Franklin.[36]

Schofield did not seem concerned about an attack from Hood, but he was worried that Forrest would cross the Harpeth River east of Franklin and drive between him and Thomas at Nashville. At 3:00 P.M. on the thirtieth, Schofield telegraphed Thomas, "I have no doubt Forrest will be in my rear tomorrow, or doing some greater mischief." That is exactly what Forrest hoped Schofield would think when he saw the enemy's impregnable line of fortification and entrenchments at Franklin.

However, it was not Forrest's call to make. General Hood would not be denied the chance to exact some sort of retribution on Schofield for escaping and on his own men for allowing it to happen. The commanding officer of the Army of Tennessee had been in a rage since sunup, and there would be hell to pay by sundown.

When Hood's infantry arrived between 1:00 and 2:00 P.M., Hood took a position under a Lim tree on Winstead's Hill and inspected the Federal line through his field glasses. His corps commanders stood by anxiously awaiting Hood's assessment of the situation. Finally, after a few minutes had passed, Hood announced, "We will make the fight."[37]

To a man, Hood's generals on the field that day adamantly disagreed with the decision to make a massive frontal assault. Hood countered their objections by stating that he believed the Union position of heavily fortified breastworks and entrenchments, which had its back to the Harpeth River, was actually a rear guard posted to hold the Confederates while the main body of enemy troops slipped away to Nashville. This was obviously not the case, and Forrest attempted to sway Hood's determination from executing such an attack. Hood was unmoved, saying, "I do not think the Federals will stand strong pressure from the front. The show of strength they are making is a feint to hold me back from a more vigorous pursuit." Forrest replied, "General Hood, if you will give me one strong division of infantry with my cavalry I will flank the Federals from their works within two hours' time."[38]

Hood felt there was no time to execute the maneuver Forrest recommended and stated, "The nature of the position was such as to render it inexpedient to attempt any further flank movement, and I therefore determined to attack him in front, and without delay."[39] Hood failed to see the logic of Forrest's suggestion or the fact that Schofield already held a very strong position and never believed that Hood would launch an all-out assault upon him at Franklin. In fact, Schofield had planned to pull out of his entrenchments at approximately 6:00 P.M. and make a run for Nashville. If General Hood had restrained himself for two more hours, one of the most suicidal and bloody charges of the Civil War would have never taken place. It was November 30, 1864.

So many stories came to an end as the sun went down on the Army of Tennessee that November 30. When it rose again on the first day of a new month, thereafter there would be no more tales to tell about the lionhearted Cleburne or eleven other Southern generals who fell on Franklin's field as victims of mere contingency.

There was no doubt that Forrest could have carried out his flanking move over the Harpeth, east of Franklin. Schofield believed it. That was the reason the Union general was itching to get to

Nashville before "that Devil Forrest" could cut him off. However, Hood would order the exact opposite of what should have been done. At Spring Hill, Hood should have launched a full-out attack against Schofield, but he did not. The last thing Hood should have ordered at Franklin was a murderous frontal assault, but he did.

Next, Hood ordered Forrest's cavalry to the extreme right in order to hold the end of the line and to be ready to fall upon the enemy when they broke and ran toward Nashville. In ordering him to the right flank, Hood probably saved Forrest's life.

As Forrest rode to the right, Cheatham and Stewart were aligning their infantry divisions on the open plain at the northern end of Winstead's Hill. Forrest's cavalry force was not that large and he was compelled to reduce its overall effectiveness by sending Chalmers and Biffle to the left of Cheatham's infantry and Buford's and Jackson's divisions to the right to close the gap between the infantry and the river. Buford's men were dismounted, and as the Confederate infantry moved up into formation they covered the ground between the Lewisburg pike and the Harpeth River on Stewart's right.[40]

The cold, overcast November sky cleared, revealing a bright and clear autumn afternoon. The Confederates had dressed their lines and the forward movement began at approximately 4:00 P.M. It was perhaps the grandest display of military grandeur during the war, as twenty thousand Confederate troops supported by five thousand cavalry began to cross the deadly two-mile expanse toward the enemy. What these troops would attempt to do at Franklin, Tennessee, was equally as reckless as the infamous "Charge of the Light Brigade." It would also exceed the feat of human courage and tenacity that was displayed by the Confederate army at Gettysburg.

Hood sat on a blanket on Winstead's Hill, just west of the Columbia Pike, two miles behind his advancing army. He had the best seat in the house for the carnival of horror that was about to be played out before the town of Franklin.

One hundred regimental flags snapped in the wind, and the bands were playing while nearly twenty-five thousand men moved northward astride the Columbia Pike that led straight into Franklin. The skyline turned blood red as the sun began to set in the south-west, and a pale moon could be seen in the southeastern sky. The grimly determined rebels marched at right shoulder shift with bayonets fixed. They were to hold their fire until they overran the advance line and began to drive the enemy into the river.

Awaiting them were Jacob D. Cox and the Twenty-third Corps of the Army of Ohio along with David S. Stanley's Fourth Corps of the Army of Cumberland. The Yankees could hardly believe their eyes as the huge gray and brown wave rumbled toward them. It was a larger force than Lee had thrown at Cemetery Ridge. At Gettysburg, Pickett's troops had made one charge across a one-mile expanse of open country and fought for fifty-five desperate minutes. At Franklin, Hood sent his men across a two-mile space with no artillery barrage to precede them and they would then fight a battle that lasted longer than two and a half hours.

Up the gut came Cleburne's, Gen. John Brown's, and Cheatham's divisions with the bands playing "Dixie" and the rebel yell echoing across the valley. As the Southerners reached artillery range, the Union barrage began. Exploding shells tore holes in the Confederate lines, which were immediately closed up without a break in the pace. The two Union lines out front of Schofield's center held their ground "until the charging rebels were almost crossing bayonets with them, but the line then broke—Conrad's brigade first, then Lane's—and men and officers made the quickest time they could to our main line." A large proportion of Lane's men came back with loaded muskets, and running at the breastworks, they fired a volley into the pressing rebels now not ten steps from them.[41]

The Federal line held its fire until most of their men had run to safety, and then at approximately one hundred paces the Union line opened fire. Brig. Gen. George W. Gordon, at the head of six Tennessee regiments, said,

> [It was as though] Hell itself had exploded in our faces! The enemy had thus long reserved their fire for the safety of their own routed comrades who were flying to them for protection, and who were just in front of and mingled with the pursuing Confederates . . . when they opened upon us (regardless of their own men who were mingled with us) such a hailstorm of shot and shell, musketry and canister, that the very atmosphere was hideous with the shrieks and messengers of death. . . . All made a scene of surpassing terror.[42]

Sheets of flame erupted and the field was soon covered in a hazy fog of black powder smoke and dust. The Army of Tennessee disappeared into the smoke as the horrific din of battle reached a crashing, thundering crescendo. A portion of the Federal line stretched across the Carters' farm. Fountain Branch Carter and twenty-three of his family and friends huddled in the basement of their home while the savage concussion of the raging battle deafened and terrified them. Some of the most vicious fighting of the day took place very near the Carter house, where the Confederates were threatening to break through. At times the combatants were unable to tell friend from foe in the thickening smoke and gathering darkness. The fight turned fiendish as both sides fought fiercely with every weapon at hand. Clubbing and stabbing, sometimes even punching and choking each other, the two armies were literally slugging it out when General Stanley arrived on the scene and ordered Col. Emerson Opdycke's Tiger Brigade to charge into the fray to check the Confederates' initiative.

At the same time that Patrick Cleburne's boys were breaking through the Union line next to the Carters' cotton gin, Opdycke's men, hidden behind a rise in the ground one hundred yards behind the main line, suddenly sprang up and rushed forward, slamming into the Confederates and plugging the temporary breach. Opdycke later stated that as he and his men charged forward, he knew "that Carter's hill was the key to it all . . . and I commenced moving the command to the left of the pike for greater security to the men and for easier maneuvering in case of need."

While en route, Opdycke said he observed "a most horrible stampede of our front troops . . . surging and rushing back past the Carter house . . . to the right and left of the pike." Opdycke remembered the scene as follows:

> Bayonets came down to a charge, the yell was raised, and the regiments rushed most grandly forward, carrying many stragglers back with them. The Rebels following our troops with great clarity and force, were met this side of the Carter house by our charge, and at once put to rout with a loss of 394 prisoners, 19 of whom were officers, 1 a colonel, and 9 battle-flags. . . . Our lines were now restored, and the battle raged with indescribable fury. The enemy hurled his masses against us with seeming desperation. . . . I never saw the dead lay near so thick.[43]

The Army of Tennessee actually penetrated the Union works, consisting of a deep ditch, parapet, and head logs. Cleburne's, Brown's, and Gordon's men had driven the Federals out of their works and back about sixty yards when the Union countercharge struck and hammered them back over the same body-littered ramparts. It was on this section of the field that Patrick Cleburne's storied career came to an end when the intrepid commander went down in a hail of lead.

Later his body was discovered to have taken forty-nine bullet wounds. Generals Brown and Gordon were both badly wounded and taken prisoner near the spot where Cleburne was killed.

It was no better on other sections of the line. In all, fifty-four regimental commanders of the Confederate army fell that evening, along with half a dozen generals. Within a few hundred yards of where Cleburne was killed, Brigadier Generals John Adams, States Rights Gist, Hiram Grandbury, and Otto Strahl all met their deaths.[44]

Into the night the struggle continued along the face of the line. Both armies were separated only by the breastworks as they unloaded everything they had on one another from point-blank range. Troopers huddled in the dark on opposite sides of the ramparts could hear men praying as they reloaded. The terror these men endured must have seemed like a nightmare from which they could never awake.

During that same afternoon and evening, Forrest's cavalry was giving a good account of themselves on both flanks. On the left, Chalmers crossed the river and drove the Federals back to their main line from behind a stone wall where they were posted. Behind them Chalmers held his position. On the right wing, Forrest, with Buford's and Jackson's horse soldiers, drove Wilson's cavalry across the Harpeth River and nearly turned the enemy's flank. However, Forrest's progress was checked by heavy reinforcements sent by Schofield upon Wilson's urgent request.

General Schofield later reported:

> Realizing the importance of holding this position, as soon as the rebel cavalry had made their appearance on the north side of the river, which properly formed the real line of defence for the Union army, I ordered Hatch and Croxton to attack the enemy with vigor and drive him into the river if possible, while Harrison, with Capron's old brigade, would look well to the left and rear. The occasion was a grave one. My subordinate commanders dismounted every man that could be spared, and went in with a rush that was irresistible. Towards the middle of the afternoon the fighting became exceedingly sharp. The enemy's troopers fought with their accustomed gallantry, but the Union cavalrymen, outnumbering their antagonists for the first time, and skillfully directed, swept everything before them. Upon this occasion, Hood made a fatal mistake, for it will be observed that he had detached Forrest, with two divisions of his corps,

on a side operation, which left him only Chalmers' division to co-operate with the main attack of his infantry. Had his whole cavalry force advanced against me [on one flank], it is possible that it would have succeeded in driving us back.[45]

The cavalry engagement on the far right carried into the night until Forrest withdrew Jackson's division back across the Harpeth under the pressure of the reinforced enemy in his quarter. Later that night, Forrest learned of the failed thrust up the middle. Around midnight, Schofield began withdrawing his troops toward the sanctuary of Nashville and Thomas's army.

By the time the fierce work of the late afternoon and early evening was over, Hood had lost approximately 7,000 men to Schofield's 2,326, and somehow, in the face of logic, Hood was able to claim a victory because the enemy had withdrawn, leaving him in command of the battlefield. History would see it rather differently, as did the demoralized troops who survived the holocaust.

On the morning of December 1, Forrest was ordered to give chase and attack the rear of Schofield's column on the way to Nashville. Hood was not ready to throw in the towel as his claim to victory would indicate. However, as he marched away from Franklin toward Nashville behind Forrest's cavalry, he marched with only 18,742 troops remaining of the 25,000 he had brought with him to that little town on the banks of the Harpeth.

Forrest galloped northward to Brentwood trying to catch up to Schofield's rear, but when he did; he was able to do little to stop the enemy column from reaching Nashville at noon on Friday, December 2. He then pitched camp a few miles outside the state capital to await the arrival of Hood's infantry, or what was left of it.

## The Battle of Nashville

Forrest's command had not been mauled at Franklin and they escaped the horrifying work that ensued on the battlefield after the guns had fallen silent. Burying the dead and caring for the wounded fell largely to the people of Franklin. In the days and months to come, the entire town of Franklin became one large hospital. Every available structure, including the Female College and courthouse, were converted into medical facilities. Six months after the battle there were still wounded men being treated at Franklin.

Hood's failure to cut off the Union force at Spring Hill and the slaughter at Franklin that ensued the next day were inexorable steps toward the coming disaster at Nashville.[46] On December 1, Stephen D. Lee's corps took the lead for Hood's army. Cheatham's corps followed on the second after spending a day in hell "burying the piles of dead, caring for the wounded and reorganizing the remains of our corps."[47]

Hood arrived at Forrest's camp outside Nashville on the second and proceeded to make another tactical error by sending Forrest to Murfreesboro, thirty miles south of Nashville. Hood wanted the railroad between Nashville and Murfreesboro torn up and also wanted Maj. Gen. Lovell Rousseau's eight thousand troops at Murfreesboro held in check so that they could not reinforce Thomas at Nashville. Sending Forrest on this mission made little difference in the lager scheme of things. General Thomas hardly needed reinforcing with the huge army he had gathered in the state capital. However, reducing his already decimated command by five thousand men in the face of Thomas's seventy thousand at Nashville could hardly be described as a stroke of strategic genius on Hood's part.

Traveling southward down the rail line, destroying track and telegraph wire as he moved, Forrest led Buford's and Jackson's cavalry divisions along with Bate's infantry division toward Murfreesboro on the afternoon of December 2. Meanwhile, Hood's ragged, shoeless eighteen-thousand-man army invested the frozen hills near Brown's Creek, three miles outside Nashville. Once there they attempted to lay siege to the city with what amounted to a long, thin picket line. Thomas was in no hurry to launch his assault and was not overly concerned about his situation. He had every right to that assessment, given the condition of Hood's army; however, Grant was not aware of the condition of the Army of Tennessee and was very concerned about what Forrest was up to. He continued to pressure Thomas to attack Hood immediately.

On December 2, fearful that Forrest would cross the Cumberland River and compel Thomas to react by retreating to Louisville to protect his rear, Grant telegraphed Secretary of War Stanton, "It looks as if Forrest would flank around Thomas until Thomas is equal to him in cavalry." It was true that Thomas was giving General Wilson more time to build the strength of the cavalry corps. Of course, it was also true that at the same time he was making Hood wait in freezing conditions, he was weakening his opponent while his own strength grew, and this strategy did not cost him a single man.

On the same day that Grant was wiring the secretary of war, Forrest struck stockade number 2 on the rail line, killing twenty men and capturing another eighty. On the fourth, he took blockhouse number 3 and thirty-two more prisoners. On the fifth, at La Vergne, the cavalry took blockhouse number 4, capturing seventy-five prisoners, two guns, several wagons, and supplies. Four miles south of La Vergne, Forrest joined General Bate's infantry, which had marched by a different route to reach the cavalry before the assault on Murfreesboro.[48]

On December 2, before moving on the chain of blockhouses farther down the railroad, Forrest had dispatched Colonel Kelley with the old regiment and four guns to Bell's Mills, six miles below Nashville, and ordered him to effect a blockade of the Cumberland River once he arrived. From the second to the fifteenth of December, until after the Battle of Nashville had begun, Colonel Kelley did just that and more by blasting hell out of six gunboats and any other Union craft that attempted to run his blockade.[49]

On the fifth, Grant wired Thomas to inquire, "Is there not danger of Forrest moving down the Cumberland to where he can cross it? It seems to me while you should be getting up your cavalry as rapidly as possible to look for Forrest, Hood should be attacked where he is." Thomas responded, "I have no doubt Forrest will attempt to cross the river, but I am in hopes the gunboats will be able to prevent him."[50]

Since the battle at Murfreesboro in 1862, the Union forces had heavily refortified the town and surrounding area with eight-foot earthen works and trenches covering the northern and western approaches. Fort Rosecrans, within these works, was two hundred acres of even more formidable defenses manned by more than eight thousand men and augmented by the firepower of fifty-seven guns. Forrest was not going to catch the Federal commanders at Murfreesboro with their pants down this time, as he had back in 1862.

Forrest arrived at Murfreesboro on December 6 and began a reconnaissance of the ground. He soon realized that a frontal assault was impractical considering that the force inside the heavily garrisoned fort was larger than his and, for the time being, well supplied. Instead, Forrest maneuvered his command around the fort in hopes of coaxing the enemy out of his barricades to engage him in the open field. He did not have long to wait. The next morning, Wednesday, December 7, Maj. Gen. Robert H. Milroy and thirty-five hundred troops marched out of Fort Rosecrans to give Forrest the fight he had hoped for.

In the coming battle, Forrest's troops would occupy the same ground the Union army held during the Battle of Stone's River on

December 31, 1863. At that engagement one hundred thousand men fought a desperate battle on this same field, and the landscape still bore the scars of the tremendous struggle. Here and there, Forrest's cavalrymen were shocked to see the polished brightness of white bones protruding from shallow graves too hastily dug.

Preparing to meet General Milroy, Forrest deployed his infantry across the Wilkinson Pike and placed his cavalry on both flanks in position to fall upon any attempt by the enemy to retreat back to the fort. At the same time he sent Buford's cavalry and Morton's guns in a wide sweep around the town to enter Murfreesboro from the east. It was a cunning move on Forrest's part, predicting that the enemy's attention would be to his front where the main body of troops was preparing to give battle.

As Milroy's column marched out of Fort Rosecrans, they suddenly veered off behind a clump of woods that hid their movements from the Confederates. General Bate later stated that he thought the enemy had changed his mind about the fight and was retreating back to the fort under the cover of the trees. Forrest apparently thought the same thing because Bate stated that Forrest ordered him to shift his line to the left to begin a pursuit of Milroy's troops. But as General Bate was realigning his formation, the Yankees burst from the tree line on his left, catching Bate and Forrest off guard and taking advantage of a "space of perhaps 75-100 yards" left between the two brigades. Forrest seemed to think that the situation was salvageable but was taken by surprise when, for one of the few times in the war, his command broke and ran in the face of the enemy.

Forrest later reported: "The enemy moved boldly forward, driving in my pickets, when the infantry, with the exception of Smith's brigade, for some cause which I cannot explain, made a shameful retreat, losing two pieces of artillery."[51] Forrest did not take the "shameful retreat" lying down. He could not believe what he was seeing, nor tolerate cowardice, and he reacted predictably.

Eyewitness accounts and reports are contradictory concerning Forrest's actions during the rout, but all agree that anyone who ran past Bedford on the way to the rear got a little more than a pep talk. As the stampede flooded to the rear, many Southerners were clubbed down or whacked with the flat of Forrest's sword as he raged and cursed them for cowards with questionable ancestry.

Spotting the colorbearer sprinting for safety with a horde of men following the battle flag to the rear along with him, Forrest charged King Phillip toward the colorbearer and demanded he halt. When the man continued to flee, Forrest either shot him down or took the colors away from him. The latter is more likely, as Forrest himself reported, "I seized the colors of the retreating troops and endeavored to rally them, but they could not be moved by any entreaty or appeal to their patriotism. Major General Bate did the same thing but was equally as unsuccessful as myself."[52]

Dismounting, Forrest waved the flag and screamed for his men to rally, taking a swipe at anyone within reach of the guidon. Some observers said that watching the fleeing men attempting to zig and zag around the cursing Forrest would have been comical if not for the seriousness of the situation. Finally, in desperation and contempt, Forrest threw the flag at the last man going by.

The story of Forrest shooting down the colorbearer is told in John Wyeth's biography of Forrest, but Wyeth's source is secondhand and directly contradicted by Judge J. P. Young. Young stated that Forrest did practically all that was humanly possible to stop the retreat short of shooting his own men. Young also reported that during the battle Sgt. Jacob Gaus had another bugle shot full of holes and ruined. It seemed as though the old sergeant's bugles were as expendable as horses ridden by Forrest.[53]

During the crisis, Forrest sent Maj. J. P. Strange with urgent dispatches for Jackson's, Armstrong's, and Ross's cavalry brigades to charge to the rescue because everything depended on their immediate response. Forrest's trusted commanders were up to the mark, and as he later reported, "they proved themselves equal to the emergency by charging on the enemy thereby checking his advance."

General Milroy began to draw his force back toward the fort once his short-lived advantage was reversed. However, there was one other reason that the Federal commander returned to Fort Rosecrans in such a hurry.

Before the attack began, Forrest had sent Buford and Morton around to the east of town to blast their way into Murfreesboro by way of the Woodbury road, which happened to be the same road Forrest took into town during his raid in 1862. Buford and Morton's raid was a shock to the troops at Murfreesboro. The Confederate horsemen and Captain Morton's flying batteries were able to charge into the center of the town, unlimber their guns, and begin shelling everything in sight, including the courthouse and the Federal garrison.

In response, Rousseau mounted aggressive countermeasures and brought his own guns to bear upon the rebel batteries. One shell exploded into Morton's position, killing six of his battery horses. Morton was able to salvage his caissons and guns by cutting the harnesses from the dead animals and pushing the field pieces off by hand.[54]

When Buford withdrew from the town and Milroy from the field, the action at Murfreesboro essentially came to an end. For the next few days Forrest foraged the area, while Rousseau was content to stay within Fort Rosecrans. Meanwhile, Hood was still waiting for Thomas to make his move. The situation was worse than anyone could have imagined. The weather dropped below zero at times and Hood's men were without winter clothing, some actually shoeless. And perhaps worst of all, the Army of Tennessee had lost faith in its commander, who was simply lost in a haze of pain and laudanum.

General Thomas seemed to realize what Grant, Lincoln, and Secretary of War Stanton did not. While his army rested in relative luxury for combat soldiers in the field, Hood's men were weakening by the day, freezing in trenches and caves. He also had allowed General Wilson, at Edgefield, north of the Cumberland, time to build the cavalry into a formidable weapon.

Thomas was finally ready to move on December 9, but a hard-freezing rain and storm clouds moved into the Nashville area, leaving the terrain covered with a sheet of ice. The delay had Grant pulling his hair out in frustration even though this latest holdup was a legitimate one. Also on the ninth, Hood called General Bate and his infantry back to Nashville to augment Cheatham's portion of the Confederate line.

While waiting for a thaw, Forrest's command was staying busy. On the thirteenth, Wirt Jackson's cavalry captured a train bound for Murfreesboro. Jackson took seventeen freight cars loaded with supplies and two hundred prisoners of the Sixty-first Illinois Infantry, commanded by Lt. Col. Daniel Grass, and then burned the train.[55]

Finally, on the morning of December 15, the Union army marched out of Nashville. The Army of Tennessee was facing north, aligned with Cheatham's corps on the right, starting at Rain's Cut on the railroad to Chattanooga. Lee's corps was in the center astride the Franklin Pike and Stewart's corps was positioned on the left, crossing the Granny White road and extending to the Hillsboro Pike.[56] Thomas's plan called for a direct advance southward against the main Confederate line, but the main maneuver was to be a long wheel move by Wilson's nine thousand cavalrymen that would strike between the end of Hood's line and the Cumberland River. Hood had no chance, outnumbered over three to one. He had hoped for reinforcements from the trans-Mississippi commander, Kirby Smith, but none were coming.

Thomas threw his left wing forward at Hood's line with the aim of holding the Confederates in their position. The gunboats on the Cumberland opened fire on Kelley's riverbank position from the cover of a dense early-morning fog that blanketed the landscape. At the same moment, Col. W. A. Johnson's Union cavalry division attacked the extreme left of the Confederate line held by Chalmers' and Rucker's cavalry. Chalmers and Rucker checked the Union advance until they discovered that they had been cut off from the rest of their army when a brigade of Confederate infantry on the Harding Pike gave way and fell back two miles to Belle Meade. Cut off from communications with Hood, Chalmers lost twenty wagons and forty men taken prisoner. He then disengaged and fell back around the rear of Hood's army.[57]

Meanwhile, Cheatham's boys, on the right and center of Hood's line, were holding their own for the first few moments of the engagement. However, on the left General Stewart's division bore the brunt of the concentrated flank and frontal attacks from a force that exceeded the total of Hood's entire army. There a whole section of the line collapsed. A moment later the rest of the Southern army was on the run. The Army of Tennessee retreated southward for about three miles beyond the Hillsboro Road and then was unceremoniously shoved back even farther past the Granny White pike. When darkness fell, Hood's newly formed line was half as long as it had been before Thomas attacked.

The night of the fifteenth, Forrest, at Murfreesboro, received a dispatch "that a general engagement was then going on at Nashville." Forrest's orders were to hold his command but be ready to move at a moment's notice. Bedford then moved his column to the Wilkinson crossroads and awaited orders on where and how General Hood wanted his troops to join in the fight at Nashville. But those orders never came.[58]

The end came for the Army of Tennessee on Friday, December 16, when Thomas executed the same type of maneuver he had used the previous day. While Thomas attacked with his left to hold the Confederate right in check, he hammered the rebel left with an overpowering force in conjunction with Wilson's nine thousand cavalrymen, who swept around and into Hood's rear. Col. William Shy was killed in action during the fight, leaving his name to Shy's Hill. The battle was over before it began. Around 4:30 P.M., during a cold winter rain, the Army of Tennessee fell completely apart.[59]

Chalmers and Rucker had rejoined Hood before daybreak on the sixteenth and were posted astride the Hillsboro pike. When Hood realized that he was about to be cut off from escape and that he faced possible annihilation, he sent a desperate message to Chalmers' and Rucker's horsemen to charge to the Granny White road and hold it, or all was lost.

Chalmers and Rucker had raced to the Granny White road and had begun to erect barricades from any material handy, but before this task was completed Brigadier General Wilson's cavalry and General Hatch's Twelfth Tennessee Cavalry (Union) were upon them. In the nearing twilight, the Union generals' men dismounted and charged Chalmers' center. It was a tooth and nail brawl as the Confederate cavalrymen fought with desperation to hold the road open for Hood's infantry to escape toward Brentwood. The division colors were captured, and Wilson later reported, "The enemy were thrown into confusion, and only the darkness saved him from a thorough rout."[60]

General Rucker's situation was indicative of the struggle. Mounted on a white stallion, Rucker found himself engaged in a close-quarter fight with Col. George Spalding and Capt. Joseph C. Boyer of the Twelfth Tennessee. Slashing away at both Union officers, Rucker somehow lost his saber but was able to wrench a sword away from one of the Yankee officers and continued to thrust and parry using his antagonist's weapon. Rucker fought on desperately until Colonel Spalding shot the general, breaking his arm and forcing his surrender.

As intense as it was, the fight on the Granny White pike had no effect on the

> disorganized masses of Confederate troops who were swept in confusion down the Franklin turnpike. The disorganized rebels retreated in the approaching darkness and drenching rain until beyond Brentwood. Eventually the fragmented commands were, in some measure, united, and bivouacked in groups for the night.[61]

By the night of December 16, Wilson was fairly sure Forrest had not been on the field. He gleaned as much from information taken from Confederate prisoners as well as from another source. General Wilson recognized that things would not have been as easy had Forrest been present. Wilson wrote:

Nothing was seen of the redoubtable Forrest himself. He was not on the field or we should certainly have known it before. . . . While it cannot be said with certainty that, had Forrest been present with his force united with that of Chalmers on the left of Hood's line he would have been able to hold it, it may well be claimed that he could have made a better and more stubborn defense than was made by Chalmers and [Gen. Matthew D.] Ector alone. . . . We should doubtless have broke through, but with Forrest resisting us we should have had much more difficult work and could hardly have pushed our turning movement far enough to reach, drive back, and take in reverse Hood's main line of defense for a mile and a half as we did.[62]

Wilson summed up the consequences of Hood's diverting Forrest to Murfreesboro during this battle as well as anyone could. Because Wilson's "turning movement" into Hood's rear had been responsible in great part for the Confederate rout, Hood's decision to divert Forrest to Murfreesboro "was not only futile but in the end frightfully costly" to the Army of Tennessee.[63]

On the evening of December 16, Rucker was taken before Brig. Gen. Edward Hatch. Rucker defiantly told Hatch, "Forrest has just arrived with all the cavalry, and will give you hell tonight. Mark what I tell you." At that opportune moment, one of Rucker's own regiments, the Seventh Alabama, made a flank attack in the darkness, driving Hatch's men a short distance back down the Granny White road. This attack, in conjunction with darkness, may have prompted Wilson to write, "Night having closed in the enemy was enabled to make his escape. The pursuit was necessarily discontinued, men and horses being worn out and hungry."[64]

Late that night Rucker was sharing quarters with Wilson and Hatch in a small farmhouse. Hatch was concerned about Rucker's health and gave up his bed to his prisoner and slept on the floor. The conscientious Union general arose several times throughout the night to attend to the feverish Confederate, whose arm would later be amputated above the elbow.[65]

Four miles south of Brentwood, Hood left a strong rear guard of cavalry posted at Hollowtree Gap. Forrest was not present, as Rucker had threatened, but he was on his way and was hoping to intercept the Confederate army approximately thirty miles north of Pulaski at the crossing over the Duck River. However, his progress was slowed because he was shepherding more than four hundred prisoners and a large heard of cattle and hogs as he moved.

At daybreak on Saturday morning, the seventeenth, Wilson continued his aggressive pursuit but was checked by Chalmers at Hollowtree Gap, which forced Wilson to deploy his command into a line of battle. The Union general described, "Chalmers made a gallant stand and compelled us to develop a full front, thus gaining precious time." However, time was all that Chalmers was hoping to buy as Hood marched through Franklin and crossed the Harpeth River.

At the next stand, made below Franklin at the crossing of the West Harpeth, the Confederate cavalry engaged in another desperate fight when they turned on their pursuers. By this time, Gen. Abe Buford and his Kentuckians, who had been sent ahead by Forrest on his own orders on December 16, rode like hell to aid Chalmers in the rear guard of Hood's army. Chalmers arrived at the crossing just as Wilson hit the main body of the Confederate army.

During the melee, General Buford, weighing in at three hundred pounds, found himself in engaged in what could be considered the definitive hand-to-hand fight from horseback. Buford found himself surrounded by three Yankee horsemen. With the last shot from his Navy Colt, he shot one down, and he then began to use the butt of the revolver as a club against the other two. He knocked the first adversary unconscious from his horse, and using his considerable strength, he grabbed the last of his assailants by the hair and dragged him from the saddle.

Stephen D. Lee stated that the "enemy's desperate attack was kept up till long after dark, but gallantly did the rear guard . . . repulse every attack with Chalmers' cavalry covering the flanks and aiding greatly in stopping the enemy."[66] The Confederates were able to make good their temporary escape and camped that night near Spring Hill "with the bitter memories of lost opportunities from only two weeks before."

Wilson's pursuit was temporarily held up on the eighteenth because he had outrun his supply line and had to wait for rations and ammunition to reach him. While waiting for supplies, Wilson and Thomas received a wire from Grant:

> The armies again operating against Richmond have fired two hundred guns in honor of your great victories. . . . In all your operations we hear nothing of Forrest. Great precautions should be taken to prevent him from crossing the Cumberland or Tennessee below East Port.

In the same breath that Grant was congratulating Thomas, he

continued to warn him and seemed to be more concerned about Forrest's whereabouts than he was any single other aspect of the campaign.

An interesting side note to the story is that when Wilson received his letter of congratulations from Grant, Col. Abel Streight was present and was doubtless a little worried himself about Forrest's current position. Forrest was the cause of his having spent the last year and a half in the Libby Prison at Richmond.[67]

At the Duck River, the full impact of the ravaged condition of his remaining troops hit Hood in the face like a cold glass of water. For all intents and purposes his army no longer existed. He had little more than one ragtag division left. The defeat had been so crushing and his men so demoralized, that crossing the Tennessee River would be the only way he could save his army from complete annihilation. First the Duck River had to be crossed, and by the time Forrest arrived on the scene, the task was almost completed. Hood and the rest of the Army of Tennessee were relieved that Forrest had arrived, all, that is, but General Cheatham, who ran into Forrest, quite literally, as the rear elements of the shattered rebel army crossed the river.

When Forrest finally arrived at the Duck River crossing he found the desperation almost palpable. Cheatham's infantry arrived at about the same time, adding to the frantic situation. Perhaps due to the confusion and apprehension, an incident occurred between the two generals that could have had disastrous ramifications. Cheatham arbitrarily decided that his men should cross the river first and either made that suggestion or actually gave an order. Exhausted and on edge, Forrest took this presumption personally. He drew his heavy Navy Colt, rode up next to Cheatham, and said, "If you are a better man than I am, General Cheatham, your troops can cross ahead of mine."

The men of both commands were fiercely loyal to their leaders, and having observed the confrontation, they prepared to come to their support. An ugly scene was averted when Stephen D. Lee, the ranking officer on the field, raced in upon his horse and quickly refereed a solution to the confrontation. The crossing was completed without further incident, and although there was no mention of it in the battle reports, rumor had it that Forrest's command crossed first.

When Hood arrived at Columbus, he "became convinced that the condition of the army made it necessary to recross the Tennessee without delay." The Army of Tennessee had been decimated during the last month and their condition was grim. Four hundred of the infantrymen were literally shoeless. So, on December 20, he started his army southward toward the Tennessee River, some eighty miles distant.

Forrest was left in command of the rear guard, which consisted of three thousand horsemen and two thousand infantry organized into eight small brigades under Maj. Gen. Edward C. Walthall.[68] From this point until the ever-nearing end of the war, Forrest would conduct one of the most fiercely contested and tenacious rear-guard actions in military history, prompting Gen. George Thomas to comment:

> Forrest and his cavalry . . . formed a powerful rear guard made up of detachments from all of his organized force, numbering about 4,000 infantry under General Walthall, and all the available cavalry and artillery under his own command. With the exception of his rear guard, Hood's army had become a disheartened and disorganized rabble of half armed barefooted men, who sought every opportunity to fall out by the wayside and desert their cause to put an end to their sufferings. The rear guard, however, was undaunted and firm, and did its work bravely to the last.[69]

Forrest set to work as soon as he received command of the rear guard. Cheatham's corps had built breastworks south of Spring Hill and was temporarily holding the enemy until Hood's wagon train crossed Rutherford Creek. Cheatham was able to buy Hood time with hard fighting then crossed the river and burned the bridge behind him. Later that day, Wilson's pursuing force crossed Rutherford Creek on a pontoon bridge and with Hatch in the lead, pressed the Confederates toward the Duck River.

At the Duck River the Union force was delayed when the components for the pontoon bridge were mistakenly sent to Nashville instead of Columbia. On the afternoon of December 20, Hatch's artillery began shelling Columbia from the north side of the river. Noncombatants who had quickly organized hospital operations for the sick and wounded Confederate soldiers occupied the town of Columbia at the time. Forrest raised a flag of truce, and from across the river, he called for a cease-fire and suggested an exchange of prisoners. Hatch refused a prisoner exchange but stopped the shelling of Columbia for the sake of the Confederate casualties.[70]

A brigade of Union infantry finally brought up the pontoons on December 22, and construction of the bridge began under the command of Forrest's old foe, Col. Abel Streight. The last time Streight and Forrest had battled over bridges, it was Forrest who was the hunter. Now the roles were reversed.

The bridge was soon completed and the Union Fourth Corps, led by Brig. Gen. Thomas J. Wood, crossed and camped for the night two miles south of Columbia. George Thomas was relying primarily on Wilson's cavalry to bring Hood to bay. He had hoped to cut Hood off from the crossing at the Tennessee River and sent Maj. Gen. James Steedman's division by train from Murfreesboro to Decatur, Alabama, to block the rebels' escape. Also, at General Thomas's request, Admiral Lee ordered a flotilla of gunboats up the Tennessee above Muscle Shoals to prevent a crossing below Decatur.[71]

Early on the morning of December 24, Wilson's cavalry came upon the Confederate rear guard at Richland Creek near Buford's Station. Forrest advanced on the enemy down the Columbia pike with his infantry covered on both flanks by the cavalry. At Buford's Station the rebels held the Federals in check for over two hours before falling back across Richland Creek. During this fight Forrest lost one man killed and nine wounded, including General Buford, whose thighbone was shattered by a bullet. Forrest then fell back to Pulaski and made temporary camp.

Gen. Wirt Jackson was left to delay the Yankees' progress while Forrest destroyed all the ammunition General Hood had been unable to carry off. He also burned two railroad trains before heading southward. Still holding the last bridge over Richland Creek, Jackson was to destroy it after the last of the Confederates had passed. Attempting to hold up the enemy as long as possible, Jackson nearly waited too long to set fire to the old covered bridge. When he did, it quickly became a tunnel of flame. The last of the Southern horsemen who dashed across and through the burning passageway singed their hair and eyebrows. However, their dramatic, daredevil stunt only slowed the Federals momentarily. Union soldiers rushed in and quickly extinguished the flames, leaving the bridge blackened but intact. As soon as a quick inspection assured that the bridge was still serviceable, the Federals continued their pursuit.

Seven miles south of Pulaski, Jackson found Forrest laying an ambush for the pursuing Federals near Anthony's Hill on the densely wooded road to Bainbridge. It was a cold and rainy Christmas morning as the lead elements of the Federal column moved cautiously forward in the gray predawn. The last of the wagons in the Confederate train were just disappearing from sight, moving ever so slowly over nearly impassable roads of deep mud. Time was the key element in a situation that could have become disastrous for the Army of Tennessee. If not for the vicious manner in which Forrest and his men would turn again and again upon the pursuing enemy force, Hood's main column would have been overtaken and crushed or captured.

Choosing an advantageous position for an ambush, Forrest sent a decoy force a half-mile ahead to draw in the enemy. The advance brigade fired a volley as the Yankees appeared and then fell rapidly back. The enemy charged forward into the V-shaped ravine as Forrest hoped they would. His infantry, artillery, and cavalry were hidden on both sides and at the front of the position. Gen. Edward C. Walthall said later that he was able to effectively conceal his troops in the dense woods. So well covered were Walthall's men that no more than a strong line of skirmishers was exposed to the eyes of the enemy. When this seemingly weak line was discovered, the Federal troops attacked, but when they found that the numbers they were facing were greater and larger than expected, their commander dismounted his troops and launched a charge on foot. Simultaneously, rebel gunners opened up with a destructive crossfire.[72]

Though it was Christmas, it was not a jolly season for the men on either side as Forrest prepared to deliver his greetings to the enemy. A Confederate soldier remembered Forrest creeping up beside him to better observe the developing drama. He was there only briefly and suddenly disappeared as the Yankees charged forward into the trap. A few moments later the same soldier remembered being startled by thundering hoofbeats as "Forrest dashes by at half speed, riding magnificently, his martial figure straight as an arrow and looking six inches taller than was his wont, the very god of war, yelling as he reached the waiting ranks: Charge! Charge!"[73]

The leading Federal brigade was driven back in a "flying mass of confusion" by the sudden onslaught. The weather was alternating between freezing rain and snow while the Confederates inflicted serious damage to the lead elements of the Union force, as Captain Morton remembered the scene. "The narrow path through the gorge seemed ringed with fire and smoke. The enemy broke in tumultuous disorder, and the Confederates charged upon them with the old time 'Rebel Yell' and spirit. A number of prisoners, several hundred horses, and one piece of artillery were captured."[74] This one captured gun was the unequal exchange of Hood's entire Tennessee campaign, in which he lost fifty of his cannon to the enemy.

In his own communiqué General Wilson wrote,

Just before sundown on Christmas Forrest, in a fit of desperation, made a stand on a heavily wooded ridge, at the head of a ravine, and by a rapid and savage counter-thrust drove back Harrison's Brigade and captured one gun, which he succeeded in carrying away as the sole trophy of that desperate campaign."[75]

Under another attack by Hatch's regrouped brigades, Forrest began his withdrawal toward Sugar Creek as darkness overtook the landscape. It was reported that several Union troopers remembered seeing bloody footprints in the snow as the Confederates fell back.

While the withdrawal was in progress, Colonel Armstrong's position was rapidly deteriorating as he attempted to hold the enemy in check on the right wing of the Confederate line. Armstrong made three separate protests to his superiors that his men were running out of ammunition and could not hold out any longer. On his third visit he rode directly up to where Forrest and Walthall were sitting on their horses. This time weeping in anger, he shouted to Walthall, "General Walthall won't you please make that damned man there on the horse see that my men are forced to retreat?" Forrest responded by quietly telling Armstrong that he was trying to give Hood a little more time to get across Sugar Creek. Forrest then looked at his pocket watch and said, "It's just about time we all got the hell out of here."[76] In all, Forrest reported killing 150 of the enemy and delaying the pursuit of Hood's column for over three hours.

A race along parallel roads then ensued between the armies as they galloped toward the next river crossing. The deadly contest continued in the dark and through a heavy snow and driving wind. Forrest's reputation for "getting there first" held as he arrived at the crossing over Sugar Creek and began to throw up breastworks, preparing to meet the pursuing Federals.

At Sugar Creek he awaited the enemy, but there was no further pursuit on the twenty-fifth. There was also no further rest or sleep for the muddy, frost-bitten rebels who had been in the saddle or in combat for more than forty-eight straight hours. General Wilson later described the circumstances and conditions of both horses and men at this juncture of the running fight:

> The men of both forces suffered dreadfully, but the poor cavalry horses fared worse than their riders. Scarcely a withered corn blade could be found for them, and thousands, exhausted by overwork, famished with hunger or crippled so that death was a

mercy, with hoofs dropping off from frost and mud, fell by the roadside, never to rise again. By the time the corps found rest on the Tennessee River, it could muster scarcely 7,000 horses fit for service.[77]

A dense fog blanketed the landscape at daybreak the next morning as Forrest made his preparations to strike the enemy again. Repeating his strategy of Christmas Day at Anthony's Hill, Forrest sent a brigade forward to engage the Federals then to fall back to the fortifications constructed on both banks of Sugar Creek just hours earlier. As before, the Yankees were drawn in and were within fifty paces of the breastworks before they could see the Confederate line through the fog. Suddenly, a sheet of flame erupted as Walthall's men rose up out of the heavy mist and fired upon their startled foes. A moment later, two mounted regiments of Ross's brigade charged through and past the rebel line, causing "the wildest confusion" as they drove the Federals back into and across Sugar Creek in "a complete rout." Forrest later reported that he had killed or wounded another 150 of the enemy, taken approximately the same number of prisoners, and destroyed about 400 horses.[78]

Forrest held his position for another two hours, but Wilson and Hatch showed no inclination for any more surprises in the fog. Fearing a possible flanking maneuver, Forrest withdrew and headed for the sanctuary of the Tennessee River. The Confederates proceeded from Sugar Creek to the Tennessee River without any further harassment from the Federals.

By the time Forrest and his men reached Richland Creek, they were encountering the ominous evidence of defeat. From there to the Tennessee the road was strewn with the wreckage of Hood's army. From the evening of December 27 through the following morning, Forrest's command utilized Hood's abandoned pontoon bridge at Bainbridge to make their easiest wartime crossing of the Tennessee ever.

The Confederates had just completed their crossing when Union admiral Samuel P. Lee's gunboats steamed through the shoals and broke through the pontoon bridge within sight of Forrest's command as the rear elements of his cavalry disappeared in the distance. Once again the enemy was one step behind him. As they moved toward their rendezvous with Hood at Tuscumbia, Alabama, one Confederate trooper displayed the humor and undaunted spirit of these men, who were suffering in "the flesh and spirit" during the march. "Ain't we in a hell of a fix," he said, "a one eyed President, a one legged General and a one hoss Confederacy."

But, as another soldier said of Forrest, they continued to march and fight in the darkness, "not by sight but by faith—faith in the man" under whose command they had come to trust with their lives.[79]

# Chapter Fifteen

# LET THE BAND
# PLAY "DIXIE"

*—Abraham Lincoln*

## Selma
## January-April 1865

A few hours after crossing the Tennessee, Forrest reported to General Hood at Tuscumbia, Alabama. One of Hood's last functions as commander of the Army of Tennessee was to send Forrest into eastern Mississippi where there would be better forage and opportunity for rebuilding the cavalry. On December 29, Forrest rode for Corinth, Mississippi, minus Roddey's detachment, which remained behind as Hood's rear guard. But shortly after Forrest departed, Roddey's cavalry was attacked near Decatur, Alabama, prompting Forrest to send Armstrong's brigade back to reinforce Roddey. Bedford arrived at Corinth on December 30, while the infantry was being transported by rail to Tupelo, forty miles southward.[1]

Hood was relieved of duty on January 10. Had the authorities in Richmond made this decision two weeks earlier, ten thousand lives might have been saved. Beauregard appointed Gen. Richard Taylor as Hood's replacement. Also, at Beauregard's suggestion, Taylor placed Forrest in command of all the cavalry forces in Alabama, Mississippi, and Louisiana. It was a vast jurisdiction with only about ten thousand poorly supplied regular Confederate cavalry troops scattered throughout. The organization of this logistical nightmare fell to Forrest.

The country to be defended by Forrest's depleted and widely dispersed corps was as devastated and shattered as were its supposed defenders. Not only had the land been ravaged by war, but roving bands of pillagers masquerading as cavalry troops also plagued the citizens.

The internal strife that had occurred while Forrest had been away with Hood's army in Tennessee was compounded by a raid launched through the heart of Mississippi by General Grierson's cavalry. Moving south through Corinth and to Verona beyond, Grierson then turned west and marched toward Vicksburg. Grierson's cavalry traveled virtually uncontested over 450 miles, tore up 80 miles of railroad track, and took six hundred Confederate prisoners.[2]

Forrest's determination to fight the Yankees at every opportunity was well known by both sides, but he reserved a special enmity for renegades of any ilk. He was determined to hunt down and to exterminate, if possible, the marauders pillaging their way across Mississippi. In a circular issued on January 28, 1865, Forrest stated his authority and put the brigands on notice. "I hereby assume command of the District of Mississippi, east Louisiana, and west Tennessee," he began, apparently deciding on his own initiative that he might as well include west Tennessee in his new jurisdiction. The remainder of the circular called for the protection of the rights and property of citizens and carried a stern warning to any guilty of "illegal operations of cavalry":

> They are in many instances nothing more or less than roving bands of deserters, absentees, stragglers, horse-thieves, and robbers . . . whose acts of lawlessness and crime demand a remedy, which I shall not hesitate to apply, even to extermination. The maxim "that kindness to bad men is cruelty to the good" is peculiarly applicable to soldiers; for all agree, without obedience and strict discipline troops cannot be made effective, and kindness to a bad soldier does great injustice to those who are faithful and true; and it is but justice to those who discharge their duties with promptness and fidelity that others who are disobedient, turbulent and mutinous, or who desert or straggle from their commands, should be promptly and effectively dealt with, as the law directs.[3]

Forrest took immediate steps to back up this threat. His brother Jesse, who had been wounded at Athens, Alabama, in September, had recently recovered from his injury and was given command of a cavalry detachment that would act very much as a posse. Jesse's mission was to lead his men into the no man's land between the picket lines and into northern Mississippi to recruit additional manpower and to track down and either capture or kill those criminals and deserters who infested "the country, robbing friend and foe indiscriminately."

Adj. Gen. Samuel Cooper and his assistants were in the same

vicinity on an inspection tour at the time. He reported that the "condition of the citizen is pitiable in the extreme . . . dismounted cavalry steal his horses, while a dastard foe robs him of food and clothing. Grain cannot be grown and food cannot be purchased." A short time later Cooper added to his report that "General Forrest, with that energy and ability which always characterize his actions . . . and with the aid of his brother, Colonel Jesse Forrest, has lately arrested and sent to their commands many of these deserters."[4]

Sherman, who was still in Savannah, Georgia, was aware that Forrest was now in command of the cavalry in the west. In late January, Sherman wrote to General Thomas at Nashville, "I would like to have Forrest hunted down and killed but doubt if we can do that just yet." Soon after, Sherman wrote to Maj. Gen. E. R. S. Canby, who commanded the Union forces at Mobile, Alabama, "It is important to prevent, as much as possible, the planting of crops this year, and to destroy their railroads, machine shops, etc."[5]

As Sherman was composing these letters, four Union expeditions organized in Memphis, Vicksburg, Baton Rouge, and Pensacola were preparing to move on the territory Forrest was assigned to defend. The greatest threat, however, was from James H. Wilson's twenty-five thousand men, organized into five cavalry divisions, in the northwestern corner of Alabama. This massive cavalry command was bivouacked along the Tennessee River where it could be readily supplied and could easily strike into Alabama or Mississippi at its discretion. To combat these invasions from Mississippi and the gulf coast Forrest attempted to pull his dispersed command into a more compact and effective force. However, within the entire vast territory entrusted to Forrest's supervision there were not more than ten thousand men who were still willing to fight for an increasingly apparent lost cause.

This buildup of forces on both sides and the gathering of intelligence in preparation for action led to a brief lull in hostilities. Gen. George Thomas took advantage of this period to send Col. John G. Parkhurst and Capt. Lewis M. Hosea to meet with Forrest. At that time over seven thousand Union soldiers were being held prisoner in Mississippi, and Thomas wanted to propose a prisoner exchange. If that was not possible, Thomas at least wanted to be allowed to send supplies to the Federal captives. Thomas was also interested in Forrest's state of mind and told Captain Hosea to "keep his eyes open" and gather as much information as was prudent.

Colonel Parkhurst would need no reminder to stay on his toes when dealing with the Wizard of the Saddle. Parkhurst's first encounter with Forrest had been in July 1862 at Murfreesboro, where he had become Forrest's prisoner. A meeting between Parkhurst and Forrest was arranged for February 23 at Rienzi. The two parties agreed to meet at the residence of a Mr. Rowland, whose small farmhouse was a short distance from the town. Sometime around nine o'clock that evening Forrest, Major Anderson, and Judge Robert Caruthers, the Confederate governor-elect of Tennessee, emerged from the darkness in the midst of a cold rain. Inside the small, one-room building where these Confederates met the Union representatives tallow candles cast a flickering glow over the five men as they took each others' measure. The conversation began in a friendly enough manner.

Captain Hosea noted the three silver stars of a lieutenant general on the collar of Forrest's fine, butternut gray uniform, though Forrest was a little premature in wearing them, as the promotion would not become official for another five days. To Forrest it probably seemed a small thing to jump rank by a few days. After all, he thought nothing of laying jurisdictional claim to half a state without the official endorsement of his superiors. His timetable did not always correspond to that of the Confederate high command.

Forrest and Parkhurst engaged in small talk as the meeting began, which gave Hosea the opportunity to carefully observe the rebel cavalryman's every move. After enough pleasantries had passed between the principals, Forrest told Parkhurst that he was "as anxious to rid the country of guerillas as was any officer in the U.S. Army, and that he would esteem it a favor if General Thomas would hang everyone he caught."[6]

Hosea's intense scrutiny did not go unnoticed by Forrest, whose understanding of human nature often bordered on mind reading. He must have realized that his presence held the Union captain somewhat in awe. Hosea later confessed in his account of the meeting, which he published in 1912, that he was impressed by Forrest's bearing and presence. He referred to him as "the great Confederate Murat":

> Forrest is a man fully six feet in height; rather waxen face; handsome; high, full forehead, and with a profusion of light gray hair thrown back from the forehead and growing down rather to a point in the middle of the same. The lines of thought and care, in an upward curve, receding are distinctly marked and add much to the dignity of expression. The general effect is suggestive of notables of the Revolutionary times with powdered hair as we see them in the portraits of that day; and to our

unaccustomed eyes the rich gray uniform with its embroidered collar (a wreath of gold on black ground enclosing three silver stars) added much to the effect produced. I could not, in the dim light afforded by tallow candles, observe the color of his eyes, but they seemed to me to be brown; pleasant-looking, lit up occasionally by a gleam of soldierly bravery. His expression, both pleasant and striking, is given to his physiognomy by the slightest possible elevation of the eyebrows. The latter are black with a slight tinge of gray, and a black moustache and chin whiskers, both cut short, add to the military bearing of the man. His face is long, and cheekbones rather prominent, eyes large, though not noticeably so, and the head full above the eyes and ears. The face indicates a decided character; and the contrast of the gray hair and waxen face and black whiskers gives a very aristocratic appearance. His habitual expression seemed rather subdued and thoughtful, but when his face is lighted up by a smile, which ripples all over his features, the effect is really charming. . . . After business, and well on toward midnight, we fell into desultory conversation one with another. Forrest expressed great admiration for soldierly qualities and especially for personal courage, and was evidently pleased at our recognition of the fame of his exploits at the head of his cavalry. . . . His language indicates a very limited education, but his impressive manner conceals many otherwise notable defects. The choice of words too plainly evidences early associations, unfortunately, and one feels sometimes disappointed at errors palpable to any schoolboy. He invariably omits the final "g" in the termination "ing" and many words are inexcusably mispronounced; and he always uses the past participle in place of the past tense of such words as "see" (as "I seen" instead of "I saw," and "holp tote," meaning to help carry), etc.

In a very short time, however, these pass unnoticed. He speaks of his successes with a soldierly vanity, and expresses the kindest feeling toward prisoners and wounded. I told him that I had the honor to present the compliments of my general, our Cavalry Murat (Wilson) to him, in the hopes of meeting him upon some future occasion. He at once accepted this as a challenge, which the friendly message might be construed to convey, and with a curl of the lip he said "Just tell General Wilson that I know the nicest little place in the world, and whenever he is ready I will fight him with any number from one to ten thousand cavalry and abide the issue. Gin'ral Wilson may pick his men and I'll pick mine. He may take his sabers and I'll take my six-shooters. I don't want nary a saber in my command—haven't got one." I replied that I had no doubt General W. would be happy to accommodate him, but that he was a West Point officer and believed in the saber. "Well," said General F. "I ain't no graduate of West Point and never rubbed my back up against any college, but Wilson may take his sabers and I'll use my six-shooters and agree to whup the fight with any cavalry he can bring."[7]

The rain came hard that night and continued for the next two days, delaying Hosea and Parkhurst's departure. Before heading back through the lines, Hosea went to the local telegraph operator and asked him to "get Judge Caruthers of Forrest's staff" on the wire. He felt that Caruthers would best understand what he wanted to say.

> When we got the O.K. signal, I shoved in and took the key, very much to the operator's surprise, and spelled out a line of Virgil in the Latin: "*Haec olin miminisse juvabit, tetgisse dextramo tyranni.*" [It will rejoice me hereafter to remember that I have touched the right hand of your leader.] And immediately mounted my horse and rode away, leaving the operator in a state of bewilderment and alarm.

Hosea concluded his account by saying that the only thing that he had actually learned from the meeting at Rowland's farmhouse was "that Forrest was mustering all his forces to 'welcome us with bloody hands to hospitable graves' when we should come in earnest."[8]

It has been rumored that the origin of Forrest's oft-quoted pronunciation "Furstest with the mostest" derived during this meeting with Parkhurst and Hosea. During the meeting Forrest did tell the two men that one of his rules of war was to always get there first with the most men. Hosea mentioned several of Forrest's peculiar mispronunciations in his later memoir, but he never mentioned the particularly outrageous "Furstest with the mostest" statement. It seems likely that Hosea would have picked up on that quote as he had Forrest's use of "holp tote." In fact, there is no evidence, testimony, or written correspondence that reports or indicates Forrest ever used words other than "first with the most," a more correct use of the English language.

As early as February 22, the week he met with Hosea and Parkhurst, Forrest was already shifting his forces in the direction of Selma. The rainy weather slowed the Confederates' progress, but one consolation was that the Federals were suffering from the same problems. Heavy rain and flooding had been holding up Wilson's advance for three weeks when he wrote Sherman on March 13 that the Tennessee River was "higher than it was ever known to be" and impassable at the present.[9]

During this time period both sides attempted to gather intelligence from their spies and continued maneuvering for position. Consequently, some of Forrest's troopers found themselves with time on their hands. While headquartered at West Point, Mississippi, all kinds of recreational games broke out among the men. It began innocently enough but soon escalated to gambling, horse racing, and indiscriminate gunfire. Forrest, known for his penchant for gambling and sport, seemed at first to join in on the fun and even placed a bet or two. He probably intended to show appreciation to his men for all they had been through with him, but the breadth of his intentions were apparently misinterpreted by some.

When a group of daredevils defiantly staked out a quarter-mile track directly in front of Forrest's tent, the party was about to end. The men hooted and hollered and were placing bets when Forrest reemerged from his tent. As he did so, the men cheered his gameness and fun-loving spirit with rebel yells and gunfire. Soon after the games had subsided and the participants began to disperse, Forrest acted. Several of the hell-raisers (one of whom was Forrest's son, Willie) were intercepted by a strong provost guard and arrested. They were then brought before Forrest, who summarily court-martialed the entire group and punished them with the duty of carrying fence rails on their shoulders for several hours until the transgressors were "exhausted and sore."[10]

On March 18, with the Tennessee having subsided, Wilson's command began to cross the river. By the twenty-third, Edward M. McCook's First Division, Brig. Gen. Eli Long's Second Division, and Gen. Emory Upton's Fourth Division were moving into Forrest territory along three separate roads. The divisional separation was designed to confuse Forrest and to increase the amount of forage for each group. Wilson was bringing approximately twenty-two thousand mounted cavalrymen, three batteries of artillery, a pontoon bridge, and a 250-wagon supply train. Fifteen hundred infantrymen guarded the supply train. More than fifteen thousand of these troopers were armed with seven-shot magazine Spencer carbines, for "this was to be no mere raid; it was to be a sustained invasion."[11]

To this point, it seemed that none of the Confederate commanders realized what type of force Wilson was bringing to bear upon them. This was something new in war. It was a precursor of the coming of the German blitzkrieg of World War II, though moving by horsepower instead of tanks, with overwhelming speed, mobility, and power to drive the resisting enemy before it.[12]

With several Union expeditions moving on him from four different directions, Forrest was unable to concentrate his scattered forces at any given position. From General Roddey's scouts, camped at Montevallo, Forrest learned that Wilson was on the move. He ordered Chalmers along with two brigades under Stark and Armstrong into Alabama. When they arrived at Pickensville, General Taylor ordered Chalmers to move on to Selma on March 23 to fend off the threat coming up against that town from Mobile. But the Confederate commanders never realized that the greatest threat of all was Wilson's massive cavalry force driving down from the north.

Forrest now had all his men and commanders on the move. Riding with his escort company toward Finch's Ferry on the Black Warrior River near Eutaw, Alabama, they crossed the Sipsey River on the morning of March 27 via one of the few remaining bridges in the area. On that same morning Forrest's point troopers took two deserters into custody. Both men admitted to being in the service and explained that they were on their way home to Kentucky. One claimed that he was actually too old for service while the other asserted that he was too young to be held responsible. Neither had furlough papers, passes, or proof of what command they had walked away from. Their pleas of innocence fell on the deaf ears of men who had remained loyal despite having been driven by the exigencies of war beyond the endurance of normal soldiers. The two were quickly court-martialed for desertion and summarily executed by firing squad.

Doctor Wyeth, author of *That Devil Forrest*, was with Forrest's command when this incident took place. He protested the execution at the time and wrote in his biography of Forrest in 1900 that later, after the execution, some sort of proof arose exonerating the two Kentuckians. However, Wyeth made no reference to how or where he came by this information. Neither did he give any explanation nor example for his determination that both men were guiltless and prematurely executed before the truth that would have saved them could be presented.[13]

Both men were laid out alongside a bridge with a sign posted over the bodies, "Shot for Desertion." The bodies were conspicuously displayed where Forrest's entire command would see the savage determination with which their general was waging this last campaign. After the column had passed solemnly over the bridge, a detachment of twenty men under the command of Gen. William H. "Red" Jackson stayed behind to guard the crossing "until the day after tomorrow, when they will bury the two men who have been shot here at the bridge today, then follow on and report to their commands." Jackson was also ordered that should "the officer left behind catch other deserters he will take them to the bridge and execute them."[14]

The night of March 30, Forrest was at Scottsville, twenty-five miles southeast of Tuscaloosa, near the Cahaba River bridge crossing at Centerville. Forrest ordered Red Jackson, then at Tuscaloosa, to "move on tonight to Centerville, as it is important that you should reach that point with as little delay as possible" and hold the bridge at all costs.[15]

General Wilson was at Jasper at about the same time when he learned that William H. Jackson's cavalry was moving in the vicinity of Tuscaloosa, heading toward his position with orders to "strike Wilson on the flank as soon as possible." Wilson then realized that Forrest knew his location, and believing that Forrest was concentrating his forces upon him, he ordered his division at a forced march for Montevallo. Wilson's route would take him through Elyton, where the steel town of Birmingham is now located.

While at Elyton, Wilson detached Gen. John Croxton's brigade, approximately eleven hundred men, and sent them seventy miles southwest to Tuscaloosa with orders to burn and destroy the University of Alabama (due to the corps of cadets on the campus) and all the bridges, factories, and government supply stores. Croxton was then to move through Centerville and rendezvous with Wilson at Selma.

When Wilson arrived at Montevallo on the thirty-first he found the town in flames. General Upton and three divisions had crossed the Cahaba at Hillsboro and entered Montevallo on the thirtieth. They immediately began burning the buildings. Soon reduced to rubble were the Red Mountain, Central, Bibb, and Columbian Iron Works along with the Cahaba Rolling Mills and nearly every other structure of importance.

After arriving at Montevallo, Wilson also learned the Confederates were just south of his position. This rebel presence was actually a small force consisting of Roddey's cavalry, Crossland's brigade, and a small detachment with Brig. Gen. Wirt Adams. Upton's division was ordered to attack immediately. Gen. Andrew J. Alexander was in the van for the Union assault.[16]

The curtain was about to go up on the final act of the American Civil War in the west. The battle for Selma, Alabama, had begun. It would be the last significant battle of the war in that quarter. This last engagement between the blue and the gray would be a running fight that would last longer than forty-eight hours, starting at Six Mile Creek, below Montevallo, and continuing all the way to Selma, more than fifty miles away.

Forrest was wounded and cornered, but he was still dangerous. Though he was perhaps acting out of a sense of futility, it was the only way he knew, and all this combined to make him an even greater threat to the Union troops pressing around him.

After reflooring a nine-hundred-foot railroad bridge near Hillsboro on March 30, Upton's division pushed hard and engaged Roddey and Adams, driving them back to Six Mile Creek near Randolph. Once there, Roddey was reinforced by Crossland's Kentuckians, who threw their small brigade across the road upon which Upton's column was approaching. The two armies slammed into one another in a hard fight, with the outnumbered Confederates stubbornly resisting.

Crossland and Roddey's men held out until they were nearly flanked on both sides. At this time, Crossland sent his mounts and horse holders to the rear and continued to fight a delaying action in which the Kentuckians would form a line, fire away, and fall back. To keep a steady front to the enemy, half the Confederate troopers would fall back and form a new line while the first line fired at the oncoming Yankees. This action would give the second line time to reload and fire as the first half fell back to the next position and prepared to fire another volley. The system effectively slowed but could not stop the Federal push.

Around 4:00 P.M., General Roddey, now north of Randolph, rallied his horse soldiers and rode to reinforce Crossland, who had been reduced from six hundred to five hundred men during the last two hours of fighting. The situation was quickly deteriorating as Forrest came riding hard from the west towards the sounds of battle.

Having crossed the Cahaba at Centerville with seventy-five men of his escort company, Forrest reached the place where the engagement had begun. Remains of men and horses littered the field, testifying to the fierceness of the battle. Forrest's escort turned onto the road, formed into a column of fours, and raced on. Fifty yards up the road he could see the rear of the Union column hammering the Southern line, which was fighting desperately to hang on. The horsemen increased their speed from a rapid trot to a gallop as their leader bellowed the order to charge. Forrest and his terrible horsemen drove a bloody wedge into the rear of the advancing Yankee cavalry column, cutting it nearly in half and breaking through.

Wheeling to the north, Forrest's escort drove a fragment of Upton's command rearward for half a mile, then turned and charged upon the remaining Federals. During the short, vicious fight that ensued on that part of the field, Forrest gathered enough information about the earlier stages of the battle and Wilson's current strength and position to realize he could not reverse the current circumstances. Consequently, he swung off to the east and eventually rendezvoused with Roddey and Adams sixteen miles south of Randolph sometime around 10:00 P.M. the night of the thirty-first.[17] Of the day's fighting, General Wilson wrote that this time they "had the bulge on Forrest and held it to the end . . . fairly turning his own rules of war against himself."[18]

At 6:00 P.M. that night, Forrest dispatched orders to William "Red" Jackson to move swiftly to Centerville and strike Wilson's right flank, harass the enemy as much as possible, and then join him before they were forced back into Selma. "Enemy moving right down the railroad," Forrest's order read, "follow them down taking the road behind them from Montevallo down [avoiding a general engagement] unless you find the balance of our forces in supporting distance of you."[19] Forrest also sent off an urgent dispatch to General Taylor in Selma about the situation and once again requested the support of General Chalmers' division. But Chalmers was twenty miles south of Randolph, making slow progress through flooded, swampy roads.

Forrest was attempting to coordinate his commands into position to strike Wilson on the front, flank, and rear, but the young Union general was not only bringing an overpowering army to bear, he also had some incredible luck. The night-riding courier, carrying the message concerning Forrest's attack plans for Jackson and other troop dispositions was captured. From that point on Wilson's four-to-one advantage in numbers was matched with inside information that doomed any remaining hope for Forrest's rear guard to stop the Union juggernaut.

Acting on this intelligence, Wilson immediately sent Brig. Gen. Edward M. McCook's and Gen. Oscar H. La Grange's brigades to Centerville to burn the bridge over the Cahaba, effectively cutting off Jackson, and then prepared to move on Forrest with his remaining nine thousand cavalrymen, confident his rear was protected.[20] With nearly five thousand Confederate troopers cut off by the destruction of the Cahaba River bridge, all that then stood in Wilson's way were a meager fifteen hundred hungry, barefooted rebels. Forrest could only bring together was what was left of Roddey's and Crossland's brigades along with some newly recruited militia troops. The odds had suddenly jumped to ten-to-one.

At daybreak on April 1, Wilson, fully aware of how weak Forrest actually was, rode to engage the famous enemy leader. When the Union advanced, the Confederates were soon forced back. For the next eight to ten miles, as they fell back Forrest and his escort turned to savagely check the enemy's forward thrust. During the combat, Forrest sent another desperate dispatch to Taylor that he would not be able to hold them for much longer. He also discovered that Chalmers was nowhere near his expected position and sent a courier to tell Chalmers to make all haste, even at the expense of leaving his train and guns behind. Supplies and cannon were of no use at this stage. All was lost if Forrest could not draw a line of battle with more troops than he had on the field at that moment.

Six miles north of Plantersville at a position near Ebenezer Church, or Bogler's Creek, it began. Grappling with the enemy in the mud and blood, Forrest contested every inch of ground as though the enemy were attacking him in his own backyard. One of Crossland's Kentuckians wrote a brief memoir after the war in which he described the fight. He said that everyone knew Forrest was a great commander, but, after observing him in action, he stated that Forrest was an even "greater close-quarter fighter" than he was a general.[21]

Sometime around noon on the first, Forrest received a dispatch that Chalmers was driving toward Dixie Station and that General Adams had established a position at the same location. The railroad and a highway intersected the new line at Dixie Station, the approach to which was commanded by steep, wooded hills. With this information in hand, Forrest's escort and about one hundred Kentucky riflemen drew up in a short line of battle to meet what, realistically, could not be matched. Of this face-to-face encounter with Forrest, Wilson wrote, "In less than an hour, although resistance was determined, the position was carried by a gallant charge and the rebels completely routed."[22]

By 4:00 P.M., Forrest was forced back to Adams' position at Bogler's Creek. There the Confederates threw out a line astride the crossroads that led to Randolph and Maplesville, with Roddey's brigade on the right and Crossland's brigade on the left. Forrest and Adams were in the center of the thirteen hundred Confederates as they braced themselves again.

Before the graybacks could catch their breaths, Gen. Eli Long's division, led by the Seventeenth Indiana Cavalry, charged Roddey's section of the line, their drawn sabers gleaming in the sunlight. Under the pressure of overwhelming numbers and the firepower of the Yankee's Spencer carbines, the rebel line began to fall apart and give way. Forrest, recognizing the potential for disaster, rushed upon the scene with his escort, turned the tide, and reestablished the line. He then charged back to the center, where his last six field pieces were located.

At about this time, Nathan Boone and his scouting party arrived from Maplesville with Gen. Emory Upton's cavalry hot on their heels. As Upton's cavalry approached, the Confederates cut loose with canister and rifle fire, "emptying a number of saddles." Upton quickly dismounted his division and resumed the attack on foot, concentrating on the Confederate right.[23] The right of the Southern line, manned primarily by the militia, gave way in great disorder and began to fall back. Although the left of the Confederate line was holding, when the right gave way the rebels suddenly found themselves in danger of being turned and cut off from the ford at Dixie Creek. Realizing he would have to withdraw to secure the crossing at the next creek, Forrest gave the order to fall back. But there was no time. As soon as the Confederates began to withdraw, Upton anticipated the move and ordered his troops to mount up and charge.

Rushing down upon the rebel gun emplacements, Upton's cavalry was within fifty yards of the Confederates when Forrest's artillerists realized they no longer had infantry support. After cutting loose with one last volley, the gunners abandoned their cannon and ran for their lives. The only thing that stood between the loss of all the remaining Confederate guns and possible annihilation was Forrest and his escort company of elite fighters.

With Forrest at the point of the mounted spear formation, the gray riders hurled themselves at the oncoming Federal cavalry and met them in a collision at the abandoned guns like two locomotives crashing head on. Battle cries could be heard floating above the deafening percussion of the impact as one unfortunate Federal cavalryman rode his horse at full speed into one of the cannon, splitting his mount's breast wide open and propelling the rider through the air like a human missile.[24]

Forrest and his small company were swallowed up and engulfed in the great blue mass. Men hacked and chopped with their sabers and fired their pistols, cursing and screaming like maddened demons. When sabers broke or firearms ran empty, they tore at each other with bare hands, blood streaming from their wounds. So tightly locked together, both sides found themselves practically paralyzed amidst the crushing mob of horses and men.

Flashes of flame could be seen through the pall of smoke that hung like a curtain over the field. Riderless horses emerged and galloped away. The ground was strewn with casualties. A few men were trampled to death as they fell beneath the hooves of the stampeding warhorses. Despite the ferocity of Forrest's countercharge, he was being swept from the field and driven into a nearby wooded area. That Devil Forrest was fighting for his life with a frenzied rage. Several Federal soldiers surrounding Forrest fell before the fire from his navy Colts, and their horses galloped away into the melee. New combatants, eager to be the man who cut down the famed Confederate warrior, soon replaced the men Forrest had shot down.

Numerous sabers hissed by his head and struck his arms and body. As Forrest attempted to parry the barrage of blows, the hammer of his pistol was sheared off by a slashing sword stroke, knocking the revolver from his hand. Impenetrable thickets on both sides of the road hemmed him in. A wagon with a two-horse team blocked his escape rearward while enemy troops poured onto the roadway to his front. It seemed that escape was impossible.

Nevertheless, with both rider and mount wounded, Forrest fiercely spurred and wheeled his horse in the direction of the wagon that blocked the road. Racing ahead, directly at the obstacle in his path, Forrest and the brave animal left the ground, rose gracefully into the air, and soared over the wagon to the amazement of all witnesses.

After clearing the wagon Forrest was set upon once again by an adversary who had recognized him and singled him out for personal combat. Capt. James D. Taylor of the Seventeenth Indiana Cavalry engaged the wounded Confederate commander "in a running fight of 200 yards" and wounded him again with the edge of his saber before Forrest was able to draw his other pistol and kill the ambitious young captain. After the war, Forrest told Wilson personally that "if that boy had known enough to give me the point of his saber instead of the edge I should not have been here to tell you about it."[25]

Capt. John Eaton, of Forrest's escort, later commented on the combat he observed around his general that day.

> Each of us was armed with a pair of six shooters, and I emptied the chambers of my two army pistols . . . not more than five paces from the Federal trooper at whom it was aimed. It seemed as though these fellows were bent upon killing the general, whom they recognized. I saw 5 or 6 slashing away at him, with their sabers at one time.

Dr. George Cowan, also of Forrest's escort, and kin to him as well, said he saw "six Federals . . . all slashing at the general, and saw one trooper who struck one of his pistols and knocked it from his hand."[26]

By this point, Forrest's artillery had been carried away, and he was forced to fall back across Dixie Creek. Without Chalmers' and Jackson's support, there was no way he could rally his men, and his own wounds had become so painful that he and his escort made for Plantersville. At Plantersville, there was barely enough time to get off a telegraph to Dick Taylor in Selma before Wilson was driving them back at a gallop toward Taylor's position.

Forrest and his remaining men practically fell out of their saddles about six miles north of Selma in the late afternoon and rested for a few precious hours. Forrest was in severe pain from several wounds, which were dressed as well as possible under the circumstances, but the hastily applied bandages could not stop the bleeding.

That night, April 1, Wilson decided to give his exhausted men a rest and made camp at Plantersville, which was only nineteen miles north of Selma. At daylight on April 2, Long's division led the Union advance on Selma, followed by Upton's division. A battalion of the Fourth Regular Cavalry moved down the railroad, burning stations, bridges, and trestles as all three corps closed on the last chief arsenal, depot, and river port containing ordinance foundries for both the Confederate army and navy.

Selma, fortified by four miles of earthworks and trenches, sat upon high bluffs on the west bank of the Alabama River. These bastions were designed to be defended with at least ten thousand men. Forrest would have about one thousand troops to cover that vast expanse of ditches and palisades.[27]

Forrest was in the saddle early that day and heading toward Selma. His wounds were still bleeding freely as he attempted to organize his decimated command for one last stand and to locate Chalmers, whom he believed to be moving southward. He reached Selma around 10:00 A.M. and reported to Gen. Richard Taylor. Both he and his horse were wounded and splattered with blood and must have seemed to his commander an apparition from an ancient battlefield. Forrest's bloody visage, combined with the desperation of the moment, prompted Taylor to write,

> Forrest appeared, horse and man covered with blood, and announced the enemy at his heels, and that I must move at once to escape capture. I felt anxious for him, but he said he was unhurt and would cut his way through, as most of his men had done, whom he had ordered to meet him west of the Cahaba.[28]

General Taylor boarded a locomotive a few minutes after meeting with Forrest and experienced a hairsbreadth escape with Federal soldiers riding alongside the train, firing at the locomotive as it pulled away. Forrest returned to the works, where hundreds of militia had turned out. Many were old men and young boys who had volunteered to bolster the pitiful force, bringing its number up to a meager twenty-two hundred troops. With four miles of works to cover and with no help from Chalmers' division in sight, Forrest knew he was facing an impossible undertaking. As Upton's and Long's divisions, nine thousand strong, came forward, Forrest must have felt some kinship with the Texans at the Alamo.[29]

The implacable Wilson reached Selma at 4:00 P.M., but he waited until nightfall to launch the assault. It was over almost before it started, as the militia in the center of the skeleton Confederate line quickly gave way. Soon after, Roddey and Adams, on each end of the line, were flanked and swept away. The outnumbered defenders found themselves fighting individually and in small groups in an attempt to escape.

Though conditions at Selma were dreadful, the situation elsewhere in the Confederacy was hardly better. Richmond was being evacuated, as Lee's line had finally broken. Sherman had burned a path of destruction across South Carolina and was currently chasing Joseph E. Johnston's twenty-thousand-man army across North Carolina. By nine o'clock that night, April 2, Wilson was in control of Selma and set about destroying "all the foundries, arsenals, arms, stores and military munitions of every kind." "The immediate fruits of our victory," Wilson reported, "were 31 field guns and one 30-pounder Parrot which had been used against us" along with huge amounts of prisoners, "including 150 officers, a number of colors, and immense quantities of stores of every kind. . . . The capture of Selma having put us in possession of the enemy's greatest depot in the Southwest was a vital blow to their cause and found most advantageous."[30]

The flames of burning Selma lit up the night sky for miles. Citizens and soldiers swirled about in the chaos sweeping the town. The evacuation became a stampede as thousands of people ran for their lives or took shelter in the basements of private homes. In the midst of this pandemonium Forrest, true to his word, cut his way out. With him were his ever-faithful escort, P. D. Roddey and Gen. Frank C. Armstrong, and a few men from their battered brigades.

Leaving by the Montgomery road, Forrest's company ran into a contingent of Federal cavalry and in the short fight that ensued, Forrest killed his last man of the war. This was the thirtieth enemy soldier he had killed in hand-to-hand combat since his first engagement at Sacramento, Kentucky, in December 1861. The enemy had killed twenty-nine of his horses with Forrest aboard, but they had failed to kill him. Forrest would later say that he was "a horse ahead" at the end of the war.

Traveling by back roads and unfamiliar pathways lit by the red glow from the burning city, this band of survivors was in a desperate and bitter state of mind. Late that night, they happened upon some Federal soldiers pillaging a local farmhouse. These looters just happened to belong to the Fourth U.S. (Regular) Cavalry, the same unit responsible for executing Captain Freeman back on April 10, 1863, following the battle at Thompson's Station. The rebels became outraged when they heard the screams of women coming from the direction of the farm and attacked. It was payback time.

> Summary was the fate of these wretches. The escort were now greatly excited and provoked by the incident, and those in the advance guard, meeting a number of these fellows, loaded down with plunder, did not hesitate to slay them on the spot. Hearing the sounds of what was happening ahead, Forrest took the advance himself to check it out. Presently capturing a picket party, he learned that it belonged to a small squadron of the Fourth Regulars, encamped near by, rearward, which he determined to surprise and capture also, small as was his own force.[31]

Each side tells very different versions of the events that transpired. The Confederate account states that after capturing more looters, Captain Jackson, commander of the escort at the time, approached Forrest, who now had one arm in a sling and was weakened by loss of blood, and requested that the general stay in the rear with the prisoners due to his condition. There was no need, Jackson suggested, for the general to risk his life in a night action, because he (Jackson) and the remaining forty Confederate horsemen could handle the situation. Forrest's personal biographers, Jordan and Pryor, wrote, "To this wish of his men who had served him so long with superb devotion and valor, Forrest properly ascended, and, halting by the wayside, directed Captain Jackson to do the work at hand."[32]

Within minutes, Jackson, George Cowan, and the rest of Forrest's men closed in on the enemy camp in the pitch-dark. The Confederate version of the action was that as they approached the camp of thirty-five to forty Federal troopers (which made the fight fairly even in numerical terms), a sentry spotted the rebels, and a gunfight erupted in the dark. The result was "35 of the enemy being either killed or wounded and five captured with the loss on the other side [the Confederates] of only one man wounded." Soon after returning to Forrest's position and resuming the march, "in the course of the next eight to ten miles, they met and captured some more of the plundering 'bummers,' so that the fruits of the night's operations were at least sixty, either killed, wounded or captured."[33]

The Union, once again, charged massacre. Wilson's report stated that Forrest found the Federal troopers "asleep in a neighboring field. . . . He charged on them in their sleep, and refusing to listen to their cries of surrender, killed or wounded the entire party, numbering 25 men." George H. Thomas said of this night, "Forrest fell upon the party with the ferocity of a wild Indian, and killed every man of it."[34] With one side losing thirty to sixty men and the other having only one man wounded, it would seem to indicate the Union soldiers were taken by surprise, although the Confederates swore that not one man was "killed after surrender."[35]

These were hard-core and bitter veterans with the recent depredations of those very Union soldiers fresh on their minds, and fighting in the dark, they could have carried the attack to excess. Given those circumstances, perhaps excesses were committed; however, the rules of engagement did not call for the Confederates to sound a warning before attacking. The gloves had come off years before this night raid occurred. Nevertheless, the next day Union troops took reprisals by burning several private homes to the ground.

A few days later, on Palm Sunday, April 8, 1865, the day before Lee surrendered at Appomattox, Wilson requested a meeting with Forrest, who was camped at Marion, Alabama. Attending this meeting was the young Captain Hosea, who had earlier met with and been so very impressed by the "great Confederate Murat." This time Hosea had a different impression of Forrest, which seems to have been primarily induced by the rumors of what had happened to Lieutenant Royce's men who had been attacked by Forrest's troops in the night raid a few days before.

> I had remarked that a subsequent interview with Forrest quite removed the favorable first impression. That first meeting occurred during a respite of war, and we saw Forrest at his best, newly shaven, in a new uniform and of tranquil mind. I next saw him in the midst of turmoil and strife wounded, defeated, savage and unkempt. Let me turn a sidelight on the interviewing conditions.[36]

The "interviewing conditions" were amidst the chaos and disorder running rampant in Selma as it fell into Union hands—hands that also carried torches:

> During the melee, Forrest and a number of his officers escaped in the darkness and by a detour crossed our line of march in rear. Here they surprised and pistoled a lieutenant Royce of the Fourth Regular Cavalry, and thirty-eight men who had been detached in observation toward the Cahaba River at our right rear. An act so cold-blooded and dastardly excited throughout the command a dangerously revengeful feeling that proved difficult to restrain.[37]

When Forrest arrived at Wilson's headquarters at noon on April 8, he was invited to dine with the Union commander. Wilson wrote that soon he and Forrest were "treating each other like old acquaintances, if not old friends." They swapped war stories and strategies of past campaigns. Forrest was wearing one arm in a sling and seemed to enjoy verbally sparring with Wilson. Wilson said that he "found him in civil life a modest, unassuming and trustworthy man of affairs." Apparently, this seemed no contradiction to Wilson, who had earlier reported that Forrest's men had killed Lieutenant Royce's detachment "to the last man in their sleep." Now, face to face with Forrest, Wilson seemed very little distressed about the Royce situation. Wilson added that he found Forrest a man of "great firmness, excellent judgment and inflexible will." After the war, Wilson and Forrest would be involved together in the business of building railroads.[38]

Captain Hosea, however, saw things quite differently as he again was observing from the sidelines. This time Hosea's pen turned poisonous, as was often the case with journalists who encountered the Jekyll and Hyde image presented by the enigmatic Forrest.

> On the 6th, Major Strange arrived from General Forrest, and through him a meeting was arranged between General Wilson and General Forrest, which took place on the 8th. My diary simply notes that Forrest "did not do justice to my first impressions of him, either in appearance or conversation"; but he had ridden far and was in a common fatigue uniform, much soiled. His hair and beard were scraggly, and he evidently had not yet calmed down from the complete and successive defeats at Plantersville, Boggler's Creek and Selma. All the brutal instincts

of the slave driver stood out unconcealed; and to these was added a sulky and guilty consciousness that we regarded him as the murderer of Royce and his party, and that his lame attempt to excuse it by putting the blame on those who accompanied him, was not believed in the face of the dying declarations of his victims that he himself set the example to his men.[39]

How brutal the attack on Royce and his men actually had been will remain a mystery, but as with Fort Pillow and many other fields of battle, controversy followed Forrest throughout his entire life like a long, dark shadow.

After the meeting with Wilson, Forrest moved his camp to Gainesville, remaining there from the fifteenth to the twenty-fifth. While bivouacked at Gainesville, information came piece-by-piece concerning the collapse of the Confederacy. Lee's surrender at Appomattox Courthouse, the fall of Mobile, and Joe Johnston's imminent surrender to Sherman came like successive body blows taking the wind out of any thoughts of sustaining the war effort. There also came the wild rumors that Lincoln had been shot by a crazed Southern actor, that Jefferson Davis was on the run toward Texas or Mexico to continue the war, and that Gen. Kirby Smith, commander of the trans-Mississippi west, also had refused to surrender. With such stories running rampant, Forrest called his men together on April 15 and gave the following speech:

Soldiers: The enemy have originated and sent through our lines various and conflicting dispatches indicating the surrender of General Robert E. Lee and the Army of Virginia. A morbid appetite for news and sensational rumors has magnified a simple flag of truce from Lieutenant General Taylor to General Canby [who had accepted the surrender at Mobile] negotiating the terms of surrender of the troops of his department. Your commanding general desires to say to you that no credence should be given to such reports. . . . On the contrary, from Southern sources and now published in our papers, it is reported that General Lee has not surrendered; that a cessation of hostilities has been agreed upon between Generals Johnston and Sherman for the purpose of adjusting the difficulties and differences between the Confederate and the United States of America. Also that since the evacuation of Richmond and the death of Abraham Lincoln, Grant has lost in battle and in desertion 100,000 men. As your commander, he further assures you that at this time, above all others, it is the duty of every man to stand firm at his post and true to his colors. . . . A few days more will determine the truth or falsity of all the reports now in circulation.[40]

The unthinkable truth would come crashing home very soon. There were hard choices to make and they were all depressing in the extreme. On the day that this report was delivered, Forrest sent a letter to his son, Willie, that reflected his current melancholy and love for his only son. "Life as you know it is uncertain, at best, and occupying the position I do it is exceedingly hazardous. I may, at no distant day, be an exile in a foreign land, and I desire to address you a few words, which I trust you will remember through life." Forrest went on to tell Willie to act as his mother's protector as he himself had done should something happen to him or "in the event the enemy overruns the country." He warned his son not to emulate his wicked and sinful ways but to strive to be an honorable man. He closed the letter by telling Willie how proud he was of him and requested that his son should "keep this letter prominently before you" on the chance that they would "meet no more on this earth."[41]

The spring of 1865 was one of mocking contrasts. As the countryside blossomed and greened, the Confederacy withered on the vine. Forrest, as well as other Confederate commanders, was looking into an abyss of a bleak and uncertain future.

On April 29, General Taylor traveled the rails by handcar from Meridian, pumping his way to Magee's Farm, twelve miles north of Mobile, Alabama, to meet Maj. Gen. E. R. S. Canby. When Taylor stepped off the rail car in Mobile, Canby's band struck up "Dixie." The two generals agreed to follow the terms of surrender set forth in the first meeting between Sherman and Joe Johnston in North Carolina.

On the same day, Forrest received word that the hostilities had ceased, but perhaps only temporarily. Upon review the U.S. government rejected the liberal terms that Sherman had given Johnston, which could be interpreted as allowing slave owners to retain their slaves. Grant insisted that all the surrendering Confederate commanders be held to the same details of surrender that he had given Lee at Appomattox. Consequently hostilities were ordered to resume in forty-eight hours. However, Taylor had no thoughts of continuing the hostilities and returned to Citronelle, Alabama, forty miles north of Mobile, and once there made the surrender official. That surrender included primarily Maury's garrison and Forrest's cavalry at Gainesville.

Concerning Forrest, Sherman was not sure if his old nemesis would ever lay down his arms. In late April, Sherman wrote to Grant, "I now apprehend that the Rebel armies will disperse. . . . We will have to deal with numberless bands of desperadoes, headed by such men as Mosby, Forrest, Red Jackson, and others, who know not and care not for danger and its consequences." A few days later, Sherman wrote to his wife,

> There is great danger of the Confederate armies breaking up into guerillas, and that is what I most fear. Such men as Wade Hampton, Forrest, Wirt Adams, etc., never will work and nothing is left for them but death or highway robbery. They will not work and their Negroes are all gone, plantations destroyed, etc.[42]

In making such predictions for their postwar employment opportunities, Sherman may have been influenced by Forrest's and Hampton's prewar wealth and power. After all they had been among the wealthiest men in the South before the war. Or perhaps Sherman was thinking that they had grown so accustomed to war that they would be unable to give it up when peace returned.

He need not have worried to what lawless pursuits Forrest and Hampton might turn. Wade Hampton would later become the governor of South Carolina and dabble in national politics. The business of railroad building and reconciliation would occupy Forrest, although during Reconstruction, Forrest would worry the Federal authorities in a much more serious manner than Sherman could ever have imagined. As lieutenant generals in the lost cause, both Hampton and Forrest were famous throughout the country. Sherman was making quite a stretch to include Forrest and Hampton in the same company with William Clarke Quantrill, "Bloody Bill" Anderson, and the James boys. To suggest a peacetime career of "highway robbery" for such men makes Sherman sound like a man dying to write fiction.

However, in Hampton's case Sherman might have had cause for concern in another respect. In early May, Hampton wrote to Davis,

> If you will allow me to do so, I can bring to your support many strong arms and brave hearts, men who will fight to Texas & will seek refuge in Mexico, rather than the Union. . . . My plan is to call the men who stick to their colors and to get to Texas. I can carry with me quite a number and I can get there.[43]

In reference to Hampton's offer, Davis wrote to his wife, "For myself, it may be that a devoted band of cavalry will cling to me, and that I can force my way across the Mississippi, and if nothing can be done there which it will be proper to do, then I can go to Mexico."[44]

After learning of Joe Johnston's imminent surrender in North Carolina, Davis escaped from Richmond and headed southwest toward Alabama and the troops commanded by Forrest and Davis's own brother-in-law, Richard Taylor. In the last week of April, the final Confederate council of war was held at Abbeville, South Carolina, where President Davis urged the continuation of the war. Five brigadier generals were present, including Gen. George Dibrell, representing Forrest's old brigade. To a man, they all disagreed with Davis and convinced him to abandon his plans to go to Mexico, although he continued to flee through Georgia under the protection of Dibrell's cavalry detachment.[45]

Back at Gainesville, Forrest's camp was in a dark mood and talk of marching to Mexico was spreading through the ranks. Their leader was not oblivious to the possibility of heading into Mexico, as a letter to his son indicated, but it was never a serious option for the Tennessean. In fact, in early May, Charles Clark and Isham G. Harris met with Forrest and urged him to reconsider surrender and to contemplate linking his command with Gen. Kirby Smith in the trans-Mississippi west and marching from there into Mexico. Forrest told them that he really wanted no part of it. "Men, you may all do as you damn please, but I'm a-going home," he told his long-suffering troops. In response to the politicians, who unintentionally challenged his honor by asking him if he did not have an army in the field ready to fight to the end, he said, "Any man who is in favor of a further prosecution of this war is a fit subject for a lunatic asylum, and ought to be sent there immediately."[46]

However, in 1868, after filing for bankruptcy, he told Norman Farrell and Thomas B. Smith, two Confederate veterans, what his plans were had he chosen to go into exile, and those plans did not sound like he had peaceful colonization in mind. Forrest was thinking more along the lines of conquest.

> Forrest said that he had been promised 20,000 muskets and that he would want 30,000 men, he could conquer the country in six months; that he would then confiscate the mines and church property; that is about $^1/_3$ of all the real estate of the country; hold possession of each state, as he advanced, by leaving four or five thousand men in each; take possession of the offices for himself and his men, among which, of course [Farrell speculated],

N.B. would get the lions share with the title of King or President; while the private got his in bullets; and then he concluded: "I would open up the country to immigration, after I had given it a free government, and would get at least 20,000 people from the southern states, besides many from Europe and the north." Smith and Farrell then added that Forrest "said there are at least 50,000 young men in the south who won't plow, but who would fight or dig for gold. I asked him if he did not think the United States would interfere with his little arrangement, but he said they would be glad to get rid of him.[47]

In the meantime, Gen. George Thomas and other members of the Union general staff had heard rumors that Forrest was intending to cut his way through Mississippi, Texas, and into Mexico. On May 3, Thomas directed Gen. Edward Hatch to send to Forrest, under a flag of truce, a "summons to surrender." Further, Hatch was to "inform him . . . of the rumors that have reached you, and that . . . if he attempts such a reckless and bloodthirsty adventure he will be treated thereafter as an outlaw, and the states of Mississippi and Alabama will be so destroyed that they will not recover for fifty years."[48]

Late at night on May 8, Forrest took a long ride with Major Anderson to contemplate the immediate future. Anderson attempted to explain to his commander that the people of Mississippi and Tennessee needed him during the coming crucible of Reconstruction. They rode in silence for a while before stopping at a fork in the road. Anderson asked, "Which way general?" Forrest replied sardonically, "Either. If one road led to Hell and the other to Mexico, I would be indifferent as to which to take."[49]

The conversation began again with Anderson reminding Forrest that it was not only he that would be going into exile, but all his men as well, and that he must think of them. Surrender for the men who stayed home would be beyond humiliation if their leader abandoned them. Having weighed Anderson's argument, Forrest stated with conviction, "That settles it." He then wheeled his horse and headed back toward camp. Besides the common sense of the decision, Forrest was now forty-four years old, wounded several times, and worn down from his super-human effort during the war.

Another aggravating circumstance was the intense scrutiny and threats he was receiving from the U.S. government. Considering the thousands of Confederates who did go to Mexico, including Kirby Smith, Jo Shelby, and Confederate secretary of the navy Matthew

Fontaine Maury, the Union authorities seemed almost paranoid concerning Forrest's postwar plans.[50]

Returning to camp, Forrest and Anderson found the men in a very agitated and worried state of mind. Forrest soon had them calmed down and the next night, May 9, 1865, he delivered his final address to his war-weary troops. They would be the last significant Confederate army east of the Mississippi River to lay down their arms.

> That we are beaten is a self-evident fact, and any further resistance on our part would be justly regarded as the very height of folly and rashness. The armies of Generals Lee and Johnston having surrendered, you are the last of all the troops of the Confederate States Army east of the Mississippi River to lay down your arms. The cause for which you have for so long and manfully struggled, and for which you have braved dangers, endured privations and sufferings, and made so many sacrifices, is today hopeless. The government which we sought to establish and perpetuate is at an end. Reason dictates and humanity demands that no more blood be shed. . . . It is your duty and mine to lay down our arms, submit to the powers to be, and to aid in restoring peace and establishing law and order throughout the land. The terms upon which you surrendered are favorable to all. They manifest a spirit of magnanimity and liberality on the part of the Federal authorities which should be met on our part by a faithful compliance with all stipulations and conditions therein expressed. . . . Civil War, such as you have just passed through, naturally engenders feelings of animosity, hatred and revenge. It is our duty to divest ourselves of all such feelings, and, so far as it is in our power to do so, to cultivate friendly feelings toward those with whom we have so long contested, and heretofore so widely but honestly differed. . . . The attempt made to establish a separate and independent confederation has failed, but the consciousness of having done your duty faithfully and to the end will in some measure repay you for the hardships you have under gone. . . . I have never on the field of battle sent you where I was unwilling to go myself, nor would I now advise you to a course which I felt myself unwilling to pursue. You have been good soldiers, you can be good citizens. Obey the laws, preserve your honor, and the government to which you have surrendered can afford to be and will be magnanimous.[51]
>
> N.B. Forrest, Lieutenant General

This speech was written as soon as Forrest and Anderson returned to camp. It was composed atop a cracker box and later set to type and copied on an old printing press. Each trooper received a personal copy. Major Anderson's inspired pen, along with Forrest's oversight, created perhaps the most eloquent and conciliatory letter of its kind from a Confederate general to his troops.[52]

# Chapter Sixteen

# SOMETHING WICKED THIS WAY COMES

*—William Shakespeare*

## Reconstruction
## May 1865-June 1871

Bearing the heavy weight of defeat and a lost cause, Forrest's troops prepared to head home. Along with their discharge papers they carried more than enough stories of courage and adventure to last a lifetime. Those who had served as members of the famed and feared Seventh Tennessee Cavalry decided to ensure that their cherished, bullet-ridden battle flag would never fall into the hands of the enemy, nor anyone else. Gathering in the darkness near their regimental headquarters, the troopers and officers cut into pieces the tattered silk banner, which had been sewn from the dress of a young girl who lived in Aberdeen, Mississippi. Each man was given a small swatch of the material to tuck away as a "testimonial to their dark and bloody glory."[1]

Forrest and the officers stayed in Gainesville for the next few days completing the muster rolls and parole process. Forrest also fulfilled a promise before handing over his command to history; he freed over forty of his slaves who had followed him into the war. He had made the promise at the beginning and still considered the covenant significant enough to recall years later when in 1871 he repeated it in testimony before a Congressional committee investigating the Ku Klux Klan conspiracy:

> I said to forty-five colored fellows on my plantation that it was a war upon slavery, and that I was going into the army; that if they would go with me, if we got whipped they would be free anyhow, and that if we succeeded and slavery was perpetuated, if they would act faithfully to me to the end of the war, I would

set them free. . . . Eighteen months before the war closed I was satisfied that we were going to be defeated, and I gave these forty-five or forty-four men of them, their free papers, for fear I might be killed.[2]

On May 13, 1865, four days after he had surrendered, Forrest attended a conference at Meridian, Alabama, along with other Confederate officers, civilians, and Union military men. While mixing among the people, Forrest was approached by a northern writer, Bryan McAlister, who engaged him in a memorable conversation after discovering from other guests that he was the infamous "Forrest of the Fort Pillow Massacre."[3] McAlister decided to keep the fact that he was actually working on the staff of a Union general to himself and played the part of a provocateur as he informally interviewed the controversial Confederate. The setting was similar to that on the night Forrest was scrutinized by Captain Hosea. "Before a large chimney-place of a small cabin . . . dimly lit by small tallow candles, I first saw Lieutenant General Nathan Bedford Forrest, commanding a corps of cavalry in the rebel army." It almost sounded like McAlister had read Hosea's essay because both reviews began practically verbatim.

Standing near the hearth of the fireplace, in the flickering candle-light, Forrest once again gave the writer plenty of ammunition that would later be fired back at Bedford in print. Upon first seeing him, McAlister described Forrest in the same heroic and mysterious fashion as Hosea. To both journalists, Forrest was "a man of fine appearance, about 6 feet in height, having dark, piercing eyes, carefully trimmed moustache, and chin whiskers, dark as night, finely cut features, and iron-gray hair." He went on to describe Forrest's physique as "lithe yet exhibiting great physical power and activity." McAlister said that if he had spotted Forrest on Broadway, he would have thought him a prominent man. However, McAlister added that other Confederate officers to whom he had talked had referred to Forrest with disgust, though grudgingly admitted he was a successful cavalry commander.

Once McAlister was able to get Forrest's attention and a somewhat private audience, he said to the cavalryman that he never imagined he would one day be engaged in a personal conversation with such a person. "Why so?" Forrest inquired. McAlister answered that Forrest's name was being mentioned everywhere he traveled. When Forrest grinned at McAlister, the writer noted that Forrest had "the finest set of white teeth I had ever seen." Perhaps aware of why his name was being mentioned everywhere, Forrest spoke through his grin and said, "I have waked up the Yankees everywhere, lately."[4]

McAlister then began to pump Forrest for information on the Fort Pillow incident and suggested that Forrest write his own account to set the record straight. Forrest told him that the Yankees had already sent investigators to examine the situation. "But, are we to believe their report General?" "Yes, if we are to believe any thing a n——— says," Forrest answered. The last question obviously touched a nerve, because Forrest launched into a profane and brutal assessment of the Fort Pillow situation, intermixed with some memorable quotes on his fighting prowess and military accomplishments.

> When I went into the war, I meant to fight. Fighting means killing. I have lost twenty-nine horses in the war, and have killed a man each time. The other day I was a horse ahead, but at Selma they surrounded me, and I killed two, jumped my horse over a wagon, and got away. . . . My Provost-Marshal's book will show that I have taken thirty-one thousand prisoners during the war. At Fort Pillow I sent a flag of truce, and demanded an unconditional surrender, or I would not answer for my men. This they refused. I could see on the river, boats loaded with troops. They sent back, asking for an hour more. I gave them twenty minutes. I sat on my horse during the whole time.
>
> The fort was filled with n——— and deserters from our army; men who lived side by side with my men. I waited five minutes after the time, and then blew my bugle for the charge. In twenty minutes my men were over the works and the firing had ceased. The citizens and Yankees had broken in the heads of whisky and lager beer barrels, and were all drunk. They kept up firing all the time as they ran down the hill. Hundreds of them rushed to the river, and tried to swim to the gunboats, and my men shot them down. The Mississippi river was red with their blood for three hundred yards. During all this, their flag was still flying, and I rushed over and cut it down, and stopped the fight. Many of the Yankees were in tents in front, and they were in their way, as they concealed my men, and some of them were set on fire. If any men were burned to death, it was in those tents. . . . I will leave it to any prisoner I have ever taken if I have not treated them well.

"You have made some rapid marches, General," said McAlister.

At that comment, Forrest changed gears from the Fort Pillow battle to his less controversial victories without missing a beat. "I have five thousand men that can whip any ten thousand in the world. . . . I meant to kill every man in Federal uniform, unless he gave up."

Speaking of Streight's raid and the epic running battle that led to Colonel Streight's capture, Forrest said it was almost a shame.

According to McAlister, Forrest said, "His [Forrest's] men rode among them and shot them down like cattle. They were mounted on sharp-edged saddles" and were worn out, and Forrest said that he killed several of them himself.

McAlister was apparently taken aback by Forrest's brutal honesty and descriptive narrative because later he added,

> But the heart sickens at the infamous conduct of this butcher. He is one of the few men that are general "blowers", and yet he will fight. Forrest is a thorough bravo—a desperate man in every respect. He was a Negro trader before the war, and in "personal affairs", as he calls them, had killed several men. He has two brothers living, one of whom is spoken of as a greater butcher than the lieutenant general. He, the lieutenant general, is a man without education or refinement, married, I believe to a very pretty wife. Any one would call him handsome. Any one hearing him talk, would call him a braggadocio. As for myself, I believe one half [of what] he said, and only dispute with him with one finger on the trigger of my pistol.

McAlister informed Forrest that the relatives of the two Kentuckians he had executed back at the Sipsey River, where he had left their bodies displayed for shock value to his remaining troops, were on his trail and had sworn to kill him. Forrest seemed unimpressed. He told his interviewer that people had been trying to do that since as long as he could remember and added that all he really wanted to do was to take a fishing trip and hoped "to see no one for twelve months."

"What a charming hero he would make for a sensational 'King of the Cannibal Islands,'" the reporter concluded.[5]

Forrest's train ride home from Meridian to Jackson was a taste of what lay ahead for the general in the next few years. Packed with civilians and soldiers, the weight of the train spread the rails of the track and caused part of the train to derail. C. B. Kilgore, who later became a judge and congressman, was a passenger on the train and gave an interesting account of the experience. Kilgore said that Forrest took command like he was still in the field and "ordered every one of us out of the cars." Forrest told them the rails could be pushed back in line and the car lifted and realigned on the track. When the first attempt to lift the car failed someone notified Forrest that there were still a few slackers who had not fallen out to lend a hand. "General," the informer said, "there are some men in the car, and if they would get out we could lift it more readily." Bedford ran up the steps of the car and opened the door to where the men who had disregarded his order were sitting. "If you damned rascals don't get out of here and help get this car on the track," he bellowed, "I'll throw every damn one of you out the windows." It was reported that the extra passengers stepped lively in "rapid fashion" as they "tumbled out" of the car to lend a hand.[6]

As the train steamed down the tracks, Forrest looked out the window of the rail car across the once-familiar landscape rushing by. It had been transformed by the ravages of four years of war and was strewn with scenes of destruction. Many ex-Confederates and civilians, pushed beyond the limits of civilized constraint by the nightmarish conditions created by the war, committed deeds unheard of when peace last existed in their land. Often starving, their homes devastated, and their families dead or scattered, thousands of these menacing relics of war wandered the countryside that had been their home for generations. In the vacuum that existed in law and order during the transition from defeated nation to military occupation, hardly any legal restraint remained to protect the honest and war-weary who wanted only to put their lives together again. The Confederacy had become a freebooter's paradise in a climate fertile for terror and bedlam.

The rebellion was over. Or was it? The military victory of the Northern armies had hardly changed the hearts and minds of those who had sought independence. Neither had it made many of those in power less aggressive toward the Southern culture and political system. The sounds of battle still echoed across the land, readily recalling offenses so recently committed. The war had ended, but in some respects the worst was yet to come, especially in the South. America had to be put back together again, and the Federal Congress assumed it should direct that undertaking. The effort was aptly called "Reconstruction." The Reconstruction period has been called the "Tragic Era," a time of revenge and a time of broken promises. It shook the country like a cataclysmic earthquake, creating tremors still felt to this day. In some ways it was the second rebellion, and to some it was a continuation of the war.

The death of Abraham Lincoln, which came even before all the guns fell silent, set events on a course that tested the fabric of America's national life. Lincoln had embarked on a plan of sectional reconciliation as early as 1864, and during the early days of

Reconstruction, Andrew Johnson, Lincoln's successor, attempted to carry out the magnanimous policies Lincoln initiated. However, Johnson found leadership difficult in Lincoln's shadow and quickly clashed with the Radical Republicans in Congress, who were motivated by an irrational fear of the rebel Southerners and their own desire to consolidate their party's national ascendancy. They attempted to thwart the Lincoln/Johnson plan at every turn, and by 1867, martial law had been established in the former Confederate states to bring about the social and political aims of the Radicals in Congress. Thus, Reconstruction, under their direction, became an "ongoing evolution of Southern society rather than a passing phenomenon."[7]

The second rebellion would bring about a radical transfer of power during which the Radicals planned to sustain this power shift by mobilizing the newly enfranchised former slaves as a Republican power base in the South. The transformation of four million slaves into free and equal citizens was more than a dramatic social and political change produced by the war. It would become a titanic struggle as Americans made a bloody attempt to live up to the political creed laid down by their forefathers. Some of the nation's darkest history was written in the 1860s and 1870s as Americans grappled with issues as old as the American republic and as contemporary as those affecting American society today.

However, analyzing Reconstruction in broad, sweeping strokes cannot do justice to the gut-wrenching experiences of the individual men, women, and children who lived through it. Nathan Bedford Forrest became in a sense the "everyman" of this postwar experience. Four years earlier, he had been worth nearly a million and a half dollars, which, by the economic standards of the twenty-first century, would have made Forrest worth a hundred times that today. The war had changed all that. Bedford stated, "I came out of the war pretty well wrecked . . . completely used up, shot all to pieces, crippled up . . . a beggar. I have given all my time since then, so far as was in my power, to try and recover."[8]

Forrest traveled to Jackson, Mississippi, on July 1, 1865, to "make application to the President for a pardon." He could not have imagined when he told his troops that the government that could "afford to be magnanimous" would deny him his parole for three years. By the time the parole finally came, at the end of 1868, Forrest had become something of a legend in both the North and the South.

Like thousands of his countrymen Forrest found it difficult to raise cash for the various enterprises he would pursue following the war, but the native business sense that had made Forrest wealthy before the war would help him survive. Though he had depleted his fortune in supplying his troops out of his own pocket, he had returned to his land and intended to make the best of what the war had left him. He immediately set about getting in his first peacetime crop of corn.

In addition, Forrest had many friends on the Union side who became his business partners and associates. "I carried seven Federal officers home with me after the war was over and rented them plantations, some of my own lands, and some of my neighborhood. . . . These men were all young men and made my house their home on Sundays."[9] Working with former enemies was not only a hospitable move, but also an astute one. "I assisted those men," Forrest said, "and found great relief with them." That relief came by way of his new friends providing help in acquiring freedmen for labor on his plantation. An official of the Freedman's Bureau reported that "the general employed the greatest number of hands of any place I visited. . . . General Forrest works about 140 hands on two plantations." Of his Union friends Bedford said, "They got me my hands, and kept my hands engaged for me."[10]

Looking for other opportunities, Bedford relinquished a 1,445-acre plantation to the original owner, Henry C. Chambers, and opened a lumber business. He placed a newspaper advertisement in September announcing his new venture: "Having thoroughly repaired my Steam Mill, situated in the lower part of Coahoma County, Mississippi, four miles back of Sunflower Landing, I can now furnish the public with lumber of every description." On the twenty-ninth, another advertisement appeared: "Wanted—Twenty good hands are wanted at the saw mill of General Nathan Bedford Forrest. The highest prices paid."[11]

The economic struggles that lay ahead were formidable, but vengeance was in the air and it soon became apparent that the end of the war had not settled all scores. It was in these early days following the war that the *Memphis Bulletin,* quoting an article from the *New York Times,* reported that "all the rebel officers concerned in the atrocious starvation of our prisoners . . . and also the Fort Pillow murder would be excluded from the benefit of the amnesty proclamation." It also reported that several Confederate officers had been taken prisoner and either spirited away or hanged.[12]

Forrest realized that he was treading on thin ice in this postwar climate, for he was becoming infamous in the North, especially regarding the near hysteria that surrounded Fort Pillow. So far he had been insulated to some degree, as some of his newer friends, such as

Union general Francis P. Blair, had political connections and could ease Bedford's transition into civilian life. Men like Blair also countered with their own personal endorsements some of the bad press and rumors concerning Forrest. Blair said of Forrest on one occasion that he was "more powerful than any man in West Tennessee." Forrest's "noble bearing since the war in accepting without complaint the result and using his powerful influence to make others accept it in the same spirit, have inspired men with respect and admiration I have not felt for any other man." In conclusion Blair said, "I have conceived a very great personal attachment for Forrest."[13]

Forrest needed all the help he could get from friends like Blair, and his charisma won him other allies as well. Even his old antagonist, Edward Hatch, described Forrest's status in the region as the reason his own former staff officer B. F. Diffenbocker went into business with Forrest. In fact, Diffenbocker would become the foreman on Forrest's plantation and would later be called as a witness in a murder trial against his new boss. General Hatch stated,

> There is no more popular man in West Tennessee today than the late rebel General Forrest. The quartermaster of my old regiment is partner with Forrest on a plantation; he said he took the plantation job because Forrest is popular, and will take care of him and his interests.[14]

In his association with business partners from the north Forrest may well have been attempting to insulate himself because, quite likely, he realized that though he was "popular" and "powerful" in west Tennessee, he had become in the North one of the most hated men to come out of the war. To his good fortune there were forces at work in the North that were advantageous to the South. The Northern business community was one of those forces. It was still understood among businessmen and bankers in the North that a good portion of the economic stability of Northern manufacturing depended on the Southern cotton crop.

Cotton was perhaps no longer king, but it still provided princely profits. And, as in those days before the war, a reliable labor force was required to work the cotton fields. Herein lay the threat to the fulfillment of the former slaves' dream of complete freedom and equality. And herein also lay one of the most despicable hypocrisies of the Reconstruction. The end of slavery was one thing; deliverance was yet another. Many in the North were no more willing to grant full suffrage and all that it entailed to blacks than were the former Confederate states. Only the strictest of the abolitionists in New England seemed willing to go that far.

As the summer of 1865 wore on, Tennessee voters abolished slavery within its borders and gave blacks the right to sue in court and to own land, but as in the North, ex-slaves were denied the right to vote. Sen. Charles Sumner of Massachusetts was prompted to describe these proceedings as nothing but a "rebel conspiracy to gain political power."[15] Given the fact that the Republican Party's best chance of "gaining political power" in the South was through the enfranchisement of the former slaves, one can see why he might have suspected some kind of conspiracy. However, the grab for power by Sumner and his colleagues in Congress probably seemed to them to be the process of a just cause.

For the time being, Forrest remained silent on the situation in Tennessee and was reconciled to joining the new Union, but "rebellion lay in his way," as Shakespeare wrote, "and he found it." Whether Forrest went looking for trouble, or whether it just found him, his independent nature and the desperate state of affairs throughout the South would soon make reconciliation almost impossible.

The newspaper business would be a contributing factor in Forrest's eventual rebellion against the new Union. Articles continually surfaced in New York, Chicago, and Memphis attacking the "butcher of Fort Pillow" and spreading dangerous rumors about Forrest's alleged activities, plans, and whereabouts. These articles, often based as they were upon innuendo, half-truths, and outright prevarication, stirred old enmities and were often downright incendiary. Forrest became a lightning rod for forces seeking a target to blame, and the threat of assassination became all too real.

Friends of the former Confederate general were so worried about his safety that they recommended he leave the country for the time being. There seems to be some substance to this apprehension on the part of Forrest's supporters. The day after Christmas 1865, the *Memphis Appeal* published an account from the *New Orleans Crescent* that Adm. Raphael Semmes, formerly of the Confederate navy, had been arrested and shipped off to the North. Actually, Semmes had only been transported from Mobile to New Orleans by steamboat, but at the time the original article appeared his whereabouts might have been unknown. It was also reported that former general Dabney Maury was detained aboard the same ship, which only underscored the widespread concern that a mass roundup of Confederate leaders was intended. Maury had personally attempted to warn Forrest a couple of days before his arrest by contacting Sam Tate, a former business associate of Forrest's, who forwarded a letter of credit to help with expenses should Forrest decide to go into exile.[16]

Although Forrest declined the letter of credit, the rumors continued along with the attacks of sensationalist newspaper journalists. On January 30, 1866, the *Memphis Avalanche* reprinted an article that had appeared a few days earlier in the *New York Tribune* proclaiming the unfairness of Admiral Semmes' arrest while Forrest remained free. Admiral Semmes, "who had shed no blood, was now, on trial for his life for a violation of the rules of civilized warfare," the article complained, "while Lieutenant General Forrest, of the Confederate Army, is peacefully running a sawmill in Mississippi. Where are our soldiers who perished at Fort Pillow?"[17]

Matthew Galloway, who had recently reopened the *Avalanche*, defended Forrest in his own editorial, concluding that Forrest was "now in all probability an exile."[18] Galloway did not seem any better informed on Forrest's plans or whereabouts than the journalists in the North.

Three weeks later, in early February 1866, when Forrest was shown a copy of these editorials, he sent a rebuttal to Galloway. Forrest stated that there was no way he "could be induced to leave the country" and that he had said nothing nor done anything that could "have furnished grounds for such a supposition." He went on to say that all his efforts were being put into "strengthening the Government . . . and uniting the people."[19]

In all probability, Forrest meant what he said, but in the spring of 1866, the frail rope with which he had tied himself to the Federal government started to unravel strand by strand. He had yet to face the bizarre treason charge that had been hanging over his head since the raid on Memphis in September 1864, so on March 13, he appeared in Memphis before the clerk of the circuit court to post a ten-thousand-dollar bond. Within days of his appearance in court, the treason charge would be marginalized in April by a grand jury indictment against him for homicide in the death of one of his employees.

Thomas Edwards was a freedman and notable character on Forrest's plantation. Edward was a man with a volatile temperament whose behavior and attitude toward his employer seemed to belie any instinct for self-preservation, considering Forrest's reputation for having killed more than thirty men in personal confrontations. The word around the Forrest plantation was that Edwards was an instigator and bully and had abused several farm animals, even having beaten one mule to death. Edwards' behavior, however, was not restricted only to the animals. On more than one occasion, Edwards was reported to have "whipped his wife so unmercifully that a physician was called to attend her."[20]

Matters escalated when Edwards had a confrontation with Forrest's plantation foreman, B. F. Diffenbocker, Union general Hatch's former quartermaster, concerning the number of hours black employees were contracted to work each day. Armed with farm tools, Edwards led a group of workers in the shrill disagreement with Diffenbocker, and although no violence erupted, threats and ultimatums were tossed about. Referring to Edwards' treatment of his wife, the foreman advised him that wife beating was against General Forrest's rules of conduct. Edwards reportedly replied,

> I will whip my wife when I damn please. I do not care a Goddamn for General Forrest or any other Goddamn man. If General Forrest or any other man attempts to interfere with me in the privilege I enjoy as regards to whipping her or beating her I'll cut his Goddamn guts out.[21]

On March 31, Forrest made a trip to the freedmen's quarters to check on some stagnant pools of water he intended to have drained because of a recent outbreak of Asiatic cholera in Memphis. When Bedford ordered Edwards to participate in the work, he stalked off to his cabin a short distance away and began screaming loudly enough for Forrest and the other workers to hear that he was going to whip his wife if his dinner was not ready. Predictably, the combination of Edwards' insolent disregard for Forrest's order and the sounds of domestic violence coming from within the cabin provoked the old cavalryman to action. Versions of the story vary as to exactly what happened when Forrest entered the Edwards cabin, as did the testimony at the trial. The result was the same in all accounts: Thomas Edwards ended up dead.

Forrest said that when he entered the cabin he told Edwards to cease abusing his wife. Forrest could be a profane man, but when Edwards launched a barrage of profanity of his own at Forrest, the general reacted characteristically. He told Edwards that no man spoke to him in such a manner and that if it continued he would do something about it. More heated words were exchanged, and suddenly Forrest struck Edwards over the head with a broom handle. Edwards then produced a hunting knife and lunged at Forrest, wounding him on the hand. Both men spotted an axe standing next to a kindling box and simultaneously made a move to get it. Forrest got there first and swung the ax, striking Edwards "on the head with the pole of the axe," killing him instantly.[22]

Local law enforcement was summoned but did not arrive at Forrest's plantation until around midnight. By the time Deputy Wirt Shaw arrived at Forrest's house, word of Edwards' death had spread throughout the area to hundreds of freedmen who had gathered and surrounded Forrest's home with bonfires. The blacks seemed determined that Forrest would not escape. Shaw first attempted to assure the crowd that the general would stand trial for his actions and then proceeded up the steps to the front door, announcing who he was and why he was there. Forrest said from behind the door, "It's alright, you've got me. Come in." The deputy found Forrest barricaded inside his home and armed with two pistols.

Other, less reliable accounts reported that before the deputy arrived, Forrest had charged out onto his porch with a pistol in each hand ordering the crowd to disperse and threatening that he would "shoot all their damned heads off."[23]

Shaw and Forrest decided it was prudent to stay inside Forrest's home for the night and attempt to make their way to the steamboat landing at Friar's Point the next morning. By sunup the crowd had dispersed and the two men, one a prisoner, made their way to the landing and boarded a steamboat bound for Memphis.

Having managed to come thus far without incident must have been cause for Deputy Shaw to breathe a sigh of relief. However, they soon realized that they had boarded a steamer filled with Union troops who might well take exception to sharing their vessel with the notorious Forrest. Expecting trouble, Bedford advised Shaw not to divulge his identity. However, Forrest's reputation was national, and his face was easily recognized. Before long the Federal soldiers discovered the identity of their famed fellow passenger, and though neither Shaw nor Forrest knew what to expect, the Yankee troops surprised them. "Instead of being insulted by them he was very much honored and lionized. Nothing on the boat was too good for him. They were dined and championed." Upon learning the reason Forrest was aboard the boat, some of the Federal troops even offered to throw Shaw into the river to help the general to escape. Forrest declined their kind offer, and the rest of the trip went without incident.

On April 11, 1866, the Coahoma Circuit Court indicted Forrest, stating the "aforesaid did willfully and of malice aforethought . . . kill and murder a certain free man of color commonly known and called by the name of Thomas Edwards." On the twentieth, the

*Coahomian* reported, "General Forrest was arraigned for the homicide of a colored free-man on his plantation a few weeks before, and was admitted to bail in the sum of $10,000 for his appearance at the next term of [the] Circuit Court."[24]

Forrest's trial was set for October 8, but first the city of Memphis would face its own trial—a trial by fire. In 1860, the black population in Memphis had been approximately eight thousand. By the spring of 1866, it had more than doubled. Many of these new residents were unemployed and often confused by their new relationships with the white population. Ex-Confederate and Unionist alike despised the armed black refugees roaming their streets and competing for the jobs exclusively reserved for the white population of the white-ruled city. Memphis had become a racial powder keg, as had many other Southern cities. Circumstances existed for an explosion of racial violence that, when it finally came, stunned North and South alike and shook the foundations of the newly reformed Union.

On May 1, 1866, Memphis erupted in a bloody race riot. Similar riots broke out across the South. From April through July in Norfolk, Virginia, Memphis, Tennessee, Charleston, South Carolina, and New Orleans, Louisiana, the former Confederacy teetered on the edge of racial Armageddon. In terms of casualties, the riots of the nineteenth century were much more violent than those in Watts and Los Angeles a century later. The riots of the twentieth century were often estimated in terms of monetary loss. As far as the cost in human lives, the riots in southern California paled by comparison to their Southern antecedents in 1866.

In Memphis on the afternoon of May 1 two horse-drawn wagons collided. One was driven by a white man, the other by a black man. When an altercation broke out the police, comprised primarily of white Unionists and ex-Confederate Irishmen, responded and promptly arrested the black man. A crowd of black ex-soldiers who had just been paid as they mustered out of the service from Fort Pickering gathered in protest. Word had it that many of the participants on both sides had been drinking or were outright drunk.

Suddenly, shots rang out, leaving two men dead in the street, one white and one black. Scores of black troops and white police and firemen joined in the melee. Soon the scene escalated into battle. The *Memphis Avalanche* reported two days later that "it was a war." The Irish-American mayor was said to be as drunk as the mob and basically did nothing. The sheriff of Shelby County deputized a one-hundred-man posse, which was joined by many more citizens who decided of their own accord to help the sheriff. The imbalance in firepower was overwhelming since several of the black troops had turned in their weapons before mustering out of the service. Many of the blacks were armed, but they were severely outgunned. The posse-mob attacked the blacks where they found them and eventually decided to invade the shantytown in south Memphis where most of the black population lived. The scene was horrendous as the white mob charged into south Memphis. The original incident, by then over two days old, was forgotten in the blood lust and racial hatred that had been ready to explode for months. The killing stopped when Mayor John Park sent Gen. George Stoneman and 150 militia troops to quell the violence. When it was finally over, forty-six blacks and two whites were dead, including two women and two children, with scores of people wounded. Five black women had been raped; hundreds of dwellings, churches, and schools were burned and destroyed.

Even worse mayhem broke out in New Orleans two months later with thirty-four blacks killed and over 100 wounded. The scenes of carnage in New Orleans were so disturbing that they prompted Hannibal Hamlin, the son of the former vice president, to write, "The wholesale slaughter and the little regard paid to human life I witnessed here surpassed anything I have seen on the battlefield."[25]

The riots could not have occurred at a worse time for President Johnson and his conciliatory policies toward the South. Conservative Radical Republicans such as Secretary of State William H. Seward and his allies in New York in conjunction with the Northern press began to turn the tide. "With moderates backing a program since the south's rejection of the 14th Amendment, radicals moved to seize the legislative initiative."[26]

Fear of a new rebel uprising gripped the North as the news kept pouring in concerning the racial violence blazing across the South. What seemed to have been forgotten was that the New York Draft Riots of 1863 had been as bad as what was now occurring in the South. The riots in New York in July 1863 occurred only a few days after the battle of Gettysburg. With barely any time to recover from one of the bloodiest battles of the war, Union troops had been quickly transported into New York by rail to quell the riot and stop the killing. In a perverse twist of fate, these Union troops found themselves attempting to stop white New Yorkers from killing the blacks for whose freedom they had just fought in Pennsylvania against white Southerners. As Shelby Foote once said, "It was a very strange war."

The racial violence and chaos would continue for years to come, demonstrating the impotence of the Reconstruction Act of 1867, which divided the ex-Confederate states into five military districts. It also demonstrated the failure of Union martial law to provide protection and order for Southern society. Lawlessness and fear swept across the South like a prairie fire, leaving many willing to accept help from any quarter.

The next decade would be marred by more lawlessness and bloodshed. For an example of how wild the times were one need only look at the tragedy that occurred in Colfax, Louisiana, a full eight years after the war ended. Had there been any vestige of law and order provided by the government through the use of local militia, what transpired in Colfax might not have happened. The fact that it did occur, and that similar incidents had been occurring for more than five years, evidenced that there was absolutely no control or protection in many cases. It should not be surprising that facing a society gone wild, organized vigilante movements such as the Ku Klux Klan sprang up all across the South. In retrospect, rampant vigilantism was probably inevitable.

The Colfax incident began when a controversy in the Louisiana election of 1872 produced rival claimants for the governorship, and freedmen in Grant Parish took up arms, fearing Democrats would seize the government. Under the leadership of black war veterans and militia officers, they barricaded the county seat of Colfax and began digging trenches. For three weeks they held their position against whites armed with new Winchester repeating rifles, revolvers, and one cannon. On Easter Sunday, the blacks were overrun and an indiscriminant slaughter followed, including the murder of some fifty men who surrendered under a flag of truce. John G. Lewis, a black legislator and teacher wrote, "They attempted armed self-defense in Colfax. The result was that on Easter Sunday of 1873, when the sun went down that night, it went down on the corpses of two hundred and eighty Negroes."[27]

For the time being, Forrest awaited his trial through the spring and summer of 1866. Things were not going well on his plantation. After posting the ten-thousand-dollar bond and selling off fifteen hundred acres, he began sharecropping on the land he had previously owned. He was in debt twenty thousand dollars to L. F. Beech of Nashville. The firm of Tate, Gill and Able handled the note, and with the bond amount tacked on, that note had reached thirty thousand dollars by April.

Forrest's bond was guaranteed by friends R. C. Brinkley and Frazier Titus, who were also prominent citizens of Memphis. Bedford had promised to pay Beech in eight $2,500 installments. If he could not meet the debt, his remaining nineteen hundred acres were to be auctioned off under the supervision of J. P. Strange. Unfortunately, Forrest's fortunes continued to decline and he eventually lost the remainder of his property.[28]

By the beginning of the summer, Forrest's crops were in danger of being ruined by the flooding of the Mississippi River. The levees had been seriously damaged during the war and could not hold back the rising water. By August he said, "I have sold my plantation in the bottom and if allowed think of making my home again in Memphis." When Forrest mentions he would move to Memphis "if allowed," he was referring to the restriction placed on him by his terms of parole.[29]

During the month of September, Forrest apparently was thinking about his death and legacy. He took out a ten-thousand-dollar life insurance policy with his wife as the sole beneficiary. About the same time he also decided he would like to record his wartime exploits and wrote to former Mississippi governor Charles Clark, "I am collecting materials for the compilation of a correct history of the operations of the cavalry serving under my orders during the war, and would be pleased to receive from you any assistance your convenience may allow you to render."[30]

As his murder trial began on October 8, 18667, the pressure on Forrest was unrelenting. The testimony during the trial was contradictory, with even Thomas Edwards' wife stating that Forrest attacked her husband without provocation. However, the overwhelming testimony to the contrary outweighed all the prosecution's evidence. The jury found that "although the defendant may have struck the first blow with the broomstick," they believed that Edwards had meant Forrest "great bodily injury," and four days after the trial began, the jury found him "not guilty in manner and form as charged in the indictment."[31]

Forrest also received an interesting endorsement from Captain Collins of the Freedman's Bureau, who had traveled up from Vicksburg to do his own investigation. Collins' report spoke in glowing terms of how Forrest ran his plantation. The *Avalanche* reported that Collins "expressed himself highly pleased with General Forrest's management of the freedmen on his land, saying that his plantation, in all its details of comfort, hours of labor and recreation had excelled any plantation in advantage of the freedmen, he had seen." Then

Collins said something concerning the supervision of the ex-slave workers that would seem to contradict everything history has led us to believe about Forrest with respect to his racist attitudes. As strange as it may sound, Forrest was accused of being too liberal and indulgent with the freedmen on his plantations. Collins was amazed at the scale of pay at Forrest's operation, saying that he has made financial "advances of too liberal a character" and he could not believe that Forrest allowed them "to purchase and carry firearms." Collins went on to conclude that he did not think the ex-slaves could handle the type of freedom and personal responsibility that Forrest was granting them and recommended that he no longer tolerate armed employees on his land. The report further suggested that this relaxed manner and forbearing treatment of the blacks on his farm and plantation was an aggravating factor in the death of Thomas Edwards.[32]

As 1866 drew to a close Forrest was involved in another business venture and traveled to Little Rock to begin the construction of the Memphis-Little Rock Railroad, which he had contracted to grade. There was an irony in this reversal in association with the railroad business, as his most recent railroad work involved their destruction. This irony was not lost on Forrest, for he said upon his arrival in Little Rock that he had come "to reverse his general practice, and build up instead of destroying railroads."[33]

On November 25, Forrest applied once again for parole and pled his case to Pres. Andrew Johnson. He also enclosed with his letter an endorsement from Frank Blair concerning his pledge "to submit to the Constitutional authority of the United States" and explaining how he had "remained faithful to his parole." Forrest desperately needed to be able to travel beyond the constraints of his parole and to acquire a thousand freedmen as laborers.

Oliver Otis Howard, the new director of the Freedman's Bureau who knew Forrest only by reputation, eventually provided the workers. During the war Howard had been a major general who commanded two corps under Sherman through the Nashville and Atlanta campaigns.[34] In December, Howard wrote the commissioner of the Freedman's Bureau in Arkansas that he believed Forrest "is disposed to do everything that is fair and right for the negroes which may be employed." However, Howard had reservations about Forrest that motivated him to add that the commissioner should "select a capable, discreet officer" to keep an eye on Forrest and his operation.[35] Forrest would have defined such an officer as a spy, but he was in no position to object to any strings attached to the deal.

In the meantime, Forrest hoped his appeal to President Johnson might win his amnesty, allowing him unfettered movement in the pursuit of his business dealings. He recognized in his letter to the president that his notoriety arising from the Fort Pillow controversy created political problems for Johnson, for which he was sympathetic, but he continued to argue his case eloquently.

Forrest included in his letter to the president a copy of Brig. Gen. Frank Blair's letter to his brother, former cabinet member Montgomery Blair, which he hoped would carry some weight. In this letter Blair covered some of the same ground he had in his *Memphis Avalanche* article, stating that "prejudice against him [Forrest] on account of Fort Pillow" was unfounded. His reference to Forrest's character commended him for "his courage," which "on more than a hundred battlefields, ought to convince any man that he is incapable of the dastardly outrage alleged against him." It might appear that Blair was overstating Forrest's case, but there was no doubt that his remarks were sincere. He wrote, Forrest's "noble bearing . . . in accepting without complaint the results of a disastrous war, and using his powerful influence to make others accept it in the same spirit, has inspired me with respect and admiration." Blair's letter concluded, "Forrest will probably write to you . . . and I hope you will aid him . . . to obtain his objects."[36]

Forrest's own letter to the president reads as follows:

> I am . . . aware that I am at this moment regarded in large communities in the north with abhorrence, as a detestable monster, ruthless and swift to take life, and guilty of unpardonable crimes in connection with the capture of Fort Pillow, on the twelfth day of April, 1864 Perhaps, at a time of political excitement so fierce and high as at present, this misjudgment of my conduct and character should not surprise me; nevertheless, it pains and mortifies me greatly; yet, if any good can be wrought from it, I am still willing to rest for a time longer under this heavy wounding weight of undeserved obloquy, without any attempt at that perfect justification before the world, of my course as a soldier and commander in the storming of Fort Pillow, which I am satisfied I can make to the conviction of all fair minded people, and in complete refutation, of the ex parte proceedings of the congressional committee, with their manifestly leading questions and willing witnesses whose prompted evidence should, thenceforward, mislead no one. I have, however, to appeal to the judgment of your excellency, in this regard, and to invoke

your advice as to my present course, and especially, whether the time is propitious or inauspicious, for an attempt on my part to throw off the load of these widely believed and injurious calamities; and I have presumed to make this appeal from a sincere desire to do nothing that shall in least contribute to those sectional animosities which now rend the country. . . . Struggling as you are, with an appalling army of forces hostile to constitutional, regulated liberty, I have been unwilling to ask you for the amnesty which I felt your own sense of right had disposed you to grant me, much as it was desirable for the proper conduct of my greatly involved private fortunes. I have preferred to endure those private embarrassments rather than to give your vindictive enemies an opportunity to misrepresent your motives were you to grant my amnesty. In conclusion, I . . . shall continue to do all that I can to assuage ill-feeling and promote a spirit of moderation and accommodation. . . . I will say further that should your excellency deem it as likely to subserve the purposes of pacification, I would even waive all immunity from investigation into my conduct at Fort Pillow that might attach to my parole. I have the honor to remain your Excellency's obedient servant. N.B. Forrest.[37]

Johnson quickly granted the extension for Forrest but predictably did not go as far as to grant Forrest amnesty. The president stated that Forrest had become a "model example of what the true restorationist of the South should be."[38]

## Forrest and Brownlow

To praise Forrest as "a true restorationist" might have been stretching things a bit. While the North was experiencing a period of unprecedented prosperity, economic devastation stalked Forrest and the South. With the state of affairs in Tennessee approaching a showdown between the ex-Confederates and the new Radical Republican governor, it would not be long before his unreconstructed nature would reassert itself.

William G. Brownlow was elected the first governor of a free Tennessee in March 1865. He would become Forrest's nemesis during Reconstruction much as Sherman had been during the war. Brownlow came to the governorship of Tennessee with an antisecessionist and Confederate-hating pedigree. His reputation had been established long before, however, as a combative Methodist minister and editor of the *Knoxville Whig*, a newspaper he used to attack any and all he considered to be his enemies, be they "democrats, abolitionists, Presbyterians," or, with the coming of secession, rebels. Already known as "the Fighting Parson" for his many crusading forays against enemies real or imagined, he assaulted secessionists and Confederate supporters with renewed zeal and kept up the attack even after Knoxville and east Tennessee came under occupation by Confederate troops.

In one of his vituperative editorials printed in the February 16, 1861, edition of the *Knoxville Whig*, he declared, "I would as soon be engaged in importing the plague from the East as in helping to build up a Southern Confederacy upon the ruins of the American Constitution."[39] That he was allowed to continue such editorial attacks for so long suggests that the Confederacy had not totally abandoned the American Constitution; freedom of speech remained intact. But when Brownlow refused to give his allegiance to the Confederate government, he became persona non grata in Tennessee and had to seek refuge with a group of North Carolina Unionists along the border between the two states.

Lured back to Knoxville by a promise of safe conduct to the north, he was arrested and briefly jailed. In a letter to Judah Benjamin, Confederate secretary of state, Brownlow challenged the government to let him go. "Just give me my passport, and I will do more for your confederacy than the devil has ever done—I will leave the country."[40]

He was allowed to move to the North in March 1862, where he became a very popular lecturer supporting the Unionist cause, especially in east Tennessee. Few in his sympathetic audiences across the North blanched at the reflection in his speeches of the bitter hatred between Unionist and Confederate that infected east Tennessee. He might have been speaking to Northerners, but his message was aimed at the Confederates, particularly those in his home state. In 1864, Brownlow wrote that he would arm "every wolf, panther, catamount, and bear in the mountains of America . . . every rattlesnake and crocodile . . . every devil in Hell and turn them loose upon the Confederacy if that's what it took to win the war."[41]

Brownlow was a man of strong partisan sentiment beneath which seethed a vengeful impulse toward anything and anyone tinged by the recent rebellion. This impulse toward retribution was partly a result of the treatment he had received from the Confederate occupation troops during the war. As governor of Tennessee he had the kind of political power he had never been able to wield in other quixotic campaigns, and he intended to use it. His harsh Reconstruction administration wasted no time declaring martial law and beginning a relentless persecution of former Confederates. To Brownlow it was the Confederate traitors who had brought the war down upon his state, and his regime moved swiftly to assert that Tennessee's Union loyalists could not be blamed if they sought to settle scores by exacting an "eye for an eye."

This was just the sort of attitude that riled a man like Forrest and got his blood up. By 1867, Forrest was no longer willing to remain the silent, content Reconstructionist, especially with his new antagonist aggravating the situation. As he saw it, "Parson Brownlow" and many other professed abolitionists had owned slaves and were no better than the worst kind of hypocrites. In fact Brownlow had been a prominent defender of slavery before the war, and his attitude toward the freedmen remained transparent as he even suggested in October 1865 that it was bad policy to give them the right to vote.

Bedford, along with a majority of Democratic Southerners, believed that the black population of Memphis, and indeed the South, had become pawns of the new radical government. Support for that belief came soon after Brownlow assumed the Tennessee governorship, when he urged Congress to carve up and set aside territory from ex-Confederate-owned lands for a new "nation of freedmen."[42] Admitting to a bit of "caste prejudice," Brownlow, nevertheless, felt it best to move the process along by being in concord with the majority of those loyal to the Union.

Such language caused concern not only among former Confederates. Many Northern politicians shared an assumption that if the former slaves were enfranchised, they would vote with their former owners. Some Northern politicians even openly questioned the Federal policy toward the freedmen and wished to be rid of the blacks altogether. Regarding this position Governor Brownlow said, "It's hard to tell which they [the Republican Unionists] hate most, the Rebels or the Negroes."[43]

As far as one particular rebel was concerned, it was not hard to tell which he hated most. The verbal war that arose between Brownlow and Forrest in 1868 made it clear where Forrest stood. Speaking to a crowd at the Democratic convention held in Brownsville on August 11, Forrest said,

> I can assure you, fellow citizens, that I for one do not want any more war . . . nor do I want to see Negroes armed to shoot down

white men. If they bring this war upon us, there is one thing I will tell you: that I shall not shoot any Negroes so long as I can see a white radical to shoot, for it is the radicals who will be to blame for bringing on this war.[44]

Forrest was not the first to sense the possibility of a renewed war. Southerners saw convincing evidence all around them that the conditions thrust upon them by Reconstruction were in many ways worse than those that had impelled them to rebellion in 1861. The dread of this looming storm spoken of by Forrest gave birth to the Ku Klux Klan and the invisible empire within which it operated. What followed became an intrastate war that would rip the social fabric of Tennessee apart. As Stanley Horn wrote, "Here was dropped into the pool the pebble whose ripples spread so far."[45]

## The Birth of the Invisible Empire

Across the silver screen came the nightriders, a blur of galloping apparitions, white robes snapping in their wake. Revolutionary filmmaker D. W. Griffith had taken Dr. Thomas Dixon's novel, *The Clansman: An Historical Romance of the Ku Klux Klan,* and transformed it into a classic of the new art form of light and shadows. America was left spellbound by Griffith's cinematic adaptation, which he called *The Birth of a Nation.* The book had appeared in 1905, but the film version, released in 1915, set the stage for the resurrection of the Ku Klux Klan and transformed the hooded mystery men into legends of Southern folklore.

On Thanksgiving night 1915, William Simmons, son of a Klansman, led a group of men to the top of Stone Mountain, just outside Atlanta, Georgia. Once atop what would become the Mount Rushmore of the South, they fired a burning cross in a ritual of mistaken symbolism—mistaken in the sense that the Klan of the Reconstruction never burned crosses. Dixon's novel and Griffith's film had revived an ancient practice from the Scottish highlands. Griffith, apparently impressed by the scenes in Dixon's book describing midnight meetings with groups of hooded ghouls gathered in circles around signal fires, recognized the cinematic possibilities.

In 1915, Rev. Thomas Dixon, author of the book, wrote to Pres. Woodrow Wilson requesting an audience with his old classmate from Johns Hopkins University. On February 18, Wilson received Dixon and Griffith into the White House for a showing in the East Room. Griffith's extraordinary mastery of cinematic technique was displayed before the president, the Secretary of the Navy Josephus Daniels, and Chief Justice Edward D. White. Before the film began, Chief Justice White leaned over and said to Dixon, "I was a member of the Klan, Sir. Through many a dark night I walked a sentinel's beat through the ugliest streets in New Orleans with a rifle on my shoulder." In anticipation, the Chief Justice inquired, "You've told the true story of that uprising of outraged manhood?" Dixon replied, "I'm sure you'll approve."

If Chief Justice White anticipated a sympathetic rendering of his former brotherhood, he was not disappointed. The groundbreaking film championed the Klan. It also established a Hollywood adage— "Tell a good story and don't let history get in the way." When the film flickered into darkness and the lights came on President Wilson was quoted in the press as having said, "It's like history written in lightning. And my only regret is that it is all so terribly true."[46]

Life, it seems, does imitate art, and so it was that over the next ten years, 1915-25, the Klan spread nationwide, becoming an army of over half a million. Riding the post-World War I wave of intolerance and fear, the Klan was generally viewed as a superpatriotic organization. It was the time of the Red Scare and the passage of antievolution laws in some states that banned teachers from presenting Darwin's theories in the classroom. Oppression plagued labor, and restrictions on immigration were growing increasingly severe. In this environment the growth of the Klan was phenomenal, its tentacles eventually reaching all the way into the nation's highest offices.

With the endorsement of numerous and powerful intellectuals, Dixon and Griffith had supplied white America with a fabulous, self-serving history. Of course, they did not invent these celluloid myths. It took civil war and Reconstruction to create the prototypical Ku Klux Klansman, but Dixon and Griffith made them accessible to millions. And they made them unforgettable. However, when the original Klan began in Pulaski, Tennessee, in May 1866, its founders were all Confederate veterans. They all came from good families, all were well educated for the times, and none of them was Nathan Bedford Forrest.

The myth of Nathan Bedford Forrest as the founding father of the Ku Klux Klan has been perpetuated to the extent that it is now accepted as fact. However, contrary to popular belief, Forrest did not originate the Klan, nor had he anything to do with its formation. For an accurate understanding of how the Klan came into being, the psychology of the times must be considered. The South's postwar paranoia was practically pathological. With militant Loyal Leagues of armed blacks roaming the countryside, encouraged by the

Freedman's Bureau to demand their rights, white Southerners resumed a two-century-old practice of nocturnal patrolling. Originally designed to police the slaves, these night-riding detachments now took to the night out of desperation to force them back into the fields to work the land and save the economy.

Incredibly, the Ku Klux Klan at its beginning was merely a small clique of bored war veterans perhaps looking for some excitement, but it was also true that their actions would not remain innocent for long. In early 1866, six young, college-educated former rebels who lived in Pulaski, Tennessee, not far below Nashville, gathered around a fireplace reminiscing about the war. They were Capt. John C. Lester, Capt. John B. Kennedy, Capt. James R. Crowe, Capt. Frank O. McCord, Richard Reed, and J. Calvin Jones. Late into the night they talked of a society cloaked in secrecy. Even their chosen name was mysterious. As the story goes, they decided upon the name of a Southern college fraternity, Kappa Alpha, or Kuklos Adelphon. Kuklos is the Greek word for circle, which they altered to the stranger sounding Ku Klux. Later they added the word Klan for phonetic purposes and perhaps because the members were predominately of Scots-Irish descent. It was also said that the sound of the words reminded them of bones rattling in a sack.

In imagination the group certainly excelled. Within a few days they donned Halloween-like costumes and mounted up for the first official ride of the Ku Klux Klan. Charging through the streets of Pulaski, they startled the citizens with their bizarre display. They also made quite an impression on the black population.

Soon they designed even more elaborate costumes and created an organizational rank structure. The titles for the various positions of responsibility were straight out of a medieval fantasy. Their meeting places became dens; the den leader would be a Grand Cyclops. His second in command was the Grand Magi, and the secretary, the Grand Scribe. Messengers were called nighthawks, and rank and file members were labeled ghouls.

For the time being, the marauders stuck with their burlesque-style raiding parties. They were soon being described as the "ghosts of the Confederate dead" due to the dramatic performances featuring a little magic to complement the terror they caused. On several occasions, in the dark of night, freedmen saw headless horsemen galloping by their farms. Ghost riders, with large bladders hidden under their robes, would suddenly appear at a chosen victim's home and demand a bucket of water to quench their thirst. The performing

Klansman would then proceed to drink the entire bucket of water, which of course, was flowing into the concealed container. Once finished, the ghoul would smack his lips and say something like, "That's the first drink I've had since I was killed at the battle of Shiloh, and you get mighty thirsty in Hell."[47]

These pranks and the recruitment of new members were the primary activities in the first few months. The recruits were kept in the dark, literally, as they were first blindfolded and taken to a secret initiation site for the formal swearing-in process. The group also grew quickly because one of the original six members, Frank O. McCord, was the editor of the Pulaski newspaper, the *Citizen*. McCord was also the Grand Cyclops in Giles County. His numerous editorials concerning the Klan's activities were great publicity.

One of the newest members was Brig. Gen. George W. Gordon, who had been captured in the center of Hood's line during the great charge at Franklin. Gordon was also an attorney. It was common for the Klan during its infancy to draw into its ranks men of standing in their communities. Usually they were men who had served in the Confederate army and who saw the political possibilities of the Klan in combating Brownlow's repressive regime.

Through late 1866 until the winter of 1867, the Klan outgrew the boundaries of Pulaski and Giles County. It was the start of something that the founders could not have foreseen. From these seeds would grow a force of underground regulators that would forever alter the image of the entire South. As the Klan evolved into its next stage of development, the leaders began to lose control. The rapid expansion had been too quick and their mission too vague to provide adequate discipline and direction. With no real agenda or criteria for membership, it was not long before "rash and imprudent men had gotten into the order."[48]

To date the Klan had spread its message through Frank McCord's newspaper, the *Citizen*. Couriers would place messages behind a loose brick in a wall of McCord's newspaper building, just across a narrow alleyway from General Gordon's law office in Pulaski. McCord would retrieve the messages and then publish them. He stated that his source was a confidential informant, a mysterious figure dressed in robes who delivered his messages at the midnight hour and then disappeared into the misty Tennessee night. The public was intrigued and the word spread.[49]

It was not long before other newspapers throughout the South began publishing McCord's articles from the *Pulaski Citizen*.

Inquiries poured in requesting more information on the under-ground movement in Giles County. The political potential of the Klan was becoming apparent and the need for reorganization and control was urgent.

Pulaski was the home of two Confederate generals: George W. Gordon and John C. Brown. Gordon, credited with writing the first prescript for the Klan, became involved early on. Brown, the brother of the antebellum governor of Tennessee and elected governor him-self in 1870, was politically connected. Evidence indicates that these two men stepped in to provide leadership in the spring of 1867.[50]

A meeting was set for April 3, 1867. The gathering of Klan officials from several states took place at the Maxwell House Hotel in Nashville. Rumors circulating had it that at an earlier date General Gordon had traveled to Memphis, where he was soon to open his new law office, and approached Forrest concerning the Klan and the possibility of attending the meeting in Nashville. Upon hearing what Gordon had to say, Forrest reportedly said, "That's a good thing; that's a damn good thing. We can use that to keep the n——— in their place."[51]

Gordon supposedly advised Forrest to seek out his former chief of artillery, John Morton, who had organized the Klan in Clarksville and was the acting Grand Cyclops of the Nashville den. If this scenario is true, it is more than coincidental that Forrest was in Nashville on the day of the meeting at the Maxwell House. In his book, written in 1909, Morton gives his account of how Forrest approached him. The facts concerning the means by which Forrest became involved in the Klan are sketchy at best. There are a few different versions, but the most reliable account does come from Captain Morton.

"When the rumors of the Ku Klux Klan first spread over Tennessee," Morton wrote, "General Forrest was quick to see its possibilities." He went on to describe spotting Forrest on the streets in Nashville, where the former Confederate general approached him and said, "John, I hear this Ku Klux Klan is organized in Nashville, and I know you are in it. I want to join." Morton continued in the third person,

> The young man avoided the issue and took his Commander for a ride. General Forrest persisted in his questions about the Klan and Morton kept smiling and changing the subject. General Forrest was somewhat vexed and swore a little: "Didn't I tell you that's what I came up here for?" Smiling at the idea of giving orders to his erstwhile commander, Captain Morton said: "Well, get out of the buggy." General Forrest stepped out of the buggy, and next received the order: "Hold up your right hand."

General Forrest did as he was ordered, and Captain Morton
solemnly administered the oath of the order. As he was finished
taking the oath General Forrest said: "John, that's the worst
swearing in that I ever did hear."

Following the impromptu ceremony, Morton took Forrest over to
meet his new fiancée. Morton reported that he overheard Forrest
say to his future wife, "Miss Annie, if you get John Morton, you take
him. I know him. He'll take care of you."

"That night the General was made a full fledged clansman, and
was soon elected Grand Wizard of the Invisible Empire."[52]

Forrest never signed the hotel registry on April 3, but neither did
several others who possibly attended the meeting. One of those who
did log in was Gen. George G. Dibrell of Forrest's old command,
who either was or would soon become the Grand Titan. Another of
the members present that day was James R. Crowe. Crowe had been
quoted as saying,

> After the order grew to large numbers, we found it necessary to
> have someone of large experience to command us. So we chose
> General N. B. Forrest. . . . He was made a member and took the
> oath in room number 10 at the Maxwell House . . . in the fallof
> 1866. The oath was administered to him by Captain J. W. Morton.[53]

Morton remembers the location of Forrest's swearing in, and either
Crowe or Morton was mistaken about the meeting being in the fall
rather than in the spring of 1866. Perhaps it was a misprint. However,
another member at the Maxwell House that day was Judge J. P. Young,
who also verified Forrest's initiation and promotion to Grand Wizard.

Later in the meeting, Young was reported to have read a letter
from Robert E. Lee concerning the Klan. Klan lore has it that Lee
was offered the leadership of the organization but declined, stating
that his health would preclude him from accepting the position. Lee
supposedly gave them his support but told them that the group
needed to be invisible. At this meeting they adopted his suggestion
and henceforth they would be the Invisible Empire. When Lee was
asked about Forrest as the second choice for commander of the
Klan, Lee reportedly said, "There is no man in the South who can
handle so large a body of men successfully. Will you pay my respects
to the General and tell him I hope he will accept."[54]

Before the meeting at the Maxwell House was adjourned, the
group ratified its new prescript. Maj. Gen. John B. Gordon, one of

Lee's most trusted generals, composed it longhand in his office at Pulaski. Nowhere in their Democratic-sounding constitution is the title Ku Klux Klan used in print. In each place those words would have appropriately appeared the author replaced the title of the organization with an asterisk. The prescript said nothing about the Klan's function or purpose but displayed its general air of mystery. The document continued by setting forth an elaborate military-style rank structure detailing each officer's duties and responsibilities. There were also revenue provisions along with an oath of secrecy for new members that held them under the threat of death.

Sometime in 1868, the prescript was revised and became more explicit about the Klan's purpose. It also added a series of ten questions each man was required to answer before he was admitted. These ten questions provided some insight into the group's expectations, which the prescript left unmentioned. The new recruits had to swear that they had never belonged to the Radical Republican Party; that they had never taken up arms against the Confederacy during the war; that they were opposed to Negro equality, either social or political; and that they favored reenfranchisement for white Southerners. There was also a new mission statement:

> This is an instrument of Chivalry, Humanity, Mercy, and Patriotism; embodying in its genius and its principles all that is chivalric in conduct, noble in sentiment, generous to the innocent, and the defenseless, from the indignities, wrongs, and outrages of the lawless, the violent, and the brutal; to relieve and assist the injured, oppressed, suffering, and unfortunate, especially widows and orphans of Confederate soldiers; and to support the United States Constitution and Constitutional Laws.[55]

Considering what the organization later degenerated into, it would be hard to imagine a more idealized description of the Klan. However, those men responsible for writing and enforcing the regulations did not intend for the Klan to become a brutal and lawless organization and, in many cases, attempted to prevent overt acts of violence. In fact they thought of themselves as champions of the cause and guardians of the people against Governor Brownlow's political oppression. Nevertheless, very soon they lost any semblance of control, and the terrorism escalated over the next few months.

It is probably no coincidence that this reorganization meeting took place in the wake of the Reconstruction Act passed by Congress on March 2, 1867. Of course, Tennessee had already reentered the Union following the 1866 ratification of the Fourteenth Amendment, but by franchise only. The other Confederate states were divided into five military districts under the rule of Union soldiers and sworn militia stationed within their respective borders.

Tennessee governor Brownlow, nemesis of Forrest and the Klan, vowed in the spring of 1867 to enforce the Disfranchisement Law to the extent that if "it becomes necessary that there shall be bloodshed and violence, so be it." Some believed the rumors that Brownlow would sanction the "forty acres and a mule" dictum for the freedmen by carving up the plantations owned by wealthy ex-Confederates. The Union League and Loyal Leagues had been demanding this and other kinds of retribution for some time.

The issue of how to deal with such a large number of former slaves went beyond the boundary of the Mason-Dixon line. For many intellectuals in the North and for men like Robert E. Lee in Virginia, where the Klan and Klan-related violence never took root as it did in other parts of the South, the problem was a philosophical one. But in Tennessee, for all intents and purposes, it was a war.[56]

Tennessee had become a dark and forbidding domain inhabited by men with a hair-trigger mentality. Later that spring, with the paranoia running at a fever pitch, Forrest met with Minor Meriwether, an ex-Confederate general, Gov. Isham G. Harris, Gen. John Gordon from Georgia, and the editor of the *Avalanche*, a Mr. Galloway, at Meriwether's home in Memphis. Lee Meriwether, the son of General Meriwether, wrote the account of the meeting in his memoirs, *My Yesterdays*, in which he said that several of his "father's friends had come to visit one night to discuss the Ku Klux Klan and how it might save Memphis from bankruptcy." It seems to have been agreed upon by those in the meeting that "the only hope of averting the bankruptcy was in the Ku Klux Klan."

Young Meriwether, in his words, continued by summarizing the general consensus of those in attendance that night. The opinion was that "ignorant ex-slaves, elected to city councils and state legislatures, and dominated by carpetbaggers who had come from the north to plunder the South, voted millions of dollars for bonds for which little or no value was received." Adding to the problem were the federal courts, "who ordered mayors of cities to levy taxes big enough to pay 100 cents on the dollar." This unlikely scenario could have forced the city of Memphis to sell or auction off all its municipal property, including the public parks and firehouses.

Meriwether said the party wrapped up with those present concluding that their only alternative was for the Klan to escalate its
"midnight parades as Ghosts" to drive the blacks away from the voting booths, even at the cost of lives. Their thinking was that this
would in turn intimidate them from attempting to gain public office
and from issuing "hundreds of millions of bonds."[57]

Desperate times inevitably led to desperate measures. That went
for both sides. Brownlow's philosophy for handling the situation
and the "hated Rebels" amounted to putting out the fire by throwing gasoline on the flames. The stage was set for a head-on collision
on a grand, statewide scale in the tradition of Fort Pillow.

The meeting at the Meriwethers' provided another documented
source of information on Forrest's position and authority within the
Klan. Minor Meriwether's wife, Elizabeth Avery Meriwhether, later
became a published author herself. In her book, *Recollections of 92
Years, 1824-1916,* written when she was ninety-two, she recounted the
evening when Forrest sat in her parlor. Elizabeth Avery wrote that
she did "not know who first thought of the Ku Klux Klan, but I do
know that General Nathan Bedford Forrest, the great cavalry soldier
who lived near us on Union Street, was the Supreme Grand Wizard;
and Minor was one of his counselors and lieutenants."[58] Minor
Meriwhether verified that claim in 1909 while practicing law in St.
Louis. He stated that he had been the Grand Scribe under Forrest
and had handled all the official correspondence.[59]

The elections in the spring and summer of 1867 were compara-
tively peaceful due to the Klan's leadership and their defensive pos-
ture. Forrest consistently disapproved of Klan violence, except in
self-defense. However, with the outcome of the election, he knew
that more aggressive action would be required, and he had never
been a man to shrink from physical force.

On May 28, another meeting took place to plan for the Klan's first
major public demonstration, set for June 5 in Pulaski. By the time
the appointed date arrived, word had spread and hundreds of citizens gathered to view the parade. At 10:00 P.M. the parade moved
through the small city. The *Pulaski Citizen* had a reporter present
who had the following to say about the event:

> The crowd impatiently waited for their approach. A closer view
> discovered their banners and transparencies with all manner of
> mottoes and devices, speers [sic], sabers, &c. The column was led
> by what we supposed to be the Grand Cyclops, who had on a flow-
> ing white robe, a white hat about eighteen inches high. . . . The

master of ceremonies was gorgiously [*sic*] caparisoned, and his "toot, toot, toot," on a very graveyard-ish sounding instrument, seemed to be perfectly understood by every ku kluxer. . . . They conversed in dutch, hebrew, or some other language which we couldn't comprehend. No two of them were dressed alike, all having on masks and some sort of fanciful costume.[60]

The elaborate shows apparently did not have the desired affect, as the elections did not turn out as the Klan had hoped. They had foolishly assumed that their former slaves would vote the conservative Democratic ticket, but instead they voted overwhelmingly Republican. In Giles County, birthplace of the Klan, the black vote was particularly heavy for the Republicans, leaving Klan organizers bitter and frustrated over their failed campaign. From this time forward, the Klan's level of intimidation and violence began to escalate in a very systematic and brutal fashion.

The first part of 1868 would see unprecedented expansion on the part of the Invisible Empire throughout the entire South. This phenomenal growth was due in no small part to Forrest. In fact, it was remarkable that wherever Forrest turned up, his visits were immediately followed by the appearance of new Ku Klux Klan dens in those states. The original prescript for the Klan charged the duty of establishing new dens throughout the empire to the Grand Wizard, and his involvement as a member of the board of directors for the Southern Life Insurance Company (managed by Lt. Gen. Wade Hampton and Sen. Benjamin H. Hill) listed him as the general traveling agent. His railroad contracting business, along with the insurance agent position, guaranteed he would be traveling far and wide. A better means to spread the Klan's message could not have availed itself to Forrest at the time, and it appears that he took full advantage of the situation.

Business for the Southern Life Company took Forrest to Georgia in March of 1868. Coincidentally, the Georgia Grand Dragon, Gen. John B. Gordon, also employed by the Southern Life Insurance Company, was there at the same time. Soon after his arrival in Atlanta, the *Intelligencer* reported on March 4 that the Klan had officially arrived in the form of Nathan Bedford Forrest. "Headquarters Mystic Order of the Ku Klux Klan, Officer Grand Cyclops, Red Legion, Office of the Grand Cross of Mystery," read the headline of the notice in the *Intelligencer*. Then, in their characteristically dramatic style, which could rival Edgar Allan Poe's darkest imagery, the public bulletin continued by notifying Georgians that their champions had ridden to the rescue and things were about to change.

It was the same story in Aberdeen, Mississippi, and in northern Alabama, Arkansas, and South Carolina. Whether on insurance business or speculating for his railroad, it seemed that wherever Forrest appeared "it was generally found that he had sown the dragon's teeth of Ku Kluxism."[61]

Forrest's travel activities were by no means purely intended as camouflage. He was actually involved in both the insurance and railroad businesses. However, that was not the whole story. At least one source during that time took notice of Forrest's surreptitious moves. Capt. John G. Stokes, editor of the *Montgomery State Journal*, charged that Forrest's business endeavors were a

> sham and a subterfuge and that while he was going around the country stump-speaking, apparently for the purposes of furthering the prospects for his railroad he was engaged in organizing the Ku Klux Klan throughout the South preparatory to pushing the country into another rebellion.[62]

The Klan began to turn up the heat with more demonstrations and a belligerent public presence that often led to armed confrontation with the authorities. Ground zero for the coming bloodshed was Giles County, Tennessee. One Klansman remembered a speech given by Forrest at one of the den meetings that spring: "Brownlow says he will bring the militia down here and get us. I say, let him fetch 'em, and you boys be ready to receive 'em." Soon after this speech, either by Forrest's tacit consent or on direct order, forty disguised men on horseback rode to confront the sheriff in Memphis. Major Dubose, an ex-Confederate officer and attorney, led the company of horsemen into the center of town.

In full regalia they rode defiantly through the streets of Memphis all the way to police headquarters. The police force was armed and gathered in front of the building as the column of ghost riders approached. Unfazed, Maj. J. J. Dubose drew his detachment up in battle formation and moved to the front of the line. He saluted the chief of police, then drew a pistol in each hand and said, "Here are the genuine Ku Klux Klan for whose arrest your governor has offered a reward. Take us." This time the authorities blinked first. The chief replied, "You can go on."[63]

This demonstration and others to come were most likely in response to the headline "Terrorism in Tennessee," which appeared April 1 in the *Knoxville Whig*, which Brownlow still controlled. A year earlier he had called for militia, now he would request regular

Federal troops and send them to Columbia. On April 15, in a signed editorial, Brownlow warned the citizens of Maury County that troops would remain in place until "the disloyal, bushwhacking, jayhawking and murderous rebels learn lessons of moderation and acquire habits of decency."[64]

Forrest's public-political stance was hardening. In May, Forrest sent the following letter to the *Memphis Avalanche* just three days prior to Andrew Johnson's narrow escape from impeachment.

> Editors Avalanche-Gents: An influence is at work in this State, as I have discovered since my recent departure from Memphis, to preclude any participation by Confederate soldiers in the coming convention of the Democracy of Tennessee . . . and in the National Democratic Convention. Upon consultation with many of my late associates in the war, I have concluded to advise against any further political emasculation of ourselves in the party movements of the State. We are already sufficiently proscribed in the constitution and statutes which now govern the State, against our consent, the proscription of which have, through the mendacious hostility of our legislative enemies, been added to time and time again, until now we barely live under the accumulated weight of disfranchisement and oppression. Shall we super-add, by our own action, to those proscriptions and exorcisms of ourselves from all participation in the assemblies of the State and National Democracy, and publish to the world a confession that we are too unworthy to intrude ourselves into the councils of the party?
>
> . . . The only hope of a restoration of a good government in this country is in the success of the National Democracy in the next Presidential campaign. I trust my late comrades will not, from expediency or other motives, absent themselves from a participation in the political exercises, which are to result in the choice of standard bearers.[65]

On June 1, 1868, Forrest and forty-nine delegates were sent to the Nashville State Convention to air their grievances concerning the rights of freedmen. Among the delegates were Minor Meriwether, J. J. Dubose (Forrest's former adjutant), Harvey Mathis, and J. P. Strange. They believed that giving blacks the vote and the right to hold office would "destroy the peace, happiness and prosperity of both black and white races." The group of delegates also believed that there were seventy thousand disfranchised white Tennesseans "emphatically in favor of a white man's government and opposed to military despotism and the Negro supremacy of the Congressional plan for reconstruction."[66]

Later during the Nashville convention, on June 9, representatives from Tennessee pushed for Forrest's election as delegate-at-large to attend the coming National Democratic convention in New York. Of course, this nomination stirred up a hornet's nest of controversy among the Unionist delegates themselves. In an attempt to defuse the situation, Forrest addressed the convention. His speech was summarized in the *Avalanche:*

> He regretted very much that any excitement should have been raised on the subject of his nomination. . . . He was one of the first men who started to go out in the rebellion, though he had never voted for the State to go out of the Union. When the State did go out, he took up arms in the State's defense. . . . He did not mean to create any discord, but would insist that those who went out and fought this thing (in rebellion) were the representative men, and were entitled to a fair representation of the offices. [Cheers.] He was willing to withdraw his name. There was no position wherein he was not willing to work. He was willing to work in the saddle, in the lead, as the off horse, or at the wheels. [Laughter.] He had not come there for self-aggrandizement, but had come without any enemies to punish and no friends to reward. He had come to harmonize with the Federal soldier and the Union man. . . [Cheers.][67]

This speech did not end the debate, but Forrest's nomination would stand. In a *Memphis Avalanche* editorial the chairman of the convention, Edmund Cooper, was quoted by Matthew Galloway as saying, "his [Forrest's] nomination as a delegate for the state at large would produce incalculable injury to the Democracy in the approaching struggle."[68]

The Klan continued its heightened public presence that spring and summer with demonstrations and parades in Murfreesboro, Columbia, and Nashville. Lee and Elizabeth Meriwether recalled their amazement when the Ku Klux Klan, in full regalia, rode by their home on Union Street in Memphis.

> The Ku Klux Klan was organized by the best men of the South. Gen. Forrest was its Grand Wizard. Father was Supreme Counsellor; other ex-Confederates were its guiding spirits. I was a small boy when the Klan came into being; nevertheless I distinctly remember the first parade of "Ghosts" in Memphis. The horses' hooves were covered with burlap to deaden the noise as they filed through the streets at midnight. Hoods concealed the

ghosts' faces, and white gowns enveloped their bodies and reached below the stirrups. Occasionally a ghost stopped before a Negro shack and demanded water. The Negroes quickly learned that "ghosts" visited such of their race as molested Whites, and inflicted punishment ranging from flogging to hanging. As a result of this drastic treatment it became safe for white women to walk on the streets. No longer were they shoved into the gutters. Some evil things were done by the Klan—or in the name of the Klan—but those evils were more than offset by the good it did in saving the South from the disastrous rule of ex-slaves and "carpet baggers." Before that rule ended the debts of Southern cities and states reached astronomical heights. The ignorant Blacks whom the "carpet baggers" elected to city councils and to state legislatures voted millions of bonds, which were sold to the "carpet baggers" at a few cents on the dollar. Redemption of the bonds at even ten cents on the dollar would have bankrupted the cities and states, but that didn't worry the "carpet baggers." They demanded payment in full, even if a city could raise the money in no other way than by selling its parks and fire engines. When cities refused to pay, Federal Courts ordered them to pay and jailed city officials who failed to levy taxes high enough to pay off the bonds.[69]

When Forrest's travels finally took him up North to New York, newspapermen in that city were practically salivating in anticipation of the arrival of "That Devil Forrest." Above the Mason-Dixon line the name of Nathan Bedford Forrest was synonymous with the bogeyman. As one might expect, his trip to New York would be an eventful one.

One incident took place in mid-June while Forrest was traveling by train to New York with a group of Democratic delegates. It seems that in one of the small towns where the train stopped on its journey into the northeast, a local brawler bent on gaining a reputation was awaiting Forrest at the depot. Basil W. Duke of Kentucky, a fellow conventioneer, told the story. Apparently, a crowd had gathered along with the loud-talking ruffian who had promised to pull Forrest off the train and "thrash" him. When the train came to a stop, the conductor approached Forrest and suggested that he remain in his seat while he tried to defuse the situation. Duke also advised Forrest not to respond to the threats, which they could easily hear coming from outside the train car. Forrest agreed to stay in his seat, "being too much accustomed to affairs of that kind to become excited."

Suddenly, the bully burst into the compartment shouting, "Where's that damn butcher Forrest? I want him." Duke then went on to describe the transformation that came over Forrest, a transformation that was all too familiar to those men who had seen him in battle. Duke said that he had never in his life "witnessed such an instantaneous transformation in anyone's appearance" as "Forrest bounded from his seat." His body "was erect . . . , his face the colour of heated bronze, and his eyes flaming, blazing. He strode rapidly down the aisle toward the approaching antagonist, his gait and manner evincing perfect, invincible determination. 'I am Forrest,' he said. 'What do you want?'"

When the rowdy challenger got a good look at the "butcher" in the flesh, "his purpose evaporated." The complete lack of fear in Forrest's demeanor sent the man running back out of the car with Forrest in pursuit, shouting for the man to stop. However, stopping was the last thing he was about to do as he "darted into and down the street with quarterhorse speed, losing his hat in his hurry, and vanished around the corner." When the train pulled away from the water depot, Forrest stood on the rear platform "receiving the cheers and plaudits of the multitude."[70]

Upon his arrival in New York, the *New York Tribune* greeted Forrest with the taunting headline "Welcome the great hero of the Massacre of Fort Pillow." The next day, Forrest was confronted by an angry woman who appeared at his hotel room early in the morning. The Bible-toting matriarch pounded on the door of the room, awakening Forrest and his son, Willie. Willie answered the knocking and was immediately assaulted with demands to see General Forrest. Rushing into the room past Willie, she demanded of Forrest, who was just rising from his bed, "Are you the Rebel General Forrest? And it is true you murdered those dear colored people at Fort Pillow? Tell me sir; I want no evasive answer."

The outraged citizen need not have worried about "an evasive answer" to her query. Rising from the bed, Forrest looked her straight in the eye and said, "Yes, madam. I killed the men and women for my soldiers' dinner and ate the babies myself for breakfast." His cynical response was said to have sent the woman running down the hallway, through the lobby, and into the street.[71]

During the convention Forrest supported Andrew Johnson as the Democratic nominee but later switched to the ticket of Horatio Seymour and Frank Blair. However, Forrest, unlike other delegates such as Wade Hampton, J. B. Gordon, and B. H. Hill, lobbied hard for Johnson. Forrest said later, "I have a letter in my pocket from Washington" stating that the president was angry because "we of the

South, who were delegates to the convention, did not press his nomination." But Forrest insisted, "I did press it and used all my influence with the Southern delegates . . . and procured him fifty votes."[72] Forrest's effort to help Johnson may also have been a part of his continuing effort to obtain his pardon. And it seems that Johnson may have taken notice, for on July 17, 1868, Forrest finally received his pardon from the president.

While the convention progressed, Forrest became the object of several editorials and cartoons, prompting him to say, "There were a great many things said in regard to myself that I looked upon as gotten up much to affect the elections in the North."[73] It was true that Forrest had become an important propaganda tool for the Republicans during the convention. His notoriety and political exposure also made Forrest a lightning rod for numerous public attacks upon his reputation. To his credit, he took most of the abuse in uncharacteristic humility; however, one particular detractor he would not overlook.

Former Union general Judson Kilpatrick had made insulting remarks about Forrest on more than one occasion, and although at first he had attempted to ignore the slights, Forrest eventually counterattacked in his usual, hot-blooded style. In a blistering tirade, Forrest responded to Kilpatrick's calumny by stating that he had used "false and mendacious representations of me" and that Kilpatrick was "criminal" in his "capacity for ribald inventions." He finished by calling Kilpatrick a blackguard, a liar, a scoundrel, and a poltroon. Forrest then suggested that their differences could be permanently resolved by a duel.

Basil Duke found himself in the uncomfortable position of middleman during the negotiations between Forrest and Kilpatrick. Treading lightly, Duke began the arrangements although dueling was illegal throughout the country. Being from Kentucky, he first attempted to set up a site for the duel in his home state. During the subsequent planning stages, Forrest contacted Duke to advise him that because he and Kilpatrick were ex-cavalrymen, he felt the duel should be fought on horseback with sabers. Before this memorable face-off could take place, however, Kilpatrick declared that he would not accept Forrest's challenge because he did not "regard him as a gentleman." Kilpatrick was, perhaps, acting the role of a gentleman, but he was also acting wisely. He not only saved his own life, but also saved Forrest from another possible murder charge.[74]

Returning home from New York, Forrest found Tennessee ready

to explode in violence. Governor Brownlow was raising the rhetoric to combat the rampant vigilantism that was escalating across his state and the rest of the South. During this time attorney George Templeton Strong in New York wrote in his diary that the Klan had grown to epidemic proportions throughout the South and was going "about nocturnally in large parties masked and disguised, shooting inconvenient niggers and uncomfortable Union men. Southern papers applaud and encourage them in a guarded and semi-ironical way."[75]

Strong was accurate with his assessment of the chaos in the South. Although the Klan did not start off as a racist and violent organization, it had become just that. The psychological trauma of war, defeat, and the coming radical Reconstruction quickly eroded their original defensive stance. The summer of 1868 produced an increasing level of violence in the South that shocked the rest of the nation.

In May, the Klan killed J. S. Webb, Republican sheriff in Georgia. Whippings and lynchings occurred practically everyday somewhere in Dixie. On June 29, over a hundred robed Klansmen charged into Pulaski and dragged a black man accused of rape out of the jail and hanged him. In Texas and Alabama, Klansmen ran nearly all of the white Republicans out of their homes at gunpoint. To many it appeared that the Klan was becoming an insurrectionist army bent on pushing the South to the brink of another war.

Much of this activity was carried on without the knowledge or consent of Klan leaders, but not all of it. It is extremely unlikely that at least some of the organized raids were not planned, or at least condoned, by the leadership. The attacks were too precisely coordinated to be the work of bogus Klansmen acting out their fantasies as purveyors of hard justice. They were, however, highly effective in ending the activities of the black Loyal Leagues under control in Tennessee. Freedmen were terrified and often made their beds in the woods to avoid being caught asleep in their homes.

On July 4, 1868, the Maury County Klan staged a mass parade in Columbia. Some three hundred Klansmen swept into Columbia that night to demonstrate their immunity to law enforcement when they were suddenly attacked by a group of armed freedmen who, seemingly unimpressed with the outlandishly dressed Klansmen, formed up, took aim, and fired into their ranks. Their aim was true, as several of the night riders dropped from their saddles. The rest formed a battle line and charged the freedmen, who had fallen back to some old fortifications.

Another volley was fired at the oncoming Klansmen, but fortunately for the freedmen, there was a company of Union army infantry stationed in Columbia. The blacks fell back to the army camp to take refuge. The long roll was beaten as the Federal troops fell out into their ranks and formed a line of battle. In the face of attacking regular army troops, and in consideration of the potential repercussions if any were killed or wounded, the Klansmen withdrew from the field.[76]

In Giles County the Klan was under slightly better control and the Pulaski Fourth of July parade came off much more smoothly, highlighted by skyrockets and celebration in the streets. But more often mob-like violence was the rule rather than the exception.

The *Pulaski Citizen* had been the covert voice of the Klan, but as the year of 1868 wore on, the partisan editorials began to change and eventually condemned the Klan's outrageous behavior. "While we do not condemn all of the acts of the Klan, yet there are many things done by them, or in their name and garb, which we do not hesitate to pronounce wrong, and which should be stopped by some means."[77]

While Forrest was at the Democratic Convention in New York, Governor Brownlow called for an "extraordinary session" of the Tennessee legislature to be held July 27, 1868. Ten days before, the *Nashville Banner* published an article by the Grand Dragon of Tennessee, George W. Gordon, demanding that all freedmen in Giles, Marshall, Maury, and Lawrence Counties disband those "military companies" they had been organizing to "make war" upon the Ku Klux Klan. The bulletin went on to state that the Klan was not "lawless," but rather "a protective organization." The article continued: "The blacks seem to be impressed with the belief that the Klan is especially their enemy. We are not the enemy of the blacks, as long as they behave themselves, make no threats upon us, and do not attack or interfere with us." Gordon promised that it was "imposters" who were perpetrating the injustices upon the freedmen and finished by emphatically stating that "whippings" were "Wrong! Wrong! Wrong! And it is denounced by this Klan, as it must be by all good and humane men."[78]

So, basically, things could be well for the freedmen as long as they did exactly what the Klan wanted them to do, which was to behave as though the plantation owners were still the masters and they the slaves. It was not going to happen. The floodgates of freedom had been opened, and once freedom is tasted, it is savored, cherished, and defended.

Gordon and the other Klan leaders found that their control and authority was much greater in theory than in practice. The men committing the acts of terrorism could be excused for some degree of confusion, for it was the officers themselves who were actually responsible in a great part for the violence. They were, however, primarily military men and being such felt that the Klan could be operated with strict military discipline as in wartime. It was a serious misjudgment. The more spectacular raids were most certainly organized and ordained by the top Klan officers.

There was obviously some miscommunication between the Klan leaders and ordinary members. Leaders had no compunctions about threatening blacks, but often they disapproved when regular members, many of them veterans who had left much of their humane sensibilities on the battlefield, carried out the threats. Since leaders had difficulty making these distinctions clear to the ordinary Klansmen, it seems to have been next to impossible to enforce them.[79]

In the summer of 1868, the Klan leadership became aware of the breakdown of the normal chain of command and began to attempt to convey their message and orders by another means—the conservative newspapers. That July, Gen. W. P. Carlin, the state commander of the Freedmen's Bureau, reported that his office continually received complaints of outrages allegedly committed by members of the Ku Klux Klan. He expressed his concerns that the "colored people" were seeking protection in great numbers, raising the specter of cities flooded with such refugees who would sorely tax the ability of local, state, and federal government to provide for them.

Carlin went on to express concern that the Klan organization was larger, better organized, and better armed than government leaders realized. These facts made it virtually impossible for the authorities to exert any influence upon them, he continued, and suggested that only armed force could stop the Klan.[80]

Governor Brownlow had come to the same conclusion, so on July 27 he declared war on the Klan. For several months Brownlow had requested Federal troops in vain. So he took matters into his own hands. During the special session of the legislature, he called for a new law regarding the use of the militia and demanded that Klansmen, whom he referred to as assassins, robbers, and outlaws, be shot as punishment for their outrages.[81]

On September 10, Brownlow got what he wanted, and more. The first new law provided a minimum penalty of five hundred dollars and five years in prison for anyone belonging to any secret organization that "prowled" by day or night threatening or terrorizing peaceable citizens of Tennessee. This law also applied to anyone attempting to intimidate voters.[82] Too, the new anti-Klan legislation authorized any victims of Klan intimidation to kill the perpetrators or sue them for punitive damages of up to ten thousand dollars. The second part of the new law empowered Brownlow to organize a state militia and send it into any county where "any ten Union men" testified that the citizens of that county needed protection from the Klan. In response to this news, blacks began to volunteer by the hundreds hoping to retaliate and wage war upon their hated keepers.

The drums of discontent were sounding through the Southern night on August 1 when thirteen ex-Confederate generals met in Nashville to voice their concerns about the impending anti-Klan movement. The group of ex-Confederates more resembled a council of war than a gathering of delegates. Those in attendance included Forrest, George W. Gordon, G. G. Dibrell Gideon Pillow, and John C. Brown, who a few days earlier had taken the incredible step of contacting Brownlow at his home in Knoxville to negotiate an agreement to stop Klan activity in return for a stand-down from the governor's position on the use of the militia. All the men in attendance were unaccustomed to backing down from a firefight, especially Forrest, who was drawn like a moth to its flame. The Klan seemed to be well represented by lawyers as well as ex-rebel generals. Others at the conference were S. R. Anderson, Thomas Benton Smith, William A. Quarles, Isham G. Harris, another attorney and judge, and Joseph B. Palmer.

Although the Southern delegation promised to stop Klan activity and "maintain the peace and order of the state . . . to uphold and support the laws," Brownlow mistrusted the rebels as much as they did him. Predictably Brownlow disregarded what he considered the delegation's hollow promises and continued his attempt to push the militia bill through the legislature as he had originally planned. A few days later, at the White House, Andrew Johnson put his stamp of approval on the bills and sent a regiment of Federal army troops to augment the militia in Tennessee.

Hoping to avoid a race war while extinguishing the Klan threat, Brownlow promised that he would rely primarily upon white Unionist recruits for his militia. This sounded as hollow to the Confederates as their guarantees did to him. In fact, Brownlow's statements concerning the use of black militiamen could have been construed as a veiled threat and was taken as such by Forrest. On

August 11 in Brownsville, Tennessee, Forrest threw political acumen to the wind by blasting Brownlow in a speech reminiscent of his motivational addresses to his troops during the war.

Forrest began his speech by informing the audience that he was ill and could only speak for a few minutes. He went on to say that he had received an urgent dispatch from General Cheatham to come to Nashville to take part in a meeting called the Council of Peace:

> Great fears had been expressed about the calling out of the militia, as many were of the opinion that it would lead to bloodshed of a very serious character. Gov. Brownlow had stated in his message to the Legislature that all those who belonged to the Ku Klux Klan were to be declared outlaws, and he declared that these Klans were composed of soldiers who had been in the Confederate army. I believe that Gov. Brownlow thinks that all Confederate soldiers, and, in fact, the whole Democratic Party in the South belong to the Ku Klux Klan. [Cheers and laughter.] All are declared outlaws, for the Governor says he has no doubt they belong to the Klan, if there is such a clan. The Legislature has passed some laws, I believe, on the subject, in which the militia are called on to shoot all Kukluxes they may find, and they need fear no prosecution for doing so. That is, simply that they may call a Confederate soldier a Kuklux, shoot him down, and no harm shall befall any of the militia who shall commit such an outrageous act; for Gov. Brownlow has proclaimed that they were all outlaws. [Applause.] When this is done, I tell you, fellow-citizens, there will be civil war. If the Radical Legislature, with Gov. Brownlow, arms the negroes, and tells them to shoot down all Confederate[s] on the grounds that they are members of the Ku Klux Klan, as they call it, and outlaws, then in my opinion, there will be civil war in Tennessee. [Applause.]

Forrest emphatically stated that he wanted no more war, but Brownlow was said to be organizing both blacks and whites into military units whose purpose was to pursue and kill all rebels suspected of belonging to the Klan. Forrest could not let that stand unchallenged:

> If they bring this war upon us, there is one thing I will tell you—that I shall not shoot any negroes so long as I see a white Radical to shoot, for it is the Radicals who will be to blame for bringing on this war. I can assure you, fellow-citizens, that I shall at all times be ready to go forward and assist the Sheriff or any other officer in carrying out the laws of the State. . . . But if they send the black men to hunt those Confederate soldiers whom

they call Kuklux, then I say to you, "Go out and shoot the Radicals." If they do want to inaugurate civil war, the sooner it comes the better that we may know what to do. [Applause.]

Forrest shifted gears and directed his remarks to the black people in the audience. He apparently saw no contradiction in his ironic statements to the freedmen and undoubtedly meant every word he said:

I wish distinctly to state that I am not against the colored man, neither have I ever been against the colored man[.] I carried forty-five of them into the war with me, and all but one remained with me during the war. . . .

. . . If, however, the [new] war should come, and I hope it never will, I want no drones in my drum of bees. [Applause.] If I am forced into a collision, I tell you that every man shall be compelled to do his duty. They have got to take sides with us or the other party. We will have no neutrals: all must show what they are. If they are not for us, then they will be against us.

I now want to say a few words to the black men who are here, before me, and what I wish to say is, to ask them to stand by the men who raised you, who nursed you when you were sick, and who took care of you when you were little children. I say, stand by them who are your real friends, and leave your Loyal Leagues, where you are taught to refuse the franchise to those who have always proved your friends. I tell you that if you will only stand by us, that we will always stand by you, and do as much for you as any white man can do for you.[83]

No one really wanted to see another war, let alone with the added dimension of a race war. It had only been three years since the surrender. Another bloody conflict might well destroy the Southern landscape and economy. Consequently, Brownlow eventually allowed Federal troops to handle the law enforcement rather than using the militia, either white or black. In response, the Klan reduced its covert activity and made a semblance at least of enforcing its new policy among the more rabid dens. Forrest himself sent specially picked men to quell the continued night riding and marauding in Madison County. Some sources reported that Forrest went so far as to order the executions of two Klansmen who disobeyed his direct orders to end the terrorism. It seemed to be working in the areas Forrest could conceivably control, which were west Tennessee and part of east Tennessee, but a permanent rift had been created in the Klan. No one at the time could have known to what it might eventually lead.

A week and a half later, still suffering from a bad cold, Forrest was interviewed by a Mr. Woodward who later vilified him in a scathing letter published in the Cincinnati and Memphis newspapers. This interview would come up again during Forrest's testimony at the Ku Klux Klan hearings in Washington. Forrest vehemently denied making many of the statements, and further, he claimed to have been misquoted and that his comments had been quoted out of context.

Woodward's letter began:

> Today, I have enjoyed "big talks" enough to have gratified any of the famous Indian chiefs who have been treating with General Sherman for the past two years. First I met General N.B. Forrest, then General Gideon Pillow, and Governor Isham G. Harris. My first visit was to General Forrest, whom I found at his office, at 8 o'clock this morning, hard at work, although complaining of an illness contracted at the New York convention.

"What are your feelings towards the Federal Government, General?" Woodward asked. Forrest told the man that he had always loved the Constitution and the old government, but the Radicals had changed all that.

"In the event of Governor Brownlow's calling out the militia, do you think there will be any resistance offered to their acts?" Woodward queried, though he apparently hadn't heard some of Forrest's latest speeches, or he would not have had to ask.

Forrest answered,

> If the militia are simply called out, and do not interfere with or molest anyone, I do not think there will be any fight. If, on the contrary, they do what I believe they will do, commit outrages, or even one outrage, upon the people, they and Mr. Brownlow's government will be swept out of existence; not a radical will be left alive. If the militia are called out, we can not but look upon it as a declaration of war, because Mr. Brownlow [Forrest, apparently, was deliberately calling Brownlow "mister" rather than "governor"] has already issued his proclamation directing them to shoot down the Ku Klux wherever they find them; and he calls all southern men Ku Klux.

This part of the interview sounded like a quote from Forrest's speech in Brownsville, and perhaps it was.

The next question to Forrest concerned the existence of the Klan. The reporter voiced doubts about whether it was a real organization or just a wild story. "Well sir," Forrest answered gravely, "there is such an organization, not only in Tennessee but all over the South, and its numbers have not been exaggerated."

"What are its numbers, general?"

"In Tennessee there are over forty thousand; in all the Southern states about five hundred thousand men."

"What is the character of the organization, may I inquire?"

"Yes, sir," Forrest replied.

> It is a protective, political, military organization. I am willing to show any man the constitution of the society. The members are sworn to recognize the Government of the United States. It does not say any thing at all about the government of the state of Tennessee. Its objects originally were protection against Loyal Leagues and the Grand Army of the Republic; but after it became general it was found that political matters and interests could best be promoted within it, and it was then made a political organization, giving its support, of course, to the Democratic Party."

Woodward then asked who was the officer commanding the Klan, and Forrest replied that he could not answer because it would be "impolitic" to do so. Woodward asked Forrest what might happen if Brownlow did decide to use the militia against the Klan. Forrest answered:

> If they attempt to carry out Governor Brownlow's proclamation by shooting down Ku Klux—for he calls all southern men Ku Klux—if they go to hunting down and shooting these men, there will be war, and a bloodier one than we have ever witnessed. I have told these radicals here what they might expect in such an event. I have no powder to burn killing negroes. I intend to kill the radicals. I have told them this and more. There is not a radical leader in this town but is a marked man; and if trouble should break out, not one of them would be left alive. I have told them that they were trying to create disturbance and then slip out and leave the consequences to fall upon the Negro; but they can't do it. . . . If militia attack us, we will resist to the last; and if necessary, I think I could raise 40,000 men in five days, ready for the field.[84]

In the final analysis, these words must have been Forrest's. It simply sounds too much like what he had been saying for the past several weeks.

On September 3, the *New York Times* republished the entire interview Forrest had given the reporter from the *Cincinnati Commercial.* Three days later they published his rebuttal, in which Forrest tried to cover his tracks with some improbable sounding interpretations of what he had reportedly said:

> I said it was reported, and I believed the report, that there are forty thousand Ku Klux in Tennessee, and I believe the organization stronger in other states. I meant to imply, when I said that the Ku Klux recognize the Federal Government, that they would obey all State laws. They recognize all laws, and will obey them, so I have been informed, in protecting peaceable citizens from oppression from any quarter. I did not say that any man's house was picketed[.] I did not mean to convey the idea that I would raise any troops, and, more than that, no man could do it in five days, even if they were organized.[85]

Despite Forrest's response, the national spotlight remained focused on him, and he was excoriated in the *Times* again on September 13 concerning Fort Pillow.

This intense scrutiny was probably the reason he turned down a request for assistance from ex-Confederate general John T. Brown back in mid-August. Brown claimed that his brother had been gunned down by "some Union men and he wanted revenge." However, the national public attention was making Forrest very cautious. The fact that he kept a copy of his own letter advising Brown to seek legal recourse rather than resort to violence, and that he burned the other one, which was probably more sympathetic to Brown's personal need for revenge, indicates that he suspected he was under surveillance.[86]

Forrest wrote the letter on August 28 in Memphis and addressed it to Mr. J. T. Brown, Esq., Humboldt, Tennessee:

> Dear Sir: Your favor of the 26th instant has been received. While I sympathize with your desire to bring those who were guilty of murdering your brother to justice, and would willingly do anything in my power to aid you in this, I cannot consent to become a party, either directly or indirectly, to any act of violence, or to the infringement of any law. On the contrary, all my efforts have been, and shall be, exerted to preserve peace and order, and to maintain the law as far a possible. . . . You will excuse me, I hope, for saying that it was very imprudent to send your letter by mail. If it had fallen into the hands of the others

it might, without some explanations, have caused some trouble to both of us. N. B. Forrest[87]

Later in September, the *New York Tribune* published an article that bore the headline "Is Forrest a Butcher?" The article claimed Forrest had murdered a "mulatto" in 1862 at Murfreesboro. The same article also included a section written by the reporter from the *Cincinnati Commercial*. In it the reporter claimed Forrest had escorted him to Fort Pillow and walked the ground with him, discussing the battle.

Forrest never gave any personal tours of Fort Pillow, let alone with a Northern newspaperman. The allegation was ridiculous, and Forrest responded by saying that he had never been to the battle site with anyone. However, he did not deny the conversation with the reporter concerning the Klan. Forrest said he could not remember all the details of the interview because he was intermittently vomiting during the conversation. He did say that the article had put words in "my mouth which I never made, and it colors others so as to change their meaning entirely." Concerning what he had actually said, Forrest rebutted the article with the following:

> I knew nothing positively of its organization, strength or objects, but that I was informed that its purpose was the protection of the people from injury, and that I was, so far at least, in sympathy with it. All the other assertions in regard to this organization which he puts into my mouth were derived from other persons, or are fabrications of his own brain. . . . I said to him . . . that . . . if the Governor should proclaim martial law in any part of the State, and attempt to enforce it . . . that . . . I thought that 40,000 or 50,000 men in this State would rise up in defense of their rights. I cannot feel that I am responsible for the misrepresentations of which he has been guilty. If all that I have said on political questions was reported correctly, I should think there would be nothing found in it which would injure the Democratic Party or the interests of the South.[88]

Forrest had been facing increasing pressure since September 2, when the Joint Military Committee passed the Anti-Ku Klux Klan Law. He was leading a double life, and it was becoming increasingly difficult to continue his role as the South's "avenging angel" and simultaneously create a new life and livelihood for his family. He was also facing the very real possibility of going to prison if convicted of conspiracy to start an insurrection through his leadership of the Klan.

Death had been a constant companion to Forrest from his birth in the wilds of west Tennessee. Even now death renewed the association on occasion. Miriam Beck Forrest Luxton died that summer of 1868 from blood poisoning caused by stepping on a rusty nail. Bedford had often said that if not for his mother's prayers, he would not have survived the war. She died in a fever-induced delirium calling for her oldest son to come to her bedside. By the time Bedford was able to get there, she was already gone.

From his adolescence in the wild frontier of west Tennessee, he had always made his own luck. During the war years it was the same, although a case could be made that he was incredibly lucky to have survived at all. He was shot four times during battle and shot at hundreds of times. And considering the number of charges, battles, and hand-to-hand struggles he survived, he seemed to have been protected by a guardian angel. Perhaps his mother's prayers did have the affect Forrest claimed. But even a cat has only the proverbial nine lives, and Forrest's luck had been just about used up by the end of the war.

Late that summer Forrest was called upon to quell a potential race riot in east Tennessee at Crawfordville (now known as Crawford) on the Mobile and Ohio Railroad. After an incident in which a white man on horseback from Crawfordville had knocked down a black man on the roadway, the blacks, some eight hundred strong, advanced on the town to seek revenge on the horseman. The townspeople had barricaded themselves and were waiting for help to arrive. The news had gotten out on the wire to West Point and Columbus, where groups of white men "had gotten all the trains they could and started down" toward the conflict at Crawfordville. Forrest was aboard one of those trains headed for Memphis when he received the news of the impending riot.

At least one house was burning when Forrest arrived on the scene. He later said that he "quickly got the white people together, organized them . . . made speeches to them . . . then got on my horse and rode over to the negroes and made a speech to them. The negroes dispersed and went home, and nothing was done; nobody was hurt, nobody molested."[89]

The wild times continued as the national elections of November 3, 1868, neared. Governor Clayton, in Arkansas, called out his militia to deal with potential problems, but the only way he could arm them was to buy guns and have them shipped from New York. The Klan's spy network discovered the plan on October 5, and soon after an article appeared in the *Memphis Avalanche*. The article claimed in part that the shipment of arms was "to be placed in the hands of the negroes of Arkansas . . . for the purpose of shooting down inoffensive citizens." Editor Galloway continued by stating that any steamboat transporting the weapons should be intercepted and destroyed. Due to the public outcry, no Southern steamboat company would accept the contract. Eventually the only Republican-operated steamboat, the *Hesper*, was chartered for the dangerous journey.

On October 15, the *Hesper* picked up its New York cargo in Memphis and steamed south toward the mouth of the Arkansas River. Heading downriver about twenty miles south of Memphis, the *Hesper's* captain, Sam Houston, noticed the tugboat *Netty Jones* was shadowing him. The *Netty Jones* was a faster craft than the *Hesper* and suddenly began to close in on her. Fearing he would be rammed, Houston deliberately ran his ship aground on the Arkansas side. The *Netty Jones* followed Houston to the shore and pulled alongside as sixty or seventy disguised Klansmen appeared and began to open fire on the crew of the *Hesper*. The ten or fifteen crewmen, along with Captain Houston, ran for their lives up and over the bank to safety. The guns were seized by the Klansmen before setting the *Hesper* adrift down the Mississippi.

The raiders had all come from Memphis and the attack had been carefully orchestrated, suggesting that Klan leadership in the Memphis area was involved. Captain Ford, of the *Netty Jones*, claimed he had been overpowered and taken prisoner by the Klansmen, but indications are that he was a member himself. The Democratic newspapers hailed the raid on their front pages, but none of them attributed the hijacking activity to the Klan, since they all refused to admit that the Klan even existed.[90]

The same night of the raid, on October 15, a party attended by several young ex-Confederate soldiers and officers was held in Memphis at the Overton Hotel. Many of the young men arrived late, and most had muddy boots. This incident received national attention that prompted Horace Greeley's *New York Tribune* to send a reporter to Memphis to investigate.

On November 2, the *Tribune* published an article stating that Forrest "in person" had led the raid and cited several reasons as to why they believed this to be so. Forrest "is recognized as the leader of the organization, proof sufficient of which is found in admissions" during his public speeches over the past few months. The article said, "No man would be so likely to be called upon to lead so desperate a venture as General N. B. Forrest." They went on to theorize that "any man in Memphis . . . will at once" identify Forrest as the man in charge of the naval operations on the day of the raid and J. J. Dubose as his accomplice in charge of the Klan's land forces.[91]

Immediately after the hijacking, Arkansas governor Clayton appealed to the secretary of war, Gen. John M. Schofield, for Federal troops. On November 1, he requested that the Arkansas legislature declare martial law. Soon, before and after the election, the Arkansas militia and the Klan engaged in open combat. Both sides were accused of committing atrocities. In fact, a small group of black militiamen were accused of robbing the home of a man in Sevier County and sexually assaulting his wife. At least one of the assailants was shot and killed and others were dishonorably discharged.[92]

No Southern governor wanted martial law or a guerilla war on his hands. Most rational Republicans were hoping the Klan would exhaust the tolerance of the Democratic community before all hell broke loose. Brownlow was no exception, but in the last days before the election he began to press hard against the Klan in response to their escalating terrorism in Tennessee.

The November election of 1868 came and went with the Republicans winning easily. The Klan, however, did play a major role in two Southern states, Georgia and Louisiana, which went Democratic. Tennessee went Republican by two to one and Brownlow still withheld enfranchisement from the ex-rebels, which in turn led to continued violence that seemed to have no end in sight.

The Klan rode on, primarily seeking retribution against those who had voted Republican. In Columbia, Tennessee, on January 11, 1869, the Klan kidnapped and hanged a man named Seymour Barmore. At Brownlow's direction, Barmore had infiltrated the Klan as a spy and as a result paid the ultimate price. He was dragged from a train traveling from Pulaski to Nashville, hanged, and his body dumped in the Duck River.[93]

Then, things suddenly began to change. A year earlier, Brownlow, his health failing, had named himself the U.S. senator from Tennessee, and his political aspirations were about to be fulfilled. In addition, as 1869 began, the Democratic outcry against the Klan began to rise. The very Southern aristocracy the Klan had been organized to protect was turning against them. The Tennessee Republican Party took advantage of this change in perception and began mobilizing to exterminate the Klan completely. On January 16, the legislature removed all restraints on Brownlow, gave him complete power to use militia, and began enlisting guardsmen to wage total war on organized Klan resistance. In a short time more than sixteen hundred militiamen were organized, mainly from eastern Tennessee, and martial law was formally declared.

This unified military operation in conjunction with Brownlow's rumored departure to the U.S. Senate may have prompted Forrest to begin considering disbandment of the Klan. Around January 25, Forrest began that process with his written order to cease all terrorism committed in the Klan's name. The order stated that evil men had gotten into the Klan for their own purposes. All costumes and Klan paraphernalia were to be "entirely abolished and destroyed." The order also stated that all "demonstrations," unless ordered directly by the Grand Titan or above, were to immediately stop. However, the proclamation added that this order was "not to be understood to dissolve the order entirely" but should hold them "more firmly together and faithfully bound to each other in any emergency that may come."[94]

On February 20, 1869, Brownlow was sworn in as the new U.S. senator and the governorship passed to the Speaker of the House, DeWitt Clinton Senter. Senter, who was a lame-duck candidate, soon declared his new policy and belief in universal suffrage, which opened the polls to thousands of ex-Confederates for the first time since the end of the war. By helping Senter to a full term as governor, the Democrats achieved re-enfranchisement and would likely see Democratic control in the state capital after his term in office. After this, there was no more Democratic need for the Klan in Tennessee.

Consequently, the disbandment order was issued, but despite Forrest's command to cease Klan activity, the proclamation had little effect outside the few counties surrounding Memphis. Even so, there is considerable doubt as to whether Forrest actually divorced himself from the Klan completely until he felt that it could no longer suit his purposes, which might have been sometime after 1870.

Others, such as John Morton, were more emphatic as to why the general put an end to things. "The order for the dissolution of the Klan, as issued by General Forrest," wrote Morton, "was in every way characteristic of the man." It was no secret that Morton admired his former commander and mentor and may have appraised Forrest's motivation in light of his warm feelings for the general. This may also have been the case when he wrote, "When the white race had redeemed six Southern states from Negro rule in 1870, the Grand Wizard knew that his mission was accomplished and issued at once his order to disband." It was the young ex-chief of artillery who had sworn Forrest into the Klan back in 1867, and if anyone had insight into the inner workings of Forrest's mind or about his motivations, it was John Morton.

Morton, a Grand Cyclops, went on to say that the execution of this order fell on his shoulders and was carried out throughout the South. However, Morton was mistaken about the order of dissolution being obeyed.[95] In the areas where it continued to operate beyond 1870, the Klan tended to be more violent and more dangerous than ever before. In 1869-70, in Alabama, Arkansas, Georgia, and Louisiana independent dens rode on. In those areas Southern conservatives had found intimidation to be an effective means of regaining political privileges.

Whether Forrest disbanded the Klan in 1869 or in 1870, reasons for the order of dissolution were probably attributable to a combination of factors. Rampant terrorism and martial law had a negative effect on business, including the railroad business. In early 1869 Forrest had bought a controlling interest in and was elected president of the Cahaba, Marion and Memphis Railroad, which a year later became the Selma, Marion and Memphis Railroad. Fortunately for Forrest's newly acquired railroad, though there are indications that the Forrest-led Klan continued to ride into 1870, the violence diminished dramatically in Tennessee after the official notice to disband was published in the newspapers throughout the state.

As John Morton related in his book, concerning Forrest's reason for disbandment, the Klan's greater political goal had been achieved. The terror it had created was a major political factor in at least eight states. The Republican vote in Georgia and Louisiana had been so decimated by Klan activity that both states wound up in the Democratic column. In reality the South was on its way to reestablishing Democratic rule and white supremacy by the end of 1871 and would achieve that goal by 1877. In 1877, the year of Forrest's death, Rutherford B. Hayes agreed to work toward withdrawing the Union troops from the South and ending Reconstruction in return for Southern Democratic support in his election to the presidency.

As the Federal government's stepped-up enforcement campaign against the remaining Klan marauders began to break the back of its organized resistance, Forrest focused his energy on his railroad business. On March 9, 1869, while traveling on a train from Jackson, Mississippi, to Memphis, Forrest gave a remarkable interview to another reporter from the *Louisville Courier*. As they passed "through beautiful tracts of country lying in waste," the reporter asked Forrest "how it could ever be repopulated." Looking out the window at the landscape, Forrest answered, "With Negroes. They are the best laborers we have ever had in the South."[96]

Apparently other ex-Confederate officers had the same opinion concerning freedmen. In 1875, Gen. James R. Chalmers found himself attempting to disperse the blacks who were rioting in Coahoma County, Mississippi. The man who had helped Forrest capture Fort Pillow was heard shouting, "Don't shoot the Negroes boys, we need cotton pickers."[97]

When the reporter asked Forrest how he intended to repopulate the South with blacks, Forrest replied, "From Africa." Forrest said they could be acquired from among prisoners taken in African tribal wars who would be "turned over to us, and emigrate and be freedmen here." His racism surfaced again as he elaborated on the wild scheme. He explained that they would "improve after getting here, [as the blacks] are the most imitative creatures in the world, and if you put them in squads of ten, with one experienced leader in each group, they will soon revive our country." Foreseeing no hope of European or Northern repopulation, "I say let's get Africans. By pursuing a liberal policy to them we can benefit them and they us."

In the same callous vein, Forrest explained that he had "an interest" in the *Wanderer*, a well-known antebellum slave ship in which, he said, he and his partners had "brought over 400" slaves and only lost "six percent" as casualties. Forrest predicted that the Federal government, once their "prejudice gets over . . . will foster this scheme; there is no need of a war of races. I want to see the whole country prosper."[98]

On March 6, 1865, Mary Chesnut had written in her diary that she had knowledge of the schooner the *Wanderer* by way of a chance meeting with the sister of the captain.

> Saw a sister of Captain [William C.] Corrie: Captain Corrie is the anachronism who tried in the 19th century to reopen the African slave trade. The captain of the "Wanderer"—Governor [James H. Adams of South Carolina] assisting . . . must be a myth. There could not be such demented benighted people in the world. I did not believe in the "Wanderer" any more than I did the "Flying Dutchman or the Red Rover or the water witch."

Perhaps Mary Chesnut did not want to believe that there were still those who contemplated and engaged in the African slave trade as late as the 1840s, but it was nevertheless true.[99]

Africans were not the only potential source of new labor. In July

1869, Forrest attended the Chinese Labor Convention in Memphis, where businessmen and civic leaders had gathered to debate the use of Chinese "coolies" as laborers. The Chinese could prove to be a less traumatized work force and Southerners might possibly gain some leverage over the existing black workers. Forrest supported the idea enthusiastically and when challenged with the notion that the blacks might feel "enmity" toward the Chinese laborers, he asserted that during a speech in Alabama "he got $1,500 in subscriptions from Negroes at the meeting, and this morning he had received a letter from there announcing that there had been stock subscribed by the county, by a vote of sixty to one, and that by the Negro vote."[100]

As Forrest spent the rest of the summer drumming up subscriptions, he had the occasion to say that "the railroads had no politics; that [he] wanted the assistance of everybody; that railroads were good for the general good of the whole country."[101] Nearing the end of 1869, Forrest had 150 workers building his rail line. Things seemed to be going well for him as 1870 approached. Although he had his typical disagreements with associates, he continued to operate the Selma, Marion and Memphis line as its president. In January 1870, he was in Greensboro, Alabama, building a depot. In July he was in New York selling railroad bonds. Then, in September, trouble found him again.

While negotiating with a group of officials from Hale County concerning the section of rail that ran through their territory, Forrest erroneously felt that Col. A. K. Shepherd, one of his contractors on the rail line, had failed to fulfill his obligations. It was similar to the Lieutenant Gould situation when Forrest next encountered the contractor face-to-face. Before the man could respond, Forrest cut loose with some rough comments that enraged Shepherd and prompted him to challenge Forrest to a duel. As was often the case, Forrest let his temper override his better judgment. After his temper had cooled overnight, and having discovered that the foreman had not fallen down on the job as he had thought, Forrest contacted the ex-colonel the next morning. Offering an apology, Forrest told Shepherd, "Colonel, I am in the wrong in this affair and have come to say so." The apology was accepted and the duel was canceled.[102]

## Mr. Forrest Goes to Washington

On June 27, 1871, Forrest was called to Washington, D.C. to testify before the Joint Congressional Committee, which was investigating the Ku Klux Klan conspiracy. Once before the committee, he suddenly developed convenient mental lapses concerning his activities over the past few years, an interesting development for a man who had a reputation for a mind like a steel trap. He also must have been kicking himself for having previously given interviews to anyone, because every word he had been quoted as saying would come back to haunt him during the hearings.

On the twenty-seventh, the *New York Times* ran a story reporting that "Gen. Forrest was before the Kuklux Committee today, and his examination lasted for hours. . . . [A]fter the examination, [he] remarked to friends that the Committee treated him with much courtesy and respect."

Forrest was aware that as he entered the hearing room that he was walking under the shadow of the Klan. He also knew that he would not be alone. The ghosts of Fort Pillow accompanied him as well. He realized that he was about to be placed under a microscope and had steeled himself for the intense scrutiny. Although he did have one ally on the panel, Sen. Francis P. Blair of Missouri, as a whole the committee was more Republican than Democrat. One of the Republican members was former Union general and radical Benjamin F. Butler from Massachusetts, who was known as the "Butcher" due to his oppressive policies during his occupation of New Orleans.

Concerning the committee's questions, Forrest's testimony varied from feigning complete ignorance to outright defiance. Had the subject not been so deadly earnest, the questions and answers at times might have seemed almost humorous. Forrest ducked, dodged, bobbed, and weaved with a nimble dexterity that would have made a firing squad look bad.

The interrogation began with questions relating to Forrest's residence and current railroad operations but quickly turned to more serious matters as a member of the committee addressed Forrest: "I have observed in one of the Western papers an account of an interview purporting to have been had with you in 1868, in which you are reported to have spoken of the organization of what has been called the Ku-Klux in Tennessee, their operations, their Constitution, the numbers of the organization; and also a correction in one or two particulars afterward made by you of the facts stated in that interview. You recollect the article to which I refer?"

"Yes, sir," Forrest replied.

Another question: "Upon what information did you make the statement in regard to the organization and constitution of the Ku Klux in Tennessee?"

Forrest answered, "Well, sir, I had but very little conversation with that party."[103]

Forrest told them that he had been very sick during the short conversation and that everything he had told the reporter was hearsay. He also denied making any statement about the fact that there were forty thousand Klansmen in Tennessee. The committee chairman then produced a copy of Forrest's complete interview with the reporter to refresh his memory. He read the entire interview to Forrest and then asked if any other portion of that statement was incorrect. Forrest answered, "Well, sir, the whole statement is wrong; he did not give anything as it took place. So far as numbers were concerned, I knew nothing about the numbers of the organization. It was reported that there was such an organization in Tennessee, in fact throughout the United States; but I knew nothing about its operations."[104]

Forrest was then asked how he came to the conclusion that there were forty thousand to fifty thousand Ku Klux members in Tennessee. He admitted he had made the statement but he had no authoritative source on that number. It was only a figure that he had heard from persons whose identity he could not recall at the moment. The committee then asked from whom he had received information about the Klan's numbers and Forrest responded by saying, "I never made that statement, because I knew nothing about how many there were."

When asked why he could not recall any specific details from the interview he had given the reporter, Forrest replied, "I did not have as much conversation with him as you and I now have had." When asked about his response to the reporter's question on the identity of the commanding officer of the Klan, which Forrest had been quoted as saying it would be "impolitic" for him to answer, Forrest snapped, "No, sir I never made that statement." Concerning the trip to Fort Pillow with the reporter, Forrest said the reporter's statements about a trip to Fort Pillow "were entirely false. I never traveled with the man ten feet in my life."[105] Asked if the entire interview was a misrepresentation of his words, Forrest said, "not all of it," but maintained that the bulk of the article was.

The chairman, Sen. John Scott of Pennsylvania, then referred to the portion of the article that dealt with the Klan's supposed disbandment and began to hammer Forrest about what he knew of the Invisible Empire. Specifically, they wanted to know how it had occurred and who had disbanded the Klan. Forrest answered, "I did not say that orders had been issued, but that I understood orders had been issued. I could not speak of anything personally."

"Will you state who they were who gave you that information?"

"One or two of the parties are dead now," Forrest answered.

"Who were they?"

"One of them was a gentleman by the name of Saunders," said Forrest.

"Did he reside in Tennessee?"

"No, sir," Forrest replied, "he resided in Mississippi then. He afterward died by poison at Asheville, North Carolina."

"Did any other person give you that information?"

"Yes, sir; I heard others say so, but I do not recollect the names now."

"Under what name is it your belief it existed at that time?"

Scott may have suspected that Forrest was attempting to be deliberately vague in his answers, and it may have been true. "Some called them Pale Faces; some called them Ku-Klux," Forrest said. "I believe they were under two names."

"What did you understand to be the purpose of the two organizations?" Scott asked.

Forrest continued: "I can tell you it was for the purpose of self-protection. . . . I think many of the organization did not have any name; parties organized themselves so as to be ready in case they were attacked. Ladies were ravished by some of those negroes, who we tried to put in the penitentiary, but were turned out in a few days afterward. There was a great deal of insecurity in the country, and I think this organization was got up to protect the weak, with no political intention at all."

After a few questions concerning the Loyal Leagues, the committee came back to what Forrest knew about the dissolution of the Klan: "Where can we get the information as to the manner of its dissolution and the time of it?"

Forrest replied, "I do not know where you can get it. I never got any positive information except that it was general[ly] understood that the organization was broken up."[106]

Later in his testimony, Forrest contradicted himself by admitting that he himself had ordered the organization to disband. It was not his only contradiction that day. The committee continued to grill him concerning who, what, when, where, and how the Klan operated. They also began to question him on the Klan's activities in other states, particularly in Mississippi. "In that portion of the State of Mississippi through which your road runs, have you any knowledge of any outrages by persons in disguise having been committed since 1867?"

Forrest told the committee that he had heard of one or two hearsay incidents, one in Greensboro, Alabama, and another in Eutaw, Alabama, in Greene County, where a man named Miller had been killed by men in disguises. But he claimed to have no recollection of where or from whom he had received that information.

Growing impatient, Sen. Job E. Stevenson from Ohio began to raise the stakes: "Then I understand you to say that this whole statement, giving the idea that you knew of your own knowledge of the organization of the Ku Klux, or that you knew of their numbers of their discipline is incorrect?"

Forrest replied, "I never said to that man that I knew anything about it."

"Had you ever a constitution of the order?"

"I saw one; yes, sir. . ."

"Who had it?"

"Well, it was sent to me in a letter."

"Have you that constitution yet?"

"No, sir. . . . Well, I burned up the one I had."

"Who sent it to you?"

"That I cannot tell," Forrest said.

When Stevenson pressed for more information, Forrest told the committee that the letter had come from somewhere in Tennessee, but he "could not recollect" exactly from where it had been sent. He told them that he had employed a secretary especially for handling the huge volume of mail he had been receiving "from all the Southern States, men complaining, being dissatisfied, persons whose friends had been killed, or their families insulted and they were writing to me to know what they ought to do."[107]

Demanding to know more about the Klan's constitution, the committee was unrelenting as Forrest attempted to satisfy them with vague and piecemeal information. The committee wanted to know about the secret nature of the Klan and its rituals, initiations, and initial distribution of its constitution. Forrest told them the Klan had "no name given to it" at the time he saw the paper. "As I recollect, there was three stars in place of a name. . . . That is when it came to the name there was a blank, and stars in the blank" in place of the name. The committee then asked if the omission of the name signified "that the name was to be kept secret?" Replying in a somewhat insolent manner, Forrest said, "You are to place your own construction on that."

When asked about the rank structure and commanding officers that may have been mentioned in the Klan constitution, Forrest slipped up when he replied: "I do not think there is anything in the prescript indicating anything of the sort." The word "prescript" had not been used up to that point in the proceedings concerning the true name of the Klan's constitution.

The interrogation became personally specific when the committee wanted to know if Forrest took part in organizing or attending meetings in any Southern states.

"Did you act upon the prescript?" they asked.

"No, sir," Forrest replied.

"Did you take any steps for organizing under it?"

"I do not think I am compelled to answer any question that would implicate me in anything. I believe the law does not require that I should do anything of the sort."

Chairman Scott then advised Forrest that he had been misinformed. He told Forrest that on January 24, 1837, Congress passed an act that compelled him to answer and proceeded to read it. Once finished, Scott said, "I will repeat the question. Did you take any steps for organizing an association or society under that prescription?"

Denied the shelter of the Fifth Amendment, Forrest had no choice. It was either lie or face the possibility of prison. After a dramatic pause, Forrest looked Scott in the eye and said, "I did not."[108]

The tension was building, as the committee seemed to be making no progress. Stevenson hammered away, "Can you now tell us who were the members, or any single member, of that organization?"

After a pause Forrest replied, "Well, that is a question I do not want to answer now."

"You decline to answer?"

"I would prefer to have a little time, if you will permit me."

When Senator Stevenson asked why he needed more time, Forrest said he needed the time to "study up" before he could reply. The chairman then wanted to know how much time Forrest needed. "Well, sir, I do not know that I could say now, as I am in the midst of this examination. I would like you to pass that over for the present and let me have some time to think about it."[109]

The committee moved back to the question of whether the Klan was still in operation or actually had been disbanded. "Were you trying to suppress the organization, or the outrages you speak of?"

Earlier, Forrest had denied knowledge of the details of the disbandment; now he made an audacious admission: "I was trying to suppress the outrages."

"Outrages committed by colored men?"

"By all people; my object was to keep peace."

"Did you want to suppress that organization?"

The committee was coming right at him, and his instinct to countercharge momentarily took over. "Yes, sir; I did suppress it."

The obvious question came next, "How?"

"I had it broken up and disbanded," Forrest confessed.

"What influence did you exert in disbanding it?"

"I talked with different people that I believed were connected with it, and urged its disbandment, that it should be broken up."

With this opening, which seemed to substantiate the article written by the *Cincinnati Commercial* reporter, the committee then wanted to know if the words he had been quoted as saying in the interview with Woodward were true. Forrest told them, "I never uttered such words; I did not talk to that man twenty words."

Then, Senator Stevenson wanted to know if Forrest's intervention had any affect on the Klan's operations. "Yes, sir; and I think they completely stopped. I do not hear of anything. . . . I think that since 1868 that organization has been disbanded. I do not think there has been any organization together; if there has been, it has been by irresponsible parties, without any organization at all."[110]

Next, the committee's questions turned to the Klan's real purpose. They wanted to know if the Klan was attempting to affect the outcome of the elections through terrorist means. "So far as you had any understanding or information, was it to act upon the elections in any shape or form?"

They were right on the money, and Forrest knew it. Nevertheless, he continued to bluff his way forward. "No, sir, I never heard it was to have anything to do with elections."

Of course, the Klan's operations had everything to do with the outcome of the elections, and everyone in the hearing room that day knew it. Because of being disenfranchised, Forrest claimed, he and most ex-Confederate officers were not interested in voting, or in the elections. Undoubtedly, no one in the courtroom believed that Forrest was unconcerned about the elections or their outcomes.

Stevenson was clearly frustrated and fired away on his favorite subject of the day: the newspaper article written by Woodward. Earlier in his testimony Forrest stated that he had not walked "ten feet" with the reporter and that their conversation had lasted only a few minutes. Forrest was asked again, "How far did you walk with him?"

This time Forrest answered, "Sixty to eighty yards."

Perhaps Stevenson believed that if he kept at it, he might get Forrest up to a quarter mile by the end of the day.

The questions changed direction when the committee wanted to know about the operations on Forrest's plantation and his opinions on Negro suffrage. Forrest said he was not against it and launched into the story of how forty-five of his slaves had followed him into the war and that he had freed them before the war ended.

The committee asked, "When was that?"

"In 1863, when the war closed I looked upon it as an act of Providence, and felt that we ought to submit to it quietly; and I have never done or said anything that was contrary to the laws that have been enacted."

In reality, Forrest did not free his slaves until after the surrender in May 1865. However, more than twenty of the ex-slaves chose to follow him home and rebuild their lives on his land as freedmen. The loyalty that some ex-slaves demonstrated toward their former masters was difficult to comprehend. This paradox in nineteenth-century Southern culture was indeed peculiar, and deep rooted.

The committee soon returned to Woodward's article. The verbal battle seesawed back and forth with Forrest feeding the panel a steady diet of "I reckon," "I can't quite recollect," "I have no idea," "I do not remember," and "That, I cannot tell." Eventually, Forrest made an admission that he had belonged to a group known as the Pale Faces and explained that the group had nothing to do with the Klan. He told them it was a club like the Masons or the Independent Order of Odd Fellows. He told them he had heard of other organizations such as the Knights of the White Camellia. The committee wanted details.

"Were they organizations of white men?"

"I suppose they were."

"Was it a secret organization?"

"I suppose it was."

The committee wanted to know who had invited Forrest into the ranks of the Pale Faces.

"Some of the members."

"Who were they?"

"I do not recollect."

"How many were there?"

"I do not recollect."

"About how many?"

"I have no idea."

"You do not remember one of them?"

"No, sir; I might if I had time to think the matter over."[111]

They wanted to know what had become of the hundreds of letters he had received requesting his counsel. "Have you any of those letters now?"

"Perhaps I have some of those; but most of the other letters I burned up, for I did not want to get them into trouble."[112]

The fear of a race war in the South was a subject the committee visited off and on during the day's proceedings. "You have said something about a war of races being apprehended. Had you any more reason to apprehend a war of the races after the rebellion was over than during the rebellion?"

Forrest answered, "A great deal more."

"Why was that?"

Forrest responded, "For the reason that during the war the negroes remained at home working and were quiet, and were not organized. After the war, they left their homes, traveled all over the country, killed all the livestock there was in the country to eat, were holding these night meetings, were carrying arms, and were making threats."

"You say there was a general apprehension throughout the whole country that there would be a war of the races?"

Forrest replied, "I think so; there was great fear. The great fear of the people at that time was that they would be dragged into a revolution something like San Domingo."

After more verbal sparring, Chairman Scott came back to the names Forrest had said he needed time to recollect. "You desired time to consider whether you would give us the names of those persons whose names were asked of you?"

"I do not recollect them."

"You gave the names of one man [Saunders] who was dead; another who was also dead you did not give the name of?"

Forrest told them, "Two of these men have gone out of the country; they are not in the country now."

"Who are they?"

"One was named Jones."

"What was his first name?"

"He has gone to Brazil, and has been there for two or three years; I cannot call his name to mind now."

The man, Saunders, was actually Benjamin E. Saunders who had been a slaveholder in Coahoma County, Mississippi. In reality, Forrest knew him very well because Saunders had commanded a company of scouts in Forrest's cavalry.[113]

Stevenson was apparently irritated by the subtle insolence he perceived and demanded, "I should like to have it understood that this witness will give us the names as soon as he can remember them, if not in person then in writing as soon as possible."

Forrest fired right back, "I tried to do my duty as a soldier, and since I have been out of the war I have tried to do my duty as a citizen. I have done more probably than any other man in the South to suppress these difficulties and keep them down. While I have been vilified and abused in the papers, and accused of things I never did while in the army and since, I have no desire to hide anything from you at all. I want this matter settled; I want our country quiet once more; and I want to see our people united and working together harmoniously."[114]

Forrest's barrage was a smoke screen. He had always enjoyed gambling, but it must have been difficult to keep a poker face as he told the committee "he had nothing to hide."

Near the closing moments of the grueling session, the committee returned to the race war issue. "Suppose the negroes had succeeded and whipped the whites?" This question from Stevenson may have been an attempt to bait Forrest.

Forrest coolly replied, "The whites would have called in more help. You would have gone, I reckon, if you had been there. I do not suppose there is a white man that would not take sides against the blacks, and with his own race."

A committee member asked, "Men at a great distance would not know which side was to blame, would they?"

Forrest replied, "But, in the case of a fight like that . . ." and left the rest unsaid, assuming that any white man would be compelled to join the white side regardless of who was to blame.

The argument continued for a few minutes more over the possibility of the white people in the North coming to the rescue of the white Southerners in the event of a race war that never took place. It seemed that Forrest had either deftly redirected the committee's focus, or they had veered completely off course on their own because the line of questioning had become completely irrelevant to the issue at hand.

Perhaps realizing that they were not going to be able to outflank the old strategist, the chairman finally asked, "I did not understand you to say whether you would send us those names by mail or not?"

It was the last question of the daylong session, and Forrest's response was uttered with a sense of finality indicative of his continuing resistance and insolence toward the committee. "I did not say whether I would or not."[115]

# Chapter Seventeen

# HE WAS, MOST VERILY, NATURE'S SOLDIER

*—Joseph Garnet Wolseley*

## June 1871-October 1877

Forrest left Washington and returned to his railroad line in Alabama. It was true that he had lied during his testimony before the committee. However, in many ways, he may have been telling them as much as he knew about the Klan's current state of affairs. He probably did not know what the remaining Klan dens were actually up to. He did tell one unnamed friend after the hearing that "he'd been lying like a gentleman."[1] It is possible that the Klan leaders who continued the night riding were still invoking his name, but the last thing a legitimate businessman needed was to be connected to the continued terrorism that plagued parts of Tennessee and the rest of the South.

Forrest definitely had inside knowledge of the Klan from 1867 to 1869. But as likely as not, he assumed his subordinates had phased out the Klan and that it no longer existed other than as renegade factions without organization. His attempts to scale back the violence and move the Klan toward a temporary truce and political toleration of conservative blacks created a huge rift among the rank and file. Hardcore members and officers divorced themselves from their original leaders, who feared the Klan's current course was jeopardizing the political progress of the conservative Democratic Party.

In the meantime, construction on the rail line was progressing slowly. As the business pressures mounted some of Forrest's old friendships began to fall apart. Minor Meriwether, who had been one of Forrest's subordinates during the war and in the Klan, began to have serious disagreements with Forrest over certain business practices. The disagreement led Meriwether, who was chief engineer, and his assistant, H. N. Pharr, to the point of quitting the entire construction project.

471

Forrest wanted Pharr removed because of his strict adherence to the codes and regulations, which Forrest believed was slowing the job and endangering future funds promised by the state and counties. When Meriwether refused to dismiss Pharr and decided to bring the matter up at the pending meeting of the board of directors, to be held at the Greenlaw Opera House, Forrest said that if Meriwether gave such a speech, "one of us will not leave the Greenlaw alive."[2]

Once again, Forrest's temper induced him to react before he thought. The threat, however, was taken very seriously in the Meriwether household. Elizabeth Meriwether remembered that "Forrest was four inches taller and forty pounds heavier than father" and that she tried to persuade her husband "to stay home." When it became obvious that Minor was going through with his speech later that night, the family mobilized like a quasi-military unit preparing for battle.

Elizabeth was a brave and hot-blooded woman who decided that she would do all she could to even the odds for her husband. She immediately sent out several notes to friends begging some of Minor's former war associates to "come to our home at seven o'clock, and to come armed." Minor's son, Lee, said his mother then went to work on sewing a concealed "pocket in the back of father's shirt . . . ten inches long and three inches wide" into which she "slipped a sharp dagger." "When Forrest attacks you," she told her husband, "you can reach up behind your neck and grab this dagger."[3]

That night at the opera house, Forrest "took a seat . . . in a box separated from the stage only by a low railing. Mother, with several friends, occupied the opposite box; in orchestra seats below her were eight of father's friends." The Meriwethers had a healthy respect for the threat Forrest had made and arrived with backup should the worst occur. When Minor took the podium the tension in the air was palpable. Lee remembered his mother "taking a pistol out of her handbag as she lifted me out of her lap and told me to lie down on the floor and go to sleep." One wonders why she would have brought the boy at all if she expected gunplay. She later told her son that she "put [Lee] out of my lap because I wanted to be free to step over the railing onto the stage. While Gen. Forrest assaulted your father I meant to jab my pistol in his back and shoot him dead."[4]

Stepping on stage, Minor "looked in Forrest's direction, drew a pistol and laid it on the table. I understand that some persons object to me speaking here tonight. If that is true, let the objections be made now!" Tense seconds ticked by as the audience "waited breathlessly to see what Forrest would do."[5]

Forrest surprised everyone by saying nothing and doing nothing. By the time of the meeting, his volcanic temper had returned to a more dormant state. Most times, when Forrest had time to consider his actions, and the circumstances, he did the right thing. This time, it was the right thing for two reasons. First, Forrest had overreacted. Secondly, if Minor Meriwether had not shot or stabbed Forrest, Mrs. Meriwether would have.

In spite of the tensions between Meriwether and Forrest, the railroad project continued for the next three years under Forrest's leadership, though construction was often delayed by accidents and weak financial backing. It would be more than three years before Forrest and Meriwether would bury the hatchet and renew their twenty-year friendship.

By the autumn of 1873, the rail project was falling apart due to unforeseen and unavoidable circumstances. The Franco-Prussian War had helped push the country into a recession, which, along with other economic factors, caused the financial panic of 1873. Soon after, an outbreak of yellow fever in Memphis exacerbated the deterioration of the Selma, Marion and Memphis Railroad project.

In the spring of 1874, Forrest's tenure as president of the rail line came to an end. The failure of the railroad project and other economic difficulties forced him to move out of a new home he had recently purchased. His health and his standard of living were declining rapidly. He had made powerful enemies in Tennessee during his life and some of them may not have gone out of their way to inspire confidence or support for his business endeavors. It could have been that some of his old Klan associates had turned on him as well since he had begun to fraternize with Republicans and had endorsed the black vote.

His financial straits affected the entire Forrest family. Willie, who had worked for Bedford's railroad and lived in his father's house along with his own wife and ten-month-old daughter had to move out and take a job with the Memphis Police Department. Bedford and Mary Ann moved into a large log cabin—actually two cabins combined—on President's Island. It was a comfortable home and nothing to be ashamed of; however, it was another step down the social ladder.

A short time before his resignation from the railroad, and with his prospects looking bleak, Forrest took a long shot at returning to the thing he knew best: war. The United States was displeased with the situation in Cuba and there was talk of war with Spain. Forrest decided to write a letter to his old nemesis, General Sherman, commander of the U.S. Army, and volunteer his services. In his letter, Forrest told Sherman he was sure he could bring one to five thousand of his former troops with him. Sherman respectfully declined his offer because he did not think any ground forces would be necessary should a war come.

He did, however, forward the letter to the War Department with a flattering endorsement. Sherman's letter stated that Forrest was

> one of the most extraordinary men developed by our Civil War, and were it left to me in the event of a war requiring cavalry, I would unhesitatingly accept his services and give him a prominent place. I believe now he would fight against our national enemies as vehemently as he did against us, and that is saying enough.[6]

Sherman's endorsement said enough about his military accomplishments, and it said a lot more about the changes in Forrest's views and loyalties. If there were any ties remaining between Forrest and the Ku Klux Klan, he shattered them in August 1874 when he volunteered to help "exterminate" those men responsible for the continued violence against the blacks. Ultimately it would do little, if any, good for his legacy because the country would never divorce his name from its association with the Klan. The offer only placed Forrest in a no man's land between the old order of Klansmen who refused to burn their robes and the general public who never completely believed his new transformation was more than a desperate attempt to salvage his name and survive financially.

Forrest's change of heart toward the Klan also failed to put an end to the violence. In the west Tennessee town of Trenton, a barbecue put on by local blacks turned ugly when some white men crashed the party, ate the food, and refused to pay for their share. A brawl ensued and sixteen black men were arrested. About 1:00 A.M. the next morning, between fifty and a hundred masked men entered the town, rode to the jail, and "forced the Sheriff to turn over his keys." The Klansmen then took the sixteen blacks from the jail and executed four of them outside of town.[7]

Southern newspapers declared it a national shame and called for action. The new governor of Tennessee was Forrest's old subordinate general and ex-Klansman John C. Brown. Forrest wrote to Brown and said that if Brown would give him the authority, "he would capture and exterminate the white marauders who disgrace their race by this cowardly murder of Negroes."[8] Governor Brown considered turning Forrest loose, but then thought again. Brown had seen Forrest in combat and decided that he would go to Trenton himself to investigate the situation and thanked Forrest for his offer.

In November another one of Forrest's generals was elected to public office, this time to a seat in Congress. George G. Dibrell, also an ex-Klansman, was able to shake off any damage to his reputation as an officer of the Invisible Empire and he managed to reestablish himself quite successfully.

Former Confederates from all over the South were also putting old animosities behind them, going on with their lives, and in many cases, moving in high social and political circles. Not so in the case of the former Grand Wizard. Forrest's gradual change of heart, which had actually begun in 1868, did little to convince the Northern newspapermen that he was anything but what they had always painted him, a butcher and a widow-maker.

Through the summer and fall of 1874, Forrest remained in the public eye, attending ceremonies, celebrations of the "lost cause," and various other functions. During that time, a former comrade in arms, Ruben Davis, requested a cannon from Forrest as a souvenir. Forrest searched throughout Memphis but could not find one. He wrote to his old colleague that he had been "looking around the city this morning, but am unable to procure one." Demonstrating his old sense of humor, Forrest continued, "Would it not be as well to employ a brass band to accompany the cannon; if so, I can order one." Then, as the nostalgia swept over him, he concluded, "If you had applied twelve or fourteen years ago, I could have furnished you with almost any sort of a cannon. . . . There is nothing like fighting at the front."[9]

Clearly Forrest still maintained a certain status with former Confederates, as seen by the many letters and visits he received, and there was one other community from which came an outpouring of respect, a community that those familiar with Forrest's newspaper reputation would never have expected. As 1875 was coming to a close, Forrest was asked to speak in a most unexpected forum. Invited to a "grand barbecue" thrown by the Pole-Bearers, a black social organization, Forrest was presented with a bouquet of flowers from Miss Lou Lewis, the black daughter of an officer in the organization. Forrest bowed deeply and thanked her. Both the blacks and the whites were exhausted from the race struggle and the flowers were "a token of reconciliation and an offering of peace and good will." Forrest, upon the urging of the crowd, stepped in front of them and gave a most revealing speech:

> Ladies and Gentlemen—I accept the flowers as a memento of reconciliation between the white and colored races of the southern states. I accept it more particularly as it comes from a colored lady, for if there is anyone on God's earth who loves the ladies I believe it is myself. (Immense applause and laughter.) . . . I came here with the jeers of some white people, who think that I am doing wrong. I believe I can exert some influence, and do much to assist the people in strengthening fraternal relations, and shall do all in my power to elevate every man—to depress none. (Applause.) I want to elevate you to take positions in law offices, in stores, on farms, and wherever you are capable of going. [This was a fairly amazing statement on Forrest's part, considering that very few Northerners went as far as recommending the Blacks seek complete equality in business and politics.] I have not said anything about politics today. I don't propose to say anything about politics. You have a right to elect whom you please; vote for the man you think best, and I think, when that is done, you and I are freemen. Do, as you consider right and honest in electing men for office. I did not come here to make you a long speech, although invited to do so by you. I am not much of a speaker, and my business prevented me from preparing myself. I came to meet you as friends, and welcome you to the white people. I want you to come nearer to us. When I can serve you I will do so. We have but one flag, one country; let us stand together. We may differ in color, but not in sentiment. . . . Many things have been said about me which are wrong, and which white and black persons here, who stood by me through the war, can contradict. I have been in the heat of battle when colored men asked me to protect them. I have placed myself between them and the bullets of my men, and told them they should go unharmed. Go to work, be industrious, live honestly and act truly, and when you are oppressed I'll come to your relief. I thank you, ladies and gentlemen, for this opportunity you have afforded me to be with you, and to assure you that I am with you in heart and in hand (Prolonged applause.)[10]

Obviously, Forrest was referring to Fort Pillow when he mentioned that he had run between his men and the black troops to stop the firing. All in all, it was quite a speech, considering his reputation among the black population in Tennessee and Mississippi. However, in a town where practically all the barbers were black, Forrest made it a point never to go to the same barber twice in a row for fear that a plot to cut his throat might be circulating.[11]

Although he was obviously attempting to tone down his warlike tendencies, he was still wrestling with control of his terrible temper. When a Memphis tailor shop was negligent in allowing one of Forrest's suits to be damaged by moths, the old warrior was irate. Charging into the shop, Forrest pulled a pistol on the poor tailor and threatened him. The startled man exclaimed, "Why, General, you would not shoot me for such a trifle as this!" "Goddamn you, yes," Forrest roared, "I'd shoot you like a rat."

As on too many occasions in his life, Forrest felt terrible after he had exploded. Returning later to the tailor shop, Forrest apologized profusely. "Good gracious!" the tailor exclaimed. "General, can you do nothing with that temper of yours?" Forrest told the truth when he answered, "No, I'll be damned if I can."[12]

He would never be able to change some aspects of his personality any more than a tiger could change its stripes. That he did struggle to control his temper is certain, but as hard as he fought to keep it in check, he returned happily to another vice. After the war, he once again began to actively gamble on horse races and card games, and he appears to have been more than an amateur; however, he now saw gambling as a necessity rather than a sport.

Mary Ann had tried to get him to stop since they were first married, but to no avail. Even the law had not been able to deter him. His last scrape with civil authority had come before the war began when on February 25, 1861, Forrest faced an indictment by a grand jury in Coahoma County, Mississippi. The indictment claimed that Bedford "unlawfully then and there did play at and bet upon a certain game of cards for money, contrary to the form and statute in such cases . . . and against the peace and dignity of the State of Mississippi." The sheriff attempted to carry out the warrant and arrest Forrest, but by that time Forrest had gone off to war, and the charges were eventually dropped.[13]

Nevertheless, neither the war nor his wife could significantly alter his appetite for the dice and cards, preferably Five Card Stud. John Morton mentioned an occasion when he ran into Forrest in Nashville. "John," the general said, "can you tell me where I can find a gambling saloon?" Morton said that he had no idea where such an institution could be found and then naively asked why he wanted one in the first place. "I found one tonight, broke the bank and have $2,500 of their money," Forrest answered, as if the evening's gambling success were a military victory. He then added,

"I thought I had time to tackle another before I went to bed."[14]

Though his wife had difficulty curtailing Forrest's gambling, as he became physically weaker, he surrendered more and more control of his life to Mary Ann. Their roles were changing because of his declining physical condition, but there were some things he did out of conviction and not to please another, even his wife. In the winter of 1875, Forrest finally made a formal spiritual commitment that seemed to profoundly affect his remaining days. This religious conversion took place at the Cumberland Presbyterian Church.[15]

The Forrests' last home was situated on President's Island, where Bedford entered his final business venture. The old warhorse leased thirteen hundred acres on President's Island, eight hundred acres of which were "cleared and in cultivation." For laborers, Forrest turned to the new Convict Lease System, which had gone into effect in Mississippi in 1866. The new system was a clever method by policymakers to return a small segment of the population to a state of virtual slavery. This system of prison labor would last for thirty years before being repealed in 1896. However, it was replaced by an equally brutal system, the chain gang. For the convicts the change brought only marginal benefits, especially when compared to the penal institutions in the North. Southern convicts died at a ratio of three to one in comparison to prisoners confined in Northern penitentiaries during the same period.

Forrest had 117 convicts segregated into "five apartments," which were more like military barracks. No records exist that tell how these convicts fared. His most well-documented trait as an employer is that he was exceedingly strict with those who worked for him. Among those convicts in his employ were eighteen black and four white female prisoners along with thirty-five white and sixty black male convicts who worked the land on Forrest's island plantation.[16]

Though his health was failing fast, Forrest still had the strength to attend a reunion of the Seventh Tennessee Cavalry on September 21, 1876, and give a speech. He spoke from horseback, fearing that if he left the saddle he would not be able to remount without assistance. "Soldiers, I was afraid I could not be here with you today," he told his former troops, "but I could not bear the thought of not meeting with you." It is well that he made the effort to be with men with whom he had made history because it would be the last time. At the next reunion, Willie went in place of his father, who was too weak to attend.[17]

With the spring of 1877, Forrest's declining health had left him all but unrecognizable to those who had known him. Although the plantation on President's Island was doing well, the swampy conditions on the island and Forrest's refusal to stop working probably aggravated his poor physical condition. In hopes of slowing the deterioration, he began to travel to the resort of Hurricane Springs, Alabama, to "take the waters," which were rumored to have medicinal properties that promoted healing. He was diagnosed with chronic dysentery brought on by some sort of malarial infection that ravaged his frame and reduced him to a one-hundred-pound skeleton of a man. Soon he could no longer make the trip to Hurricane Springs and stopped his traveling altogether to stay home where "the only food he could keep down was Mary Ann's 'beef tea.'"[18]

Returning from his last trip to the hot springs in September 1877, he had to be carried from the carriage to the Memphis home of his brother, Jesse, to which he had moved to spend his final days. Over the next month Forrest was visited by a wide array of former soldiers and officers who made the trip to see the old general before it was too late. None of them could believe how badly his condition had worsened. Maj. Charles Anderson noted "that he didn't appear to me to be the same man I used to know so well." Forrest was aware of how he had changed and told Anderson, "Major, I am not the man you were with so long ago and I knew so well. I hope I am a better man. I've joined the Church and am trying to live a Christian life. . . . I want you to know that between me and . . . the face of my Heavenly Father, not a cloud intervenes."[19]

At the end of October, Minor Meriwether and his son, Lee, came to pay their respects. To them Forrest looked like a ghost, and he spoke with great effort to Minor's son. "Don't be afraid, Lee. . . . Your father is my friend. Come closer [and] let me look at you." Forrest ran his fingers through Lee's hair and said, "A fine boy, Colonel . . . I hope he will live to be a true son of the South."

Lee later wrote that when father and son left Forrest that day, his father's eyes suddenly "brimmed with tears." Minor told his son, "The man you just saw dying will never die. He will live in the memory of men who love patriotism, and who admire genius and daring."[20]

The former president of the Confederacy, Jefferson Davis, came by to see Forrest on October 29, but Bedford was passing into and out of consciousness and hardly recognized his old commander in chief. After Davis departed, Minor Meriwether returned and volunteered to keep the deathwatch until Forrest's last enemy came for him.

Nearing 7:30 P.M. that evening, October 29, 1877, Meriwether heard the final words ever spoken by the Wizard of the Saddle. Momentarily regaining consciousness, Forrest said, "Call my wife." Then he let out his last breath and passed into legend.

They all came out to honor him at his funeral. The politicians were there, and the citizens, the generals and the soldiers. Some three thousand African-Americans also were there, perhaps as a reminder that, after all, Forrest had also been a man of vision on their behalf, calling for their civil rights a hundred years before it became fashionable.

The size of his funeral procession befitted such a man: business-man, civic leader, warrior, and reconciler. In spite of the other things he was—slave trader, racist, rebel, and, some would say, murderer—the tribute was appropriate. It affirmed, as those who have sought to understand him have said ever after, that in the end any attempt to fully understand such a man remains a search for the enigma that was Nathan Bedford Forrest.

# AFTERWORD

In researching the life of Nathan Bedford Forrest we seemed to be trying continually to unravel one mystery or another about the man. It appears to us that for almost every side of his character, and there are many, there is an opposite; in short the word we found ourselves trying to work around is "enigma." Many who have written about Forrest have been adamant that whatever he was, he was certainly not an enigma or a mystery, and those writers have felt comfortable with that assessment. Their conclusions have often been one dimensional: murderer, legendary warrior, boaster, man of peace. Our conclusion is that it is practically impossible to categorize him and his actions. In attempting to be impartial in presenting readers and students with yet another Forrest tome, we found much to admire about the man. Yet, in another situation his actions give us pause.

One of the most elusive mysteries about Forrest is what appears to be a mighty change of heart near the end of his life and the significance of that transformation. The change we speak of is his attitude toward the former slaves whose bondage he was deeply involved in as a slave trader before the war. As early as 1865, he spoke of a covenant between himself and his slaves that led him to promise those who went to war with him that they would have their freedom no matter what the outcome of the war.

Not long before his death he addressed an organization of African-Americans known as the Pole-Bearers. His obviously heartfelt words were ahead of their time. He said things about the opportunities and rights of freedmen that even Lincoln had not said, nor had those in Congress and other anti-slavery organizations. Though his words have often been cynically dismissed, if one takes his speech at face value he seems to be visionary in his call for full citizenship, education, and an equal place for freedmen in the new postwar society.

As Forrest's health began to fail he opened himself to religion. Could this be a factor in his change of heart toward the former slaves? His wife, Mary Ann, must have prayed mightily for his conversion, and in her happiness when it came she asked no questions. Or might Forrest have again been showing a very human side of his character in seeking peace and forgiveness in religion? Many do become more religious as they approach the end of their lives.

It is easy for some to dismiss this late life conversion as the desires of an old, sick man to be absolved of his sins. But this is a shallow judgment, for no one can read the mind and heart of another. So we take his religious experience, and the peace it obviously brought him, for what it is. Among his last professions in this life were those of faith and his sense of God's forgiveness. But there is some evidence that this vision was not the product of a deathbed repentance.

Shortly after the war Forrest sought to regain at least a part of his prewar fortune in whatever enterprise he could. He tried building railroads instead of wrecking them as he had proved so adept during the war. There was a short stint in insurance, which took him across the South and probably provided cover for his Klan-organizing activities. And, of course, he returned to the soil and cotton. At one point he was in partnership with former Union officers and employed a number of black farm laborers.

His kindnesses to these former slaves caused concern, just as his prewar slave trading had brought him critical attention. He paid his laborers more for their services than did other farmers in western Tennessee, and he allowed many of them to have guns. Both of these actions caused some anxiety not only among Southern neighbors, but also among Union officials. Captain Collins, a representative of the Freedman's Bureau, visited Forrest and told him that he was highly pleased with Forrest's management of his laborers and his farm. He noted that Forrest's operation exceeded any advantage for freedmen on any other plantation he had seen.

Forrest was so far ahead of his neighbors in the way he treated and paid his black employees that Captain Collins seemed duty bound to qualify his earlier praise by pointedly questioning the wisdom in treating freedmen so. Surely, the official implied, Forrest could see that the wages he paid his laborers was unhealthy for the local economy; and to put guns in the hands of blacks?

Even though he was at that time being recruited for leadership in the Ku Klux Klan, Forrest seems to have been slowly developing a more enlightened outlook. If one sees a progression in Forrest's attitude change, it is reasonable to assume that that change began some ten years before he "got religion" and called for the rights of the freedmen of the South before the Pole-Bearers Association in 1875. And yet, the mystery again arises when in that same speech he inexplicably brought up Fort Pillow, certainly the one event in his military career for which there has been no absolution in the eyes of his critics. To the blacks who listened attentively to his speech, he appeared to be imploring them to understand that he also acted nobly at Fort Pillow by rushing between his men and the Union soldiers with pistol and saber drawn in an effort to stop the killing frenzy.

If the reader seeks evidence that Forrest was a predictable, one-dimensional character, easy to understand and to brand as a mean and hateful image of the dark side of the Southern cause, then this observation fails to explain Forrest's complexity. Are his assertions of faith and acceptance of the new realities following the war, his support of black rights, and loyalty to the United States proof of a sincere and profound change in his life? In these pages we have attempted to present the complete Forrest: survivor of a harsh frontier boyhood, dedicated family man, civic leader, businessman, unequaled warrior, would-be reconciler.

We leave to the reader to divine, if it is possible, Forrest's true nature. Perhaps Shakespeare said it as well as can be said when he gave Marc Antony the following words to speak over the body of Brutus in *Julius Caesar:* "The elements [were] so mix'd in him that Nature might stand up and say to all the world, 'This was a man!'"[1]

# NOTES

## Chapter One

1. "Speeches of Abraham Lincoln, at Springfield, June 17, 1858," *The Writings of Abraham Lincoln,* ed. Arthur Brooks Lapsley (New York: G. P. Putnam's Sons, 1906), 1-13.
2. Thomas Jordan and J. P. Pryor, *The Campaigns of Lieutenant General N. B. Forrest and of Forrest's Cavalry* (1868; reprint, Dayton, Ohio: Morningside Bookshop, 1977), 18.
3. Desoto County Chancery Clerk's Records, Book H, 43-44, quoted in Jack Hurst, *Forrest: A Biography* (New York: Random House, 1993), 390; Jordan and Pryor, 18-20.
4. Robert Selph Henry, *First with the Most* (1944; New York: Konecky and Konecky, 1992), 13. (All citations referencing Henry hereafter refer to this citation unless otherwise noted.)
5. Henry, 13-14.
6. Jordan and Pryor, 20.
7. John A. Wyeth, *That Devil Forrest* (1899; reprint, Baton Rouge and London: Louisiana State UP, 1989), 12-13.
8. Brian Steel Wills, *A Battle from the Start* (New York: HarperCollins 1992), 11-12.
9. Ibid., 12.
10. Wyeth, 8-9.
11. Jordan and Pryor, 21-22.
12. Wills, 377; "General Forrest's Illness," *Atlanta Daily Constitution,* 3 September 1877.
13. Jordan and Pryor, 22-23.
14. Wyeth, 23; Jordan and Pryor, 22-23.
15. Jack Hurst, *Forrest: A Biography* (New York: Random House, 1993), 25; Wyeth, 19.

16. Hurst, 17.

17. Jordan and Pryor, 25.

18. Hurst, 17; Wyeth, 14; Henry, 25.

19. Jordan and Pryor, 25.

20. Ibid.

21. Jordan and Pryor, 26-27; Wyeth, 15-16; Thomas Hugh, *The Slave Trade: The Story of the Atlantic Slave Trade, 1440-1870* (New York: Simon and Schuster, 1997), 570.

22. Jordan and Pryor, 27-28; Wills, 27-28.

23. Jordan and Pryor, 29.

24. Hurst, 36; Shelby County Register's Records, Book 42, 163, as quoted in Hurst.

25. Jordan and Pryor, 26-27.

26. Ibid., 26.

## Chapter Two

1. *The Rebellion Record,* vol. 1, ed. Frank Moore (New York, 1861), 3-4.

2. *Mary Chestnut's Civil War,* ed. C. Vann Woodward (New Haven, Conn.: Yale UP, 1981), 46.

3. Ibid., 217.

4. John Milton Hubbard, *Notes of a Private,* (St. Louis: Nixon-Jones Printing Co., 1911), 15.

5. Jordan and Pryor, 41-44; Wyeth, 24-28.

6. C. W. Button, Mrs., *Confederate Veteran* (September 1897): 478.

7. Jordan and Pryor, 42-43.

8. D. C. Kelley, *The Methodist Review* 49 (March-April 1900): 221.

9. *The War of the Rebellion: A Compilation of the Official Records of the Union and Confederate Armies,* series 4, 179-92 (hereafter cited as O.R.).

10. Henry, 38-39.

11. Ibid., 40.

12. Hurst, 77; Henry, 41; O.R., series 1, vol. 7, 333.

13. Wyeth, 26.

14. Ibid., 27.

15. Ibid.

16. O.R., series 1, vol. 7, 295.

17. Henry, 44.

18. O.R., series 1, vol. 7, 65.

19. Henry, 45; Jordan and Pryor, 53; O.R., series 1, vol. 7, 65.

20. O.R., series 1, vol. 7, 65.

21. William Stier, "Fury Takes the Field," *Civil War Times* 38

(December 1999): 27.

22. O.R., series 1, vol. 7, 62-66.

23. Jordan and Pryor, 53-54.

24. O.R., series 1, vol. 7, 62-66.

25. O.R., series 1, vol. 7, 62-66; Stier, 28; Adam R. Johnson, *The Partisan Raiders of the Confederate States Army* (Louisville, Ky., 1904), 42-43.

26. Jordan and Pryor, 54; Wyeth, 33; Lonnie E. Maness, *An Untutored Genius: The Military Career of General Nathan Bedford Forrest* (Oxford, Miss.: University of Tennessee at Martin; Guild Bindery Press, 1990), 29.

27. Wyeth, 32.

28. Ibid.

29. O.R., series 1, vol. 7, 362-72; Maness, 30.

30. Henry, 49-50.

31. O.R., series 1, vol. 7, 601.

32. Henry, 51-52.

33. O.R., series 1, vol. 7, 183, 383-84; Wyeth, 37.

34. O.R., series 1, Vol. 7, 384.

35. Ibid.; Wyeth, 37; Jordan and Pryor, 64.

36. Jordan and Pryor, 64.

37. Ibid.

38. Maness, 35; Henry, 53.

39. O.R., series 1, vol. 7, 262-63, 395; Wyeth, 36; Maness, 39.

40. O.R., series 1, vol. 7, 262-63, 395.

41. Jordan and Pryor, 67-69.

42. O. R., series 1, vol. 7, 384; Maness, 39; Jordan and Pryor, 68.

43. Jordan and Pryor, 68.

44. Wyeth, 40.

45. O.R., series 1, vol. 7, 263; Maness, 39.

46. O.R., series 1, vol. 7, 263.

47. Maness, 40.

48. Jordan and Pryor, 71.

49. Ibid., 72-73.

50. O.R., series 1, vol. 7, 384-87; Henry, 55.

51. O.R., series 1, vol. 7, 186, 243, 248, 282, 340, 343, 374: Maness, 42.

52. Henry, 55.

53. Jordan and Pryor, 76.

54. Ibid., 77-78.

55. O.R., series 1, vol. 7, 167-68, 186-87, 200, 244; Maness, 43; Jordan and Pryor, 84-85.

56. Jordan and Pryor, 82-83.
57. Ibid., 86-87.
58. Henry, 55.
59. O.R., series 1, vol. 7, 318, 332-33; Maness, 45.
60. Jordan and Pryor, 87-88.
61. Robert T. Johnson and Clarence C. Buel, eds., *Battles and Leaders of the Civil War*, 4 vol. (New York, 1956), 419: Maness, 46.
62. Henry, 56.
63. Jordan and Pryor, 84.
64. Ibid., 88.
65. O.R., series 1, vol. 7, 269, 287-88, 295-98, 300, 333, 386.
66. O.R., series 1, vol. 7, 386; Maness, 50.
67. Jordan and Pryor, 90-92.
68. O.R., series 1, vol. 7, 204-98, 300; Wyeth, 52; Maness, 48; Jordan and Pryor, 91-92.
69. Henry, 56-59.
70. O.R., series 1, vol. 7, 294-98, 300, 334, 386; Henry, 59.
71. O.R., series 1, vol. 7, 295; Wyeth, 53.
72. Jordan and Pryor, 92-94.
73. O.R., series 1, vol. 7, 295, 396; Jordan and Pryor, 92-93.

**Chapter Three**

1. Basil W. Duke, *Morgan's Cavalry* (New York: Doubleday, 1906), 113; Maness, 54.
2. Stanley F. Horn, *The Army of Tennessee* (Norman: University of Oklahoma Press, 1952), 103; O.R., series 1, vol. 7, 427-49.
3. O.R., series 1, vol. 7, 428-32.
4. Horn, 103.
5. William Preston Johnson, *The Life of General Albert Sidney Johnston* (New York: Appleton, 1878), 497, 512; Maness, 57.
6. O.R., series 1, vol. 8, 27.
7. Jordan and Pryor, 107; Maness, 59.
8. Henry, 75.
9. Isham G. Harris to Col. William Preston, 6 April 1862, as quoted in Henry, 31.
10. Henry, 77.
11. O.R., series 1, part 1, vol. 10, 454-55; Jordan and Pryor, 127-28.
12. Maness, 63; O.R., series 1, part 1, vol. 10, 135-37.
13. Jordan and Pryor, 127-28; Wyeth, 62.
14. O.R., series 1, part 1, vol. 10, 355; Henry, 79.
15. O.R., series 1, part 1, vol. 10, 135-37.

16. Jordan and Pryor, 134-35.
17. James R. Chalmers (speech before the Southern Historical Society, August 15, 1879), *Southern Historical Society Papers*, vol. VII, no. 10, 458.
18. Wills, 69.
19. Henry, 79.
20. Ibid., 79-80.
21. Ibid., 80-81; Jordan and Pryor, 143-48.
22. Gilbert V. Rambaut, "Forrest at Shiloh" (paper read before the Confederate Historical Society at Memphis, Tenn., 14 January 1896) in *Commercial Appeal,* 19 January 1896, 5-6, as quoted in Henry, *As They Saw Forrest,* 54-65.
23. Henry, 81; O.R., series 1, part 1, vol. 10, 639-41.
24. Henry, 82.
25. *Memphis Appeal,* June 1862; Henry, 82.
26. Hurst, 95.

**Chapter Four**

1. Hurst, 96.
2. Jordan and Pryor, 159-73; Hurst, 96; Alfred Roman, *Military Operations of General Beauregard,* vol. 1 (New York, 1884), 402.
3. Jordan and Pryor, 159-73.
4. Wills, 72.
5. O.R., series 1, part 1, vol. 16, 810; Hurst, 97.
6. O.R., series 1, part 1, vol. 16, 774-75; Maness, 71.
7. Wyeth, 72; Wills, 71-72.
8. Wyeth, 73; Henry, 87.
9. Charles F. Bryan, "I Mean to Have Them All: Forrest's Murfreesboro Raid," *Civil War Times Illustrated* (January 1974): 30; Maness, 73.
10. Hurst, 99-100.
11. O.R., series 1, part 1, vol. 16, 802, 810; Hurst, 97; Wyeth, 73-74.
12. O.R., series 1, part 1, vol. 16, 805.
13. Ibid., 806.
14. Ibid., 798-811.
15. Ibid., 809, 811.
16. Ibid., 806-7; Hurst, 102; Jordan and Pryor, 170.
17. Jordan and Pryor, 170.
18. D. S. Stanley, "Is Forrest a Butcher? A Little Bit of History," *New York Times,* September 14, 1868.
19. Wills, 77; Tennessee Cavalry, Regiment Fourth, Folder 13,

Military Units, Confederate Collection, Civil War Collection, Box 17, Tennessee State Library and Archives, Nashville, as quoted in Wills, 77.

20. Wills, 78; *The Heavens Are Weeping: The Diaries of George Richard Browder, 1852-1886,* ed. Richard L. Troutman (Grand Rapids, Mich.: Zondervan Publishing House, 1987), 125.

21. Hurst, 103.

22. Wyeth, 81.

23. O.R., series 1, part 1, vol. 16, 809-11.

24. Robert Selph Henry, *As They Saw Forrest* (Jackson, Tenn.: McCowat-Mercer Press, 1956), 40-41.

## Chapter Five

1. O.R., series 1, part 2, vol. 16, 716, 721, 728-29.

2. Henry, *First with the Most,* 91-92.

3. Ibid., 92.

4. Jordan and Pryor, 178.

5. O.R., series 1, part 2, vol. 16, 234; Henry, 92-94.

6. O.R., series 1, part 2, vol. 16, 266; Maness, 79.

7. O.R., series 1, part 2, vol. 16, 906-52: Henry, 98-99; Maness, 80.

8. Jordan and Pryor, 180 (Forrest's notes).

9. Jordan and Pryor, 180-81.

10. O.R., series 1, part 2, vol. 16, 754; Jordan and Pryor, 181-82.

11. Jordan and Pryor, 182-83; Maness, 81-82.

12. O.R., series 1, part 2, vol. 16, 748-49; Hurst, 105.

13. O.R., series 1, part 2, vol. 16, 833; Jordan and Pryor, 183.

14. Jordan and Pryor, 183-84.

15. Ibid., 187-88; Hurst 107.

16. Jordan and Pryor, 189.

17. Morton, John. *The Artillery of Nathan Bedford Forrest's Cavalry* (Marietta, Ga.: R. Bemis Publishing Ltd., 1995), 45.

18. Morton, 45-46; Hurst, 103-4.

19. O.R., series 1, part 1, vol. 17, 592; Maness, 88.

20. Henry, 108.

21. Wyeth, 92.

22. O.R., series 1, part 2, vol. 17, 423; Andrew Nelson Lytle, *Bedford Forrest and His Critter Company* (New York: Herald Tribune, 1931), 117-18.

23. Jordan and Pryor, 195; Maness, 89; Hurst, 108.

24. O.R., series 1, part 1, vol. 17, 553.

25. *Confederate Veteran* 15 (January 1909): 54; Maness, 91.
26. Jordan and Pryor, 196.
27. *Confederate Veteran* 15 (January 1909): 54; Maness, 91.
28. O.R., series 1, part 1, vol. 17, 594; Jordan and Pryor, 196-97.
29. Jordan and Pryor, 197-98; O.R., series 1, vol. 17, 593-98.
30. Jordan and Pryor, 199; Maness, 93.
31. O.R., series 1, part 1, vol. 17, 593-94; Jordan and Pryor, 199.
32. Jordan and Pryor, 199-200.
33. Jordan and Pryor, 201.
34. *Trenton Herald Democrat* (beginning with the issue of September 25, 1903), as reported in Culp and Ross, Gibson County, 40, as quoted in Maness, 96-97; Jordan and Pryor, 202.
35. *Trenton Herald Democrat,* as quoted in Maness, 96-97.
36. Morton, 60-61.
37. Morton, 59; Hurst, 109.
38. O.R., series 1, part 1, vol. 17, 593-96, 598; Jordan and Pryor, 204; Morton, 60.
39. Jordan and Pryor, 205; Morton, 60-61.
40. Logan report, December 27, 1862; O.R., series 1, part 1, vol. 17, 562-68; Wills, 90.
41. O.R., series 1, part 1, vol. 17, 594.
42. Henry, 115.
43. Morton, 61-62.
44. O.R., series 1, part 1, vol. 17, 495; Henry, 115.
45. Henry, 115; Morton, 62; Jordan and Pryor, 207.
46. O.R., series 1, part 1, vol. 17, 595; Jordan and Pryor, 206-8.
47. O.R., series 1, part 2, vol. 17, 505.
48. Henry, 116-17.
49. Ibid., 116.
50. Jordan and Pryor, 209.
51. O.R., series 1, part 1, vol. 17, 480, 569, 573; Jordan and Pryor, 210-11.
52. Wyeth, 107; Jordan and Pryor, 209-11; Maness, 105.
53. Maness,106-7.
54. Wills, 95.
55. Henry, 487; Hurst, 112.
56. Jordan and Pryor, 212.
57. Ibid., 217.
58. Ibid., 212.
59. O.R., series 1, part 1, vol. 17, 588-89; Maness, 108.
60. Wills, 94.

61. Morton, 66-67.
62. Jordan and Pryor, 214.
63. Henry, 118-19.
64. Maness, 111; O.R., series 1, part 1, vol. 17, 570.
65. O.R., series 1, part 1, vol. 17, 552.
66. Henry, 120.

**Chapter Six**

1. Maness, 118.
2. Henry, 126.
3. Ibid., 124.
4. Ibid.,125-26.
5. O.R., series 1, part 1, vol. 23, 38, 41; Jordan and Pryor, 229.
6. Maness, 121.
7. Wyeth, 127.
8. Henry, 126-27.
9. Wyeth, 133.
10. O.R., series 1, part 1, vol. 35, 65; Henry, 127.
11. Henry, 128.
12. O.R., series 1, part 2, vol. 23, 718.
13. O.R., series 1, part 1, vol. 23, 86-87; Henry, 129.
14. Robert C. Cheeks, "Federal Fiasco at Thompson's Station," *America's Civil War* (November 1999): 29.
15. Ibid., 29-30.
16. O.R., series 1, part 1, vol. 23, 87-89, 116, 120; Wyeth, 157-59.
17. O.R., series 1, part 1, vol. 23, 86-87, 116.
18. O.R., series 1, part 1, vol. 23, 116-19.
19. Henry, 130; O.R., series 1, part 1, vol. 23, 190.
20. Wyeth, 141; O.R., series 1, part 1, vol. 23, 83-85.
21. Cheeks, 28-30.
22. Henry, 130.
23. Ibid., 129; Wyeth, 158-60.
24. O.R., series 1, part 1, vol. 23, 89, 117-20.
25. O.R., series 1, part 1, vol. 23, 83-84, 117, 119, 120-21.
26. Henry, 131.
27. Cheeks, 29-31.
28. Henry, 131.
29. Jordan and Pryor, 238-41; O.R., series 1, part 1, vol. 23, 193.
30. O.R., series 1, part 1, vol. 34, 150-51; Henry, 132.
31. Henry, 133; Wyeth, 149-51.

32. O.R., series 1, part 1, vol. 23, 187-89, 193.
33. Wyeth, 149.
34. Ibid., 150.
35. Ibid.; Henry, 131-33.
36. Wyeth, 149-51.
37. Ibid., 151-53.
38. Henry, 134.
39. Henry, 134-35.
40. O.R., series 1, part 1, vol. 23, 192-95; Henry, 135.
41. Wyeth, 154.
42. Ibid., 154-55; Henry, 135.
43. Henry, 136.
44. Ibid., 137-38; O.R., series 1, part 1, vol. 23, 239-40.
45. O.R., series 1, part 1, vol. 23, 222, 227.
46. Viscount Wolseley, "General Forrest," *The United Service Magazine* n.s., 5 (1892): 121; Henry, 137.
47. Wolseley, as quoted in Henry, 137.
48. Wyeth, 162-63.
49. Hurst, 116.
50. Wills, 107; Henry, 143.
51. Henry, 143-44; *A Soldier's Honor, By His Comrades: The Memoirs of General Van Dorn* as told by his fellow officers (New York, 1902), 276-79.
52. Albert Castel, *Articles of War: Winners, Losers, and Some Who Were Both During the Civil War* (Mechanicsburg, Pa.: Stackpole Books, 2001), 113.

## Chapter Seven

1. Wyeth, 169; Henry, 144.
2. Wills, 109-10.
3. Ibid., 110.
4. Ibid.; Wyeth, 168-70.
5. Henry, 145.
6. Henry, 146; Lt. A. C. Roach, *The Prisoner of War* (Indianapolis, 1865), 21.
7. O.R., series 1, part 1, vol. 23, 288-89.
8. Henry, 147; Wills, 112.
9. Henry, 148-51.
10. Ibid., 149; Wills, 113.
11. Henry, 148.

12. O.R., series 1, part 1, vol. 23, 289-90; Jordan and Pryor, 254.

13. Wills, 114-15.

14. O.R., series 1, part 1, vol. 23, 289-91.

15. Henry, 151; Wyeth, 210-12.

16. Jordan and Pryor, 267-69; Wyeth, 210-12; Henry, l50-51.

17. Jordan and Pryor, 269.

18. Ibid., 269-70.

19. Wills, 116; Jordan and Pryor, 269; Wyeth, 210-12.

20. Jordan and Pryor, 162.

21. Jordan and Pryor, 270.

22. Henry, 154.

23. Henry, 155; Roach, 37-39.

24. O.R., series 1, part 1, vol. 23, 290.

25. O.R., series 1, part 1, vol. 23, 292; Maness, 144.

26. O.R., series 1, part 1, vol. 23, 291-92.

27. Henry, 157.

28. Wyeth, 221-22; Maness, 146.

29. Wills, 121; Wyeth, 198.

30. Wills, 120-21.

31. Henry, 159; Jordan and Pryor, 279-80.

32. Carl Von Clausewitz, *On War* (Princeton, N.J.: Princeton UP, 1976), 605.

33. Frank E. Moran, "Colonel Rose's Tunnel at Libby Prison," *Century Illustrated Monthly Magazine* (March 1888): 770-90; "Particulars of the Escape of the Yankee Officers from the Libby Prison," *Charleston Mercury* (February 16, 1864): 2.

34. Henry, 160-61; O.R., series 1, part 1, vol. 23, 827; Jordan and Pryor, 284.

35. Jordan and Pryor, 286; Wyeth, 226-27.

36. Henry, 162; Morton, 102-5.

37. Morton, 102-5.

38. Henry, 162; Hurst, 128; Morton, 119-22.

39. Hurst, 128.

40. Wills, 125; Henry, 162.

41. Hurst, 129-31; *Nashville Banner* 29 April 1911.

42. Hurst, 130; Lytle, 181.

43. Wyeth, 202.

## Chapter Eight

1. O.R., series 1, part 2, vol. 23, 459-61.

2. Wyeth, 208-9.

3. W. C. Dodson, *Campaigns of Wheeler and His Cavalry* (Guild Bindery Press, 1899), 89-94; John P. Dyer, *Fightin' Joe Wheeler* (Baton Rouge: Louisiana State UP, 1941), 106-7.

4. O.R., series 1, part 1, vol. 23, 534-41.

5. Morton, 110.

6. O.R., series 1, part 2, vol. 23, 507-9; Hurst, 131.

7. O.R., series 1, part 2, vol. 23, 403-9.

8. O.R., series 1, part 4, vol. 30, 588.

9. Henry, 148.

10. Ibid.

11. O.R., series 1, part 4, vol. 30, 610-11, 615, 628; Henry, 173-75.

12. O.R., series 1, part 2, vol. 30, 528.

13. Jordan and Pryor, 306-7.

14. O.R., series 1, part 2, vol. 30, 528; Jordon and Pryor, 308.

15. Henry, 183.

16. Wyeth, 222-23; Henry, 174-75.

17. Wyeth, 224-25.

18. Henry, 183-84.

19. Don Piatt and H. V. Boynton, *The Life of General George H. Thomas* (Cincinnati, 1883), 109, as quoted in Henry, 185-86.

20. Henry, 183-84.

21. Maness, 173-74.

22. O.R., series 1, part 2, vol. 30, 658-60.

23. O.R., series 1, part 2, vol. 30, 525.

24. G. A. Hanson, *Minor Incidents of the Late War* (Bartown, Fla.: 1887), 60.

25. Wyeth, 235-36.

26. Ibid., 236.

27. Ibid., 237; Henry 193-94.

28. Henry, 189-90.

29. Maness, 176.

30. Tully Brown, as quoted in Henry, 193.

31. Henry, 193-94.

32. Ibid., 194.

33. Ibid., 196; Wyeth, 246-47.

34. Henry, 198; Wyeth, 264; Jordan and Pryor, 357.

35. Dr. J. B. Cowan, as quoted in Wyeth, 146-47.

36. Dr. J. B. Cowan, as quoted in Wyeth, 147.

37. Horn, 264-65.

38. Wyeth, 245.

## Chapter Nine

1. O.R., series 1, part 3, vol. 31, 604; Wills, 148-49.
2. O.R., series 1, part 3, vol. 31, 641.
3. O.R., series 1, part 3, vol. 31, 646; Maness, 186; Henry, 203-4.
4. Jordan and Pryor, 362-63.
5. Wyeth, 254.
6. O.R., series 1, part 1, vol. 31, 187, 242-43, 336, 343; Wyeth, 253; Jordon and Pryor, 372-73.
7. Maness, 188-89; William Henderson, ed., "Forrest's March Out of West Tennessee: Recollections of a Private John Johnston," *The West Tennessee Historical Society Papers,* no. XII (1958), 139.
8. Wyeth, 255; O.R., series 1, part 3, vol. 31, 789-90.
9. Wyeth, 255-57; O.R., series 1, part 3, vol. 31, 789-90.
10. Wyeth, 255-56.
11. Henry, 205-7.
12. O.R., series 1, part 3, vol. 31, 443-46, 450-51, 456, 473; Henry, 206.
13. O.R., series 1, part 3, vol. 31, 844-45, 853-54.
14. Wyeth, 258-59.
15. Henry, 259-61.
16. Wyeth, 259-60; Henry, 174-75.
17. Wyeth, 260.
18. Maness, 192.
19. Henry, 209; Wyeth, 262.
20. Henry, 209.
21. Ibid.; Wyeth, 262.
22. O.R., series 1, part 1, 31, 853.
23. Henry, 209.
24. Henry, 208-10; Wyeth, 202-4.
25. Henry, 208-9.
26. Ibid., 210.
27. Wyeth, 262-64; Henry, 209-11.
28. Wyeth, 261-63.
29. O.R., series 1, part 1, vol. 31, 608, 615-17; Henry, 210; Wyeth, 263.
30. Henry, 211.
31. Wyeth, 261-63; O.R., series 1, part 1, vol. 31, 618-20.
32. Henry, 211; O.R., series 1, part 1, vol. 31, 620.
33. Henry, 212.
34. Ibid., 213.
35. From Grierson's and Morgan's official reports, as cited in Henry, 500-1.

36. Wyeth, 265-66.
37. O.R., series 1, part 2, vol. 32, 512-13, 617; Maness, 196; Henry, 213-16.
38. Jordan and Pryor, 382-83; Maness, 197.
39. Henry, 217.
40. Wyeth, 258.
41. Henry, 219.
42. O.R., series 1, part 2, vol. 32, 673, 680-81, 683-85; Maness, 197.
43. Robert G. Domer, "Sooy Smith and That Devil Forrest," *America's Civil War* (May 1988): 37.
44. Henry, 221; O.R., series 1, part 2, vol. 32, 315-16.
45. Henry, 215.
46. Ibid.; Wyeth, 259-61.
47. O.R., series 1, part 2, vol. 32, 315-18.
48. Henry, 222.
49. Hurst, 148; O.R., series 1, part 2, vol. 32, 567, 575, 639, 648.
50. Maness, 201; Henry, 222; O.R., series 1, part 2, vol. 32, 173, 177, 187-89.
51. Henry, 223.
52. Henry, 213-16; Maness, 196-98.
53. Henry, 223; Morton, 145-47.
54. Hurst, 147; O.R., series 1, part 1, vol 32, 181-82.
55. Maness, 202; O.R., series 1, part 2, vol. 32, 431; O.R., series 1, part 1, vol. 32, 257.
56. Henry, 224; O.R., series 1, part 2, vol. 32, 703; O.R., series 1, part 1, vol. 32, 348.
57. Maness, 202; Domer, 38.
58. Morton, 146-49.
59. *Memoirs of General William T. Sherman,* vol. 1 (New York: Charles Webster and Co., 1892), 389-90.
60. Morton, 146-47.
61. Henry, 225; O.R., series 1, part 1, vol. 32, 256-57.
62. Jordan and Pryor, 391-93.
63. Henry, 226; Wyeth, 299-302.
64. Wills, 161; Wyeth, 301-3.
65. Wyeth, 279-80.
66. Jordan and Pryor, 392; John Preston Young, *The Seventh Tennessee Cavalry, C.S.A.: A History* (Dayton, Ohio: Morningside Bookshop, 1976), 77.
67. Henry, 227; Hurst, 151; O.R., series 1, part 1, vol. 32, 350, 353.
68. Henry, 227; O.R., series 1, part 1, vol. 32, 268.

69. Jordan and Pryor, 392.

70. O.R., series 1, part 1, vol. 32, 353; *Sergeant R. Hancock's Diary, or a History of the Second Tennessee Cavalry, C.S.A.* (Dayton, Ohio: Morningside Bookshop,1981), 322-23.

71. Henry, 228; O.R., series 1, part 1, vol. 32, 353; Hancock, 322-23.

72. *Memphis Appeal,* 1 November 1877; Henry, 228.

73. Henry, 229; Hurst, 151; Jordan and Pryor, 392-99; O.R., series 1, part 1, vol. 32, 353.

74. Henry, 229; O.R., series 1, part 1, vol. 32, 351-53.

75. O.R., series 1, part 1, vol. 32, 302-4.

76. Hurst, 152; Jordan and Pryor, 396-97.

77. Jordan and Pryor, 396.

78. Hurst, 153; Henry, 230; Maness, 209; Jordan and Pryor, 396; O.R., series 1, part 1, vol. 32, pp. 354-55.

79. Wyeth, 290-91.

80. Hurst, 153; Wyeth, 290-91.

81. Henry, 230; Wyeth, 291-92.

82. O.R., series 1, part 1, vol. 32, 354; Jordan and Pryor, 399-400.

83. Hurst, 154; O.R., series 1, part 1, vol. 32, 354.

84. Jordan and Pryor, 397-99.

85. Wyeth, 291-93; Jordan and Pryor, 397-99.

86. William Witherspoon, *Reminiscences of a Scout, Spy and Soldier of Forrest's Cavalry* (Jackson, Tenn.: McCowat-Mercer Press, 1910), 97.

87. Ibid., 97-98.

88. Ibid., 97-99.

89. Ibid., 99.

90. O.R., series 1, part 1, vol. 32, 354.

91. Witherspoon, 98-100.

92. Ibid., 100-1.

93. Henry, 232; Maness, 210; Hurst, 154-55; O.R., series 1, part 1, vol. 32, 354.

94. Witherspoon, 34-36.

95. O.R., series 1, part 1, vol. 32, 289, 252.

96. *Personal Memoirs of U.S. Grant,* vol. 2 (New York: Charles L. Webster and Co., 1886), 108-10.

## Chapter Ten

1. Henry, 239.

2. House Committee on the Conduct of the War, *Fort Pillow Massacre Report,* 38th Congress, 1st sess., 1864, H. Rept. 65, 3-4.

3. O.R., series 1, part 1, vol. 32, 549, 551-52; Henry, 239; Wyeth, 306-7.

4. Henry, 240-41.

5. Eddy W. Davison and Daniel L. Foxx, "A Journey to the Most Controversial Battlefield in America," *Confederate Veteran* 6 (2001): 17; Henry, 241-43.

6. O.R., series 1, part 1, vol. 32, 612.

7. Henry, 242.

8. O.R., series 1, part 1, vol. 32, 608-9.

9. Henry, 242; O.R., series 1, part 1, vol. 32, 184.

10. O.R., series 1, part 1, vol. 32, 607-10.

11. Jordan and Pryor, 420-21.

12. Wyeth, 307; O.R., series 1, part 1, vol. 32, 609.

13. *Fort Pillow Massacre Report*, 66.

14. Jordan and Pryor, 422-23.

15. Wyeth, 313; *Fort Pillow Massacre Report*, 65.

16. Maness, 245; *Fort Pillow Massacre Report*, 3-4; Henry, 252.

17. Davison and Foxx, 17-20.

18. Henry, 251.

19. O.R., series 1, part 1, vol. 32, 585-88; *Fort Pillow Massacre Report*, 38; Charles W. Anderson, "The True Story of Fort Pillow," *Confederate Veteran* 3 (November 1895): 322-26.

20. Maness, 245-46.

21. Jordan and Pryor, 431-32; O.R., series 1, part 1, vol. 32, 561, 615.

22. Maness, 246; Davison and Foxx, 19-20.

23. Henry, 253; Anderson, 322.

24. *Fort Pillow Massacre Report*, 38-40.

25. Ibid., 39-41.

26. Maness, 250; Henry, 264-65; Wyeth, 434-35.

27. O.R., series 1, part 1, vol. 32, 614-15; James Dinkins, "The Capture of Fort Pillow," *Confederate Veteran* 33 (December 1925): 460-62; John Cimprich and Robert C. Mainfort, Jr., ed., "Dr. Fitch's Report on the Fort Pillow Massacre," *The Tennessee Historical Quarterly* 44 (Spring 1985): 27-39.

28. Hurst, 171; Jordan and Pryor, 435; O.R., series 1, part 1, vol. 32, 535, 561.

29. O.R., series 1, part 1, vol. 32, 615.

30. *Fort Pillow Massacre Report*, 37-38; Henry, 255; O.R., series 1, part 1, vol. 32, 561.

31. O.R., series 1, part 1, vol. 32, 523, 566; Hancock, 363-64, as quoted in Henry, 508-9.

32. *Fort Pillow Massacre Report*, 36-39; Henry, 254-55.

33. Henry, 256; Hancock, 368.

34. Hurst, 176; Cimprich and Mainfort, 30; *Official Naval Records of the War of the Rebellion: A Compilation of the Official Naval Records of the Union and Confederate Navies,* series 1, vol. 26, 224-25 (hereafter cited as O.R. Navies).

35. Wills, 188-89; Hurst, 176-77.

36. Henry, 264.

37. Cimprich and Mainfort, 30-34; *Fort Pillow Massacre Report,* 85-87.

38. O.R., series 1, part 1, 32, 597-98; *Fort Pillow Massacre Report,* 86.

39. Henry, 257.

40. *Fort Pillow Massacre Report,* 90-91.

41. Henry, 257.

42. *Fort Pillow Massacre Report,* 83.

43. O.R., series 1, part 1, 32, 558.

44. Henry, 255-58.

45. *Fort Pillow Massacre Report,* 8.

46. Hancock, as quoted in Henry, 256.

47. A witness at the Congressional hearings in Cairo, Illinois, reported that a Negro woman came to one of the gunboats with a bullet wound to the knee. See *Fort Pillow Massacre Report,* 82.

48. Maness, 255.

49. Wyeth, 333.

50. Henry, 261.

51. "Between April 1867 and February 1868, 243 bodies of Union soldiers from Fort Pillow were relocated to the National Cemetery in Memphis. Of these bodies, 192 are classified as unknown, while 51 are casualties of units previously garrisoned at Fort Pillow. But if we sum up the relocated, the wounded and the prisoners taken, the total is 558 men, the reported strength of the garrison during the battle. Did the Federal Government inflate the actual casualties or falsely report the killing of civilians?" Althea Sayers, "Fort Pillow: What the Federal Government Didn't Tell," *The Online Civil War Magazine* (http://ehistory.osu.edu/uscw/features/articles/9905/ftpillow.cfm): 4.

52. Ibid., 9.

53. Hurst, 175.

54. *Fort Pillow Massacre Report,* 90-91.

55. Cimprich and Mainfort, 306; *Fort Pillow Massacre Report,* 13, 15, 20-21.

56. Henry, 262-63 (Sergeant Clark's letter supplied by Mrs. Sidney S. Crockett, Sergeant Clark's daughter, of Nashville, Tenn.).

57. Hurst, 177.
58. O.R., series 1, part 1, vol. 32, 610; *Fort Pillow Massacre Report*, 45.
59. O.R., series 1, part 1, vol. 32, 531; *Fort Pillow Massacre Report*, 37-39.
60. *Fort Pillow Massacre Report*, 38-40.
61. Ibid., 32-33.
62. Ibid., 35-38.
63. Hurst, 173.
64. O.R., series 1, part 1, vol. 32, 570; Henry, 256.
65. *Fort Pillow Massacre Report*, 101-2; O.R., series 1, part 1, vol. 32, 619.
66. Henry, 269-70.
67. Ibid.
68. O.R., series 1, part 1, vol. 32, 618-20.
69. *Chicago Tribune*, 4 May 1864, 3.

**Chapter Eleven**

1. Henry, 22-23, 271.
2. Edwin C. Bearss, *Forrest at Brice's Crossroads and in Northern Mississippi in 1864* (Dayton, Ohio: Morningside Bookshop, 1979), 4. (All citations referencing Bearss hereafter refer to this source unless otherwise noted.)
3. O.R., series 1, part 3, vol. 32, 441.
4. O.R., series 1, part 3, vol. 32, 521, 527.
5. O.R., series 1, part 3, vol. 32, 536.
6. O.R., series 1, part 1, vol. 39, 91, 162, 200, 207.
7. O.R., series 1, part 3, vol. 32, 527, 536.
8. Henry, 283.
9. Wills, 203; O.R., series 1, part 1, vol. 39, 91.
10. Wyeth, 350; Edwin C. Bearss, "Brice's Cross Roads," *The Blue and Gray* (summer 1999): 19.
11. Bearss, 67-68.
12. Ibid., 68; O.R., series 1, part 1, vol. 39, 223.
13. Bearss, 69; O.R., series 1, part 1, vol. 39, 132, 135.
14. Wills, 206.
15. John M. Hubbard, *Private Hubbard's Notes* (Memphis, 1909), as quoted in Bearss, 69.
16. O.R., series 1, part 2, vol. 39, 637; Bearss, 71.
17. O.R., series 1, part 1, vol. 39, 141, 204, 223; Hubbard, as quoted in Henry, *As They Saw Forrest,* 162-63.

18. Bearss, 75-76; Morton, 179.

19. Morton, 178-79.

20. Ibid., 179.

21. Ibid., 179-80.

22. Wills, 212-14; Wyeth, 366.

23. Bearss, 101-2.

24. Henry, 293.

25. Bearss, 99-100.

26. Henry, 294.

27. Hurst, 297.

28. O.R., series 1, part 1, vol. 39, 105, 125-26, 181, 210, 213, as cited in Henry, 297.

29. Ibid.

30. Henry, 297.

31. Ibid., 299-300.

32. E. Hunn Hanson, "Forrest's Defeat of Sturgis at Brice's Cross Roads" (June 10, 1864), as quoted in Bearss, 197.

33. Bearss, 133.

34. O.R., series 1, part 1, vol. 39, 214; Henry, 300; Bears, 137-38.

35. Ezra J. Warner, *Generals in Blue; Lives of the Union Commanders* (Baton Rouge: Louisiana State UP, 1964), 486-87.

36. Witherspoon, 124, as quoted in Henry, 66-110; Wills, 215.

37. Henry, 301; O.R., series 1, part 1, vol. 39, 171.

38. Henry, 302; *Home Letters of General Sherman*, ed. M. A. DeWolfe Howe (New York: Charles Scribner's Sons, 1909), 297.

39. Bearss, 137; Howe, 297-98.

40. Bearss, 148; O.R., series 1, part 1, vol. 39, 226-28.

41. Wyeth, 376; O.R., series 1, part 1, vol. 38, 72.

42. Bears, 138; Wyeth, 376; O.R., series 1, vol. 38, 910.

43. Bruce Catton, *Centennial History of the Civil War, Vol. 3: Never Call Retreat* (New York: Doubleday and Co., Inc., 1965), 334-35.

44. Catton, 336.

45. Wyeth, 377; Johnson and Buel, vol. 4, 276.

## Chapter Twelve

1. Maness, pp. 278-79; Johnson and Buel, vol. 4, 276.

2. O.R., series 1, part 2, vol. 39, 651.

3. O.R., series 1, part 1, vol. 39, 325; Wyeth, 379.

4. Bearss, 159-60.

5. Ibid., 162-63.

6. Wyeth, 634; O.R., series 1, part 2, vol. 39, 671.

7. O.R., series 1, part 2, vol. 52, 679-80, 682; Henry, 312.

8. Bearss, 169-70.

9. Ibid., 170.

10. O.R., series 1, part 1, vol. 39, 304-9, Bearss, 173.

11. Henry, 314; Bearss 174-75.

12. Bearss, 179.

13. Ibid., 184; O.R., series 1, part 1, vol. 39, 251, 326.

14. O.R., series 1, part 1, vol. 39, 251-52, 322-23; Wyeth, 384-85.

15. Morton, 204-5.

16. Wyeth, 382-83, Henry, 316, quoting O.R., series no. 77, 372.

17. Henry, 316-17.

18. Wyeth, 386-87, Henry, 316-17, quoting O.R., series no. 77, 322.

19. Henry, 317, quoting from a letter dated February 18, 1902, to John Morton, published in *Memphis Commercial Appeal.*

20. *Southern Historical Society Papers,* vol. 7, 476-77, as quoted in Henry, 317; Wyeth, 388.

21. O.R., series 1, part 1, vol. 39, 322; Henry, 320.

22. Wyeth, 388.

23. Wyeth, 390; Henry, 321.

24. Wyeth, 390-91.

25. O.R., series 1, part 1, vol. 39, 322.

26. Henry, 321-22; O.R., series 1, part 1, vol. 39, 322.

27. Morton, 207-8.

28. Wyeth, 388-89.

29. Henry, 321-22; O.R., series 1, part 1, vol. 39, 322.

30. O.R., series 1, part 1, vol. 38, 281, 286, 295, 301, 323, 327; Bearss, 213-14.

31. Hancock, 434-34, as quoted in Bearss, 215.

32. Hurst, 207; O.R., series 1, part 1, vol. 39, 320; Lytle, 315.

33. Henry, 323, quoting Mississippi Valley Historical Society Publications, vol. 6, 45-47.

34. Henry, 324; Bearss, 215-16.

35. Henry, 324.

36. Ibid., 325.

37. Bearss, 225.

38. Ibid., 226, O.R., series 1, part 1, vol. 39, 288-90, 292-93.

39. Henry, 325.

40. O.R., series 1, part 1, vol. 39, 327-28, 344.

41. Wyeth, 398.

42. Ibid.

43. O.R., series 1, part 2, vol. 39, 201.

44. O.R., series 1, part 1, vol. 78, 202-4; Bearss, 229-31; Hurst, 209-12.

45. O.R., series 1, part 1, vol. 78, 202, 204.

46. Wyeth, 461.

47. Bearss, 237-38.

48. Ibid., 237-44.

49. Wyeth, 408-9; Henry, 330-31.

50. Henry, 330-31.

51. Bearss, 262; O.R., series 1, part 2, vol. 39, 235-36, 764.

52. Henry, 332.

53. Bearss, 268; O.R., series 1, part 2, vol. 39, 767.

54. Henry, 331-32.

55. Jordan and Pryor, 534; Henry, 333.

56. O.R., series 1, part 2, vol. 39, 783.

57. Wyeth, 470; O.R., series 1, part 2, vol. 39, 787-88.

58. Dinkins, 180, as quoted in Henry, 335.

59. Bearss, 285-87.

60. Henry, 337.

61. Ibid., 336-37.

62. Ibid., 337.

63. Bearss, 287-88; Henry, 337-38.

64. Bearss, 288.

65. Henry, 338; Bearss, 289; O.R., series 1, part 1, vol. 39, 469, 472-73.

66. Henry, 339.

67. Bearss, 339.

68. Henry, 339; Bearss, 294.

69. Henry, 340; Bearss, 294-95.

70. Henry, 340-41.

71. O.R., series 1, part 2, vol. 39, 470; Henry, 341.

72. Jordan and Pryor, 550-51; Henry, 341.

73. O.R., series 1, part 1, vol. 39, 481-84, as quoted in Bearss, 297-98.

74. Henry, 342, quoting O.R., serial no. 77, 320, 325.

75. Henry, 343, quoting O.R., serial no. 77, 320, 325.

76. *Memphis Commercial Appeal,* 12 March 1939, as quoted in Henry, 343-44.

**Chapter Thirteen**

1. Henry, 348; O.R., series 1, part 2, vol. 39, 731-32.

2. Richard Taylor, *Destruction and Reconstruction* (New York:

Appleton, 1879), 198-99.

3. Young, 97

4. O.R., series 1, part 2, vol. 39, 845; Jordan and Pryor, 557.

5. Henry, 347.

6. Ibid., 352.

7. Ibid.

8. Wyeth, 430.

9. Ibid., 430-31.

10. O.R., series 1, part 1, vol. 39, 542-43.

11. O.R., series 1, part 1, vol. 39, 519, 521; Hurst, 217.

12. Morton, 227.

13. Ibid., 228-30.

14. Ibid., 227-28; O.R., series 1, part 2, vol. 39, 522.

15. O.R., series 1, part 1, vol. 39, 513-14, 543-44.

16. Morton, 230; O.R., series 1, part 1, vol. 39, 523-26, 528.

17. Morton, 231.

18. Ibid., 232.

19. O.R., series 1, part 1, vol. 39, 514, 544-45.

20. Morton, 234; Jordan and Pryor, 569-70.

21. Maness, 300; Henry, 355.

22. O.R., series 1, part 1, vol. 39, 544-45.

23. Ibid., 545.

24. Wyeth, 437.

25. Ibid., 438.

26. Ibid.

27. Ibid., 440.

28. O.R., series 1, part 1, vol. 39, 545-46.

29. Henry, 358-59.

30. Morton, 239-40; Henry, 358.

31. Henry, 359; O.R., series 1, part 1, vol. 39, 517.

32. Wyeth, 443.

33. Henry, 360.

34. Ibid., 361-62.

35. Ibid., 362; O.R., series 1, part 3, vol. 39, 20, 28, 40, 57-60, 79.

36. O.R., series 1, part 1, vol. 39, 547-48.

37. Henry, 363; Wyeth, 507-8.

38. O.R., series 1, part 1, vol. 39, 547-48.

39. O.R., series 1, part 1, vol. 39, 546, 548-49.

40. Henry, 365.

41. O.R., series 1, part 3, vol. 39, 815-16.

42. Henry, 369.

43. O.R., series 1, part 2, vol. 39, 810, 815-16.
44. Henry, 366; O.R., series 1, part 1, vol. 39, 807.
45. Henry, 371.
46. Morton, 245.
47. Jordan and Pryor, 591-92.
48. Morton, 246-48.
49. Henry, 373.
50. Jordan and Pryor, 597; Wyeth, 461.
51. Morton, 249.
52. Henry, 374.
53. Henry, 374-75.
54. O.R. Navies, series 1, vol. 26, 610, 615, 624; O.R., series 1, part 1, vol. 39, 861, 869, 874.
55. O.R. Navies, series 1, vol. 26, 610; Henry, 376.
56. Morton, 253.
57. Shelby Foote, *The Civil War: A Narrative* (New York: Random House, 1958), 619-20; Henry, 376.
58. Henry, 377.
59. Ibid.; Foote, 619-20.
60. Henry, 378; Morton, 255-56.
61. Henry, 378; O.R., series 1, part 2, vol. 52, 777.
62. Jordan and Pryor, 605.
63. Ibid., 659; Henry, 381.
64. Grant, vol. 2, 633-34.
65. Hurst, 229; O.R., series 1, part 1, vol. 39, 915.

**Chapter Fourteen**

1. Henry, 380-81.
2. Ibid.; O.R., series 1, part 2, vol. 39, 694-97, 709-10.
3. O.R., series 1, part 1, vol. 39, 808.
4. Ibid.; Hurst, 231.
5. Hurst, 230.
6. Henry, 384-85.
7. Albert Castel, *Decision in the West: The Atlanta Campaign of 1864* (Lawrence: University of Kansas Press, 1992), 60-63.
8. Grant, vol. 2, 632-33.
9. Morton, 14.
10. O.R., series 1, part 1, vol. 45, 752.
11. Henry, 385-86.
12. Jordan and Pryor, 614-16.

13. Henry, p. 386.

14. O.R., series 1, part 1, vol. 45, 753.

15. Henry, 389; O.R., series 1, part 1, vol. 45, 113-14, 550, 558.

16. Hurst, 232; O.R., series 1, part 1, vol. 45, 753.

17. Henry, 387.

18. Ibid., 389.

19. O.R., series 1, part 1, vol. 45, 753; Maness, 328.

20. Henry, 388.

21. Ibid., 390.

22. Irving A. Buck, *Cleburne and His Command* (New York, 1903), 320.

23. O.R., series 1, part 1, vol. 45, 114.

24. Henry, 391-92.

25. O.R., series 1, part 1, vol. 45, 742.

26. Henry, 392.

27. O.R., series 1, part 1, vol. 45, 652-53, 712-13; Henry, 392-93.

28. O.R., series 1, part 1, vol. 45, 652-53, 712-13.

29. Ibid.

30. O.R., series 1, part 1, vol. 45, 742.

31. Henry, 393-94.

32. O.R., series 1, part 1, vol. 45, 742.

33. *Collected Works of Ambrose Bierce*, vol. 1 (New York and Washington, 1909), 318; Henry, 527.

34. O.R., series 1, part 1, vol. 45, 769-70.

35. O.R., series 1, part 1, vol. 45, 763-64; John B. Hood, *Advance and Retreat with the Army of Tennessee* (New Orleans, 1880), 290.

36. Jordan and Pryor, 624-25; O.R., series 1, part 1, vol. 45, 753, 764.

37. O.R., series 1, part 1, vol. 45, 342.

38. Jordan and Pryor, 625-26; Wyeth, 544.

39. O.R., series 1, part 1, vol. 45, 342.

40. Henry, 398.

41. Hurst, 234-35; O.R., series 1, part 1, vol. 45, 116.

42. Ibid.

43. Hurst, 236; O.R., series 1, part 1, vol. 45, 116.

44. Henry, 399.

45. Wyeth, 482-83.

46. Henry, 401.

47. Ibid., 400-2; O.R., series 1, part 1, vol. 45, 731.

48. O.R., series 1, part 1, vol. 45, 754-55.

49. Henry, 403; O.R., series 1, part 1, vol. 45, 764.

50. Wyeth, 485.

51. O.R., series 1, part 1, vol. 45, 613, 755-56; Henry, 404.

52. Henry, 404.

53. Wyeth, 552; Henry, 529.

54. Henry, 405.

55. O.R., series 1, part 1, vol. 45, 756.

56. Ibid., 654-55, 756; Maness, 344-45.

57. Henry, 407.

58. Ibid., 410-11.

59. Ibid., 408; O.R., series 1, part 1, vol. 45, 756.

60. Johnson and Buel, 552, 578; Henry, 409.

61. Henry, 409; O.R., series 1, part 1, vol. 45, 750.

62. James Harrison Wilson, *Under the Old Flag,* vol. 1 ( New York: Appleton, 1912), 119-20; Henry, 409.

63. Henry, 410.

64. Jordan and Pryor, 642-43.

65. Ibid.

66. Ibid., 644; O.R., series 1, part 1, vol. 45, 552-53, 689-90, 766.

67. Henry, 412.

68. O.R., series 1, part 1, vol. 45, 655, 728-29.

69. Morton, 292.

70. Henry, 413.

71. O.R., series 1, part 1, vol. 45, 136-37, 726-27, 757.

72. Henry, 415.

73. O.R., series 1, part 1, vol. 45, 727.

74. Morton, 299.

75. Ibid.

76. Morton, 297.

77. O.R., series 1, part 1, vol. 45, 727.

78. O.R., series 1, part 1, vol. 45, 727-28; Hurst, 244.

79. Clark, 155, as quoted in Henry, 416.

**Chapter Fifteen**

1. Jordan and Pryor, 655-56.

2. Henry, 420.

3. O.R., series 1, part 1, vol. 49, 930.

4. Ibid., 950, 1032; Wyeth, 513-14.

5. O.R., series 1, part 2, vol. 45, 622; Henry, 421.

6. Henry, 423.

7. Lewis Hosea, *Some Sidelights on the War for the Union* (Cleveland 1912), 8-11. The reference to Forrest as the Confederate Murat is a comparison with Marshal Joachim Murat, the celebrated cavalry leader in Napoleon's army. Like Forrest, Murat also rose from the

military ranks to command a legendary cavalry force.

8. Hosea, 11-14.
9. O.R., series 1, part 1, vol. 49, 909.
10. Henry, 426; Maness, 364.
11. Henry, 427; Maness, 358.
12. Henry, 428.
13. Wyeth, 521.
14. Henry, 428; Wyeth, 521-22; O.R., series 1, part 1, vol. 49, 1172.
15. O.R., series 1, part 1, vol. 49, 383-84, 357.
16. Ibid., 357-58.
17. Jordan and Pryor, 662-63.
18. Wilson, vol. 1, 209-18.
19. O.R., series 1, part 1, vol. 49, 357-58; Henry, 430.
20. O.R., series 1, part 1, vol. 49, 351, 359; Maness, 363.
21. Jordan and Pryor, 663-64;Henry, 430.
22. O.R., series 1, part 1, vol. 49, 354; Henry, 431.
23. Jordan and Pryor, 667.
24. O.R., series 1, part 1, vol. 49, 351-59.
25. Ibid., 359; Henry, 431; Maness, 363.
26. O.R., series 1, part 1, vol. 49, 359; Hurst, 250-51.
27. Wyeth, 603.
28. Henry, 431; Taylor, 219-20.
29. Jordan and Pryor, 672.
30. O.R., series 1, part 1, vol. 49, 361-62.
31. Jordan and Pryor, 676-77.
32. Ibid.
33. Ibid., 677-78.
34. Piatt and Boynton, 614, as quoted in Wyeth, 539.
35. Wyeth, 538-39; Henry, 433.
36. Hosea, 15.
37. Ibid., 16.
38. Wilson, vol. 11, 240-45.
39. Hosea, 17.
40. O.R., series 1, part 2, vol. 49, 1206-7, 1224-25, 1229, 1263-64.
41. Wills, 312-13; J. Hamilton Eckenrode, *Life of Nathan B. Forrest* (Richmond, Va.: B. F. Johnson Co., 1918), 169-70.
42. Wills, 314; Howe, 346; Henry, 436.
43. Rowland Dunbar, *Jefferson Davis, Constitutionalist: His Letters, Papers and Speeches* (Jackson, Miss.: 1923), 553-54, as quoted in Henry, 436.
44. Ibid.
45. *Reminiscences of General Basil W. Duke, C. S. A.* (New York, 1911),

385; Henry, 437.

46. Henry, 452-53.

47. Wyeth, 610-11.

48. Wills, 316; Jason Niles Diary, Southern Historical Collection, University of North Carolina, Chapel Hill; Dan T. Carter, *When the War Was Over: The Failure of Self-Reconstruction in the South 1865-1867* (Baton Rouge: Louisiana State UP, 1985), 9.

49. Hurst, 257; O.R., series 1, part 2, vol. 49, 552, 569.

50. Henry, 437.

51. O.R., series 1, part 2, vol. 49, 1259-90, as quoted in Henry, 437-38.

52. Hurst, 257-58; Jordan and Pryor, 602-3.

## Chapter Sixteen

1. Hurst, 260; Morton, 319; Young, *The Seventh Tennessee Cavalry*, 138.

2. Henry, 439.

3. Bryan McAlister, "Forrest on Fort Pillow" in *The Rebellion Record: A Diary of American Events: Documents and Narratives, Etc.*, ed. Frank Moore (New York, 1865), 3-4.

4. Ibid., 5.

5. Ibid., 3-4.

6. Hurst, 265; Wyeth, 615-16.

7. Eric Foner, preface to *Reconstruction: America's Unfinished Revolution* (New York: Harper and Row, 1988), xxiii.

8. *Ku Klux Conspiracy Report of the Joint Select Committee to Inquire into the Condition of Affairs in the Late Insurrectionary States, Made to the Two Houses of Congress. February, 1872*, 42nd Cong., 2nd Sess., S. Rept. 41, vol. 13 (Washington, D.C.: U.S. Government Printing Office), 24 (Hereafter referred to as *Ku Klux Conspiracy*).

9. Ibid., 24.

10. Ibid.

11. *Friar's Point Coahomian*, 29 September 1865.

12. Hurst, 267.

13. Henry, 440-41.

14. Hatch's testimony, January 25, 1866, *Report of the Joint Committee on Reconstruction, at the First Session, Thirty-ninth Congress*, 1866.

15. Hurst, 268.

16. *Memphis Appeal*, 26 and 28 December 1865, 2; Wyeth, 616-17.

17. Hurst, 270; *Memphis Appeal*, 26 December 1865, 2.

18. *Memphis Avalanche*, 30 January 1866, 2.

19. Ibid; *Memphis Avalanche*, 22 February 1866, 2.

20. Wills, 326.

21. *Report on the Joint Committee on Reconstruction at the First Session Thirty-Ninth Congress* (Washington, D.C.: U.S. Government Printing Office, 1866), 130-32; Wills, 326. 22. *Memphis Appeal,* 5 April 1866, 2.

23. Ibid.

24. *Friar's Point Coahomian,* 20 April 1866; Wills, 329-30.

25. Foner, 262-63; Iver Bernstein, *The New York City Draft Riots* (New York: Oxford UP, 1990), 5.

26. Foner, 273.

27. Foner, 437.

28. Coahoma County Land Deeds, Book G, 821-22; Henry, 442; Hurst, 271.

29. Forrest to Walter, August 14, 1866, Harvey W. Walters Papers, Southern Historical Society Collection, University of North Carolina, Chapel Hill; Wills, 332.

30. Forrest to Clark, September 4, 1866, Clark Papers, Mississippi Department of Archives and History, Jackson Tennessee; Wills, 333.

31. Coahoma County Circuit Court, Final Record, Book E, 454-55.

32. *Memphis Avalanche,* 10 April 1866, 2.

33. William W. White, *The Confederate Veteran* (Tuscaloosa, Ala.: Confederate Veteran Publishing Company, 1962), 54; Wills, 333.

34. Grant, vol. 11, 637.

35. Hurst, 283.

36. Ibid., 281; *Memphis Avalanche,* 22 September 1866, 1-2.

37. Hurst, 284; Forrest to Johnson, November 25, 1866, N. B. Forrest Papers. William R. Perkins Library, Drake University, Durham, N.C.

38. Hurst, 284.

39. E. Merton Coulter, *William G. Brownlow: Fighting Parson of the Southern Highlands* Chapel Hill, 1937; Knoxville: University of Tennessee Press, 1999), 126-28.

40. Ibid.; Foner, 186.

41. Foner, 17.

42. Ibid., 45.

43. Ibid., 187.

44. *Memphis Bulletin,* 12 August 1868, 2.

45. Horn, 20; Jordon and Pryor, 394-95.

46. Richard Schickel, *D. W. Griffith: An American Life* (New York: Simon and Schuster, 1984), 269-70; Robert Lang, ed., *The Birth of a Nation: Director D. W. Griffith* (Library of Congress, 1957), 251.

47. Horn, 7-12; Alan Trelease, *White Terror: The Ku Klux Klan Conspiracy and Southern Reconstruction* (Baton Rouge: Louisiana State UP, 1971), 4.

48. Trelease, 11.

49. Horn, 33.

50. Trelease, 13-14.

51. Horn, 314-15.

52. Morton, 344-45.

53. Hurst, 285; Morton, 344.

54. Horn, 312-13.

55. Horn, 395-409; Trelease, 17.

56. Hurst, 275; Lytle, 385; Horn, 312-13.

57. Lee Meriwether, *My Yesterdays: An Autobiography* (Webster Groves, Mo., 1942), 59-64.

58. J. Mathes, *General Forrest* (New York: Appleton, 1902), 20-21; Meriwether, 204.

59. Trelease, 21.

60. *Pulaski Citizen,* 5 June 1867.

61. Horn, 193.

62. Horn, 324; L. Wilmer Jones, *After the Thunder: Fourteen Men Who Shaped Post-Civil War America* (Landham, Md.: Taylor Trade Publishing, 2000), 219-21.

63. Horn, 96.

64. Trelease, 32.

65. Hurst, 296; *Memphis Avalanche,* 20 May 1868, 2.

66. Hurst, 297; *Memphis Appeal,* 2 June 1868, 3.

67. Hurst, 298-99.

68. *Memphis Avalanche,* 10 June 1868, 3, as quoted in Henry, 298.

69. Meriwether, 66-69.

70. Duke, *Reminiscences,* 348-49.

71. Lytle, 381; *Memphis Appeal,* 10 July 1868, *Memphis Appeal,* 19 July 1868, 3.

72. *New York Times,* 17 August 1868.

73. Wills, 347.

74. Duke, *Reminiscences,* 351-54.

75. Trelease, 109; Lytle, 383.

76. Trelease, 31.

77. *Pulaski Citizen,* 26 June 1868, as quoted in Trelease, 28; Horn, 363-65.

78. *Nashville Republican Banner,* 17 July 1868, as quoted in Trelease, 41-42; Hurst, 307.

79. Trelease, 41.

80. Ibid., 43.

81. Ibid.

82. Ibid.

83. *Ku Klux Conspiracy,* 4-5, 19, 21; Horn, 95.

84. Henry, 450; *New York Times,* 17 August 1868 (reprinted from the *Memphis Avalanche*).

85. Horn, 415-16.

86. *Ku Klux Conspiracy,* 27; Hurst, 316.

87. Letter from N. B. Forrest to Mr. J. T. Brown, as quoted in Hurst, 315-16.

88. Hurst, 317-18; *New York Times* 14 September 1868, 2, 5.

89. *Ku Klux Conspiracy,* 31; Hurst; 319.

90. Trelease, 157-58; *Memphis Avalanche,* as quoted in *Memphis Evening Post,* 17 October 1868.

91. Horn, 250-51; Hurst, 320.

92. Trelease, 163.

93. Trelease, 175-77.

94. Horn, 357; Henry, 449; Morton, 345.

95. Morton, 345-46.

96. *Memphis Daily Appeal,* 12 March 1869.

97. "Outlaw Days," Mrs. Mary Fisher Robinson interview, "Riot of 1875," Mrs. Geo. S. Robinson interview, Carnegie Public Library, Clarksdale, Mississippi, as quoted in Wills, 359.

98. *New York Times,* 15 March, 1869, 5.

99. Chestnut, 748.

100. *Memphis Daily Appeal,* 15-16 July 1869.

101. *Ku Klux Conspiracy,* 17.

102. Wyeth, 617-19.

103. *Ku Klux Conspiracy,* 2-4.

104. Ibid., 3-5.

105. Ibid., 5.

106. Ibid., 7.

107. Ibid., 9.

108. Ibid.,11.

109. Ibid.

110. Ibid., 12.

111. Ibid., 24.

112. Ibid., 26-27.

113. Ibid., 29-30; Wills, 364.

114. *Ku Klux Conspiracy,* 29-30.

115. Ibid., 31.

**Chapter Seventeen**

1. Horn, 316.
2. Hurst, 346.
3. Ibid., 347.
4. Lee, 59-62.
5. Ibid.; Hurst, 347-49.
6. *New York Times,* 9 August 1873, 1; Hurst, 360.
7. Hurst, 361; *Memphis Public Ledger,* 26 August 1874, 2.
8. *Philadelphia Bulletin,* as quoted in the *Memphis Appeal,* 10 September 1874, 1.
9. Wills, 370; Hurst, 368.
10. Hurst, 366-67.
11. *Memphis Appeal,* 6 July 1875, 1, as quoted in Hurst, 366.
12. Hurst, 369.
13. Wills, 372.
14. Coahoma County Circuit Court, Final Record, Book E, Clarksdale, Mississippi, 355-56.
15. Wills, 372-73; "Two Confederate Heroes," *Charleston (S.C.) Sunday-News,* 27 September 1903.
16. Henry, 459; Fred T. Wooten, Jr., "Religious Activity in Civil War Memphis," *Tennessee Historical Quarterly* 3 (September 1944).
17. Wills, 374; "President's Island," *Memphis Daily Appeal,* 5 May 1876.
18. Wills, 373-74; Hurst, 371-72; "Last Speech of General Forrest," *Confederate Veteran* 29 (January 1921): 25.
19. *Atlanta Daily Constitution,* 3 September 1877; Hurst, 378-79.
20. Hurst, 375; Meriwether, 64.

**Afterword**

1. Shakespeare, William. *Julius Caesar.* act 5, scene 5.

# BIBLIOGRAPHY

**Books**

Bartlett, Irving H. *John C. Calhoun*. New York: W. W. Norton & Company, 1993.

Bearss, Edwin C. *Forrest At Brice's Crossroads and in Northern Mississippi in 1864*. Dayton, Ohio: Morningside Bookshop, 1979.

Bernstein, Iver. *The New York City Draft Riots*. New York: Oxford UP, 1990.

Bierce, Ambrose. *Collected Works of Ambrose Bierce*. Vol. 1. New York and Washington, 1909.

Browder, George Richard. *The Heavens Are Weeping: The Diaries of George Richard Browder 1852-1886*. Edited by Richard L. Troutman. Grand Rapids, Mich.: Zondervan Publishing House, 1987.

Buck, Irving A. *Cleburne and His Command*. New York, 1903.

Carter, Dan T. *When the War Was Over: The Failure of Self-Reconstruction in the South 1865-1867*. Baton Rouge: Louisiana State UP, 1985.

Castel, Albert. *Articles of War: Winners, Losers and Some Who Were Both During the Civil War*. Mechanicsburg, Pa.: Stackpole Books, 2001.

——. *Decision in the West: The Atlanta Campaign of 1864*. Lawrence: University of Kansas Press, 1992.

Catton, Bruce. *Centennial History of the Civil War*. Vol. 3, *Never Call Retreat*. New York: Doubleday and Co., Inc., 1965.

Dixon, Thomas Jr. *The Clansman*. New York: Doubleday, 1905.

Dodson, W. C. *Campaigns of Wheeler and His Cavalry*. Guild Bindery Press, 1899.

Duke, Basil W. *Morgan's Cavalry*. New York: Doubleday, 1906.

Dyer, John P. *Fightin' Joe Wheeler*. Baton Rouge: Louisiana State UP, 1941.

Eckenrode, Hamilton J. *The Life of Nathan Bedford Forrest*. Richmond,

Va.: B. F. Johnson Co., 1918.

Foner, Eric. *Reconstruction: America's Unfinished Revolution*. New York: Harper and Row, 1988.

Hancock, R. R. *A History of the Second Tennessee Cavalry, C. S. A.* Dayton, Ohio: Morningside Bookshop, 1981.

Hanson, G. A. *Minor Incidents of the Late War*. Bartow, Florida, 1887.

Hart, Liddell B. H. *Strategy: The Classic Book on Military Strategy*. London: Faber and Faber, Ltd., 1954.

Hearn, Chester G. *Admiral David Dixon Porter: The Civil War Years*. Annapolis, Md.: Naval Institute Press, 1996.

Henry, Robert Selph. *First with the Most*. New York: Konecky and Konecky, 1992.

———. *As They Saw Forrest*. Jackson, Tenn.: McCowat-Mercer Press, 1956.

Hood, John B. *Advance and Retreat with the Army of Tennessee*. New Orleans, 1880.

Horn, Stanley F. *The Army of Tennessee*. Norman: University of Oklahoma Press, 1952.

———. *The Invisible Empire: The Story of the Ku Klux Klan 1866-1871*. Boston: Houghton Mifflin Co., 1939.

Hosea, Lewis. *Some Sidelights on the War for the Union*. Cleveland, 1912.

Hubbard, John Milton. *Notes of a Private*. Nixon-Jones Printing Co., 1911.

Hurst, Jack. *Forrest: A Biography*. New York: Random House, 1993.

Johnson, Adam R. *The Partisan Raiders of the Confederate States Army*. Louisville, Kentucky, 1904.

Johnson, Robert T., and Clarence C. Buel, eds. *Battles and Leaders of the Civil War*. 4 Vols. New York, 1956.

Johnson, William Preston. *The Life of General Albert Sidney Johnston*. New York: Appleton, 1878.

Jones, Wilmer L. *After the Thunder: Fourteen Men Who Shaped Post-Civil War America*. Landham, Md.: Taylor Trade Publishing, 2000.

Jordan, Thomas, and J. P. Pryor *The Campaigns of Lieutenant General N. B. Forrest and of Forrest's Cavalry*. Dayton, Ohio: Morningside Bookshop, 1977.

Lang, Robert, ed. *The Birth of a Nation: Director D.W. Griffith* Library of Congress, 1957.

Leeke, Jim. *Smoke, Sound and Fury: The Civil War Memories of Major General Lew Wallace, U.S. Volunteers*. Strawberry Hill Press, 1988.

Lincoln, Abraham. *The Writings of Abraham Lincoln*. 8 Vols. Edited by Arthur Brooks Lapsley. New York: G. P. Putnam's Sons, 1906.

Lytle, Andrew. *Forrest and His Critter Company.* New York: Herald Tribune, 1931.

Maness, Lonnie E. *An Untutored Genius: The Military Career of General Nathan Bedford Forrest.* Oxford, Miss.: The University of Tennessee at Martin; The Guild Bindery Press, 1990.

Mathes, J. *General Forrest.* New York: Appleton, 1902.

Meriwether, Lee. *My Yesterdays: An Autobiography.* Webster Groves, Mo., 1942.

Merton, Coulter E. *William G. Brownlow: Fighting Parson of the Southern Highlands.* Chapel Hill, 1937; Knoxville: University of Tennessee Press, 1999.

Moore, Frank, ed. *The Rebellion Record.* New York, 1865.

Morton, John. *The Artillery of Nathan Bedford Forrest's Cavalry.* Marietta, Ga.: R. Bemis Publishing, Ltd., 1995.

Niven, John. *John C. Calhoun and the Price of Union.* Baton Rouge: Louisiana State UP, 1988.

Petersen, Merril D. *The Great Triumvirate.* New York: Oxford UP, 1987.

Piatt, Donn, and H. V. Boyton. *General George H. Thomas.* Cincinnati, 1893.

Roach, A. C. *The Prisoner of War.* Indianapolis, 1865.

Roman, Alfred. *Military Operations of General Beauregard.* New York, 1884.

Schickel, Richard. *D. W. Griffith: An American Life.* New York: Simon and Schuster, 1984.

Seitz, Don C. *Braxton Bragg, General of the Confederacy.* Columbia, S.C., 1924.

Shelby, Foote. *The Civil War: A Narrative.* 3 vol. New York: Random House, 1958.

Taylor, Richard. *Destruction and Reconstruction.* New York: Appleton, 1879.

Thomas, Hugh. *The Slave Trade: The Story of the Atlantic Slave Trade 1440-1870.* New York: Simon and Schuster, 1997.

Trelease, Alan. *White Terror: The Ku Klux Klan Conspiracy and Southern Reconstruction.* Baton Rouge: Louisiana State UP, 1971.

Troutman, Richard L., ed. *The Heavens Are Weeping: The Diaries of George Richard Browder, 1852-1886.* Grand Rapids, Mich: Zondervan Publishing House, 1987.

Von Clausewitz, Carl. *On War.* Princeton, N.J.; Princeton UP, 1976.

Wallace; Lew. *An Autobiography 1822-1925.* 2 Vol. Harper and Brothers, 1960.

Wills, Brian Steel. *A Battle from the Start.* New York: HarperCollins, 1992.

Willett, Robert L. *The Lightning Mule Brigade: Abel Streight's 1863 Raid into Alabama.* Guild Press, 1999.

Wilson, James Harrison. *Under the Old Flag.* 2 Vol. New York: Appleton, 1912.

Witherspoon, William. *Reminiscences of a Scout, Spy and Soldier of Forrest's Cavalry.* Jackson, Tenn., 1910.

Wyeth, John Allen. *That Devil Forrest.* Baton Rouge and London: Louisiana State UP, 1989.

Young, John Preston. *The Seventh Tennessee Cavalry, CSA.* Dayton, Ohio: Morningside Bookshop, 1976.

## Articles

Bearss, Edwin C. "Brice's Crossroads." *The Blue and Gray* 26 (summer 1999).

Bryan, Charles F. "I Mean to Have Them All: Forrest's Murfreesboro Raid." *Civil War Times Illustrated* (January 1974).

Button, Mrs. C. W. *Confederate Veteran* (September 1897).

Castel, Albert. "The Fort Pillow Massacre: A Fresh Examination of the Evidence." *Civil War History* (March 1958).

Chalmers, James R. "Brigadier General before the Southern Historical Society, August 15, 1879." Southern Historical Society Papers, 7, no. 10, 458.

Cimprich, John, and Robert C. Mainfort, Jr., ed. "Fort Pillow Revisited: New Evidence about an Old Controversy." *Civil War History* (winter 1982).

*Confederate Veteran* 15 (January 1909): 54.

*Confederate Veteran* 2 (1885).

Cheeks, Robert C. "Federal Fiasco at Thompson's Station." *American Civil War* (November 1999).

Davison, Eddy W., and Daniel L. Foxx. "A Journey to the Most Controversial Battlefield in America." *Confederate Veteran* 6 (2001).

Dinkins, James. "The Capture of Fort Pillow." *Confederate Veteran* 33 (December 1925).

"Dr. Fitch's Report on the Fort Pillow Massacre." *The Tennesee Historical Quarterly* 44 (Spring 1985).

Jordan, John L. "Was There a Massacre at Fort Pillow?" *The Tennessee Historical Quarterly* 6 (1947).

Henderson, William, ed. "Forrest's March Out of West Tennessee: Recollections of Private John Johnston." The West Tennessee Historical Society Papers 12, (1958): 127.

Kelley, D. C. "The Methodist Review" 49 (March-April 1900).

Maness, Lonnie E. "The Capture of Union City." The West Tennessee Historical Society Papers, 30 (1976).

Sayers, Althea. "Fort Pillow: What the Federal Government Didn't Tell." *The Online Civil War Magazine* (http://ehistory.osu.edu/uscw/features/articles/9905/ftpillow.cfm).

Stier, William. "Fury Takes the Field." *Civil War Times* 38 (December 1999).

Wolseley, Viscount. "General Forrest." *United Service Magazine* (London) n.s., 5 (1892): 21.

Wooten, Fred T., Jr. "Religious Activity in Civil War Memphis." *The Tennessee Historical Quarterly* 3 (September 1944).

Wyeth, John A. "The Storming of Fort Pillow." *Harpers Magazine* 99 (September, 1899).

## Government Records

Congress Joint Committee on Reconstruction. *Report on the Joint Committee on Reconstruction.* 39th Cong., 1st sess. Washington, D.C.: Government Printing Office, 1866.

Congress Joint Select Committee. *Ku Klux Conspiracy: Report of the Joint Select Committee to Inquire into the Condition of Affairs in the Late Insurrectionary States, Made to the Two Houses of Congress.* 42nd Cong., 2nd sess., S. Rept. 41, Vol. 13. Washington, D.C.: Government Printing Office, 1872.

House Committee on the Conduct of the War. *Reports of the Committee on the Conduct of the War: Fort Pillow Massacre.* 38th Cong., 1st sess., H. Rept. 65. Washington, D.C.: Government Printing Office, 1864.

*Official Naval Records of the War of the Rebellion: A Compilation of the Official Naval Records of the Union and Confederate Navies.* 30 Vol. Washington, D.C.: Government Printing Office, 1894-1927.

*The War of the Rebellion: A Compilation of the Official Records of the Union and Confederate Armies,* 128 Vol. Washington, D.C.: United States Printing Office, 1880-1901.

## Memoirs

*A Soldier's Honor, By His Comrades: The Memoirs of General Van Dorn,* as told by his fellow officers. New York, 1902.

Davis, Jefferson. *The Rise And Fall of the Confederate Government.* 2 Vol. New York: D Appleton Co., 1881.

Dunbar, Rowland, ed. *Jefferson Davis, Constitutionalist: His Letters, Papers and Speeches.* 10 Vol. Jackson, Mississippi, 1923.

Grant, Ulysses S. *Personal Memoirs of U.S. Grant.* New York: Charles L. Webster and Co., 1886.

Hubbard, John Milton. *Notes of a Private (7th Tennessee Cavalry Regiment, Forrest's Cavalry Corps).* St. Louis: Nixon-Jones Printing Co., 1911.

Porter, David Dixon. *The Naval History of the Civil War.* New York: The Sherman Publishing Co., 1886.

Sherman, William T. *Home Letters of General Sherman.* Edited by M. A. DeWolfe Howe. New York: Charles Scribner's Sons, 1909.

Sherman, William T. *Memoirs of General William T. Sherman.* New York: Charles Webster and Co., 1892.

Watkins, Sam R. *"Co. Aytch," Maury Grays, First Tennessee Regiment; or, A Side Show of the Big Show.* Chattanooga, 1900.

Witherspoon, William. *Reminiscences of a Scout, Spy and Soldier of Forrest's Cavalry.* Jackson, Tennessee, 1910.

Woodward, C. Vann, ed. *Mary Chestnut's Civil War.* New Haven, Conn.: Yale UP, 1981.

## Collections

Southern Historical Collection; University of North Carolina, Chapel Hill.

Nathan Bedford Forrest Papers, William Perkins Library, Drake University, Durham, North Carolina.

## Newspapers

*Memphis Appeal*
*Memphis Avalanche*
*Memphis Bulletin*
*Memphis Eagle and Enquirer*
*New York Times*
*Chicago Tribune*
*Nashville Banner*
*Trenton Herald Democrat*
*Pulaski Citizen*
*Atlanta Daily Constitution*
*Friar's Point Coahomian*
*Cincinnati Commercial*
*Phenix, Hernando, Mississippi*

# INDEX

On 6·14·1861,
Nathan Bedford
Forrest enlisted as
a Private at age 40.
In early October, he
was elected Lt. Col.
and organized and
led his 1st command on
its 1st campaign as
depicted on this
map.

III      2002

ILL.

Ohio River

Cairo      Paducah

Columbus

FT. DONELS.

Ft. Her

Union City

Paris

Obion River

Forked Deer Creek

Trenton      McLemoresv

So. Fork

Humboldt

Mississippi River

Sharron's Ferry

Ft. Pillow

Browns ville

Jackson

Hatchie

River

Memphis

Somerville

Wolf

Moscow

Grand Jct.

Shiloh Church

Pi

To Memphis by

and back rail

River

Montery

MISS.

Corinth

Scale in Miles

0    3.5    7    10.5    14    17.8    21    24.5    28